TEACH YOURSELF ACCESS 97 VISUALLY™

IDG's 3-D Visual™ Series

IDG Books Worldwide, Inc.
An International Data Group Company
Foster City, CA • Indianapolis • Chicago • Southlake, TX

Teach Yourself Access 97 VISUALLY™

Published by
IDG Books Worldwide, Inc.
An International Data Group Company
919 E. Hillsdale Blvd., Suite 400
Foster City, CA 94404

Library of Congress Catalog Card No.: 97-072426

ISBN: 0-7645-6026-3

Printed in the United States of America
10 9 8 7 6 5 4 3

XX/XX/XX/XX/XX

Distributed in the United States by IDG Books Worldwide, Inc.

Distributed by Transworld Publishers Limited in the United Kingdom; by IDG Norge Books for Norway; by IDG Sweden Books for Sweden; by Woodslane Pty. Ltd. for Australia; by Woodslane Enterprises Ltd. for New Zealand; by Longman Singapore Publishers Ltd. for Singapore, Malaysia, Thailand, and Indonesia; by Simron Pty. Ltd. for South Africa; by Toppan Company Ltd. for Japan; by Distribuidora Cuspide for Argentina; by Livraria Cultura for Brazil; by Ediciencia S.A. for Ecuador; by Addison-Wesley Publishing Company for Korea; by Ediciones ZETA S.C.R. Ltda. for Peru; by WS Computer Publishing Corporation, Inc., for the Philippines; by Unalis Corporation for Taiwan; by Contemporanea de Ediciones for Venezuela; by Computer Book & Magazine Store for Puerto Rico; by Express Computer Distributors for the Caribbean and West Indies. Authorized Sales Agent: Anthony Rudkin Associates for the Middle East and North Africa.

For corporate orders, please call maranGraphics at 800-469-6616.
For general information on IDG Books Worldwide's books in the U.S., please call our Consumer Customer Service department at 800-762-2974.
For reseller information, including discounts and premium sales, please call our Reseller Customer Service department at 800-434-3422.
For information on where to purchase IDG Books Worldwide's books outside the U.S., please contact our International Sales department at 415-655-3200 or fax 415-655-3295.
For information on foreign language translations, please contact our Foreign & Subsidiary Rights department at 415-655-3021 or fax 415-655-3281.
For sales inquiries and special prices for bulk quantities, please contact our Sales department at 415-655-3200.
For information on using IDG Books Worldwide's books in the classroom or for ordering examination copies, please contact our Educational Sales department at 800-434-2086 or fax 817-251-8174.
For press review copies, author interviews, or other publicity information, please contact our Public Relations department at 415-655-3000 or fax 415-655-3299.
For authorization to photocopy items for corporate, personal, or educational use, please contact maranGraphics at 800-469-6616.

Trademark Acknowledgments

The 3-D illustrations are the copyright of maranGraphics, Inc.

U.S. Corporate Sales
Contact maranGraphics at (800) 469-6616 or Fax (905) 890-9434.

U.S. Trade Sales
Contact IDG Books at (800) 434-3422 or (415) 655-3000.

Welcome to the world of IDG Books Worldwide.

IDG Books Worldwide, Inc., is a subsidiary of International Data Group, the world's largest publisher of computer-related information and the leading global provider of information services on information technology. IDG was founded more than 25 years ago and now employs more than 8,500 people worldwide. IDG publishes more than 270 computer publications in over 75 countries (see listing below). More than 90 million people read one or more IDG publications each month.

Launched in 1990, IDG Books Worldwide is today the #1 publisher of best-selling computer books in the United States. We are proud to have received eight awards from the Computer Press Association in recognition of editorial excellence and three from Computer Currents' First Annual Readers' Choice Awards. Our best-selling ...For Dummies® series has more than 25 million copies in print with translations in 30 languages. IDG Books Worldwide, through a joint venture with IDG's Hi-Tech Beijing, became the first U.S. publisher to publish a computer book in the People's Republic of China. In record time, IDG Books Worldwide has become the first choice for millions of readers around the world who want to learn how to better manage their businesses.

Our mission is simple: Every one of our books is designed to bring extra value and skill-building instructions to the reader. Our books are written by experts who understand and care about our readers. The knowledge base of our editorial staff comes from years of experience in publishing, education, and journalism - experience which we use to produce books for the '90s. In short, we care about books, so we attract the best people. We devote special attention to details such as audience, interior design, use of icons, and illustrations. And because we use an efficient process of authoring, editing, and desktop publishing our books electronically, we can spend more time ensuring superior content and spend less time on the technicalities of making books.

You can count on our commitment to deliver high-quality books at competitive prices on topics you want to read about. At IDG Books Worldwide, we continue in the IDG tradition of delivering quality for more than 25 years. You'll find no better book on a subject than one from IDG Books Worldwide.

John Kilcullen
President and CEO
IDG Books Worldwide, Inc.

IDG Books Worldwide, Inc., is a subsidiary of International Data Group, the world's largest publisher of computer-related information and the leading global provider of information services on information technology. International Data Group publishes over 276 computer publications in over 75 countries. Ninety million people read one or more International Data Group publications each month. International Data Group's publications include: Argentina: Annuario de Informatica, Computerworld Argentina, PC World Argentina; Australia: Australian Macworld, Client/Server Journal, Computer Living, Computerworld, Computerworld 100, Digital News, IT Casebook, Network World, On-line World Australia, PC World, Publishing Essentials, Reseller, WebMaster; Austria: Computerwelt Osterreich, Networks Austria, PC Tip; Belarus: PC World Belarus; Belgium: Data News; Brazil: Annuário de Informática, Computerworld Brazil, Connections, Super Game Power, Macworld, PC Player, PC World Brazil, Publish Brazil, Reseller News; Bulgaria: Computerworld Bulgaria, Networkworld/Bulgaria, PC & MacWorld Bulgaria; Canada: CIO Canada, Client/Server World, ComputerWorld Canada, InfoCanada, Network World Canada; Chile: Computerworld Chile, PC World Chile; Colombia: Computerworld Colombia, PC World Colombia; Costa Rica: PC World Centro America; The Czech and Slovak Republics: Computerworld Czechoslovakia, Elektronika Czechoslovakia, Macworld Czech Republic, PC World Czechoslovakia; Denmark: Communications World, Computerworld Danmark, Macworld Danmark, PC Privat Danmark, PC World Danmark, PC World Danmark Supplements, TECH World; Dominican Republic: PC World Republica Dominicana; Ecuador: PC World Ecuador; Egypt: Computerworld Middle East, PC World Middle East; El Salvador: PC World Centro America; Finland: MikroPC, Tietoverkko, Tietoviikko; France: Distributique, Golden, Hebdo-Distributique, Info PC, Le Guide du Monde Informatique, Le Monde Informatique, Reseaux & Telecoms; Germany: Computer Partner, Computerwoche, Computerwoche Extra, Computerwoche Focus, I/M Information Management, Macwelt, PC Welt; Greece: GamePro, Multimedia World; Guatemala: PC World Centro America; Honduras: PC World Centro America; Hong Kong: Computerworld Hong Kong, PCWorld Hong Kong, Publish in Asia; Hungary: ABCD CD-ROM, Computerworld Szamitastechnika, PC & Mac World Hungary, PC-X Magazine; Iceland: Tolvuheimur/PC World Island; India: Information Systems Computerworld, PC World India, Publish in Asia; Indonesia: InfoKomputer PC World, Komputek Computerworld, Publish in Asia; Ireland: ComputerScope, PC Live!; Israel: People & Computers; Italy: Computerworld Italia, Computerworld Italia Special Editions, Macworld Italia, Networking Italia, PC Shopping, PC World Italia, PC World/Walt Disney; Japan: DTP World, HP Open World Japan, Macworld Japan, Nikkei Personal Computing, Open World Japan, OS/2 World Japan, SunWorld Japan, Windows World Japan; Kenya: East African Computer News; Korea: Hi-Tech Information/Computerworld, Macworld Korea, PC World Korea; Macedonia: PC World Macedonia; Malaysia: Computerworld Malaysia, PC World Malaysia, Publish in Asia; Mexico: Computerworld Mexico, Macworld, PC World Mexico; Myanmar: PC World Myanmar; Netherlands: Computer! Totaal, LAN Magazine, LanWorld Buyers Guide, Macworld, Net Magazine, Totaal! Beurskrant; New Zealand: Absolute Beginner's Guide, Computer Buyer, Computer Industry Directory, Computerworld New Zealand, MTB, Network World, PC World New Zealand; Nicaragua: PC World Centro America; Nigeria: PC World Nigeria; Norway: Computerworld Norge, Computerworld Privat (Datamagasinet), CW Rapport Norge, IDG's KURSGUIDE, Macworld Norge, Multimediaworld, PC World Ekspress, PC World Nettverk, PC World Norge, PC World's Produktguide, Windows World Spesial; Pakistan: Computerworld Pakistan, PC World Pakistan; Panama: PC World Panama; P. R. of China: China Computer Users, China Computerworld, China Infoworld, China Telecom World Weekly, Computer & Communication, Electronic Design China, Electronics Today, Electronics Weekly, Game Camp, Game Soft, Network World China, PC World China, Popular Computer Weekly, Software Weekly, Software World, Telecom World; Peru: Computerworld Peru, PC World Profesional Peru, PC World Peru; Poland: Computerworld Poland, Computerworld Special Report, Macworld, Networld, PC World Komputer; Philippines: Computerworld Philippines, PC World Philippines, Publish in Asia; Portugal: Cerebro/PC World, Computerworld/Correio Informático, Dealer World Portugal, Mac*In/PC*In, Multimedia World Portugal; Puerto Rico: PC World Puerto Rico; Romania: Computerworld Romania, PC World Romania, Telecom Romania; Russia: Computerworld Russia, Mir PK, Sety; Singapore: Computerworld Singapore, PC World Singapore, Publish in Asia; Slovenia: MONITOR; South Africa: Computing S.A., InfoWorld S.A., Network World S.A., Software World; Spain: Computerworld Espa-a, COMUNICACIONES WORLD, Dealer World, Macworld Espa-a, PC World Espa-a; Sweden: CAP&Design, Computer Sweden, Corporate Computing, MacWorld, Maxi Data, MikroDatorn, Nätverk & Kommunikation, PC/Aktiv, PC World, Windows World; Switzerland: Computerworld Schweiz, Macworld Schweiz, PCtip; Taiwan: Computerworld Taiwan, Macworld Taiwan, PC World Taiwan, Publish Taiwan, Windows World; Thailand: Thai Computerworld, Publish in Asia; Turkey: Computerworld Turkiye, MACWORLD Turkiye, PC WORLD Turkiye; Ukraine: Computerworld Kiev, Computers & Software, Multimedia World Ukraine, PC World Ukraine; United Kingdom: Acorn User, Amiga Action, Amiga Computing, Appletalk, Computing, GamePro, Macworld, Network News, Parents and Computers, PC Advisor, PC Home, PSX Pro UK, The WEB; United States: Cable in the Classroom, CD Review, CIO Magazine, Computerworld, Computerworld Client/Server Journal, Digital Video Magazine, DOS World, Federal Computer Week, GamePro, InfoWorld, I-Way, JavaWorld, Macworld, Multimedia World, Netscape World Online, Network World, PC Entertainment, PC World, Publish, SunWorld Online, SWATPro Magazine, Video Event, WebMaster; Uruguay: PC World Uruguay; Venezuela: Computerworld Venezuela, PC World Venezuela; and Vietnam: PC World Vietnam.

Every maranGraphics book represents
the extraordinary vision and commitment of a unique family:
the Maran family of Toronto, Canada.

Back Row (from left to right): *Sherry Maran, Rob Maran, Richard Maran, Maxine Maran, Jill Maran.*

Front Row (from left to right): *Judy Maran, Ruth Maran.*

Richard Maran is the company founder and its inspirational leader. He developed maranGraphics' proprietary communication technology called "visual grammar." This book is built on that technology—empowering readers with the easiest and quickest way to learn about computers.

Ruth Maran is the Author and Architect—a role Richard established that now bears Ruth's distinctive touch. She creates the words and visual structure that are the basis for the books.

Judy Maran is the Project Coordinator. She works with Ruth, Richard and the highly talented maranGraphics illustrators, designers and editors to transform Ruth's material into its final form.

Rob Maran is the Technical and Production Specialist. He makes sure the state-of-the-art technology used to create these books always performs as it should.

Sherry Maran manages the Reception, Order Desk and any number of areas that require immediate attention and a helping hand.

Jill Maran is a jack-of-all-trades and dynamo who fills in anywhere she's needed anytime she's back from university.

Maxine Maran is the Business Manager and family sage. She maintains order in the business and family—and keeps everything running smoothly.

CREDITS

Author & Architect:
Ruth Maran

Copy Development and Screen Captures:
Kelleigh Wing

Project Coordinator:
Judy Maran

Editors:
Peter Lejcar
Tina Veltri

Proofreaders:
Brad Hilderley
Wanda Lawrie
Carol Barclay
Roxanne Coppens

Layout Designer:
Christie Van Duin

Layout Revisions & Illustrations:
Jamie Bell

Illustrations & Screens:
Chris K.C. Leung
Russell C. Marini
Ben Lee
Jeff Jones
Tamara Poliquin

Indexer:
Kelleigh Wing

Post Production:
Robert Maran

ACKNOWLEDGMENTS

Thanks to the dedicated staff of maranGraphics, including Carol Barclay, Jamie Bell, Roxanne Coppens, Francisco Ferreira, Brad Hilderley, Jeff Jones, Wanda Lawrie, Ben Lee, Peter Lejcar, Chris K.C. Leung, Michael W. MacDonald, Jill Maran, Judy Maran, Maxine Maran, Robert Maran, Sherry Maran, Russell C. Marini, Tamara Poliquin, Christie Van Duin, Tina Veltri, Paul Whitehead and Kelleigh Wing.

Finally, to Richard Maran who originated the easy-to-use graphic format of this guide. Thank you for your inspiration and guidance.

TABLE OF CONTENTS

CHAPTER *1* *Getting Started*

Introduction....4

Parts of a Database....6

Planning a Database....8

Using the Mouse....10

Start Access....11

CHAPTER *2* *Create a Database*

Create a Database Using the Wizard....14

Minimize a Window....20

Maximize a Window....21

Switch Between Windows....22

Close a Window....23

Using the Database Window....24

Display or Hide a Toolbar....26

Exit Access....27

Create a Blank Database....28

Open a Database....30

Getting Help....32

CHAPTER 3 *Create Tables*

Create a Table 36

Rename a Field 40

Rearrange Fields 41

Add a Field 42

Delete a Field 43

Close a Table 44

Open a Table 45

Rename a Table 46

Delete a Table 47

Create a Table Using the Wizard 48

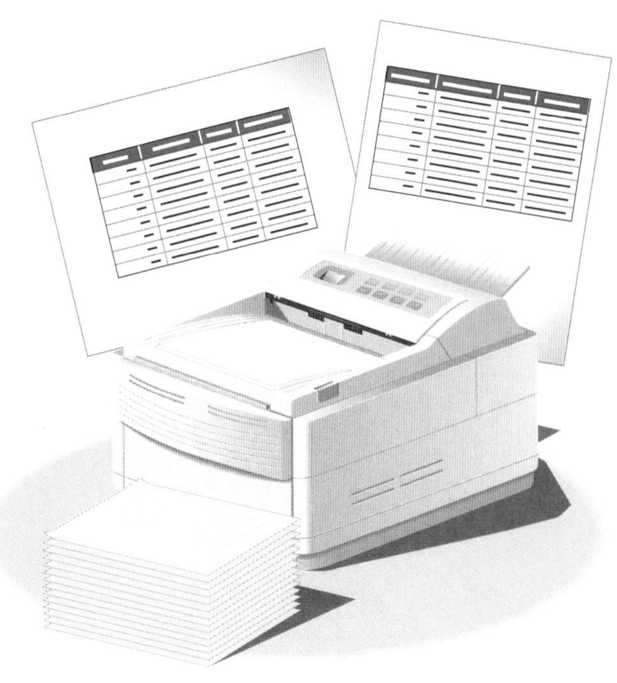

CHAPTER 4 *Edit Tables*

Move Through Records 56

Select Data 58

Scroll Through Data 60

Zoom Into a Cell 61

Add a Record 62

Delete a Record 63

Edit Data 64

Move or Copy Data 66

Check Spelling 68

Change Column Width 70

Change Row Height 71

Change Font of Data 72

Change Cell Appearance 74

Hide a Field 76

Freeze a Field 78

CHAPTER 5 *Print*

Preview Before Printing 82

Change Page Setup 84

Print Information 86

Create Mailing Labels 88

TABLE OF CONTENTS

CHAPTER 6 *Design Tables*

Change View of Table 96

Add a Field 98

Delete a Field..100

Rearrange Fields..101

Add a Field Description..102

Display Field Properties 103

Change a Data Type..104

Select a Format 106

Change the Field Size 108

Add a Caption..110

Add a Default Value..111

Data Entry Required..112

Allow Zero-Length Strings 114

Change Number of Decimal Places 115

Add a Validation Rule..116

Create a Yes/No Field 118

Create an Index 120

Create a Lookup Column..122

Add Pictures to Records 126

Create an Input Mask..130

CHAPTER 7 *Establish Relationships*

Set the Primary Key....................136

Start a New Relationship....................138

Enforce Referential Integrity....................142

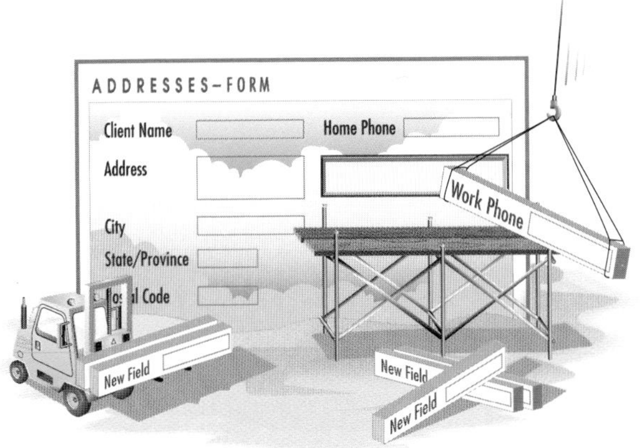

CHAPTER 8 *Create Forms*

Create a Form Using an AutoForm....................146

Change View of Form....................148

Move Through Records....................150

Add a Record....................152

Delete a Record....................153

Edit Data....................154

Close a Form....................156

Open a Form....................157

Rename a Form....................158

Delete a Form....................159

Create a Form Using the Form Wizard....................160

CHAPTER 9 *Design Forms*

Move a Control....................170

Resize a Control....................171

Delete a Control....................172

Add a Field....................173

Change Format of Field....................174

Change Control Color....................175

Add a Label....................176

Change Label Text....................177

Change Fonts....................178

Change Size of Form....................180

Select an AutoFormat....................181

Add a Picture....................182

CHAPTER 10 *Find Data*

Find Data....................186

Replace Data....................188

Sort Records....................190

Filter by Selection....................192

Filter by Exclusion....................194

Filter by Form....................196

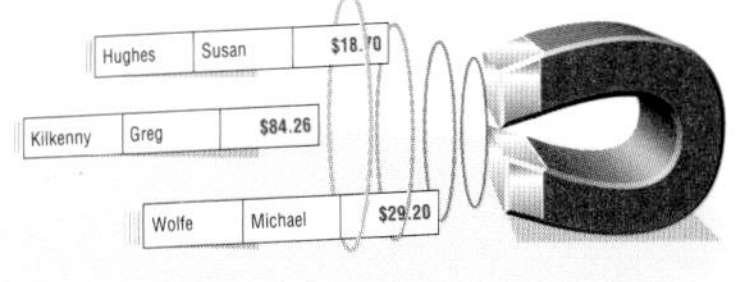

TABLE OF CONTENTS

CHAPTER *11* *Create Queries*

Create a Query 202

Change View of Query 206

Sort the Records 208

Set Criteria 209

Examples of Criteria 210

Delete a Field 212

Hide a Field 213

Rearrange Fields 214

Clear the Grid 215

Select All Fields 216

Close a Query 218

Open a Query 219

Rename a Query 220

Delete a Query 221

Using the Simple Query Wizard 222

CHAPTER 12 Advanced Queries

Display Top or Bottom Values 230
Perform Calculations 232
Change Format of Calculated Field 234
Using Parameters 236
Change the Join Type 238
Using Multiple Criteria 240
Summarize Data 244
Find Unmatched Records 250

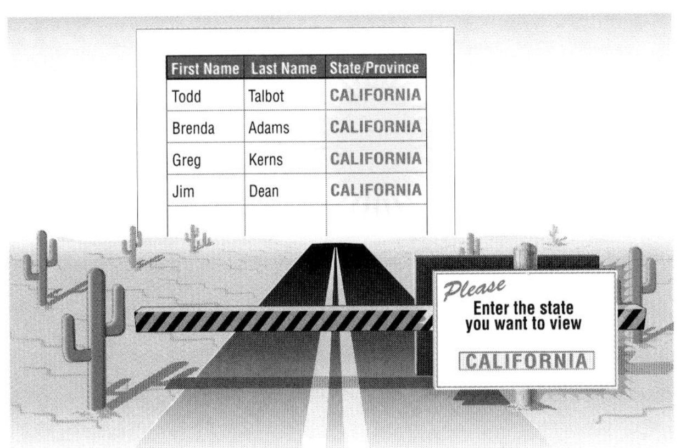

CHAPTER 13 Create Reports

Create a Report Using an AutoReport 256
Change View of Report 260
Close a Report 262
Open a Report 263
Rename a Report 264
Delete a Report 265
Create a Report Using the Report Wizard 266

CHAPTER 14 Access and the Internet

Display the Web Toolbar 276
Display the Start or Search Page 277
Insert a Hyperlink 278
Move Between Documents 282
Refresh a Document 283
Open a Document 284
Stop the Connection 285
Add a Database to Favorites 286
Publish Your Database 288

REPORTS
QUERIES
FORMS
PUPPY MEAL
Nutritious Food fo
PUPPY MEAL
Nutritious Food for Pup
BULK PETS Inc.
Proud Suppliers of Quality Pet Food
ORDERS Table
Order ID
Company Name
Product
Quantity
Unit Price
1 Pet Superstore
2 Petterson Inc.
3 Martin Vet Supplies
4 Greg's Pet Store
5 Pet Superstore
6 Feline Foods Inc.
7 Weasels R Us
8 Purrrfect Portions
9 Doggone Yummy Inc.
10 Jim's Pets
11 Allen's Dog Kennel
12 B&T Food Suppliers
13 Pet Superstore
14 Kitty-Mart
15 Canine Nutrition Inc.
Vitamins
Bulk Dry Food
Diet Dog Food
5-Variety Biscuits
Canned Dog Food
Dry Cat Food
Ferret Pellets
Dry Cat Food
Steak-flavored Bones
Hamster Treats
Puppy Kibble
Gerbil Mix
Parrot Food
Dry Cat Food
Rawhide Chew Sticks
12
15
30
50
24
40
30
24
40
30
20
35
25
35
15
$20.00
$18.00
$10.00
$3.50
$3.00
$4.00
$6.50
$4.00
$1.25
$5.00
$8.50
$4.50
$17.00
$4.00
$2.00
BULK PETS Inc.
Proud Suppliers of Quality Pet Food
BILL TO:
Martin Vet Supplies
68 Cracker Ave.
San Francisco
CA 94110
ORDER #
12340
ORDER DATE
April 4 1997
P.O. NUMB
34499
PRODUCT
Diet Dog Food
BULK PETS Inc.
Proud Suppliers of Quality Pet Food
Susan Hughes
Sales Manager
(555) 555-3234
1820 Unit B, Daphne Crescent, Los Angeles, CA 90030
1820

CHAPTER 1

Getting Started

Do you want to learn how to use Microsoft Access 97? This chapter will help you get started.

Introduction....................4

Parts of a Database....................6

Planning a Database....................8

Using the Mouse....................10

Start Access....................11

INTRODUCTION

Microsoft Access is a database program that allows you to store and manage large collections of information. Access provides you with all the tools you need to create an efficient and effective database.

WHY WOULD I USE A DATABASE?

Personal Use

Many people use a database to store personal information such as addresses, music and video collections, recipes or a wine list. Using a database to store and organize information is much more efficient than using sheets of paper or index cards.

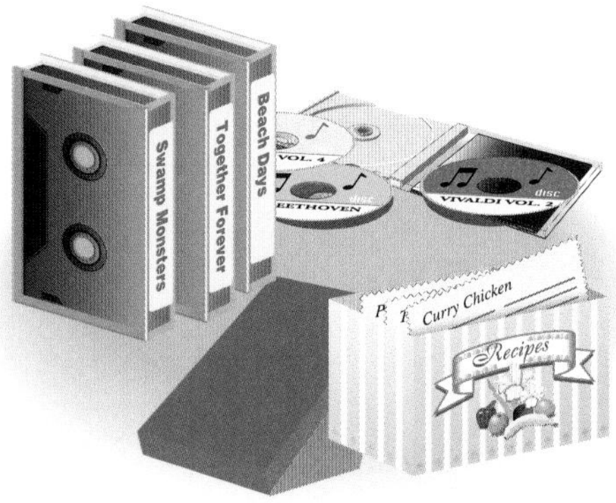

Business Use

Companies use a database to store information such as mailing lists, billing information, client orders, expenses, inventory and payroll. Access helps companies effectively manage information that is constantly being reviewed and updated.

DATABASE APPLICATIONS

Store Information

A database stores and manages a collection of information related to a particular subject or purpose.

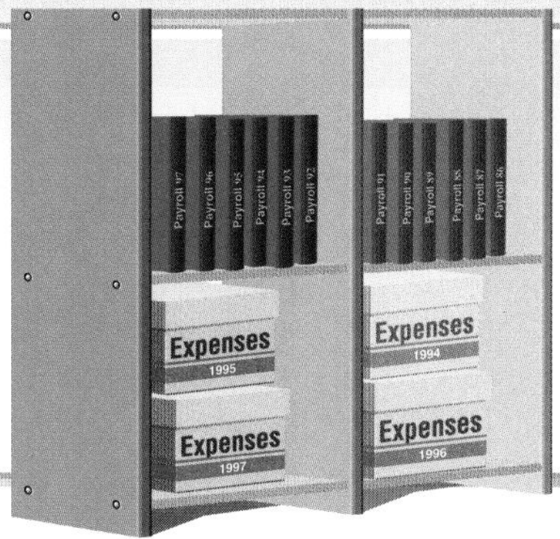

You can efficiently and accurately add, update, view and organize the information stored in a database.

Find Information

You can instantly locate information of interest in a database. For example, you can find all clients with the last name Smith.

You can also perform more advanced searches, such as finding all clients who live in California and who purchased more than $100 of supplies last year.

Analyze and Print Information

You can perform calculations on the information in a database to help you make quick, accurate and informed decisions.

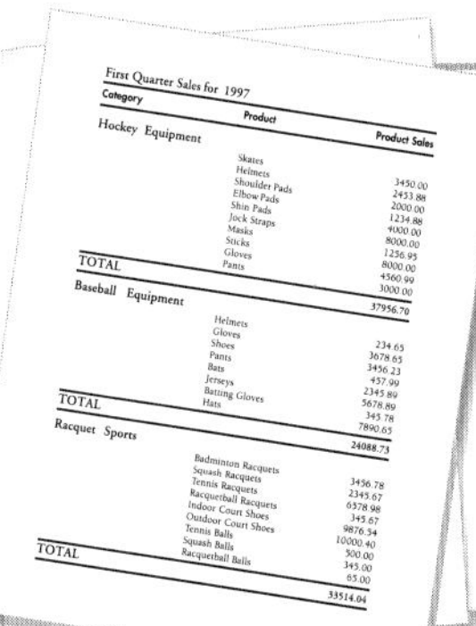

You can neatly present the information in professionally designed reports.

PARTS OF A DATABASE

A database is a collection of information related to a particular topic. Databases consist of tables, forms, queries and reports.

A database is like a filing cabinet full of folders and papers.

Tables

A table is a collection of information about a specific topic, such as a mailing list. You can have one or more tables in a database.

Address ID	First Name	Last Name	Address	City	State/Province	Postal Code
1	Jim	Schmith	258 Linton Ave.	New York	NY	10010
2	Brenda	Petterson	50 Tree Lane	Boston	MA	02117
3	Todd	Talbot	68 Cracker Ave.	San Francisco	CA	94110
4	Chuck	Dean	47 Crosby Ave.	Las Vegas	NV	89116
5	Melanie	Robinson	26 Arnold Cres.	Jacksonville	FL	32256
6	Susan	Hughes	401 Idon Dr.	Nashville	TN	37243
7	Allen	Toppins	10 Heldon St.	Atlanta	GA	30375
8	Greg	Kilkenny	36 Buzzard St.	Boston	MA	02118
9	Jason	Marcuson	15 Bizzo Pl.	New York	NY	10020
10	Jim	Martin	890 Apple St.	San Diego	CA	92121

A table consists of fields and records.

Field

A field is a specific category of information in a table. For example, a field can contain the first names of all your clients.

Record

A record is a collection of information about one person, place or thing in a table. For example, a record can contain the name and address of one client.

Forms

Forms provide a quick way to view, enter and change information in a database by presenting information in an easy-to-use format.

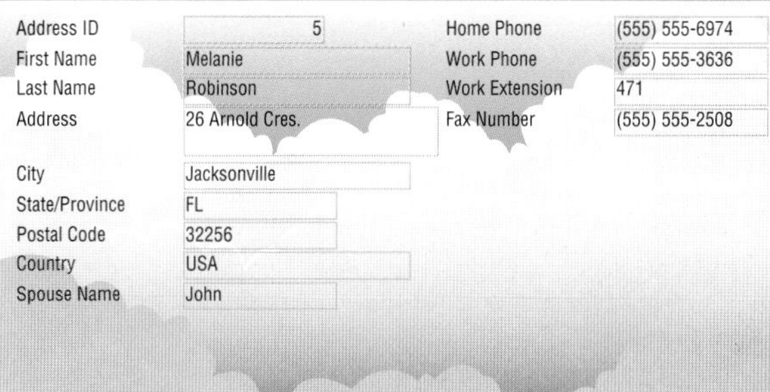

A form displays boxes that clearly show you where to enter information and allows you to focus on one record at a time.

Queries

When you create a query, you ask a database to find information that meets the criteria, or conditions, you specify. Queries let you quickly gather information of interest.

Address ID	First Name	Last Name
10	Jim	Martin
11	Kathleen	Matthews
3	Todd	Talbot
13	John	Thyfault
14	Michael	Wolfe

For example, you can create a query to find all clients who live in California.

Reports

Reports allow you to create professionally designed, printed copies of information in your database.

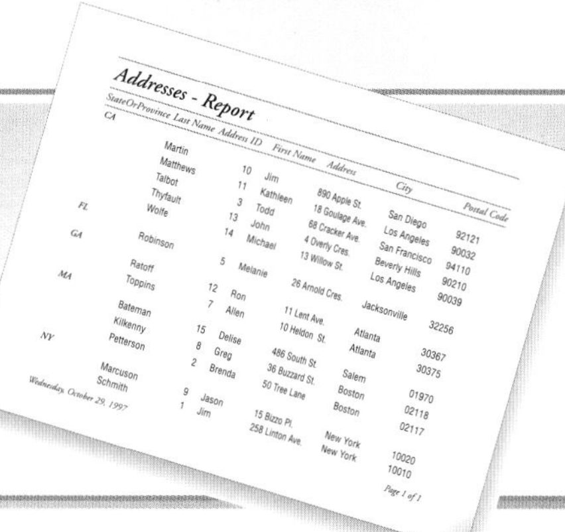

You can perform calculations, such as averages or totals, in a report to summarize information.

PLANNING A DATABASE

Make sure you take time to properly design your database. A good database design ensures that you will be able to perform tasks efficiently and accurately.

Determine the Purpose of the Database

Decide what you want the database to do and how you plan to use the information. Talk to the people who will use the database to determine the questions the database will need to answer. Consider what information you need to make the database complete.

Determine the Tables You Need

Gather all the information you want to store in the database and then divide the information into separate tables. A table should contain information for only one subject.

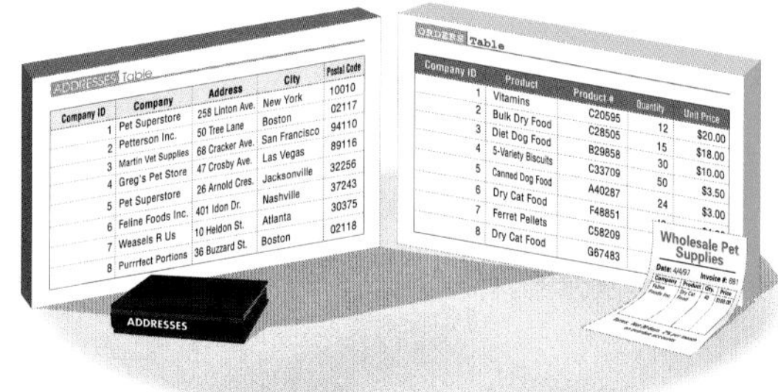

Information should not appear in more than one table in your database. This allows you to work more efficiently and reduces errors since you only need to update information in one place.

Determine the Fields You Need

Determine which fields you need to work with the table effectively.

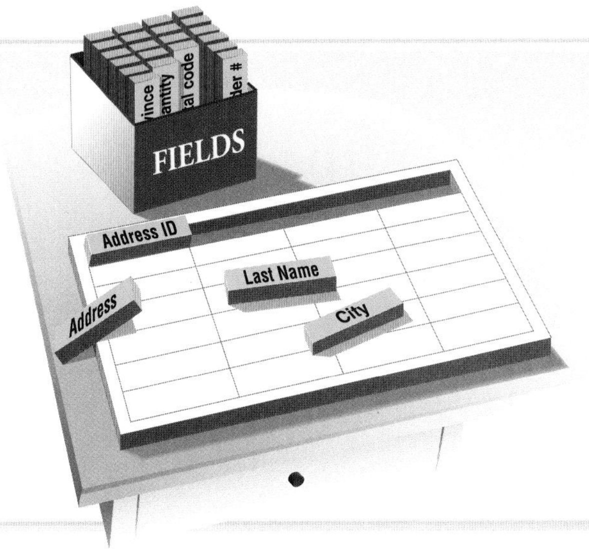

- Each field should relate directly to the subject of the table.
- Make sure you break information down into its smallest parts. For example, break down the Name field into two fields called First Name and Last Name.
- Do not include a field containing data you calculate from other fields.

Determine the Primary Key

A primary key is one or more fields that uniquely identifies each record in a table.

Social Security ID	First Name	Last Name	Address	City	State/Province	Postal Code
11-1111	Jim	Schmith	258 Linton Ave.	New York	NY	10010
2-22-2222	Brenda	Petterson	50 Tree Lane	Boston	MA	02117
33-33-3333	Todd	Talbot	68 Cracker Ave.	San Francisco	CA	94110
444-44-4444	Chuck	Dean	47 Crosby Ave.	Las Vegas	NV	89116
600-60-6000	Melanie	Robinson	26 Arnold Cres.	Jacksonville	FL	32256
777-77-7777	Susan	Hughes	401 Idon Dr.	Nashville	TN	37243
888-88-8888	Allen	Toppins	10 Heldon St.	Atlanta	GA	30375
999-99-9999	Greg	Kilkenny	36 Buzzard St.	Boston	MA	02118
000-00-0000	Jason	Marcuson	15 Bizzo Pl.	New York	NY	10020
000-11-2222	Jim	Martin	890 Apple St.	San Diego	CA	92121

For example, the primary key for a table of employees could be the social security number for each employee.

Determine the Relationships Between Tables

A relationship tells Access how to bring together related information stored in separate tables.

ADDRESSES Table

Company ID	Company Name	Address	City	Postal Code
1	Pet Superstore	258 Linton Ave.	New York	10010
2	Petterson Inc.	50 Tree Lane	Boston	02117
3	Martin Vet Supplies	68 Cracker Ave.	San Francisco	94110
4	Greg's Pet Store	47 Crosby Ave.	Las Vegas	89116
5	Pet Superstore	26 Arnold Cres.	Jacksonville	32256
6	ine Foods Inc.	401 Idon Dr.	Nashville	37243
7	easels R Us	10 Heldon St.	Atlanta	30375
8	urrrfect Portions	36 Buzzard St.	Boston	02118

ORDERS Table

Company ID	Product	Product Number	Quantity	Unit Price
1	Vitamins	C20595	2	$20.00
2	Bulk Dry Food	C28505	2	$18.00
3	Diet Dog Food	B29858	1	$10.00
4	5-Variety Biscuits	C33709	3	$3.50
5	nned Dog Food	A40287	7	$3.00
6	ry Cat Food	F48851	2	$4.00
7	erret Pellets	C58209	1	$6.50
8	Dry Cat Food	G67483	3	$4.00

You can use the primary key to match the records in one table with the records in another table to form a relationship between the tables.

The mouse is a hand-held device that lets you select and move items on your screen.

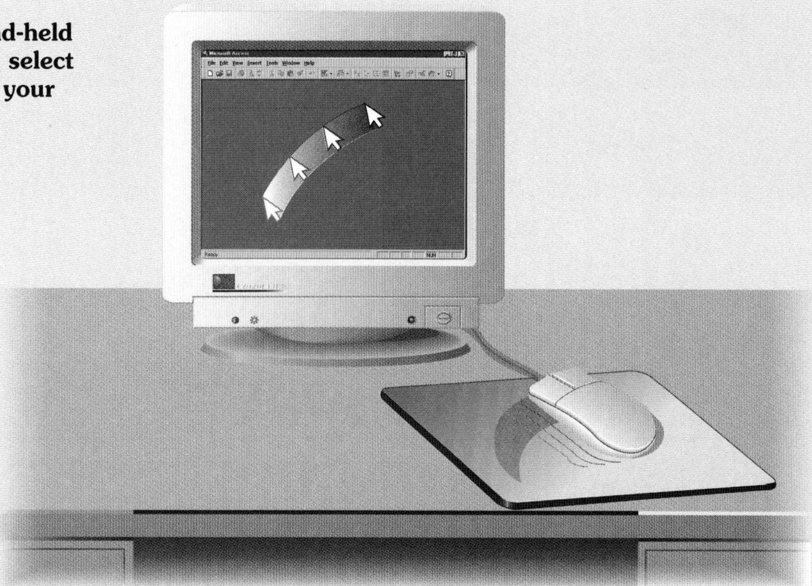

When you move the mouse on your desk, the mouse pointer on your screen moves in the same direction. The mouse pointer assumes different shapes (example: ↖, I) depending on its location on your screen and the task you are performing.

Resting your hand on the mouse, use your thumb and two rightmost fingers to move the mouse on your desk. Use your two remaining fingers to press the mouse buttons.

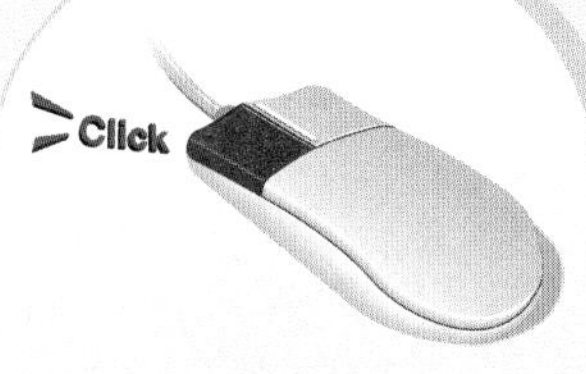

Click
Press and release the left mouse button.

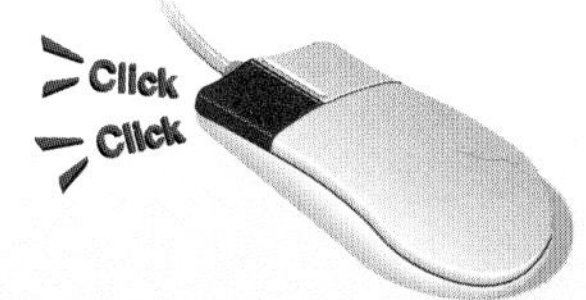

Double-click
Quickly press and release the left mouse button twice.

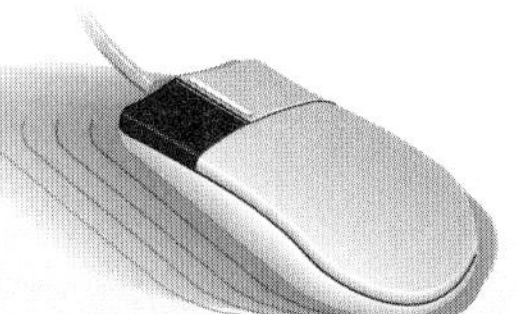

Drag
When the mouse pointer is over an object on your screen, press and hold down the left mouse button. Still holding down the mouse button, move the mouse to where you want to place the object and then release the mouse button.

START ACCESS

You can start Access to create a new database or work with a database you previously created.

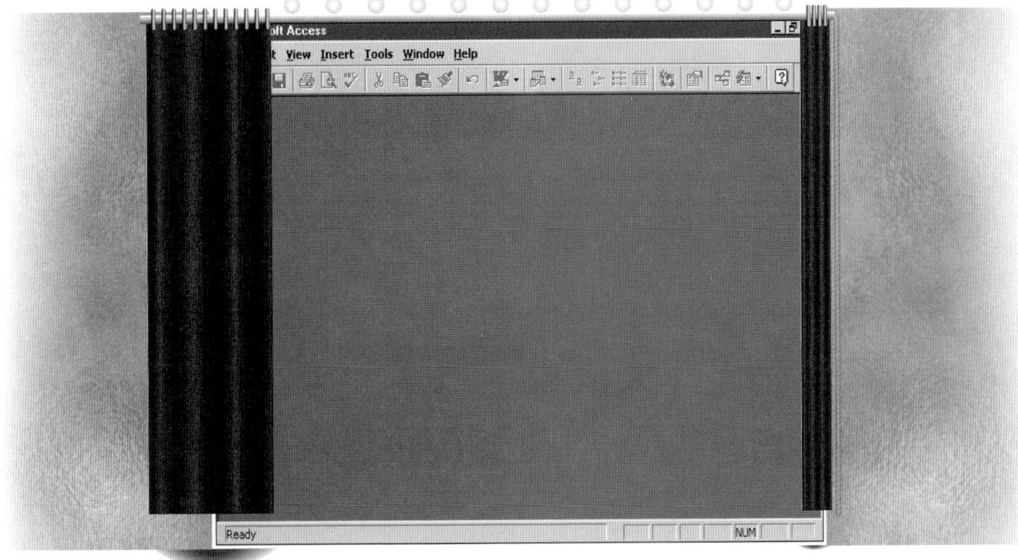

START ACCESS

1 Click **Start**.

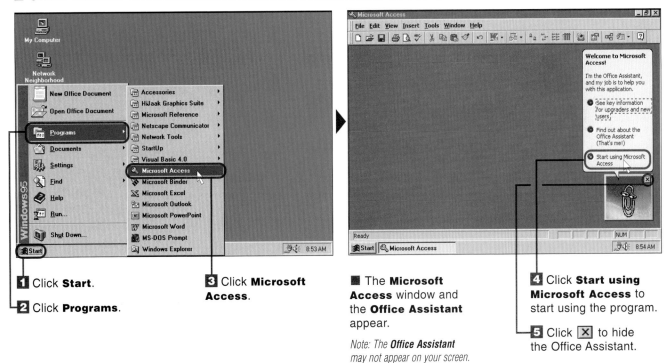

2 Click **Programs**.

3 Click **Microsoft Access**.

■ The **Microsoft Access** window and the **Office Assistant** appear.

*Note: The **Office Assistant** may not appear on your screen.*

4 Click **Start using Microsoft Access** to start using the program.

5 Click ☒ to hide the Office Assistant.

Company Information
Invoices
Customers
Shipping
Products
Payments
Customers
Products
Shipping
Payments
Clients
Employees
Company Information
Invoices

CHAPTER 2

Create a Database

Are you ready to start your database? This chapter will teach you how to create a database, switch between windows, and much more.

Create a Database Using the Wizard................14

Minimize a Window 20

Maximize a Window 21

Switch Between Windows.............................22

Close a Window 23

Using the Database Window 24

Display or Hide a Toolbar 26

Exit Access 27

Create a Blank Database 28

Open a Database 30

Getting Help 32

CREATE A DATABASE USING THE WIZARD

The Database Wizard lets you create a database quickly and efficiently. The wizard saves you time by providing ready-to-use tables, queries, forms and reports.

You can use the Database Wizard to quickly create databases for many types of information, such as addresses, expenses, music collections, recipes and wine lists.

CREATE A DATABASE USING THE WIZARD

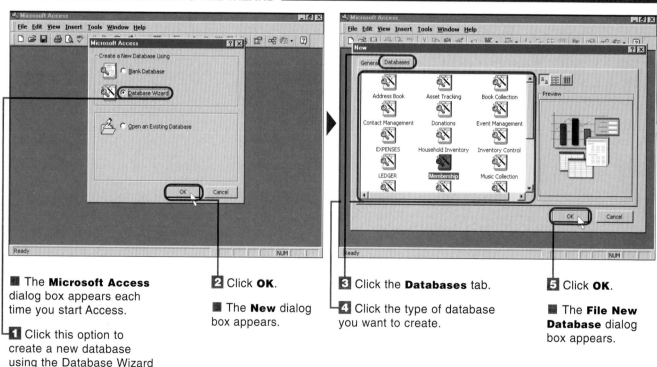

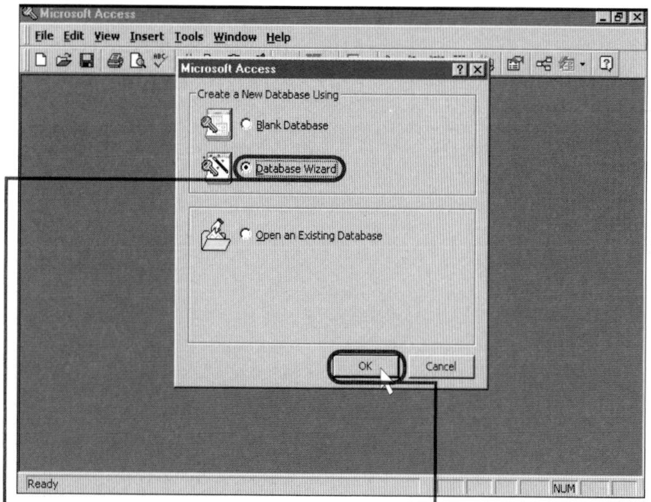

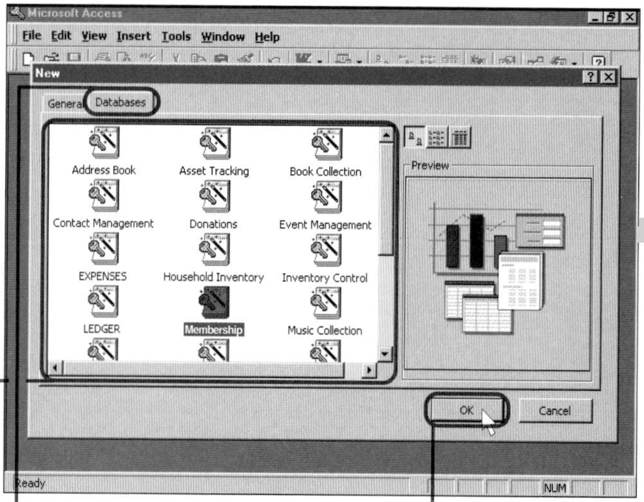

■ The **Microsoft Access** dialog box appears each time you start Access.

1 Click this option to create a new database using the Database Wizard (○ changes to ◉).

2 Click **OK**.

■ The **New** dialog box appears.

3 Click the **Databases** tab.

4 Click the type of database you want to create.

5 Click **OK**.

■ The **File New Database** dialog box appears.

?

Is there another way to start the Database Wizard?

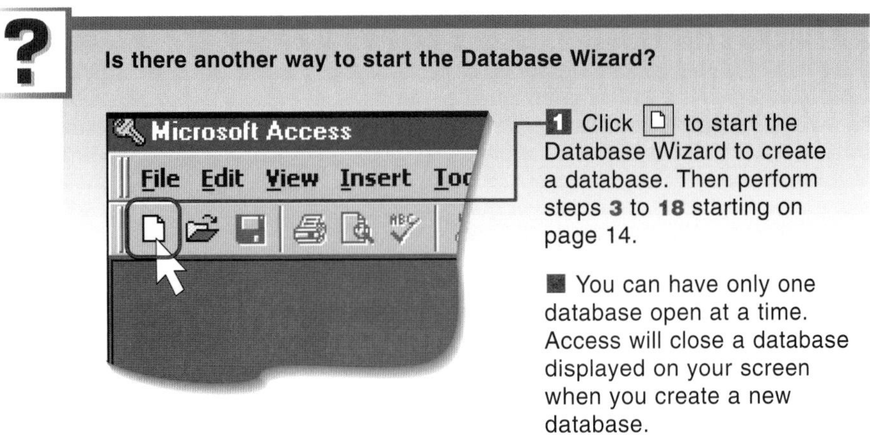

1 Click [new] to start the Database Wizard to create a database. Then perform steps **3** to **18** starting on page 14.

■ You can have only one database open at a time. Access will close a database displayed on your screen when you create a new database.

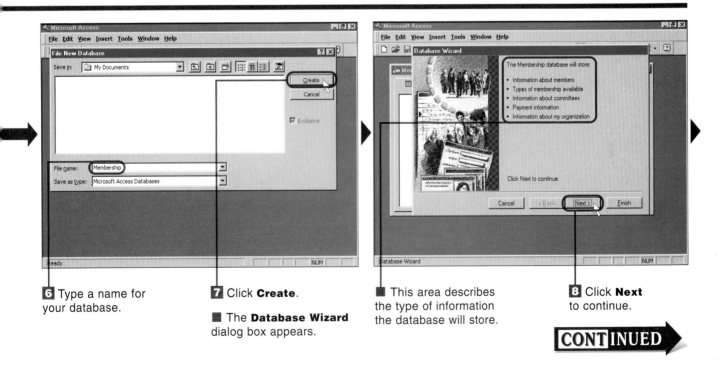

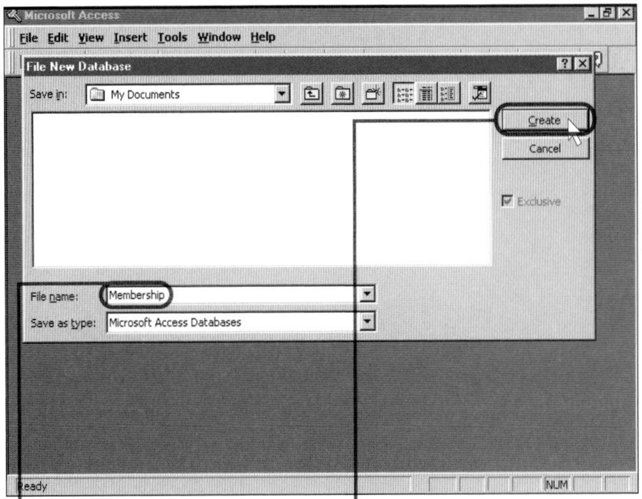

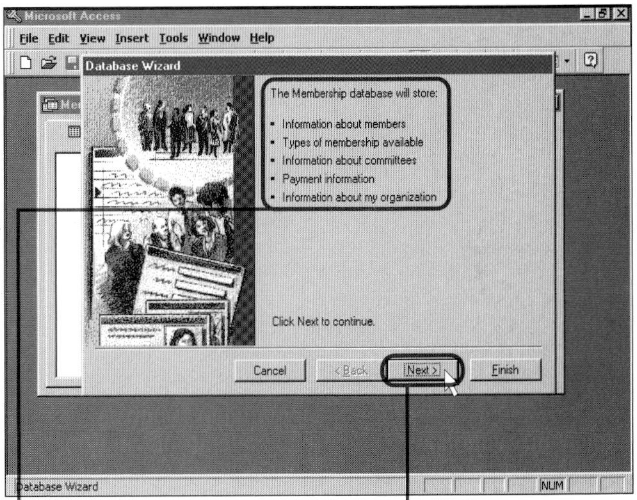

6 Type a name for your database.

7 Click **Create**.

■ The **Database Wizard** dialog box appears.

■ This area describes the type of information the database will store.

8 Click **Next** to continue.

CONTINUED

When using the Database Wizard to create a database, the wizard displays the fields that will be included in each table. You can choose to include other optional fields.

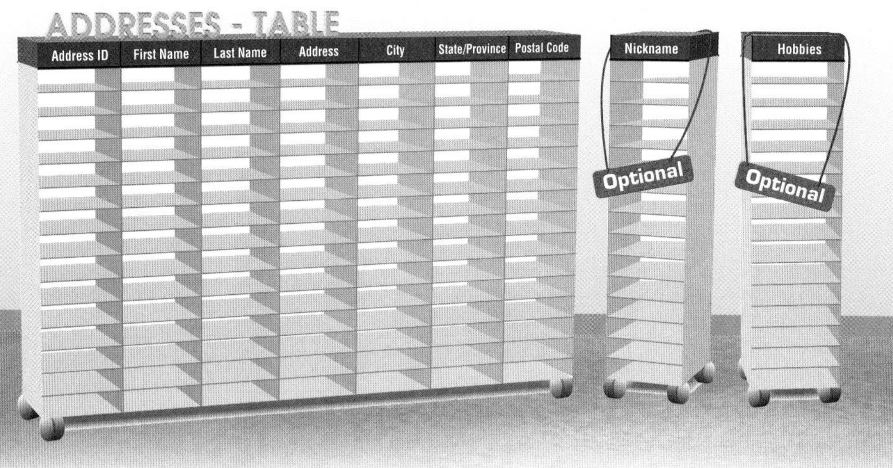

CREATE A DATABASE USING THE WIZARD (CONTINUED)

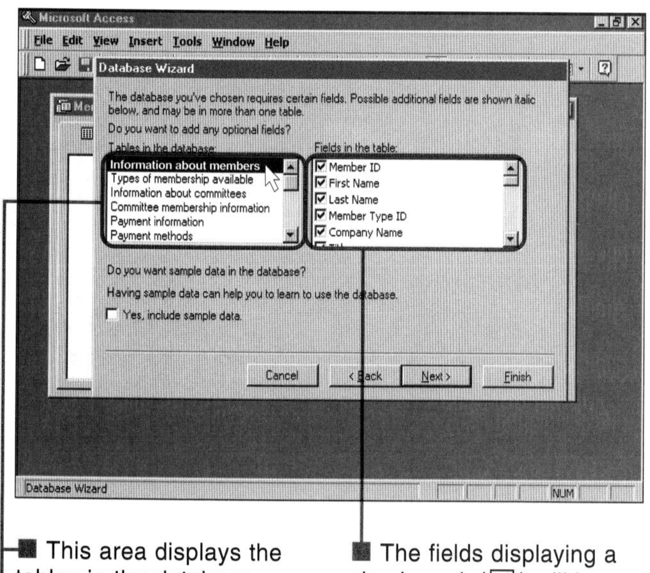

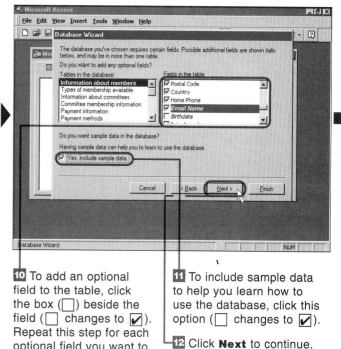

■ This area displays the tables in the database.

9 To display the fields that will be included in a table, click the table.

■ The fields displaying a check mark (☑) will be included in the table. The other fields are optional.

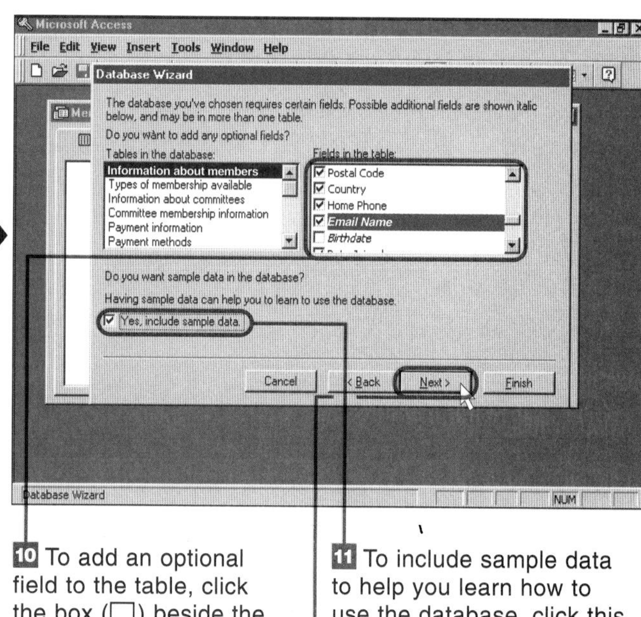

10 To add an optional field to the table, click the box (☐) beside the field (☐ changes to ☑). Repeat this step for each optional field you want to add.

11 To include sample data to help you learn how to use the database, click this option (☐ changes to ☑).

12 Click **Next** to continue.

What styles does the wizard offer for screen displays and printed reports?

Here are some of the styles the wizard offers:

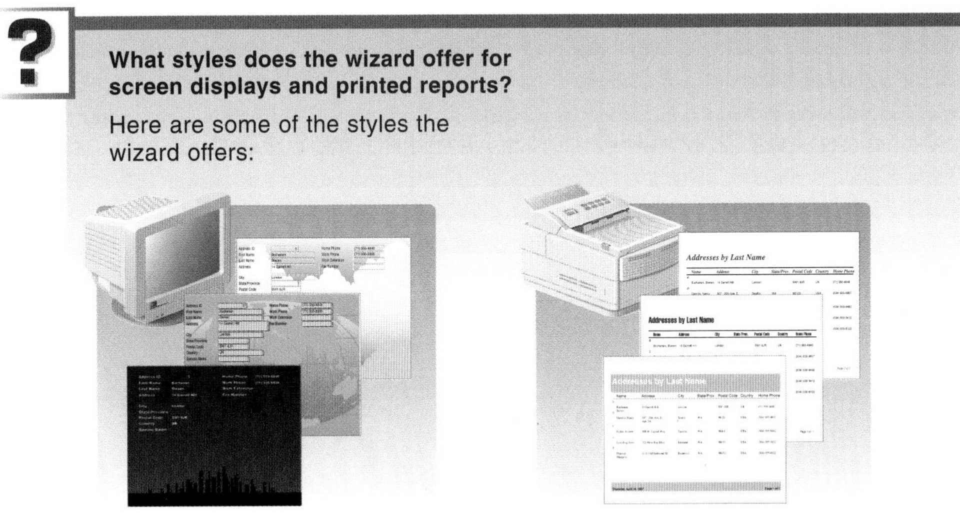

Screen Displays

Printed Reports

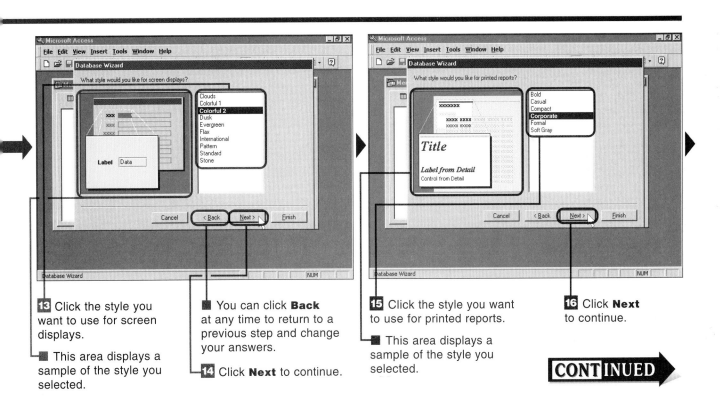

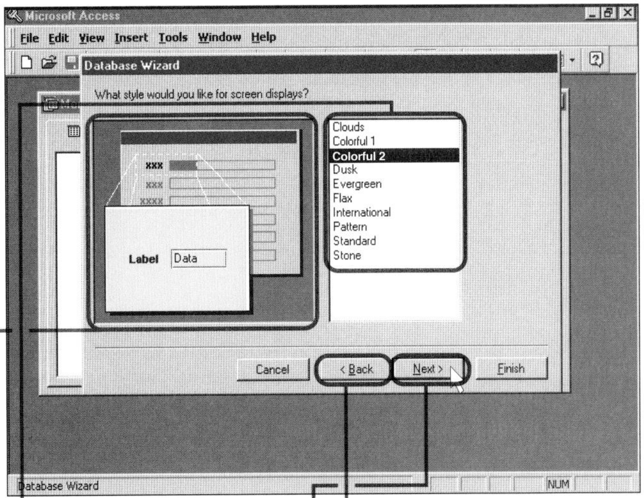

13 Click the style you want to use for screen displays.

■ This area displays a sample of the style you selected.

■ You can click **Back** at any time to return to a previous step and change your answers.

14 Click **Next** to continue.

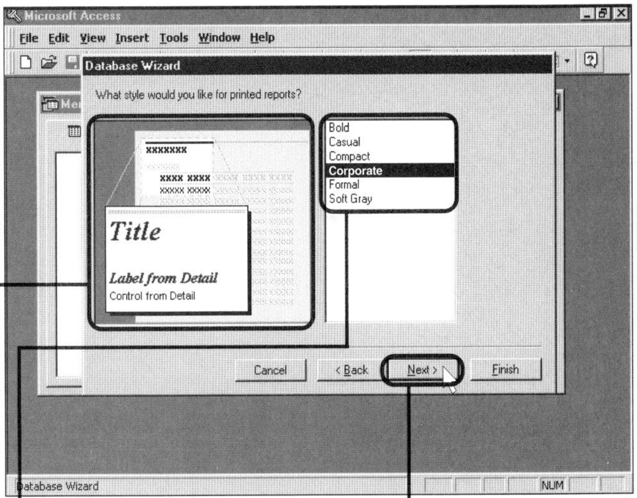

15 Click the style you want to use for printed reports.

■ This area displays a sample of the style you selected.

16 Click **Next** to continue.

CONTINUED

When you finish creating a database, Access displays a switchboard to help you perform common tasks in the database.

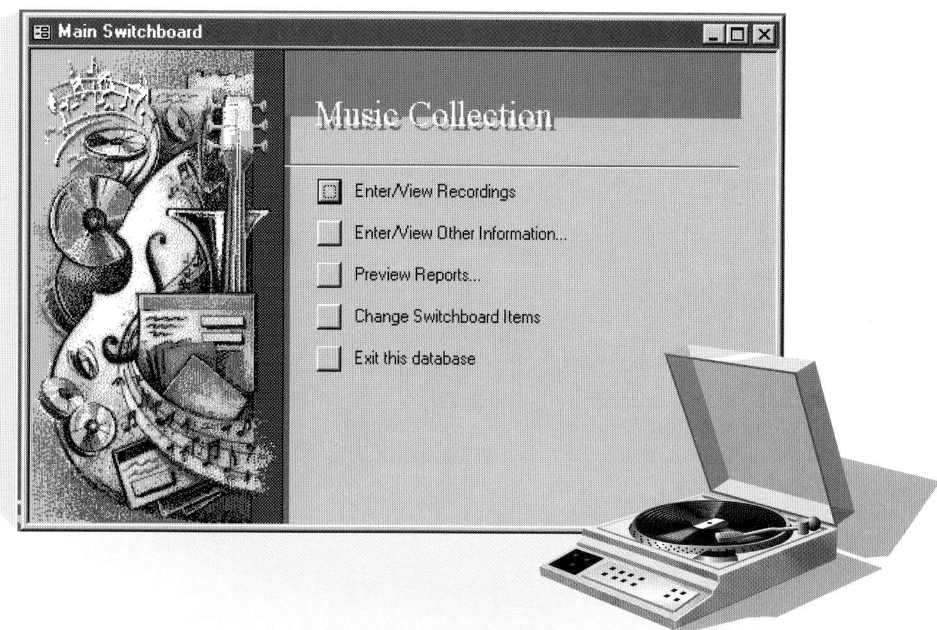

CREATE A DATABASE USING THE WIZARD (CONTINUED)

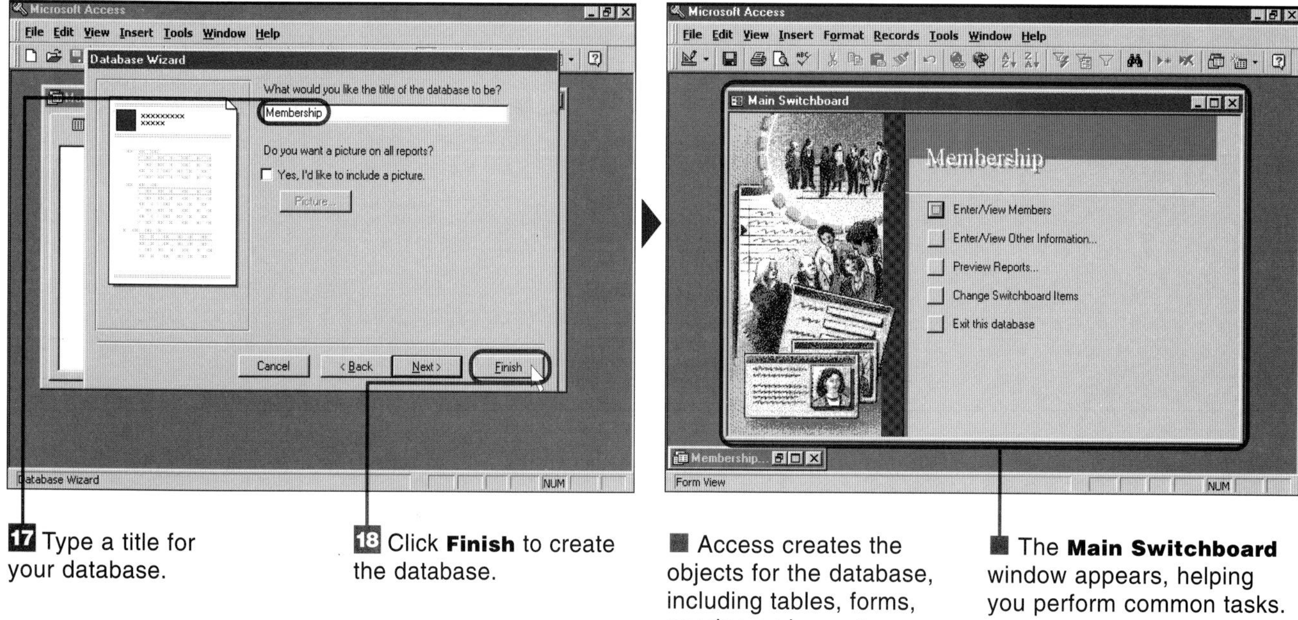

17 Type a title for your database.

18 Click **Finish** to create the database.

■ Access creates the objects for the database, including tables, forms, queries and reports.

■ The **Main Switchboard** window appears, helping you perform common tasks.

?

How else can I work with objects such as tables, forms, queries and reports in my database?

Instead of using the switchboard, you can use the Database window to view and work with all the objects in your database. For information on using the Database window, refer to page 24.

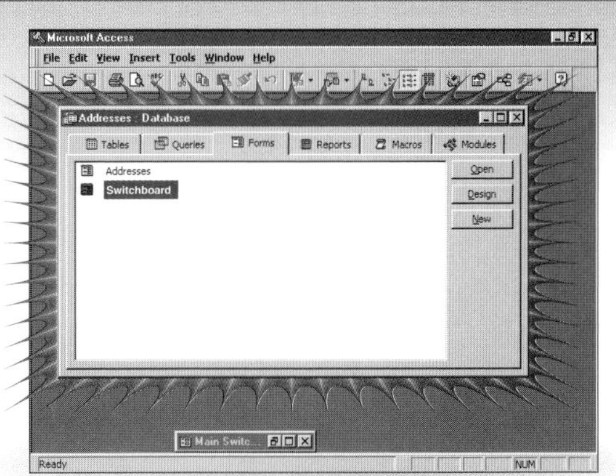

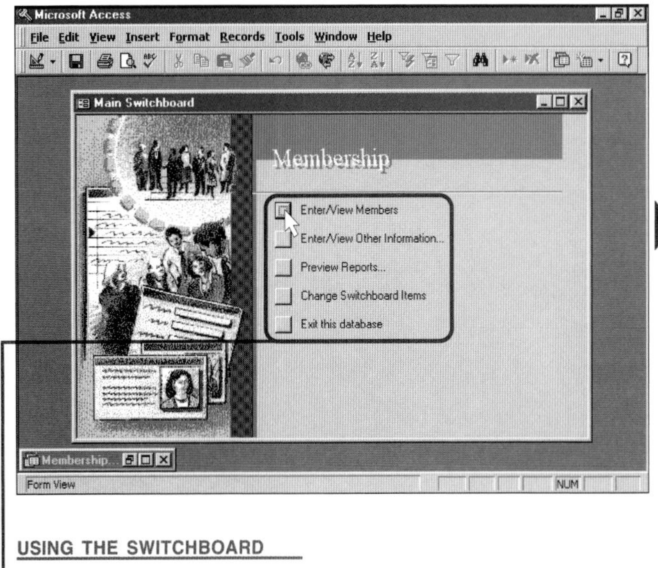

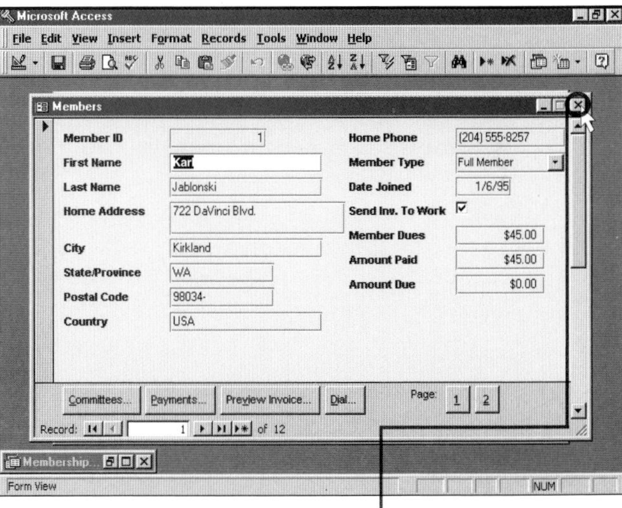

USING THE SWITCHBOARD

1 To use the switchboard to perform a task, click the task you want to perform.

■ The object in the database that allows you to perform the task appears.

■ To close the object and return to the switchboard, click ☒.

MINIMIZE A WINDOW

If you are not using a window, you can minimize the window to temporarily remove it from your screen. You can redisplay the window at any time.

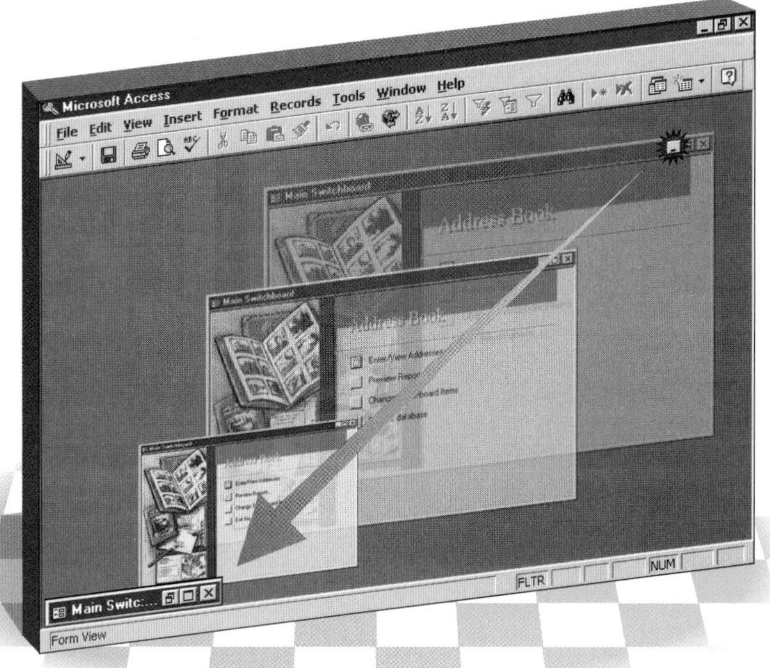

MINIMIZE A WINDOW

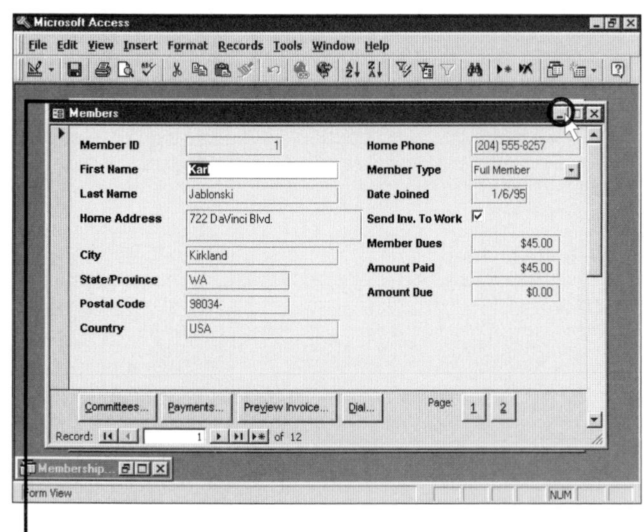

■1 Click [minimize button] in the window you want to minimize.

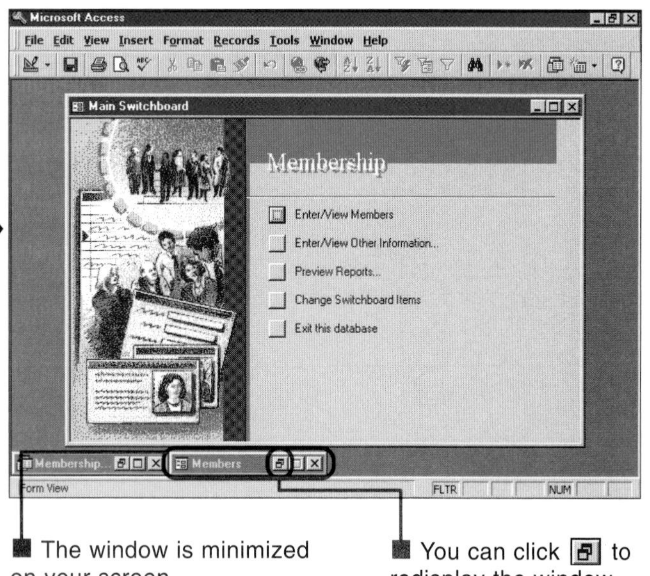

■ The window is minimized on your screen.

■ You can click [restore button] to redisplay the window.

MAXIMIZE A WINDOW

You can enlarge a window to fill your screen. This lets you view more of the contents of the window.

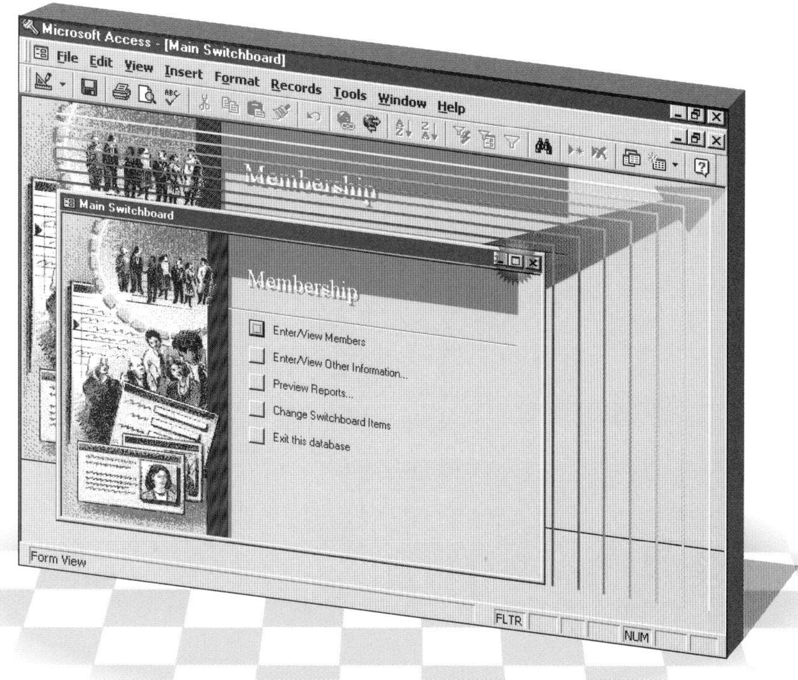

MAXIMIZE A WINDOW

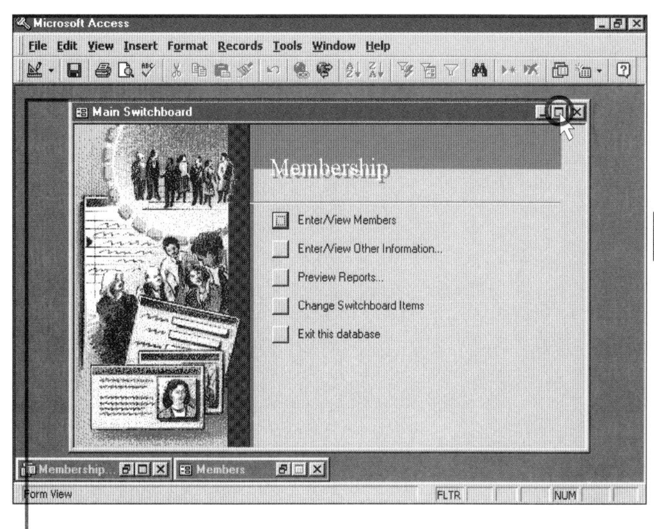

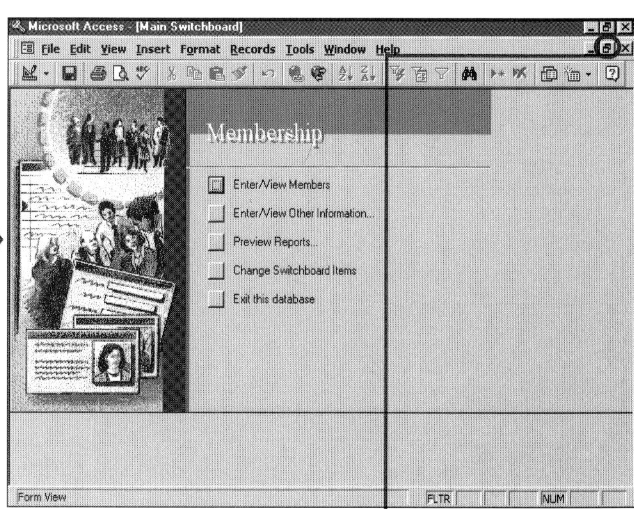

1 Click ▢ in the window you want to maximize.

■ The window fills your screen.

■ You can click ⧉ to restore the window to its previous size.

SWITCH BETWEEN WINDOWS

You can have more than one window open at a time. You can easily switch between all your open windows.

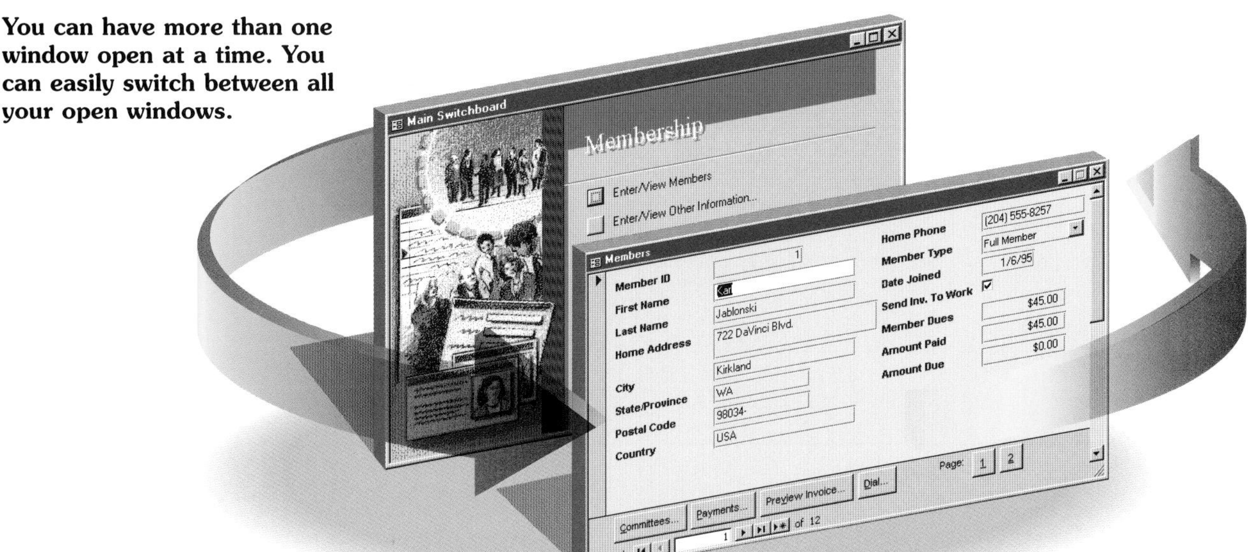

SWITCH BETWEEN WINDOWS

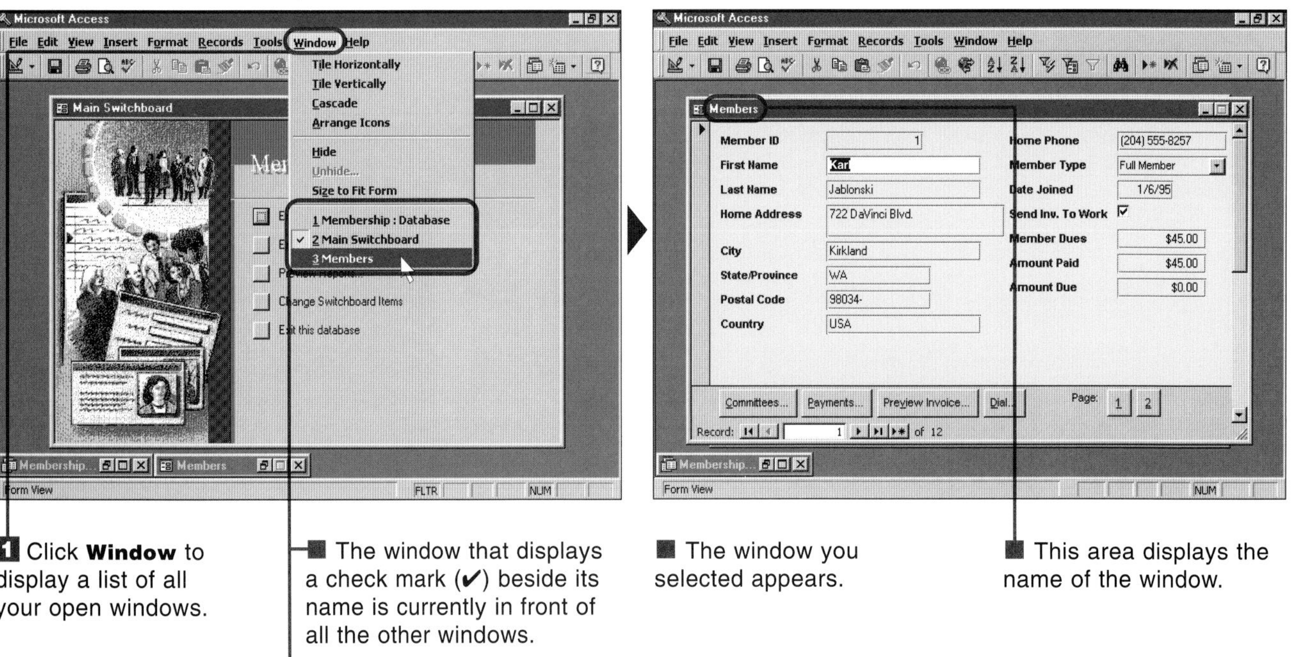

1 Click **Window** to display a list of all your open windows.

■ The window that displays a check mark (✔) beside its name is currently in front of all the other windows.

2 Click the window you want to display.

■ The window you selected appears.

■ This area displays the name of the window.

CLOSE A WINDOW

When you finish working with a window, you can close the window to remove it from your screen.

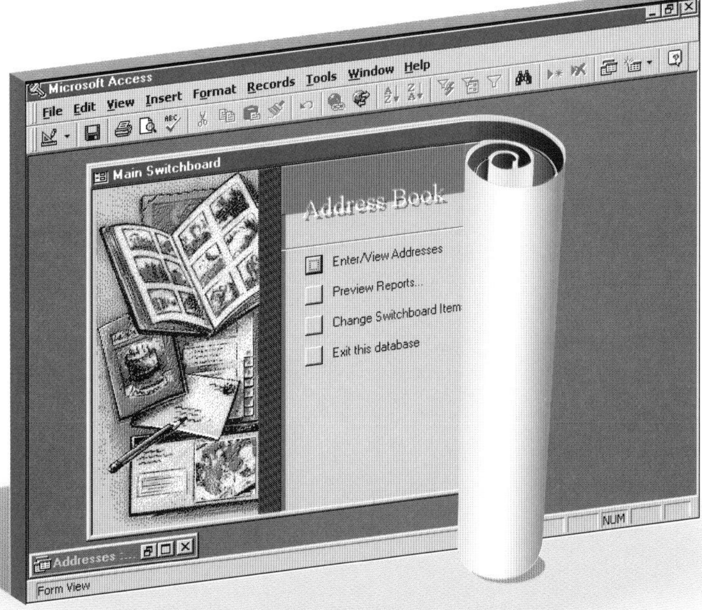

CLOSE A WINDOW

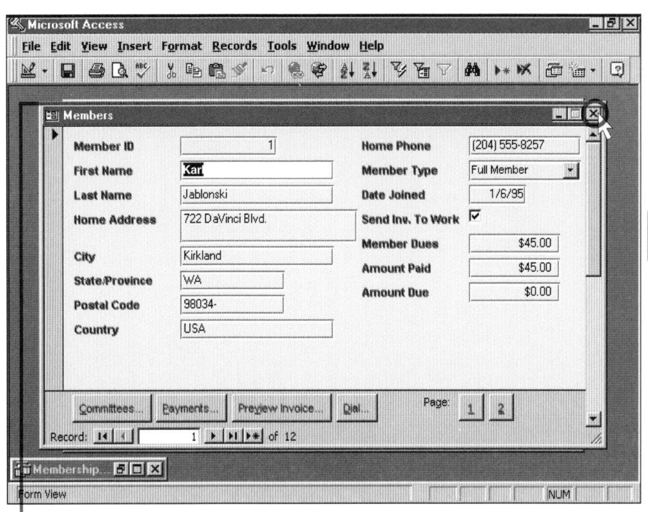

1 Click ☒ in the window you want to close.

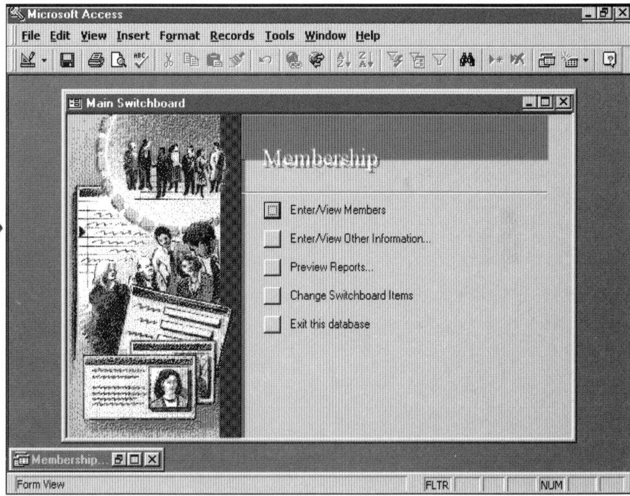

■ The window disappears from your screen.

USING THE DATABASE WINDOW

You can use the Database window to view and work with all the objects in your database, including tables, queries, forms and reports.

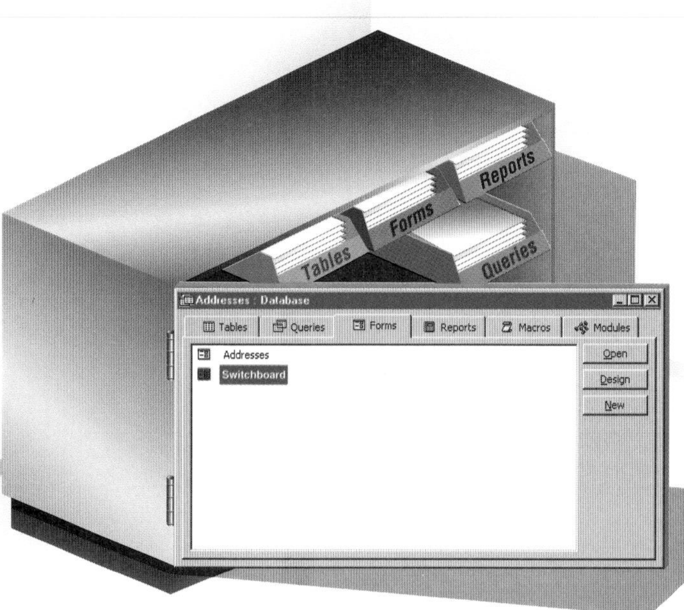

USING THE DATABASE WINDOW

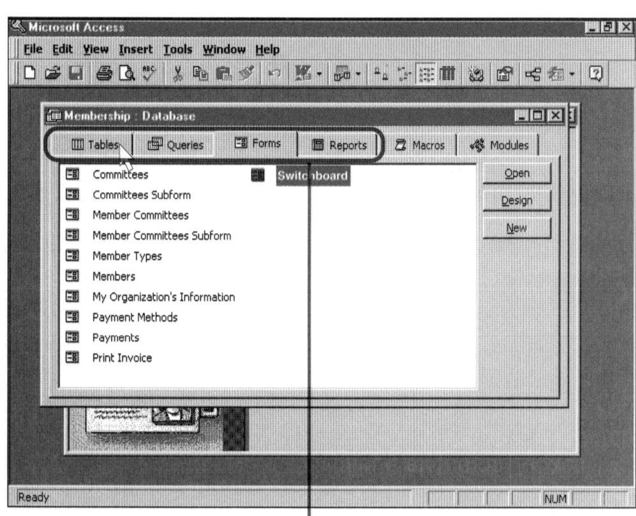

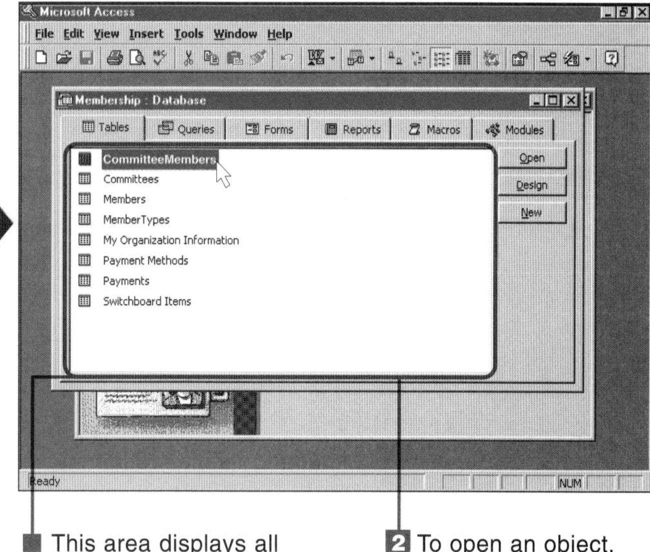

■ Each table, query, form and report in the database will appear in your Database window.

Note: If the Database window is hidden behind other windows, you can press **F11** *on your keyboard to display the window.*

■ The Database window displays a tab for each type of object in the database.

1 Click the tab for the type of object you want to view.

■ This area displays all the objects for the type you selected.

2 To open an object, double-click the object.

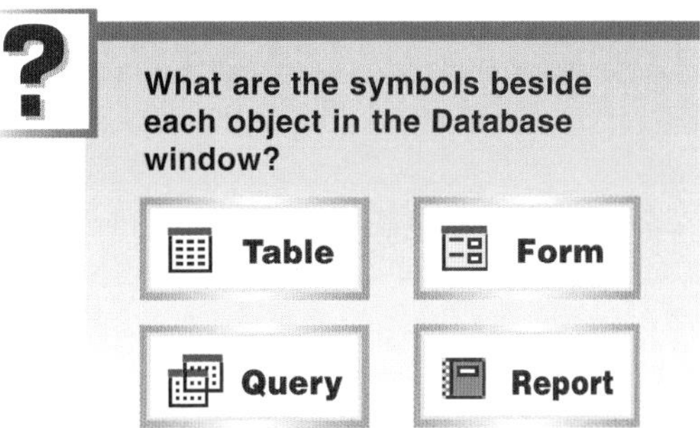

?
What are the symbols beside each object in the Database window?
Table
Form
Query
Report

The symbols beside each object in the Database window identify the type of object.

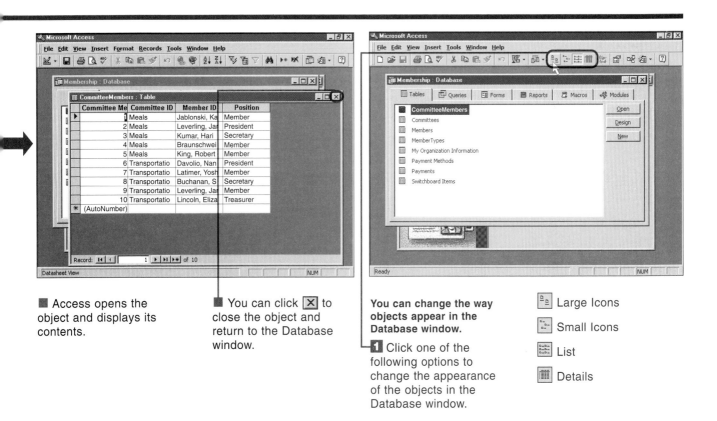

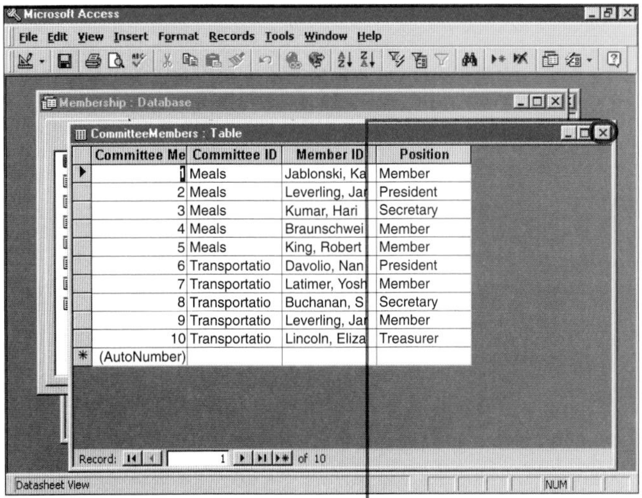

■ Access opens the object and displays its contents.

■ You can click [X] to close the object and return to the Database window.

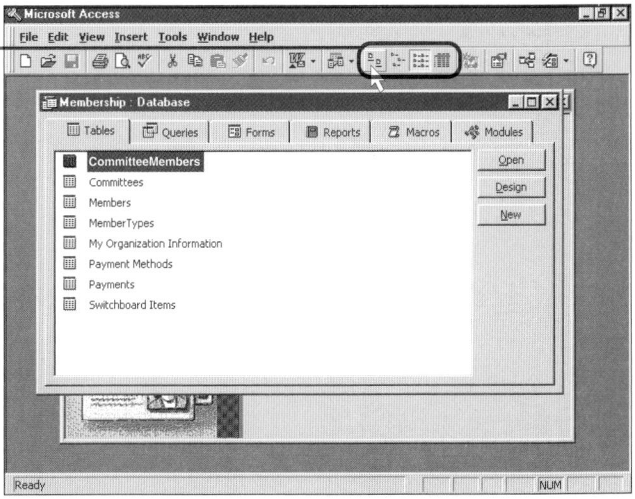

You can change the way objects appear in the Database window.

1 Click one of the following options to change the appearance of the objects in the Database window.

- Large Icons
- Small Icons
- List
- Details

DISPLAY OR HIDE A TOOLBAR

Access offers several toolbars you can display or hide at any time. Each toolbar contains buttons that help you quickly perform common tasks.

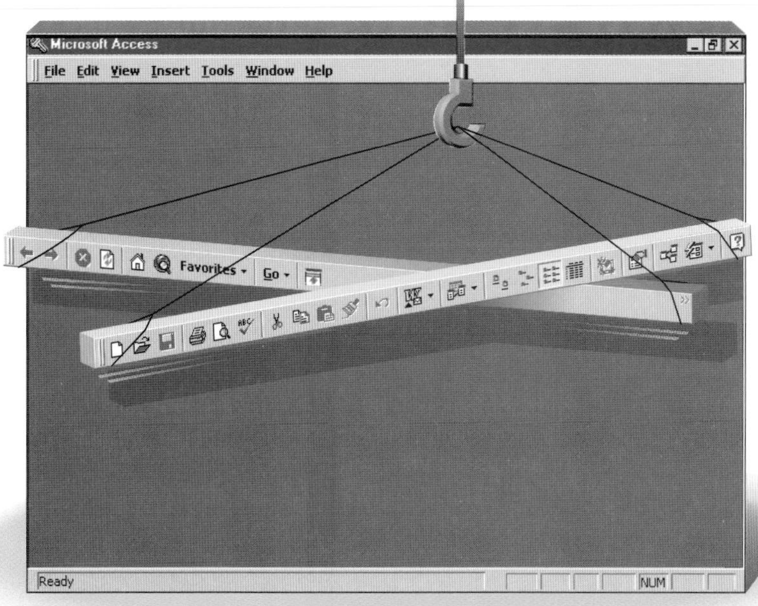

The available toolbars depend on the task you are performing.

DISPLAY OR HIDE A TOOLBAR

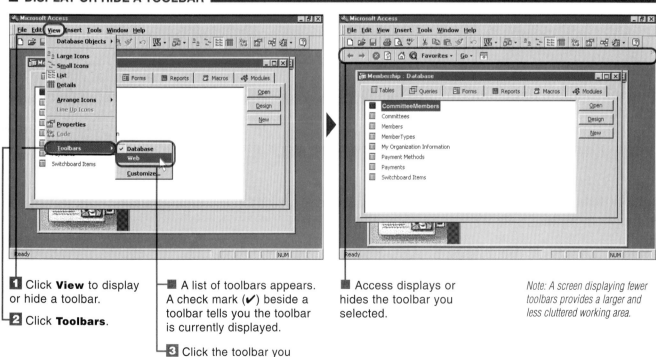

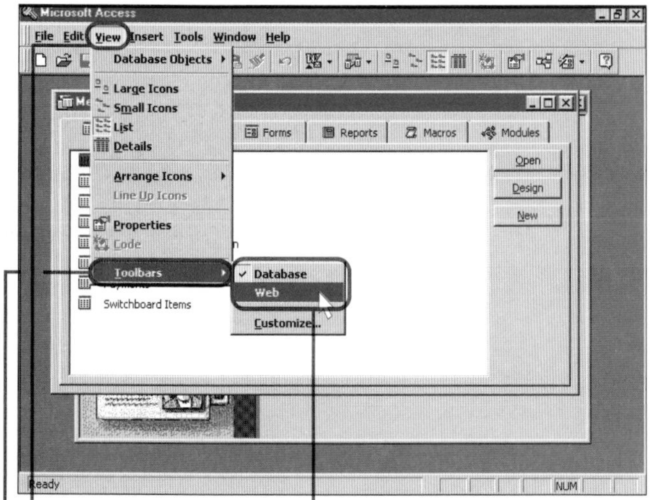

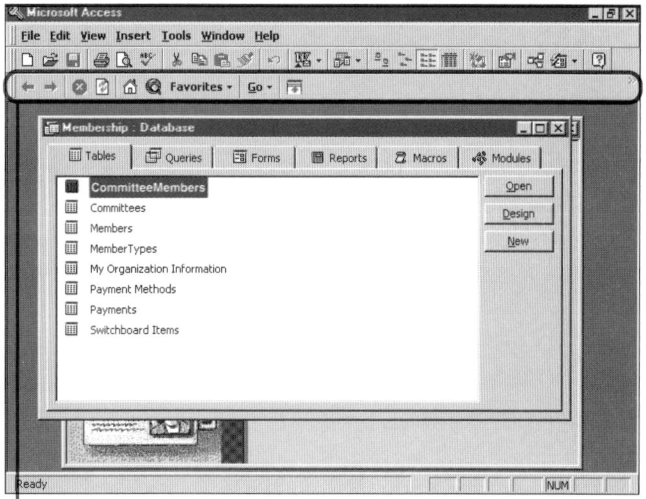

1 Click **View** to display or hide a toolbar.

2 Click **Toolbars**.

■ A list of toolbars appears. A check mark (✔) beside a toolbar tells you the toolbar is currently displayed.

3 Click the toolbar you want to display or hide.

■ Access displays or hides the toolbar you selected.

Note: A screen displaying fewer toolbars provides a larger and less cluttered working area.

EXIT ACCESS

When you finish using Access, you can exit the program.

You should exit all programs before turning off your computer.

EXIT ACCESS

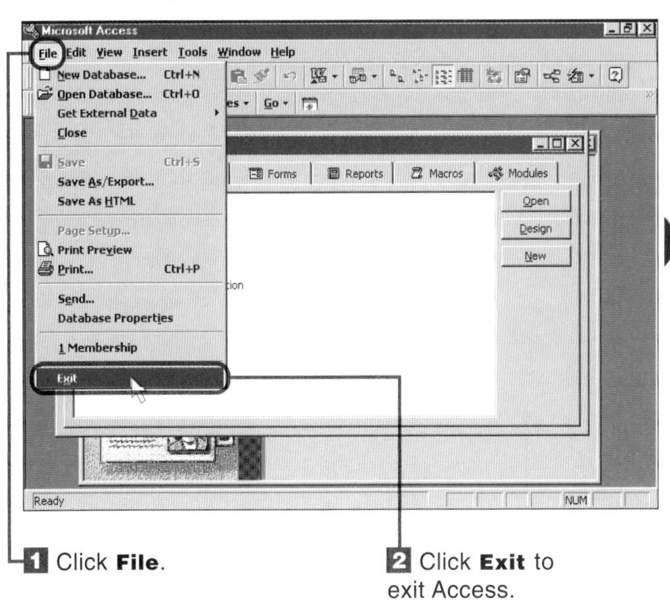

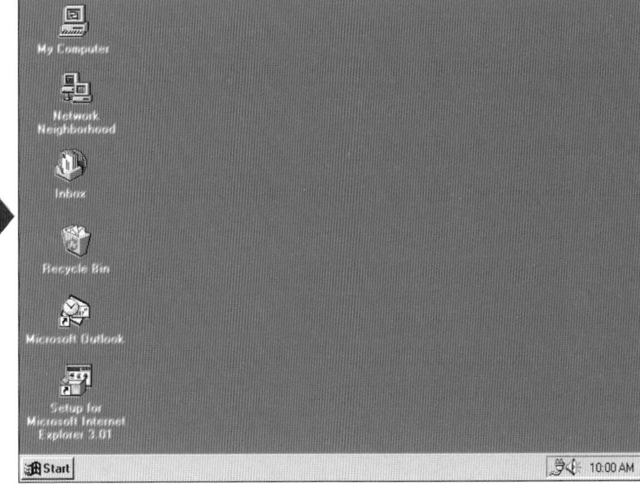

1 Click **File**.

2 Click **Exit** to exit Access.

■ The Access window disappears from your screen.

Note: To restart Access, refer to page 11.

CREATE A BLANK DATABASE

If you want to design your own database from scratch, you can create a blank database. Designing your own database gives you the most flexibility and control.

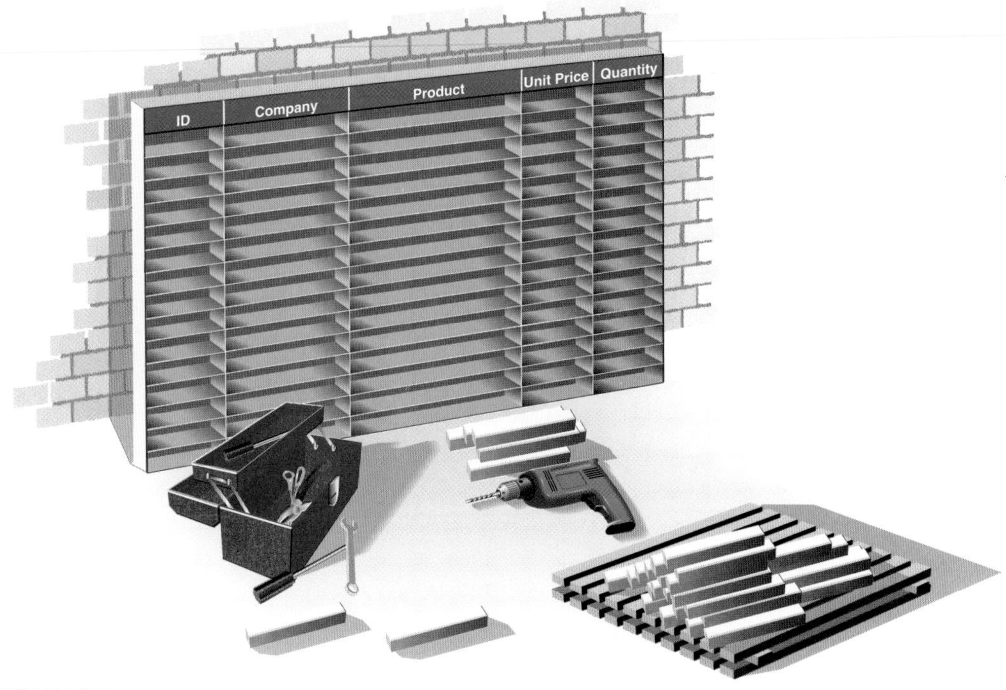

CREATE A BLANK DATABASE

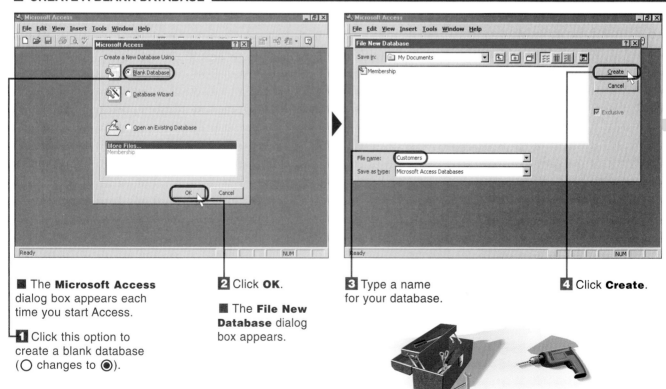

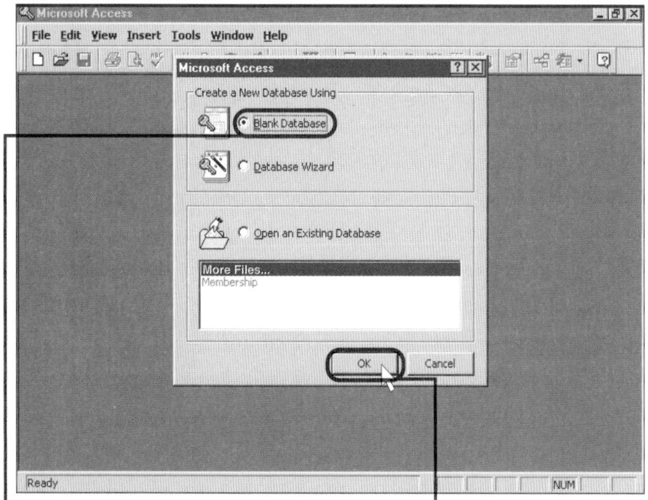

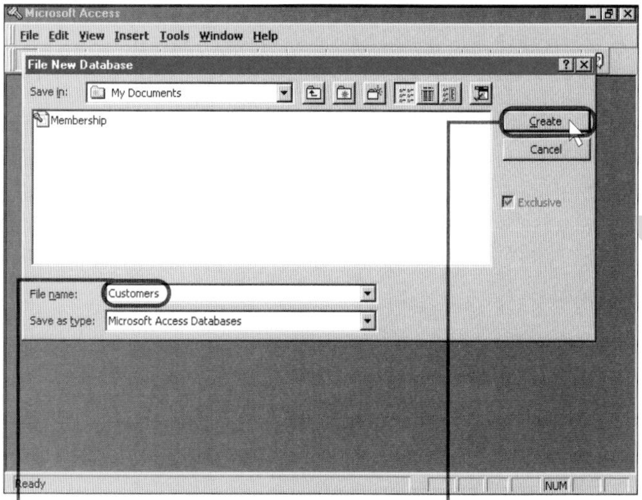

■ The **Microsoft Access** dialog box appears each time you start Access.

1 Click this option to create a blank database (○ changes to ◉).

2 Click **OK**.

■ The **File New Database** dialog box appears.

3 Type a name for your database.

4 Click **Create**.

Can I have more than one database open at a time?

You can have only one database open at a time. Access will close the database displayed on your screen when you create or open another database.

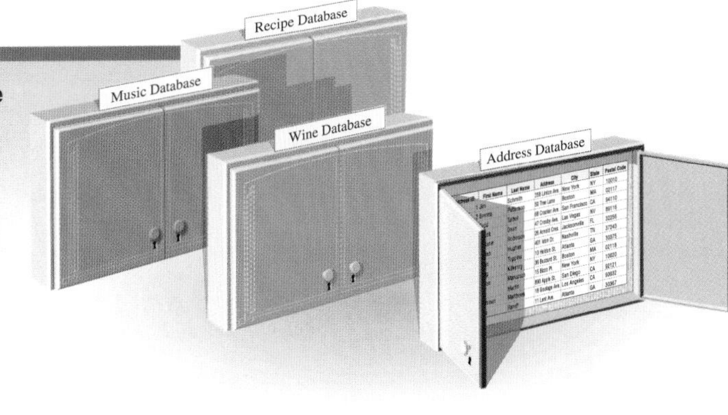

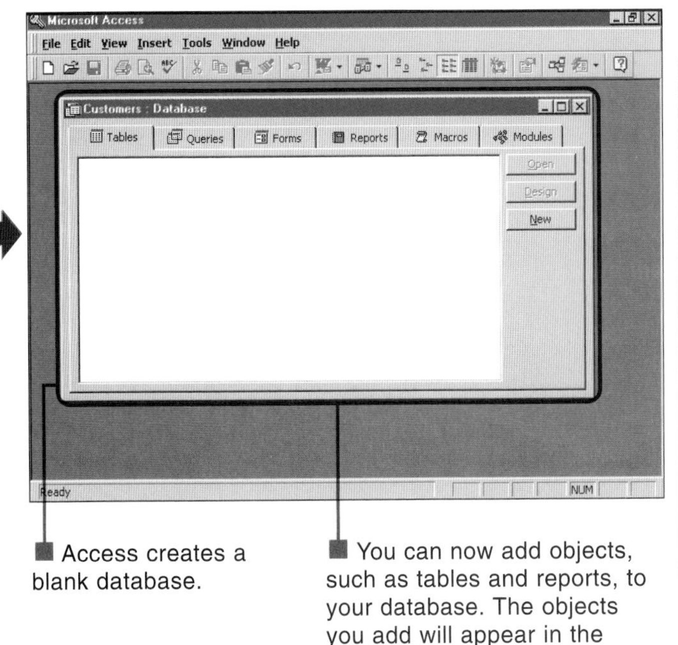

■ Access creates a blank database.

■ You can now add objects, such as tables and reports, to your database. The objects you add will appear in the Database window.

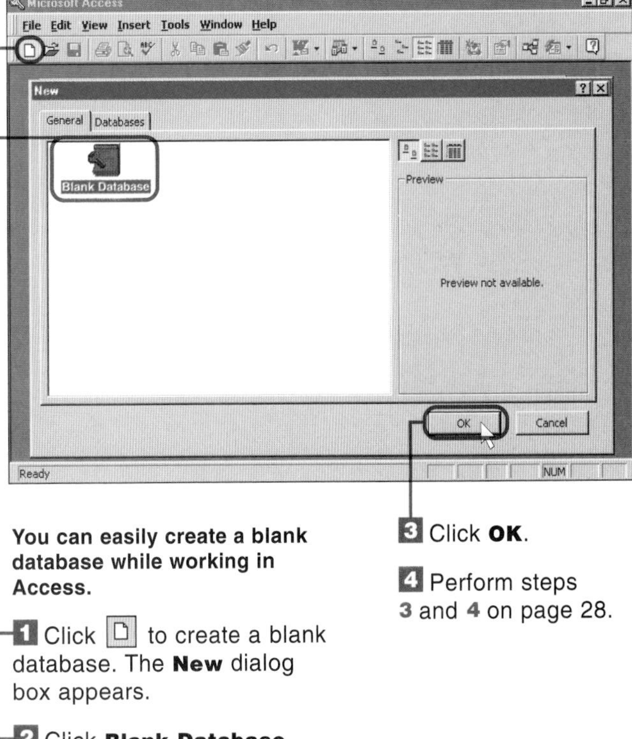

You can easily create a blank database while working in Access.

1 Click [icon] to create a blank database. The **New** dialog box appears.

2 Click **Blank Database**.

3 Click **OK**.

4 Perform steps **3** and **4** on page 28.

OPEN A DATABASE

You can open a database you previously created and display it on your screen. This lets you review and make changes to the database.

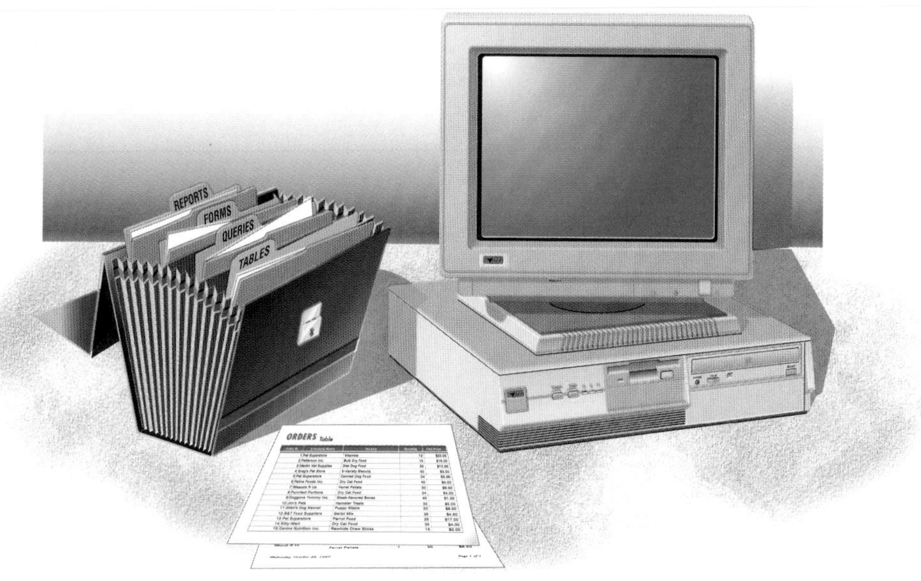

OPEN A DATABASE

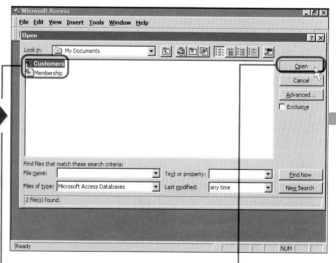

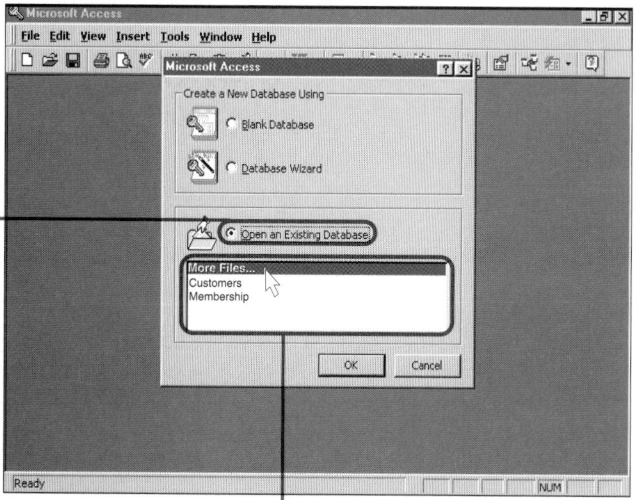

■ The **Microsoft Access** dialog box appears each time you start Access.

1 Click this option to open a database you previously created (○ changes to ◉).

■ This area displays the names of the last databases you worked with. To quickly open one of these databases, double-click the name of the database.

2 To display a list of all the databases you have created, double-click **More Files**.

■ The **Open** dialog box appears.

3 Click the name of the database you want to open.

4 Click **Open**.

?

How can I quickly open one of the last databases I worked with?

The File menu displays the names of the last four databases you worked with. When you are working in Access, you can quickly open any of these databases.

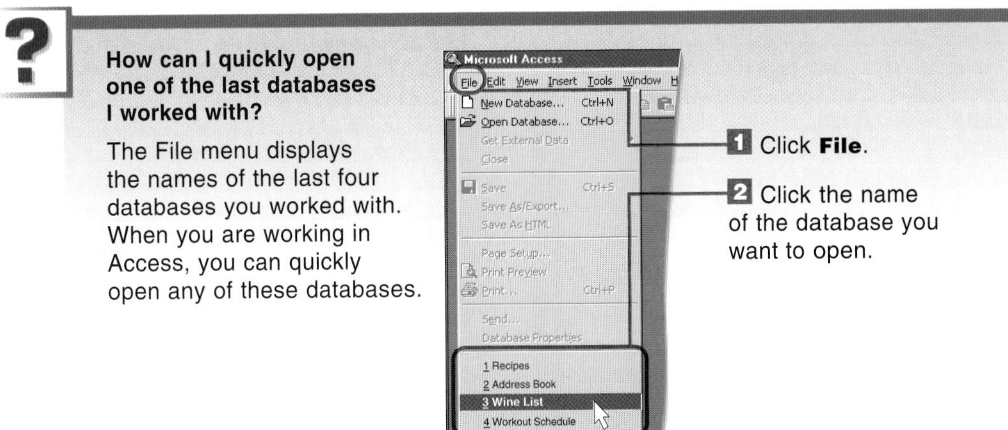

1 Click **File**.

2 Click the name of the database you want to open.

■ The database you selected opens.

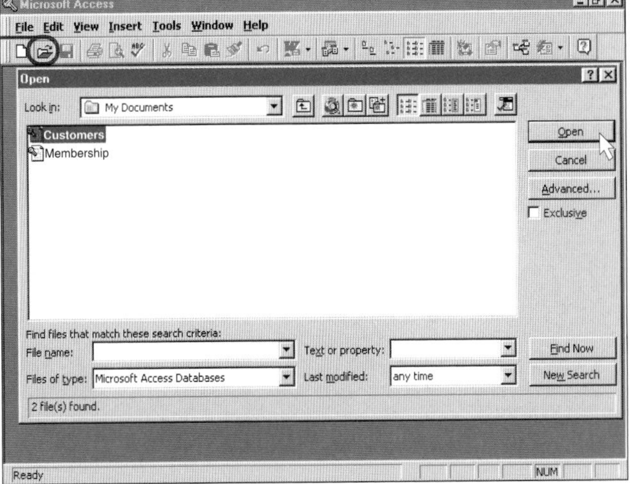

While working in Access, you can easily open a database you previously created.

1 Click [open icon] to open a database you previously created. Then perform steps **3** and **4** on page 30.

■ You can have only one database open at a time. Access will close a database displayed on your screen when you open another database.

GETTING HELP

If you do not know how to perform a task in Access, you can ask the Office Assistant for help.

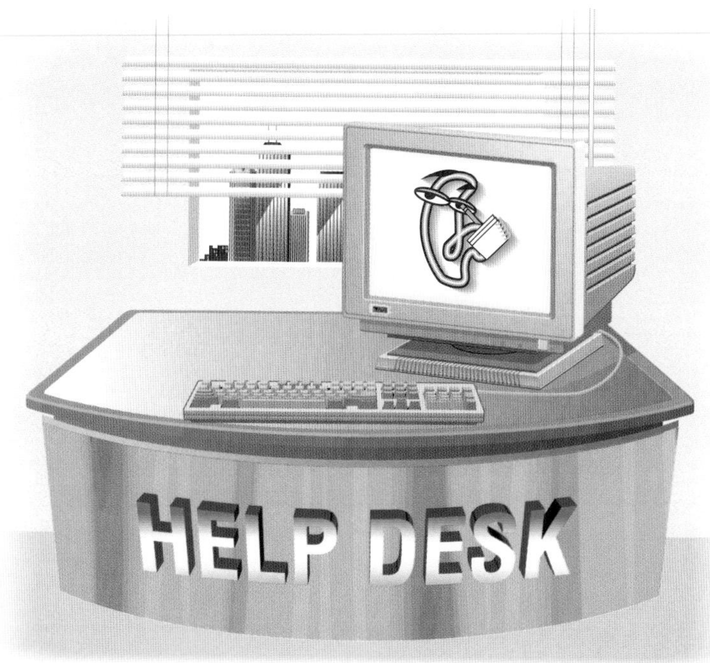

GETTING HELP

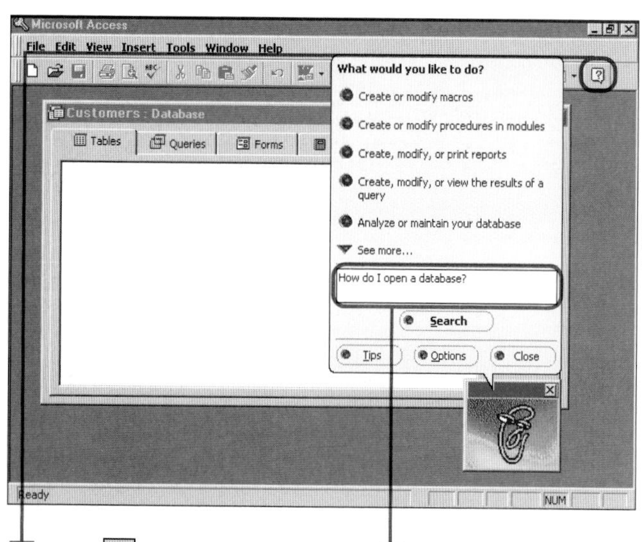

1 Click [?] to display the Office Assistant.

2 Type the question you want to ask and then press Enter on your keyboard.

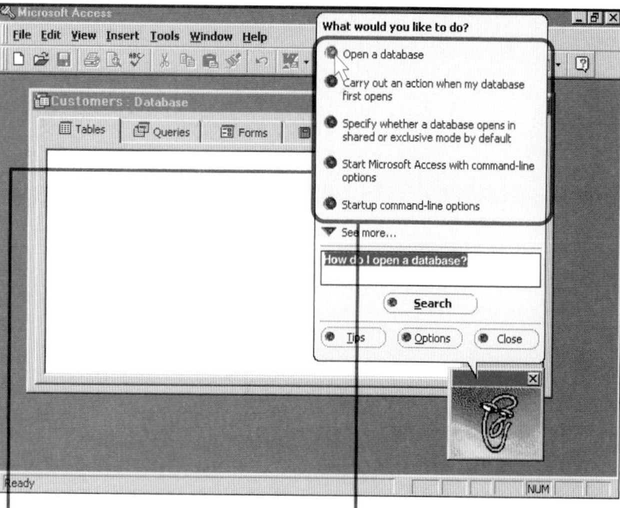

■ The Office Assistant displays a list of help topics that relate to the question you asked.

Note: If you do not see a help topic of interest, try rephrasing your question. Type the new question and then press Enter *on your keyboard.*

3 Click the help topic you want information on.

How can I display the name of a toolbar button?

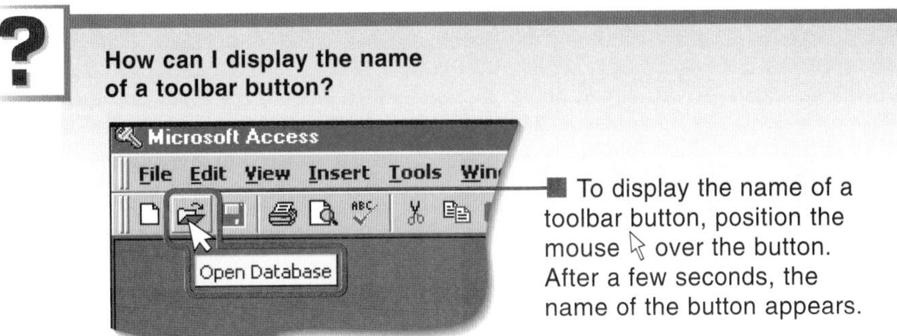

■ To display the name of a toolbar button, position the mouse over the button. After a few seconds, the name of the button appears.

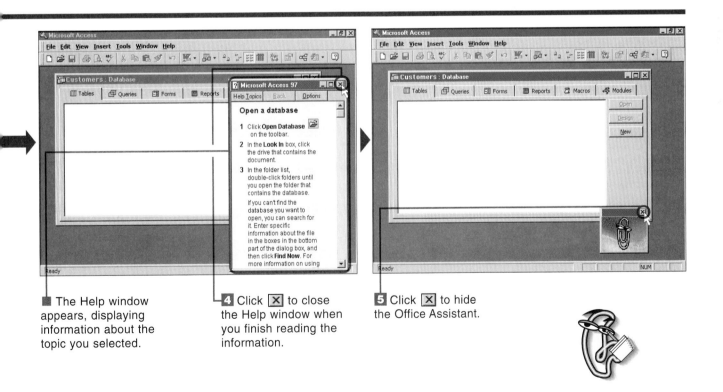

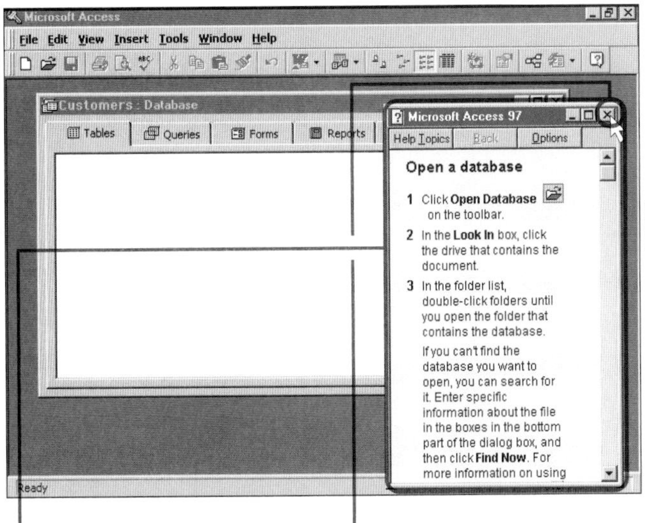

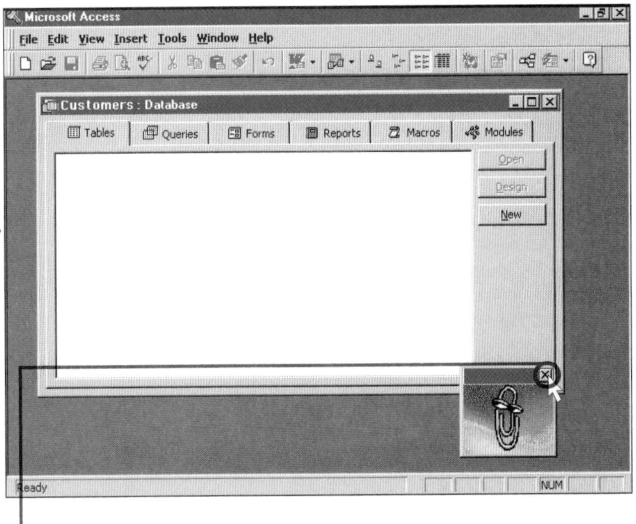

■ The Help window appears, displaying information about the topic you selected.

4 Click ☒ to close the Help window when you finish reading the information.

5 Click ☒ to hide the Office Assistant.

Recipe Table
Recipe ID
Recipe Name
Meal
Vegetarian
1 Chicken Stir-fry Dinner No
2 Omelet Breakfast Yes
3 Veggie Pizza Lunch Yes
4 Lasagna Dinner No
5 Pancakes Breakfast Yes
6 Pork Chops Dinner No
7 Garden Salad Lunch Yes
8 Fruit Salad Breakfast Yes
ADDRESSES Table
Address ID
First Name
Last Name
Address
City
1 Jim Schmith 258 Linton Ave. New York NY
2 Brenda Petterson 50 Tree Lane Boston MA
3 Todd Talbot 68 Cracker Ave. San Francisco CA
4 Chuck Dean 47 Crosby Ave. Las Vegas NV
5 Melanie Robinson 26 Arnold Cres. Jacksonville FL
6 Susan Hughes 401 Idon Dr. Nashville
Table
Film ID
Customer's First Name
Customer's Last Name
Date Dropped Off
1 Kathleen Matthews 5/9/97
2 Ron Ratoff 5/11/97
3 Chuck Dean 5/12/97
4 Jim Martin 5/17/97
5 Carol Brown 5/20/97
6 Michael Wolfe 5/21/97
7 Jeremy Chivers 5/25/97
8 Randy Coyle 5/30/97
ORDERS Table
Order ID
Company Name
Product
1 Pet Superstore Vitamins
2 Petterson Inc. Bulk Dry Food
3 Martin Vet Supplies Diet Dog Food
4 Greg's Pet Store 5-Variety Biscuits
5 Pet Superstore Canned Dog Food
6 Feline Foods Inc. Dry Cat Food
7 Weasels R Us Ferret Pellets

CHAPTER 3

Create Tables

How can I create a table in my database? This chapter teaches you how to create and work with tables.

Create a Table 36

Rename a Field 40

Rearrange Fields....................41

Add a Field 42

Delete a Field 43

Close a Table 44

Open a Table....................45

Rename a Table 46

Delete a Table 47

Create a Table Using the Wizard 48

CREATE A TABLE

A table stores a collection of information about a specific topic, such as a list of recipes. You can create a table to store new information in your database.

Recipe ID	Recipe Name	Meal	Vegetarian
1	Chicken Stir-fry	Dinner	No
2	Omelet	Breakfast	Yes
3	Veggie Pizza	Lunch	Yes
4	Lasagna	Dinner	No
5	Pancakes	Breakfast	Yes
6	Pork Chops	Dinner	No
7	Garden Salad	Lunch	Yes
8	Fruit Salad	Breakfast	Yes

CREATE A TABLE

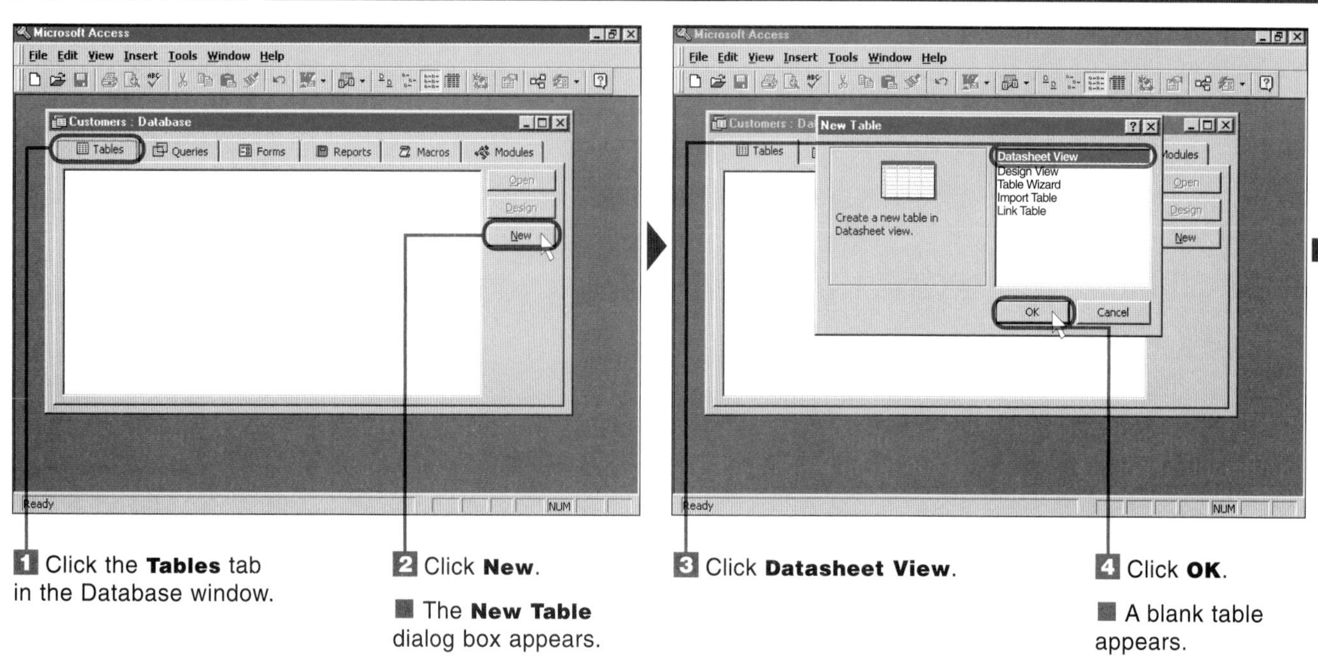

1 Click the **Tables** tab in the Database window.

2 Click **New**.

■ The **New Table** dialog box appears.

3 Click **Datasheet View**.

4 Click **OK**.

■ A blank table appears.

What are records and fields?

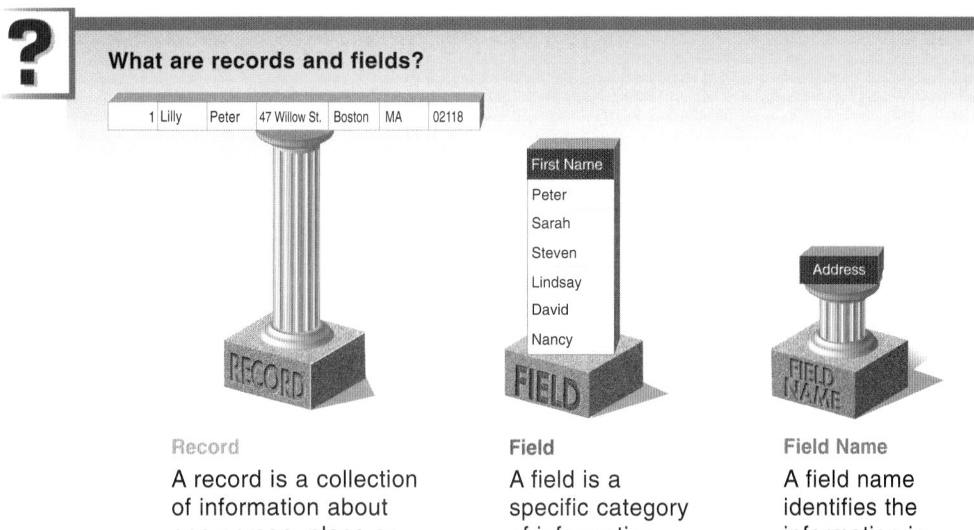

Record
A record is a collection of information about one person, place or thing.

Field
A field is a specific category of information.

Field Name
A field name identifies the information in a field.

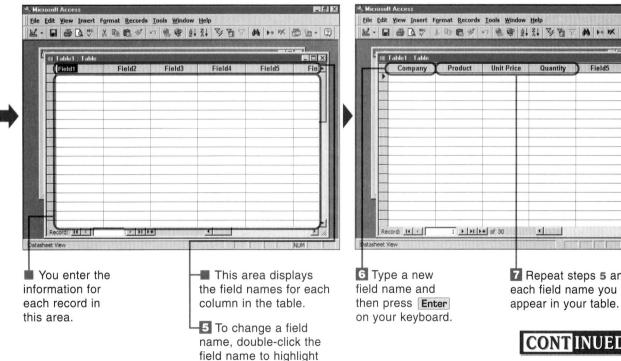

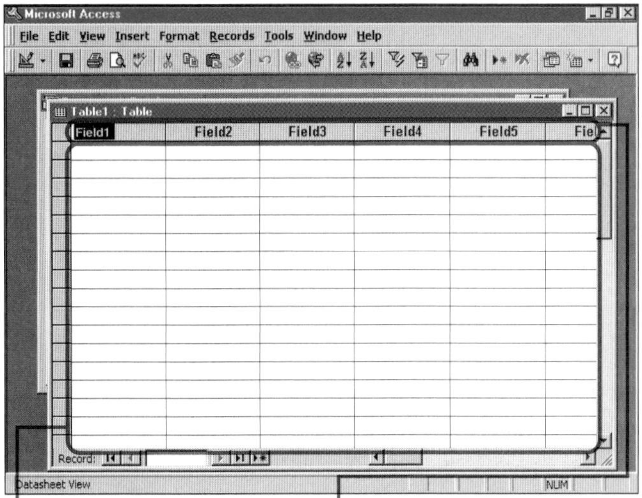

■ You enter the information for each record in this area.

■ This area displays the field names for each column in the table.

5 To change a field name, double-click the field name to highlight the name.

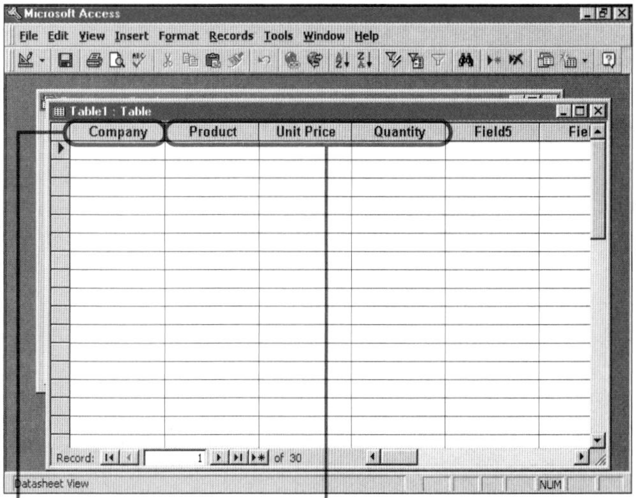

6 Type a new field name and then press Enter on your keyboard.

7 Repeat steps 5 and 6 for each field name you want to appear in your table.

CONTINUED

You can have Access set a primary key in your table for you. A primary key is one or more fields that uniquely identifies each record in a table, such as an ID number.

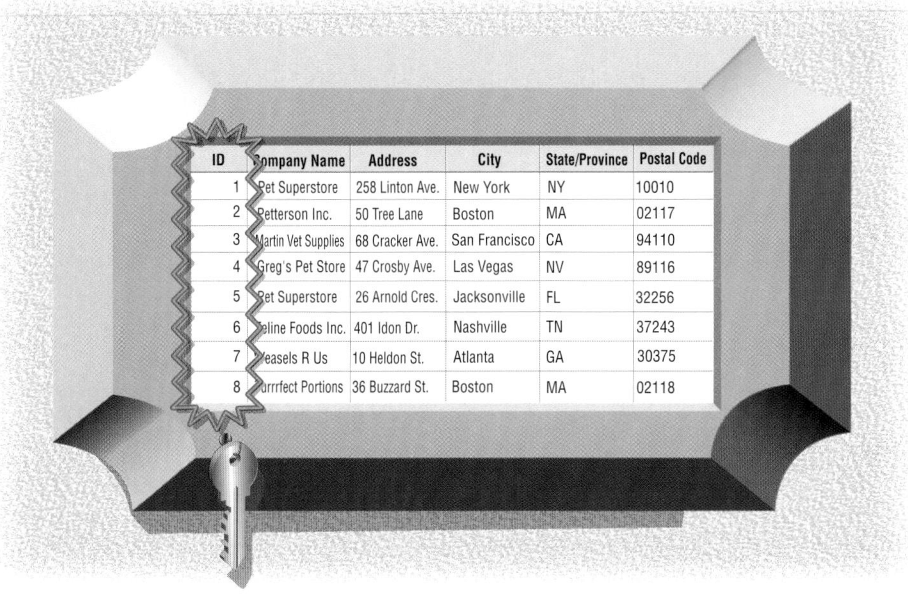

ID	Company Name	Address	City	State/Province	Postal Code
1	Pet Superstore	258 Linton Ave.	New York	NY	10010
2	Petterson Inc.	50 Tree Lane	Boston	MA	02117
3	Martin Vet Supplies	68 Cracker Ave.	San Francisco	CA	94110
4	Greg's Pet Store	47 Crosby Ave.	Las Vegas	NV	89116
5	Pet Superstore	26 Arnold Cres.	Jacksonville	FL	32256
6	Feline Foods Inc.	401 Idon Dr.	Nashville	TN	37243
7	Weasels R Us	10 Heldon St.	Atlanta	GA	30375
8	Purrrfect Portions	36 Buzzard St.	Boston	MA	02118

CREATE A TABLE (CONTINUED)

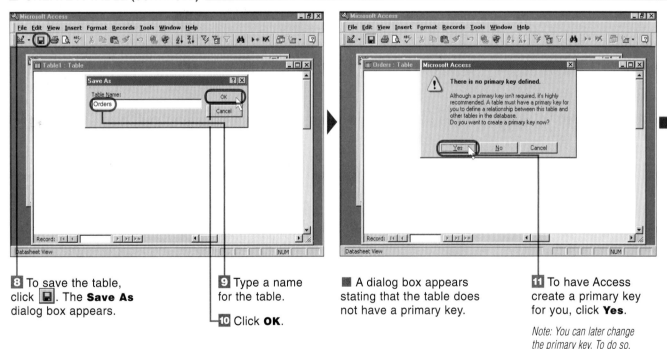

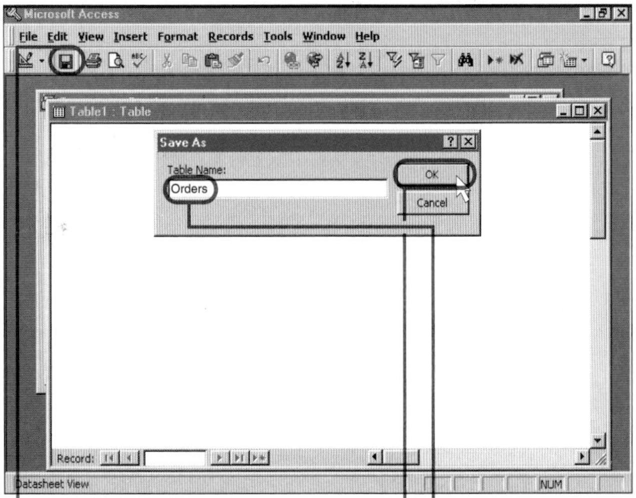

8 To save the table, click ▣. The **Save As** dialog box appears.

9 Type a name for the table.

10 Click **OK**.

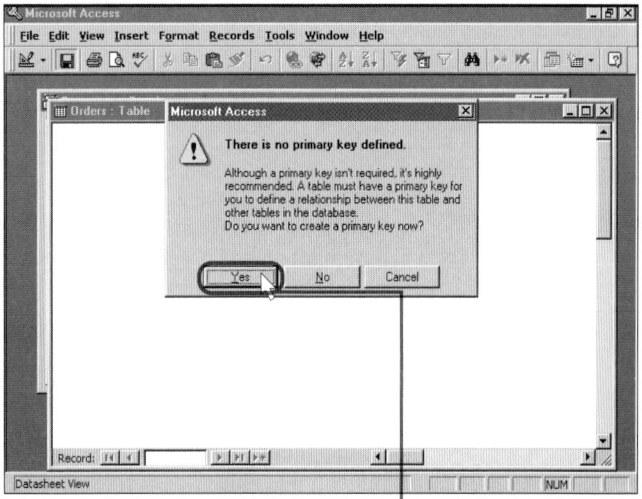

■ A dialog box appears stating that the table does not have a primary key.

11 To have Access create a primary key for you, click **Yes**.

Note: You can later change the primary key. To do so, refer to page 136.

How can I avoid wrist strain when entering data?

You can avoid wrist strain when entering data by keeping your elbows level with the keyboard and keeping your wrists straight and higher than your fingers.

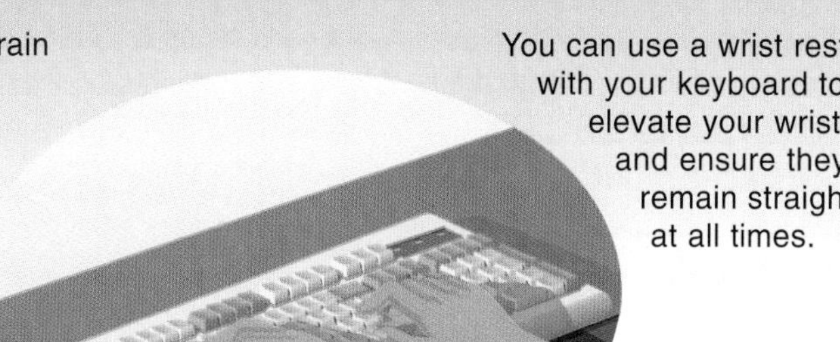

You can use a wrist rest with your keyboard to elevate your wrists and ensure they remain straight at all times.

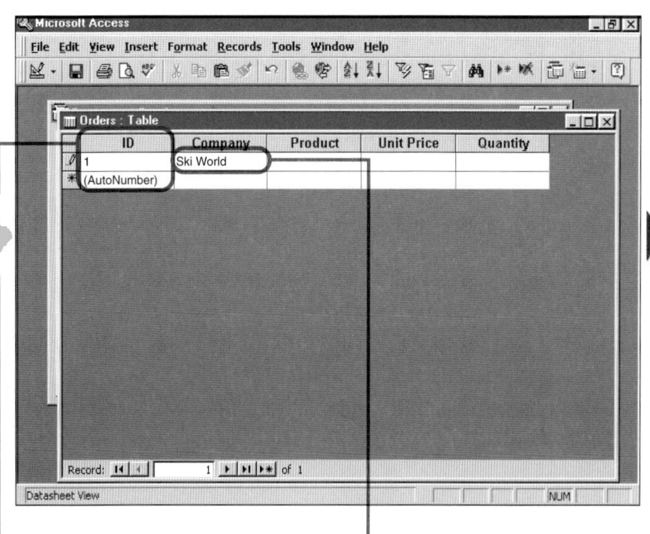

■ Access removes the rows and columns that do not contain data.

■ If you selected **Yes** in step **11**, Access adds an **ID** field to the table to serve as the primary key. The **ID** field will number each record you add to the table.

12 To enter the data for the first record, click the first empty cell in the row. Then type the data that corresponds to the field.

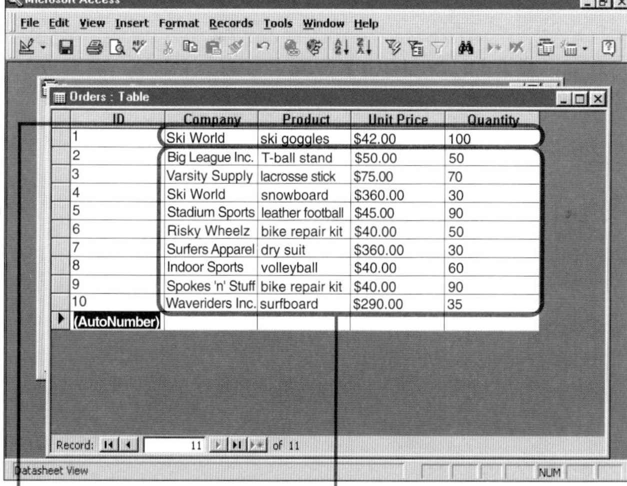

13 Press **Enter** on your keyboard to enter the data and move to the next cell. Then type the data that corresponds to the next field. Repeat this step until you finish entering all the data for the record.

14 Repeat steps **12** and **13** for each record. Access automatically saves each record you enter.

RENAME A FIELD

You can easily give a field a different name to more accurately describe the contents of the field.

Preparation Time
RECIPES Table
Recipe ID
Recipe Name
Time
Meal
Servings
1
Chicken Stir-fry
25 minutes
Dinner
4
2
Omelet
15 minutes
Breakfast
1
3
Veggie Pizza
45 minutes
Lunch
6
Lasagna
45 minutes
Dinner
10 minutes

If you rename a field that is used in other objects in your database, such as a form or report, you will need to update all references to the field.

RENAME A FIELD

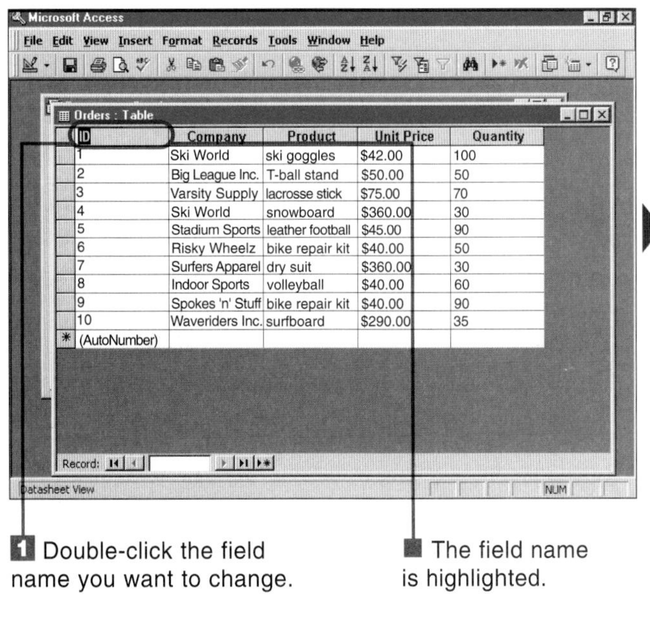

ID	Company	Product	Unit Price	Quantity
1	Ski World	ski goggles	$42.00	100
2	Big League Inc.	T-ball stand	$50.00	50
3	Varsity Supply	lacrosse stick	$75.00	70
4	Ski World	snowboard	$360.00	30
5	Stadium Sports	leather football	$45.00	90
6	Risky Wheelz	bike repair kit	$40.00	50
7	Surfers Apparel	dry suit	$360.00	30
8	Indoor Sports	volleyball	$40.00	60
9	Spokes 'n' Stuff	bike repair kit	$40.00	90
10	Waveriders Inc.	surfboard	$290.00	35
(AutoNumber)				

1 Double-click the field name you want to change.

■ The field name is highlighted.

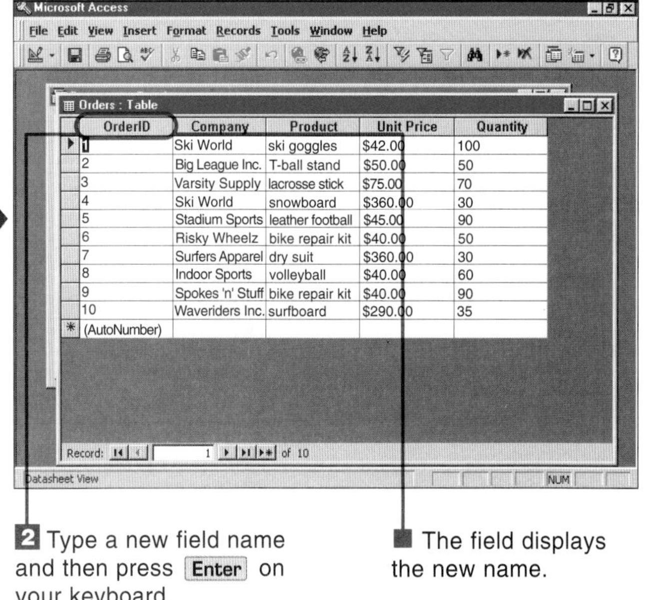

OrderID	Company	Product	Unit Price	Quantity
1	Ski World	ski goggles	$42.00	100
2	Big League Inc.	T-ball stand	$50.00	50
3	Varsity Supply	lacrosse stick	$75.00	70
4	Ski World	snowboard	$360.00	30
5	Stadium Sports	leather football	$45.00	90
6	Risky Wheelz	bike repair kit	$40.00	50
7	Surfers Apparel	dry suit	$360.00	30
8	Indoor Sports	volleyball	$40.00	60
9	Spokes 'n' Stuff	bike repair kit	$40.00	90
10	Waveriders Inc.	surfboard	$290.00	35
(AutoNumber)				

2 Type a new field name and then press **Enter** on your keyboard.

■ The field displays the new name.

REARRANGE FIELDS

You can change the order of fields to better organize the information in your table.

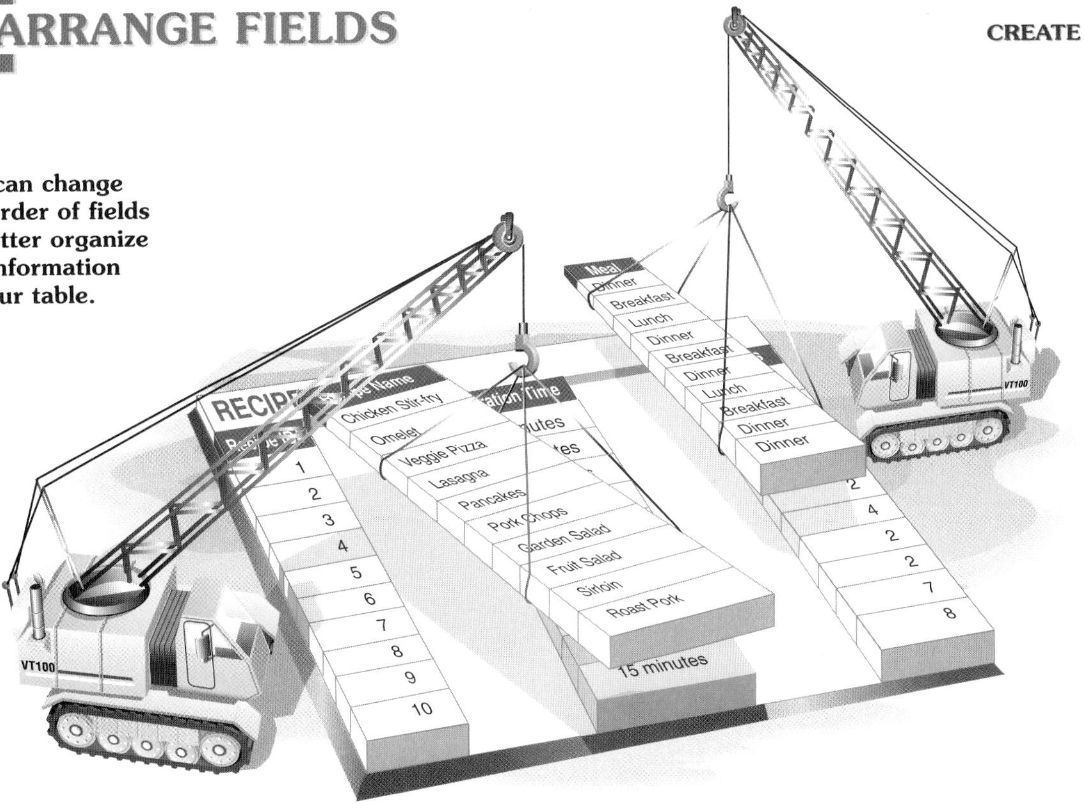

REARRANGE FIELDS

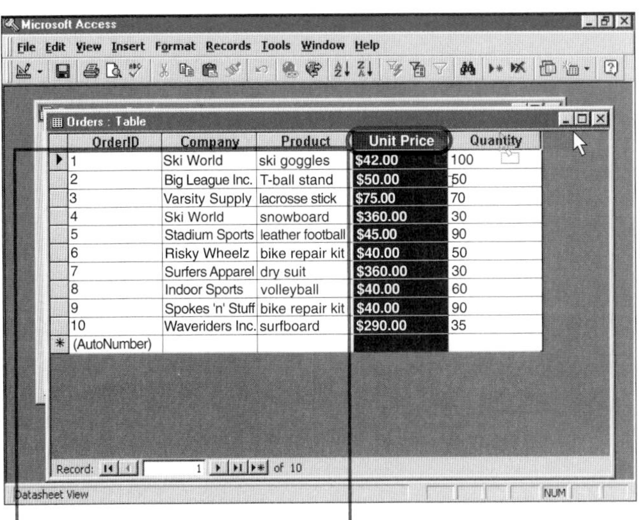

OrderID	Company	Product	Unit Price	Quantity
1	Ski World	ski goggles	$42.00	100
2	Big League Inc.	T-ball stand	$50.00	50
3	Varsity Supply	lacrosse stick	$75.00	70
4	Ski World	snowboard	$360.00	30
5	Stadium Sports	leather football	$45.00	90
6	Risky Wheelz	bike repair kit	$40.00	50
7	Surfers Apparel	dry suit	$360.00	30
8	Indoor Sports	volleyball	$40.00	60
9	Spokes 'n' Stuff	bike repair kit	$40.00	90
10	Waveriders Inc.	surfboard	$290.00	35
(AutoNumber)				

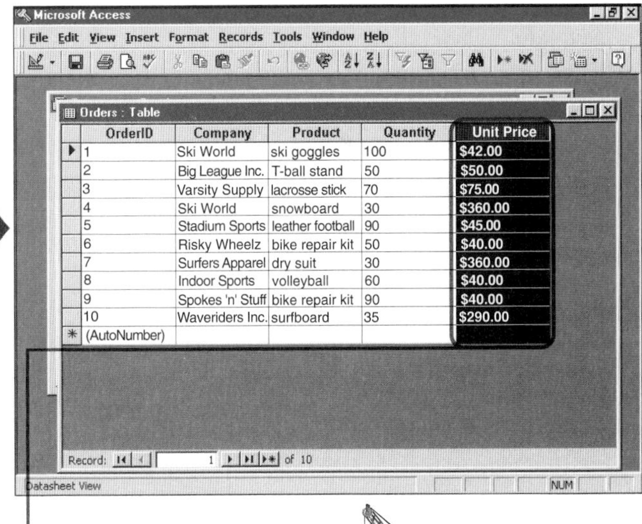

OrderID	Company	Product	Quantity	Unit Price
1	Ski World	ski goggles	100	$42.00
2	Big League Inc.	T-ball stand	50	$50.00
3	Varsity Supply	lacrosse stick	70	$75.00
4	Ski World	snowboard	30	$360.00
5	Stadium Sports	leather football	90	$45.00
6	Risky Wheelz	bike repair kit	50	$40.00
7	Surfers Apparel	dry suit	30	$360.00
8	Indoor Sports	volleyball	60	$40.00
9	Spokes 'n' Stuff	bike repair kit	90	$40.00
10	Waveriders Inc.	surfboard	35	$290.00
(AutoNumber)				

1 To select the field you want to move, click the name of the field.

2 Position the mouse over the field name and then drag the field to the new location.

Note: A thick line shows where the field will appear.

■ The field appears in the new location.

ADD A FIELD

You can easily add a field to your table when you want to include an additional category of information.

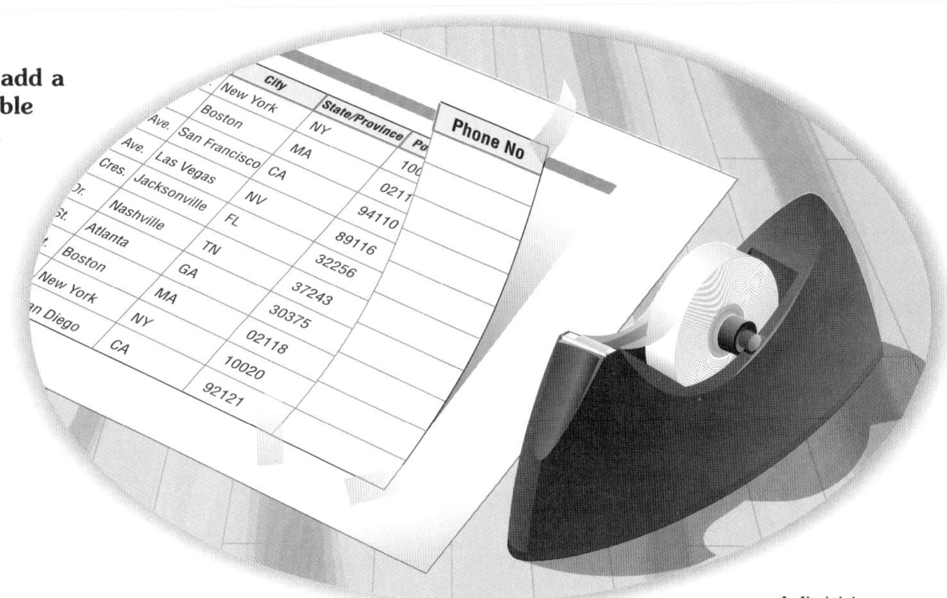

A field is a specific category of information in a table. For example, a field can contain the phone numbers of all your clients.

ADD A FIELD

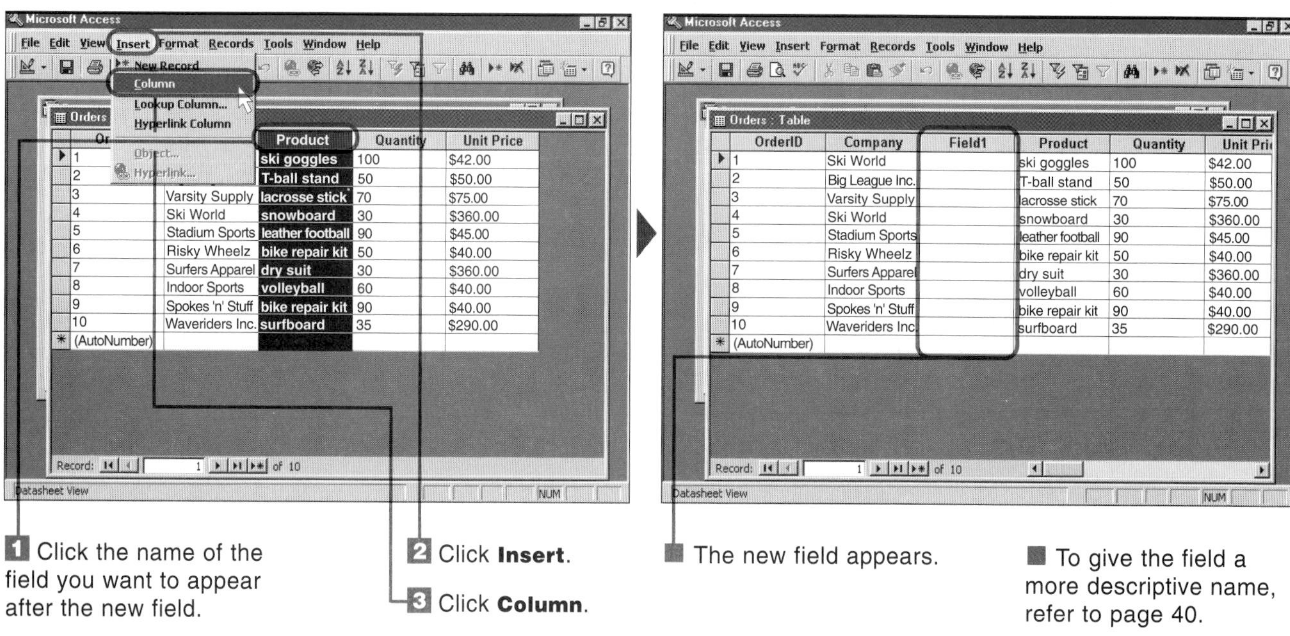

1 Click the name of the field you want to appear after the new field.

2 Click **Insert**.

3 Click **Column**.

■ The new field appears.

■ To give the field a more descriptive name, refer to page 40.

DELETE A FIELD

If you no longer need a field, you can permanently delete the field from your table.

Before you delete a field, make sure the field is not used in any other objects in your database, such as a form, report or query.

DELETE A FIELD

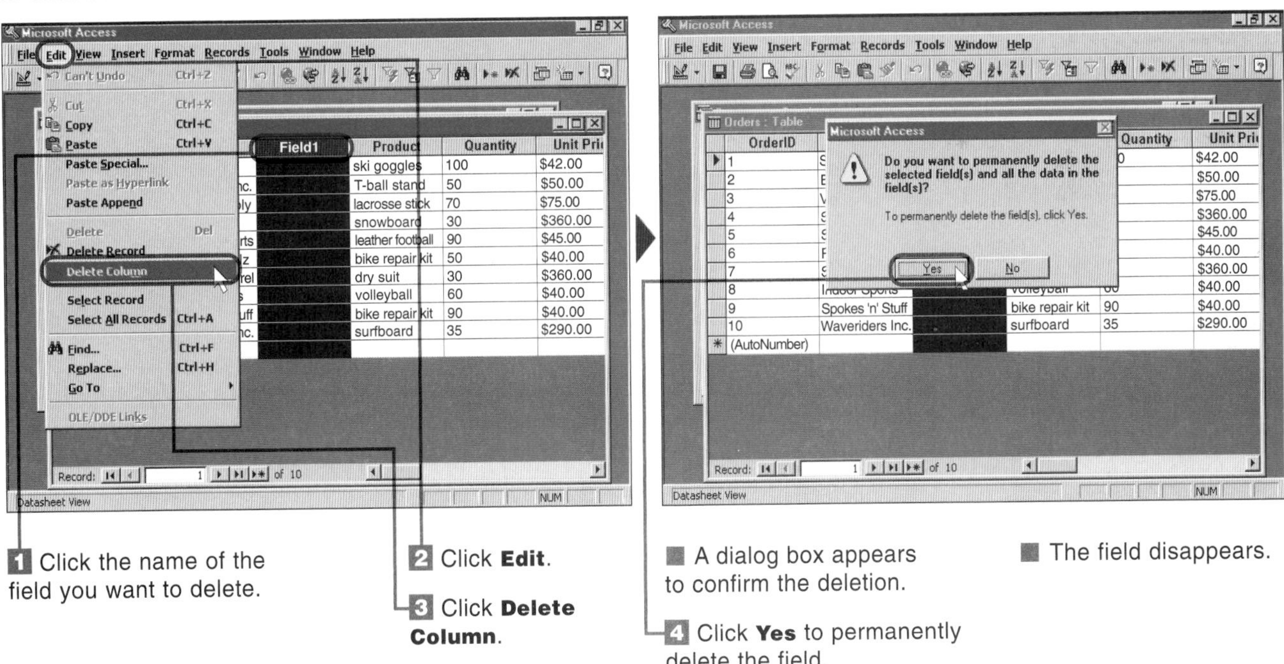

1 Click the name of the field you want to delete.

2 Click **Edit**.

3 Click **Delete Column**.

■ A dialog box appears to confirm the deletion.

4 Click **Yes** to permanently delete the field.

■ The field disappears.

CLOSE A TABLE

When you have finished working with a table, you can close the table to remove it from your screen.

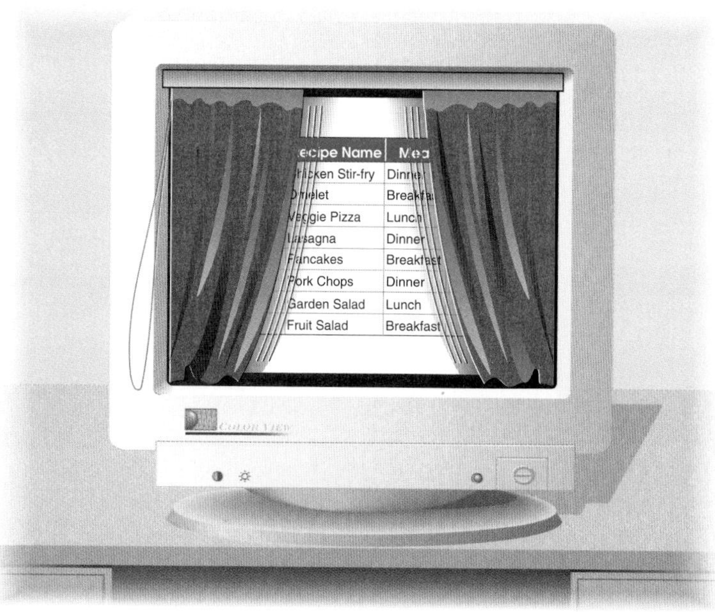

CLOSE A TABLE

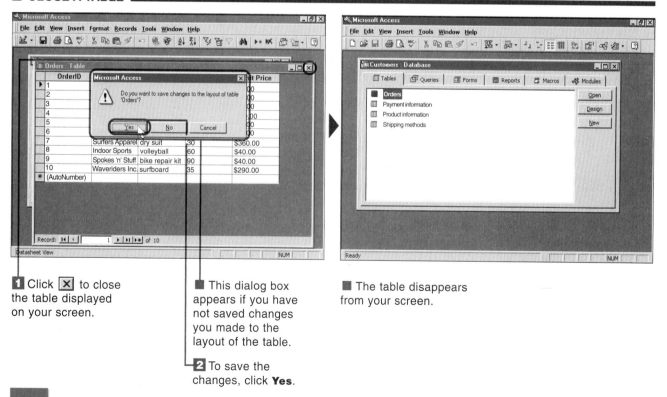

1 Click ☒ to close the table displayed on your screen.

■ This dialog box appears if you have not saved changes you made to the layout of the table.

2 To save the changes, click **Yes**.

■ The table disappears from your screen.

OPEN A TABLE

You can open a table to display its contents on your screen. This lets you review and make changes to the table.

OPEN A TABLE

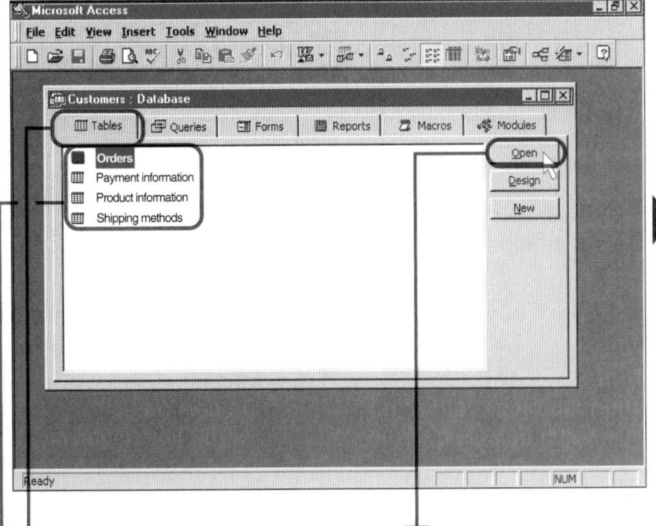

1 Click the **Tables** tab in the Database window to display a list of your tables.

2 Click the table you want to open.

3 Click **Open**.

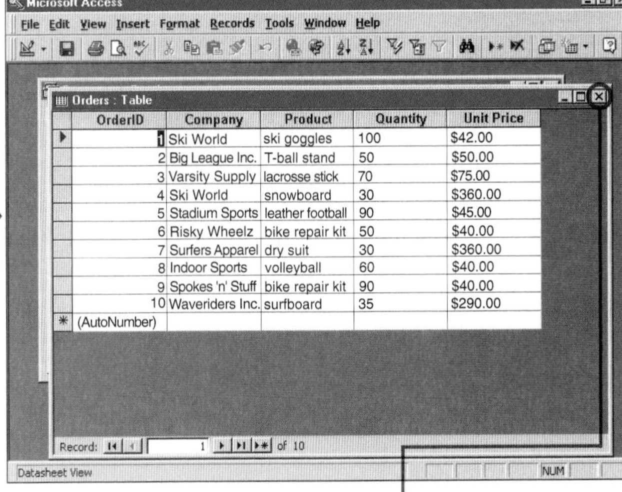

OrderID	Company	Product	Quantity	Unit Price
1	Ski World	ski goggles	100	$42.00
2	Big League Inc.	T-ball stand	50	$50.00
3	Varsity Supply	lacrosse stick	70	$75.00
4	Ski World	snowboard	30	$360.00
5	Stadium Sports	leather football	90	$45.00
6	Risky Wheelz	bike repair kit	50	$40.00
7	Surfers Apparel	dry suit	30	$360.00
8	Indoor Sports	volleyball	60	$40.00
9	Spokes 'n' Stuff	bike repair kit	90	$40.00
10	Waveriders Inc.	surfboard	35	$290.00
(AutoNumber)				

■ The table opens. You can now review and make changes to the table.

■ You can click ☒ to close the table.

RENAME A TABLE

You can change the name of a table to help you remember what data the table includes.

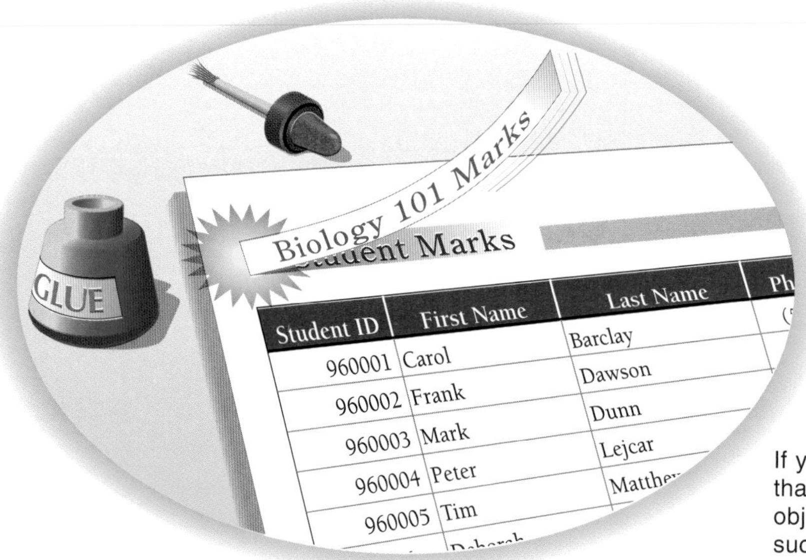

If you rename a table that is used in other objects in your database, such as a form or report, you will need to update all references to the table.

RENAME A TABLE

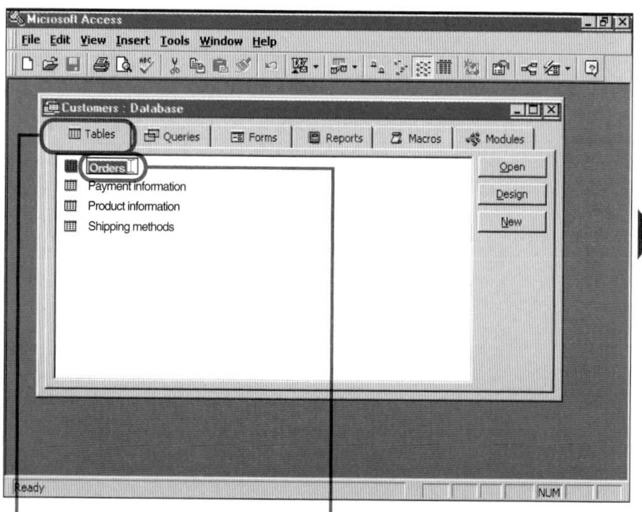

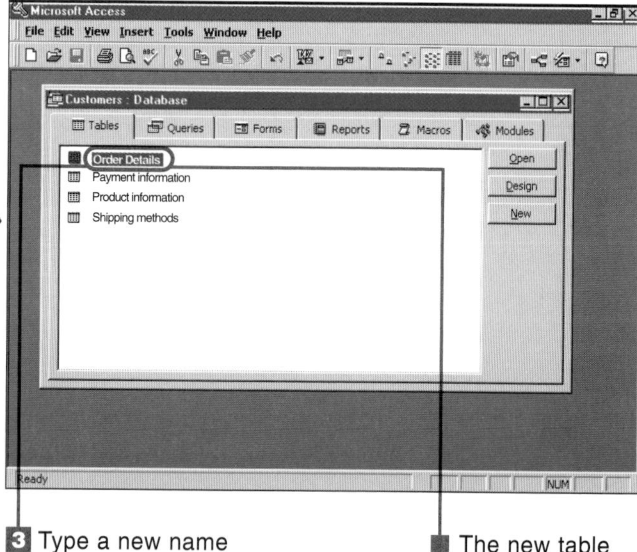

1 Click the **Tables** tab in the Database window to display a list of your tables.

2 Click the name of the table you want to change. After a few seconds, click the name of the table again. A black border appears around the table name.

Note: If you accidentally double-click the name of a table, the table will open.

3 Type a new name for the table and then press Enter on your keyboard.

■ The new table name appears.

DELETE A TABLE

If you no longer need the information stored in a table, you can permanently delete the table from your database.

Before you delete a table, make sure the table is not used by any other objects in your database, such as a form or report.

DELETE A TABLE

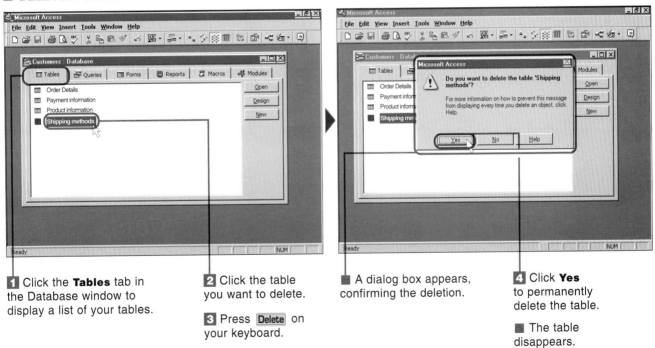

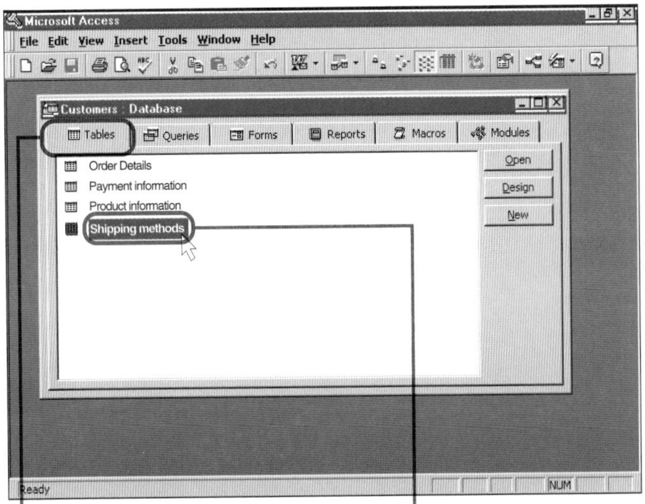

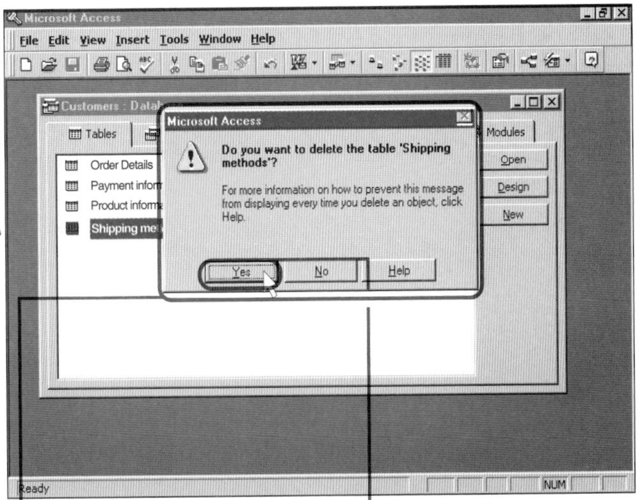

1 Click the **Tables** tab in the Database window to display a list of your tables.

2 Click the table you want to delete.

3 Press Delete on your keyboard.

■ A dialog box appears, confirming the deletion.

4 Click **Yes** to permanently delete the table.

■ The table disappears.

CREATE A TABLE USING THE WIZARD

The Table Wizard helps you quickly create a table that suits your needs.

The Table Wizard asks you a series of questions and then sets up a table based on your answers.

CREATE A TABLE USING THE WIZARD

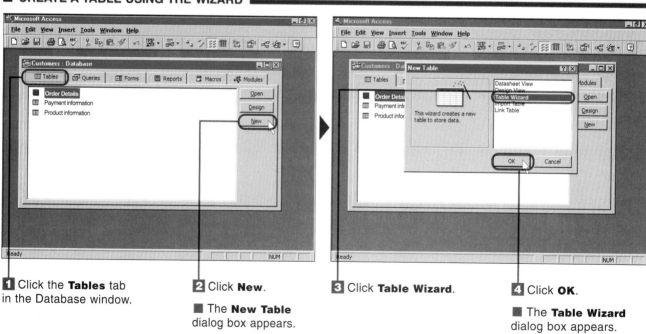

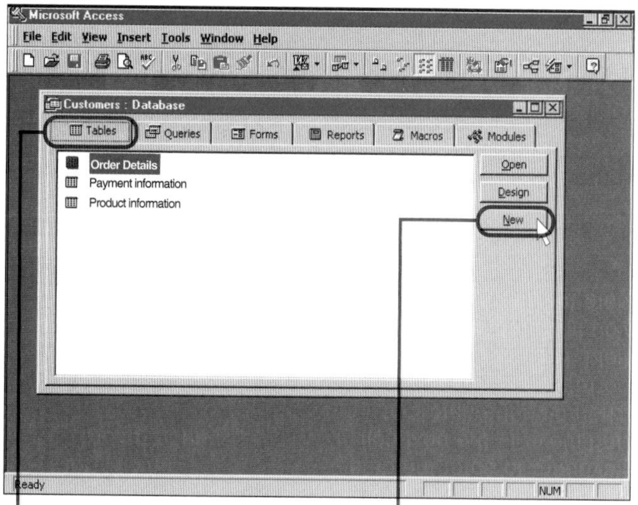

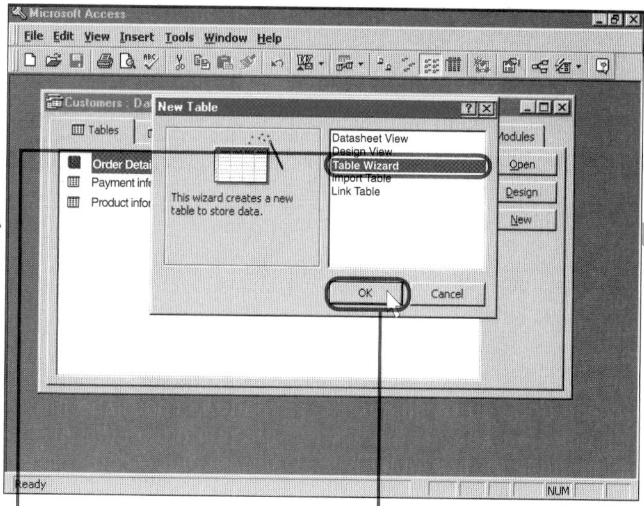

1 Click the **Tables** tab in the Database window.

2 Click **New**.

■ The **New Table** dialog box appears.

3 Click **Table Wizard**.

4 Click **OK**.

■ The **Table Wizard** dialog box appears.

What kinds of tables does the Table Wizard help me create?

The Table Wizard offers many tables for both business and personal use.

Business

Customers

Products

Orders

Deliveries

Personal

Recipes

Plants

Wine List

Investments

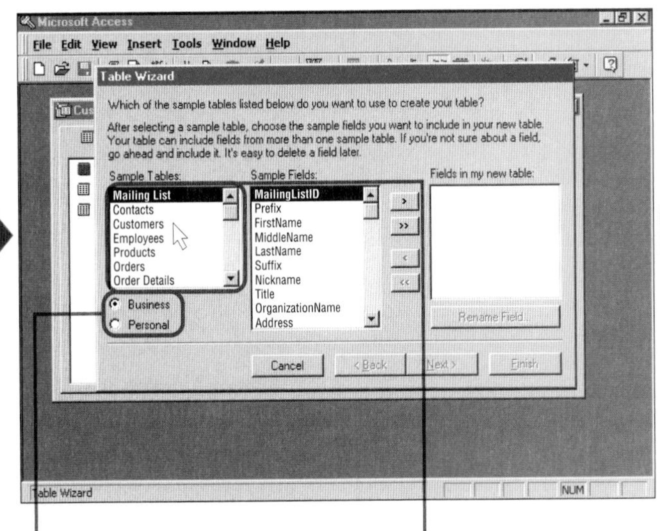

5 Click one of these options to specify whether the table is for business or personal use (○ changes to ◉).

6 Click the sample table that best describes the table you want to create.

*Note: The available sample tables depend on the option you selected in step **5**.*

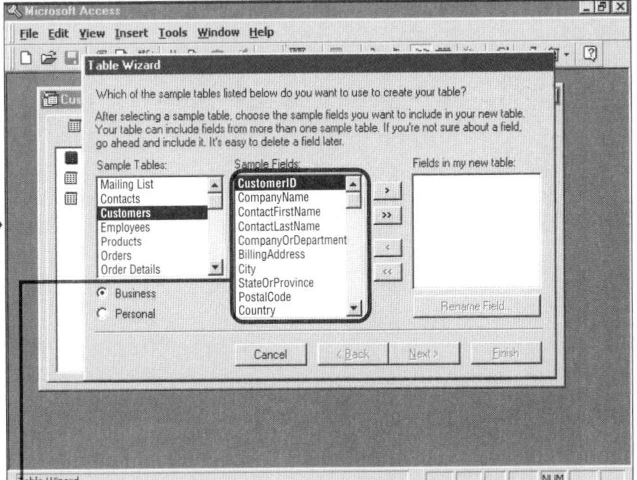

■ This area displays the available fields for the sample table you selected.

CONTINUED

You can decide exactly which fields you want to include in your new table. Make sure each field you select relates directly to the subject of the table.

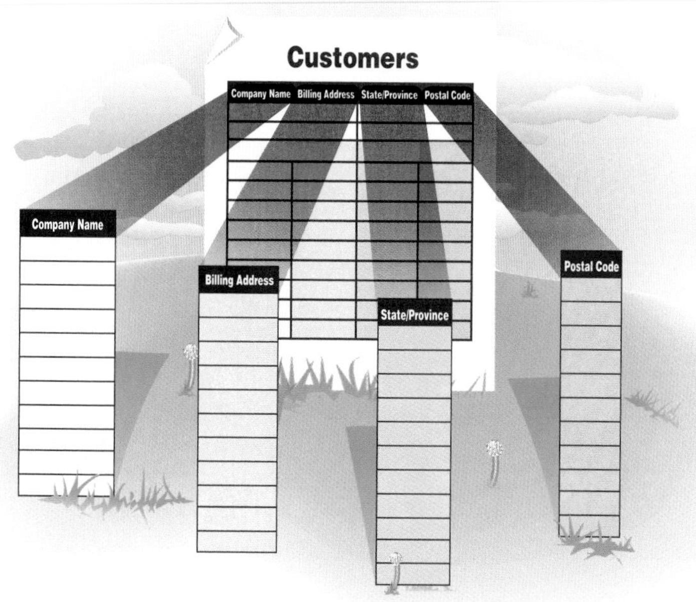

CREATE A TABLE USING THE WIZARD (CONTINUED)

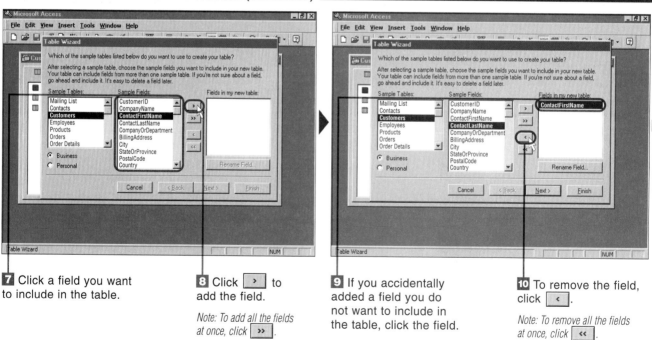

7 Click a field you want to include in the table.

8 Click [>] to add the field.

Note: To add all the fields at once, click [>>].

9 If you accidentally added a field you do not want to include in the table, click the field.

10 To remove the field, click [<].

Note: To remove all the fields at once, click [<<].

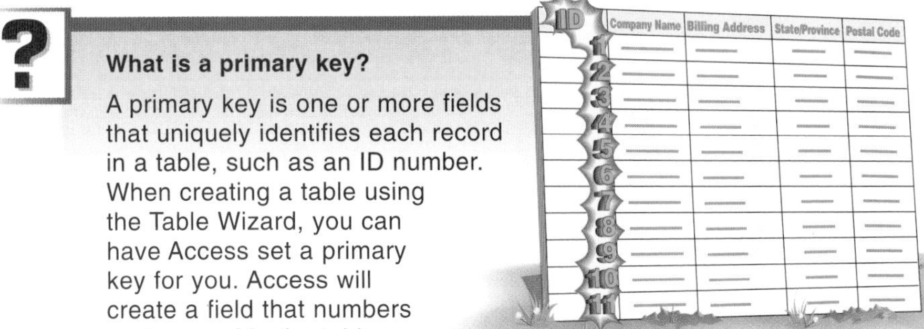

What is a primary key?

A primary key is one or more fields that uniquely identifies each record in a table, such as an ID number. When creating a table using the Table Wizard, you can have Access set a primary key for you. Access will create a field that numbers each record in the table.

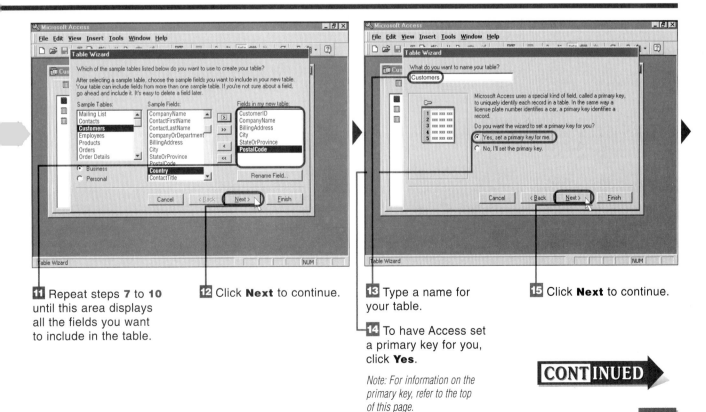

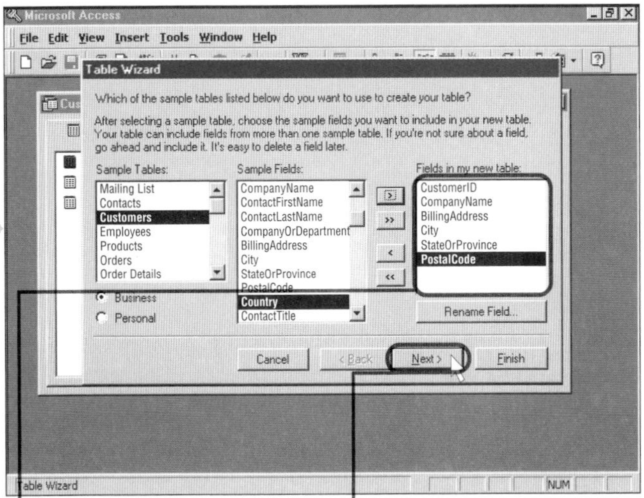

11 Repeat steps **7** to **10** until this area displays all the fields you want to include in the table.

12 Click **Next** to continue.

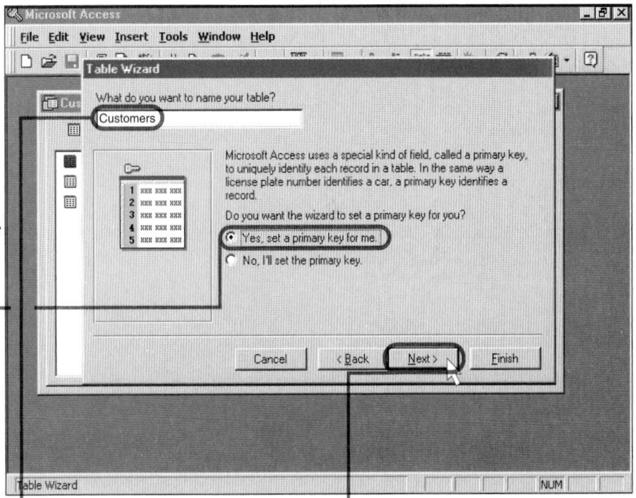

13 Type a name for your table.

14 To have Access set a primary key for you, click **Yes**.

Note: For information on the primary key, refer to the top of this page.

15 Click **Next** to continue.

CONTINUED

CREATE A TABLE USING THE WIZARD

When creating a table, the wizard will show you how the new table relates to all the other tables in your database. Related tables have matching records.

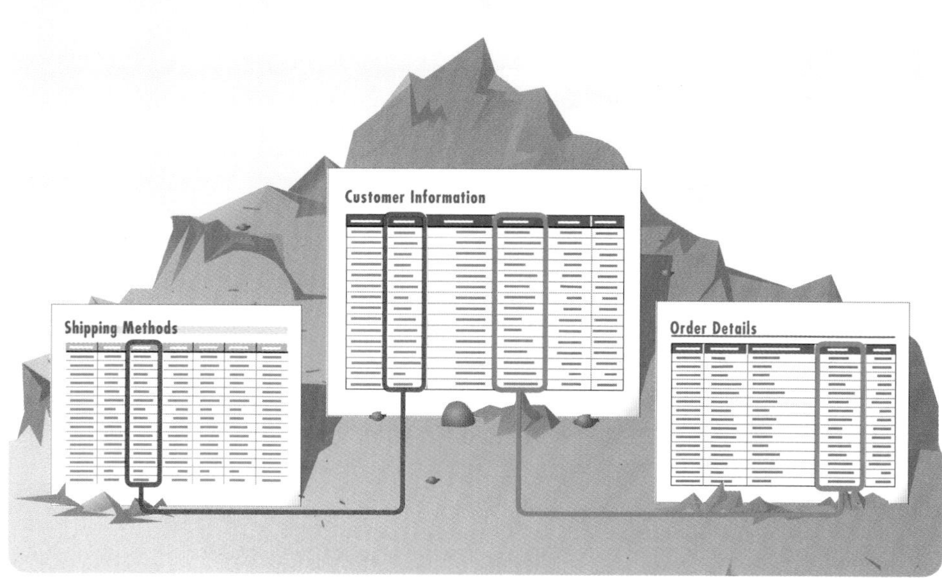

CREATE A TABLE USING THE WIZARD (CONTINUED)

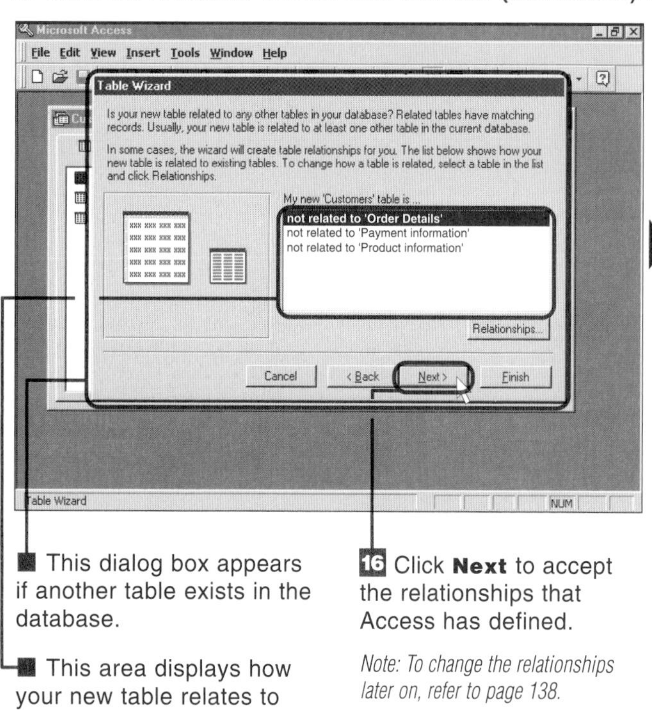

■ This dialog box appears if another table exists in the database.

■ This area displays how your new table relates to the existing tables.

16 Click **Next** to accept the relationships that Access has defined.

Note: To change the relationships later on, refer to page 138.

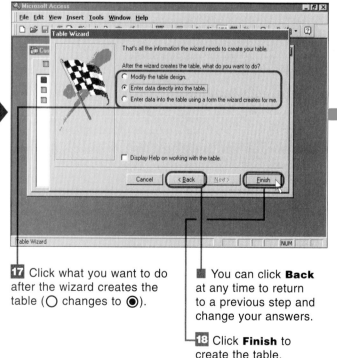

17 Click what you want to do after the wizard creates the table (○ changes to ◉).

■ You can click **Back** at any time to return to a previous step and change your answers.

18 Click **Finish** to create the table.

? Do I need to save the records I add to a table?

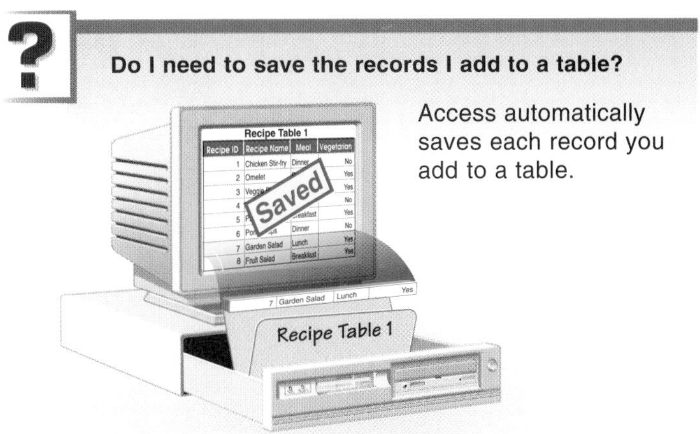

Access automatically saves each record you add to a table.

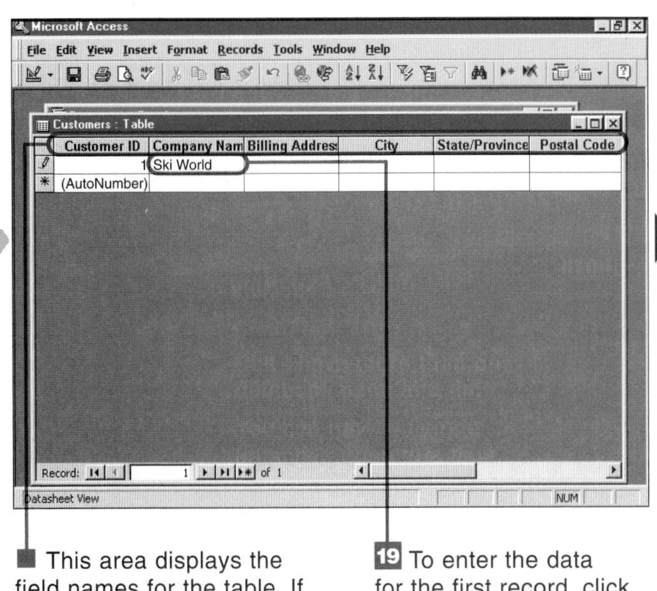

■ This area displays the field names for the table. If you selected **Yes** in step **14**, Access adds an **ID** field to the table to serve as the primary key. The **ID** field will number each record you add to the table.

19 To enter the data for the first record, click the first empty cell in the row. Then type the data that corresponds to the field.

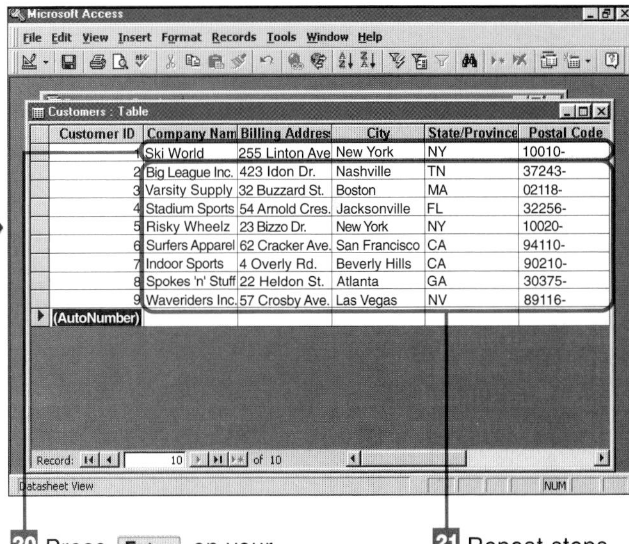

20 Press **Enter** on your keyboard to enter the data and move to the next cell. Then type the data that corresponds to the next field. Repeat this step until you finish entering all the data for the record.

21 Repeat steps **19** and **20** for each record.

ADDRESSES TABLE

me	Address	City	State/Province
	258 Linton Ave.	New York	NY
son	26 Arnold Cres.	Jacksonville	FL
ns	10 Heldon St		GA
cuson	15 Bizzo P		NY
tthews	18 Goul	geles	CA
		Beverly Hills	CA

Edit Tables

Do you want to change the appearance of your tables? This chapter shows you how to edit data, check your spelling, and much more.

Move Through Records 56

Select Data 58

Scroll Through Data 60

Zoom Into a Cell 61

Add a Record 62

Delete a Record 63

Edit Data 64

Move or Copy Data 66

Check Spelling 68

Change Column Width 70

Change Row Height 71

Change Font of Data 72

Change Cell Appearance 74

Hide a Field 76

Freeze a Field 78

MOVE THROUGH RECORDS

You can easily move through the records in your table when reviewing and editing information.

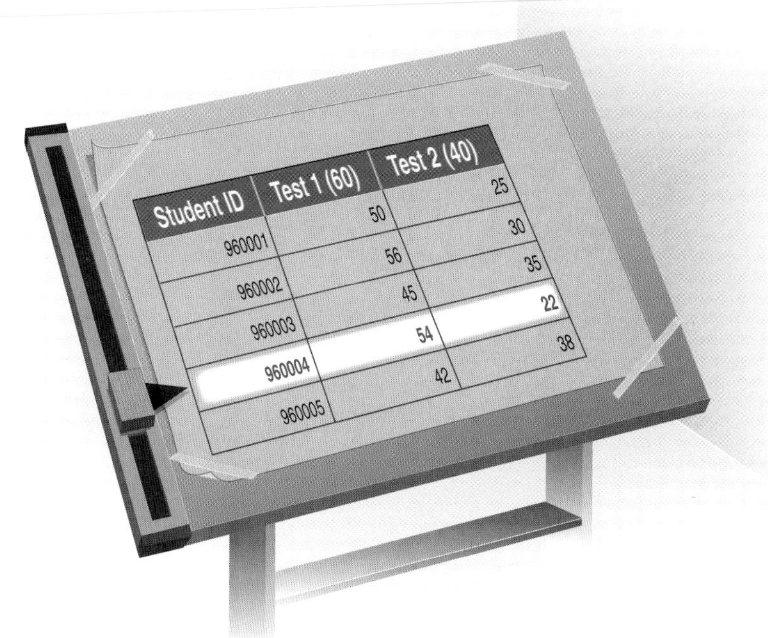

MOVE THROUGH RECORDS

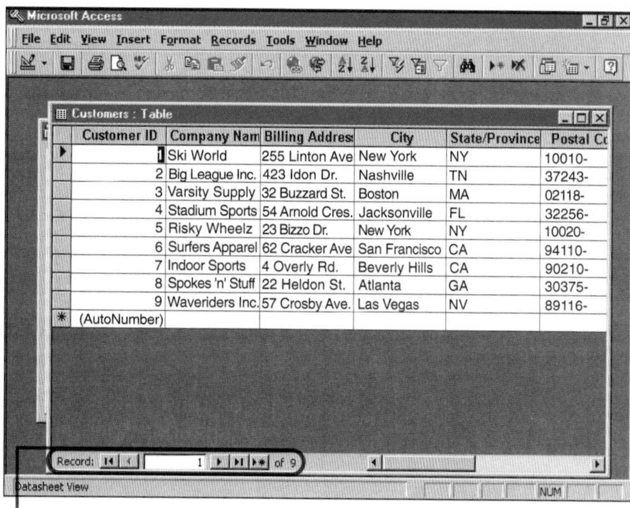

■ This area displays the number of the record containing the insertion point and the total number of records in the table.

Note: The insertion point is the flashing line on your screen that indicates where text you type will appear.

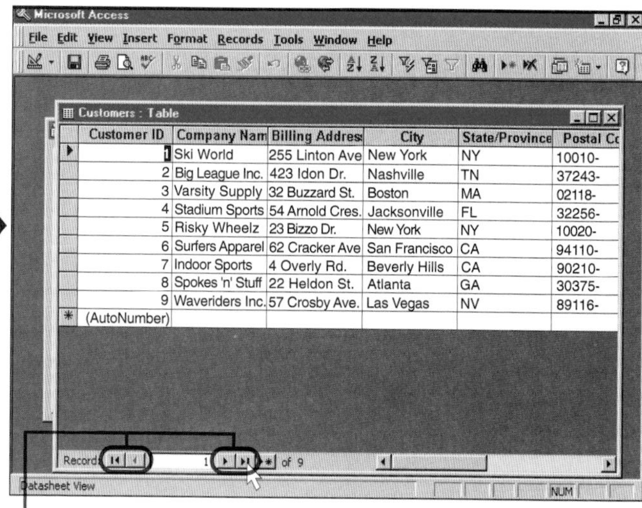

1 To move the insertion point to another record, click one of the following options.

- First Record
- Previous Record
- Next Record
- Last Record

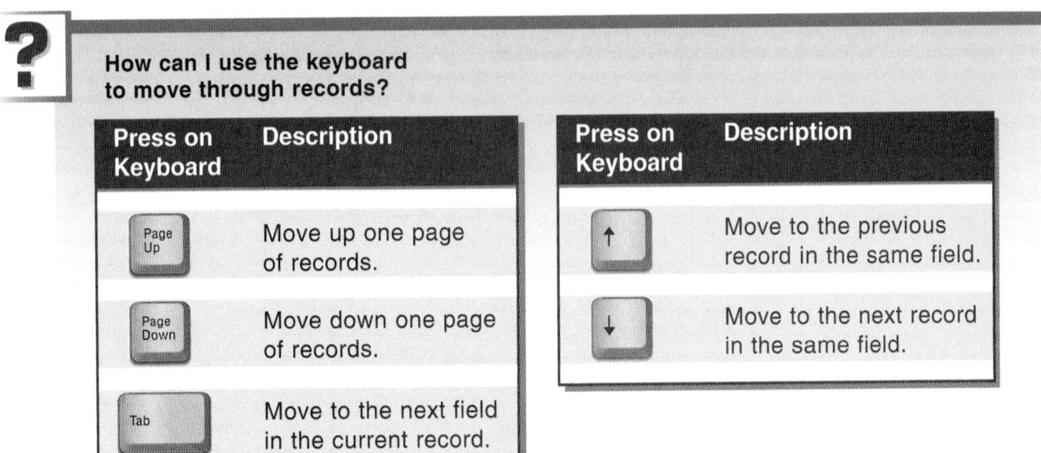

How can I use the keyboard to move through records?

Press on Keyboard	Description
Page Up	Move up one page of records.
Page Down	Move down one page of records.
Tab	Move to the next field in the current record.

Press on Keyboard	Description
↑	Move to the previous record in the same field.
↓	Move to the next record in the same field.

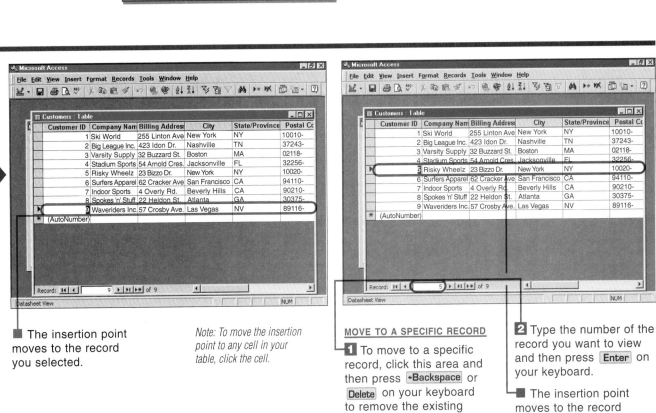

■ The insertion point moves to the record you selected.

Note: To move the insertion point to any cell in your table, click the cell.

MOVE TO A SPECIFIC RECORD

1 To move to a specific record, click this area and then press ←Backspace or Delete on your keyboard to remove the existing number.

2 Type the number of the record you want to view and then press Enter on your keyboard.

■ The insertion point moves to the record you selected.

SELECT DATA

Before performing many tasks in a table, you must select the information you want to work with. Selected information appears highlighted on your screen.

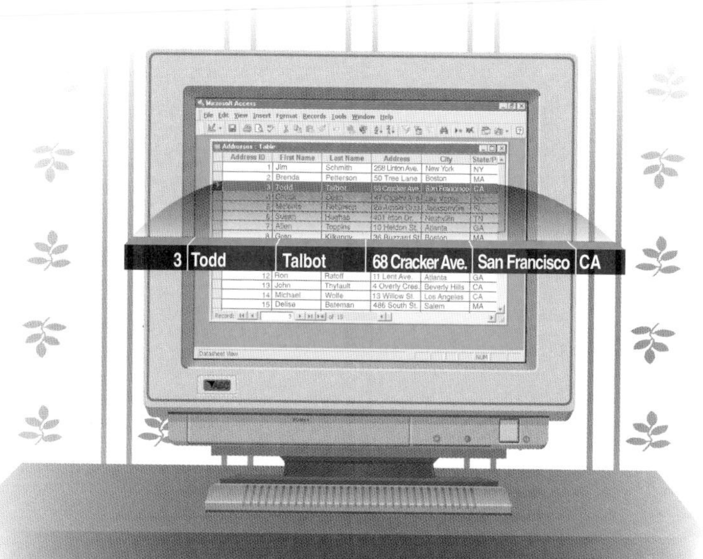

To deselect information in a table at any time, click anywhere in the table.

SELECT DATA

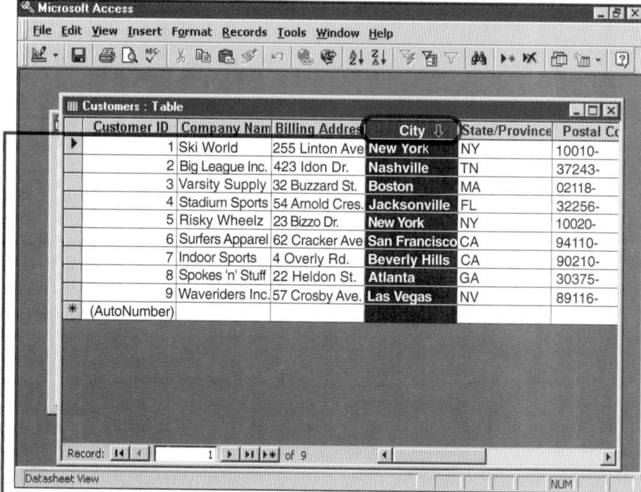

Customer ID	Company Nam	Billing Addres	City	State/Province	Postal Co
1	Ski World	255 Linton Ave	New York	NY	10010-
2	Big League Inc.	423 Idon Dr.	Nashville	TN	37243-
3	Varsity Supply	32 Buzzard St.	Boston	MA	02118-
4	Stadium Sports	54 Arnold Cres.	Jacksonville	FL	32256-
5	Risky Wheelz	23 Bizzo Dr.	New York	NY	10020-
6	Surfers Apparel	62 Cracker Ave	San Francisco	CA	94110-
7	Indoor Sports	4 Overly Rd.	Beverly Hills	CA	90210-
8	Spokes 'n' Stuff	22 Heldon St.	Atlanta	GA	30375-
9	Waveriders Inc.	57 Crosby Ave.	Las Vegas	NV	89116-
(AutoNumber)					

SELECT A FIELD

1 Position the mouse ↖ over the name of the field you want to select (↖ changes to ↓) and then click to select the field.

■ To select multiple fields, position the mouse ↖ over the first field name (↖ changes to ↓). Then drag the mouse until you highlight all the fields you want to select.

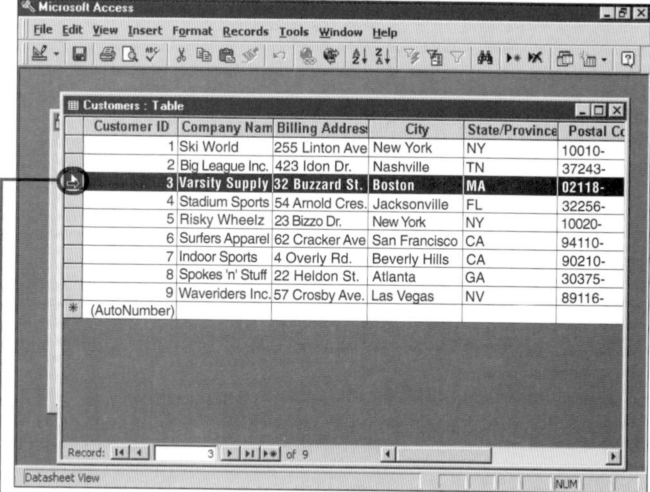

Customer ID	Company Nam	Billing Addres	City	State/Province	Postal Co
1	Ski World	255 Linton Ave	New York	NY	10010-
2	Big League Inc.	423 Idon Dr.	Nashville	TN	37243-
3	Varsity Supply	32 Buzzard St.	Boston	MA	02118-
4	Stadium Sports	54 Arnold Cres.	Jacksonville	FL	32256-
5	Risky Wheelz	23 Bizzo Dr.	New York	NY	10020-
6	Surfers Apparel	62 Cracker Ave	San Francisco	CA	94110-
7	Indoor Sports	4 Overly Rd.	Beverly Hills	CA	90210-
8	Spokes 'n' Stuff	22 Heldon St.	Atlanta	GA	30375-
9	Waveriders Inc.	57 Crosby Ave.	Las Vegas	NV	89116-
(AutoNumber)					

SELECT A RECORD

1 Position the mouse ↖ over the area to the left of the record you want to select (↖ changes to ➡) and then click to select the record.

■ To select multiple records, position the mouse ↖ over the area to the left of the first record (↖ changes to ➡). Then drag the mouse until you highlight all the records you want to select.

?

How do I select the entire table?

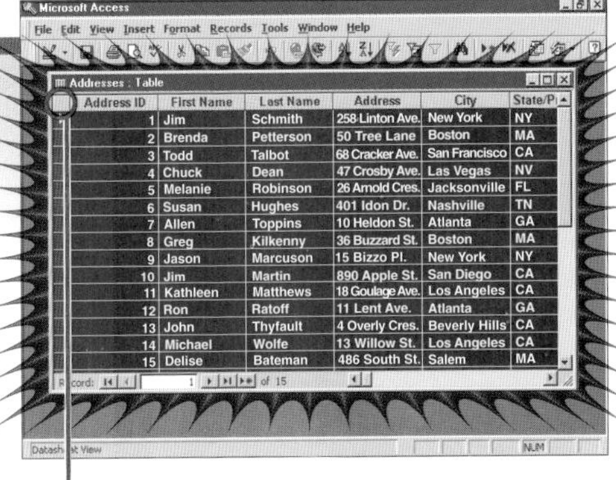

■ To select the entire table, click the area to the left of the field names.

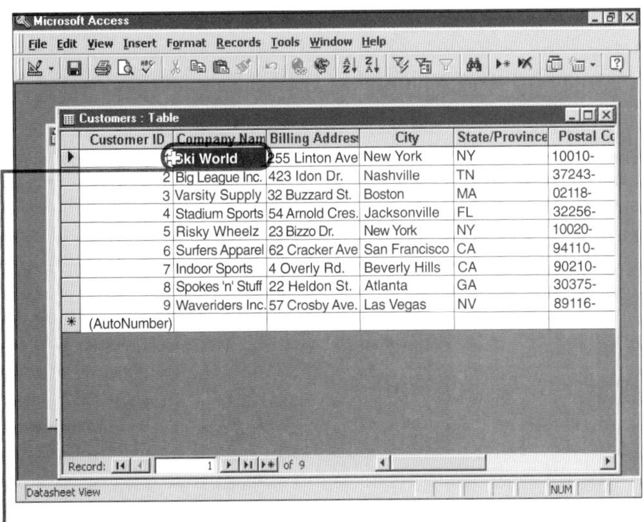

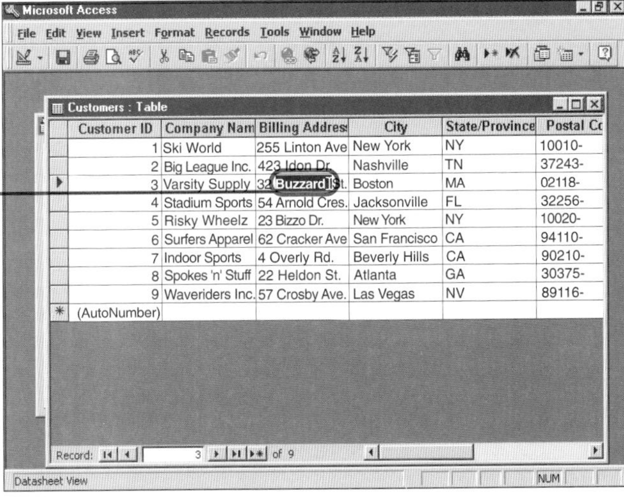

SELECT A CELL

1 Position the mouse I over the left edge of the cell you want to select (I changes to ✚) and then click to select the cell.

■ To select multiple cells, position the mouse I over the left edge of the first cell (I changes to ✚). Then drag the mouse until you highlight all the cells you want to select.

SELECT DATA WITHIN A CELL

1 Position the mouse I over the data. Then drag the mouse until you highlight all the data you want to select.

SCROLL THROUGH DATA

If your screen cannot display all of your records and fields at once, you can scroll through your data to view other areas of the table.

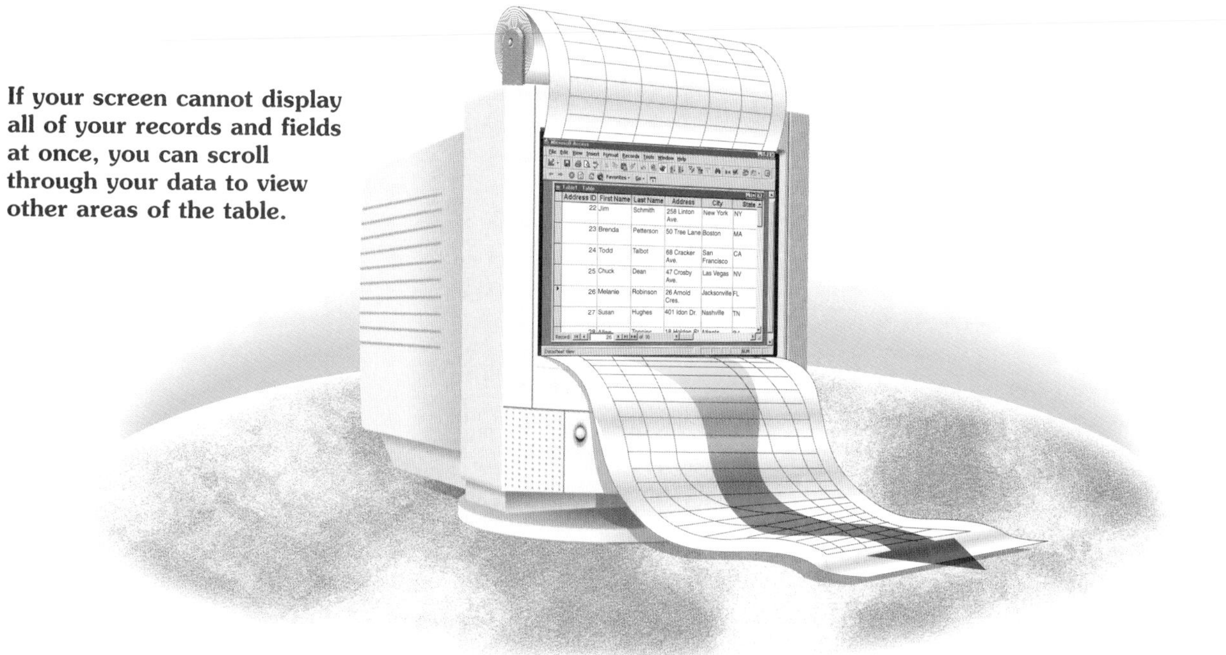

SCROLL THROUGH DATA

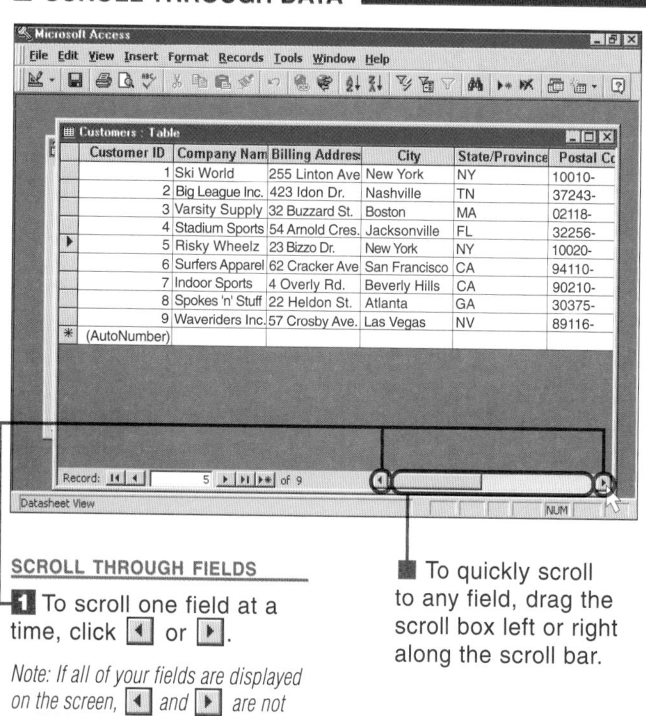

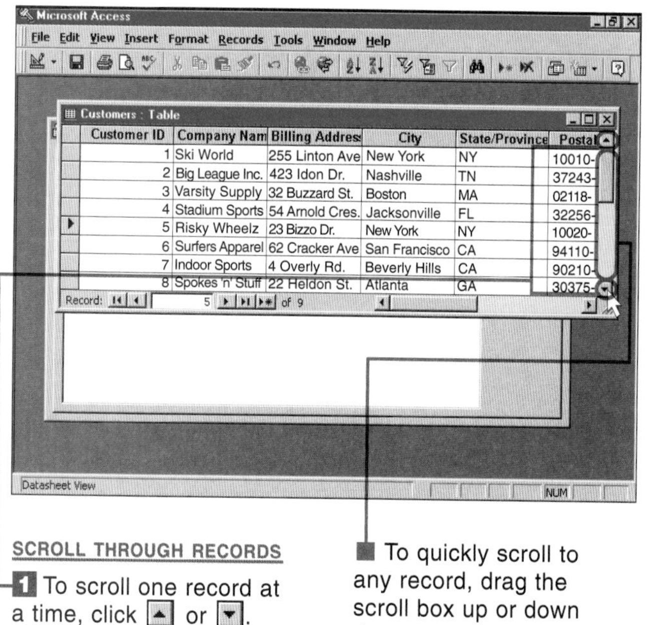

SCROLL THROUGH FIELDS

1 To scroll one field at a time, click ◀ or ▶.

Note: If all of your fields are displayed on the screen, ◀ and ▶ are not available.

■ To quickly scroll to any field, drag the scroll box left or right along the scroll bar.

SCROLL THROUGH RECORDS

1 To scroll one record at a time, click ▲ or ▼.

Note: If all of your records are displayed on the screen, ▲ and ▼ are not available.

■ To quickly scroll to any record, drag the scroll box up or down the scroll bar. As you drag the scroll box, Access indicates which record will appear at the top of your screen.

ZOOM INTO A CELL

You can zoom into a cell to make the contents of the cell easier to review and edit. Zooming into a cell is useful if a column is not wide enough to display all the data in a cell.

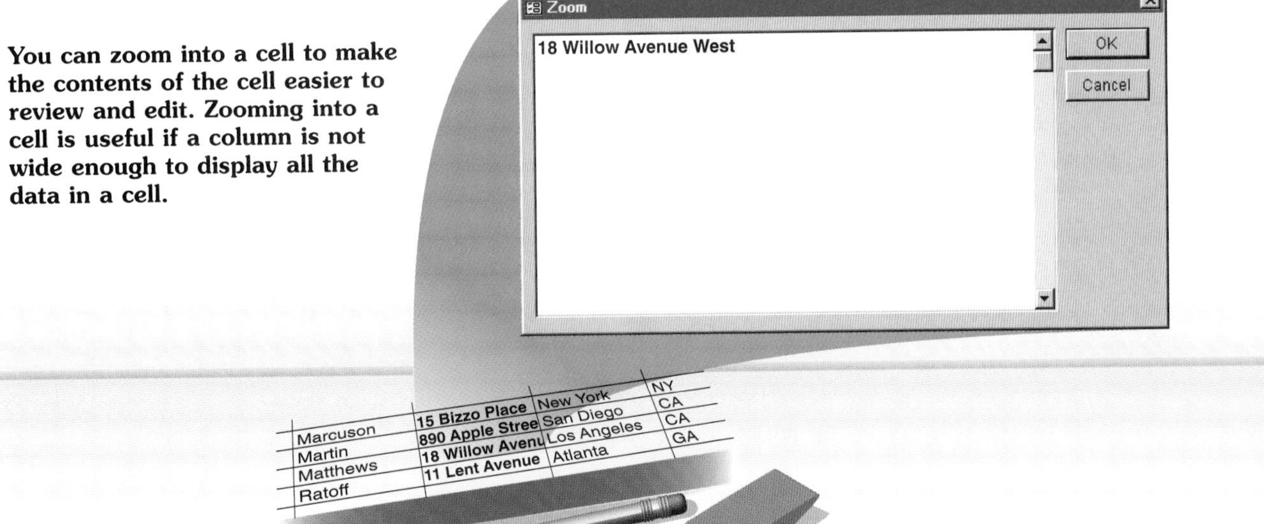

ZOOM INTO A CELL

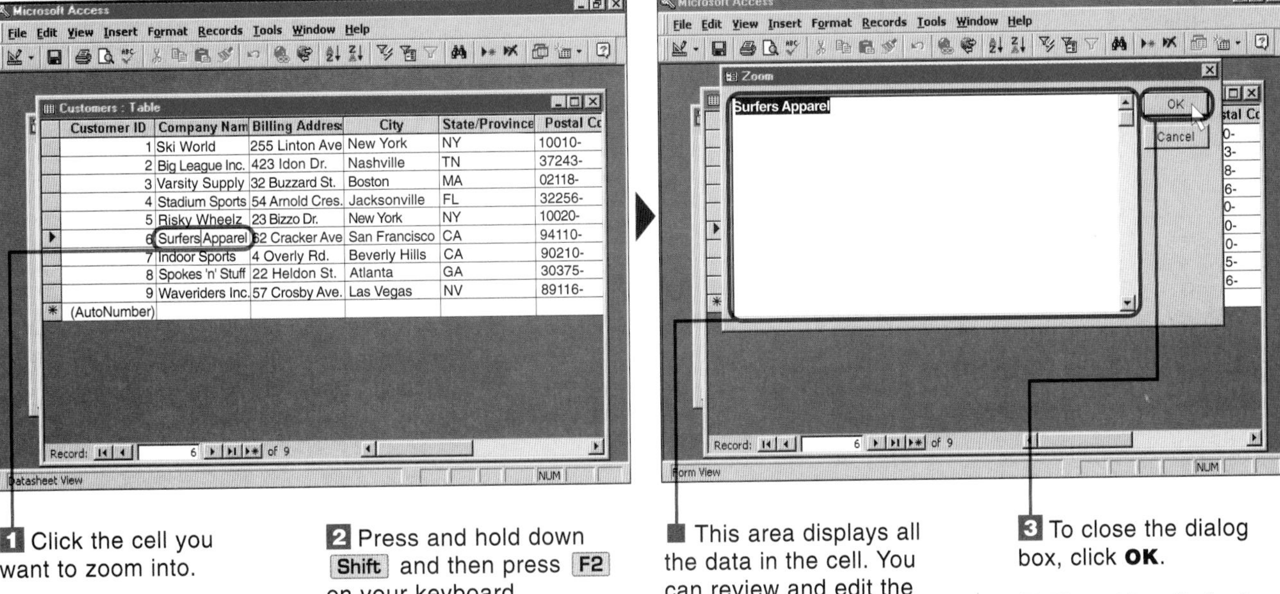

1 Click the cell you want to zoom into.

2 Press and hold down Shift and then press F2 on your keyboard.

■ The **Zoom** dialog box appears.

■ This area displays all the data in the cell. You can review and edit the data in this area.

3 To close the dialog box, click **OK**.

■ The table will display any changes you made to the data.

ADD A RECORD

You can add a new record to insert additional information into your table. For example, you may want to add a new customer.

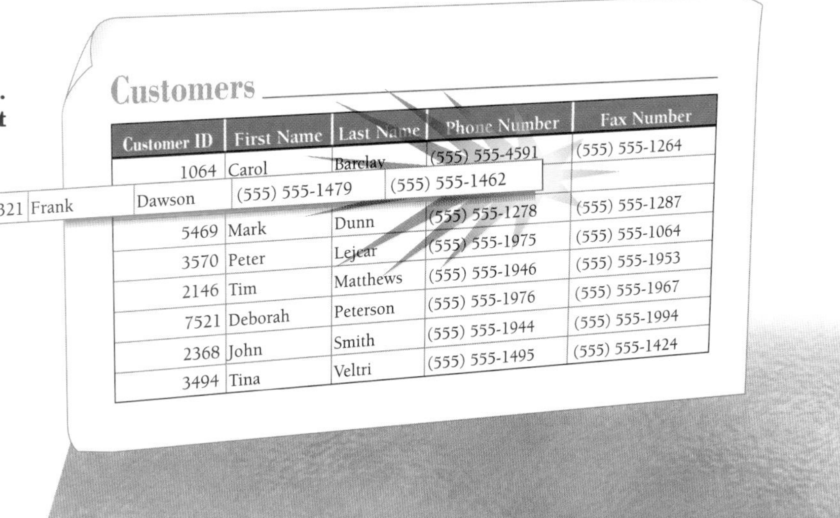

Customers
Customer ID | First Name | Last Name | Phone Number | Fax Number
1064 Carol Barclay (555) 555-4591 (555) 555-1264
7321 Frank Dawson (555) 555-1479 (555) 555-1462
5469 Mark Dunn (555) 555-1278 (555) 555-1287
3570 Peter Lejear (555) 555-1975 (555) 555-1064
2146 Tim Matthews (555) 555-1946 (555) 555-1953
7521 Deborah Peterson (555) 555-1976 (555) 555-1967
2368 John Smith (555) 555-1944 (555) 555-1994
3494 Tina Veltri (555) 555-1495 (555) 555-1424

ADD A RECORD

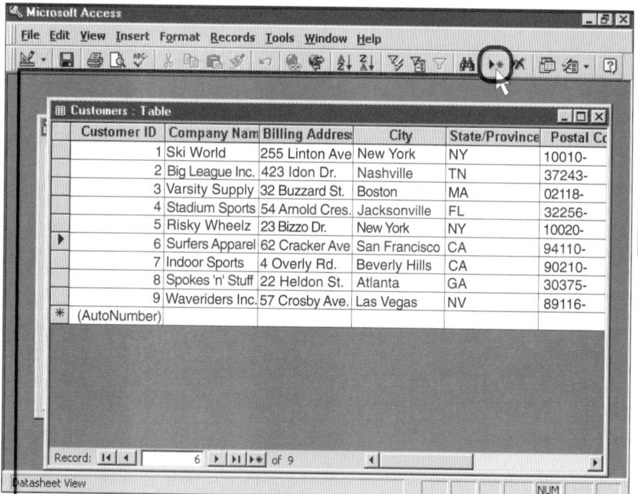

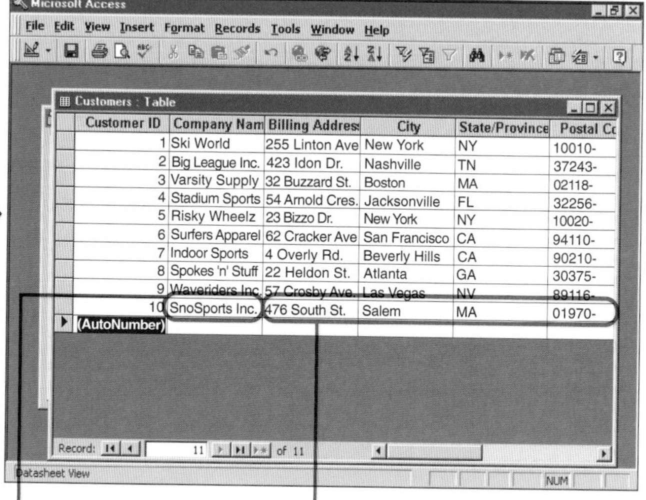

1 Click ▸* to add a new record to your table.

2 Click the first empty cell in the row. Then type the data that corresponds to the field.

3 Press Enter on your keyboard to enter the data and move to the next cell. Then type the data that corresponds to the next field. Repeat this step until you finish entering all the data for the record.

Note: Access automatically saves each new record you add to the table.

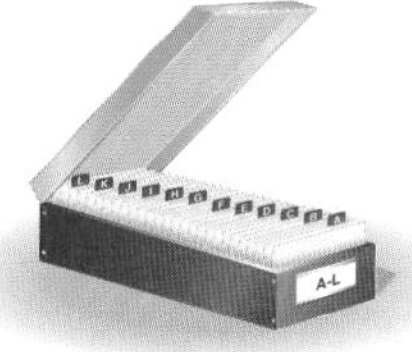

DELETE A RECORD

You can delete a record to remove information you no longer need. For example, you may want to remove an item you no longer offer from a product listing.

DELETE A RECORD

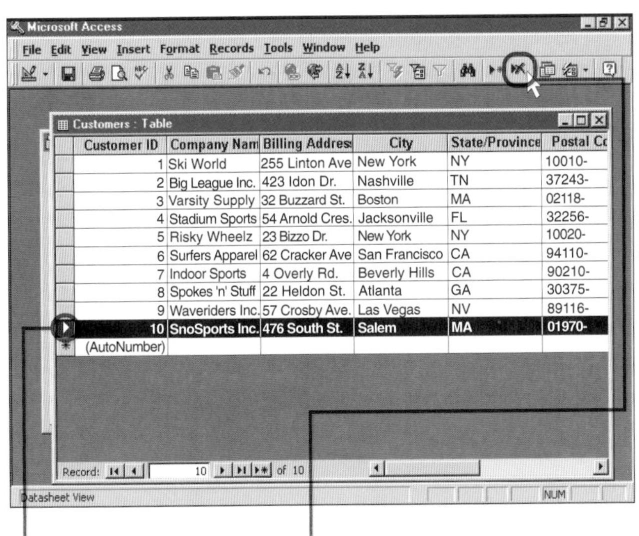

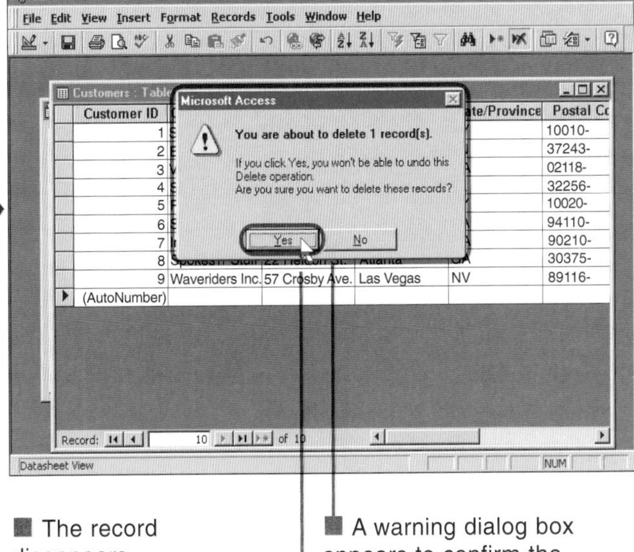

1 Position the mouse over the area to the left of the record you want to delete (changes to ➡) and then click to select the record.

Note: To delete more than one record at once, select all the records you want to delete. To select multiple records, refer to page 58.

2 Click to delete the record.

■ A warning dialog box appears to confirm the deletion.

3 Click **Yes** to permanently delete the record.

■ The record disappears.

EDIT DATA

After you enter data into your table, you can change the data to correct a mistake or update the data.

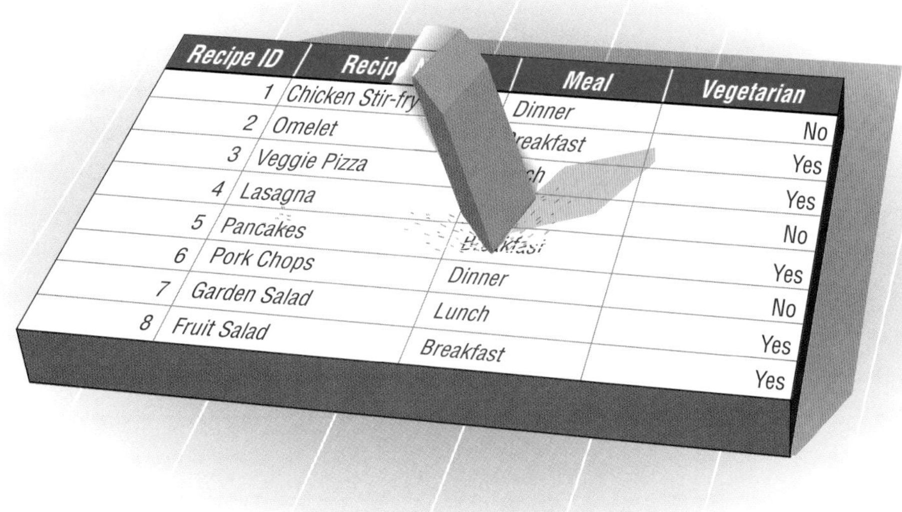

EDIT DATA

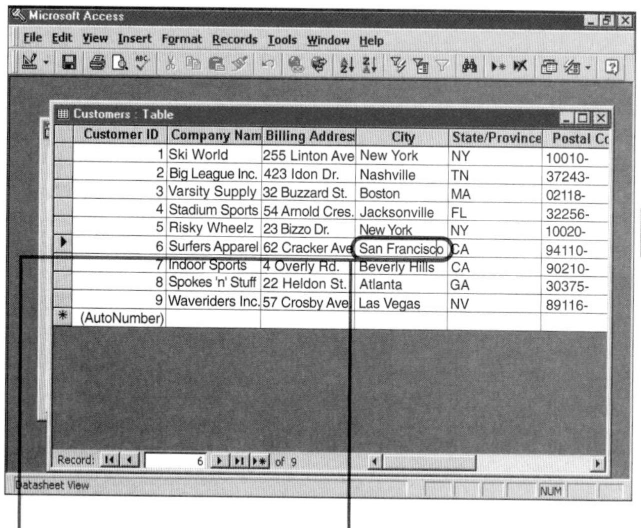

1 Click the location in the cell where you want to change the data.

■ A flashing insertion point appears in the cell.

Note: You can press ← or → on your keyboard to move the insertion point to where you want to change the data.

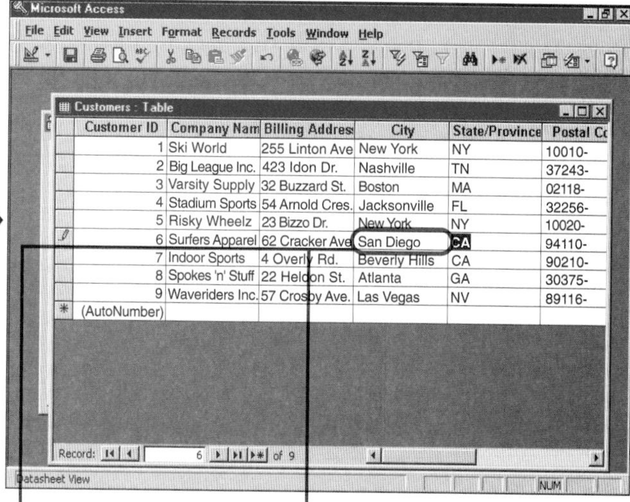

2 To remove the character to the left of the insertion point, press Backspace on your keyboard.

3 To insert data where the insertion point flashes on your screen, type the data.

4 When you finish making changes to the data, press Enter on your keyboard.

What are the symbols that appear to the left of the records?

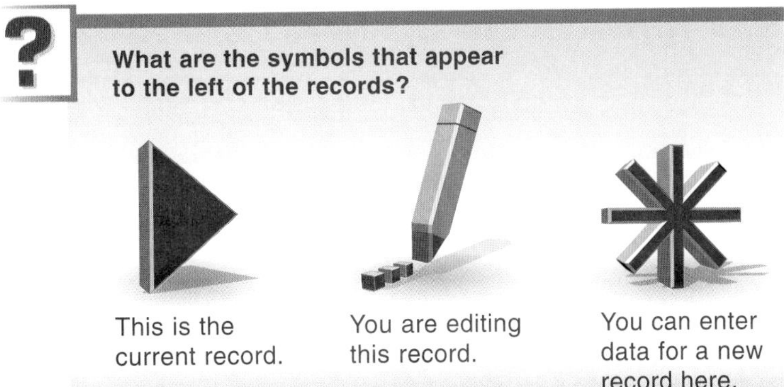

This is the current record.

You are editing this record.

You can enter data for a new record here.

REPLACE ALL DATA IN A CELL

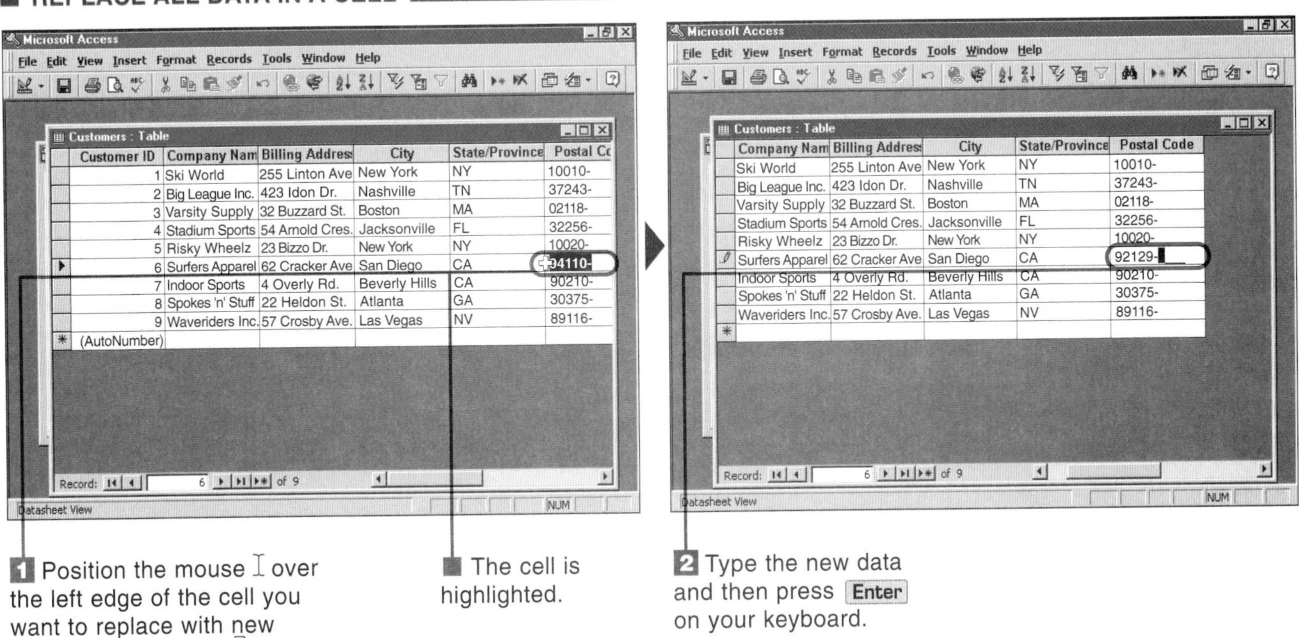

1 Position the mouse I over the left edge of the cell you want to replace with new data (I changes to ✚) and then click to select the cell.

■ The cell is highlighted.

2 Type the new data and then press **Enter** on your keyboard.

MOVE OR COPY DATA

You can easily place data from one location in a table in another location. Moving or copying data helps you quickly reorganize your table and saves you from retyping information.

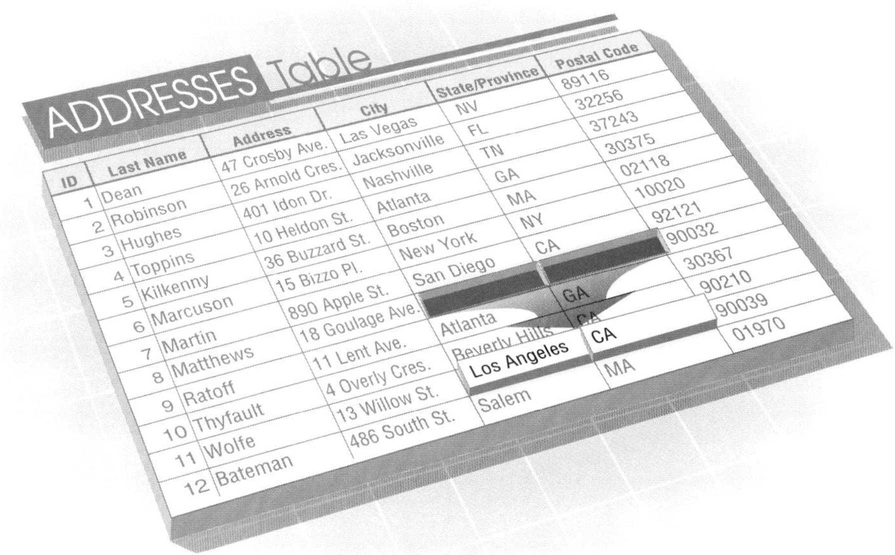

MOVE OR COPY DATA

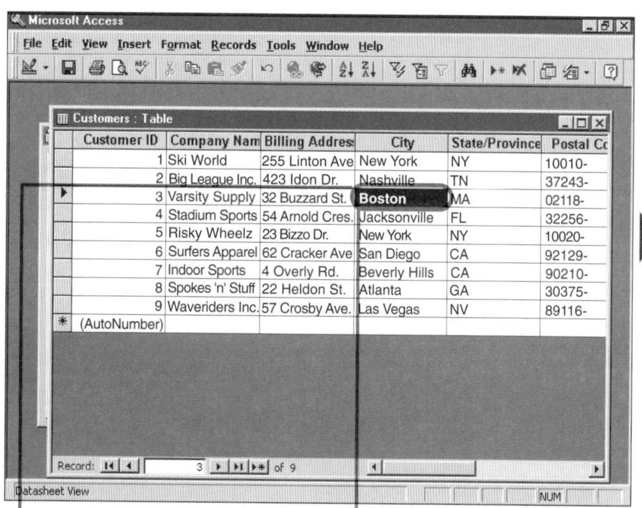

1 To copy an entire cell, position the mouse I over the left edge of the cell you want to copy (I changes to ✚) and then click to select the cell.

Note: You cannot move an entire cell.

■ To move or copy data within a cell, position the mouse I over the data. Then drag the mouse until you highlight all the data you want to move or copy.

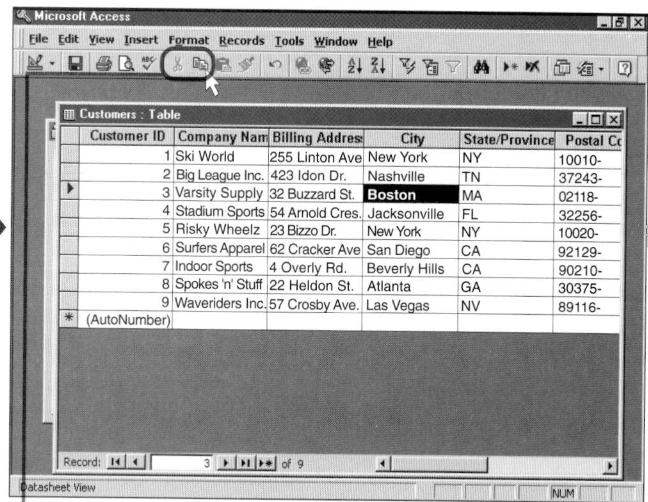

2 Click one of the following options.

✂ Move the data.

⎘ Copy the data.

What is the difference between moving and copying data?

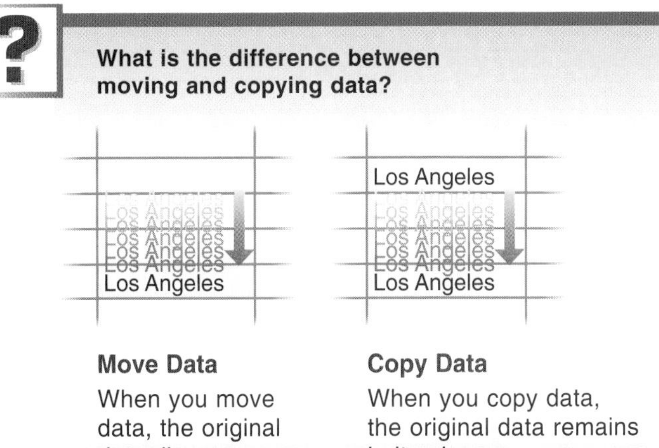

Move Data

When you move data, the original data disappears.

Copy Data

When you copy data, the original data remains in its place.

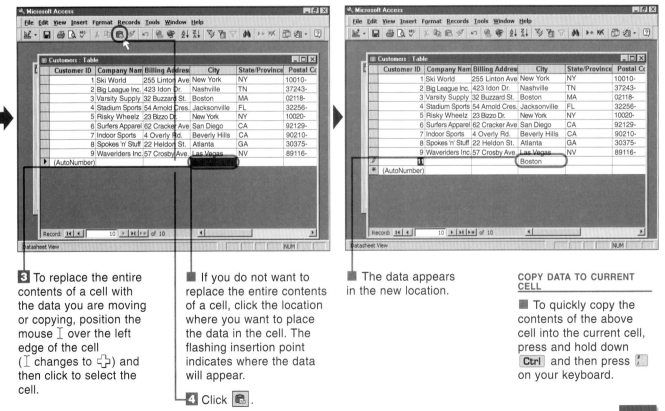

3 To replace the entire contents of a cell with the data you are moving or copying, position the mouse I over the left edge of the cell (I changes to ✚) and then click to select the cell.

■ If you do not want to replace the entire contents of a cell, click the location where you want to place the data in the cell. The flashing insertion point indicates where the data will appear.

4 Click 📋.

■ The data appears in the new location.

COPY DATA TO CURRENT CELL

■ To quickly copy the contents of the above cell into the current cell, press and hold down Ctrl and then press ' on your keyboard.

CHECK SPELLING

You can quickly find and correct all the spelling errors in your table.

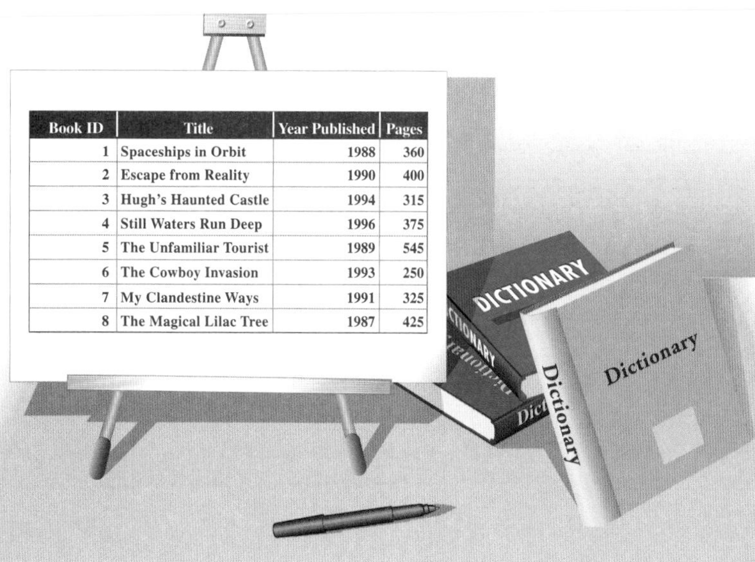

Book ID	Title	Year Published	Pages
1	Spaceships in Orbit	1988	360
2	Escape from Reality	1990	400
3	Hugh's Haunted Castle	1994	315
4	Still Waters Run Deep	1996	375
5	The Unfamiliar Tourist	1989	545
6	The Cowboy Invasion	1993	250
7	My Clandestine Ways	1991	325
8	The Magical Lilac Tree	1987	425

Access compares every word in your table to words in its dictionary. If a word does not exist in the dictionary, Access considers the word misspelled.

CHECK SPELLING

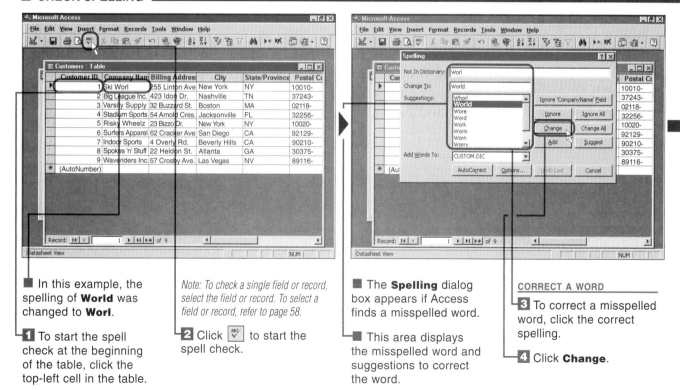

■ In this example, the spelling of **World** was changed to **Worl**.

1 To start the spell check at the beginning of the table, click the top-left cell in the table.

Note: To check a single field or record, select the field or record. To select a field or record, refer to page 58.

2 Click [spelling button] to start the spell check.

■ The **Spelling** dialog box appears if Access finds a misspelled word.

■ This area displays the misspelled word and suggestions to correct the word.

CORRECT A WORD

3 To correct a misspelled word, click the correct spelling.

4 Click **Change**.

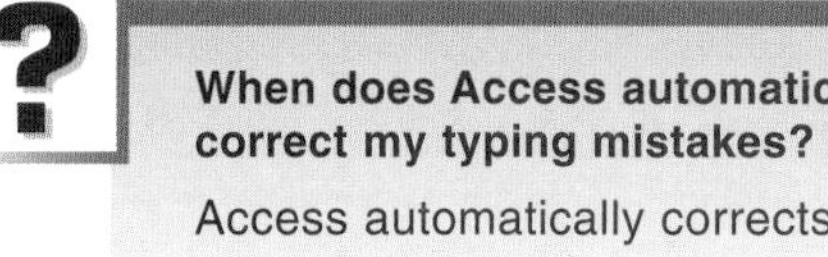

When does Access automatically correct my typing mistakes?

Access automatically corrects common errors as you type.

abotu → about
adn → and
comittee → committee
nwe → new
occurence → occurrence
recieve → receive
seperate → separate
smoe → some
teh → the

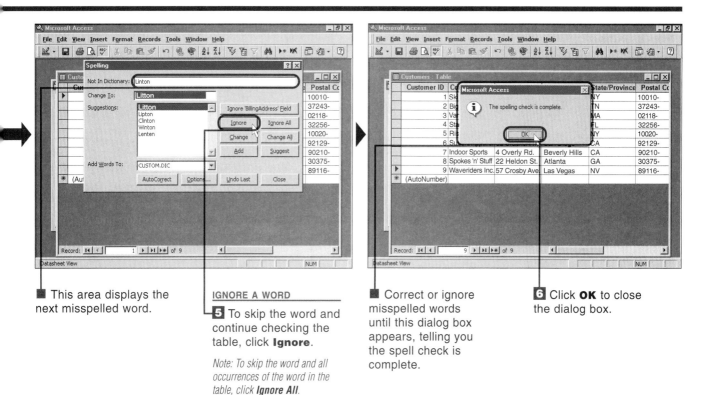

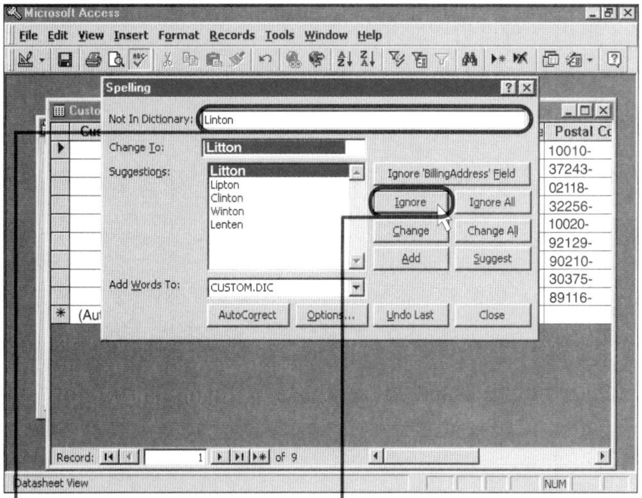

■ This area displays the next misspelled word.

IGNORE A WORD

5 To skip the word and continue checking the table, click **Ignore**.

*Note: To skip the word and all occurrences of the word in the table, click **Ignore All**.*

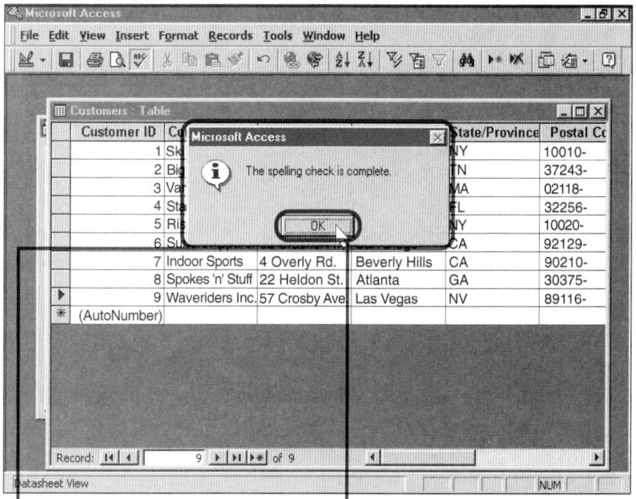

■ Correct or ignore misspelled words until this dialog box appears, telling you the spell check is complete.

6 Click **OK** to close the dialog box.

CHANGE COLUMN WIDTH

You can improve the appearance of your table by changing the width of columns. Changing the width of a column also lets you view data that is too long to display in a column.

Address	First Na	Last Na	Address	City	State/Pr	Postal
1	Jim	Schmith	258 Linton Ave.	New Yor	NY	1001
2	Brenda	Petterso	50 Tree Lane	Boston	MA	0211
3	Todd	Talbot	68 Cracker Ave	San Fra	CA	9411
4	Chuck	Dean	47 Crosby Ave.	Las Veg	NV	8911
5	Melanie	Robinso	26 Arnold Cres.	Jackson	FL	3225
6	Susan	Hughes	401 Idon Dr.	Nashvill	TN	3724
7	Allen	Toppins	10 Heldon St.	Atlanta	GA	3037
8	Greg	Kilkenny	36 Buzzard St.	Boston	MA	0211

CHANGE COLUMN WIDTH

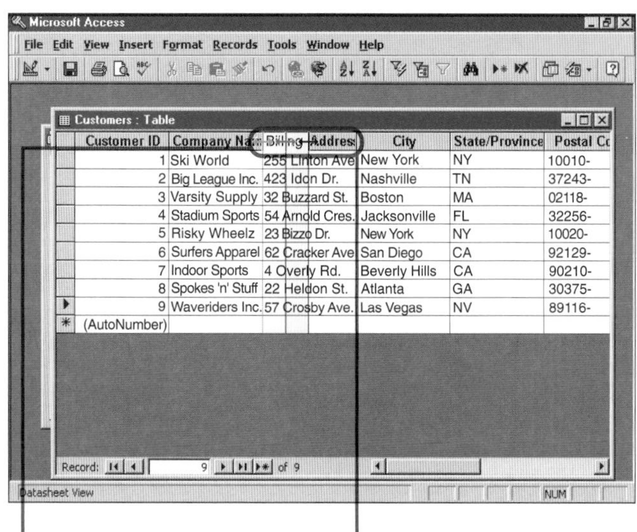

1 To change the width of a column, position the mouse ↖ over the right edge of the column heading (↖ changes to ↔).

2 Drag the column edge until the line displays the column width you want.

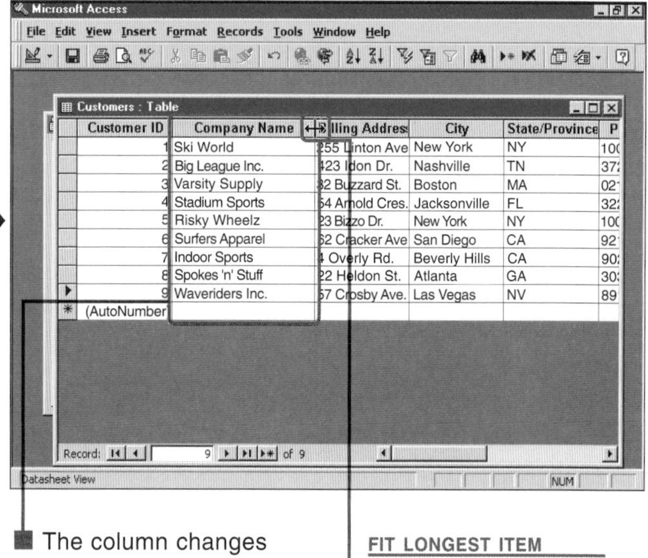

■ The column changes to the new width.

FIT LONGEST ITEM

You can have Access change a column width to fit the longest item in the column.

1 Double-click the right edge of the column heading.

CHANGE ROW HEIGHT

You can change the height of all the rows in your table at once to add space between the rows. This can make the information in the table easier to read.

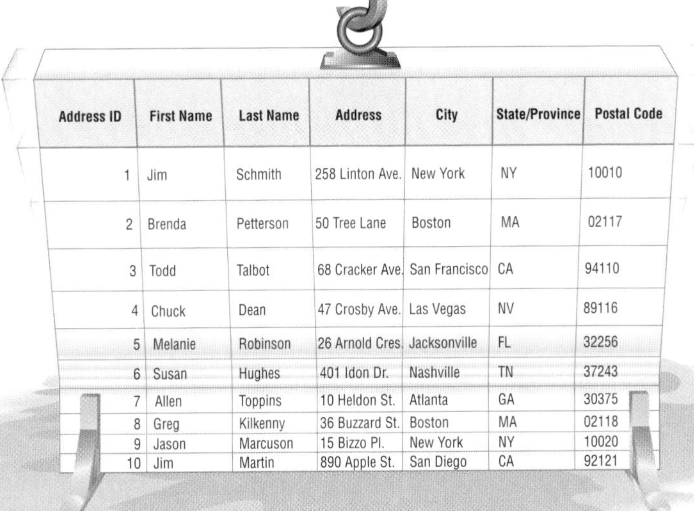

Address ID	First Name	Last Name	Address	City	State/Province	Postal Code
1	Jim	Schmith	258 Linton Ave.	New York	NY	10010
2	Brenda	Petterson	50 Tree Lane	Boston	MA	02117
3	Todd	Talbot	68 Cracker Ave.	San Francisco	CA	94110
4	Chuck	Dean	47 Crosby Ave.	Las Vegas	NV	89116
5	Melanie	Robinson	26 Arnold Cres.	Jacksonville	FL	32256
6	Susan	Hughes	401 Idon Dr.	Nashville	TN	37243
7	Allen	Toppins	10 Heldon St.	Atlanta	GA	30375
8	Greg	Kilkenny	36 Buzzard St.	Boston	MA	02118
9	Jason	Marcuson	15 Bizzo Pl.	New York	NY	10020
10	Jim	Martin	890 Apple St.	San Diego	CA	92121

CHANGE ROW HEIGHT

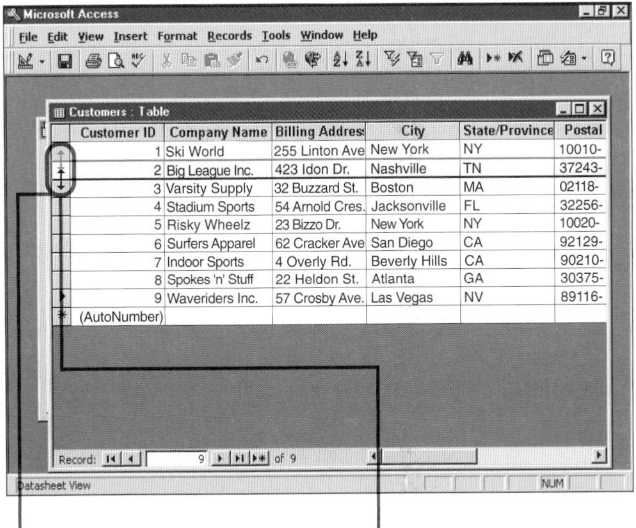

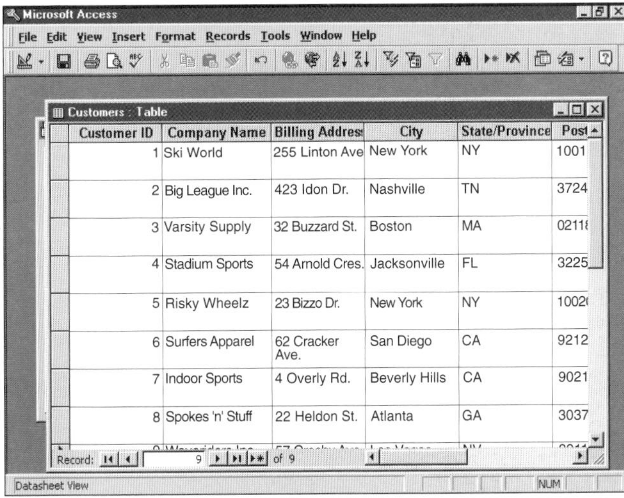

1 To change the height of all the rows, position the mouse ↖ over the bottom edge of a row in this area (↖ changes to ‡).

2 Drag the row edge until the line displays the row height you want.

■ All the rows change to the new height.

CHANGE FONT OF DATA

You can change the design, style and size of data to enhance the appearance of your table.

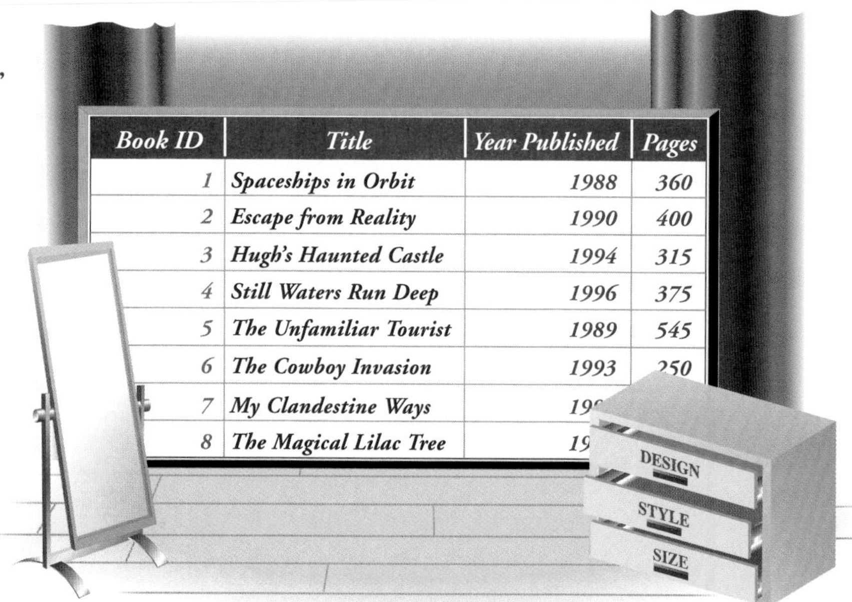

Book ID
Title
Year Published
Pages
1 Spaceships in Orbit 1988 360
2 Escape from Reality 1990 400
3 Hugh's Haunted Castle 1994 315
4 Still Waters Run Deep 1996 375
5 The Unfamiliar Tourist 1989 545
6 The Cowboy Invasion 1993
7 My Clandestine Ways
8 The Magical Lilac Tree
DESIGN
STYLE
SIZE

CHANGE FONT OF DATA

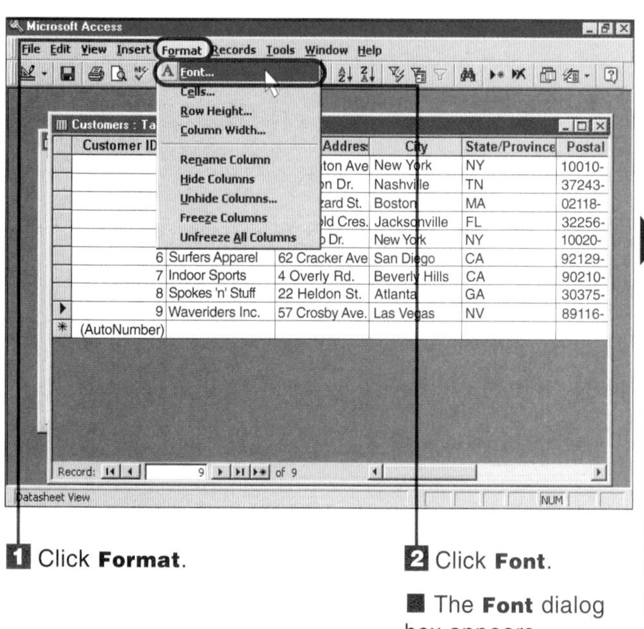

1 Click **Format**.

2 Click **Font**.

■ The **Font** dialog box appears.

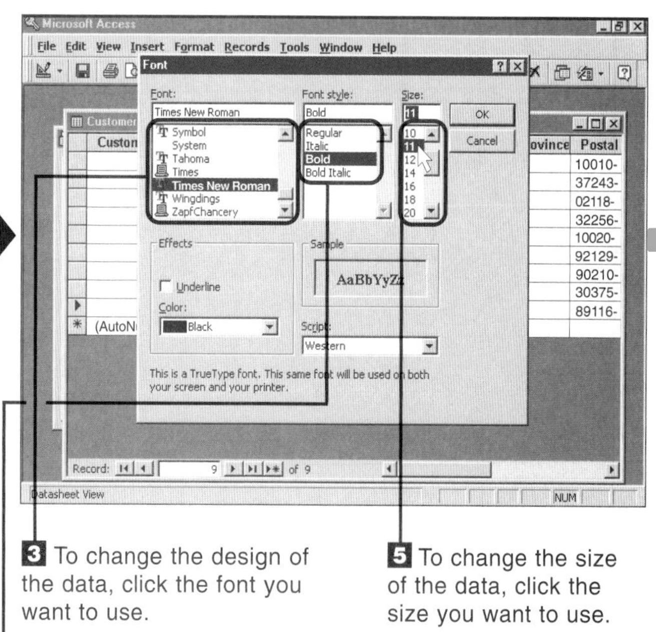

3 To change the design of the data, click the font you want to use.

4 To change the style of the data, click the font style you want to use.

5 To change the size of the data, click the size you want to use.

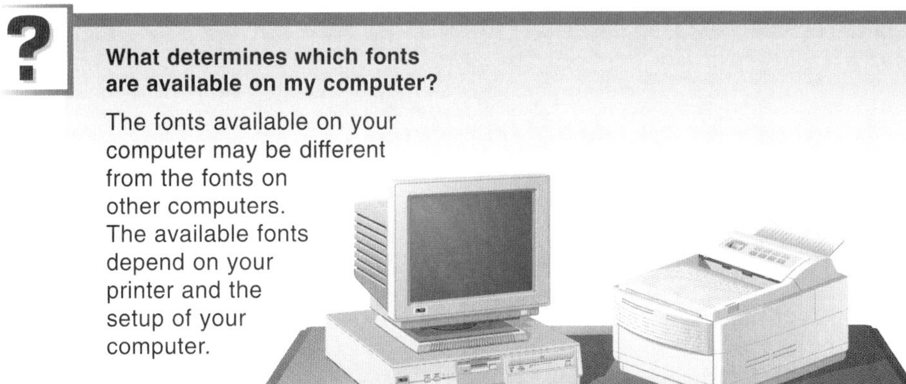

What determines which fonts are available on my computer?

The fonts available on your computer may be different from the fonts on other computers. The available fonts depend on your printer and the setup of your computer.

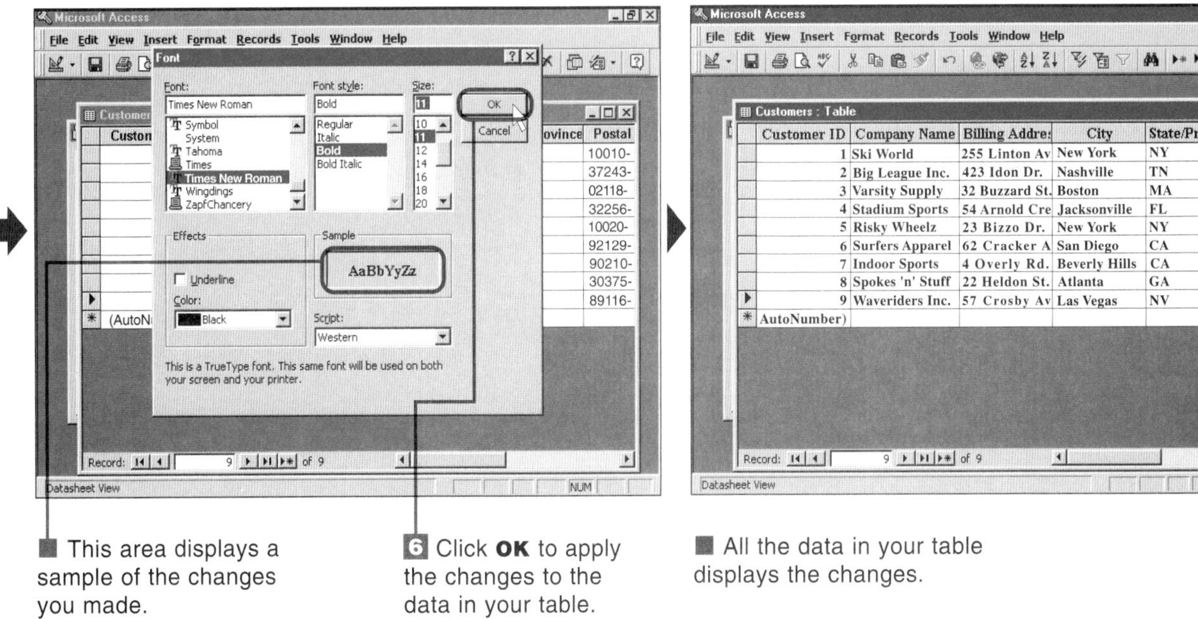

■ This area displays a sample of the changes you made.

6 Click **OK** to apply the changes to the data in your table.

■ All the data in your table displays the changes.

CHANGE CELL APPEARANCE

You can make a table more attractive by changing the appearance of cells.

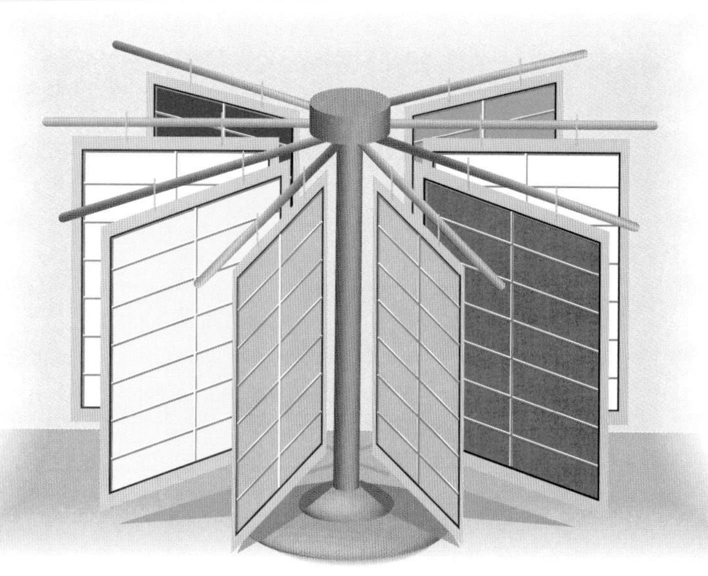

CHANGE CELL APPEARANCE

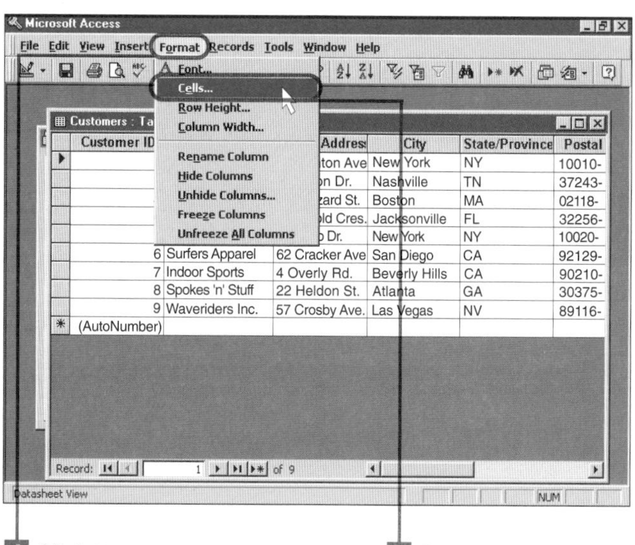

1 Click **Format**.

2 Click **Cells**.

■ The **Cells Effects** dialog box appears.

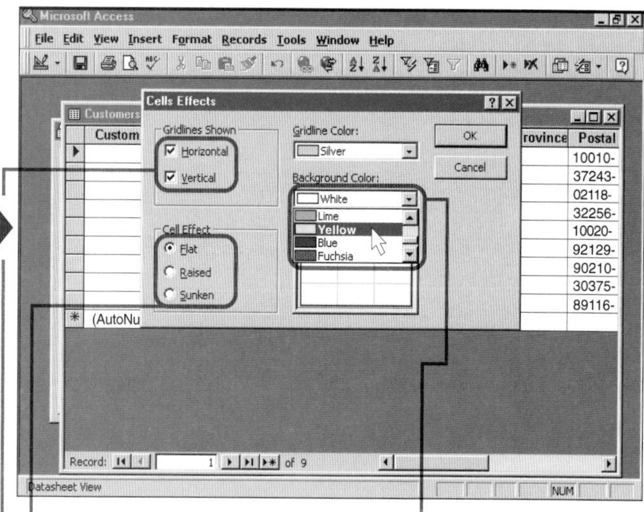

3 Click the cell effect you want to use (○ changes to ◉).

4 To remove gridlines, click the gridline you want to remove (☑ changes to ☐). These options are only available if you selected **Flat** in step **3**.

5 To change the background color, click this area. Then click the color you want to use.

How can I change the appearance of cells in a table?

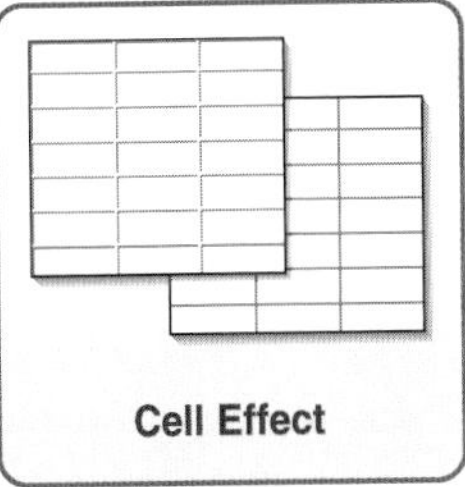
Cell Effect

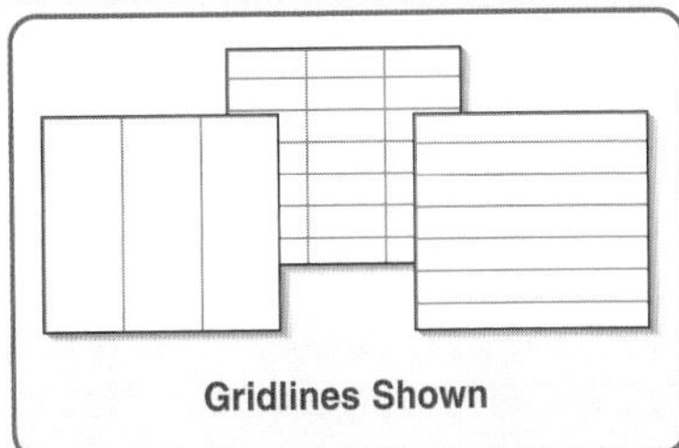
Gridlines Shown

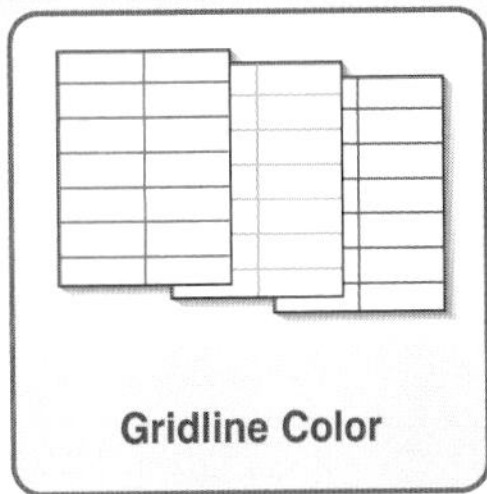
Gridline Color

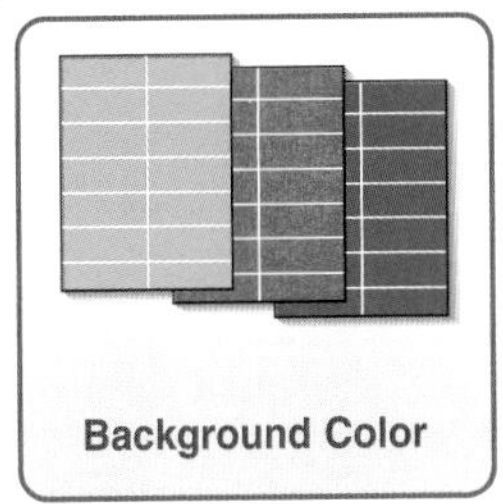
Background Color

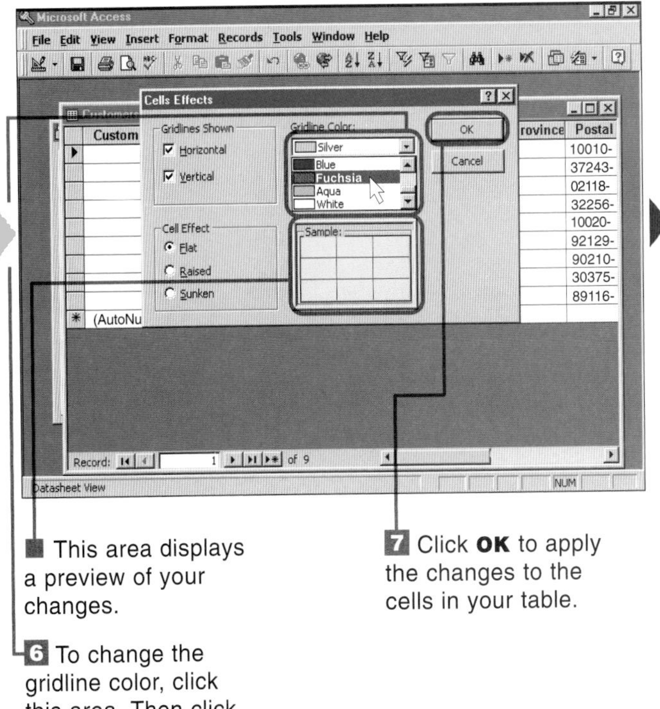

■ This area displays a preview of your changes.

6 To change the gridline color, click this area. Then click the color you want to use.

7 Click **OK** to apply the changes to the cells in your table.

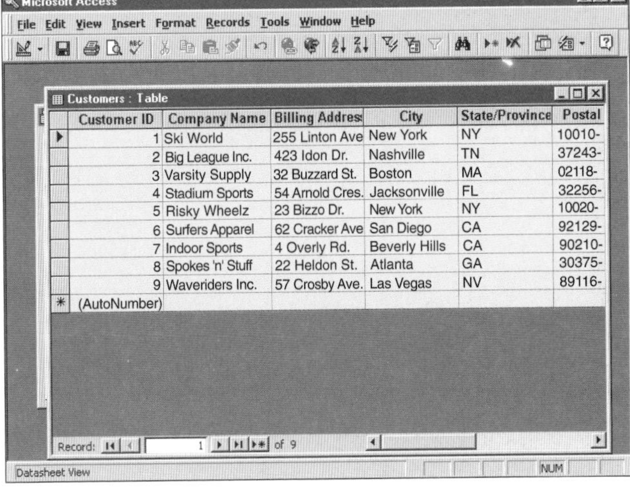

■ The cells in your table display the changes.

HIDE A FIELD

You can temporarily hide a field in your table and then redisplay the field at any time.

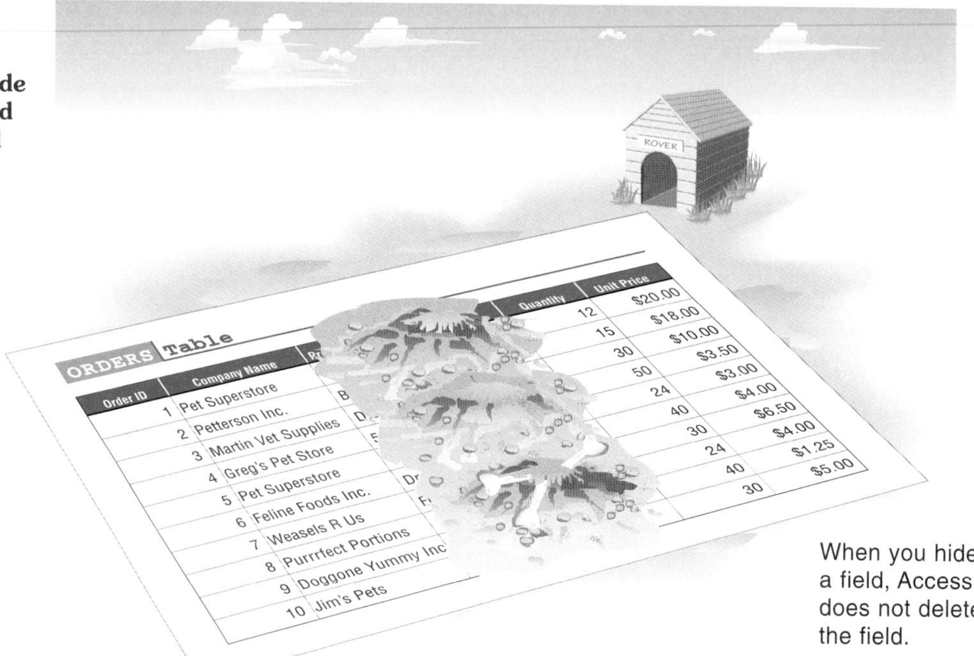

When you hide a field, Access does not delete the field.

HIDE A FIELD

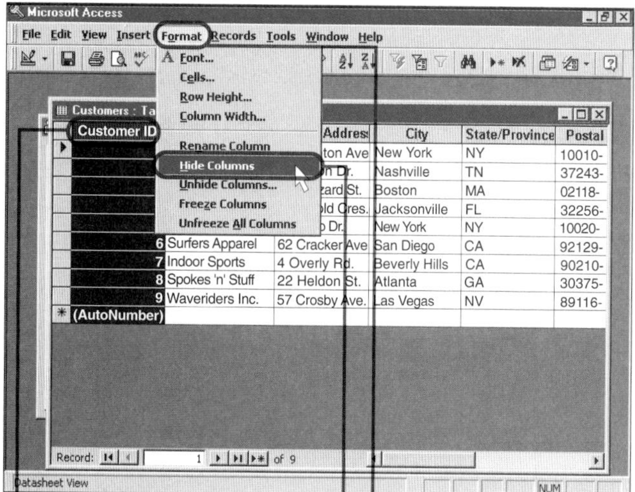

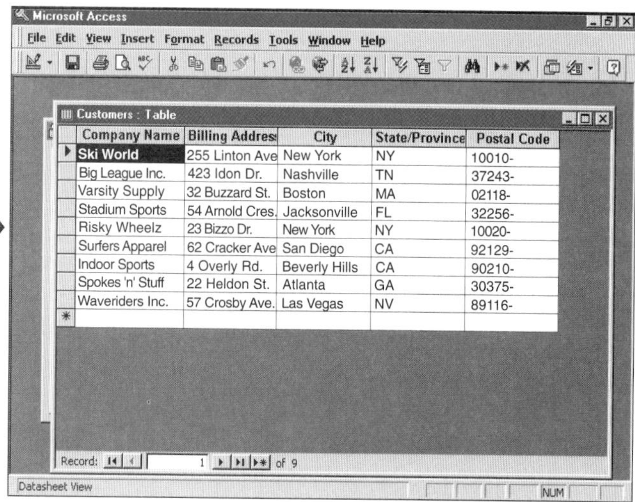

1 Click the name of the field you want to hide.

Note: To hide more than one field, select all the fields you want to hide. To select multiple fields, refer to page 58.

2 Click **Format**.

3 Click **Hide Columns**.

■ The field disappears.

When would I hide a field?

Hiding a field reduces the clutter on your screen and allows you to review only the fields of interest. For example, if you want to browse through only the names and telephone numbers of your students, you can hide all the fields displaying other information.

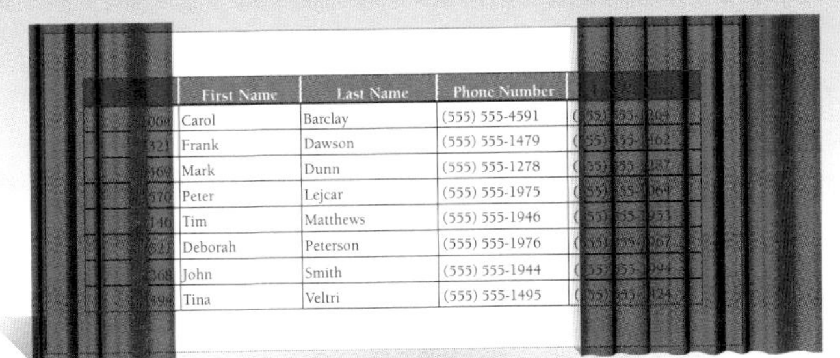

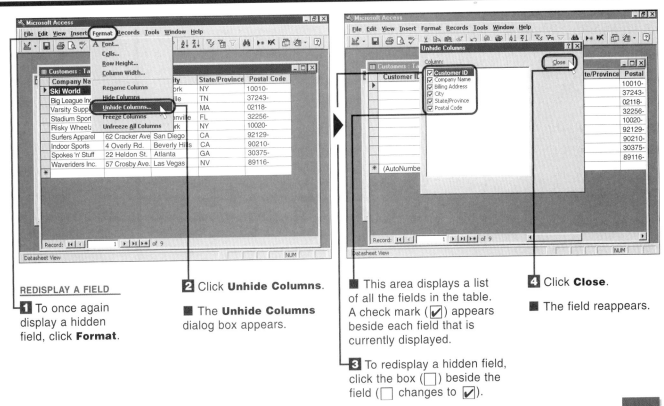

REDISPLAY A FIELD

1 To once again display a hidden field, click **Format**.

2 Click **Unhide Columns**.

■ The **Unhide Columns** dialog box appears.

■ This area displays a list of all the fields in the table. A check mark (☑) appears beside each field that is currently displayed.

3 To redisplay a hidden field, click the box (☐) beside the field (☐ changes to ☑).

4 Click **Close**.

■ The field reappears.

FREEZE A FIELD

You can freeze a field so it will remain on your screen at all times.

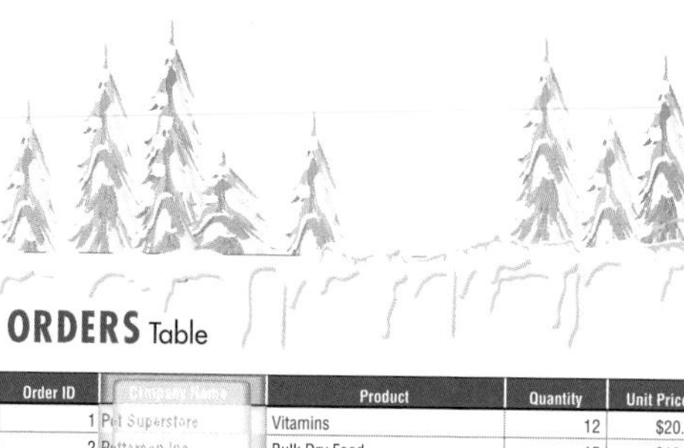

Freezing a field lets you keep important data on the screen as you move through data in a large table.

FREEZE A FIELD

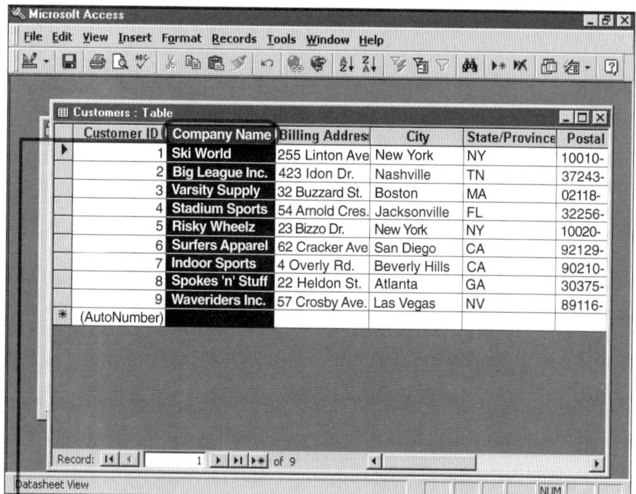

1 Click the name of the field you want to freeze.

Note: To freeze more than one field, select the fields you want to freeze. To select multiple fields, refer to page 58.

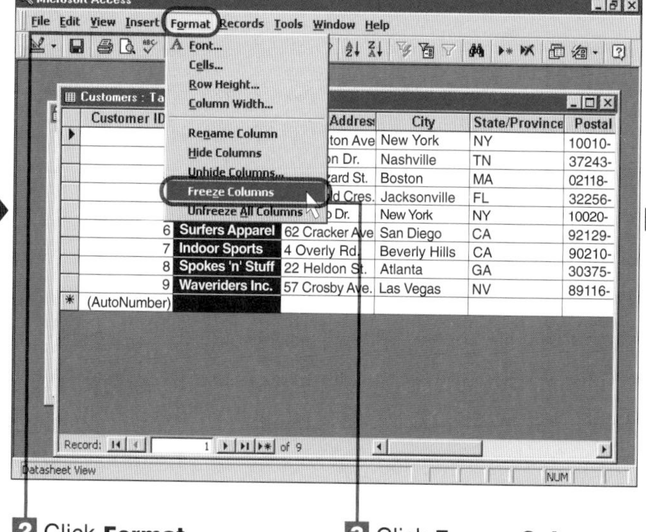

2 Click **Format**.

3 Click **Freeze Columns**.

How do I unfreeze a field?

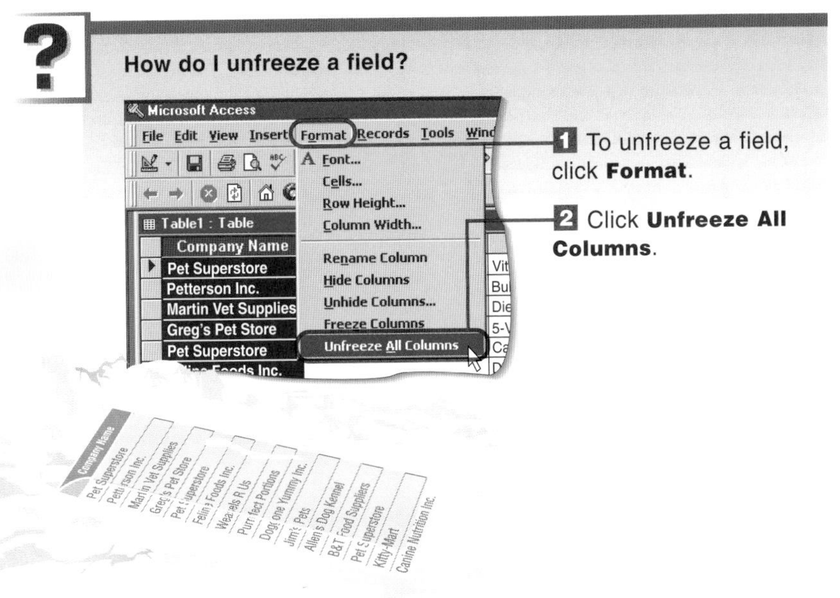

1 To unfreeze a field, click **Format**.

2 Click **Unfreeze All Columns**.

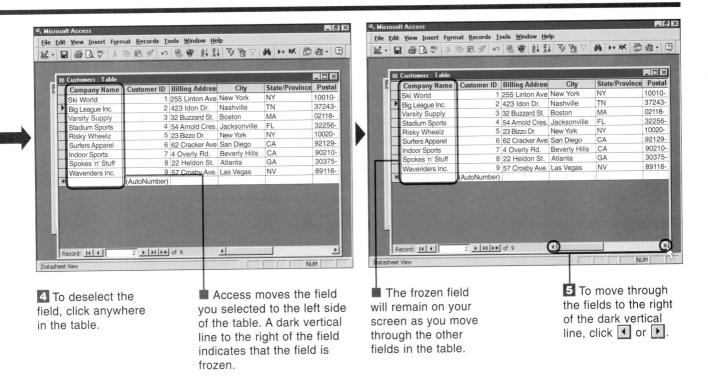

4 To deselect the field, click anywhere in the table.

■ Access moves the field you selected to the left side of the table. A dark vertical line to the right of the field indicates that the field is frozen.

■ The frozen field will remain on your screen as you move through the other fields in the table.

5 To move through the fields to the right of the dark vertical line, click ◂ or ▸.

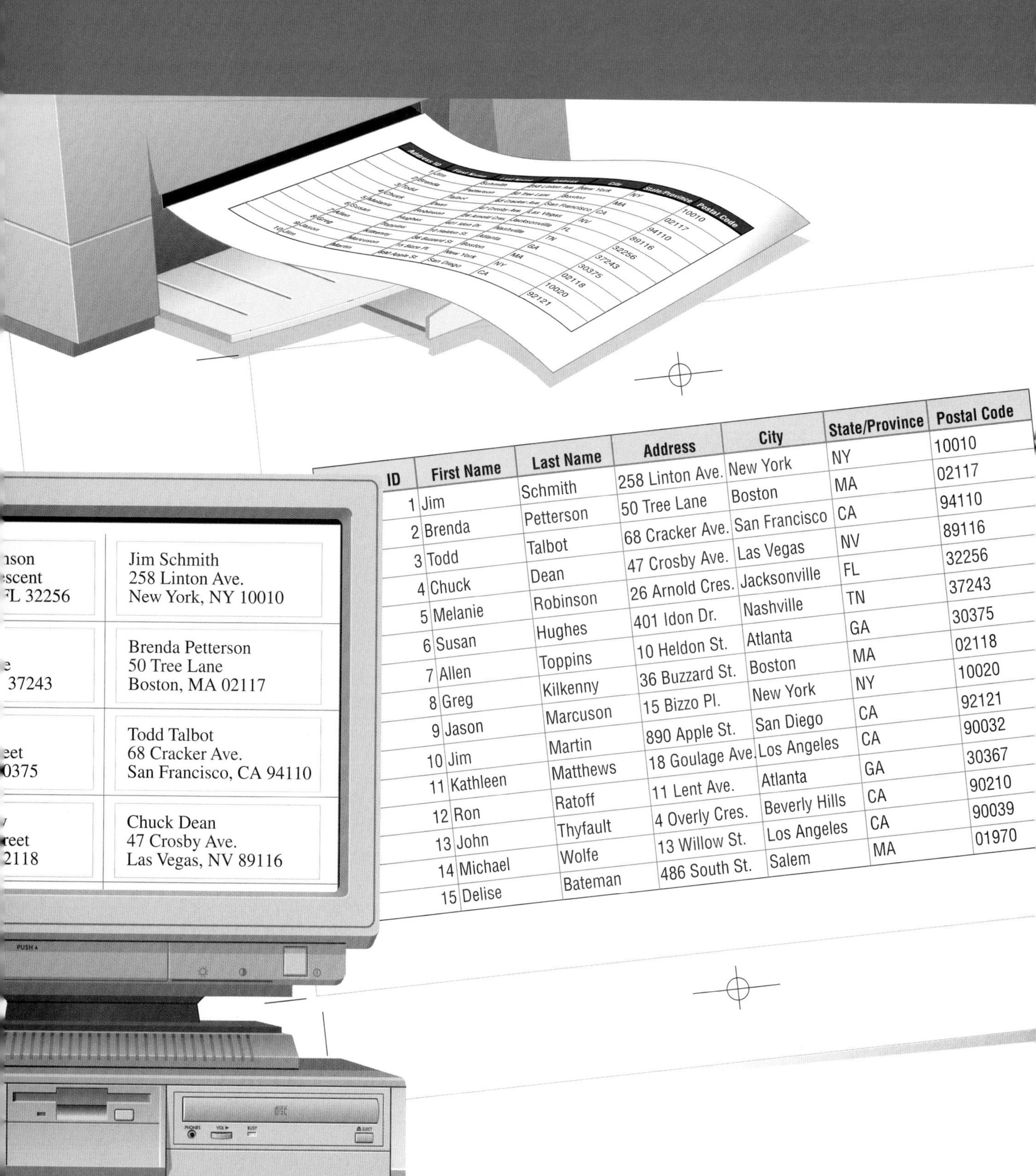
ID First Name Last Name Address City State/Province Postal Code
1 Jim Schmith 258 Linton Ave. New York NY 10010
2 Brenda Petterson 50 Tree Lane Boston MA 02117
3 Todd Talbot 68 Cracker Ave. San Francisco CA 94110
4 Chuck Dean 47 Crosby Ave. Las Vegas NV 89116
5 Melanie Robinson 26 Arnold Cres. Jacksonville FL 32256
6 Susan Hughes 401 Idon Dr. Nashville TN 37243
7 Allen Toppins 10 Heldon St. Atlanta GA 30375
8 Greg Kilkenny 36 Buzzard St. Boston MA 02118
9 Jason Marcuson 15 Bizzo Pl. New York NY 10020
10 Jim Martin 890 Apple St. San Diego CA 92121
11 Kathleen Matthews 18 Goulage Ave. Los Angeles CA 90032
12 Ron Ratoff 11 Lent Ave. Atlanta GA 30367
13 John Thyfault 4 Overly Cres. Beverly Hills CA 90210
14 Michael Wolfe 13 Willow St. Los Angeles CA 90039
15 Delise Bateman 486 South St. Salem MA 01970
Jim Schmith
258 Linton Ave.
New York, NY 10010
Brenda Petterson
50 Tree Lane
Boston, MA 02117
Todd Talbot
68 Cracker Ave.
San Francisco, CA 94110
Chuck Dean
47 Crosby Ave.
Las Vegas, NV 89116

CHAPTER 5

Print

Are you ready to print your work? This chapter teaches you how to print tables, queries, forms and reports. You will also learn how to create and print mailing labels.

Preview Before Printing 82

Change Page Setup......................................84

Print Information 86

Create Mailing Labels 88

PREVIEW BEFORE PRINTING

You can use the Print Preview feature to see how information will look when printed.

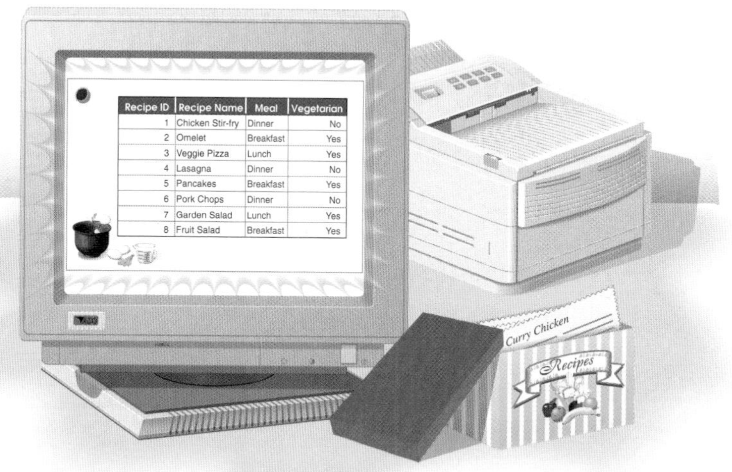

You can save time and paper by previewing your work to make sure the printed pages will look the way you want them to.

PREVIEW BEFORE PRINTING

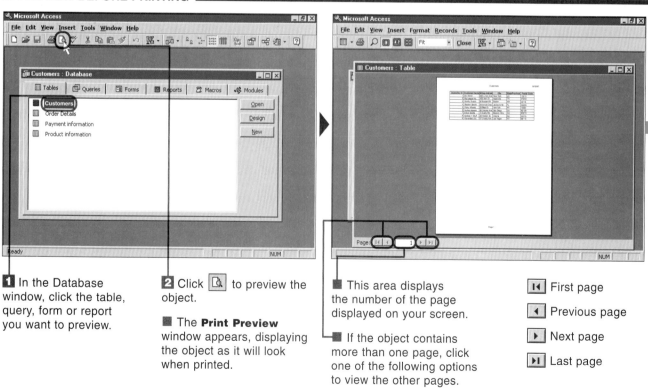

1 In the Database window, click the table, query, form or report you want to preview.

2 Click [Print Preview] to preview the object.

■ The **Print Preview** window appears, displaying the object as it will look when printed.

■ This area displays the number of the page displayed on your screen.

■ If the object contains more than one page, click one of the following options to view the other pages.

- [⏮] First page
- [◀] Previous page
- [▶] Next page
- [⏭] Last page

How can I display more than one page in the Print Preview window?

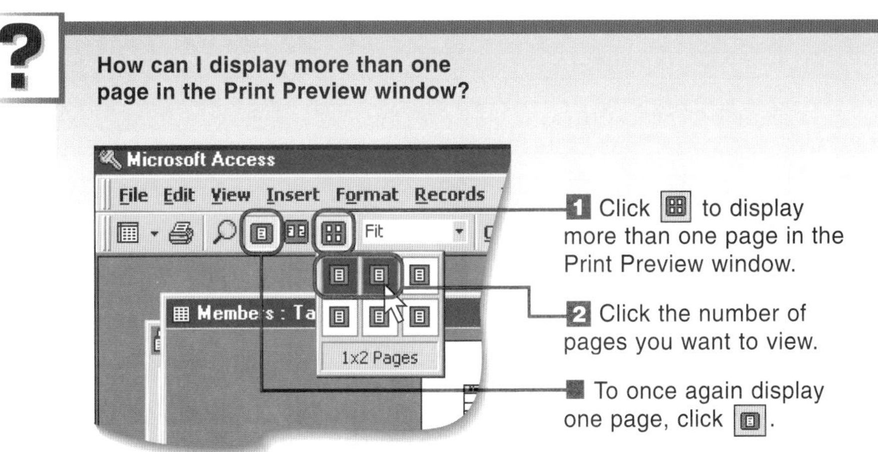

1 Click ⊞ to display more than one page in the Print Preview window.

2 Click the number of pages you want to view.

■ To once again display one page, click ▣.

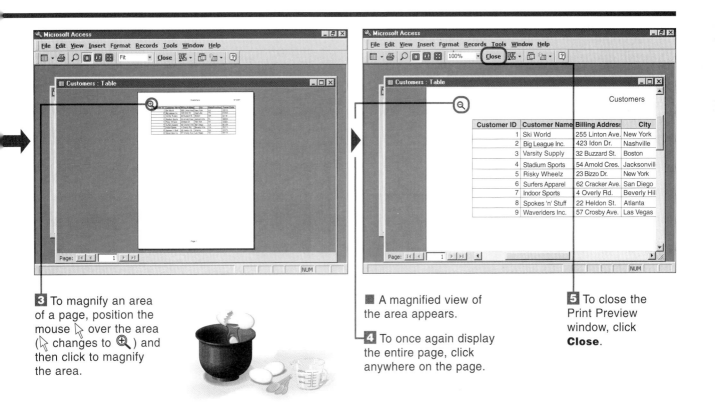

3 To magnify an area of a page, position the mouse ↖ over the area (↖ changes to 🔍) and then click to magnify the area.

■ A magnified view of the area appears.

4 To once again display the entire page, click anywhere on the page.

5 To close the Print Preview window, click **Close**.

CHANGE PAGE SETUP

You can change the way information appears on a printed page. Access offers these page setup options.

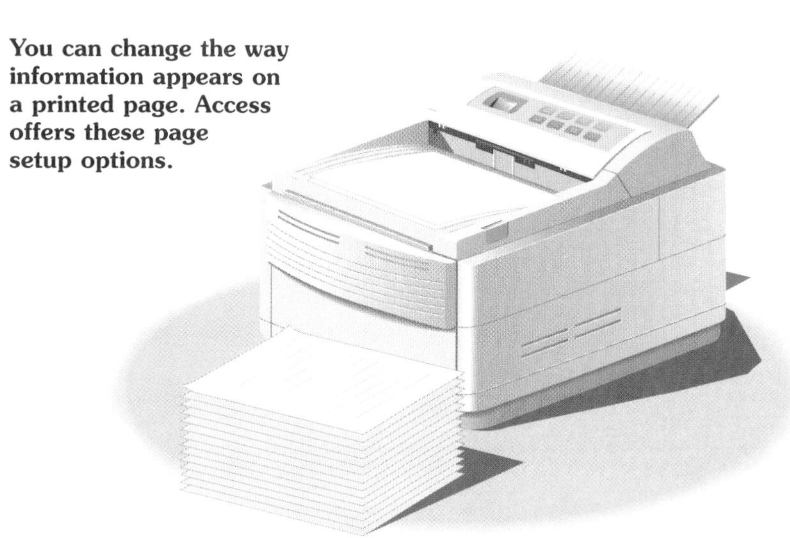

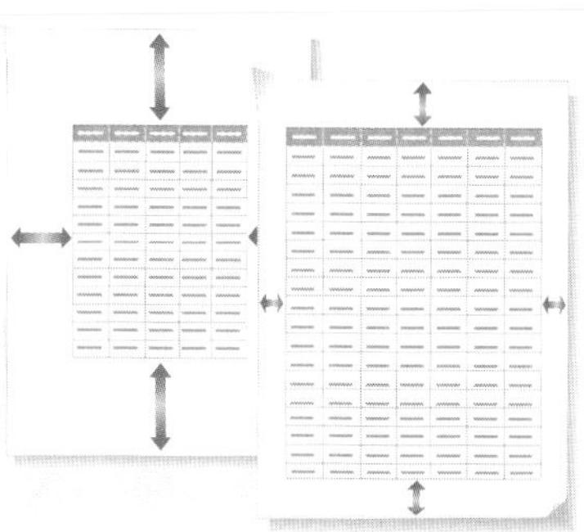

Margins

Determines the amount of space between data and the edges of the paper.

CHANGE PAGE SETUP

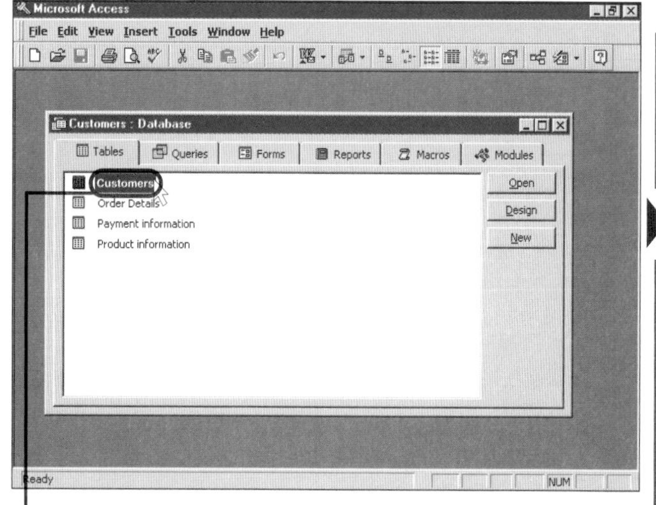

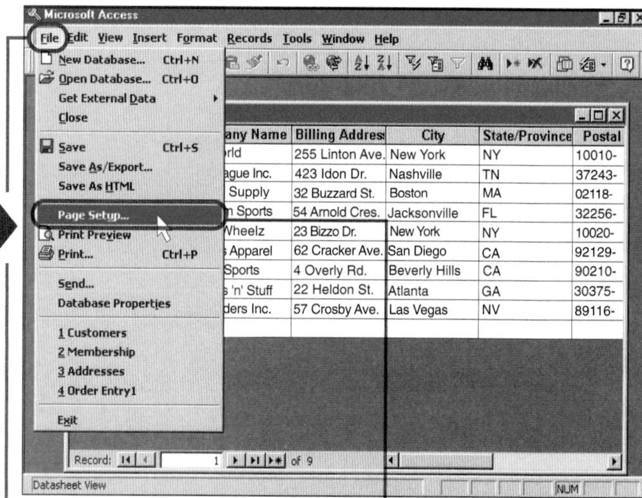

1 In the Database window, double-click the table, query, form or report you want to print differently.

■ The object opens.

2 Click **File**.

3 Click **Page Setup**.

■ The **Page Setup** dialog box appears.

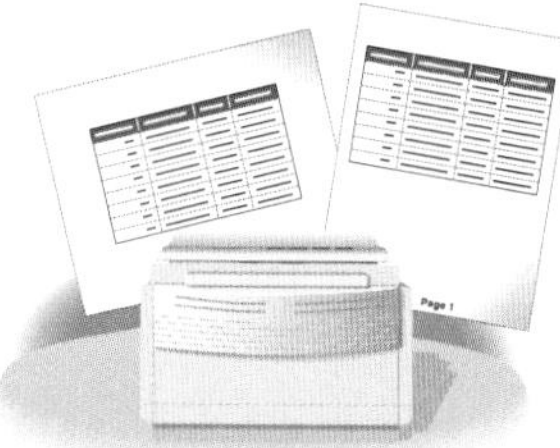

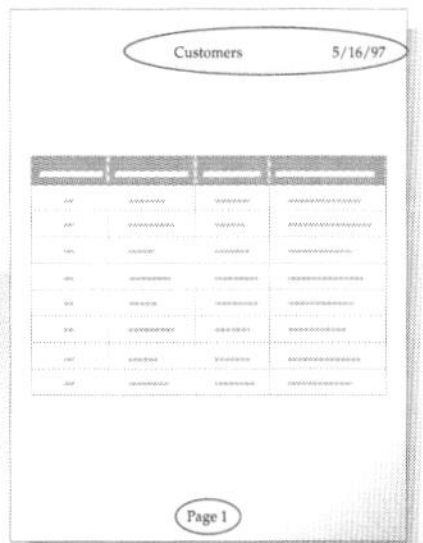

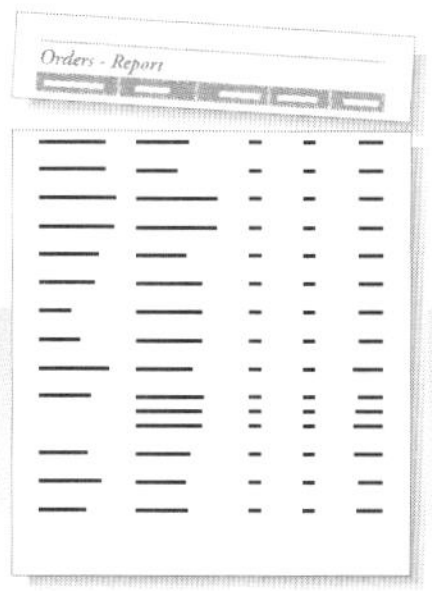

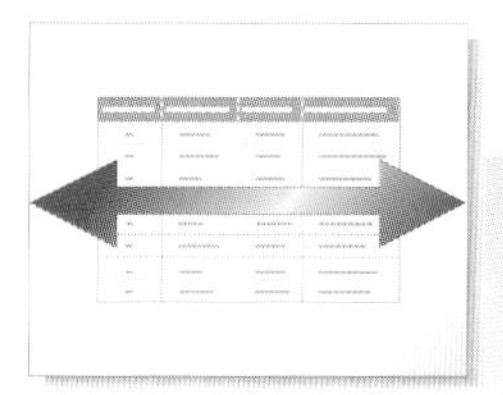

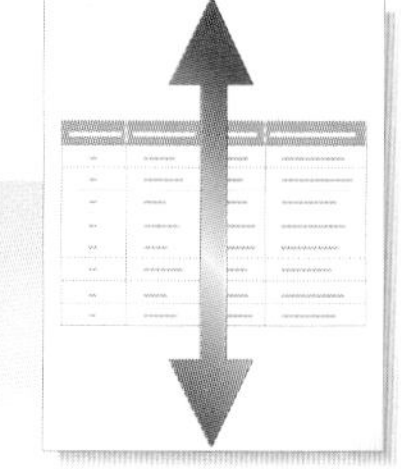

Print Headings
Prints headings which include the title, date and page number. This option is usually available for tables and queries.

Print Data Only
Prints the data without the title, date, page number or field names. This option is only available for forms and reports.

Orientation
Determines which direction information prints on a page.

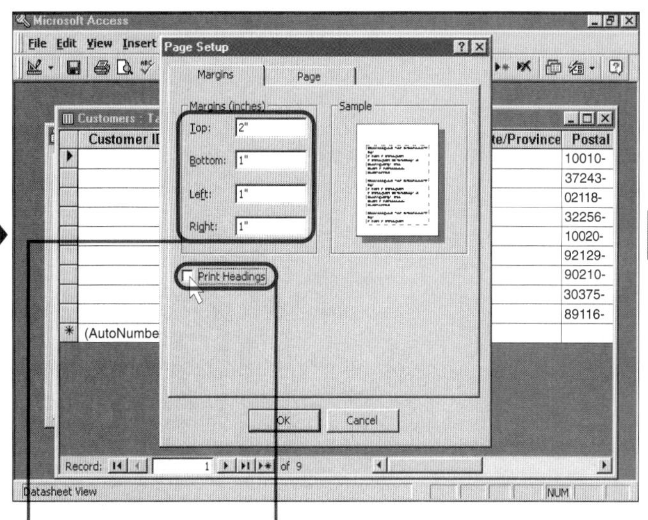

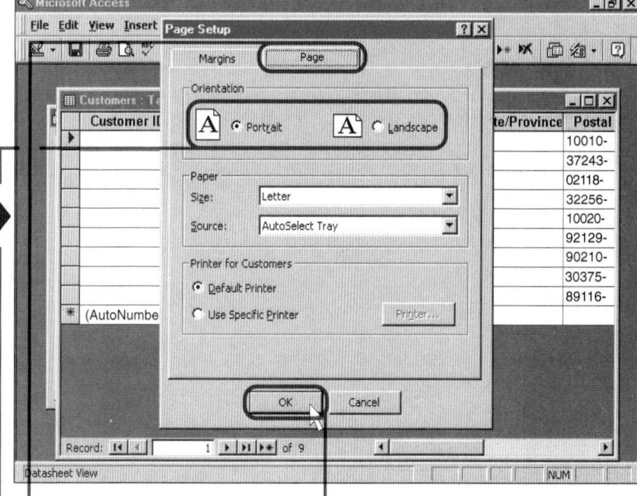

4 To change a margin, double-click the box beside the margin. Then type a new margin.

5 If you do not want to print the title, date or page numbers, click **Print Headings** (☑ changes to ☐).

■ If this area displays the **Print Data Only** option and you do not want to print the title, date, page numbers or field names, click the option (☐ changes to ☑).

6 To change the orientation of the page, click the **Page** tab.

7 Click the orientation you want to use (○ changes to ◉).

8 Click **OK** to confirm all of your changes.

■ You can use the Print Preview feature to preview the changes you made. For more information, refer to page 82.

PRINT INFORMATION

You can produce a paper copy of a table, query, form or report.

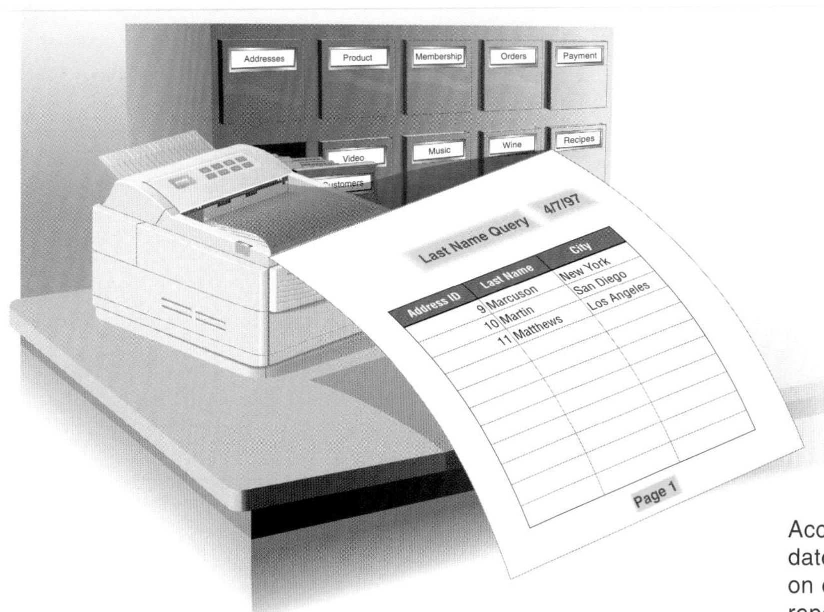

Access includes the title, date and page number on each table, query or report you print.

PRINT INFORMATION

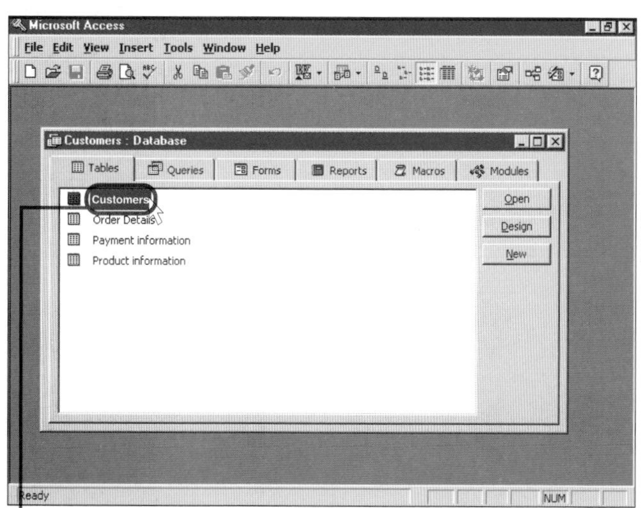

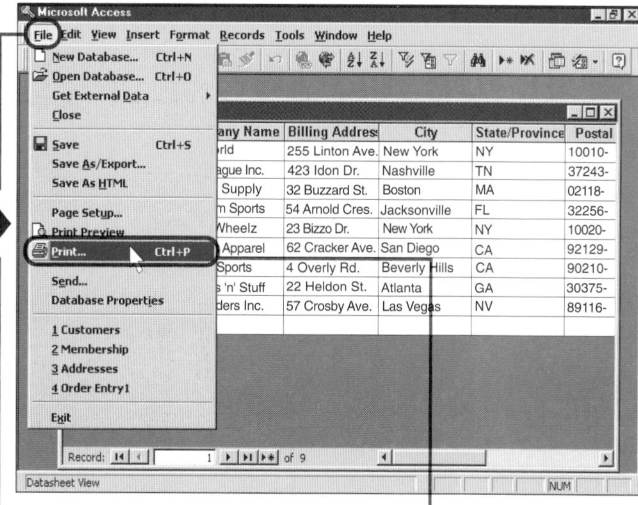

1 In the Database window, double-click the table, query, form or report you want to print.

■ The object opens.

■ If more than one record appears on your screen and you only want to print a few records, select the records you want to print. To select records, refer to page 58.

2 Click **File** to print the information.

3 Click **Print**.

■ The **Print** dialog box appears.

What information can I print?

You can choose to print all or some of your records.

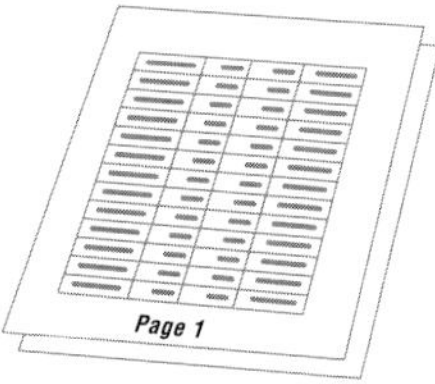

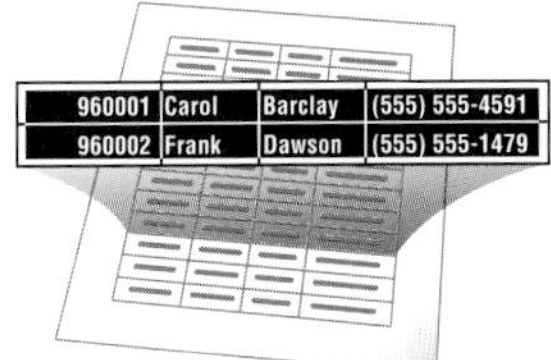

All
Prints all records.

Pages
Prints the pages you specify.

Selected Record(s)
Prints the record(s) you selected.

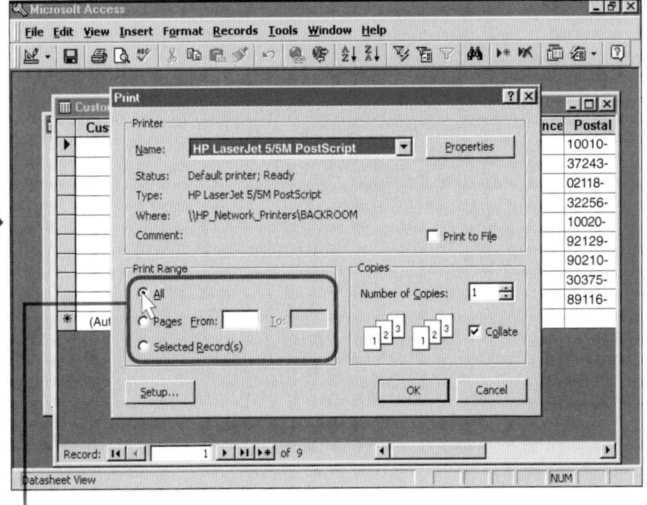

4 Click the print option you want to use (○ changes to ◉).

Note: For information on the print options, refer to the top of this page.

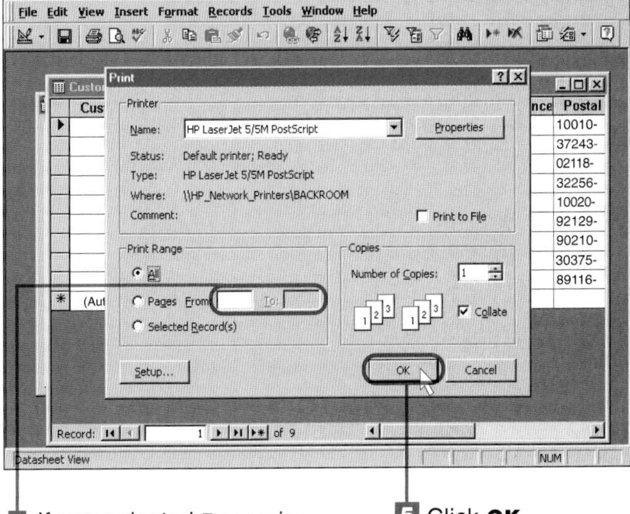

■ If you selected **Pages** in step **4**, type the number of the first page you want to print. Then press Tab on your keyboard and type the number of the last page you want to print.

5 Click **OK**.

QUICKLY PRINT ALL RECORDS

1 Click [print icon] to quickly print all the records.

CREATE MAILING LABELS

You can create a mailing label for every customer in a table.

CREATE MAILING LABELS

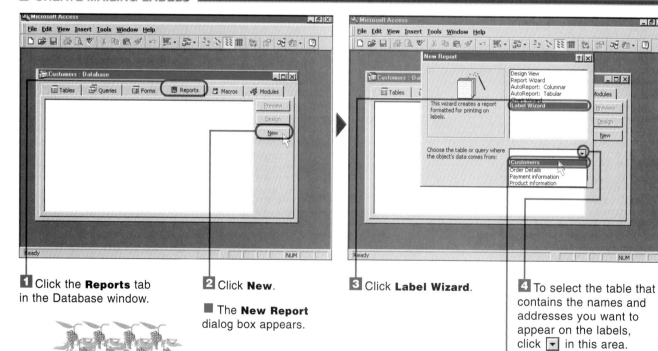

1 Click the **Reports** tab in the Database window.

2 Click **New**.

■ The **New Report** dialog box appears.

3 Click **Label Wizard**.

4 To select the table that contains the names and addresses you want to appear on the labels, click ▼ in this area.

5 Click the table you want to use.

? What types of labels are available?

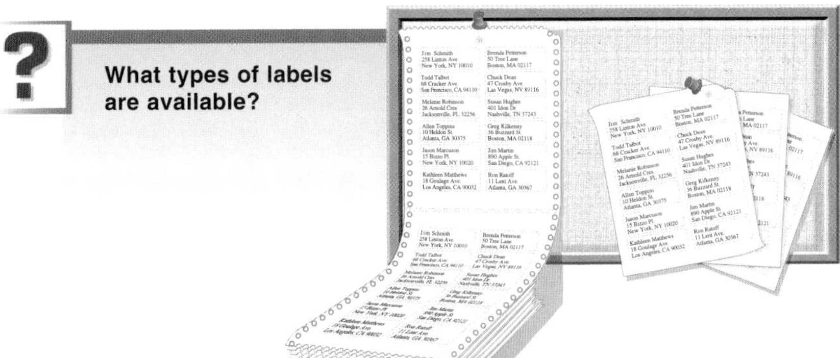

Continuous

Connected sheets of labels, with holes punched along each side.

Sheet feed

Individual sheets of labels.

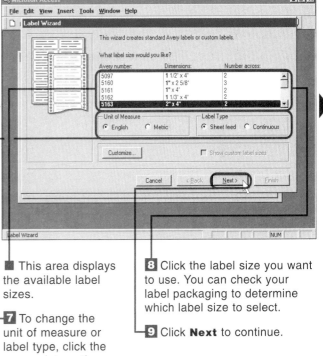

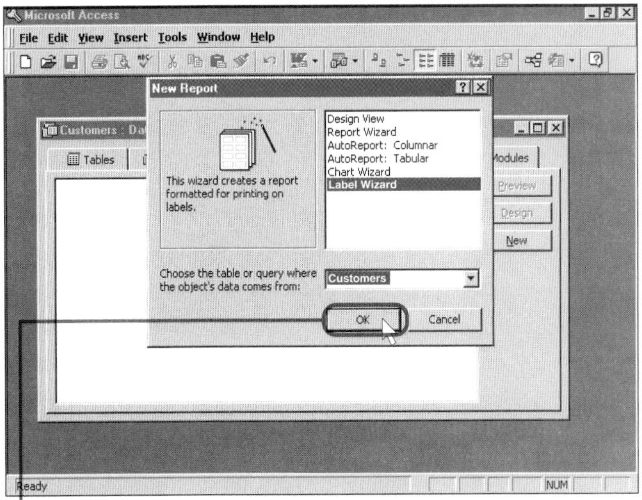

6 Click **OK**.

■ The **Label Wizard** dialog box appears.

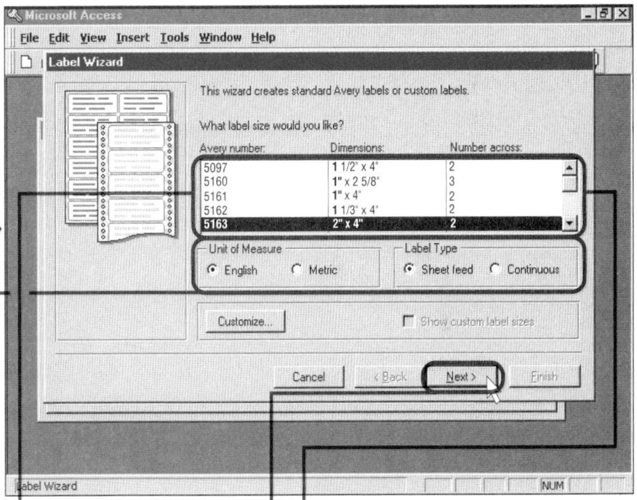

■ This area displays the available label sizes.

7 To change the unit of measure or label type, click the appropriate option (○ changes to ◉).

8 Click the label size you want to use. You can check your label packaging to determine which label size to select.

9 Click **Next** to continue.

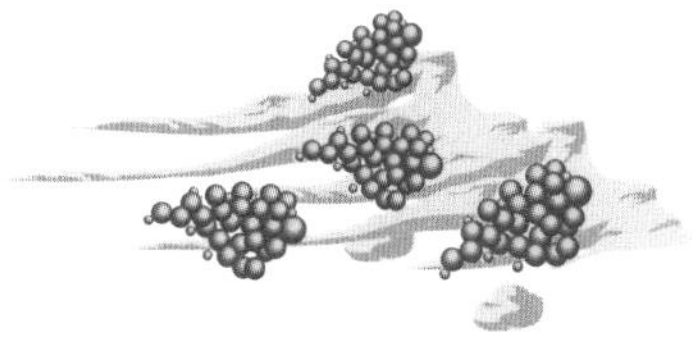

CONTINUED

CREATE MAILING LABELS

You can change the appearance of the text on your labels. You can choose between various fonts, sizes and weights.

The text appearance you choose affects all the text on every label. You cannot change the text appearance for part of a label.

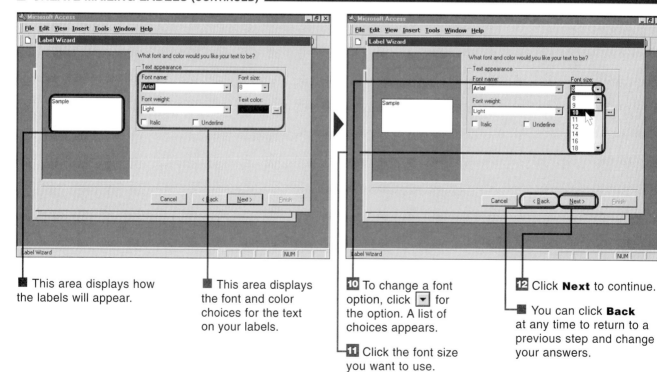

CREATE MAILING LABELS (CONTINUED)

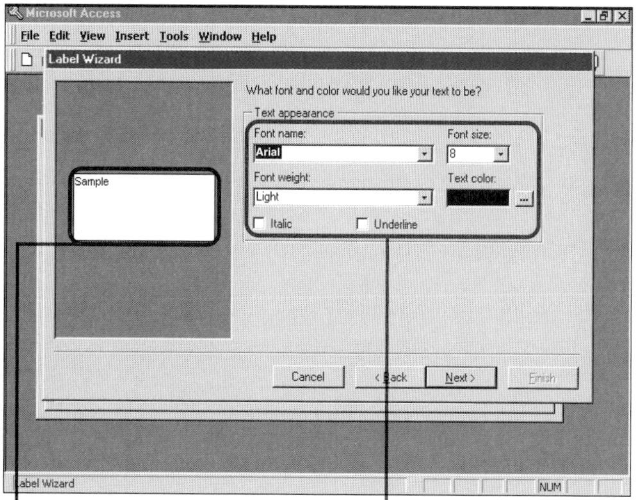

■ This area displays how the labels will appear.

■ This area displays the font and color choices for the text on your labels.

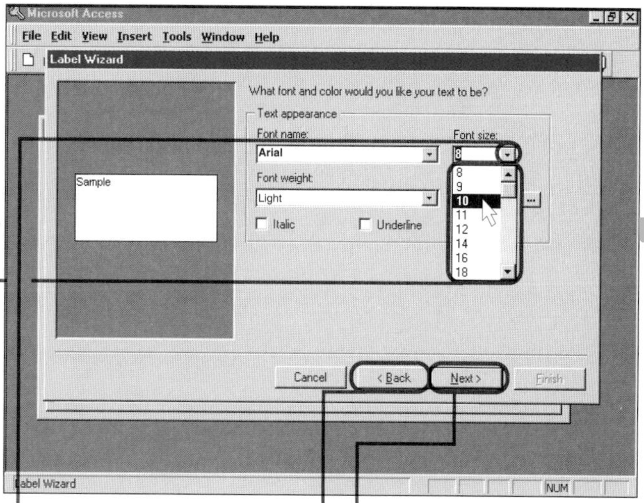

10 To change a font option, click ▼ for the option. A list of choices appears.

11 Click the font size you want to use.

12 Click **Next** to continue.

■ You can click **Back** at any time to return to a previous step and change your answers.

? How can I use the labels that I create?

You can use labels for items such as envelopes, packages, file folders and name tags.

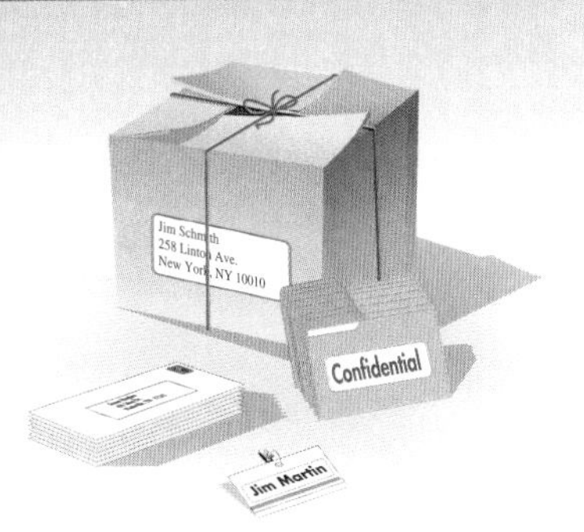

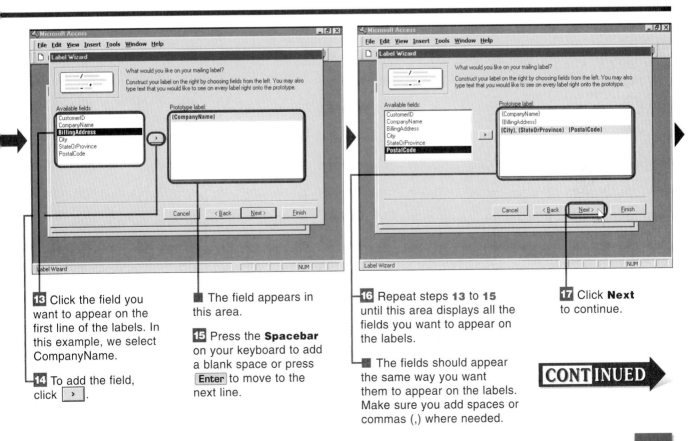

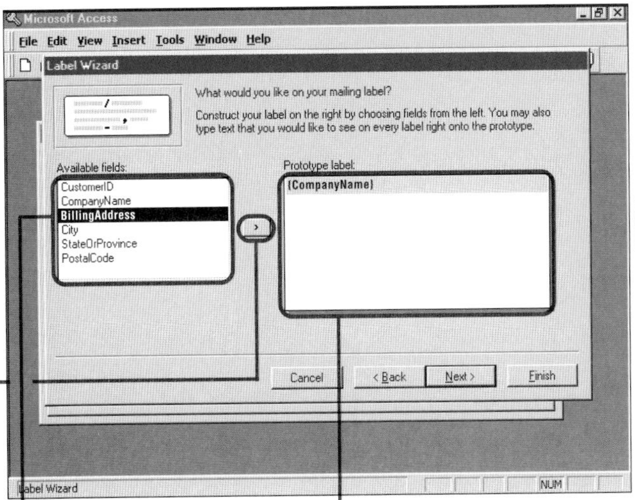

13 Click the field you want to appear on the first line of the labels. In this example, we select CompanyName.

14 To add the field, click [>].

■ The field appears in this area.

15 Press the **Spacebar** on your keyboard to add a blank space or press Enter to move to the next line.

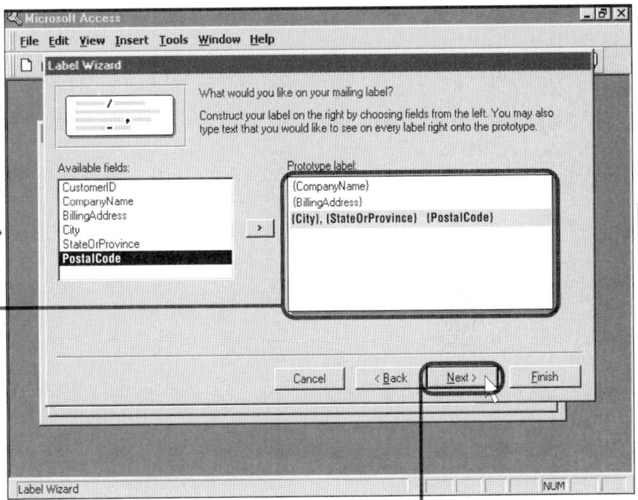

16 Repeat steps **13** to **15** until this area displays all the fields you want to appear on the labels.

■ The fields should appear the same way you want them to appear on the labels. Make sure you add spaces or commas (,) where needed.

17 Click **Next** to continue.

CONTINUED

You can specify how you want to sort your mailing labels. Sorting the labels determines the order that Access arranges the labels.

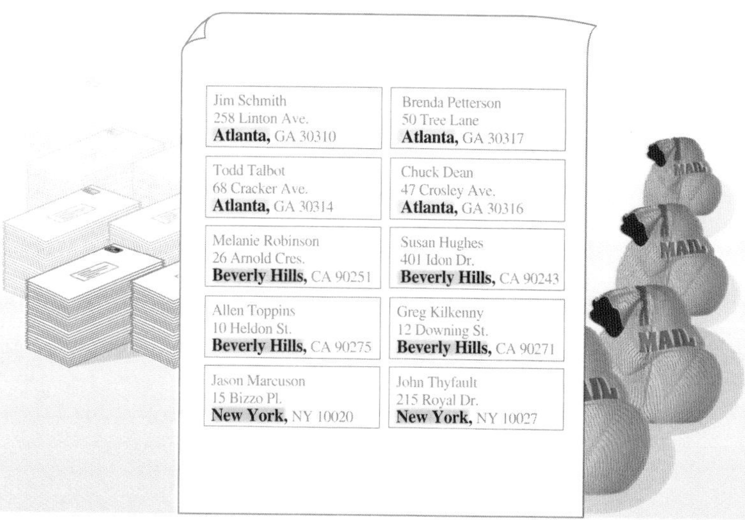

For example, you may want to sort your mailing labels by city to place all labels for the same city together.

CREATE MAILING LABELS (CONTINUED)

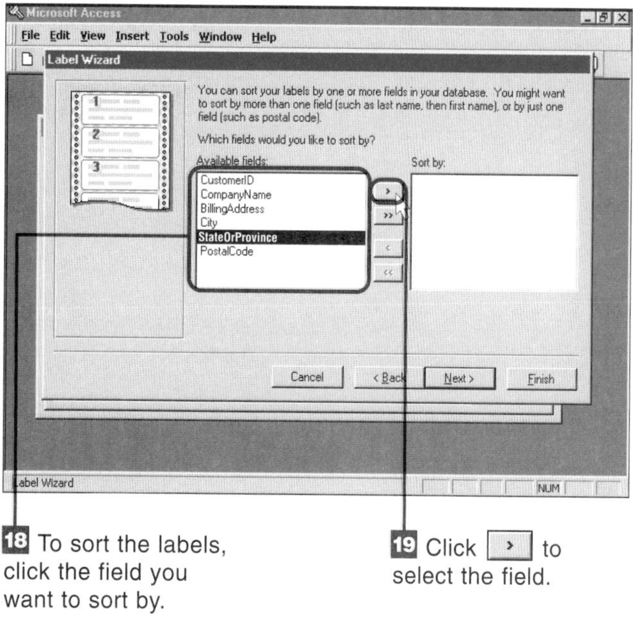

18 To sort the labels, click the field you want to sort by.

19 Click > to select the field.

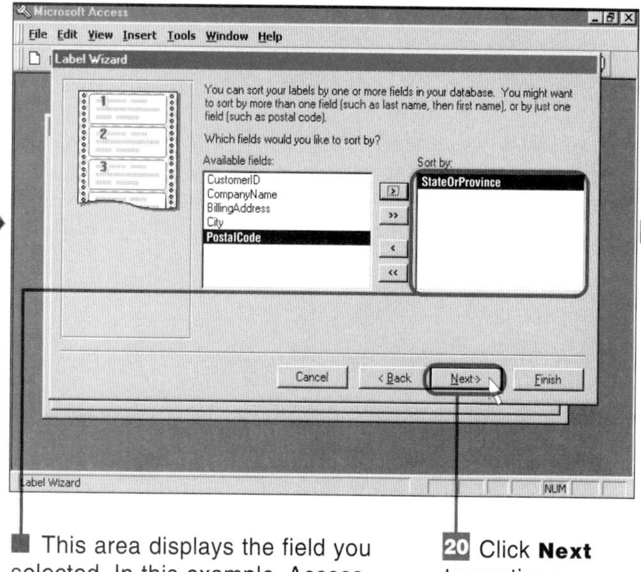

■ This area displays the field you selected. In this example, Access will sort the labels by state.

■ If the field you selected has matching information, you can repeat steps **18** and **19** to sort by a second field. For example, if you have clients who live in the same state, you can perform a secondary sort by last name.

20 Click **Next** to continue.

? Where will I find the mailing labels I created?

Access saves your mailing labels as a report. You will find your mailing labels by clicking on the Reports tab in the Database window.

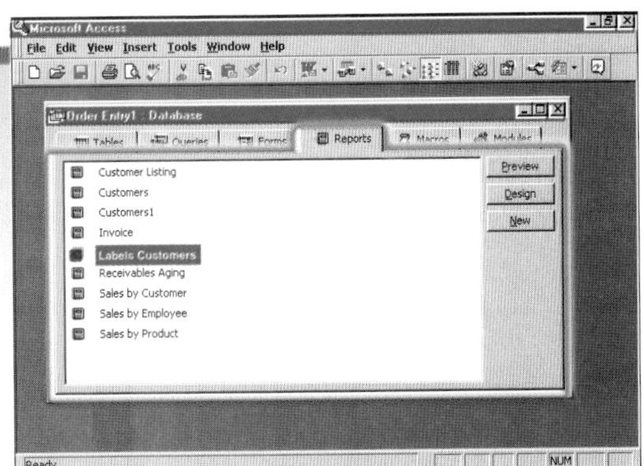

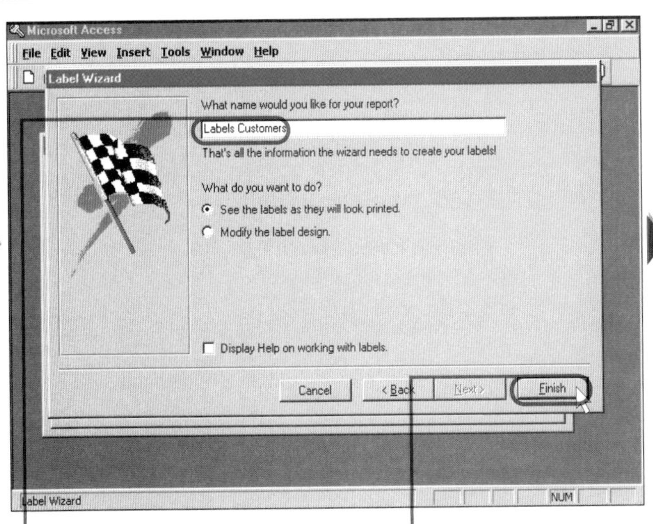

21 Type a name for the mailing labels.

22 Click **Finish** to create the labels.

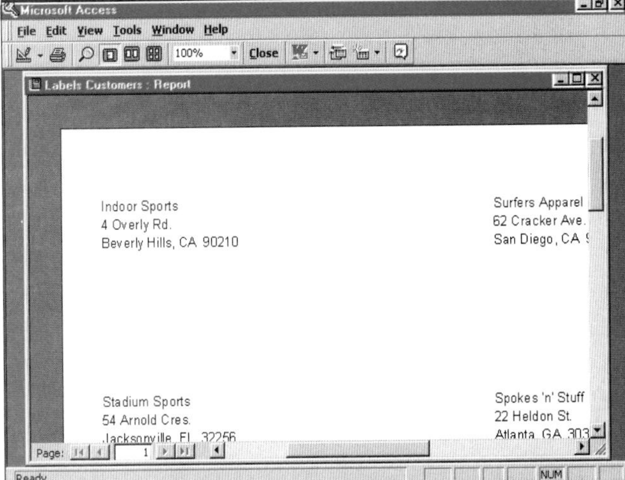

■ The labels appear as they will look when printed.

Note: To print the labels, refer to page 86.

Add field d

Address ID	First Name	Last Name	Address	City	Sta
1	Jim	Schmith	258 Linton Ave.	New York	NY
2	Brenda	Petterson	50 Tree Lane	Boston	MA
3	Todd	Talbot	68 Cracker Ave.	San Francisco	CA
4	Chuck	Dean	47 Crosby Ave.	Las Vegas	NV
5	Melanie	Robinson	26 Arnold Cres.	Jacksonville	FL
9	Jason	Marcuson	15 Bizzo Pl.	New York	NY
10	Jim	Martin	Apple	San Diego	CA
11	Kathleen	Matthews	18 Goulage Ave	s Angeles	
12	Ron	Ratoff		nta	G
13	John	Thyfault	11 Lent Ave.	erly Hills	C
14	Michael	Wolfe		os Angeles	CA
15	Delise	Bateman	486 South St.	Salem	MA

increase field size?

CHAPTER 6

Design Tables

Would you like to design a table tailored to your specific needs? Find out how in this chapter.

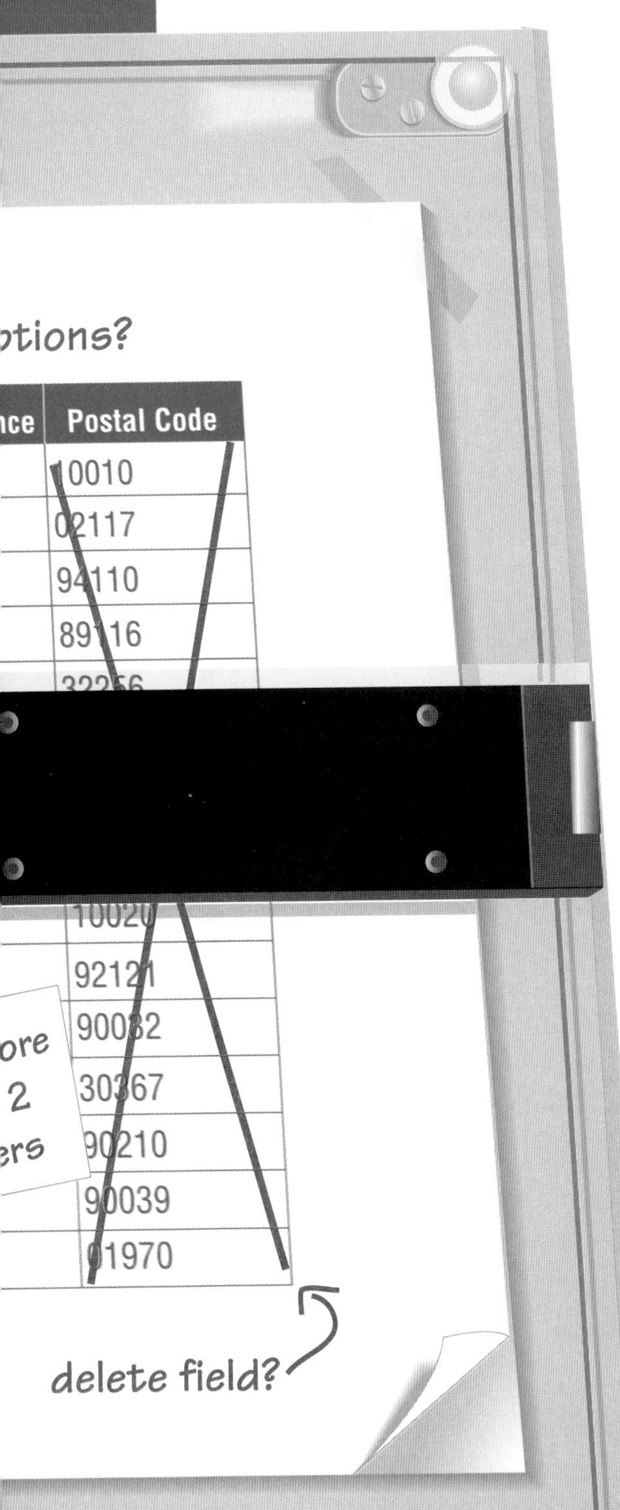

Change View of Table 96

Add a Field 98

Delete a Field 100

Rearrange Fields....................................101

Add a Field Description 102

Display Field Properties 103

Change a Data Type 104

Select a Format 106

Change the Field Size 108

Add a Caption 110

Add a Default Value....................................111

Data Entry Required 112

Allow Zero-Length Strings 114

Change Number of Decimal Places 115

Add a Validation Rule 116

Create a Yes/No Field 118

Create an Index 120

Create a Lookup Column....................................122

Add Pictures to Records 126

Create an Input Mask 130

CHANGE VIEW OF TABLE

There are two ways you can view a table. Each view allows you to perform a different task.

CHANGE VIEW OF TABLE

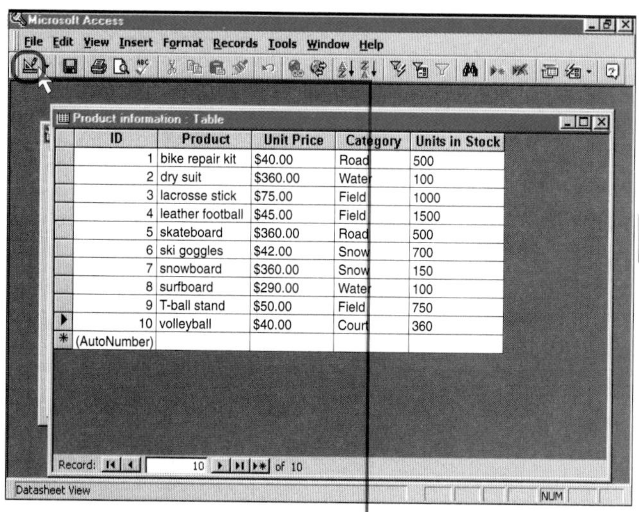

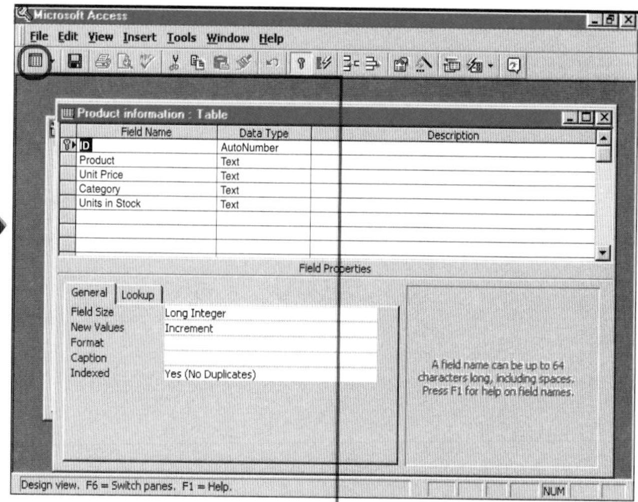

■ When you open a table, the table appears in the Datasheet view.

1 To display the table in the Design view, click .

■ The table appears in the Design view.

■ The View button changes to . You can click the View button to quickly switch between the Design ( ) and Datasheet ( ) views.

THE TABLE VIEWS

DATASHEET VIEW

The Datasheet view displays all the records in a table. You can enter, edit and review records in this view.

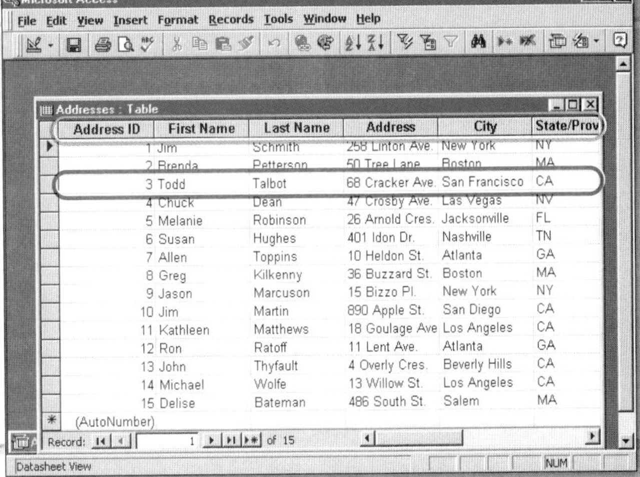

Field Name

A field name identifies the information within a field.

Record

A record is a collection of information about one person, place or thing.

DESIGN VIEW

The Design view displays the structure of a table. You can change the settings in this view to specify the kind of information you can enter in a table.

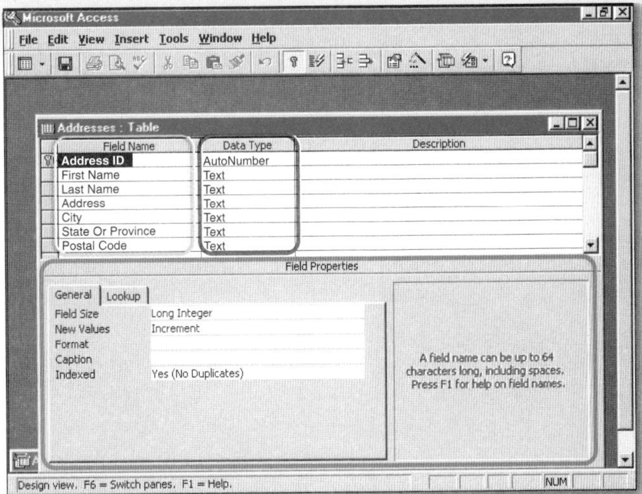

Field Name

A field name identifies the information within a field.

Data Type

The data type determines the kind of information you can enter in a field. Specifying a data type helps ensure that you enter information in the correct form. For example, you cannot enter text in a field that has the Number data type.

Field Properties

The field properties are a set of characteristics that provide additional control over the kind of information you can enter in a field. For example, you can specify the maximum number of characters a field will accept.

ADD A FIELD

You can insert a new field to include an additional category of information in your table.

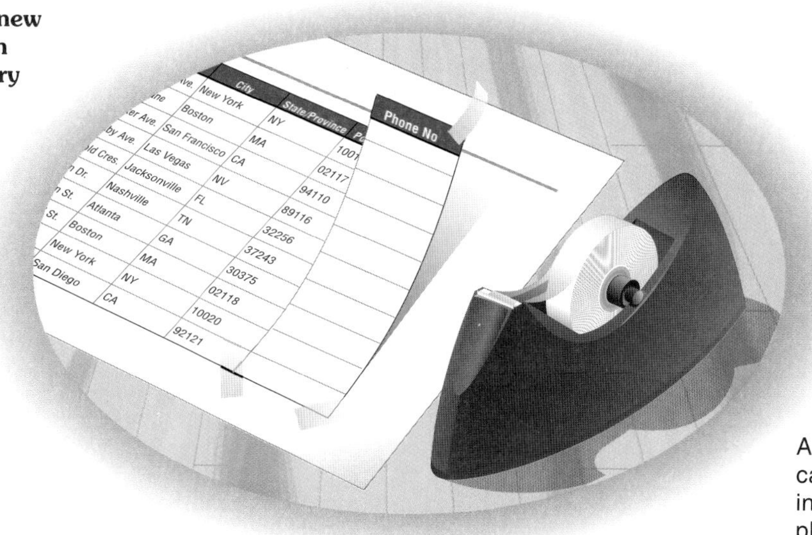

A field is a specific category of information in a table, such as the phone numbers of all your clients.

ADD A FIELD

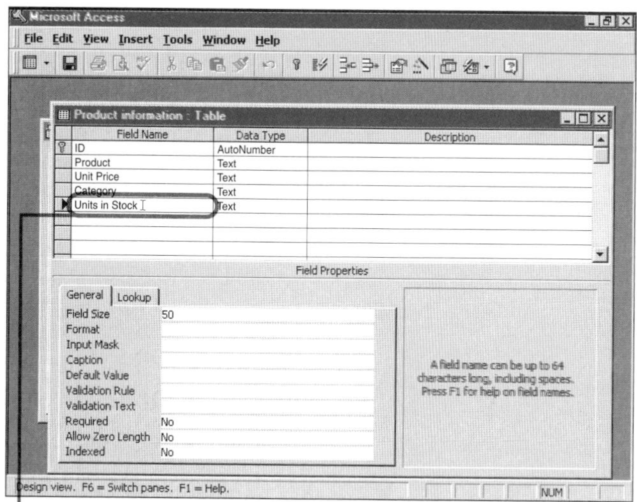

1 Click the name of the field you want to follow the new field.

■ To add a field to the end of the table, click the area directly below the last field name. Then skip to step **3**.

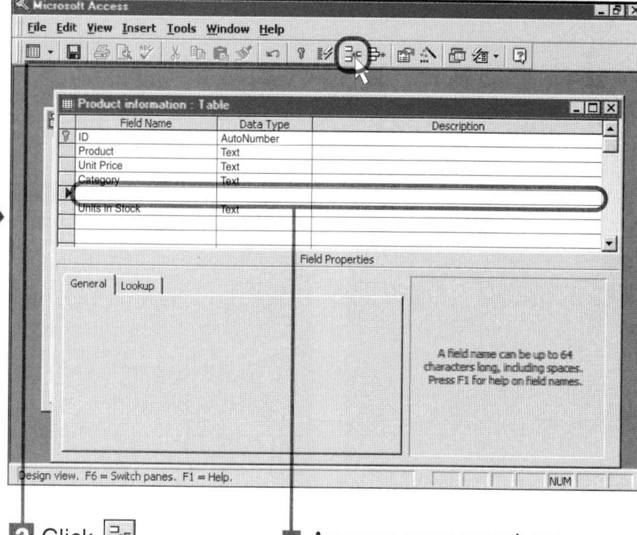

2 Click .

■ An area appears where you can enter information for the new field.

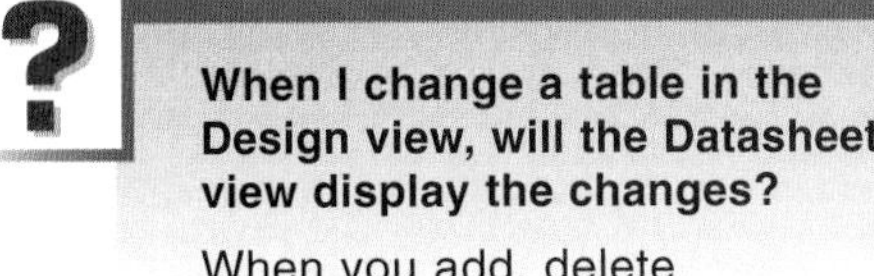

When I change a table in the Design view, will the Datasheet view display the changes?

When you add, delete or rearrange fields in the Design view, the table will also display the changes in the Datasheet view.

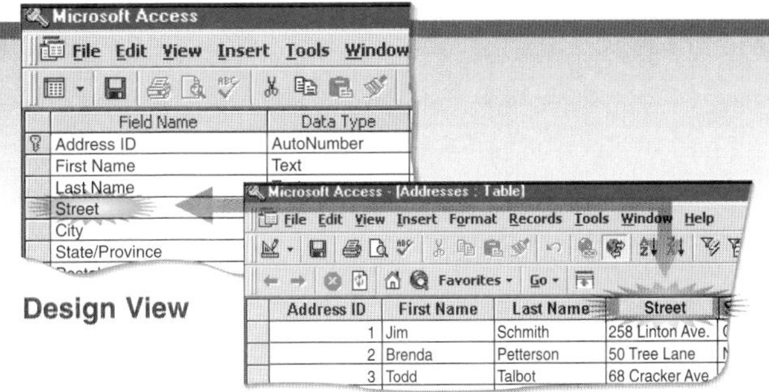

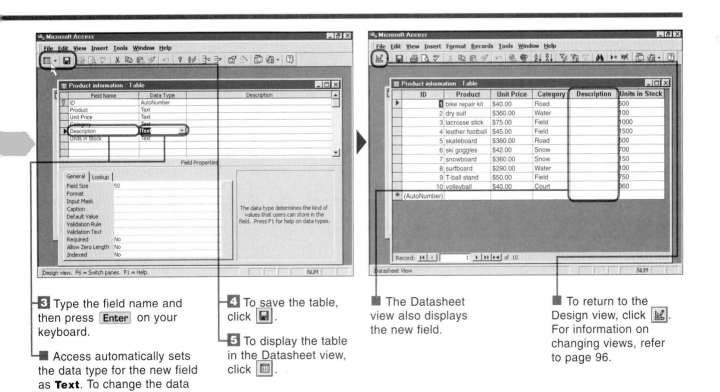

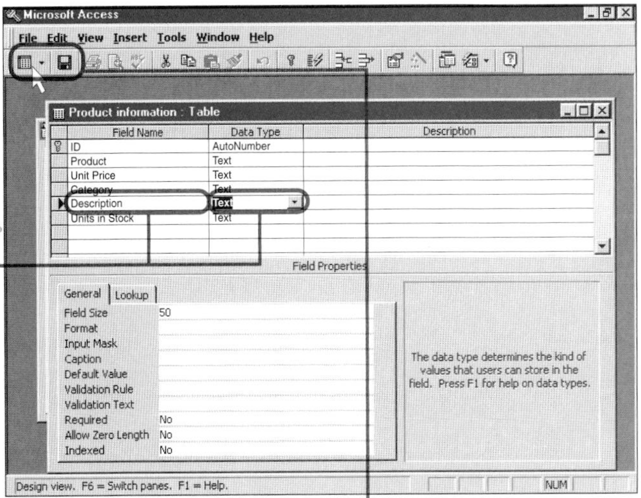

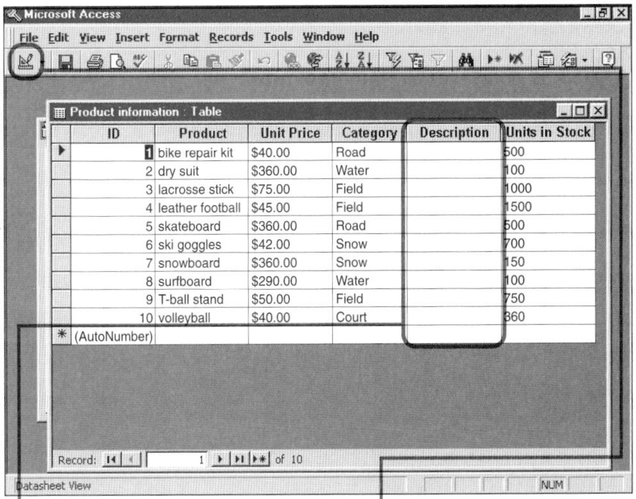

3 Type the field name and then press Enter on your keyboard.

■ Access automatically sets the data type for the new field as **Text**. To change the data type, refer to page 104.

4 To save the table, click 💾.

5 To display the table in the Datasheet view, click ▦.

■ The Datasheet view also displays the new field.

■ To return to the Design view, click 📐. For information on changing views, refer to page 96.

DELETE A FIELD

You can delete a field from a table to remove information you no longer need.

Before you delete a field, make sure the field is not used in any other objects in your database, such as a form or report.

When you delete a field in the Design view, the field is also deleted from the table in the Datasheet view.

DELETE A FIELD

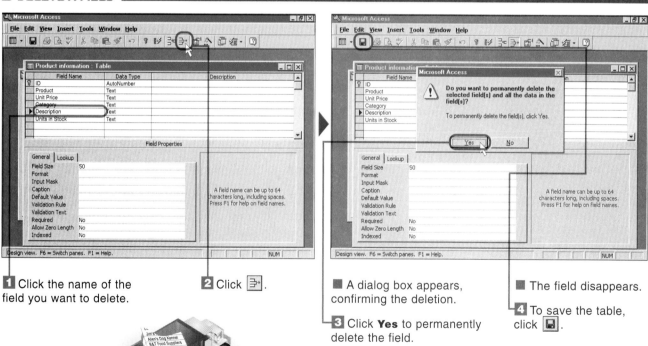

1 Click the name of the field you want to delete.

2 Click [Delete Rows button].

■ A dialog box appears, confirming the deletion.

3 Click **Yes** to permanently delete the field.

■ The field disappears.

4 To save the table, click [Save button].

REARRANGE FIELDS

You can rearrange the fields in a table to better organize your information.

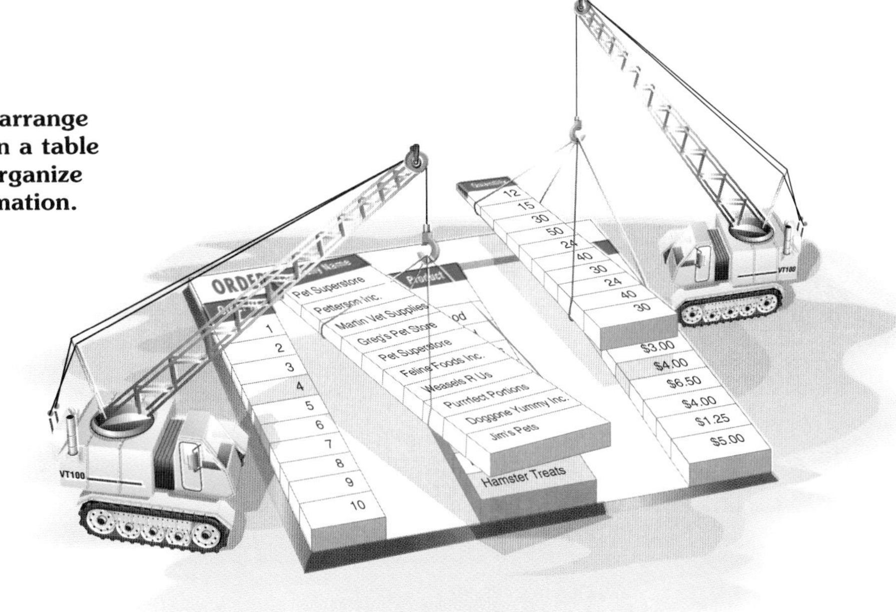

When you rearrange fields in the Design view, the fields are also rearranged in the Datasheet view.

REARRANGE FIELDS

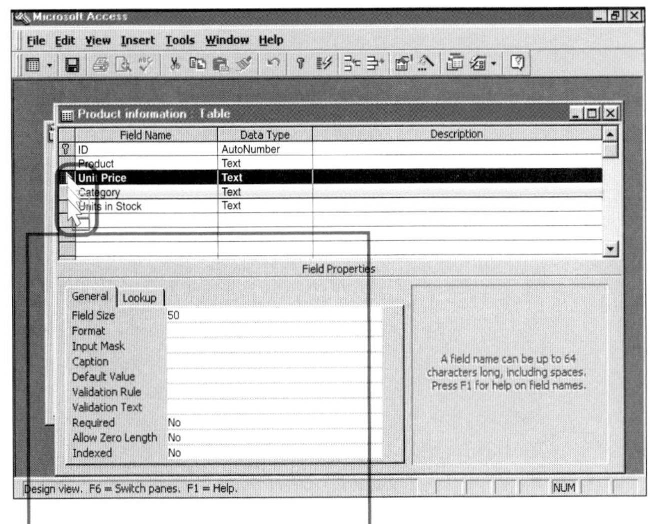

1 Click the area to the left of the field you want to move.

2 Position the mouse I over the area to the left of the field name (I changes to ↖) and then drag the field to a new location.

Note: A thick line shows where the field will appear.

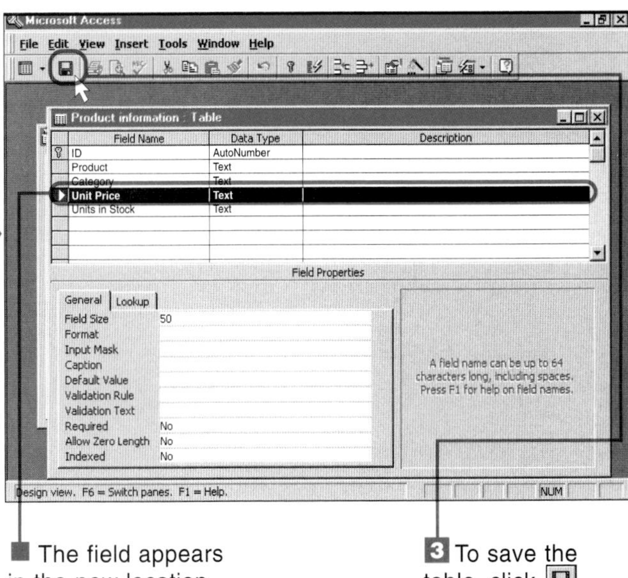

■ The field appears in the new location.

3 To save the table, click 💾.

ADD A FIELD DESCRIPTION

You can add a description to help you remember what information to enter in a field.

ADD A FIELD DESCRIPTION

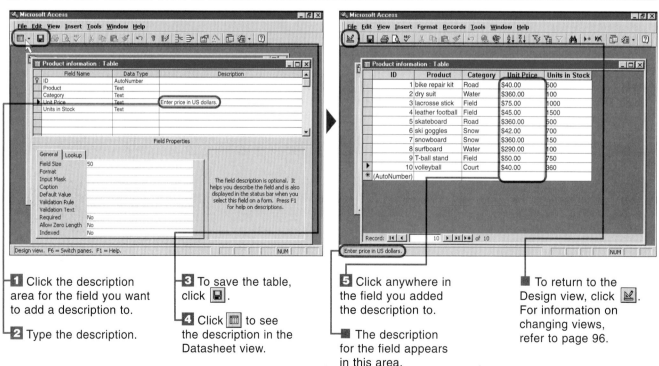

1 Click the description area for the field you want to add a description to.

2 Type the description.

3 To save the table, click the save button.

4 Click the Datasheet View button to see the description in the Datasheet view.

5 Click anywhere in the field you added the description to.

■ The description for the field appears in this area.

■ To return to the Design view, click the Design View button. For information on changing views, refer to page 96.

DISPLAY FIELD PROPERTIES

The field properties are a set of characteristics that provide additional control over the kind of information you can enter in a field.

For example, a field property can tell Access the maximum number of characters a field will accept.

DISPLAY FIELD PROPERTIES

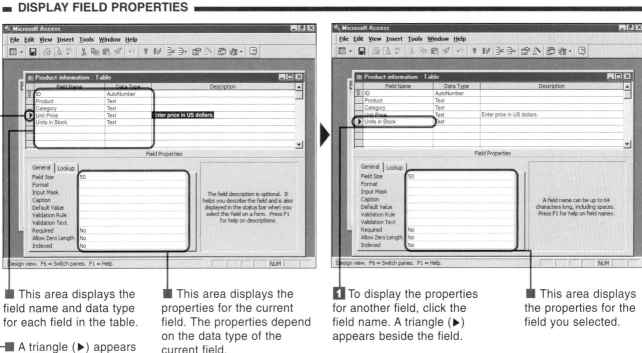

■ This area displays the field name and data type for each field in the table.

■ A triangle (▶) appears beside the current field.

■ This area displays the properties for the current field. The properties depend on the data type of the current field.

1 To display the properties for another field, click the field name. A triangle (▶) appears beside the field.

■ This area displays the properties for the field you selected.

CHANGE A DATA TYPE

You can easily change the type of data you can enter in a field.

Changing the data type helps prevent errors when entering data. Access will not accept entries that do not match the data type.

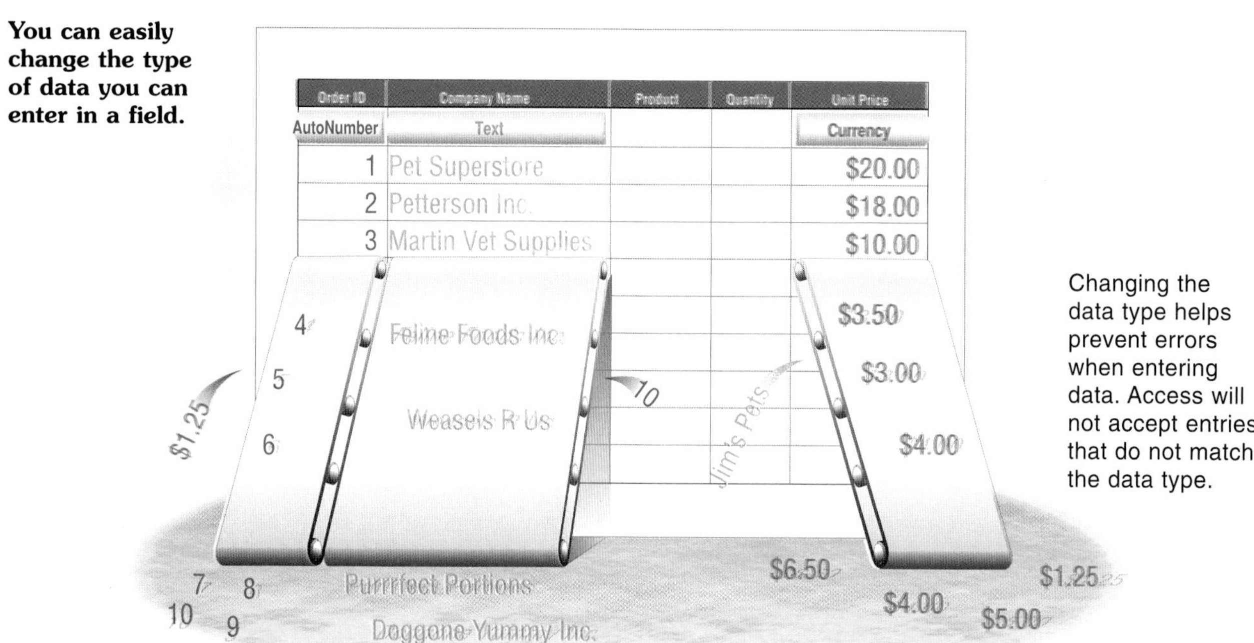

CHANGE A DATA TYPE

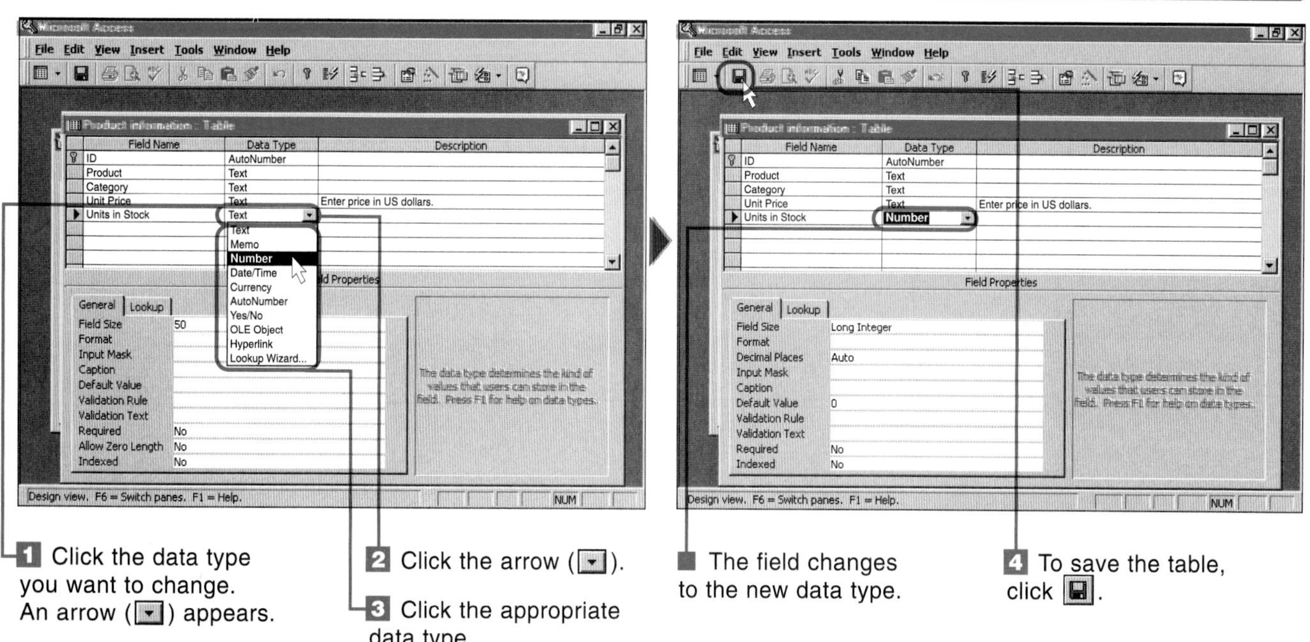

1 Click the data type you want to change. An arrow (▾) appears.

2 Click the arrow (▾).

3 Click the appropriate data type.

■ The field changes to the new data type.

4 To save the table, click 💾.

DATA TYPES

Text

Accepts entries up to 255 characters long that include text and numbers. Make sure you use this data type for numbers you will not use in calculations, such as phone numbers or postal codes.

AutoNumber

Automatically numbers each record for you.

Memo

Accepts entries over 255 characters long that include text and numbers, such as notes or descriptions.

Yes/No

Accepts only one of two values—Yes/No, True/False or On/Off.

Number

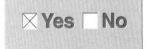

Accepts numbers you want to use in calculations.

OLE Object

Accepts objects created in other programs, such as documents, spreadsheets, pictures or sounds.

Date/Time

Accepts only dates and times.

Hyperlink

Accepts hyperlinks you can select to jump to another document or Web page.

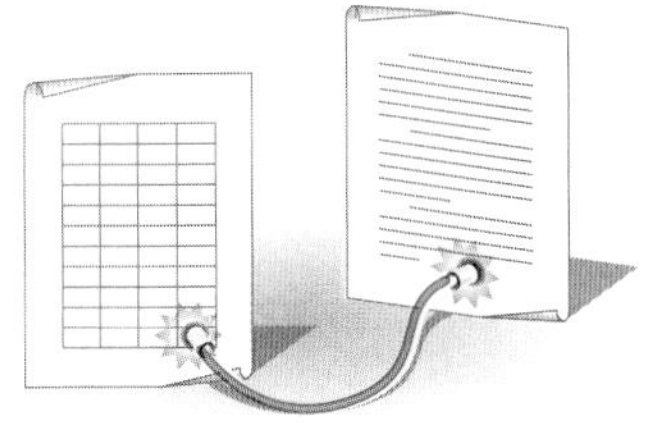

Currency

Accepts only monetary values.

Lookup Wizard

Starts the Lookup Wizard so you can create a list of items to choose from when entering information in a field. For more information, refer to page 122.

SELECT A FORMAT

You can customize the way information appears in your database. You can choose a format that suits your own personal preference.

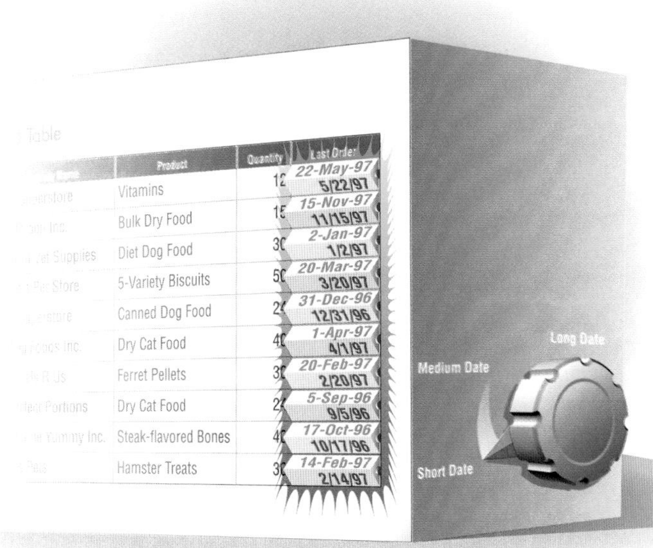

For example, you can select how you want to display dates.

SELECT A FORMAT

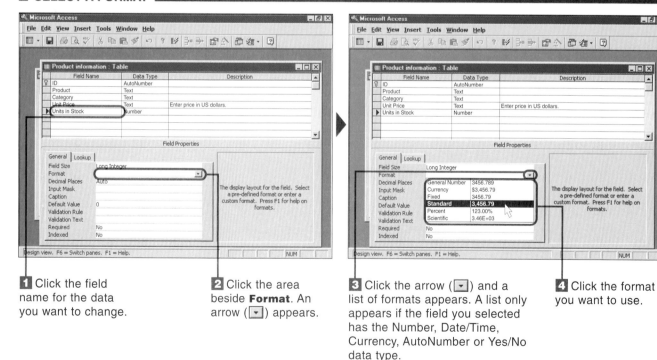

1 Click the field name for the data you want to change.

2 Click the area beside **Format**. An arrow (▼) appears.

3 Click the arrow (▼) and a list of formats appears. A list only appears if the field you selected has the Number, Date/Time, Currency, AutoNumber or Yes/No data type.

Note: For information on some of the available formats, refer to the top of page 107.

4 Click the format you want to use.

What formats are available?

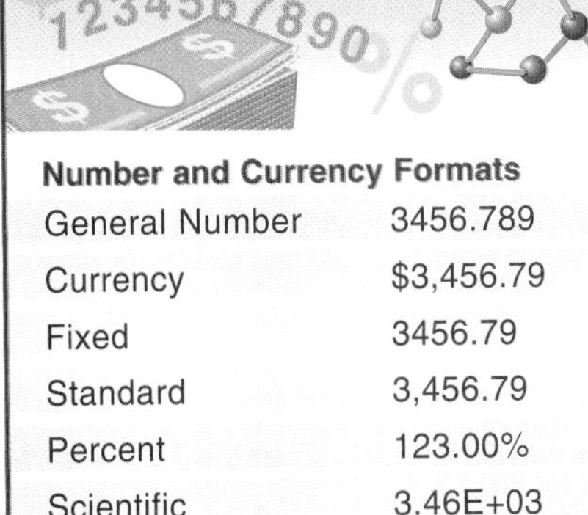

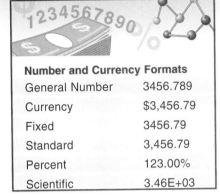

Number and Currency Formats

Format	Example
General Number	3456.789
Currency	$3,456.79
Fixed	3456.79
Standard	3,456.79
Percent	123.00%
Scientific	3.46E+03

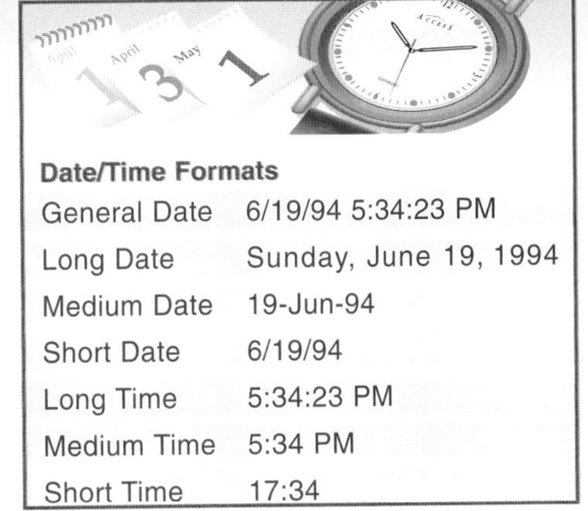

Date/Time Formats

Format	Example
General Date	6/19/94 5:34:23 PM
Long Date	Sunday, June 19, 1994
Medium Date	19-Jun-94
Short Date	6/19/94
Long Time	5:34:23 PM
Medium Time	5:34 PM
Short Time	17:34

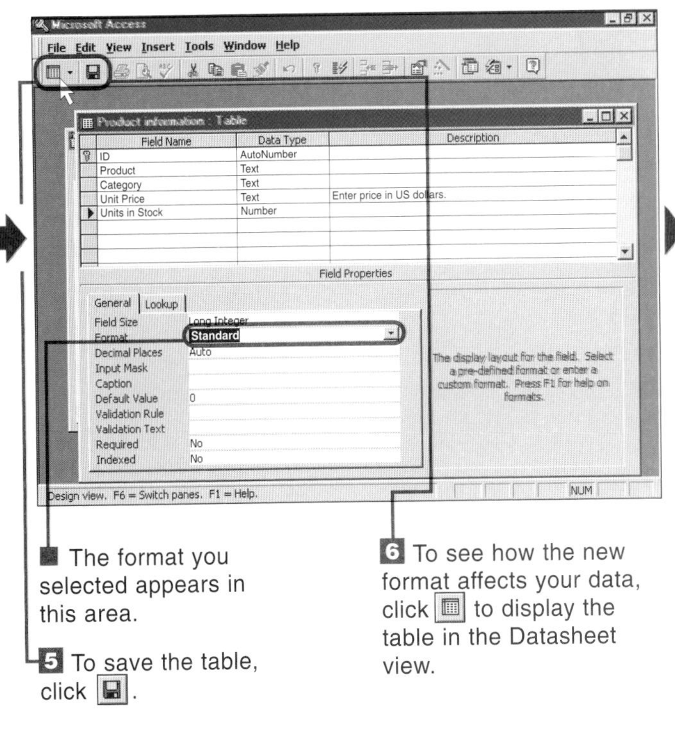

■ The format you selected appears in this area.

5 To save the table, click 💾.

6 To see how the new format affects your data, click ▦ to display the table in the Datasheet view.

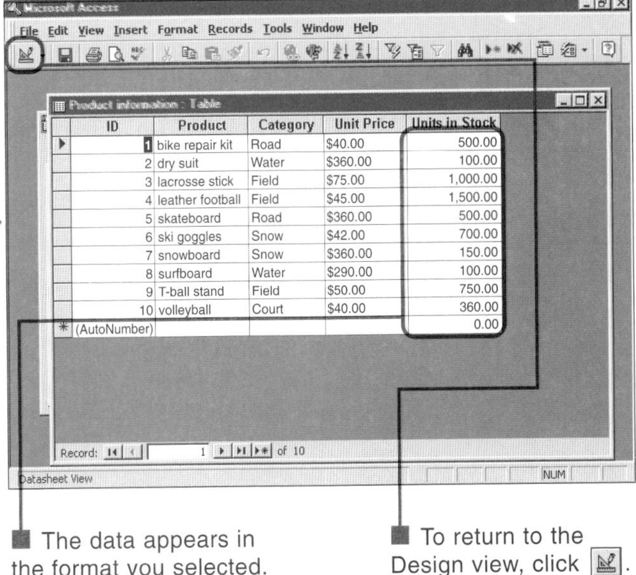

■ The data appears in the format you selected.

■ Access will automatically change any data you enter to the correct format. For example, Access can automatically change **6/22/97** to **22-Jun-97** or **1234** to **$1,234.00**.

■ To return to the Design view, click ✎. For information on changing views, refer to page 96.

CHANGE THE FIELD SIZE

You can reduce errors by changing the maximum number of characters you can enter in a field. Access can process smaller field sizes quicker.

First Name
Last Name
City
State
Jim
Schmith
New York
N Y
Brenda
Petterson
Boston
M A
Jim
Martin
San Diego
C A
Melanie
Robinson
Jacksonville
F L
Susan
Hughes
Nashville
T N
Allen
Toppins
Atlanta
G A

For example, if you set the field size to 2, you can enter CA but not California.

TEXT FIELDS

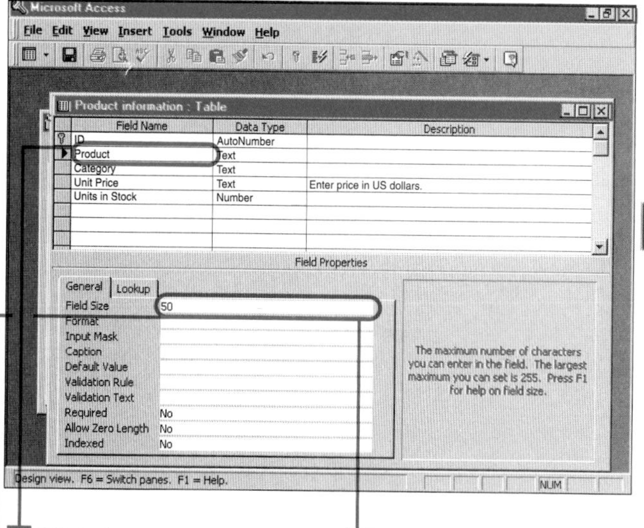

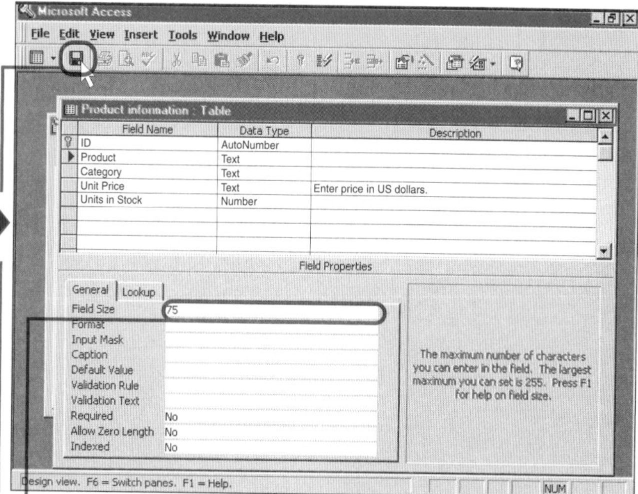

1 Click the name of the field you want to accept a maximum number of characters.

■ This area displays the maximum number of characters you can currently type in the field.

2 Click the area beside **Field Size** to change the number.

3 Press Backspace or Delete on your keyboard to remove the existing number.

4 Type the maximum number of characters you want the field to accept. You can enter a number from 0 to 255.

5 To save the table, click 💾.

■ A warning dialog box appears if you typed a smaller field size and the field contains data. Access will cut off any characters that exceed the new field size. To continue, click **Yes**.

What field sizes are available for numbers?

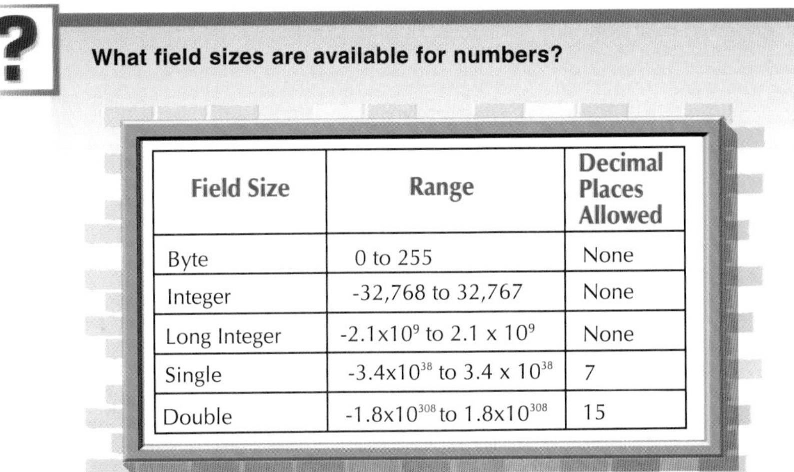

Field Size	Range	Decimal Places Allowed
Byte	0 to 255	None
Integer	-32,768 to 32,767	None
Long Integer	-2.1×10^{9} to 2.1×10^{9}	None
Single	-3.4×10^{38} to 3.4×10^{38}	7
Double	-1.8×10^{308} to 1.8×10^{308}	15

NUMBER FIELDS

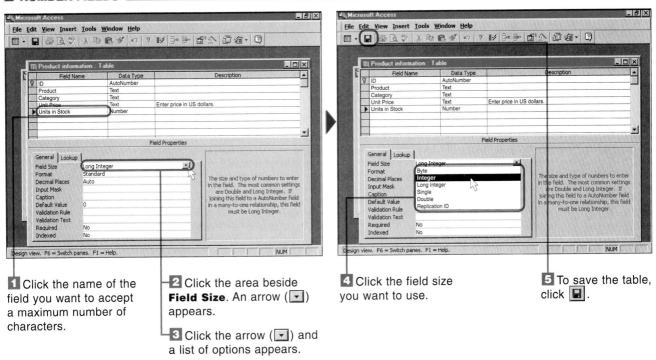

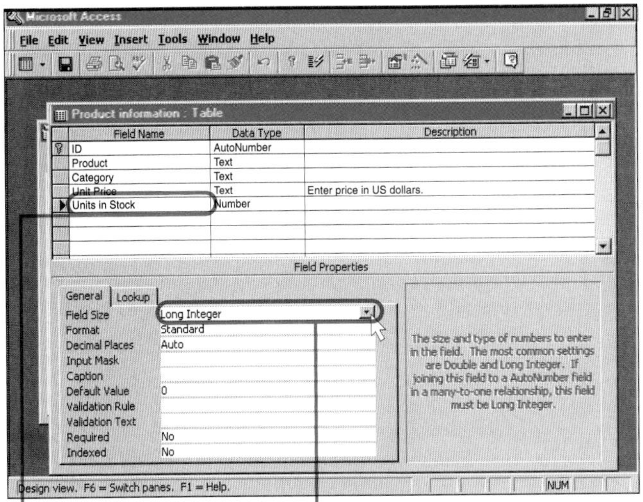

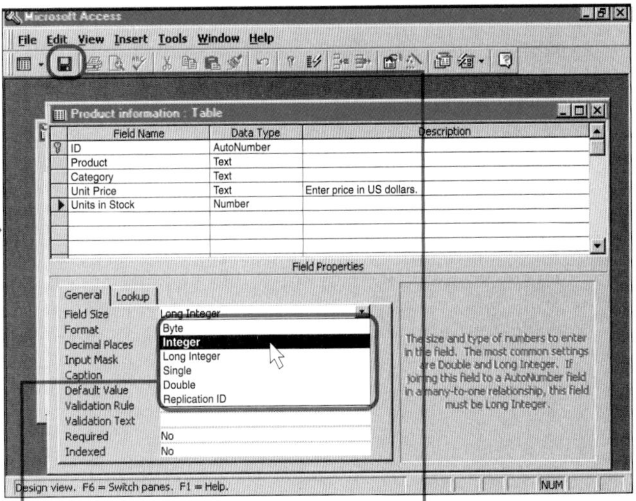

1 Click the name of the field you want to accept a maximum number of characters.

2 Click the area beside **Field Size**. An arrow (▾) appears.

3 Click the arrow (▾) and a list of options appears.

4 Click the field size you want to use.

5 To save the table, click 💾.

ADD A CAPTION

You can create a caption to appear as a heading instead of a field name. A caption can be longer and more descriptive than a field name, which is useful when you are entering or reviewing data.

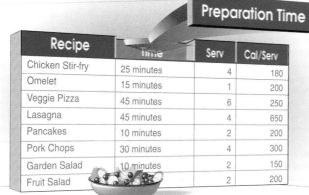

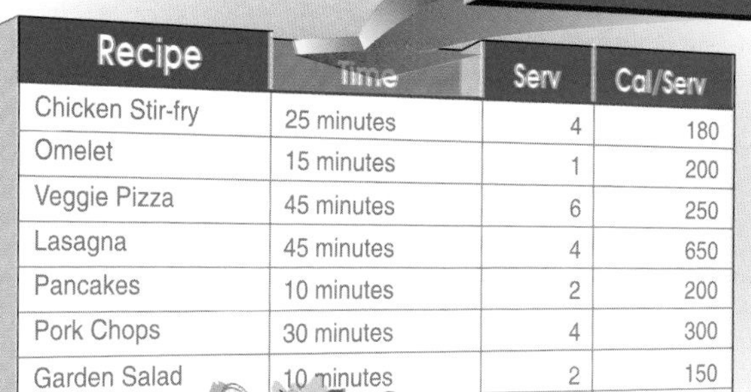

Preparation Time
Recipe
Time
Serv
Cal/Serv
Chicken Stir-fry
25 minutes
4
180
Omelet
15 minutes
1
200
Veggie Pizza
45 minutes
6
250
Lasagna
45 minutes
4
650
Pancakes
10 minutes
2
200
Pork Chops
30 minutes
4
300
Garden Salad
10 minutes
2
150
Fruit Salad
2
200

If you do not add a caption, the field name will appear as a heading for the field.

ADD A CAPTION

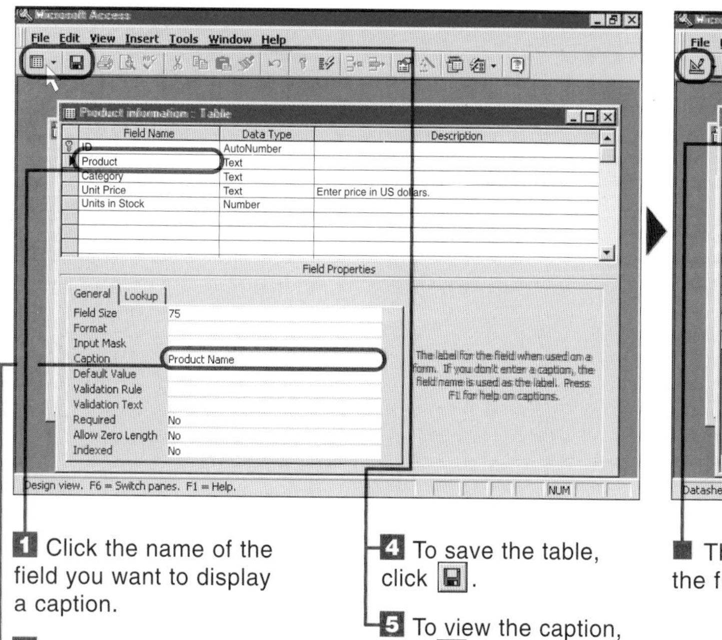

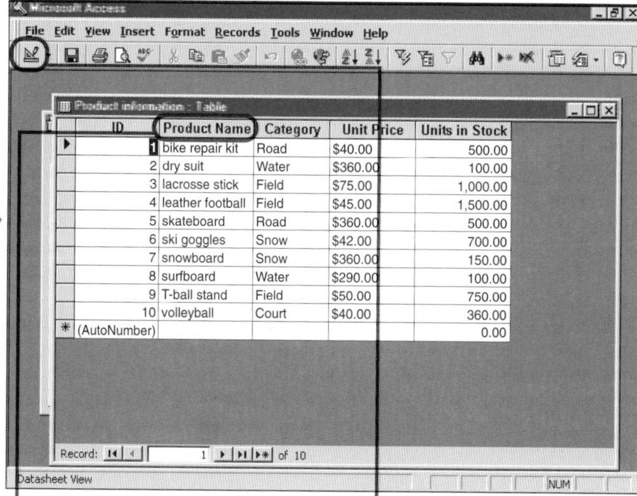

1 Click the name of the field you want to display a caption.

2 Click the area beside **Caption**.

3 Type the text you want to use as the caption.

4 To save the table, click .

5 To view the caption, click to display the table in the Datasheet view.

■ The caption replaces the field name.

■ To return to the Design view, click . For information on changing views, refer to page 96.

ADD A DEFAULT VALUE

You can specify a value that you want to appear automatically in a field each time you add a new record. This prevents you from having to retype the same information.

For example, you can set California (CA) as the default value in a field. When entering data, you can accept California (CA) or type another value.

ADD A DEFAULT VALUE

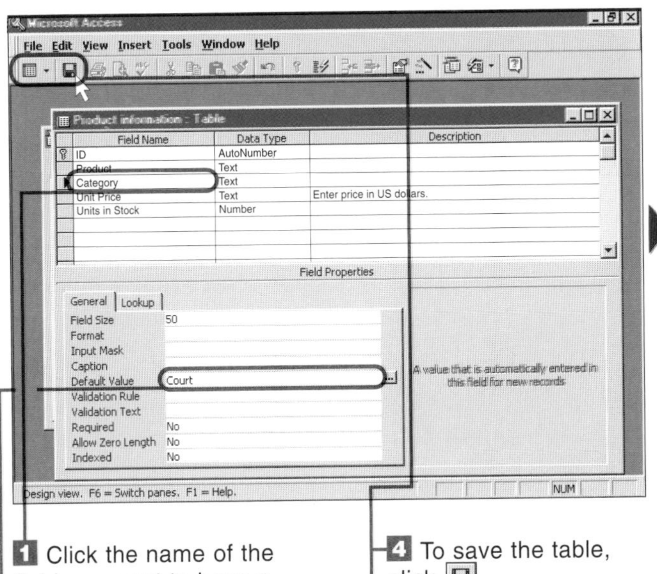

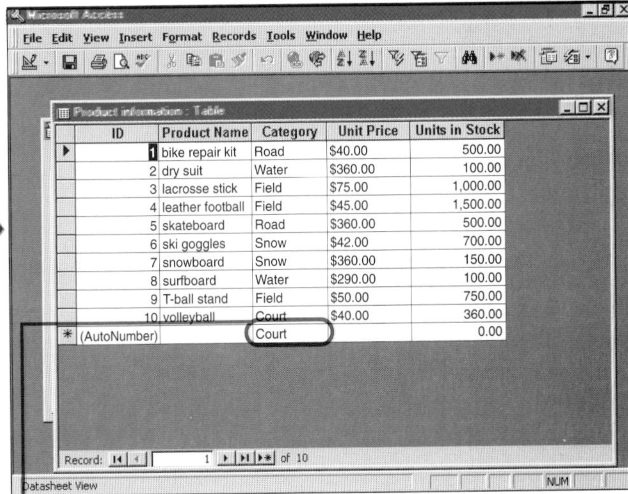

1 Click the name of the field you want to have a default value.

2 Click the area beside **Default Value**.

3 Type the text or number you want to set as the default value.

4 To save the table, click [save icon].

5 To display the table in the Datasheet view, click [datasheet icon].

■ The default value automatically appears in the field each time you add a new record. You can accept the default value or type another value.

Note: You can type ***=Date()*** *in step* ***3*** *to set the current date as the default value in a date field. Each time you add a new record, Access will insert the current date.*

DATA ENTRY REQUIRED

You can specify that a field must contain data for each record. Records that require data prevent you from leaving out important information.

	Qty	Amount	Invoice #
...et Dog Food	505	$60.00	16437
...iety Biscuits	736	$12.95	16438
...d Dog Food	377	$4.99	16439
...ry Cat Food	638	$15.49	16440
...mster Treats	894	$89.99	16441

DATA ENTRY REQUIRED

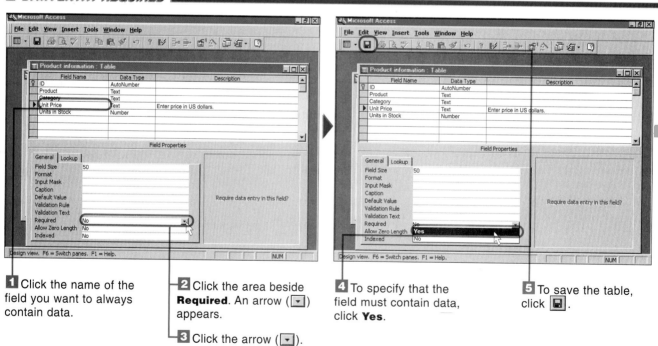

1 Click the name of the field you want to always contain data.

2 Click the area beside **Required**. An arrow (▾) appears.

3 Click the arrow (▾).

4 To specify that the field must contain data, click **Yes**.

5 To save the table, click 💾.

Will the field properties I specify for a table also be used in forms?

Properties you specify for a table will also apply to forms that use data from the table. For example, if you specify that a field in a table must contain data, the field in the form must also contain data. Make sure you set all the field properties for a table before creating any forms.

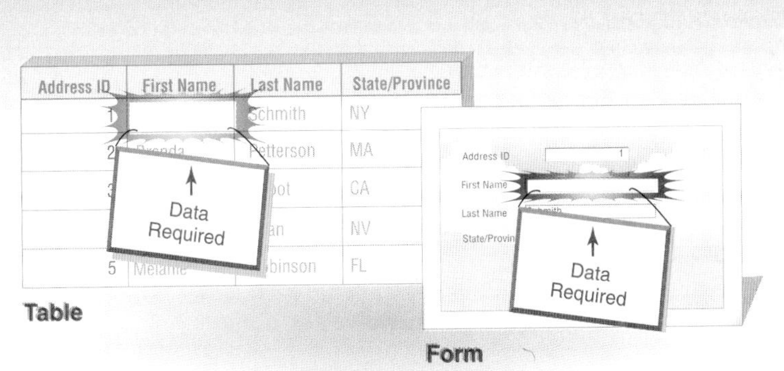

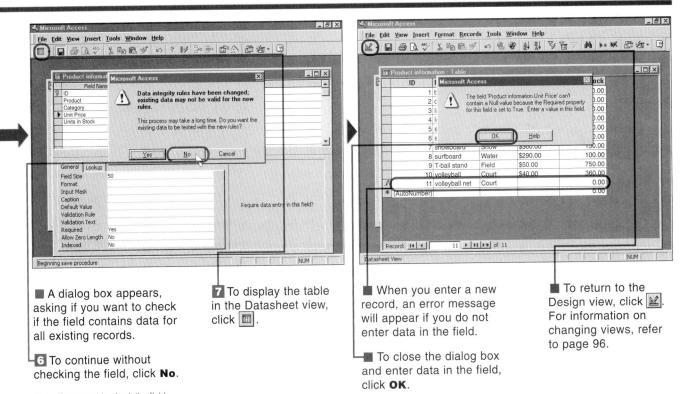

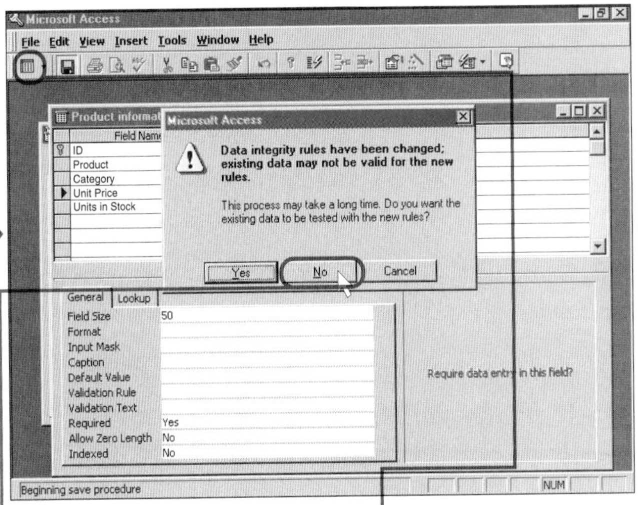

■ A dialog box appears, asking if you want to check if the field contains data for all existing records.

6 To continue without checking the field, click **No**.

Note: If you want to check the field, click ***Yes****.*

7 To display the table in the Datasheet view, click .

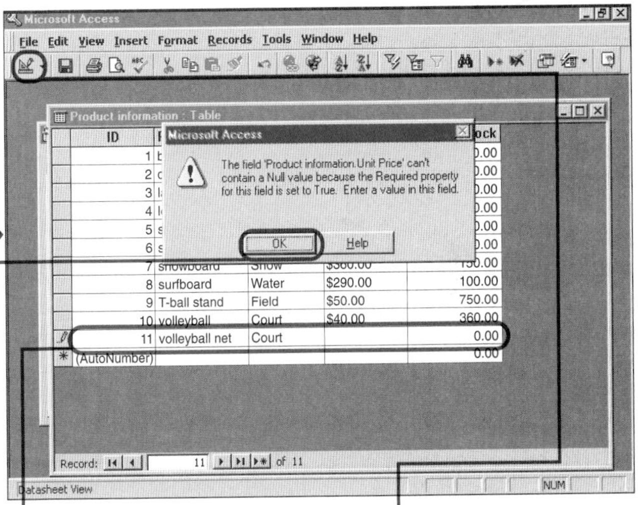

■ When you enter a new record, an error message will appear if you do not enter data in the field.

■ To close the dialog box and enter data in the field, click **OK**.

■ To return to the Design view, click . For information on changing views, refer to page 96.

ALLOW ZERO-LENGTH STRINGS

You can specify that a field may contain a zero-length string (""). A zero-length string is an entry containing no characters.

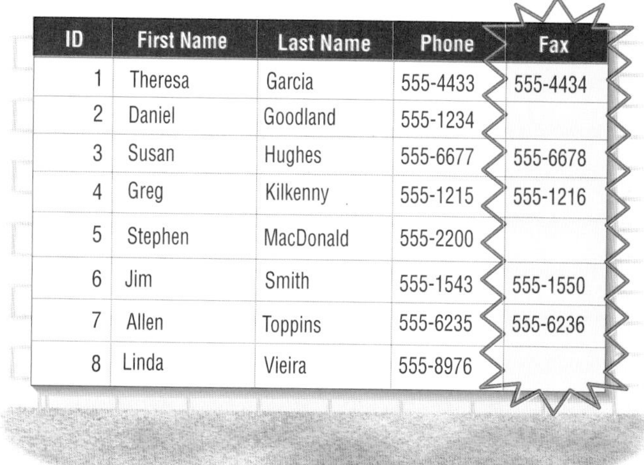

ID	First Name	Last Name	Phone	Fax
1	Theresa	Garcia	555-4433	555-4434
2	Daniel	Goodland	555-1234	
3	Susan	Hughes	555-6677	555-6678
4	Greg	Kilkenny	555-1215	555-1216
5	Stephen	MacDonald	555-2200	
6	Jim	Smith	555-1543	555-1550
7	Allen	Toppins	555-6235	555-6236
8	Linda	Vieira	555-8976	

CAN CONTAIN ZERO-LENGTH STRINGS

The zero-length string is useful if you must enter data in a field, but no data exists. For example, if the Fax Number field must contain data, but a client does not have a fax machine, you can enter a zero-length string in the field.

ALLOW ZERO-LENGTH STRINGS

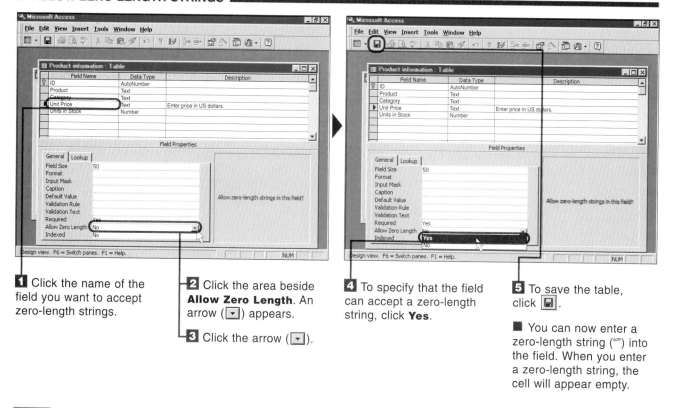

1 Click the name of the field you want to accept zero-length strings.

2 Click the area beside **Allow Zero Length**. An arrow (▾) appears.

3 Click the arrow (▾).

4 To specify that the field can accept a zero-length string, click **Yes**.

5 To save the table, click 💾.

■ You can now enter a zero-length string ("") into the field. When you enter a zero-length string, the cell will appear empty.

CHANGE NUMBER OF DECIMAL PLACES

You can specify how many decimal places Access uses to display numbers in a field.

CHANGE NUMBER OF DECIMAL PLACES

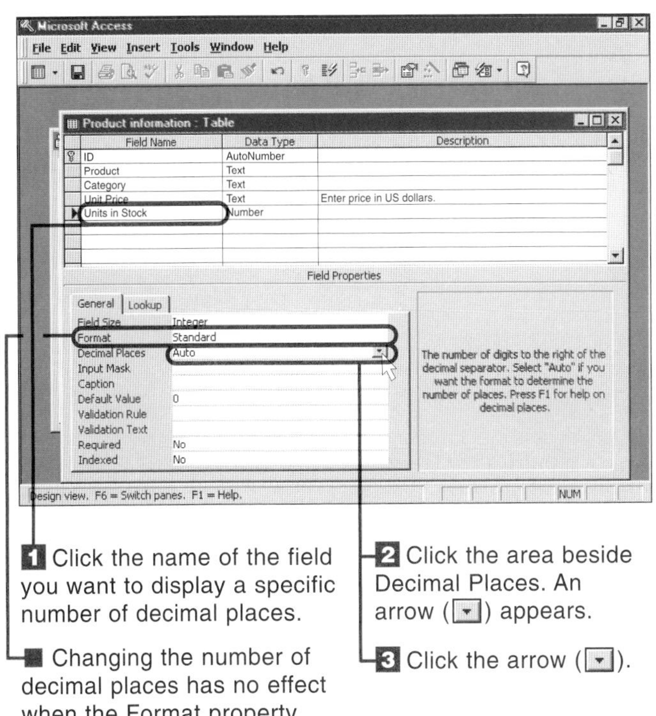

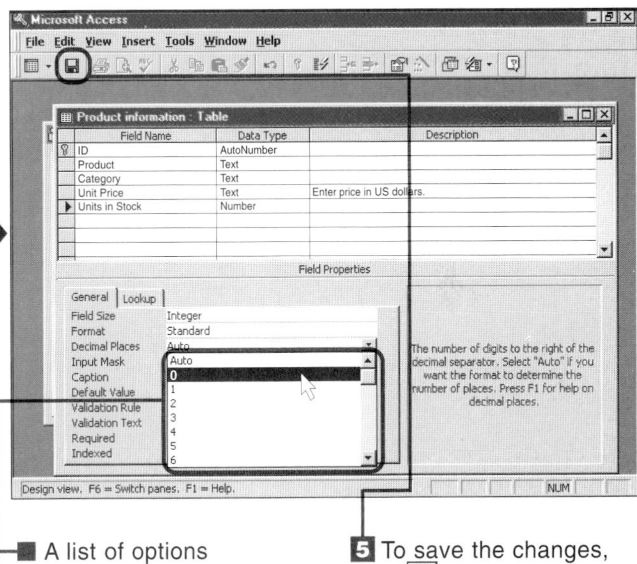

1 Click the name of the field you want to display a specific number of decimal places.

■ Changing the number of decimal places has no effect when the Format property is blank or set to General Number. To change the format, refer to page 106.

2 Click the area beside Decimal Places. An arrow (▾) appears.

3 Click the arrow (▾).

■ A list of options appears.

4 Click the number of decimal places you want the numbers in the field to display.

5 To save the changes, click 💾.

■ Access will display the number of decimal places you specified for all the numbers in the field.

ADD A VALIDATION RULE

You can reduce errors when entering data in a field by only accepting data that meets certain requirements. An error message appears if the data you enter does not meet the requirements.

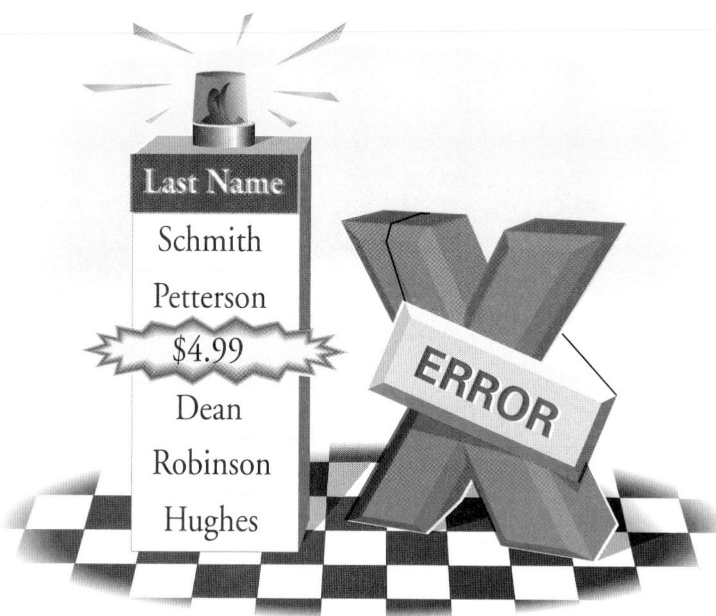

ADD A VALIDATION RULE

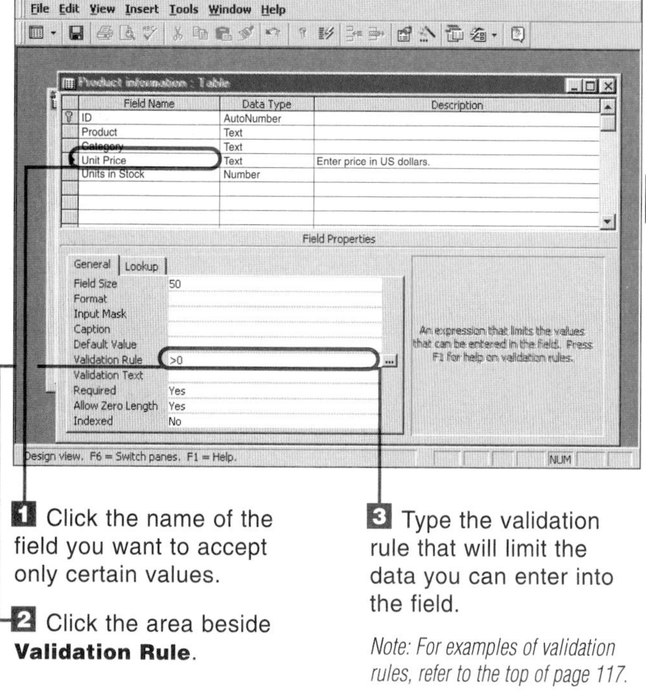

1 Click the name of the field you want to accept only certain values.

2 Click the area beside **Validation Rule**.

3 Type the validation rule that will limit the data you can enter into the field.

Note: For examples of validation rules, refer to the top of page 117.

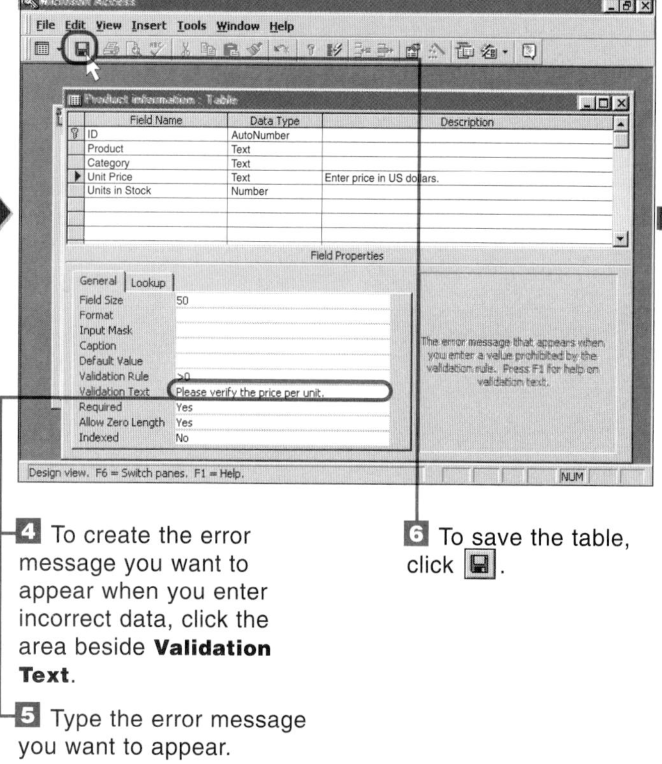

4 To create the error message you want to appear when you enter incorrect data, click the area beside **Validation Text**.

5 Type the error message you want to appear.

6 To save the table, click 💾.

What validation rules can I use?

Here are some examples of validation rules.

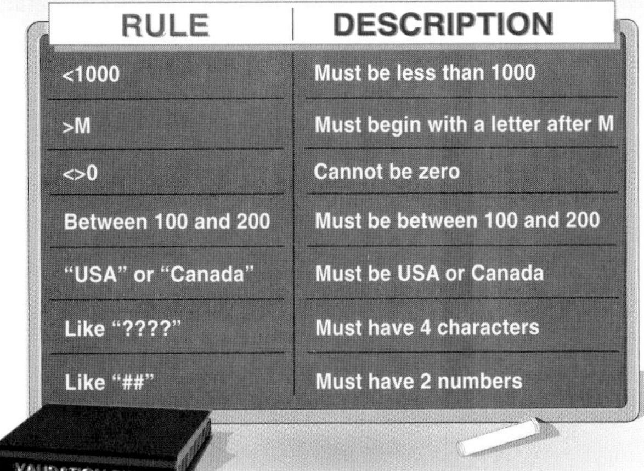

RULE	DESCRIPTION
<1000	Must be less than 1000
>M	Must begin with a letter after M
<>0	Cannot be zero
Between 100 and 200	Must be between 100 and 200
"USA" or "Canada"	Must be USA or Canada
Like "????"	Must have 4 characters
Like "##"	Must have 2 numbers

Note: For more examples, refer to pages 210 to 211.

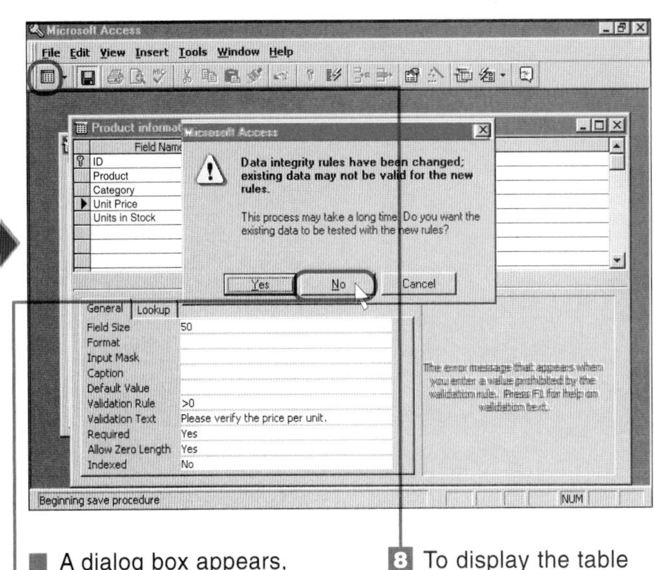

■ A dialog box appears, asking if you want to check if the existing data meets the new requirements.

7 To continue without checking existing data, click **No**.

Note: If you want to check existing data, click ***Yes****.*

8 To display the table in the Datasheet view, click ▦.

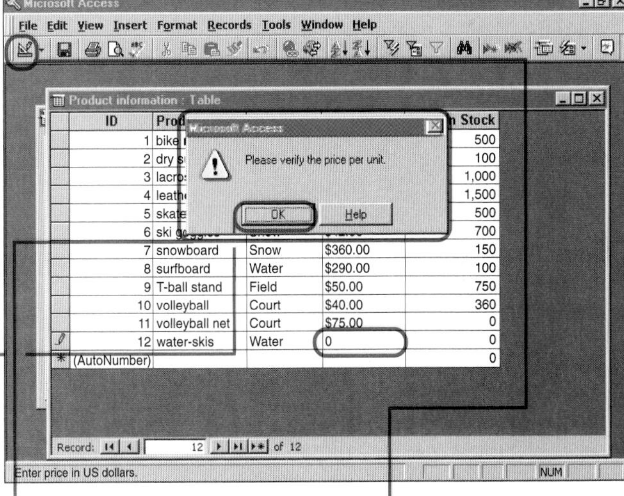

■ When you enter data that does not meet the requirements of the field, the error message you typed in step 5 will appear.

■ To close the dialog box and retype the data, click **OK**.

■ To return to the Design view, click ✎. For information on changing views, refer to page 96.

CREATE A YES/NO FIELD

You can create a field that accepts only one of two values, such as Yes/No, True/False or On/Off.

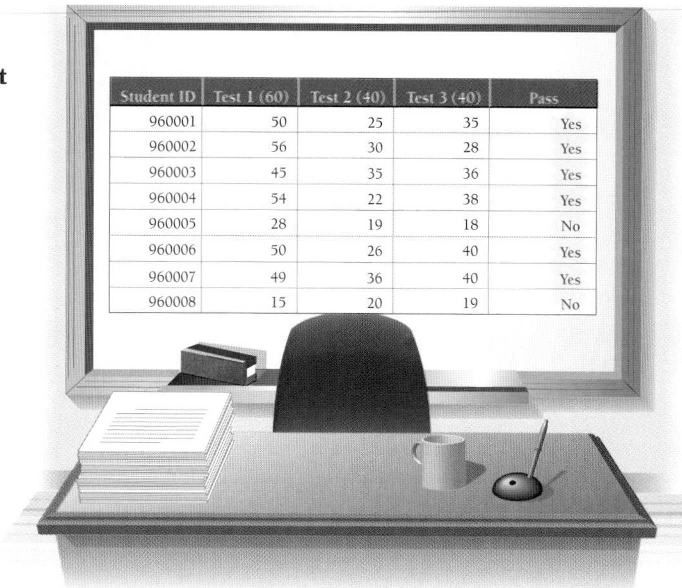

Student ID
Test 1 (60)
Test 2 (40)
Test 3 (40)
Pass
960001 50 25 35 Yes
960002 56 30 28 Yes
960003 45 35 36 Yes
960004 54 22 38 Yes
960005 28 19 18 No
960006 50 26 40 Yes
960007 49 36 40 Yes
960008 15 20 19 No

For example, you can create a Yes/No field that specifies whether or not each student passed the course.

CREATE A YES/NO FIELD

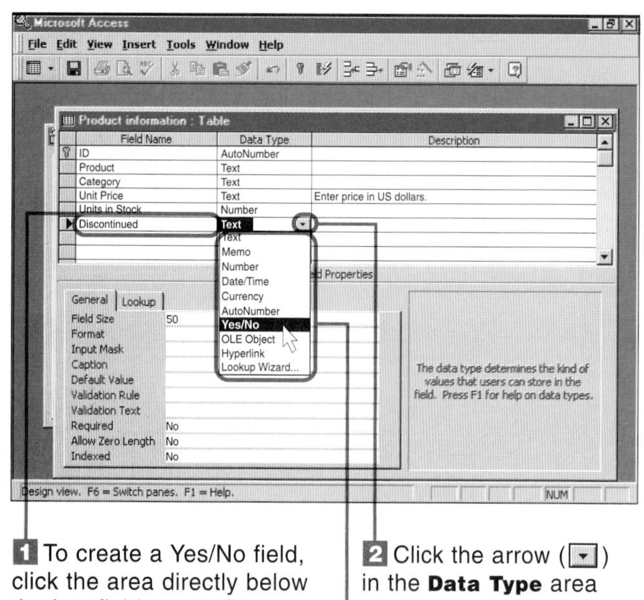

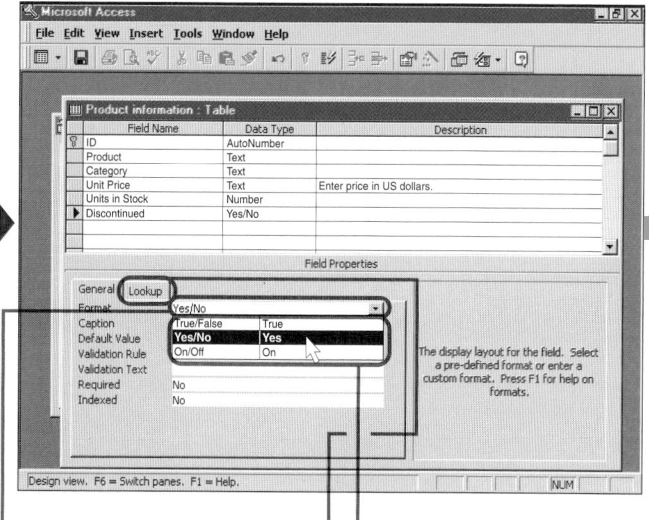

1 To create a Yes/No field, click the area directly below the last field name. Type a name for the field and then press Enter on your keyboard.

Note: To add a field between existing fields, refer to page 98.

2 Click the arrow (▾) in the **Data Type** area to change the data type of the field.

3 Click **Yes/No**.

4 To change the format of the field, click the area beside **Format**. An arrow (▾) appears.

5 Click the arrow (▾) and a list of formats appears.

6 Click the format you want to use.

7 To change the way data will appear in the field, click the **Lookup** tab.

*Note: You can click the **General** tab at any time to return to the general properties.*

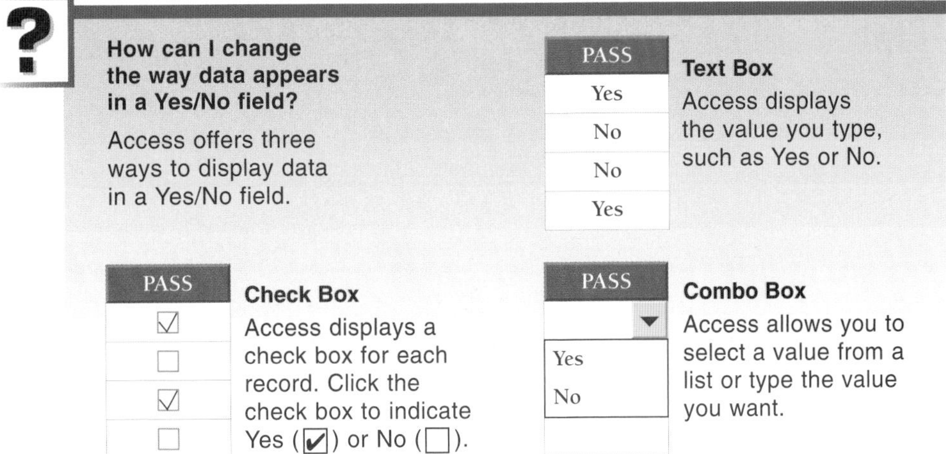

How can I change the way data appears in a Yes/No field?

Access offers three ways to display data in a Yes/No field.

Text Box
Access displays the value you type, such as Yes or No.

Check Box
Access displays a check box for each record. Click the check box to indicate Yes (☑) or No (☐).

Combo Box
Access allows you to select a value from a list or type the value you want.

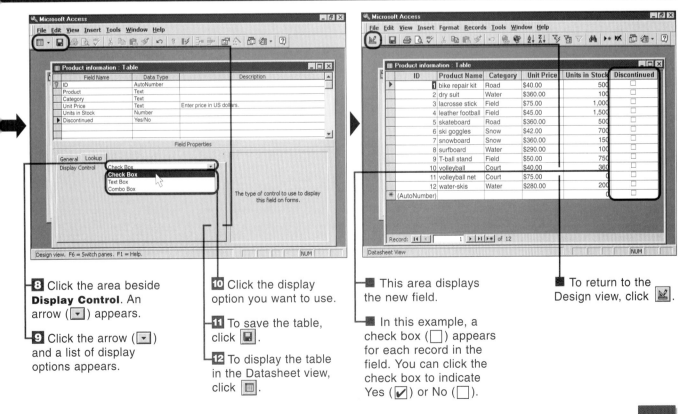

8 Click the area beside **Display Control**. An arrow (▾) appears.

9 Click the arrow (▾) and a list of display options appears.

10 Click the display option you want to use.

11 To save the table, click 💾.

12 To display the table in the Datasheet view, click ▦.

■ This area displays the new field.

■ In this example, a check box (☐) appears for each record in the field. You can click the check box to indicate Yes (☑) or No (☐).

■ To return to the Design view, click ✎.

CREATE AN INDEX

You can create an index for a field to speed up searching and sorting information in a table.

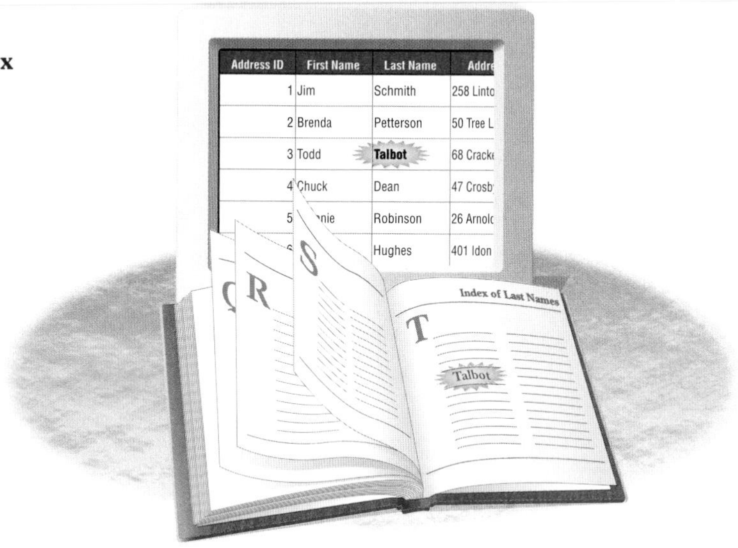

Access uses the index to find the location of information. Using the index is quicker than searching each individual record.

For example, you can create an index for the Last Name field to search for specific last names quicker.

CREATE AN INDEX

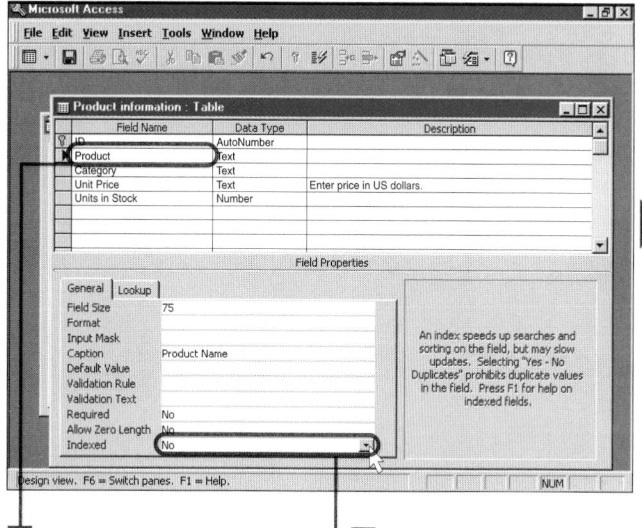

1 Click the name of the field you want to index.

2 Click the area beside **Indexed**. An arrow (▼) appears.

3 Click the arrow (▼).

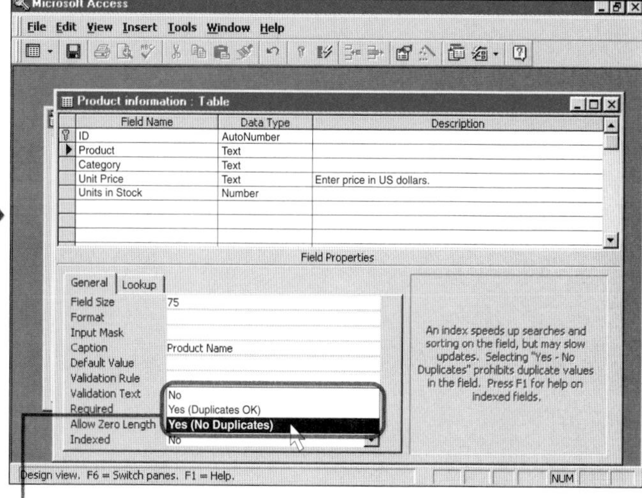

4 Click the index option you want to use.

Note: For information on the index options, refer to the top of page 121.

What index options does Access offer?

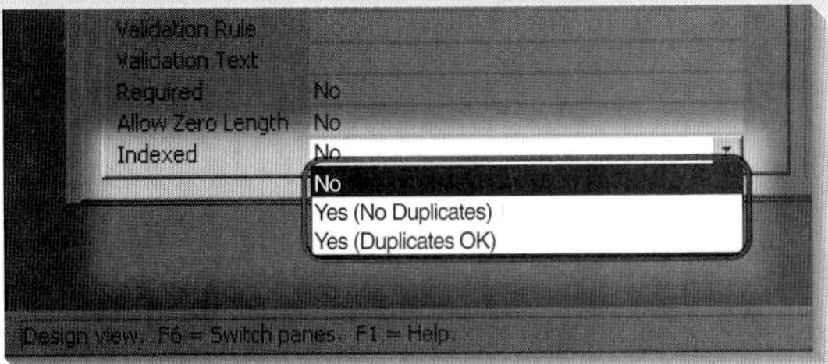

No

Do not index the information.

Yes (No Duplicates)

Index the information. You cannot enter the same information in more than one record.

Yes (Duplicates OK)

Index the information. You can enter the same information in more than one record.

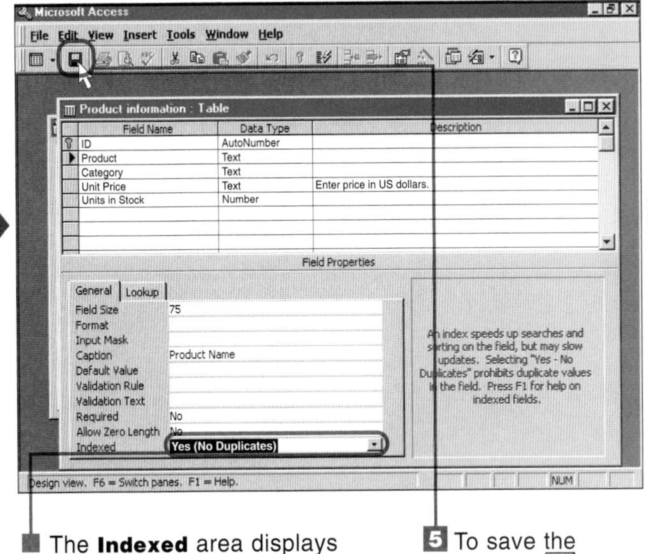

■ The **Indexed** area displays the index option you selected. Access indexes the information in the field. When you sort or search for information in the field, Access will now perform the task more quickly.

5 To save the table, click 💾.

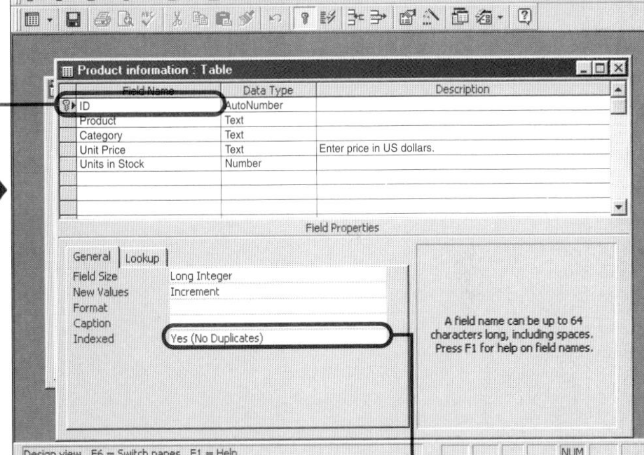

THE PRIMARY KEY

The primary key is a field that uniquely identifies each record in a table. The primary key is automatically indexed.

1 To display the Index property for the primary key, click the field name of the primary key. The primary key displays a key symbol (🔑).

■ The index for the primary key is automatically set to **Yes (No Duplicates)**.

CREATE A LOOKUP COLUMN

You can create a list of values that you can choose from when entering information in a field.

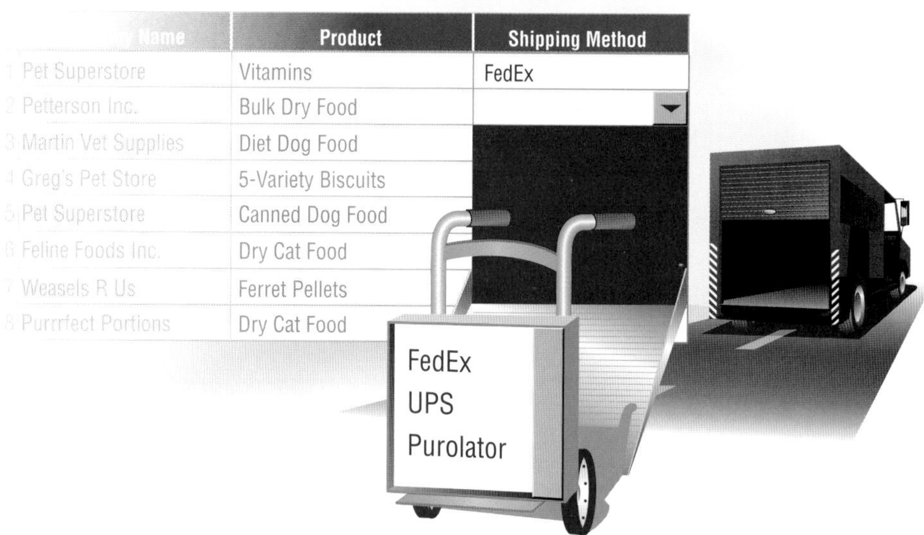

Product
Shipping Method
Pet Superstore
Vitamins
FedEx
Petterson Inc.
Bulk Dry Food
Martin Vet Supplies
Diet Dog Food
Greg's Pet Store
5-Variety Biscuits
Pet Superstore
Canned Dog Food
Feline Foods Inc.
Dry Cat Food
Weasels R Us
Ferret Pellets
Purrrfect Portions
Dry Cat Food
FedEx
UPS
Purolator

CREATE A LOOKUP COLUMN

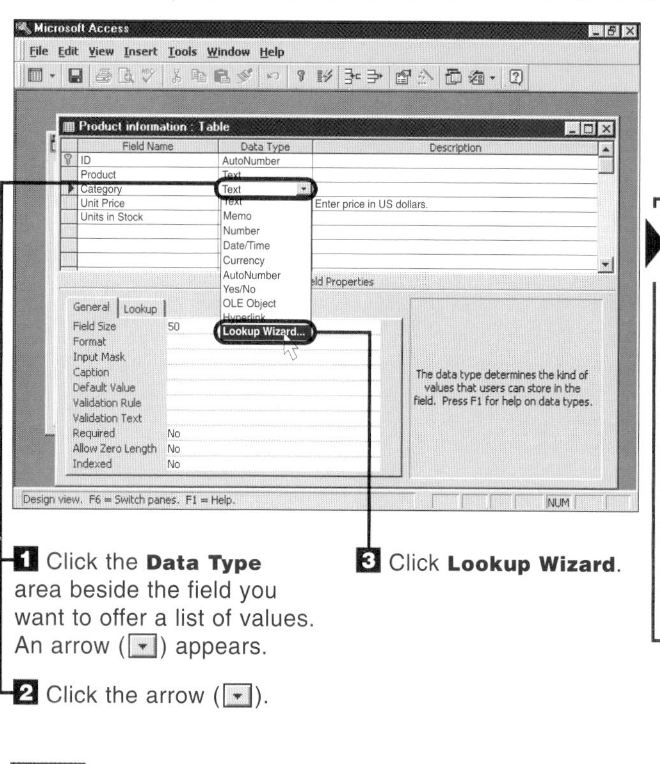

1 Click the **Data Type** area beside the field you want to offer a list of values. An arrow (▾) appears.

2 Click the arrow (▾).

3 Click **Lookup Wizard**.

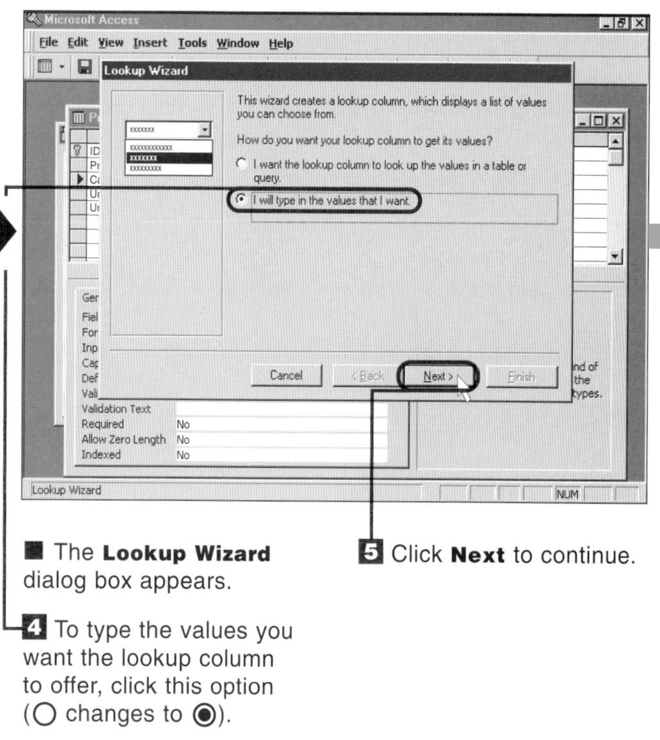

■ The **Lookup Wizard** dialog box appears.

4 To type the values you want the lookup column to offer, click this option (○ changes to ◉).

5 Click **Next** to continue.

Why would I create a lookup column?

Creating a lookup column is very useful if you repeatedly enter the same values in a field. For example, if you always use one of three methods to ship your orders, you can create a lookup column that displays the three shipment methods.

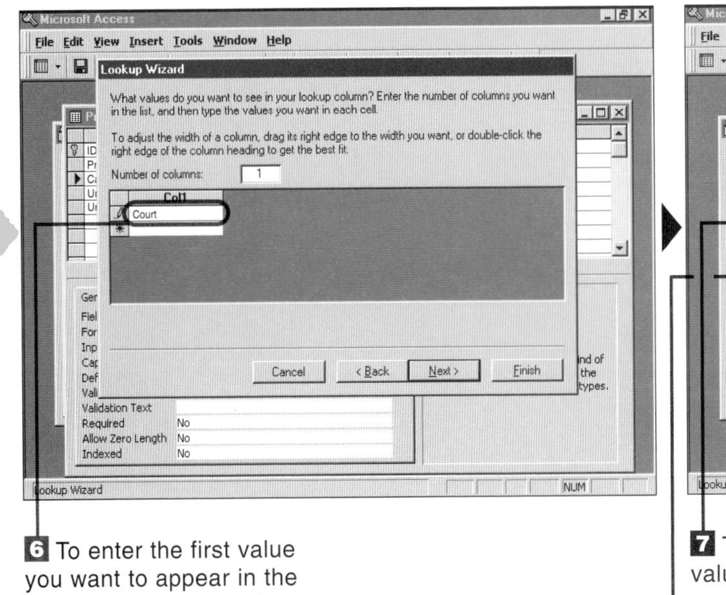

6 To enter the first value you want to appear in the list, click this area and then type the value.

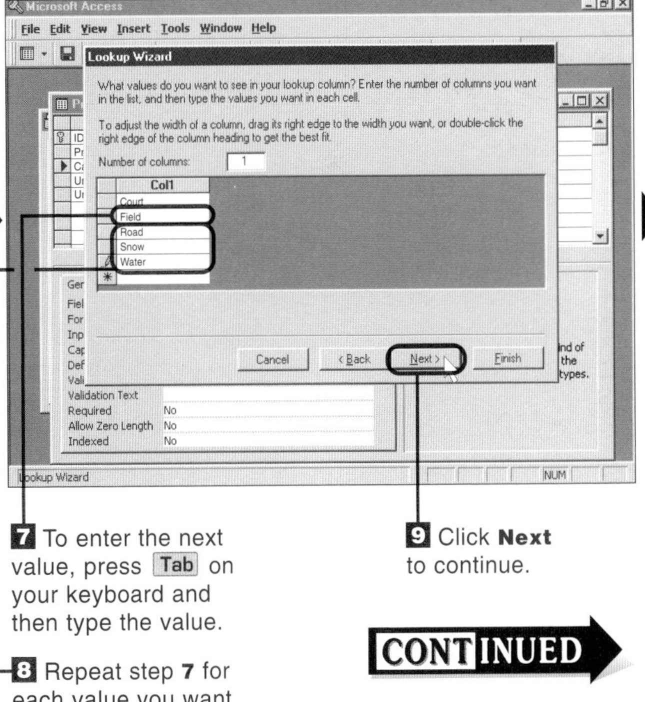

7 To enter the next value, press **Tab** on your keyboard and then type the value.

8 Repeat step **7** for each value you want to appear in the list.

9 Click **Next** to continue.

CONTINUED

CREATE A LOOKUP COLUMN

You can save time and reduce errors when entering information by selecting a value from a lookup column you created.

Order ID
Company Name
Product
Qty
Ship
1 Pet Superstore Vitamins 12 Ground
2 Petterson Inc. Bulk Dry Food 15 1 Day Air
3 Martin Vet Supplies Diet Dog Food 30 4 Day Air
4 Greg's Pet Store 5-Variety Biscuits 50 4 Day Air
5 Pet Superstore Canned Dog Food 24 1 Day Air
6 Feline Foods Inc. Dry Cat Food 40
7 Weasels R Us Ferret Pellets 30
Ground
1 Day Air
2 Day Air
4 Day Air

CREATE A LOOKUP COLUMN (CONTINUED)

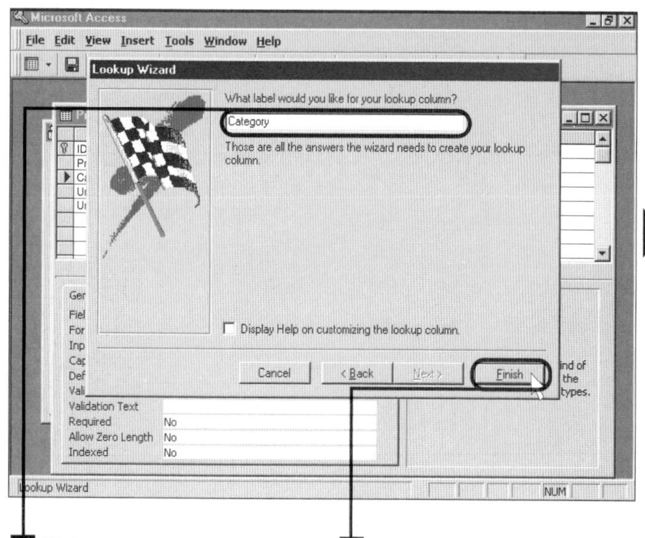

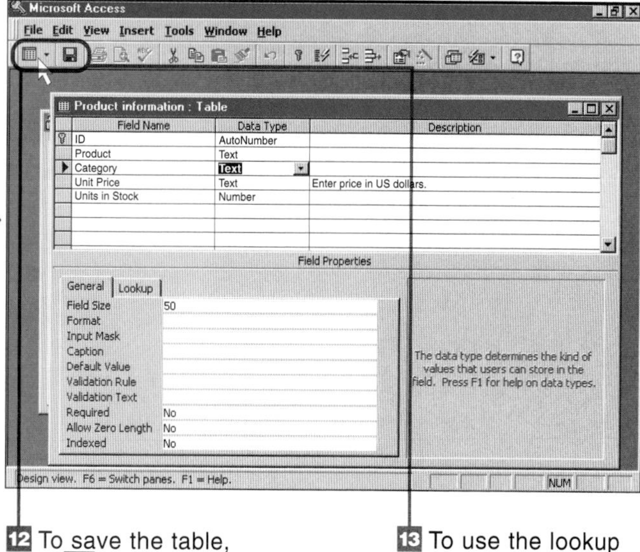

10 This area displays the name of the field that will provide the lookup column. To change the field name, type a new name.

11 Click **Finish** to create the lookup column.

12 To save the table, click 💾.

13 To use the lookup column, click ▦. The table appears in the Datasheet view.

? Do I have to select a value from a lookup column?

If the lookup column does not display a value you want to use, you can type another value. To hide a lookup column you displayed without selecting a value from the list, click outside the list.

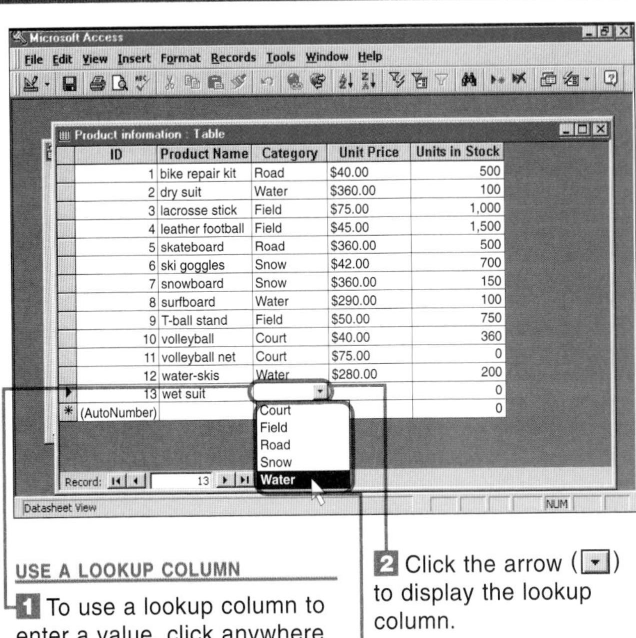

Microsoft Access — Product information : Table

ID	Product Name	Category	Unit Price	Units in Stock
1	bike repair kit	Road	$40.00	500
2	dry suit	Water	$360.00	100
3	lacrosse stick	Field	$75.00	1,000
4	leather football	Field	$45.00	1,500
5	skateboard	Road	$360.00	500
6	ski goggles	Snow	$42.00	700
7	snowboard	Snow	$360.00	150
8	surfboard	Water	$290.00	100
9	T-ball stand	Field	$50.00	750
10	volleyball	Court	$40.00	360
11	volleyball net	Court	$75.00	0
12	water-skis	Water	$280.00	200
13	wet suit	Water		0
(AutoNumber)				0

Record: 13 of 13

Datasheet View NUM

USE A LOOKUP COLUMN

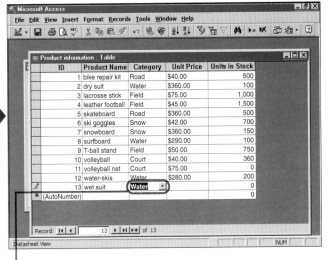

1 To use a lookup column to enter a value, click anywhere in the field that provides the lookup column. An arrow (▾) appears.

2 Click the arrow (▾) to display the lookup column.

3 Click the value you want to enter in the field.

■ Access enters the value you selected from the lookup column.

ADD PICTURES TO RECORDS

You can add a picture to each record in a table. For example, you can include pictures of employees, houses for sale, artwork, recipes or products.

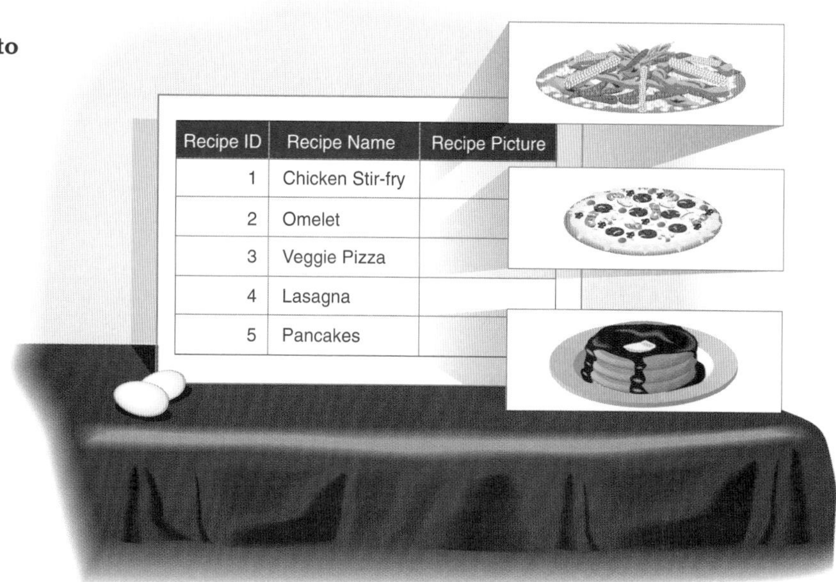

Recipe ID
Recipe Name
Recipe Picture
1
Chicken Stir-fry
2
Omelet
3
Veggie Pizza
4
Lasagna
5
Pancakes

ADD PICTURES TO RECORDS

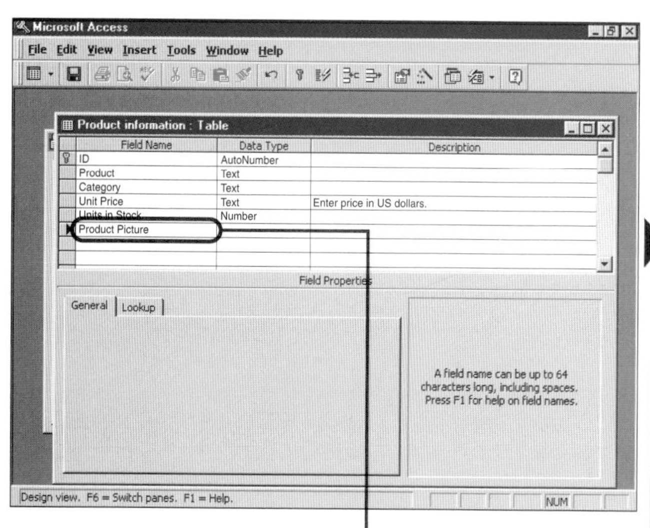

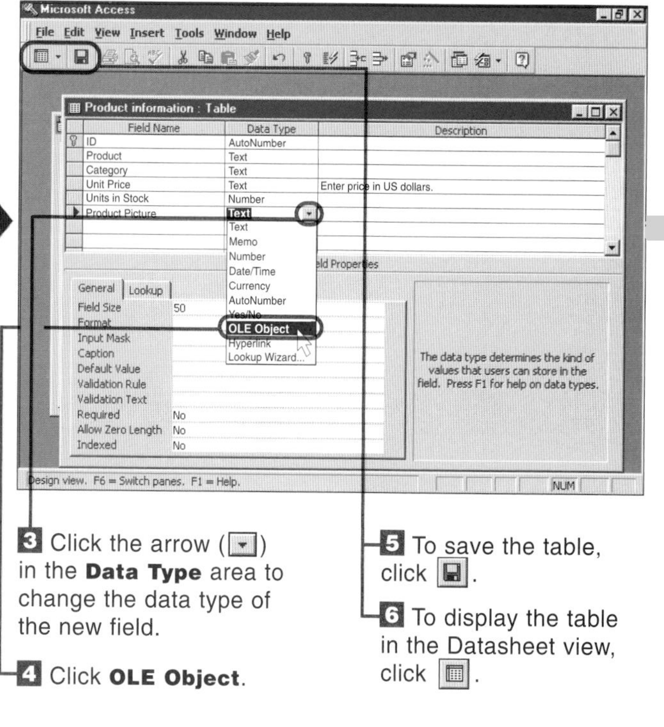

1 Open the table you want to add the pictures to and display the table in the Design view.

2 To create a field you will add the pictures to, click the area directly below the last field name. Type a name for the field and then press Enter on your keyboard.

Note: To add a field between existing fields, refer to page 98.

3 Click the arrow (▾) in the **Data Type** area to change the data type of the new field.

4 Click **OLE Object**.

5 To save the table, click 💾.

6 To display the table in the Datasheet view, click ▦.

?

Can I add objects other than pictures to a table?

You can add many types of objects to a table. For example, you can include Word documents, Excel worksheets, sounds and even video files.

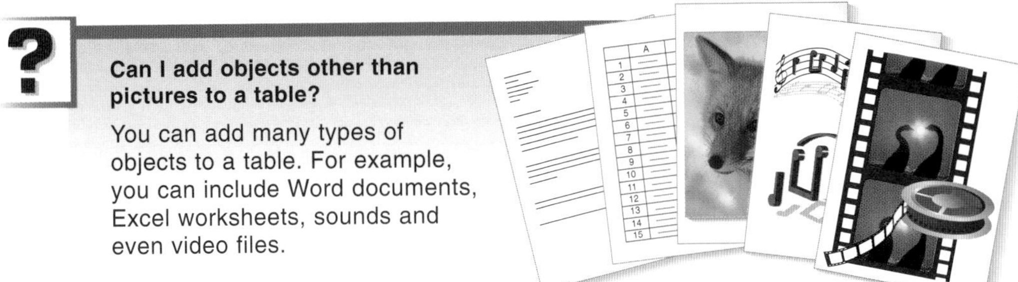

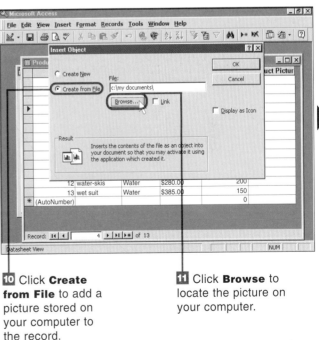

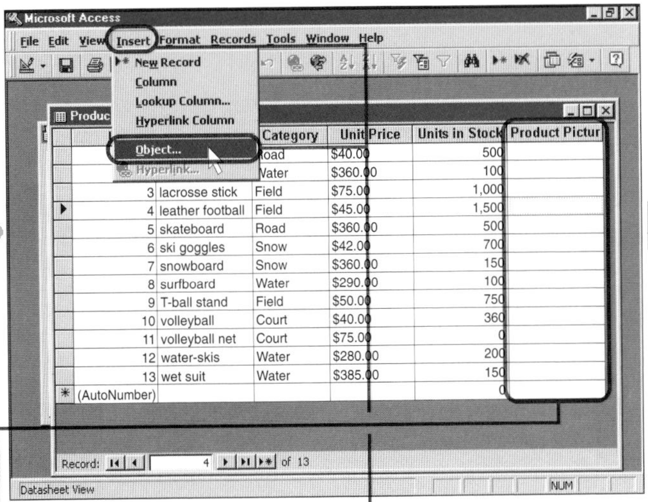

■ This area displays the new field.

7 Click the cell where you want to add a picture.

8 Click **Insert**.

9 Click **Object**.

■ The **Insert Object** dialog box appears.

10 Click **Create from File** to add a picture stored on your computer to the record.

11 Click **Browse** to locate the picture on your computer.

CONTINUED

ADD PICTURES TO RECORDS

When you add pictures to a record in a table, you can open and display the pictures at any time.

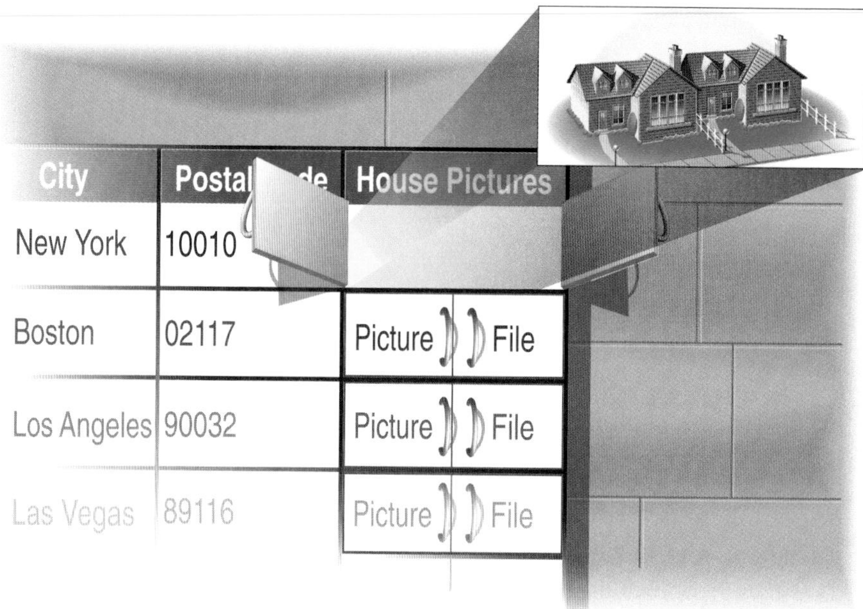

ADD PICTURES TO RECORDS (CONTINUED)

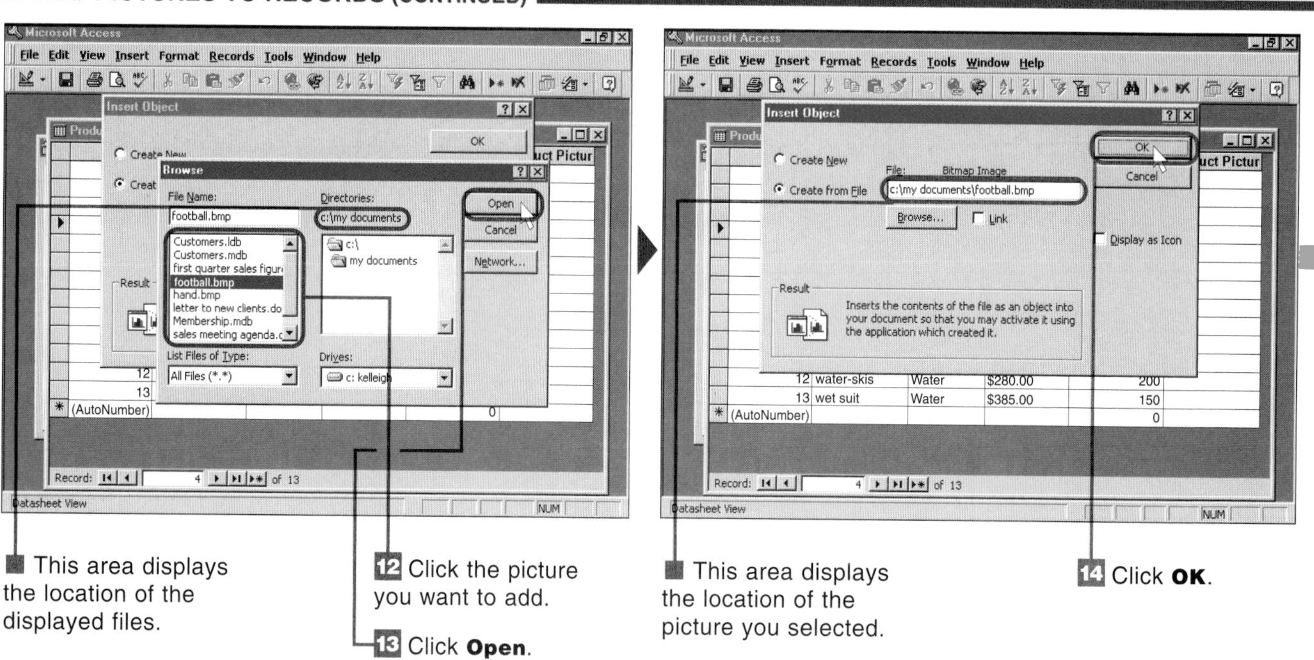

■ This area displays the location of the displayed files.

12 Click the picture you want to add.

13 Click **Open**.

■ This area displays the location of the picture you selected.

14 Click **OK**.

?

Will a picture appear in a form?

When you create a form based on a table that includes pictures, the form will also display the pictures.

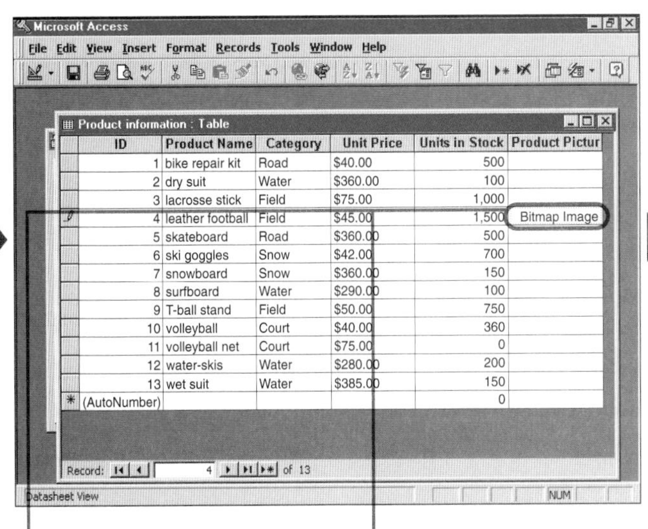

ID	Product Name	Category	Unit Price	Units in Stock	Product Pictur
1	bike repair kit	Road	$40.00	500	
2	dry suit	Water	$360.00	100	
3	lacrosse stick	Field	$75.00	1,000	
4	leather football	Field	$45.00	1,500	Bitmap Image
5	skateboard	Road	$360.00	500	
6	ski goggles	Snow	$42.00	700	
7	snowboard	Snow	$360.00	150	
8	surfboard	Water	$290.00	100	
9	T-ball stand	Field	$50.00	750	
10	volleyball	Court	$40.00	360	
11	volleyball net	Court	$75.00	0	
12	water-skis	Water	$280.00	200	
13	wet suit	Water	$385.00	150	
(AutoNumber)				0	

■ Access displays the type of picture you added to the table.

■ Repeat steps 7 to 14 starting on page 127 for each cell you want to add a picture to.

VIEW A PICTURE

1 To view a picture, double-click the cell displaying the picture type.

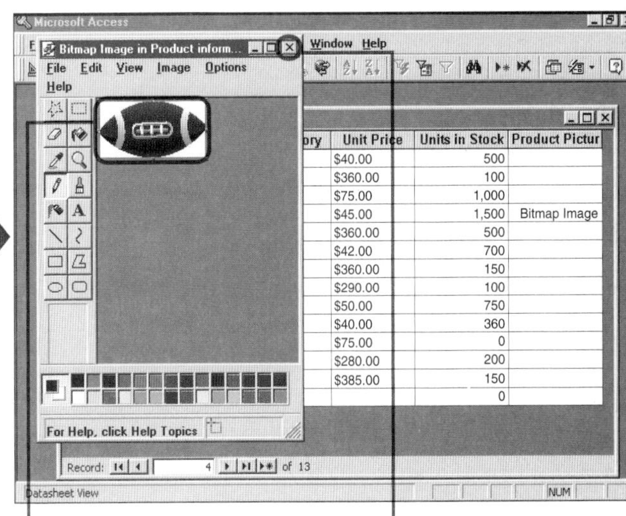

■ The program used to create the picture opens, displaying the picture.

■ When you finish viewing the picture, click ☒ to close the picture.

CREATE AN INPUT MASK

You can create an input mask to limit the type of information you can enter in a field. Input masks reduce errors and ensure data has a consistent appearance.

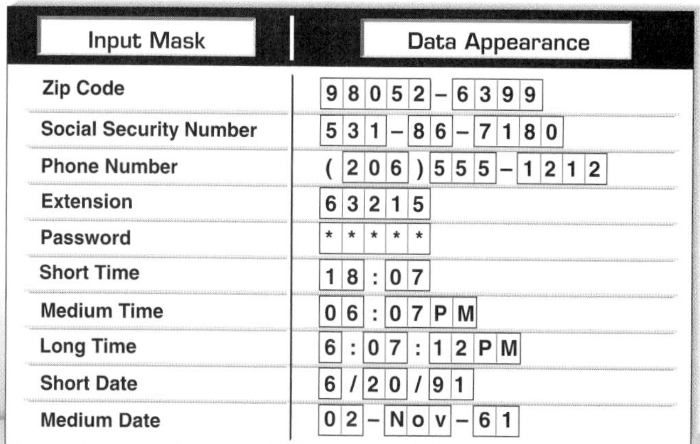

Input Mask	Data Appearance
Zip Code	98052-6399
Social Security Number	531-86-7180
Phone Number	(206)555-1212
Extension	63215
Password	*****
Short Time	18:07
Medium Time	06:07PM
Long Time	6:07:12PM
Short Date	6/20/91
Medium Date	02-Nov-61

The Input Mask Wizard provides you with common input masks.

CREATE AN INPUT MASK USING THE WIZARD

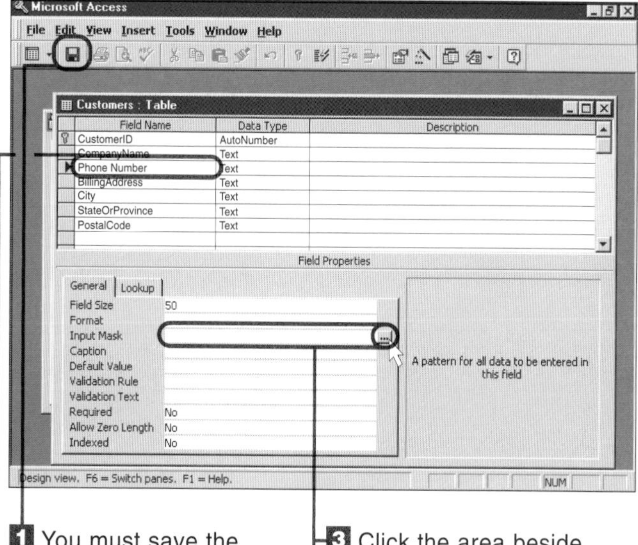

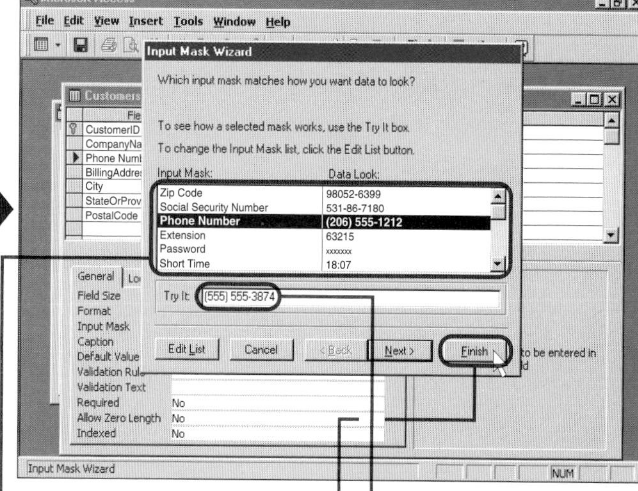

1 You must save the table before starting the Input Mask Wizard. To save the table, click 💾.

2 Click the name of the field you want to create an input mask for.

Note: The Phone Number field was added for this example. To add a field, refer to page 98.

3 Click the area beside **Input Mask**. A button (...) appears.

4 Click the button (...).

■ The **Input Mask Wizard** dialog box appears.

■ This area displays the available input masks and how the data will appear on your screen.

5 Click the input mask you want to use.

6 To try the input mask you selected, press Tab on your keyboard and then type the appropriate data.

7 Click **Finish** to select the input mask.

?

Why does this error message appear?

This error message appears if the Input Mask Wizard is not available on your computer. You need to install the Advanced Wizards feature from the Microsoft Access or Microsoft Office Setup program if you want to use the wizard to create input masks.

Microsoft Access
This feature isn't installed.
To install this feature, rerun the Microsoft Access or Microsoft Office Setup program, click Add/Remove, and then click the Advanced Wizards check box.
OK

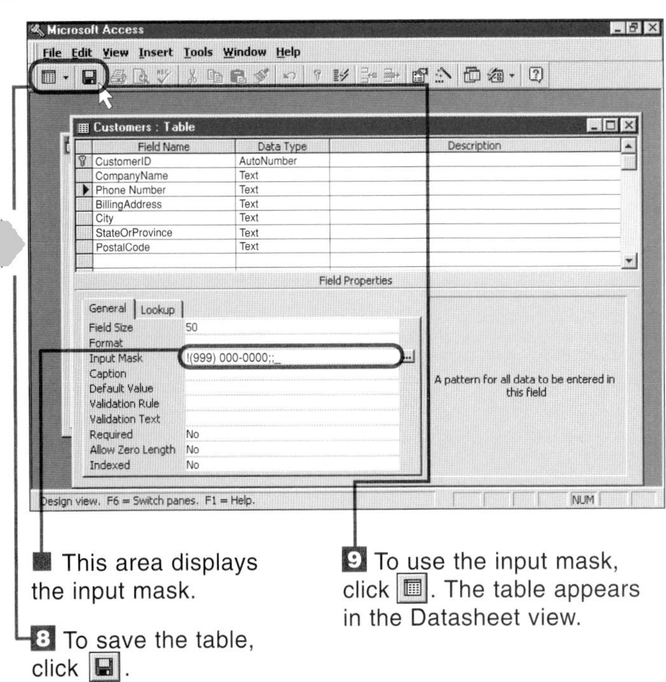

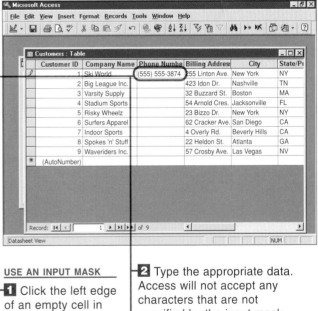

■ This area displays the input mask.

8 To save the table, click 💾.

9 To use the input mask, click ▦. The table appears in the Datasheet view.

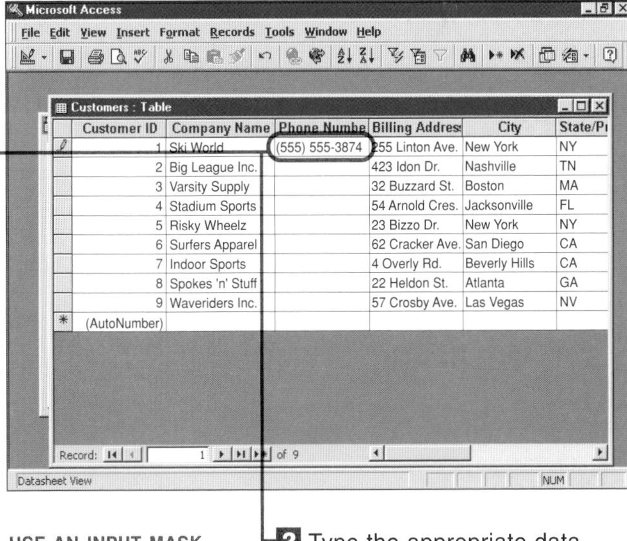

USE AN INPUT MASK

1 Click the left edge of an empty cell in the field that uses the input mask.

2 Type the appropriate data. Access will not accept any characters that are not specified by the input mask.

■ When you use an input mask to enter data, the input mask automatically enters some characters such as slashes (/) and hyphens (-) for you.

CREATE AN INPUT MASK

You can create your own personalized input masks to establish a pattern for information entered in a field.

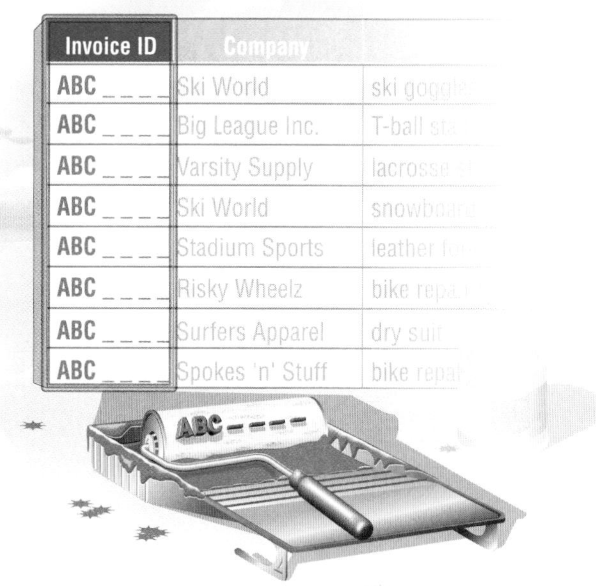

Invoice ID
Company
ABC
Ski World
Big League Inc.
Varsity Supply
Ski World
Stadium Sports
Risky Wheelz
Surfers Apparel
Spokes 'n' Stuff

Input masks save you time by automatically entering some characters for you. For example, if your invoice numbers always begin with **ABC**, you can have the input mask automatically enter these characters for you.

CREATE A PERSONALIZED INPUT MASK

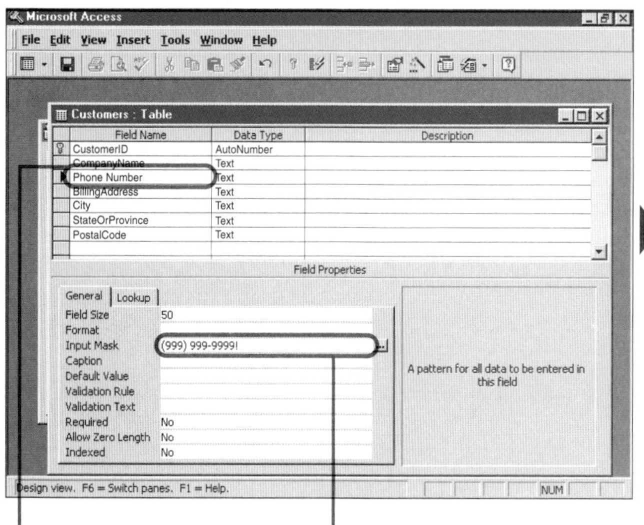

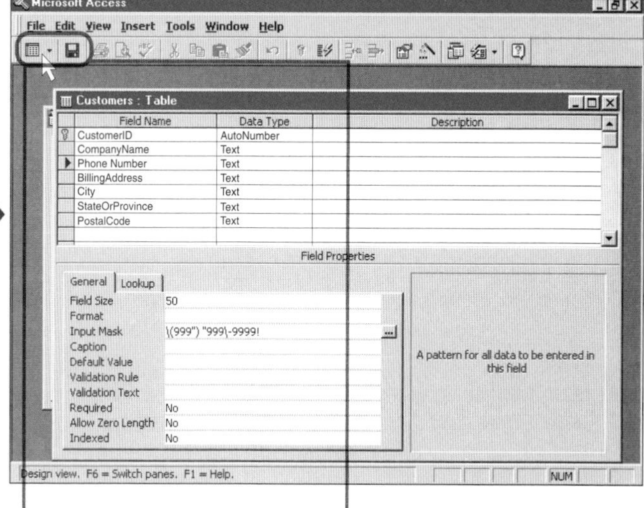

1 Click the name of the field you want to create an input mask for.

Note: The Phone Number field was added for this example. To add a field, refer to page 98.

2 Click the area beside **Input Mask**.

3 Type the input mask to specify the kind of data you want the field to accept.

4 To save the table, click 💾.

5 To use the input mask, click ▦ to display the table in the Datasheet view.

When would I create a personalized input mask?

You may want to create a personalized input mask if the wizard does not offer an input mask that suits the data you want to enter. To use the wizard, refer to page 130. Here are some examples of input masks.

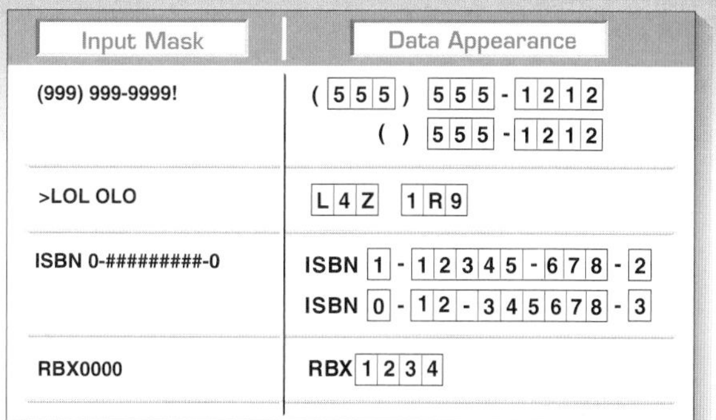

Input Mask	Data Appearance
(999) 999-9999!	(555) 555-1212 ( ) 555-1212
>LOL OLO	L4Z 1R9
ISBN 0-#########-0	ISBN 1-12345-678-2 ISBN 0-12-345678-3
RBX0000	RBX1234

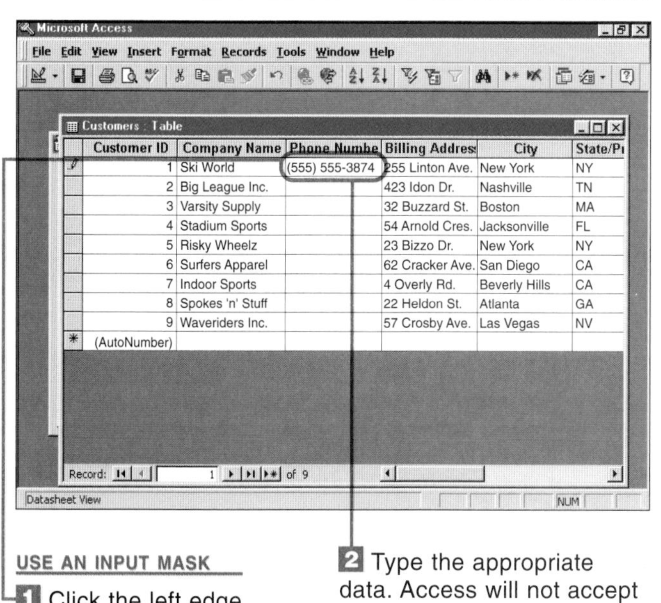

USE AN INPUT MASK

1 Click the left edge of an empty cell in the field that uses the input mask.

2 Type the appropriate data. Access will not accept any characters that are not specified by the input mask.

These characters allow you to create a personalized input mask.

Character	Description
0	Numbers 0 to 9, required
9	Number or space, optional
#	Number or space, optional, plus and minus signs allowed
L	Letters A to Z, required
?	Letters A to Z, optional
A	Letter or number, required
a	Letter or number, optional
&	Character or space, required
C	Character or space, optional
.	Decimal point
,	Thousands separator
: - /	Date and time separators
<	Convert all characters that follow to lowercase
>	Convert all characters that follow to uppercase
!	Display characters from right to left in the cell, rather than from left to right
\	Displays the next character. Used to display input mask characters (using **\&** will display **&**)
Password	Displays an asterisk (*) for each character you type

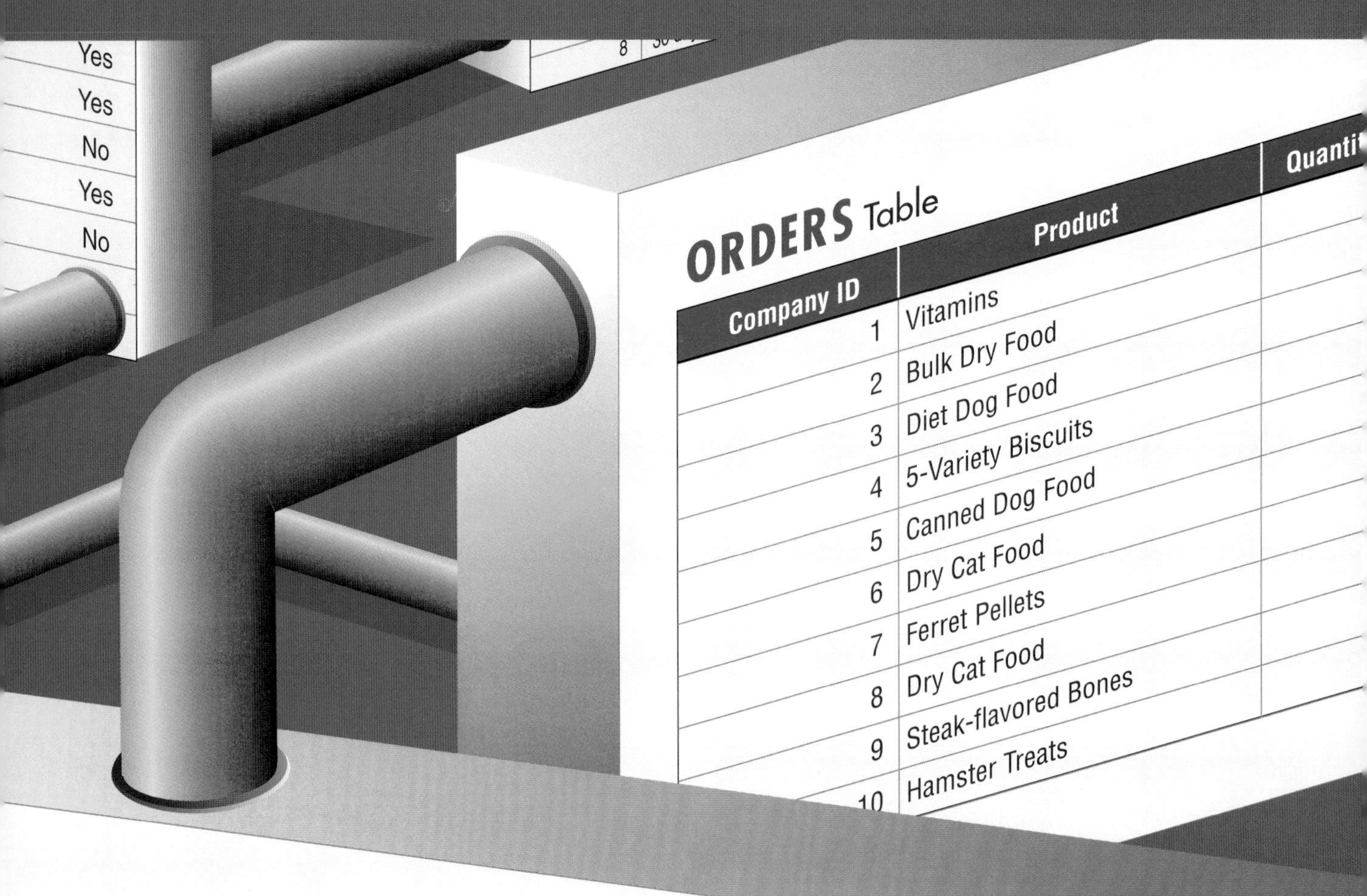
Yes
Yes
No
Yes
No
ORDERS Table
Company ID
Product
Quantit
1 Vitamins
2 Bulk Dry Food
3 Diet Dog Food
4 5-Variety Biscuits
5 Canned Dog Food
6 Dry Cat Food
7 Ferret Pellets
8 Dry Cat Food
9 Steak-flavored Bones
Hamster Treats
ESSES Table
Company Name
1 Feline Foods Inc.
2 Martin Vet Supplies
3 Doggone Yu
4 Pet S
/Province
Postal Code
NY
10010
MA
02117
San Francisco

CHAPTER 7

Establish Relationships

Are you ready to establish relationships between your tables? This chapter teaches you how to set a primary key, start a new relationship and more.

Set the Primary Key 136

Start a New Relationship 138

Enforce Referential Integrity 142

SET THE PRIMARY KEY

A primary key is one or more fields that uniquely identifies each record in a table. Each table in your database should have a primary key.

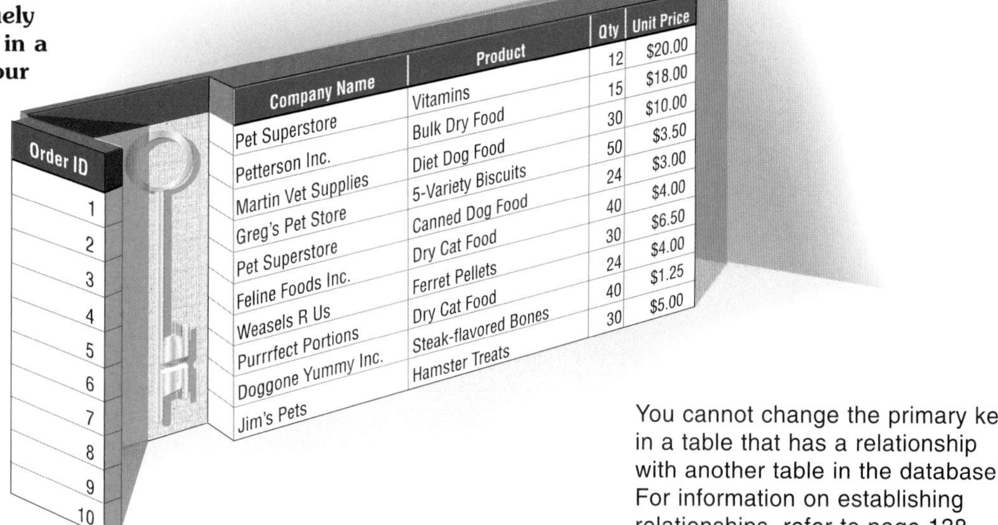

You cannot change the primary key in a table that has a relationship with another table in the database. For information on establishing relationships, refer to page 138.

SET THE PRIMARY KEY

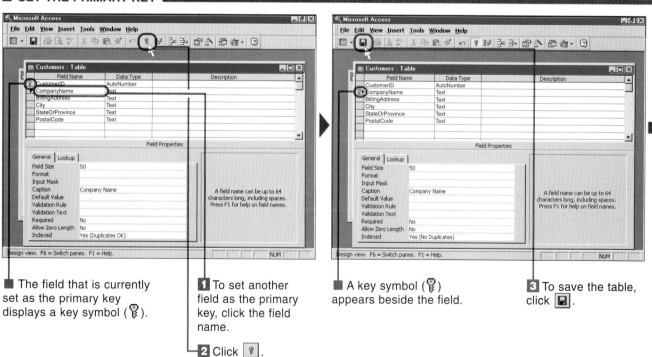

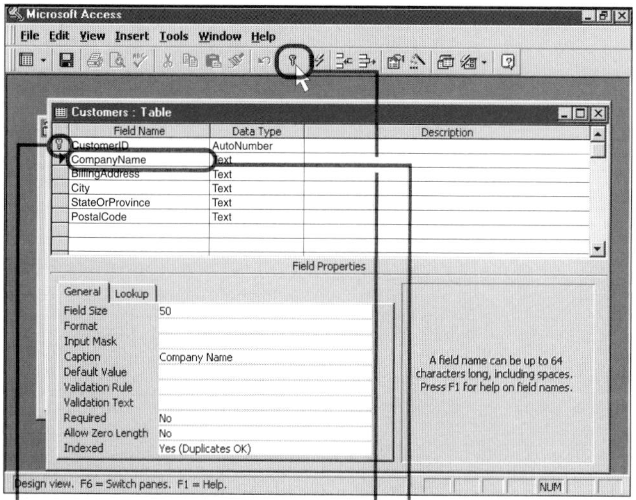

■ The field that is currently set as the primary key displays a key symbol (🔑).

1 To set another field as the primary key, click the field name.

2 Click 🔑.

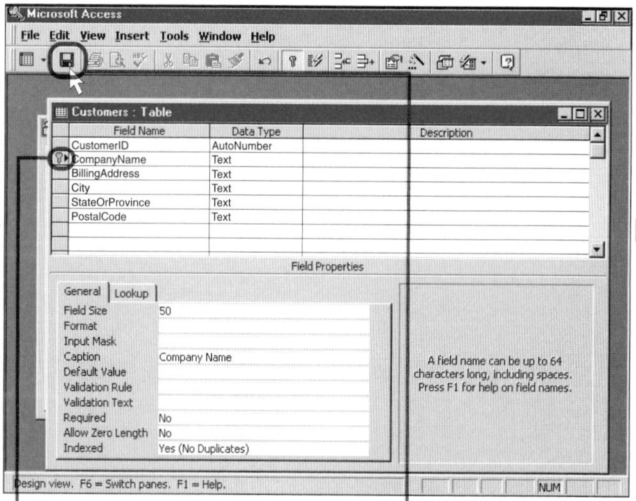

■ A key symbol (🔑) appears beside the field.

3 To save the table, click 💾.

?

What types of primary keys can I create?

AutoNumber
A field that automatically assigns a unique number to each record.

AutoNumber
ID
1
2
3
4

Note: When you create a table, Access can create an AutoNumber primary key for you. To create a table, refer to page 36.

Single-Field
A field that contains a unique value for each record, such as an invoice number or social security number.

Single-Field
Invoice No
6218
7410
8611
9431

Multiple-Field
Two or more fields that together make up a unique value for each record.

Multiple-Field	
Name	Appt Time
Johnson	9:15 AM
Smith	11:30 AM
Petterson	2:45 PM
Lee	3:30 PM

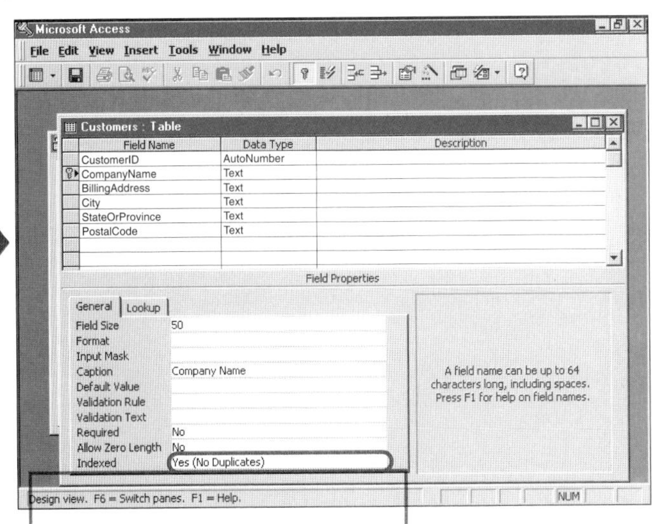

■ Access sets the Indexed property of the field to **Yes (No Duplicates)**. Access indexes the information in the field so you can sort or search for information in the field quicker.

■ The phrase **No Duplicates** indicates that Access will not allow you to enter the same value in the field more than once.

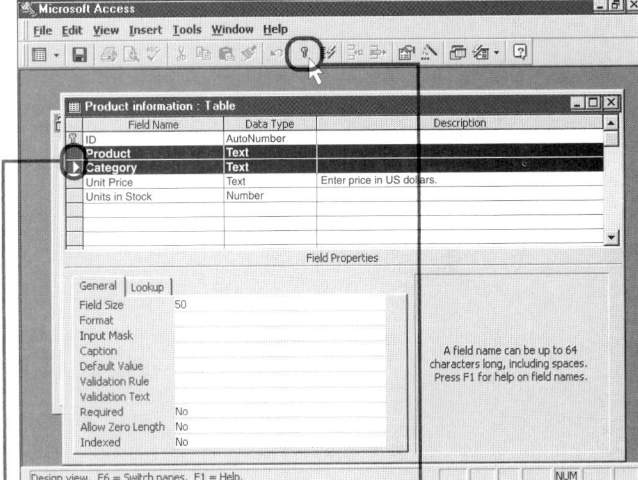

You can set a primary key with more than one field.

1 Press and hold down Ctrl on your keyboard.

2 Still holding down Ctrl, click the area to the left of each field you want to set as the primary key.

3 Click the primary key button.

■ A key symbol appears beside each field.

START A NEW RELATIONSHIP

You can create relationships between tables to bring together related information.

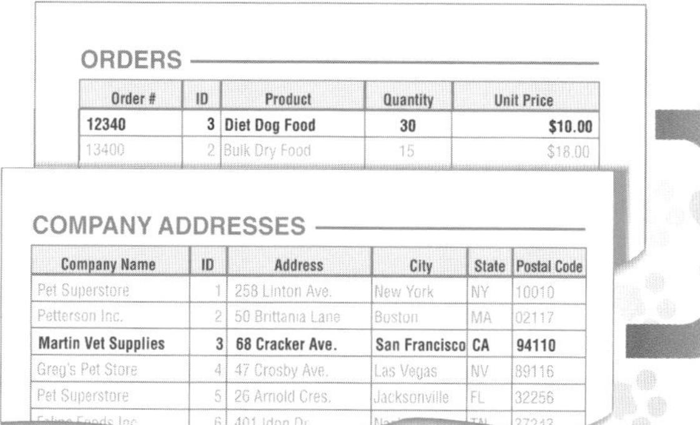

ORDERS

Order #	ID	Product	Quantity	Unit Price
12340	3	Diet Dog Food	30	$10.00
13400	2	Bulk Dry Food	15	$18.00

COMPANY ADDRESSES

Company Name	ID	Address	City	State	Postal Code
Pet Superstore	1	258 Linton Ave.	New York	NY	10010
Petterson Inc.	2	50 Brittania Lane	Boston	MA	02117
Martin Vet Supplies	3	68 Cracker Ave.	San Francisco	CA	94110
Greg's Pet Store	4	47 Crosby Ave.	Las Vegas	NV	89116
Pet Superstore	5	26 Arnold Cres.	Jacksonville	FL	32256
[illegible]	6	401 Idon Dr.	[illegible]	[illegible]	37243

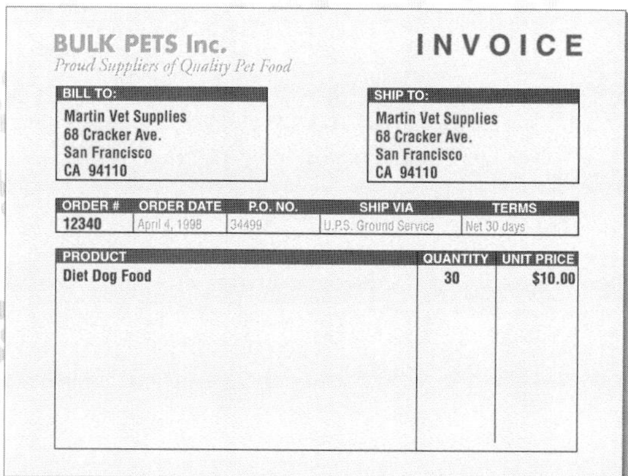

BULK PETS Inc.
Proud Suppliers of Quality Pet Food

INVOICE

BILL TO:	SHIP TO:
Martin Vet Supplies 68 Cracker Ave. San Francisco CA 94110	Martin Vet Supplies 68 Cracker Ave. San Francisco CA 94110

ORDER #	ORDER DATE	P.O. NO.	SHIP VIA	TERMS
12340	April 4, 1998	34499	U.P.S. Ground Service	Net 30 days

PRODUCT	QUANTITY	UNIT PRICE
Diet Dog Food	30	$10.00

START A NEW RELATIONSHIP

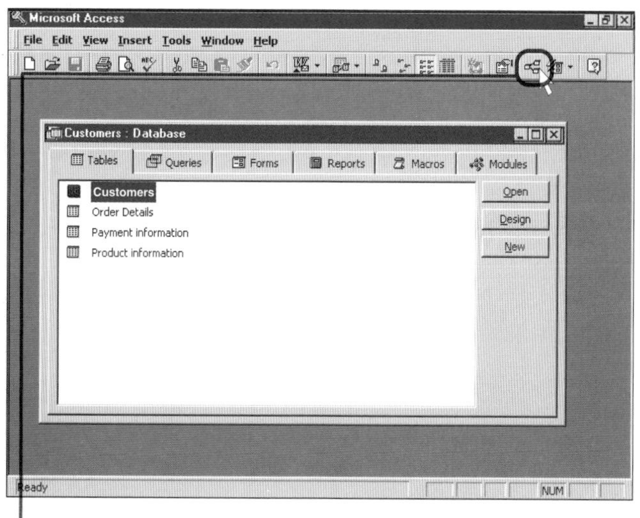

1 Click to display the **Relationships** window.

Note: If is not available, make sure the Database window is open and you do not have any other windows open on your screen.

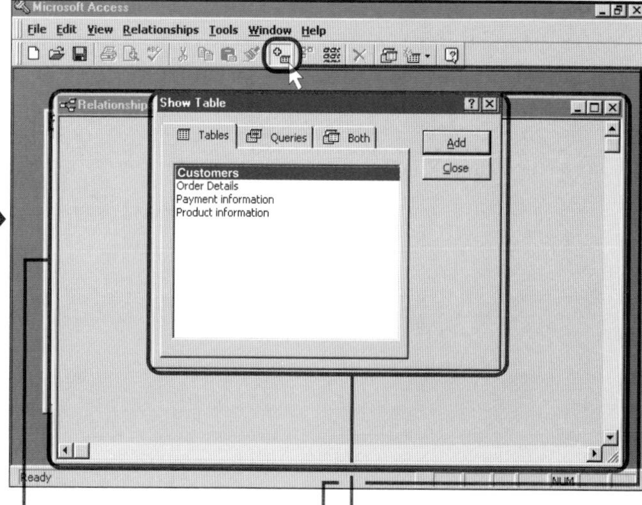

■ The **Relationships** window appears. If any relationships exist between the tables in your database, the tables will appear in the window.

■ The **Show Table** dialog box may also appear, displaying all the tables in your database.

2 If the **Show Table** dialog box is not displayed, click to display the dialog box.

? Why do I need to establish relationships between the tables in my database?

Relationships between tables are essential when you want to create a form, report or query that uses information from more than one table in a database.

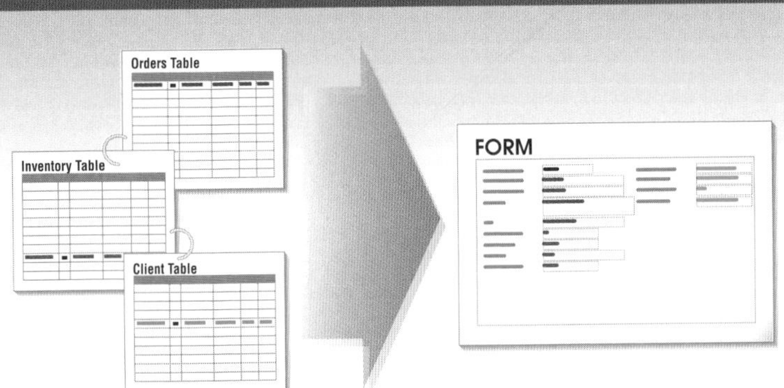

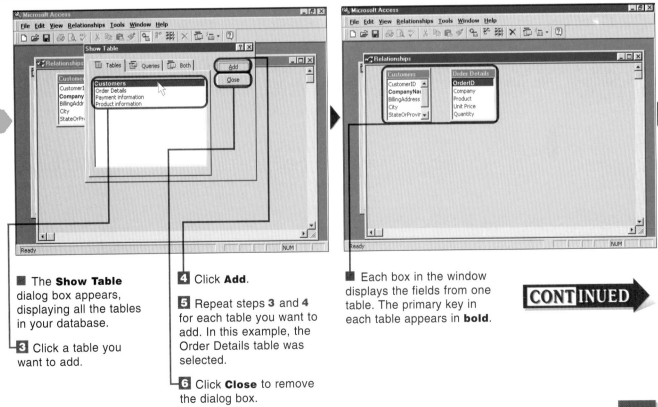

■ The **Show Table** dialog box appears, displaying all the tables in your database.

3 Click a table you want to add.

4 Click **Add**.

5 Repeat steps **3** and **4** for each table you want to add. In this example, the Order Details table was selected.

6 Click **Close** to remove the dialog box.

■ Each box in the window displays the fields from one table. The primary key in each table appears in **bold**.

CONTINUED

START A NEW RELATIONSHIP

You establish a relationship by identifying matching fields in two tables.

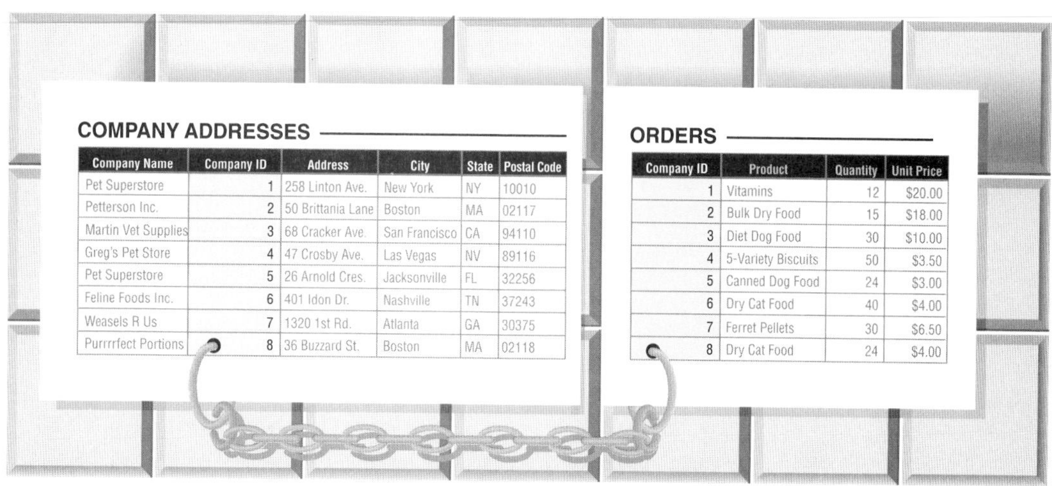

COMPANY ADDRESSES

Company Name	Company ID	Address	City	State	Postal Code
Pet Superstore	1	258 Linton Ave.	New York	NY	10010
Petterson Inc.	2	50 Brittania Lane	Boston	MA	02117
Martin Vet Supplies	3	68 Cracker Ave.	San Francisco	CA	94110
Greg's Pet Store	4	47 Crosby Ave.	Las Vegas	NV	89116
Pet Superstore	5	26 Arnold Cres.	Jacksonville	FL	32256
Feline Foods Inc.	6	401 Idon Dr.	Nashville	TN	37243
Weasels R Us	7	1320 1st Rd.	Atlanta	GA	30375
Purrrfect Portions	8	36 Buzzard St.	Boston	MA	02118

ORDERS

Company ID	Product	Quantity	Unit Price
1	Vitamins	12	$20.00
2	Bulk Dry Food	15	$18.00
3	Diet Dog Food	30	$10.00
4	5-Variety Biscuits	50	$3.50
5	Canned Dog Food	24	$3.00
6	Dry Cat Food	40	$4.00
7	Ferret Pellets	30	$6.50
8	Dry Cat Food	24	$4.00

You will usually relate the primary key in one table to a matching field in the other table. The fields do not need to have the same name, but they do in most cases.

Note: The table in a relationship that contains the primary key is referred to as the primary table.

START A NEW RELATIONSHIP (CONTINUED)

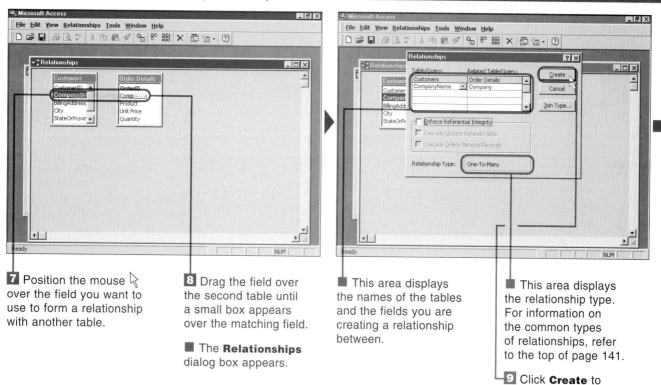

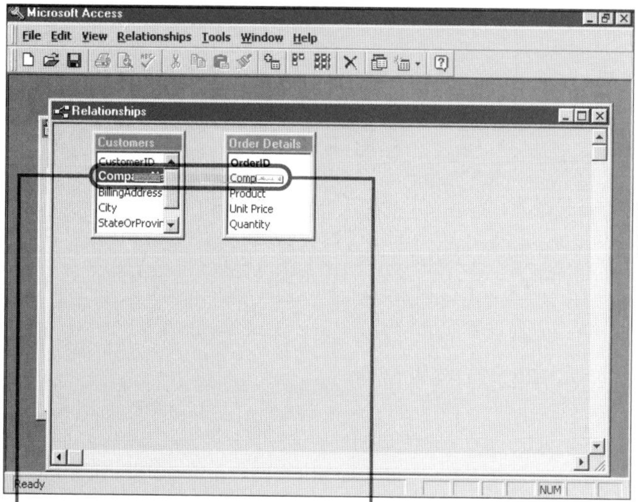

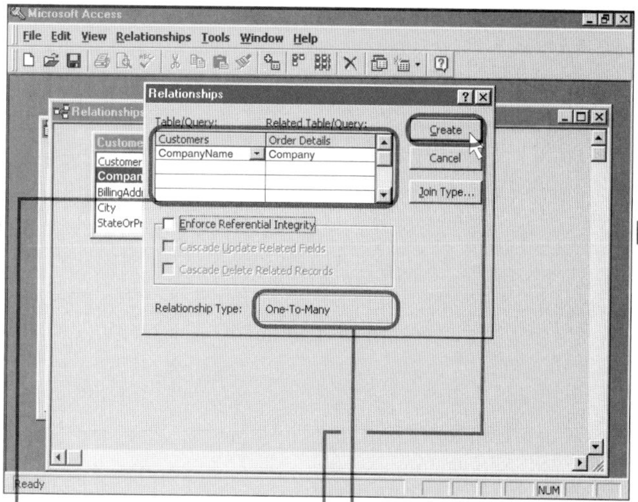

7 Position the mouse over the field you want to use to form a relationship with another table.

8 Drag the field over the second table until a small box appears over the matching field.

■ The **Relationships** dialog box appears.

■ This area displays the names of the tables and the fields you are creating a relationship between.

■ This area displays the relationship type. For information on the common types of relationships, refer to the top of page 141.

9 Click **Create** to establish the relationship.

What are the common types of relationships?

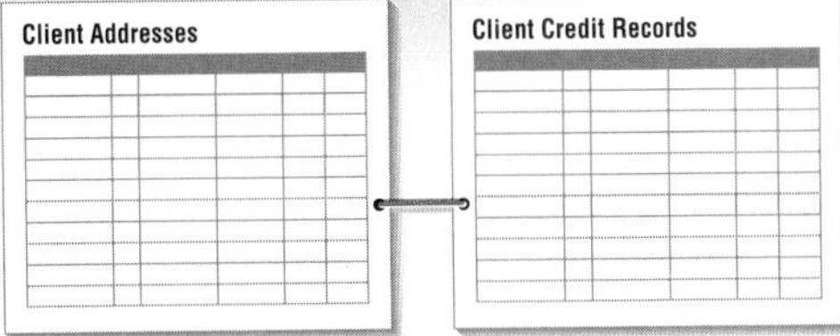

Client Addresses | Client Orders

One-To-One

Each record in one table relates to just one record in another table. For example, each client has only one credit record.

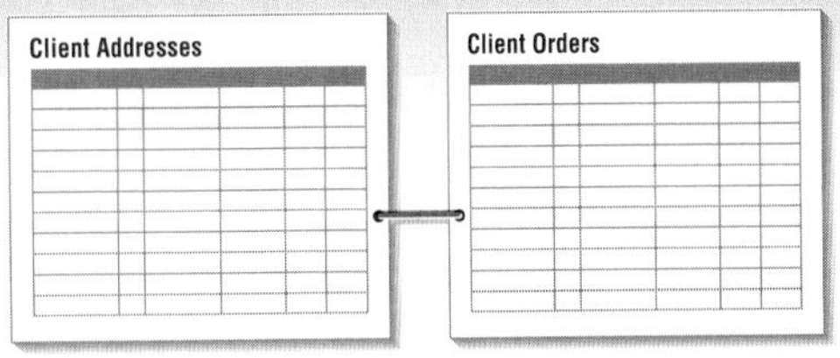

One-To-Many

Each record in one table relates to one or more records in another table. This is the most common type of relationship. For example, each client can have more than one order.

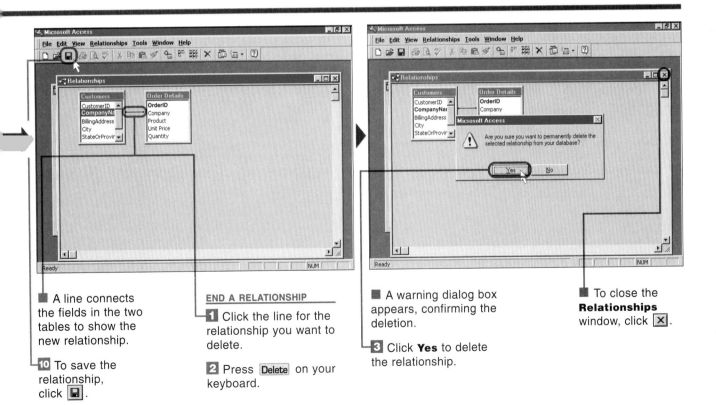

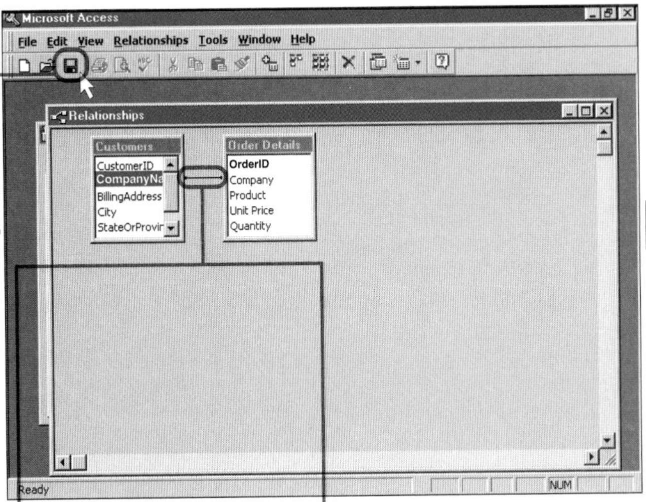

■ A line connects the fields in the two tables to show the new relationship.

10 To save the relationship, click 💾.

END A RELATIONSHIP

1 Click the line for the relationship you want to delete.

2 Press Delete on your keyboard.

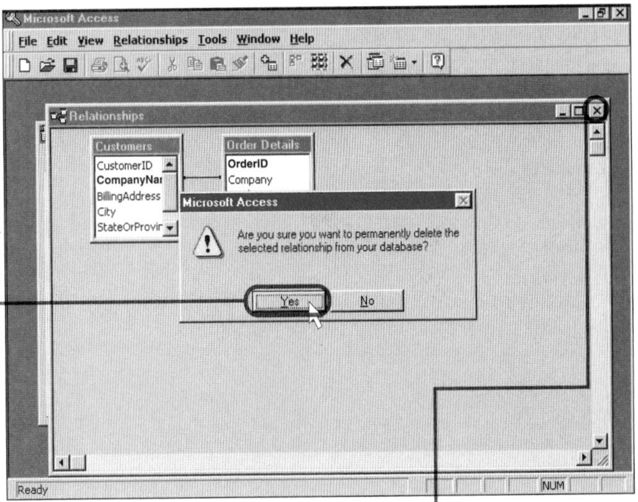

■ A warning dialog box appears, confirming the deletion.

3 Click **Yes** to delete the relationship.

■ To close the **Relationships** window, click ☒.

ENFORCE REFERENTIAL INTEGRITY

Referential integrity is a set of rules that protect data from accidental changes or deletions. These rules prevent you from changing or deleting a record if matching records exist in a related table.

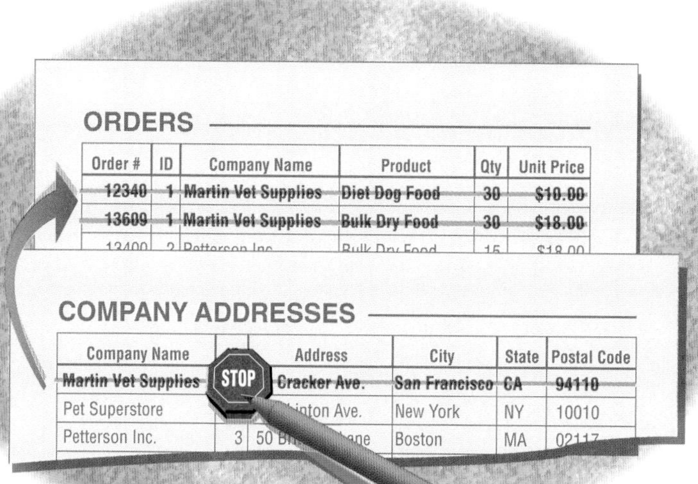

For example, if a client still has orders, referential integrity prevents you from deleting the client.

ENFORCE REFERENTIAL INTEGRITY

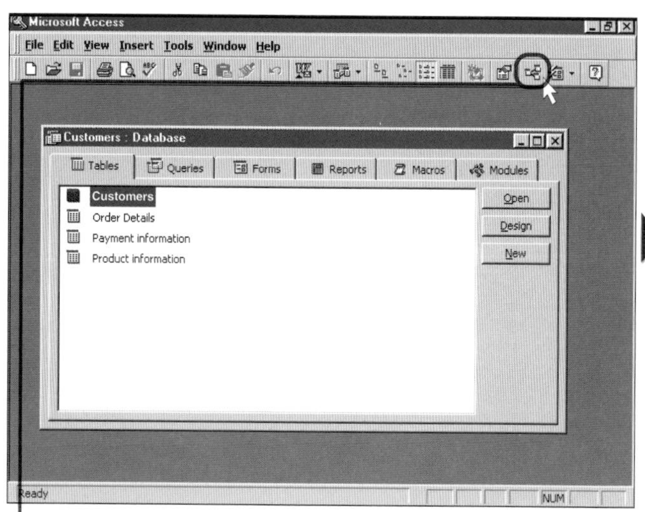

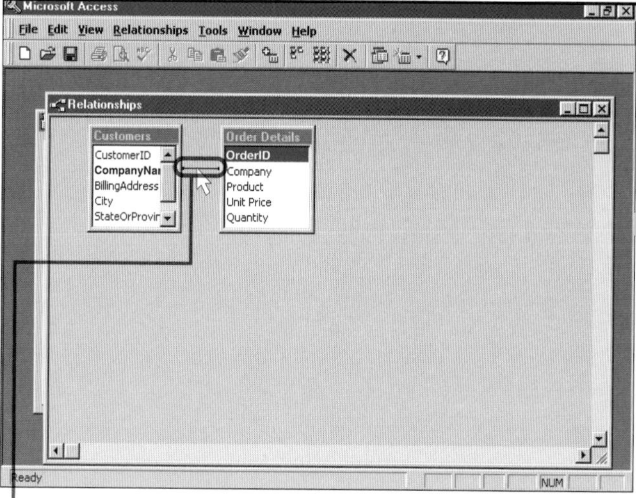

1 Click [icon] to display the **Relationships** window.

Note: If [icon] is not available, make sure the Database window is open and you do not have any other windows open on your screen.

2 To enforce referential integrity between two tables, double-click the line that connects the tables.

■ The **Relationships** dialog box appears.

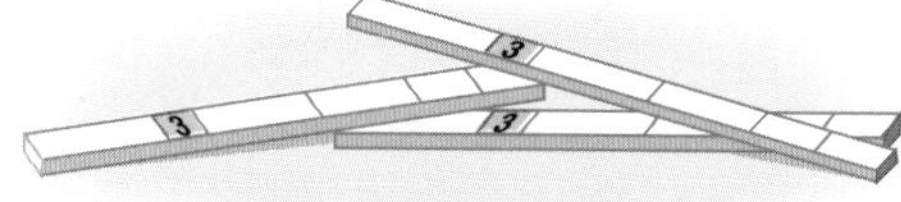

Access provides two options that let you override the rules of referential integrity but still protect data from accidental changes or deletions.

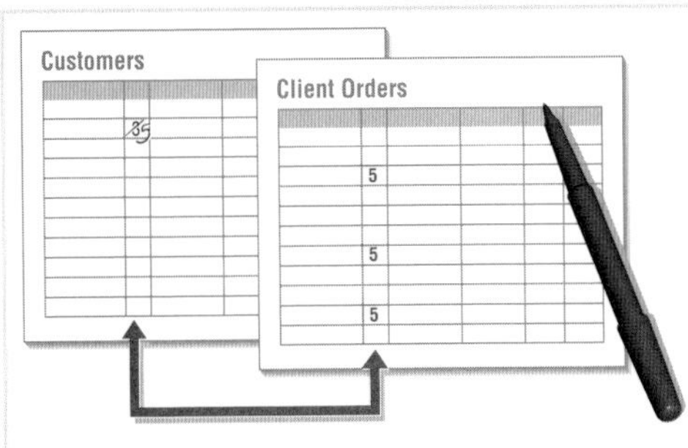

Cascade Update Related Fields

When you change data in the primary key, Access will automatically update the matching data in all related records.

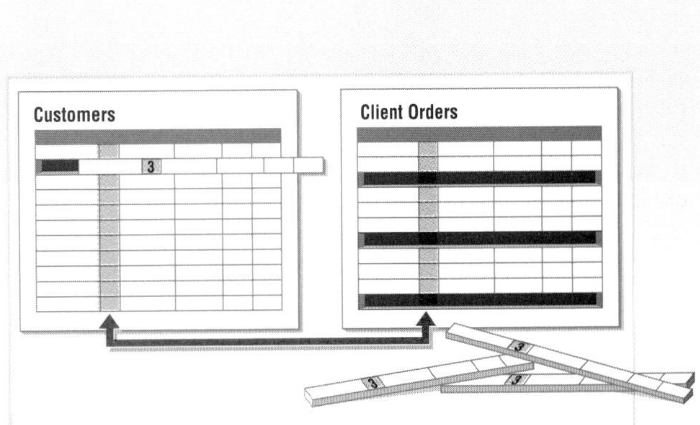

Cascade Delete Related Records

When you delete a record in the primary table, Access will automatically delete matching records in the related table.

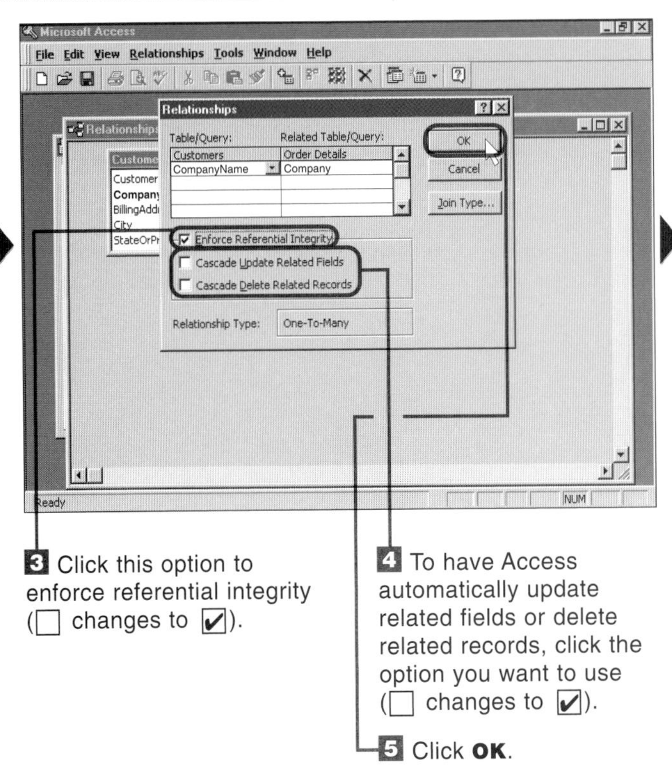

3 Click this option to enforce referential integrity (☐ changes to ☑).

4 To have Access automatically update related fields or delete related records, click the option you want to use (☐ changes to ☑).

5 Click **OK**.

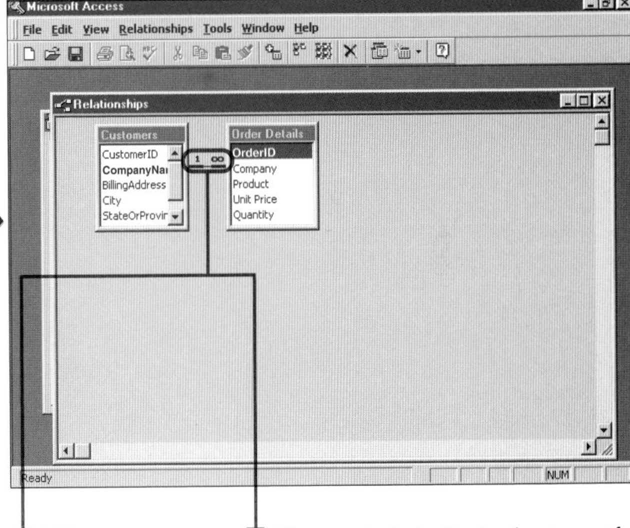

■ When you enforce referential integrity, the black line connecting the tables becomes thicker.

■ The symbols indicate the type of relationship. In this example, a single record in the Customers table (**1**) relates to one or more records in the Order Details table (**∞**). For information on the common types of relationships, refer to the top of page 141.

ESSES FORM
Addr
5
First Name
Melanie
Last Name
Robinson
Address
26 Arnold Cres.
City
Jacksonville
State/Province
FL
Postal Code
32256
Country
USA
Home Phone
(555) 555-6974
Work Phone
(555) 555-3636
Work Extension
471
Fax Number
(555) 555-2508
Spouse Name
John

Create Forms

Do you want to learn how to create forms? This chapter will teach you how to present information in an easy-to-use format so you can quickly view, enter and change information.

Create a Form Using an AutoForm 146

Change View of Form 148

Move Through Records 150

Add a Record 152

Delete a Record 153

Edit Data...154

Close a Form 156

Open a Form 157

Rename a Form 158

Delete a Form 159

Create a Form Using the Form Wizard............160

CREATE A FORM USING AN AUTOFORM

The AutoForm Wizard provides the fastest and simplest way to create a form.

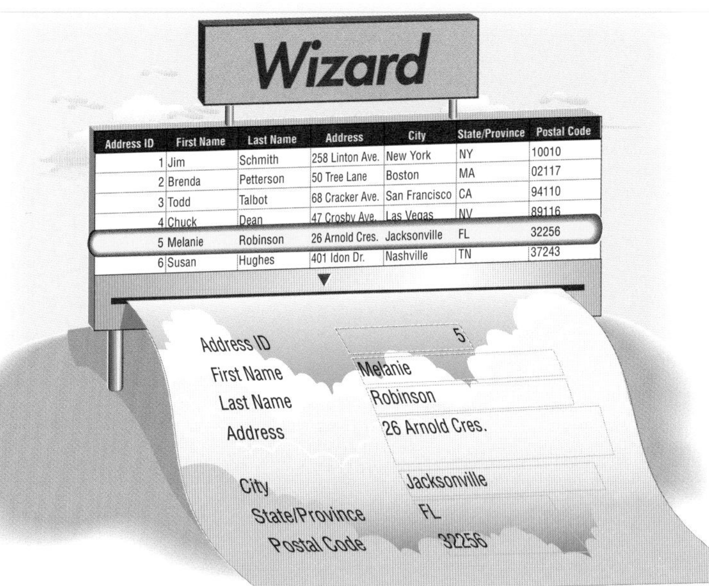

Forms present information in an easy-to-use format so you can quickly view, enter and change information.

CREATE A FORM USING AN AUTOFORM

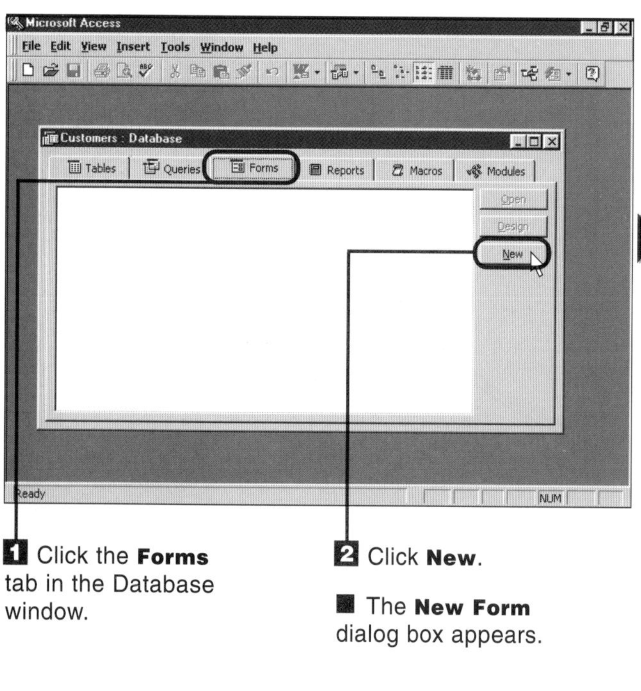

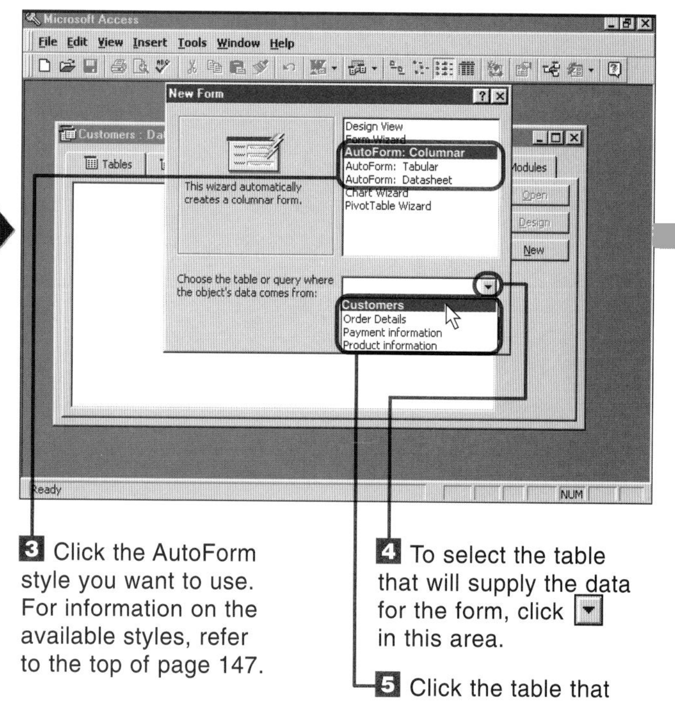

1 Click the **Forms** tab in the Database window.

2 Click **New**.

■ The **New Form** dialog box appears.

3 Click the AutoForm style you want to use. For information on the available styles, refer to the top of page 147.

4 To select the table that will supply the data for the form, click ▼ in this area.

5 Click the table that will supply the data.

What AutoForm styles are available?

Access provides three AutoForm styles that you can choose from.

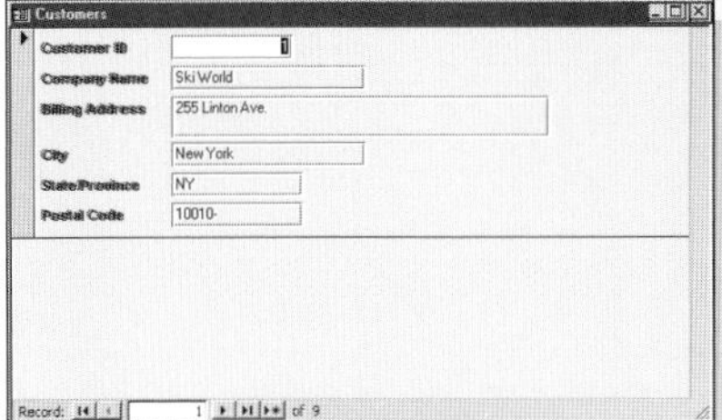

Columnar

Displays one record at a time.

Tabular

Displays many records at a time.

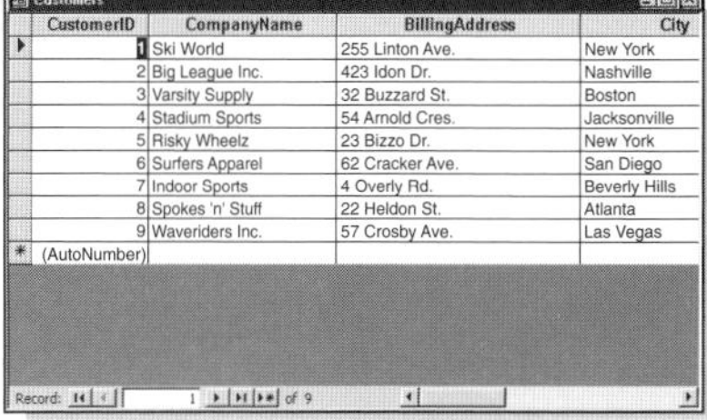

Datasheet

Displays many records at a time. This style is similar to the Datasheet view for tables.

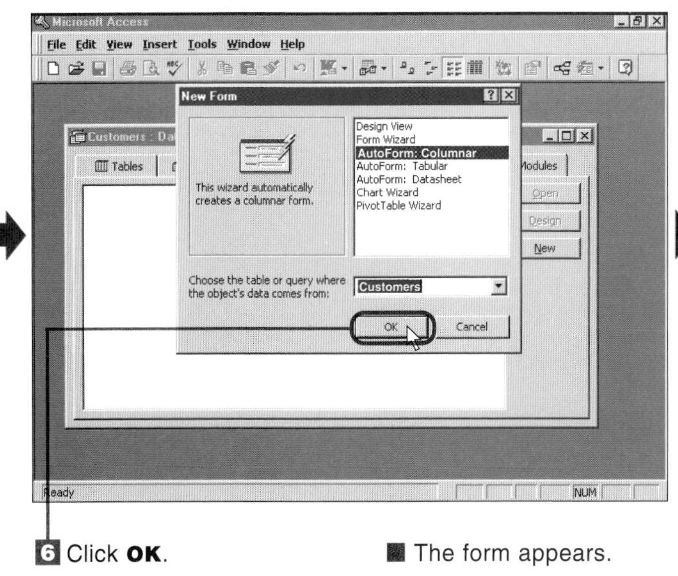

6 Click **OK**.

■ The form appears.

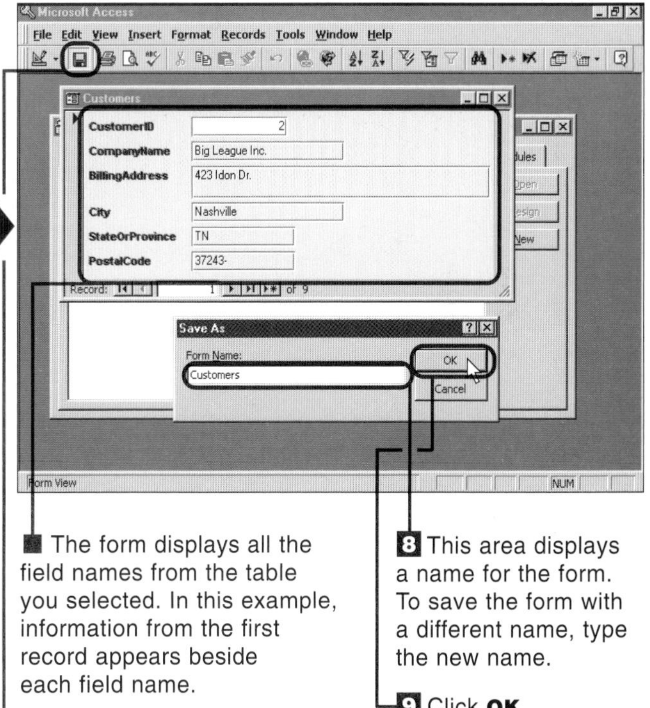

■ The form displays all the field names from the table you selected. In this example, information from the first record appears beside each field name.

7 Click 💾 to save the form.

■ The **Save As** dialog box appears.

8 This area displays a name for the form. To save the form with a different name, type the new name.

9 Click **OK**.

CHANGE VIEW OF FORM

There are three ways you can view a form. Each view allows you to perform a different task.

CHANGE VIEW OF FORM

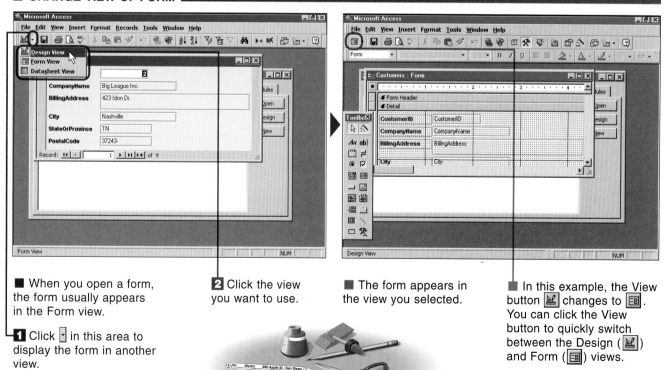

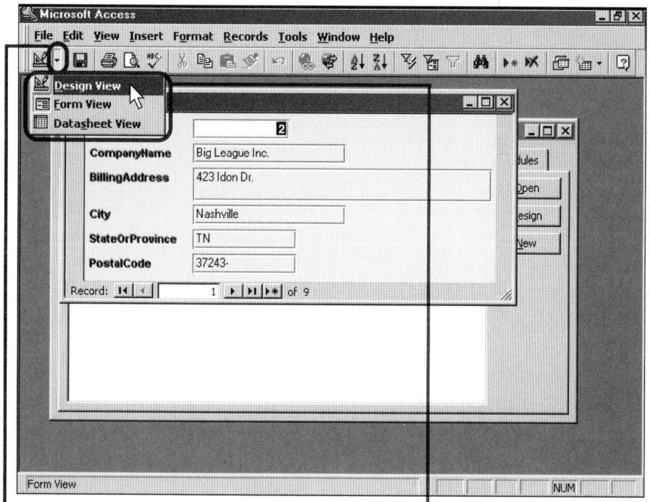

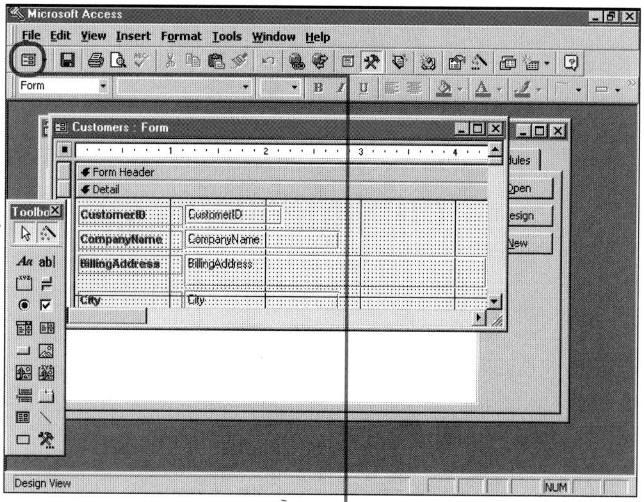

■ When you open a form, the form usually appears in the Form view.

1 Click ▾ in this area to display the form in another view.

2 Click the view you want to use.

■ The form appears in the view you selected.

■ In this example, the View button changes to . You can click the View button to quickly switch between the Design () and Form () views.

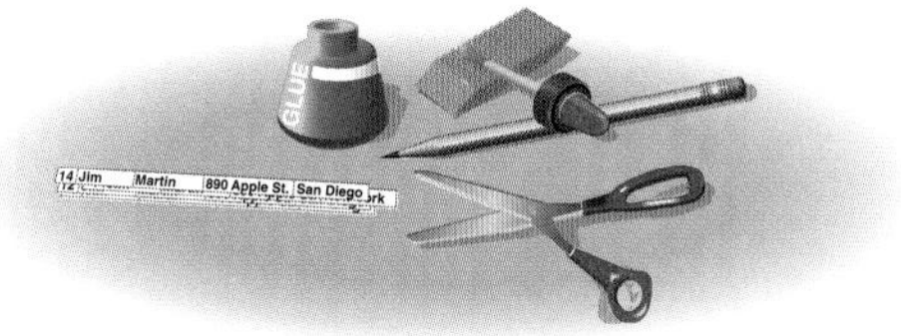

THE FORM VIEWS

Design View

The Design view allows you to change the design of a form.

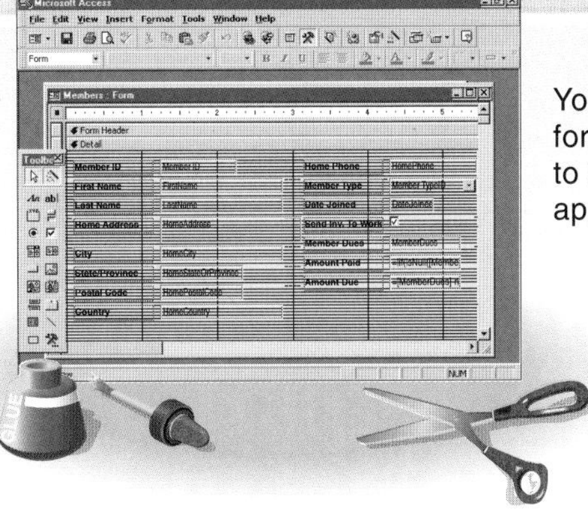

You can customize the form to make it easier to use or enhance the appearance of the form.

Form View

The Form view usually displays one record at a time in an organized and attractive format.

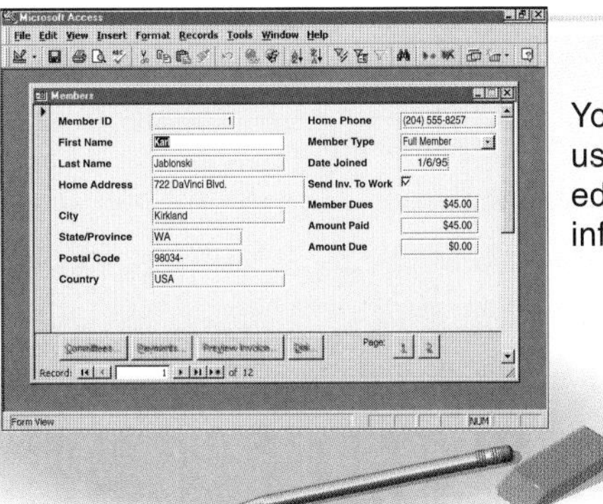

You will most often use this view to enter, edit and review your information.

Datasheet View

The Datasheet view displays all the records at once. You can enter, edit and review the records in this view.

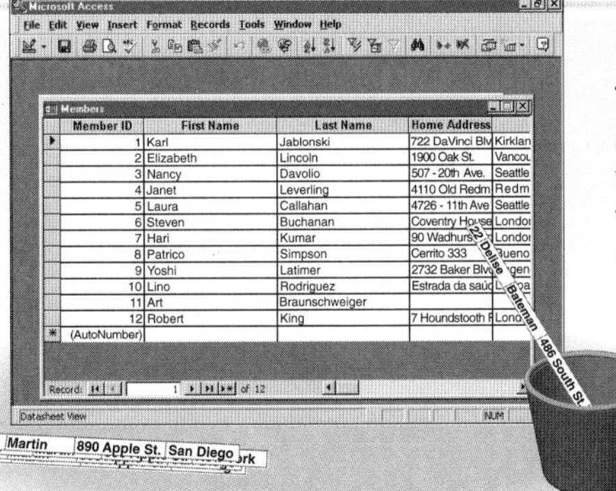

The field names appear across the top of the window. Each row shows the information for one record.

MOVE THROUGH RECORDS

You can easily move through the records in a form to review or edit information.

MOVE THROUGH RECORDS

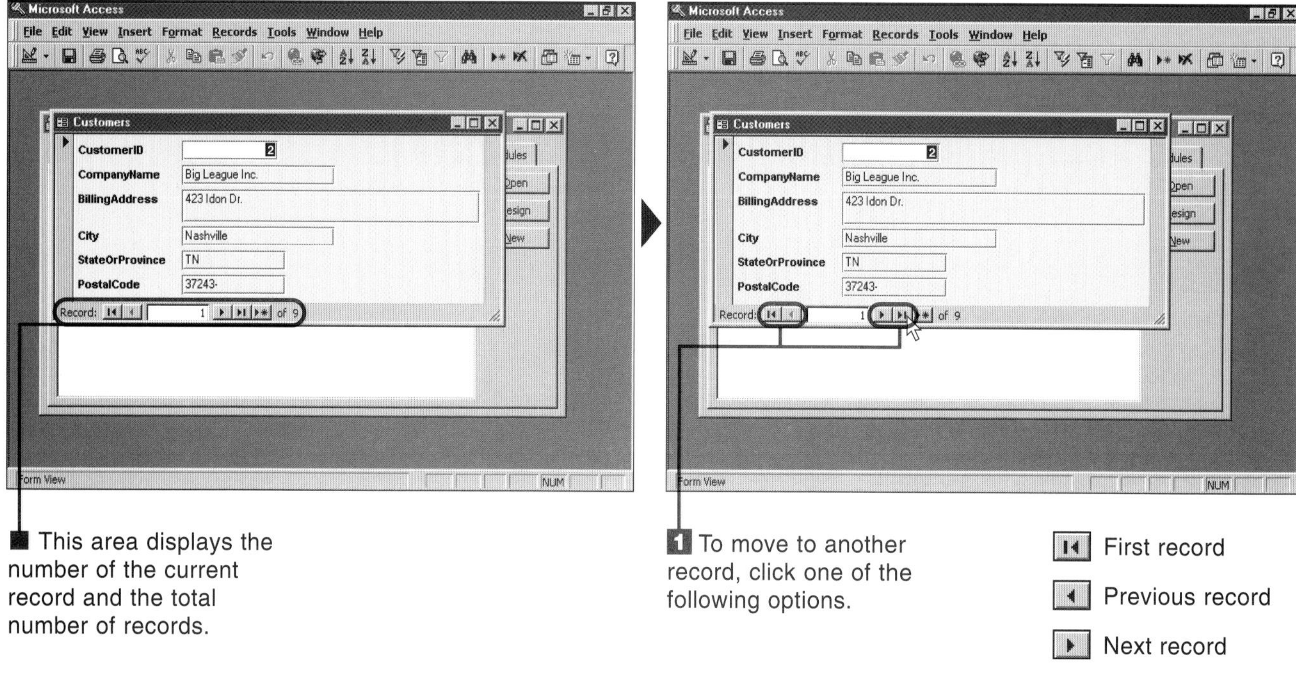

■ This area displays the number of the current record and the total number of records.

1 To move to another record, click one of the following options.

- First record
- Previous record
- Next record
- Last record

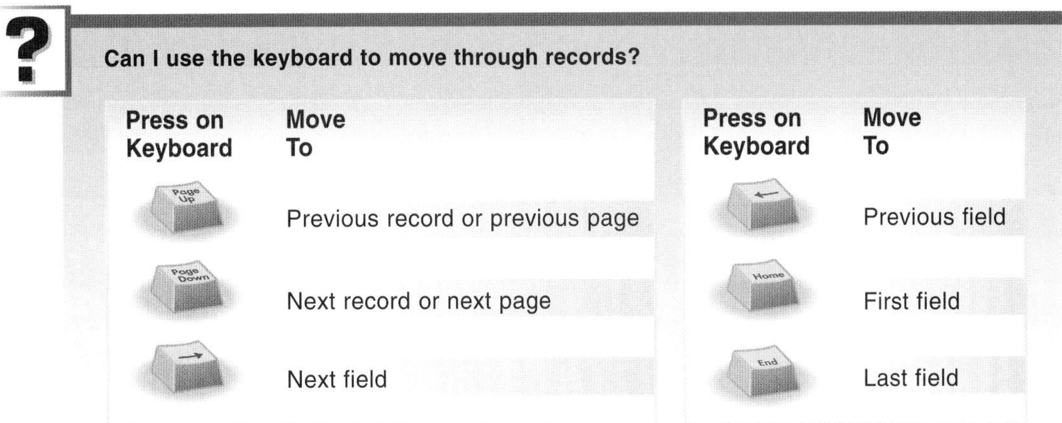

Can I use the keyboard to move through records?

Press on Keyboard	Move To
Page Up	Previous record or previous page
Page Down	Next record or next page
→	Next field
←	Previous field
Home	First field
End	Last field

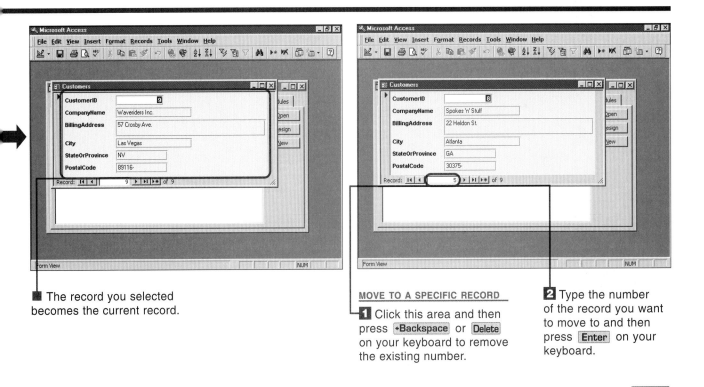

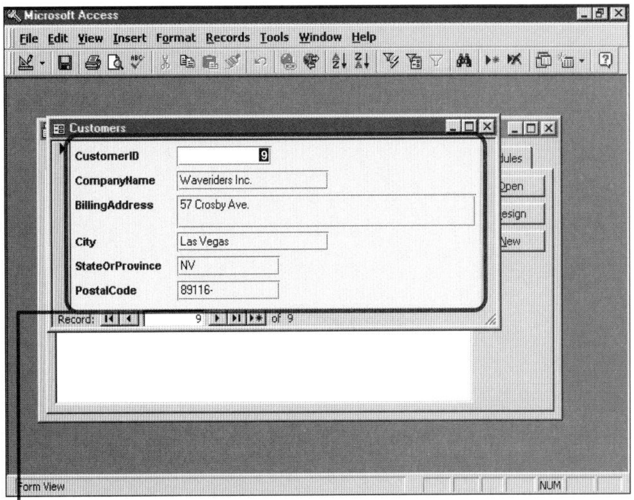

■ The record you selected becomes the current record.

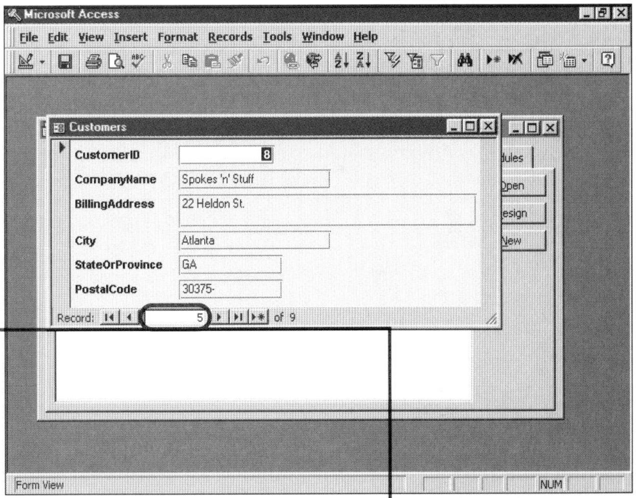

MOVE TO A SPECIFIC RECORD

1 Click this area and then press ←Backspace or Delete on your keyboard to remove the existing number.

2 Type the number of the record you want to move to and then press Enter on your keyboard.

ADD A RECORD

You can add a record to insert new information into your form.

For example, you may want to add information about a new client.

ADD A RECORD

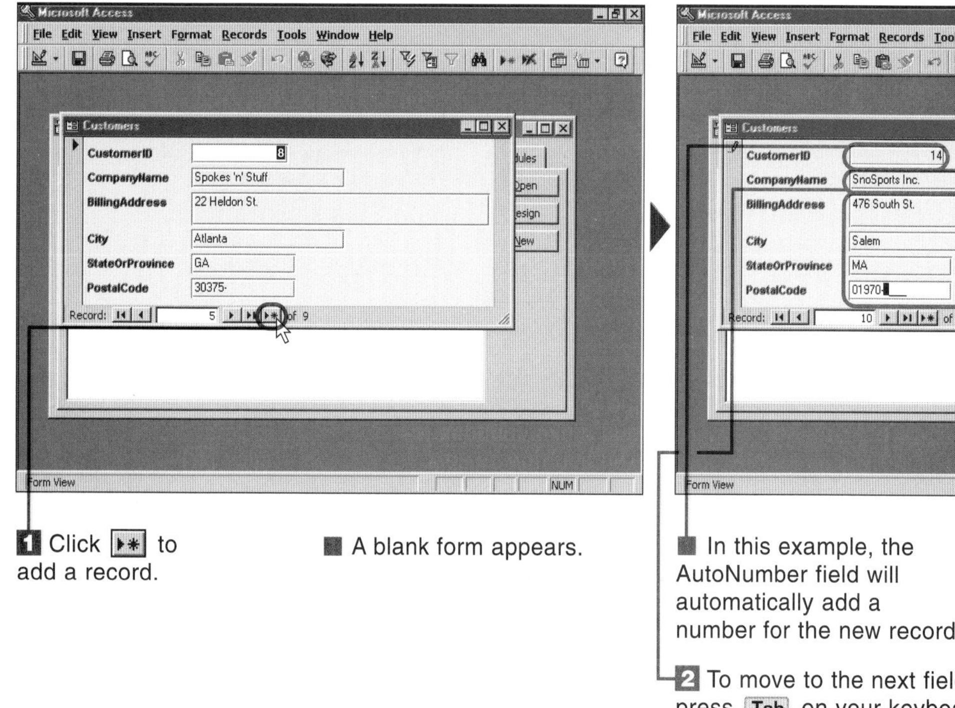

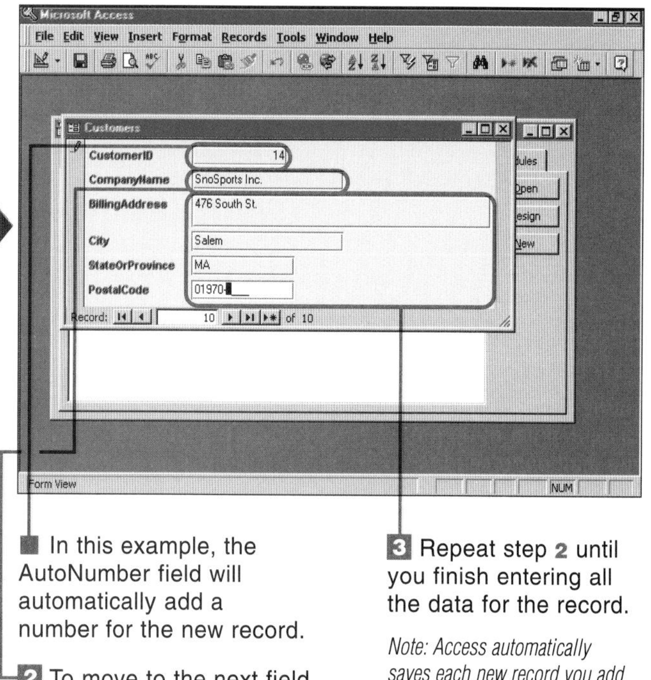

1 Click ▸* to add a record.

■ A blank form appears.

■ In this example, the AutoNumber field will automatically add a number for the new record.

2 To move to the next field, press Tab on your keyboard. Then type the data that corresponds to the field.

3 Repeat step **2** until you finish entering all the data for the record.

Note: Access automatically saves each new record you add to the table.

DELETE A RECORD

You can delete a record to remove information you no longer need. Deleting records saves storage space on your computer and makes your database less cluttered.

For example, you may want to remove a client who no longer orders your products.

DELETE A RECORD

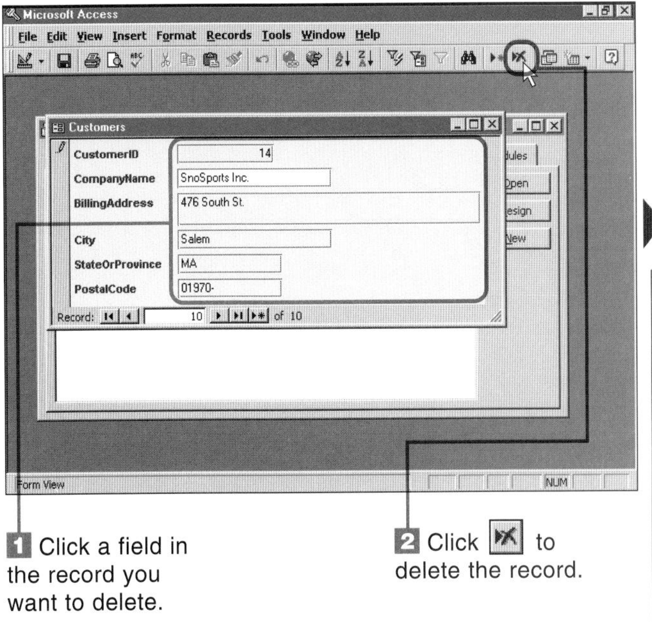

1 Click a field in the record you want to delete.

2 Click [delete record button] to delete the record.

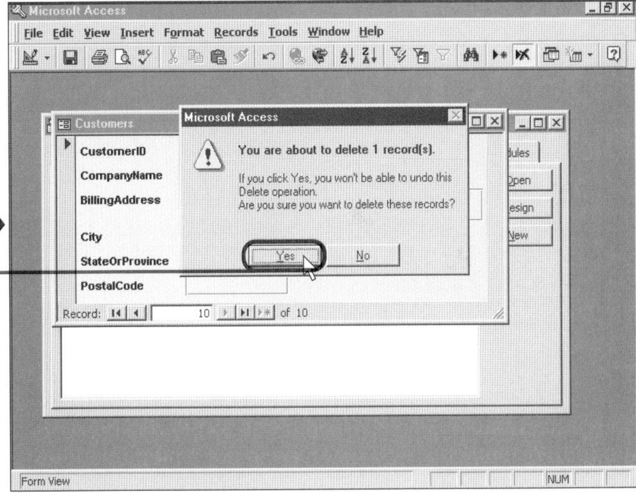

■ A warning dialog box appears, confirming the deletion.

3 Click **Yes** to permanently delete the record.

■ The record disappears.

EDIT DATA

You can change data in a record to correct a mistake or update the data.

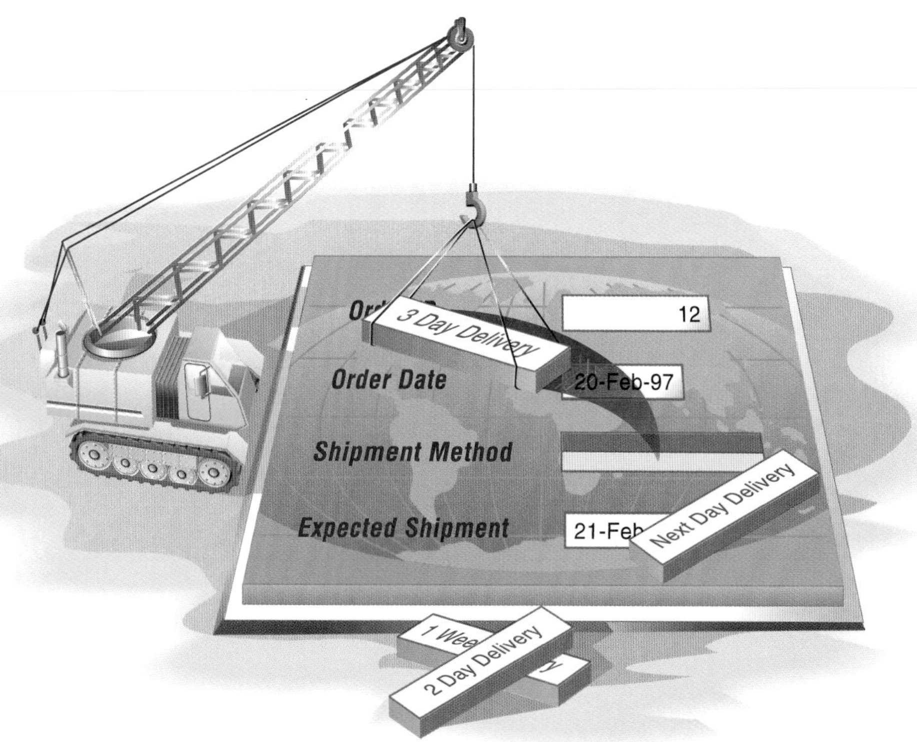

EDIT DATA

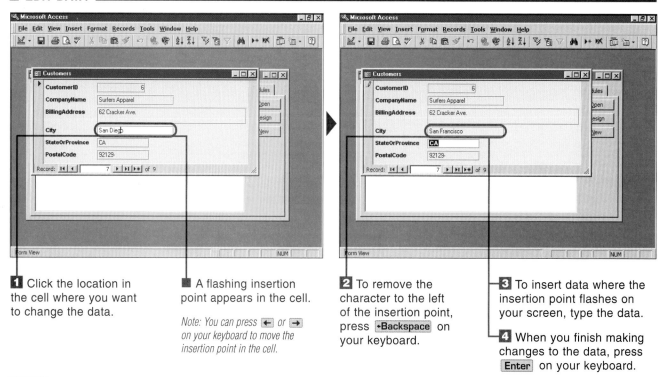

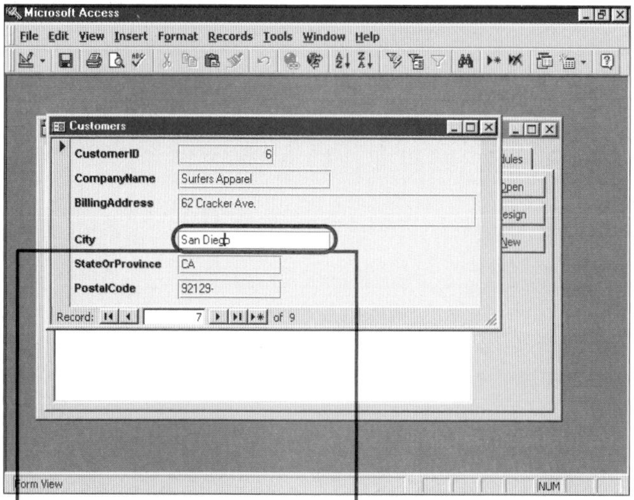

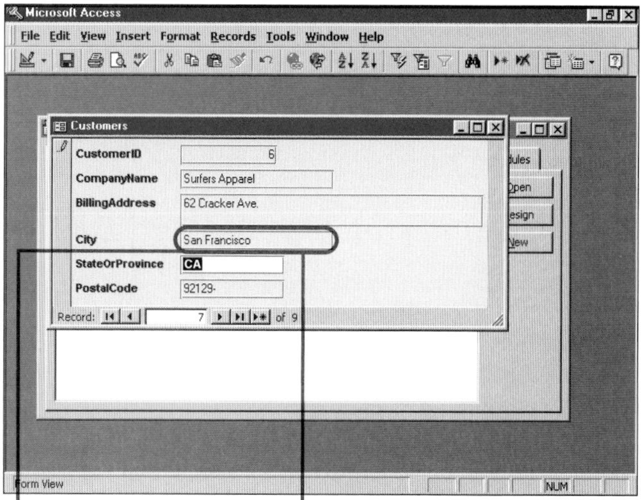

1 Click the location in the cell where you want to change the data.

■ A flashing insertion point appears in the cell.

Note: You can press ← or → on your keyboard to move the insertion point in the cell.

2 To remove the character to the left of the insertion point, press **Backspace** on your keyboard.

3 To insert data where the insertion point flashes on your screen, type the data.

4 When you finish making changes to the data, press **Enter** on your keyboard.

If I make a mistake while editing data, can I undo my changes?

Access remembers the changes you made to a record. If you make a mistake while editing data, you can use the Undo feature to immediately undo the changes.

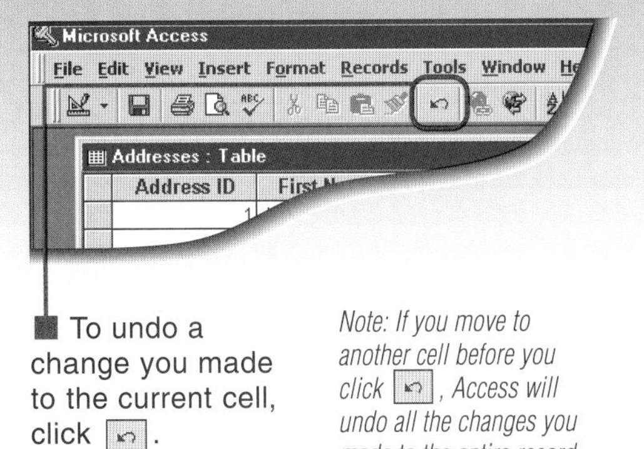

■ To undo a change you made to the current cell, click .

Note: If you move to another cell before you click , Access will undo all the changes you made to the entire record.

■ REPLACE ALL DATA IN A CELL

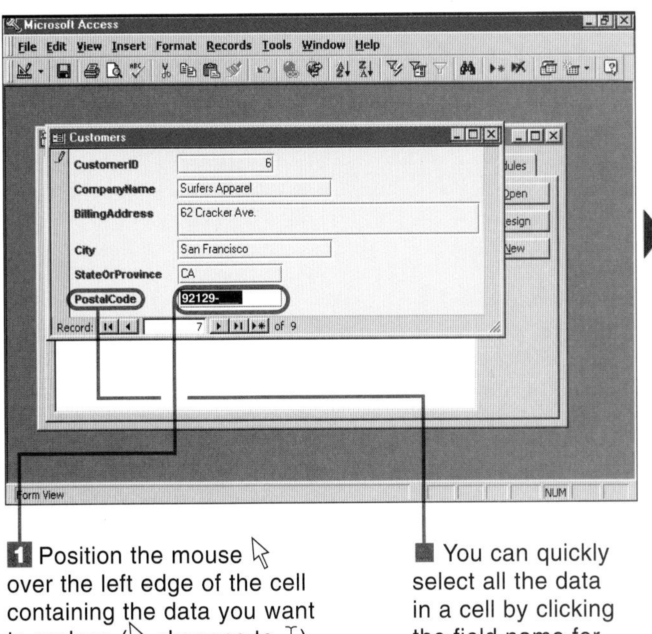

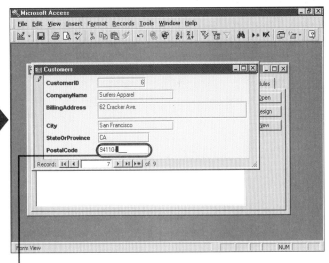

1 Position the mouse over the left edge of the cell containing the data you want to replace (changes to I). Then drag the mouse I until you highlight all the data in the cell.

■ You can quickly select all the data in a cell by clicking the field name for the data.

2 Type the new data and then press **Enter** on your keyboard.

CLOSE A FORM

When you finish working with a form, you can close the form to remove it from your screen.

CLOSE A FORM

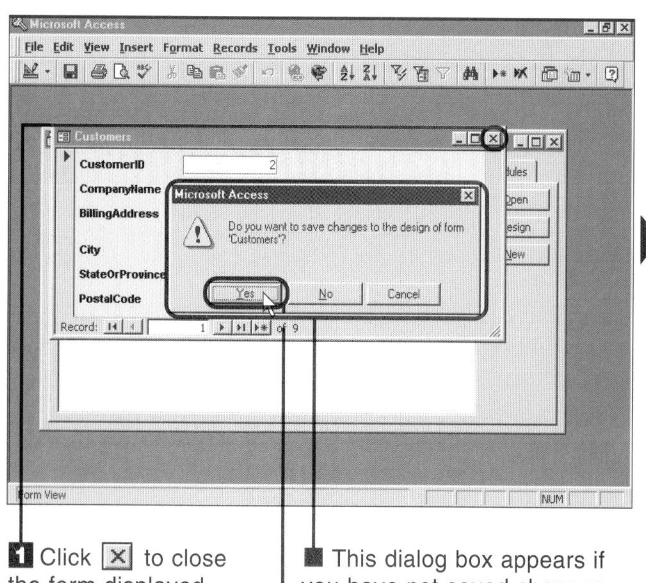

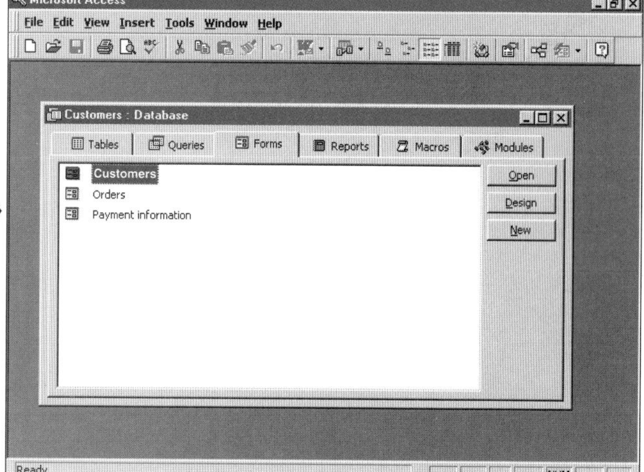

1 Click ☒ to close the form displayed on your screen.

■ This dialog box appears if you have not saved changes you made to the design of the form.

2 To save the changes, click **Yes**.

■ The form disappears from your screen.

OPEN A FORM

You can open a form to display its contents on your screen. This lets you review and make changes to the form.

OPEN A FORM

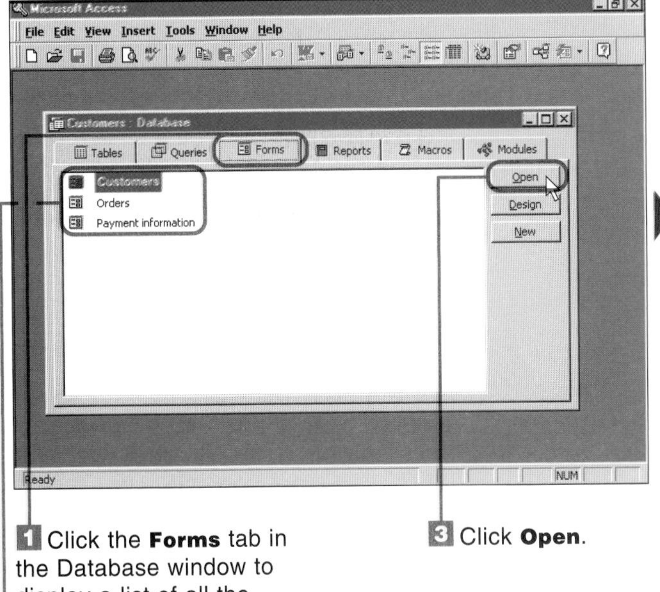

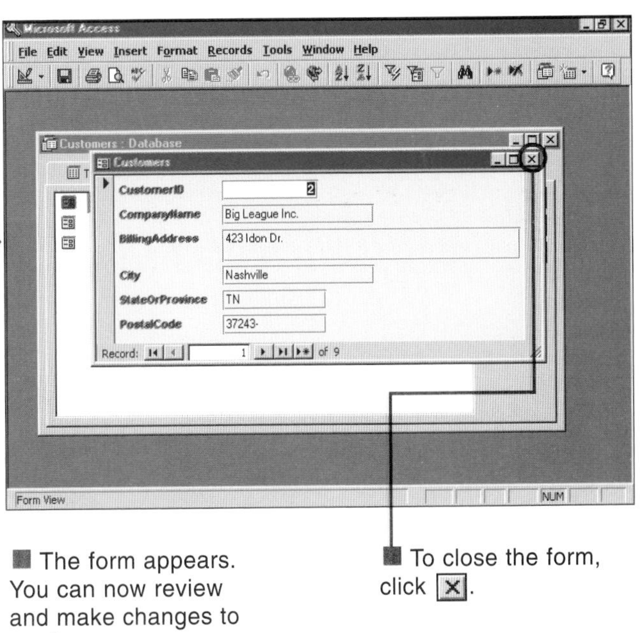

1 Click the **Forms** tab in the Database window to display a list of all the forms in your database.

2 Click the form you want to open.

3 Click **Open**.

■ The form appears. You can now review and make changes to the form.

■ To close the form, click ☒.

RENAME A FORM

You can change the name of a form to better describe the type of information the form contains.

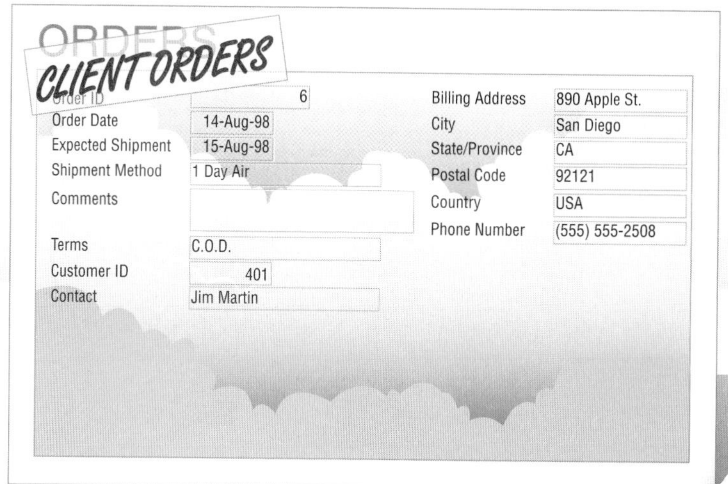

RENAME A FORM

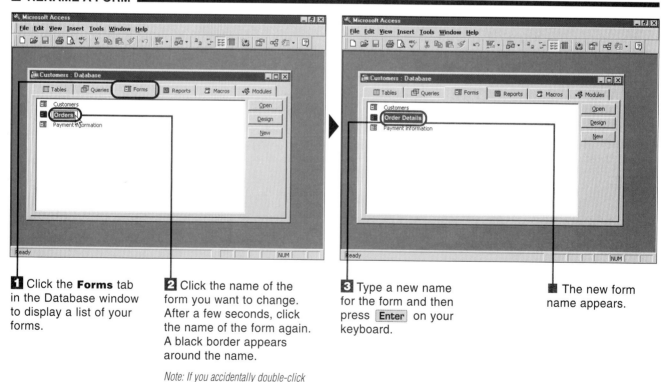

1 Click the **Forms** tab in the Database window to display a list of your forms.

2 Click the name of the form you want to change. After a few seconds, click the name of the form again. A black border appears around the name.

Note: If you accidentally double-click the name of a form, the form will open.

3 Type a new name for the form and then press **Enter** on your keyboard.

■ The new form name appears.

DELETE A FORM

If you are sure you will no longer need a form, you can permanently delete the form from your database.

DELETE A FORM

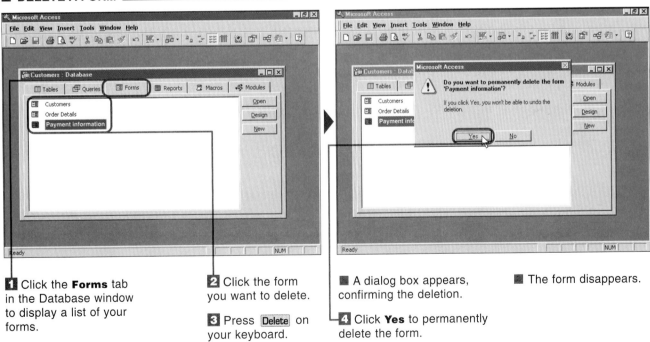

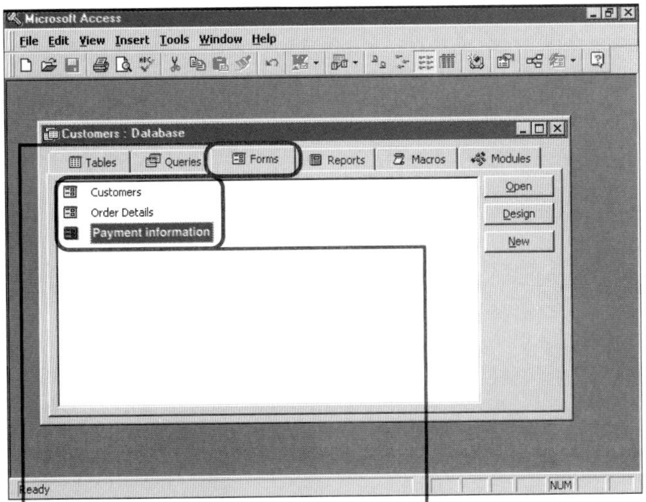

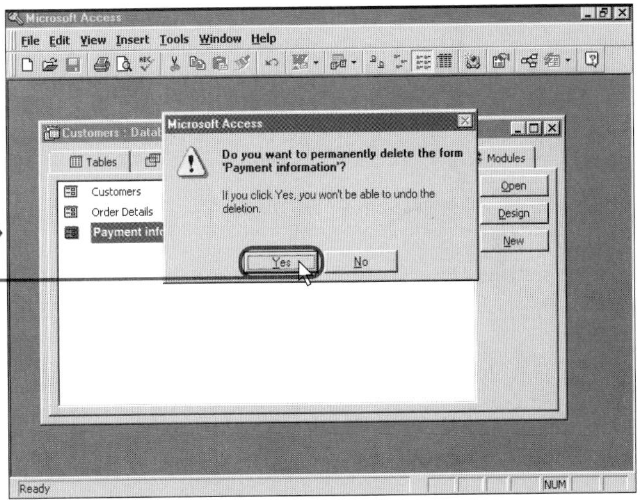

1 Click the **Forms** tab in the Database window to display a list of your forms.

2 Click the form you want to delete.

3 Press Delete on your keyboard.

■ A dialog box appears, confirming the deletion.

4 Click **Yes** to permanently delete the form.

■ The form disappears.

CREATE A FORM USING THE FORM WIZARD

The Form Wizard helps you create a form that suits your needs. The wizard will ask you a series of questions and then set up a form based on your answers.

A form presents information in an easy-to-use format. You can quickly view, enter and change information in a form.

CREATE A FORM FROM ONE TABLE

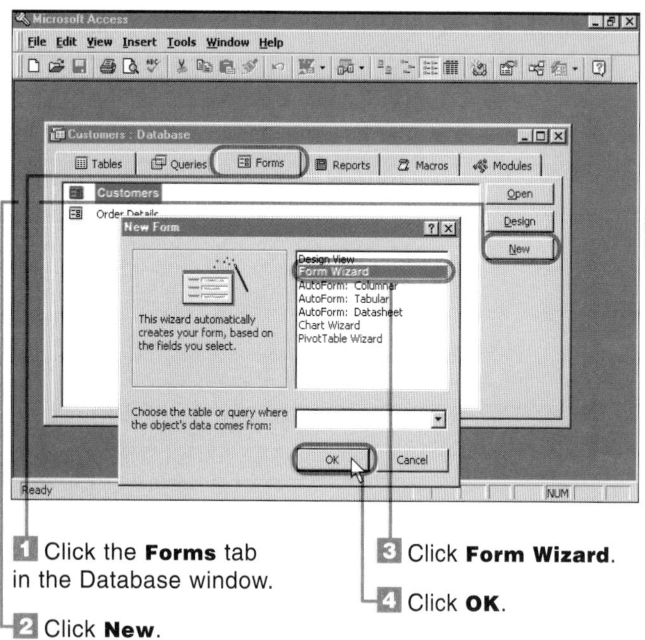

1 Click the **Forms** tab in the Database window.

2 Click **New**.

■ The **New Form** dialog box appears.

3 Click **Form Wizard**.

4 Click **OK**.

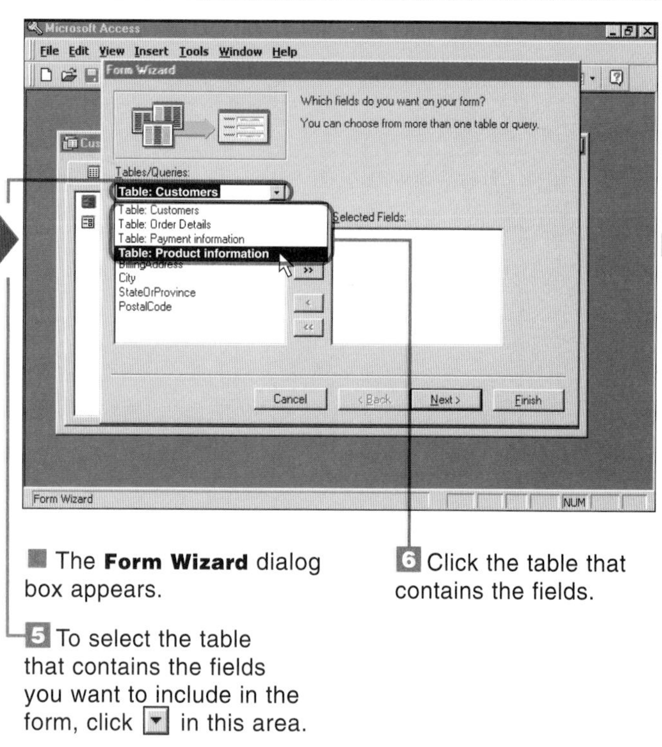

■ The **Form Wizard** dialog box appears.

5 To select the table that contains the fields you want to include in the form, click ▾ in this area.

6 Click the table that contains the fields.

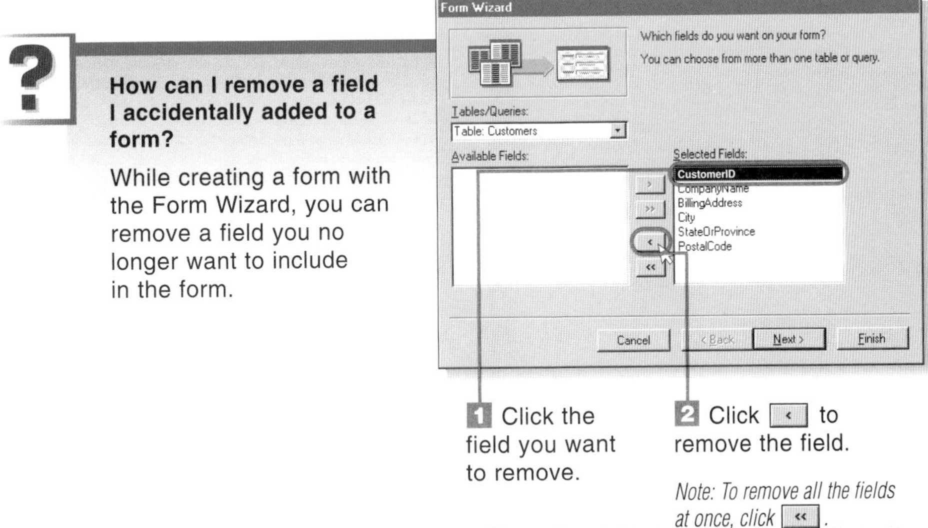

How can I remove a field I accidentally added to a form?

While creating a form with the Form Wizard, you can remove a field you no longer want to include in the form.

1 Click the field you want to remove.

2 Click [<] to remove the field.

Note: To remove all the fields at once, click [<<].

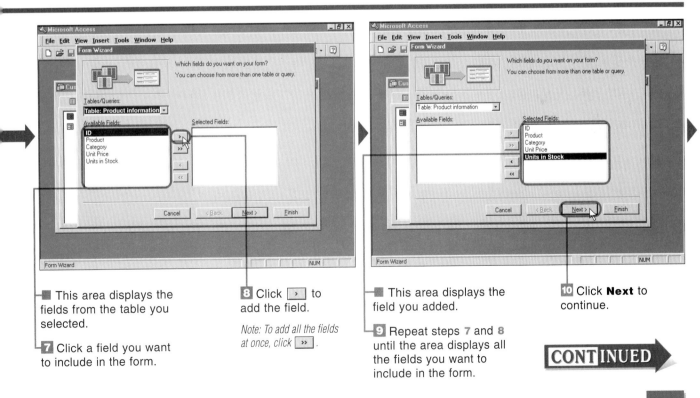

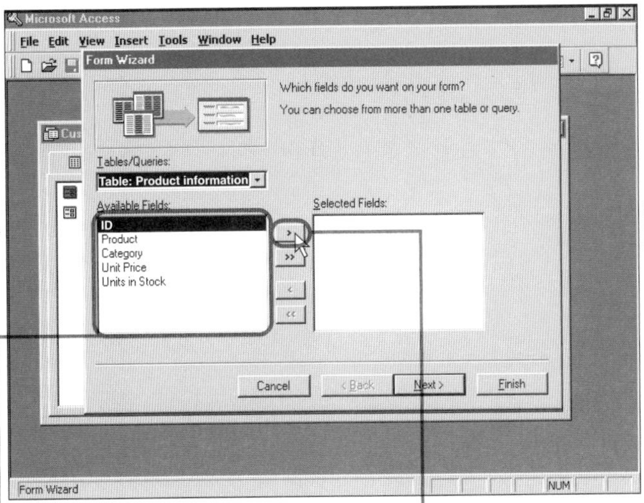

- This area displays the fields from the table you selected.

7 Click a field you want to include in the form.

8 Click [>] to add the field.

Note: To add all the fields at once, click [>>].

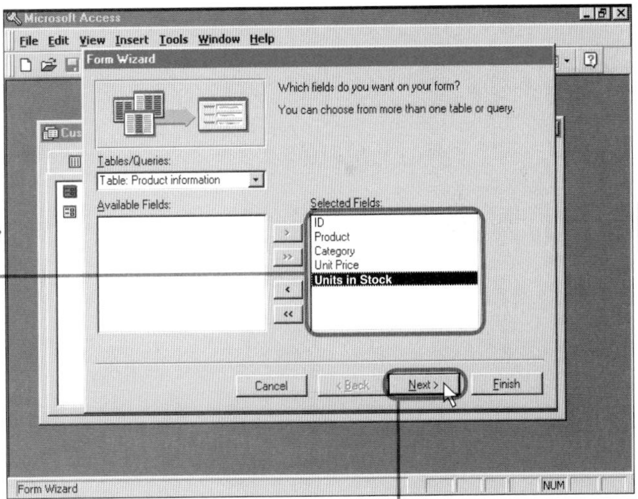

- This area displays the field you added.

9 Repeat steps **7** and **8** until the area displays all the fields you want to include in the form.

10 Click **Next** to continue.

CONTINUED

CREATE A FORM USING THE FORM WIZARD

You can choose between several layouts for your form. The layout of a form determines the arrangement and position of information on the form.

CREATE A FORM FROM ONE TABLE (CONTINUED)

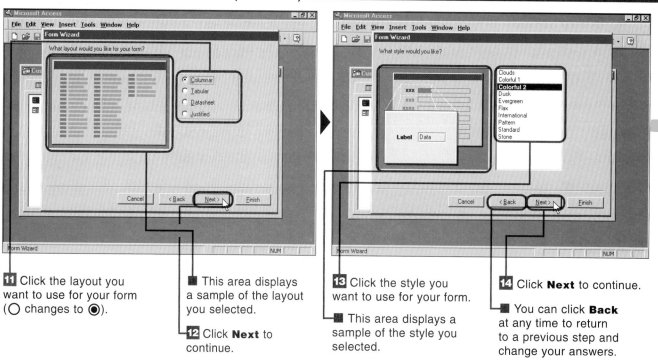

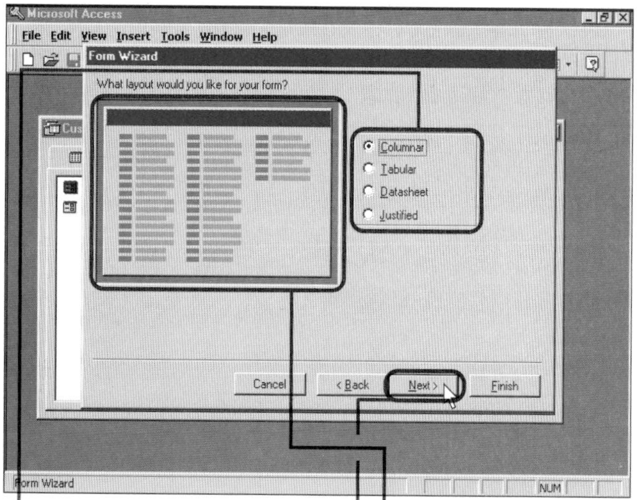

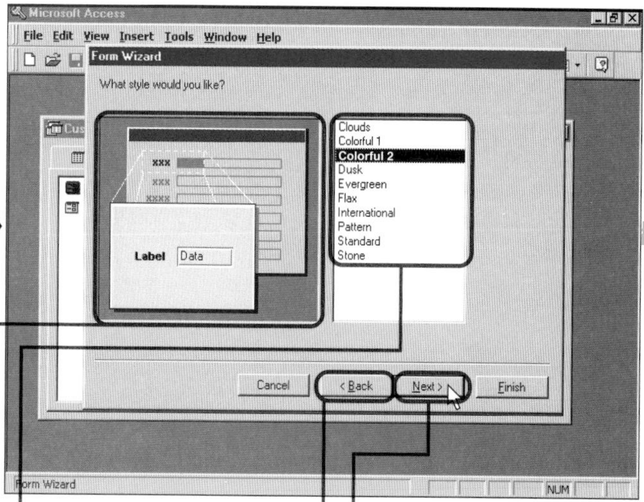

11 Click the layout you want to use for your form (○ changes to ◉).

■ This area displays a sample of the layout you selected.

12 Click **Next** to continue.

13 Click the style you want to use for your form.

■ This area displays a sample of the style you selected.

14 Click **Next** to continue.

■ You can click **Back** at any time to return to a previous step and change your answers.

What styles are available for my forms?

These are some of the styles you can choose from to personalize the appearance of your forms.

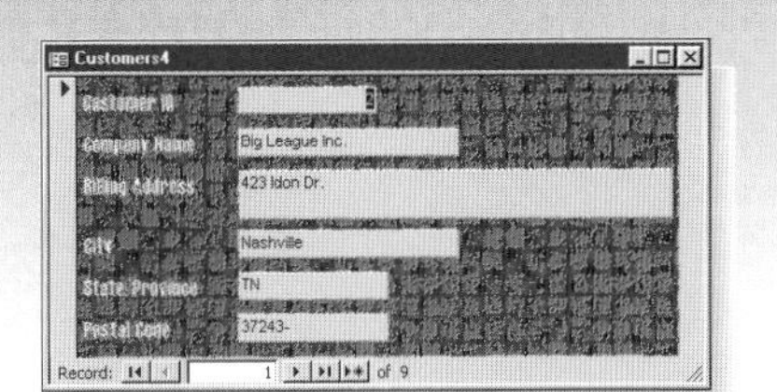

Pattern

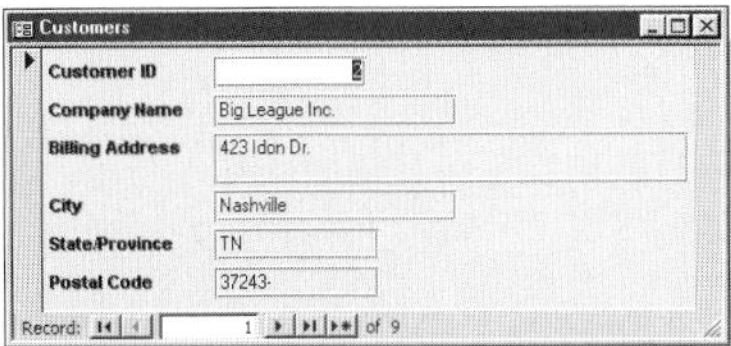

Colorful 2

Stone

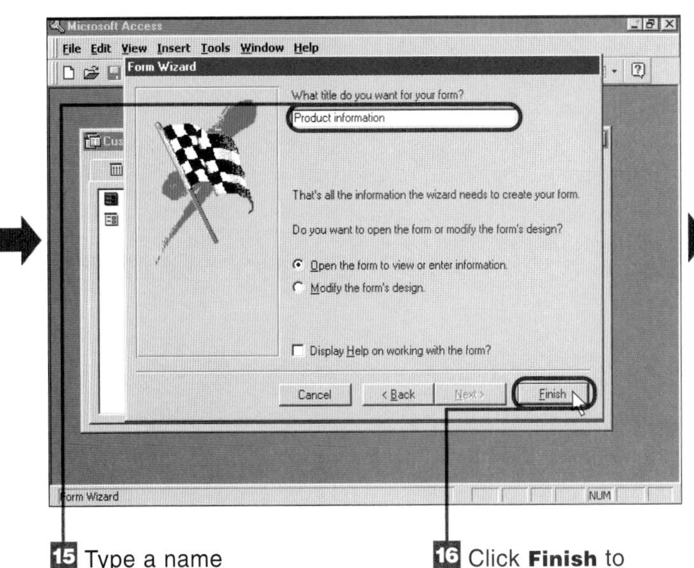

15 Type a name for your form.

16 Click **Finish** to create the form.

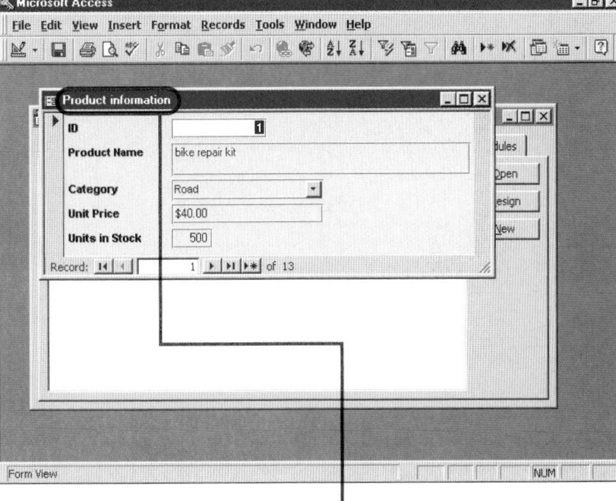

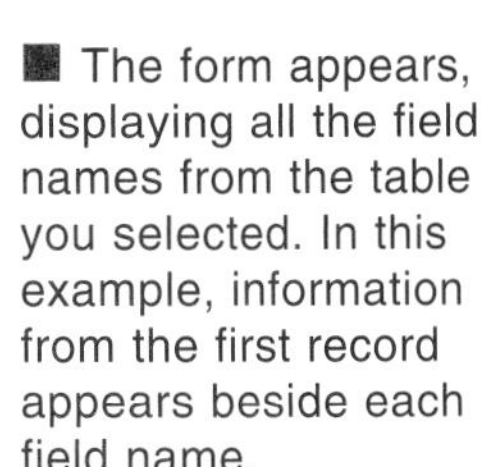

■ The form appears, displaying all the field names from the table you selected. In this example, information from the first record appears beside each field name.

■ The name of the form appears in this area.

CREATE A FORM USING THE FORM WIZARD

You can use the Form Wizard to create a form that displays information from more than one table.

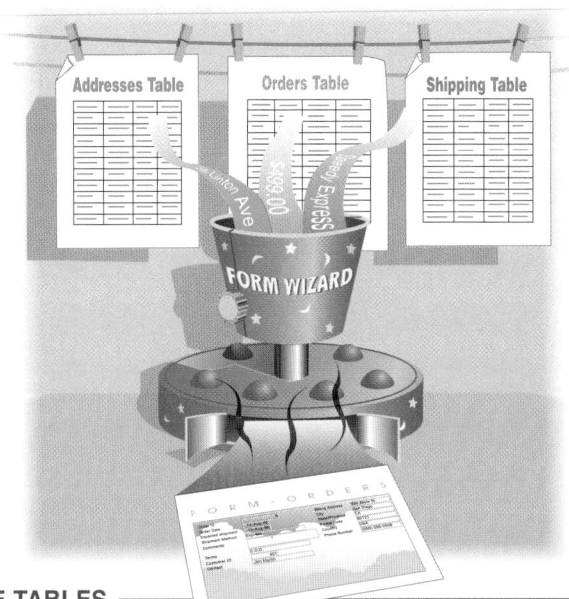

The tables you want to use to create a form must be related. For information on establishing relationships between tables, refer to page 138.

CREATE A FORM FROM MULTIPLE TABLES

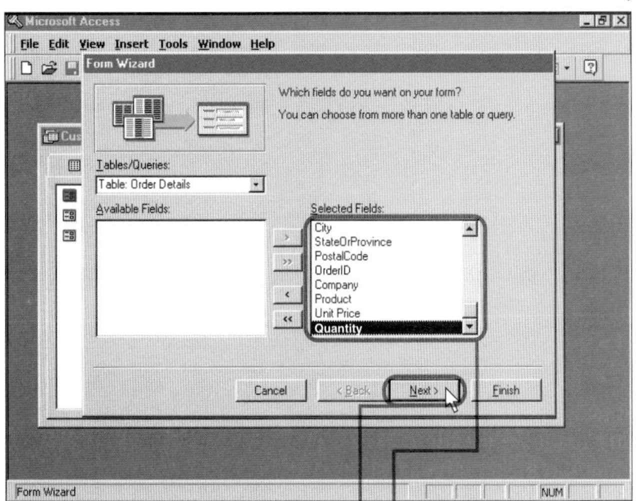

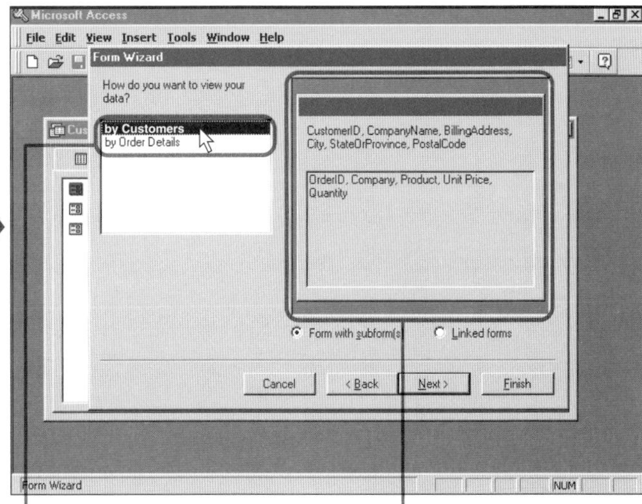

1 To start the Form Wizard and select the fields you want to include from one table, perform steps 1 to 9 starting on page 160.

2 To select the fields you want to include from another table, repeat steps 5 to 9 starting on page 160.

■ This area displays all the fields the form will include. In this example, we select all the fields from the Customers and Order Details tables.

3 Click **Next** to continue.

4 Click the way you want to view the data on the form. You can view the data from each table in separate sections or together in one section.

■ This area displays the way the data will appear on the form.

How can I organize the data on a form?

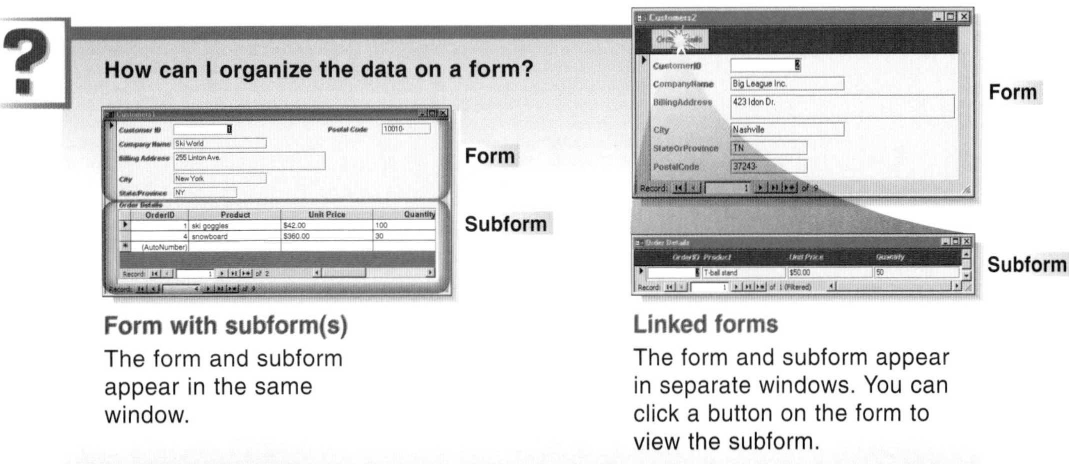

Form with subform(s)
The form and subform appear in the same window.

Linked forms
The form and subform appear in separate windows. You can click a button on the form to view the subform.

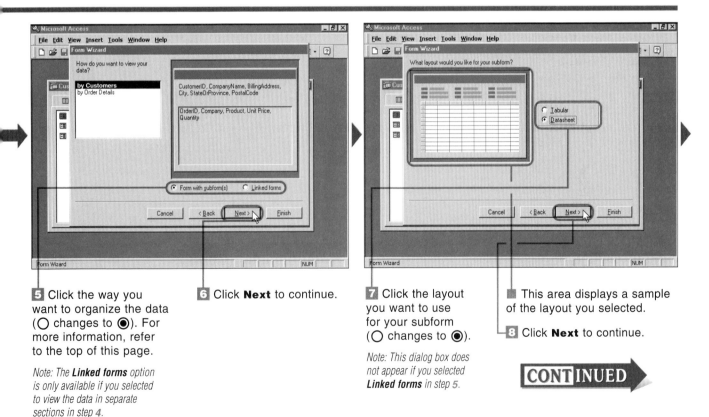

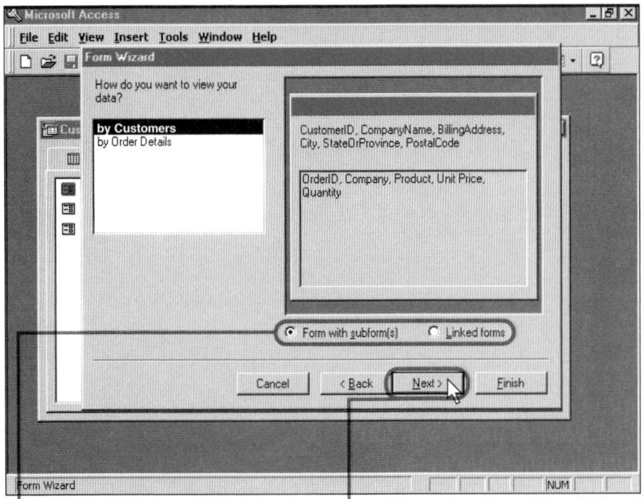

5 Click the way you want to organize the data (○ changes to ◉). For more information, refer to the top of this page.

*Note: The **Linked forms** option is only available if you selected to view the data in separate sections in step **4**.*

6 Click **Next** to continue.

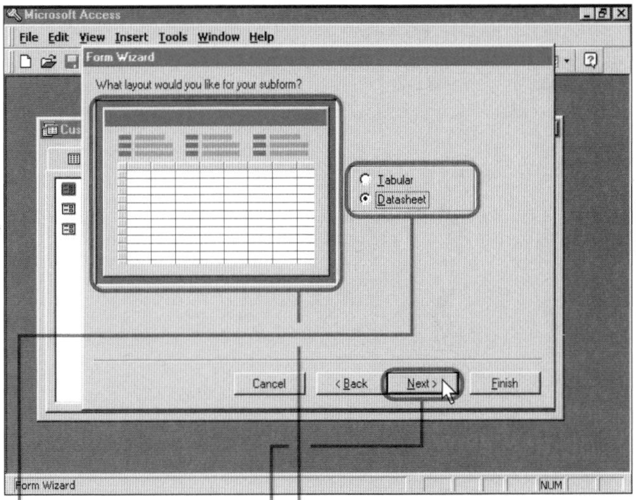

7 Click the layout you want to use for your subform (○ changes to ◉).

*Note: This dialog box does not appear if you selected **Linked forms** in step **5**.*

■ This area displays a sample of the layout you selected.

8 Click **Next** to continue.

CONTINUED

When you create a form using information from more than one table, you need to name both the main form and the subform.

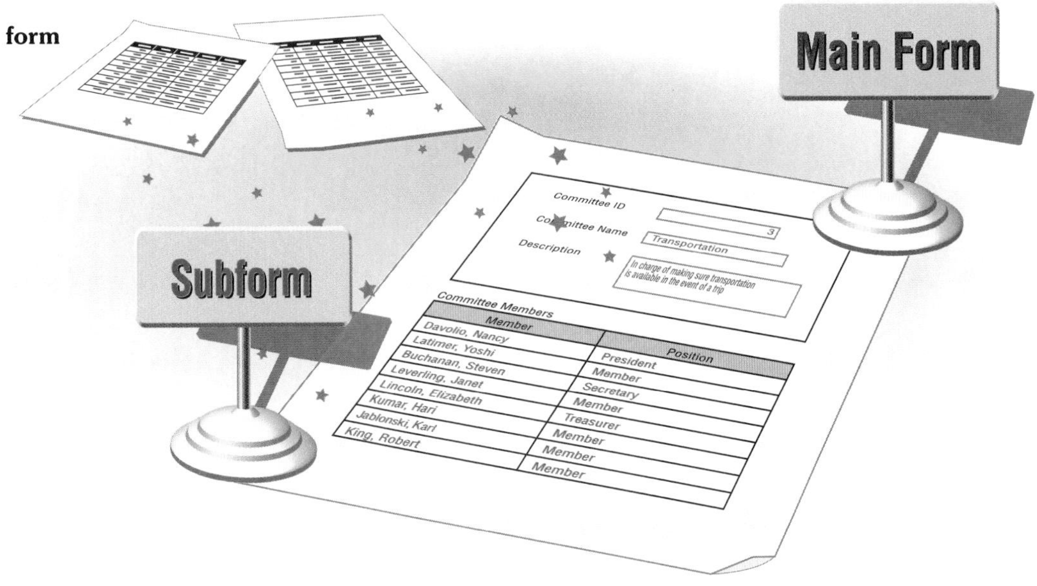

CREATE A FORM FROM MULTIPLE TABLES (CONTINUED)

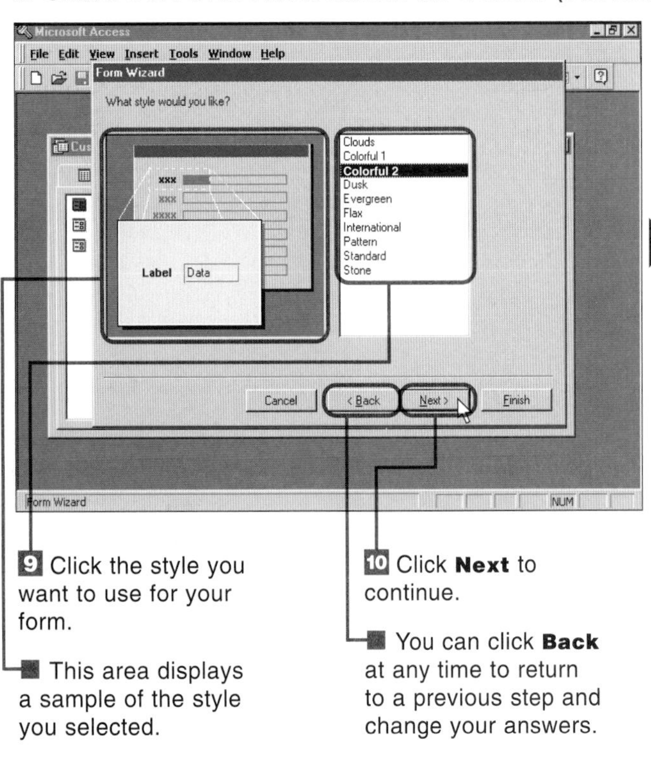

9 Click the style you want to use for your form.

■ This area displays a sample of the style you selected.

10 Click **Next** to continue.

■ You can click **Back** at any time to return to a previous step and change your answers.

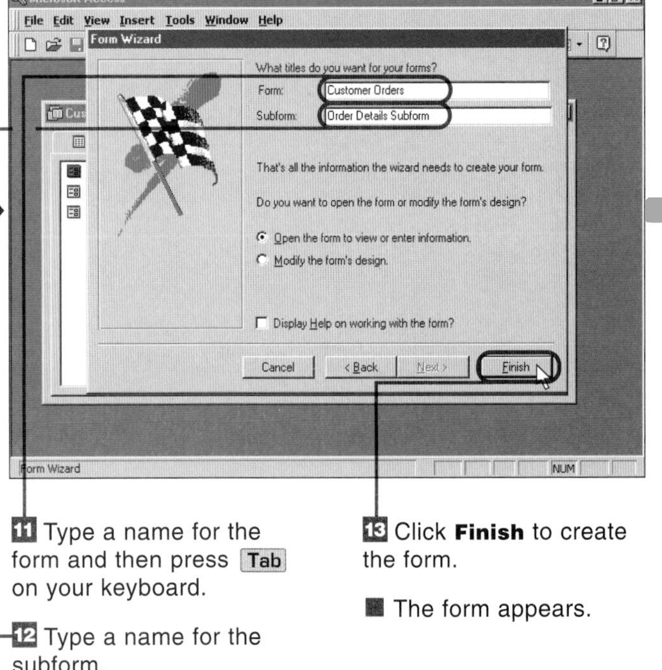

11 Type a name for the form and then press Tab on your keyboard.

12 Type a name for the subform.

Note: You do not need to name a subform if you chose to view all the data in one section in step ***4***.

13 Click **Finish** to create the form.

■ The form appears.

How will my new form appear in the Database window?

If you created a form that contains a subform, the main form and subform will both be listed in the Database window. When you open the main form, you will be able to work with the contents of both the main form and the subform.

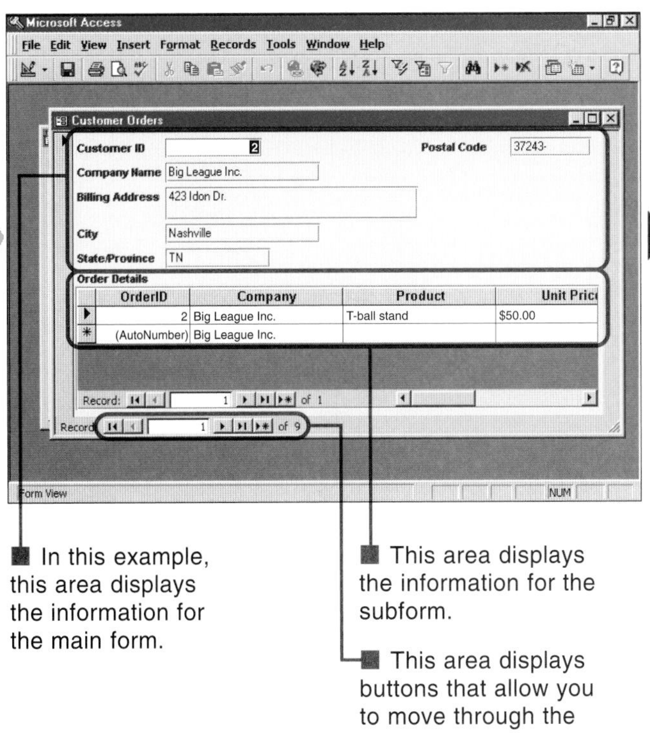

■ In this example, this area displays the information for the main form.

■ This area displays the information for the subform.

■ This area displays buttons that allow you to move through the records in the main form.

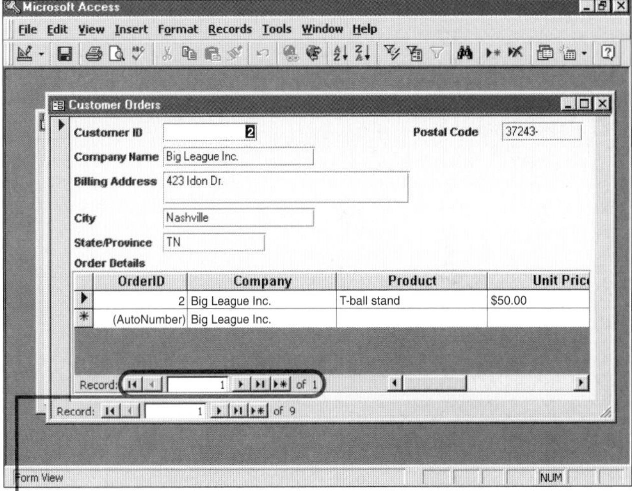

■ This area displays buttons that allow you to move through the records in the subform.

Note: To use the buttons to move through the records, refer to page 150.

■ As you move through the records in the main form, the information in the subform changes. For example, when you select another client, the orders for the client appear in the subform.

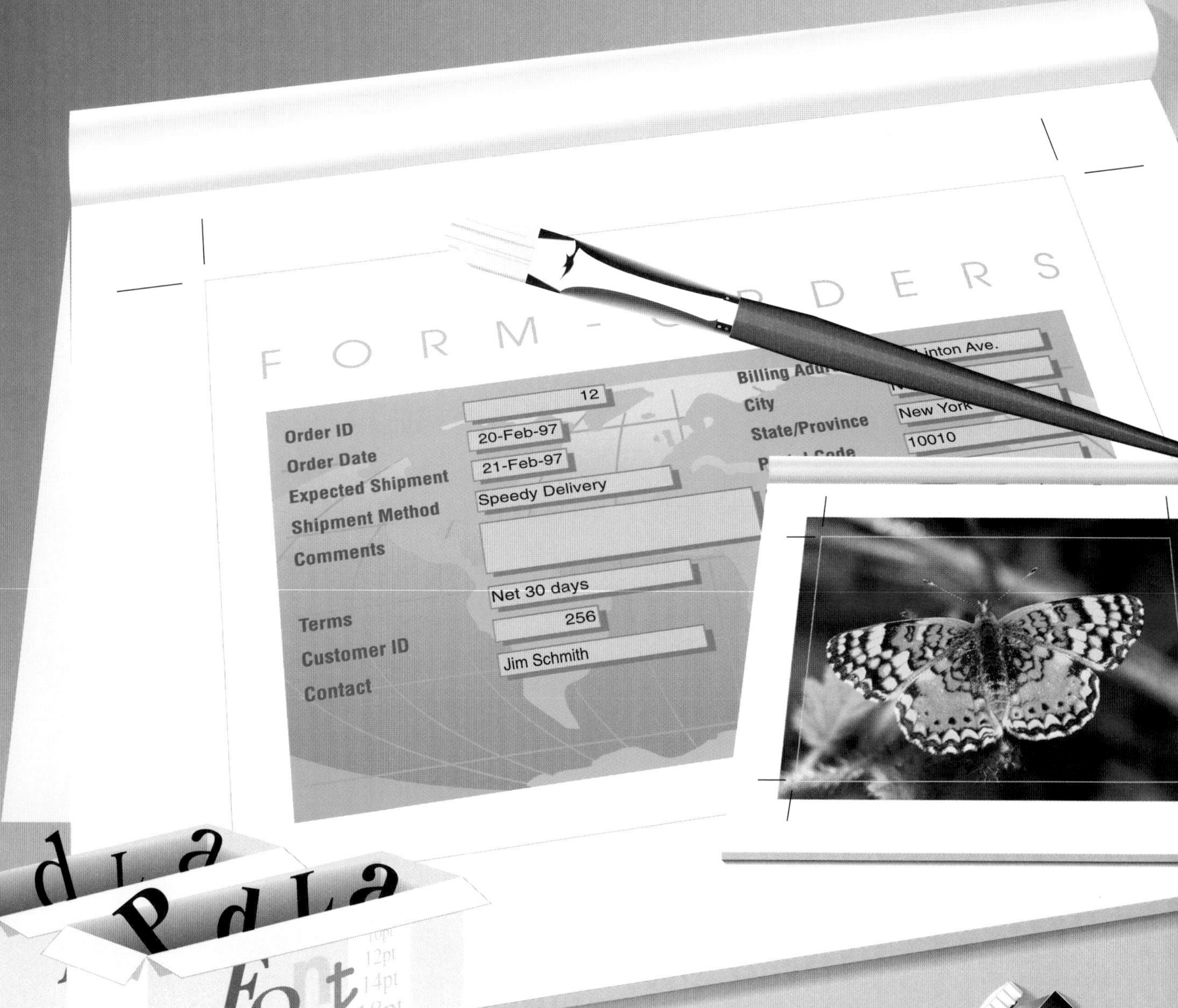
Order ID
12
Order Date
20-Feb-97
Expected Shipment
21-Feb-97
Shipment Method
Speedy Delivery
Comments
Terms
Net 30 days
Customer ID
256
Contact
Jim Schmith
City
New York
State/Province
10010
12pt
14pt
18pt
Times
New Roman
Times
New Roman
Acrylic

Design Forms

Would you like to learn how to design forms? This chapter will teach you the skills you need to design a personalized form. You will learn how to change fonts, add a picture and much more.

Move a Control....170

Resize a Control....171

Delete a Control....172

Add a Field....173

Change Format of Field....174

Change Control Color....175

Add a Label....176

Change Label Text....177

Change Fonts....178

Change Size of Form....180

Select an AutoFormat....181

Add a Picture....182

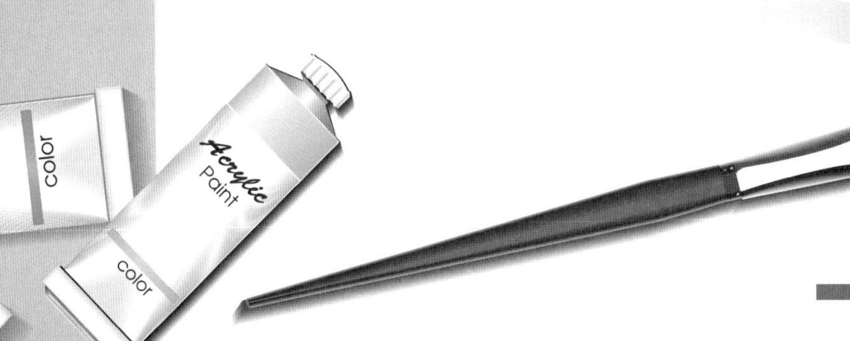

MOVE A CONTROL

You can change the location of a control on a form. Moving controls allows you to change the order of information on a form.

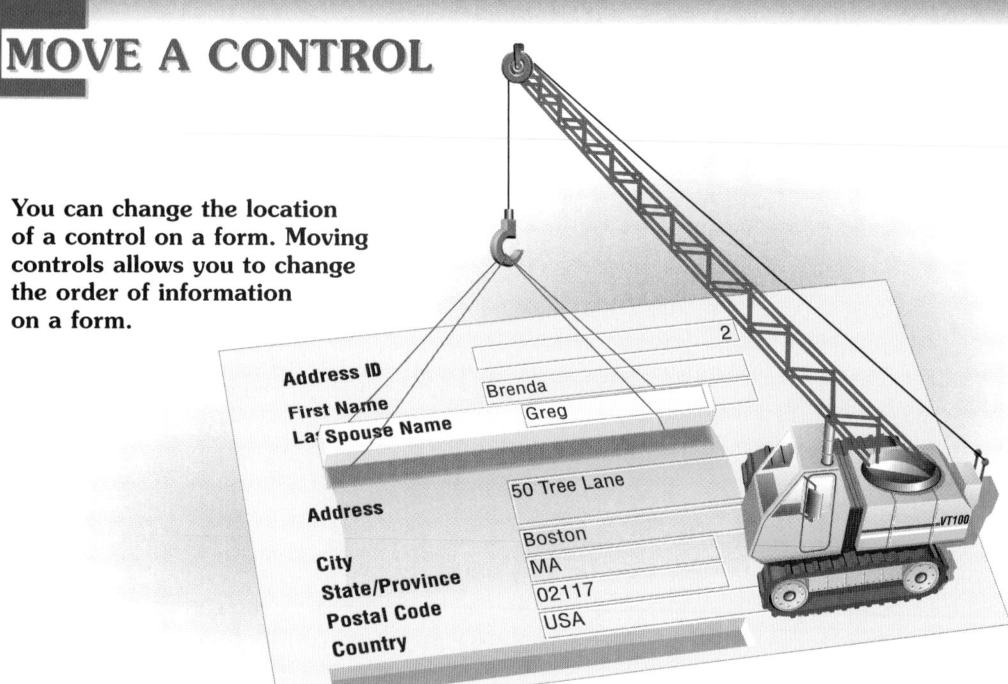

A control is an item on a form, such as a label that displays a field name or a text box that displays information from a record.

MOVE A CONTROL

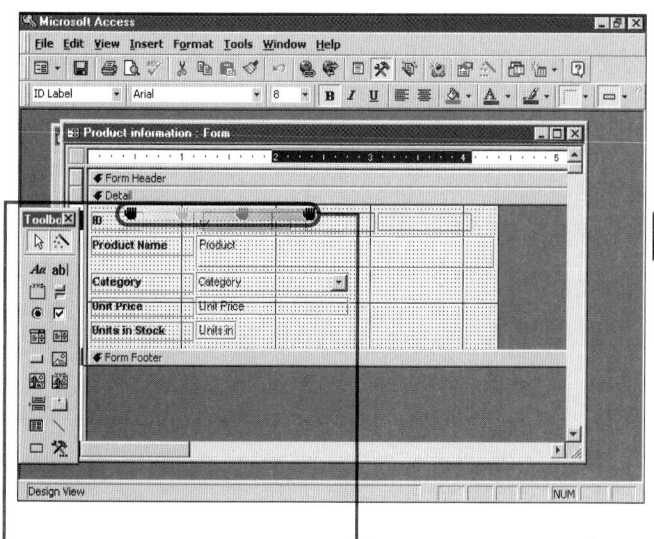

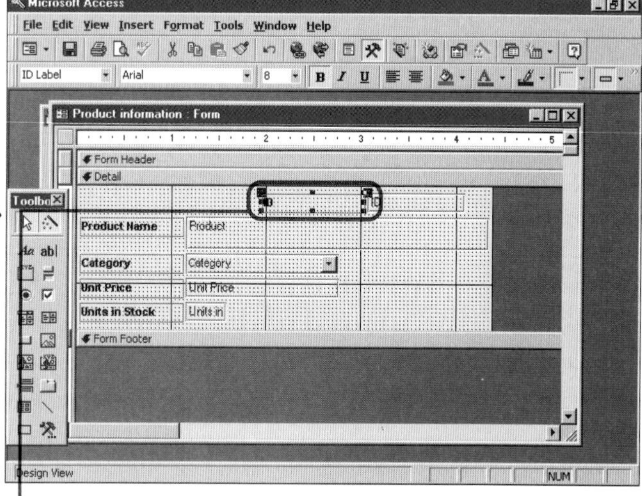

■ Display the form you want to change in the Design view. To do so, refer to page 148.

1 Click the control you want to move. Squares (■) appear around the control.

2 Position the mouse over the border of the control (changes to ✋) and then drag the control to a new location.

■ In this example, the text box and corresponding label appear in the new location.

■ If you want to move a text box or label individually, position the mouse over the large square (■) at the top left corner of the text box or label in step **2** (changes to ☝).

RESIZE A CONTROL

You can change the size of controls on a form. Increasing the size of controls allows you to display longer entries.

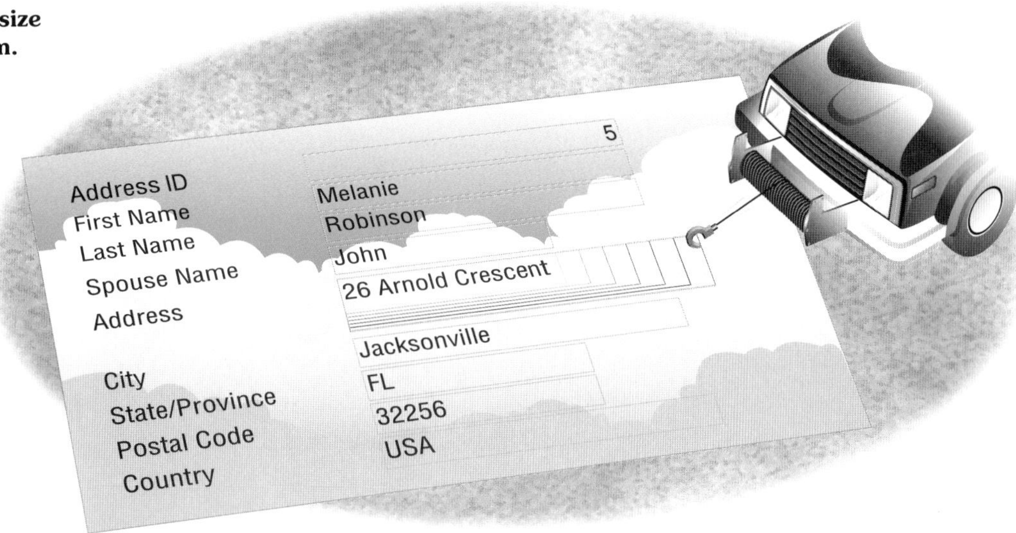

RESIZE A CONTROL

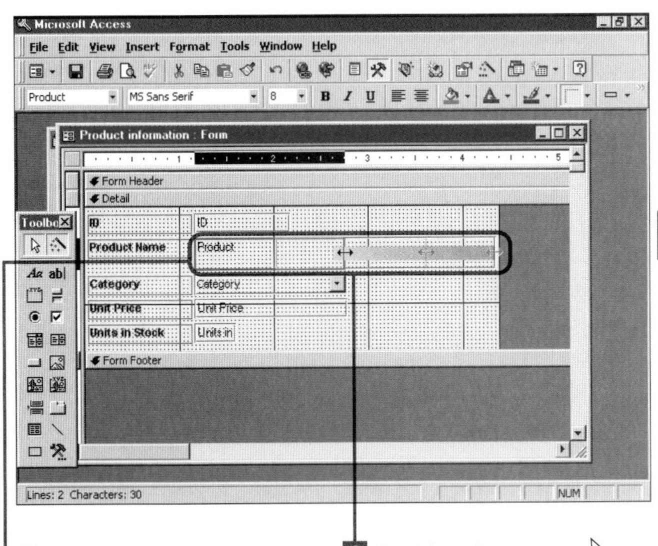

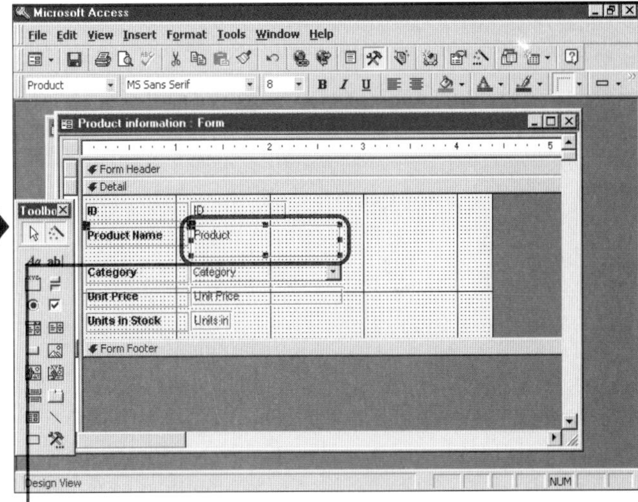

■ Display the form you want to change in the Design view. To do so, refer to page 148.

1 Click the control you want to resize. Squares (■) appear around the control.

2 Position the mouse over a square around the control (↖ changes to ↕ or ↔) and then drag the mouse until the control is the size you want.

■ The control appears in the new size.

Note: If you want to change the size of several controls at once, you must first select the controls. To select multiple controls, hold down **Shift** *on your keyboard as you click each control you want to resize.*

DELETE A CONTROL

You can delete a control you no longer want to appear on a form.

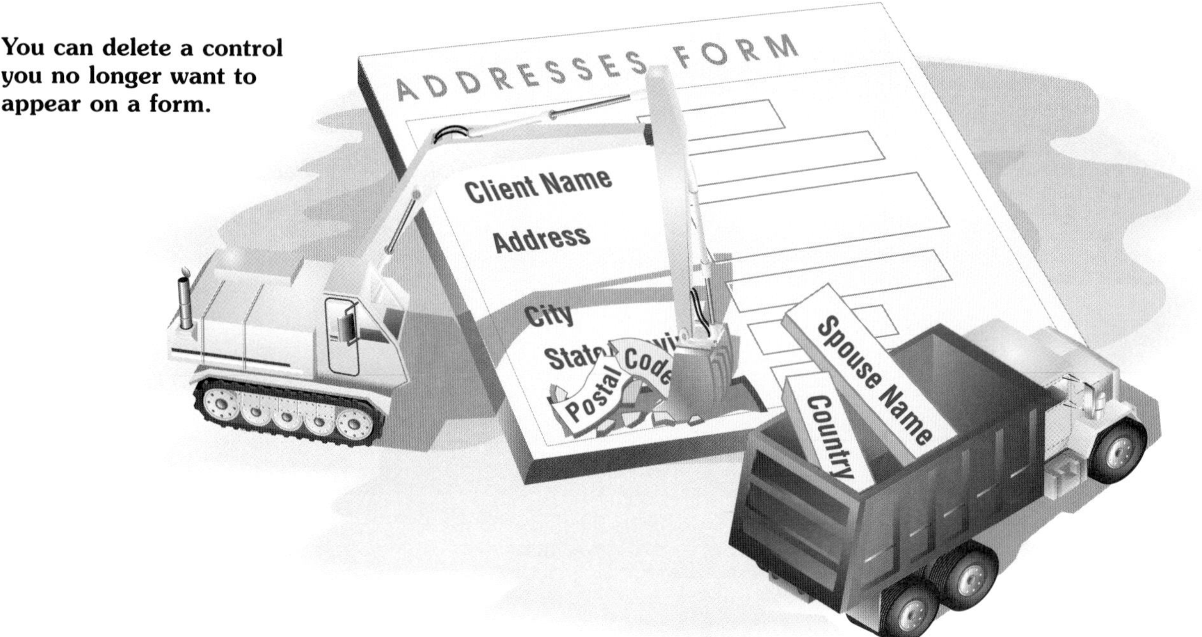

DELETE A CONTROL

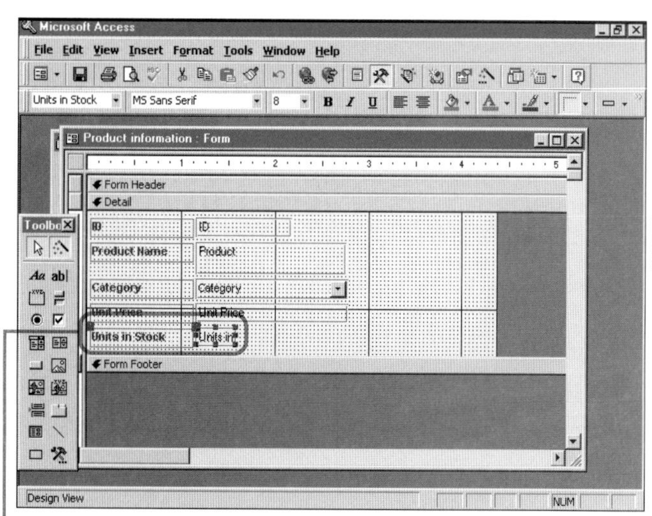

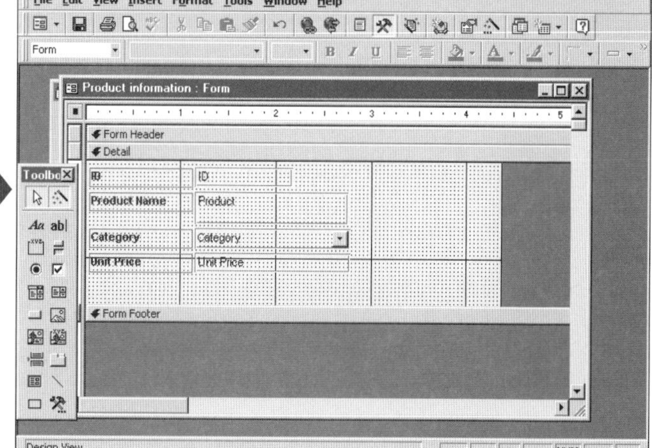

■ Display the form you want to change in the Design view. To do so, refer to page 148.

1 Click the control you want to delete. Squares (■) appear around the control.

2 Press Delete on your keyboard.

■ In this example, the text box and corresponding label disappear.

■ If you want to delete just the label, click the label and then press Delete on your keyboard.

ADD A FIELD

If you left out a field when you created a form, you can easily add the field later.

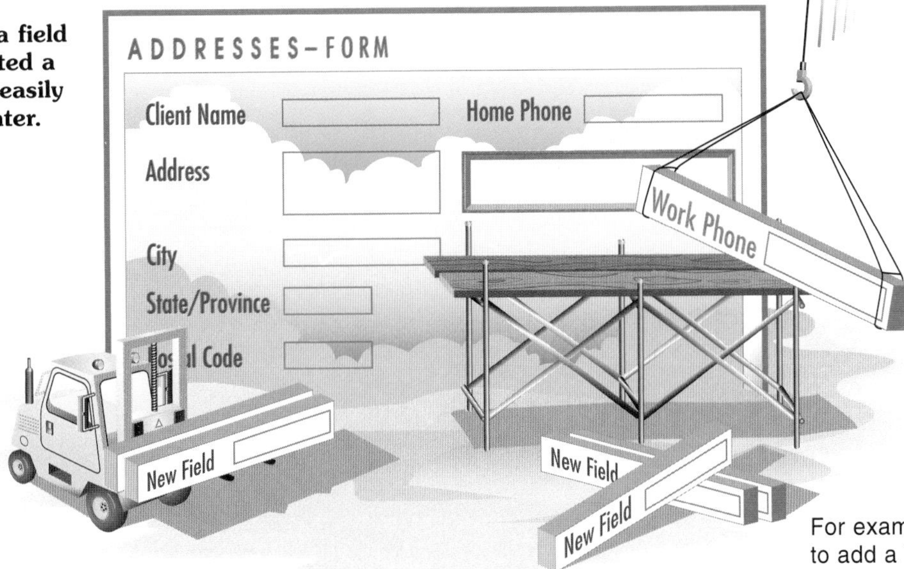

For example, you may want to add a Telephone Number field to a form that displays client addresses.

ADD A FIELD

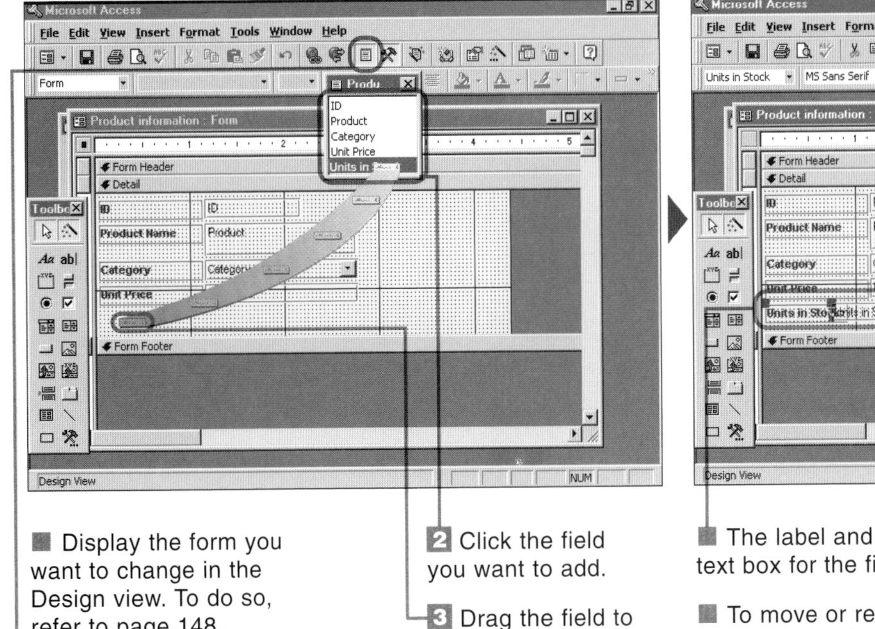

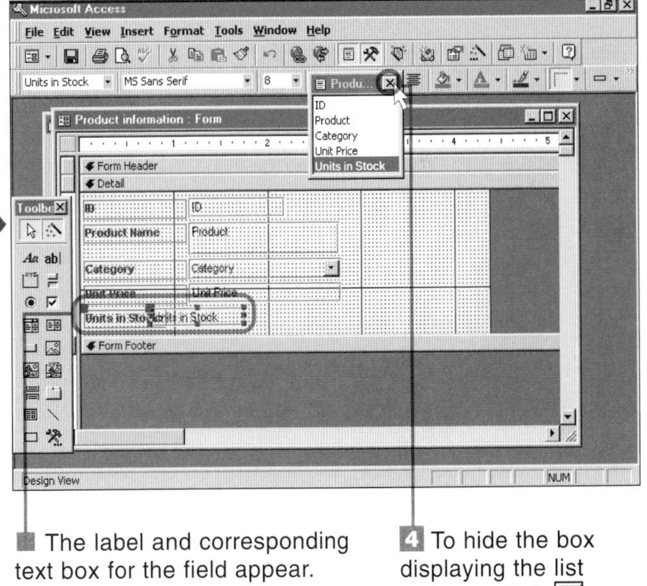

■ Display the form you want to change in the Design view. To do so, refer to page 148.

1 Click ▤ to display a list of fields from the table you used to create the form.

2 Click the field you want to add.

3 Drag the field to where you want to place the field on the form.

■ The label and corresponding text box for the field appear.

■ To move or resize the label or text box, refer to pages 170 to 171.

4 To hide the box displaying the list of fields, click ☒.

CHANGE FORMAT OF FIELD

You can customize the way numbers, dates and times appear on a form.

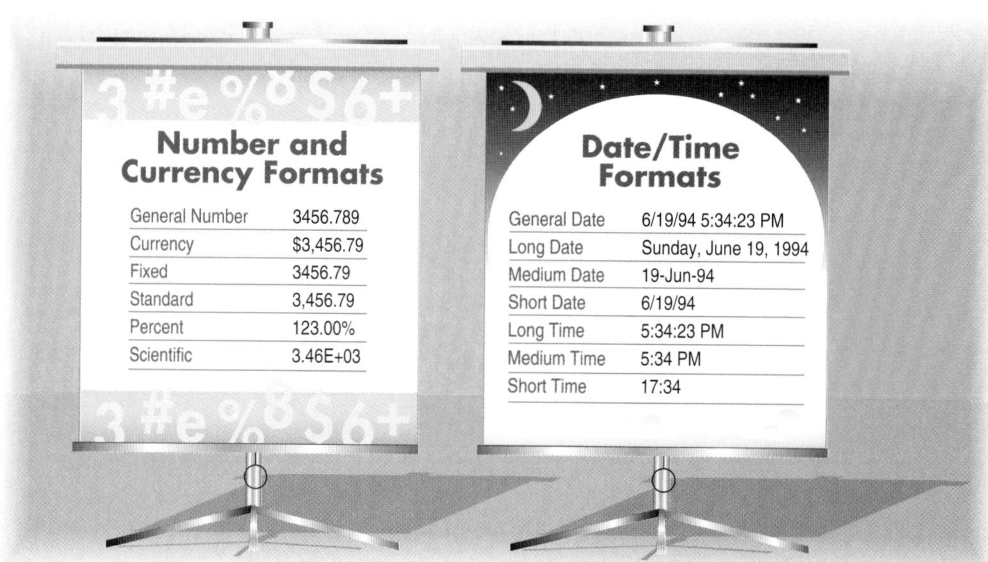

Number and Currency Formats
General Number 3456.789
Currency $3,456.79
Fixed 3456.79
Standard 3,456.79
Percent 123.00%
Scientific 3.46E+03
Date/Time Formats
General Date 6/19/94 5:34:23 PM
Long Date Sunday, June 19, 1994
Medium Date 19-Jun-94
Short Date 6/19/94
Long Time 5:34:23 PM
Medium Time 5:34 PM
Short Time 17:34

CHANGE FORMAT OF FIELD

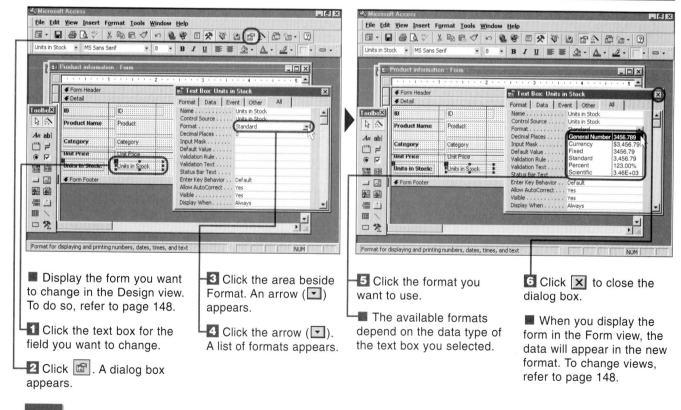

■ Display the form you want to change in the Design view. To do so, refer to page 148.

1 Click the text box for the field you want to change.

2 Click [Properties button]. A dialog box appears.

3 Click the area beside Format. An arrow ([▾]) appears.

4 Click the arrow ([▾]). A list of formats appears.

5 Click the format you want to use.

■ The available formats depend on the data type of the text box you selected.

6 Click [X] to close the dialog box.

■ When you display the form in the Form view, the data will appear in the new format. To change views, refer to page 148.

CHANGE CONTROL COLOR

You can change the text and background color of a control to emphasize information on a form.

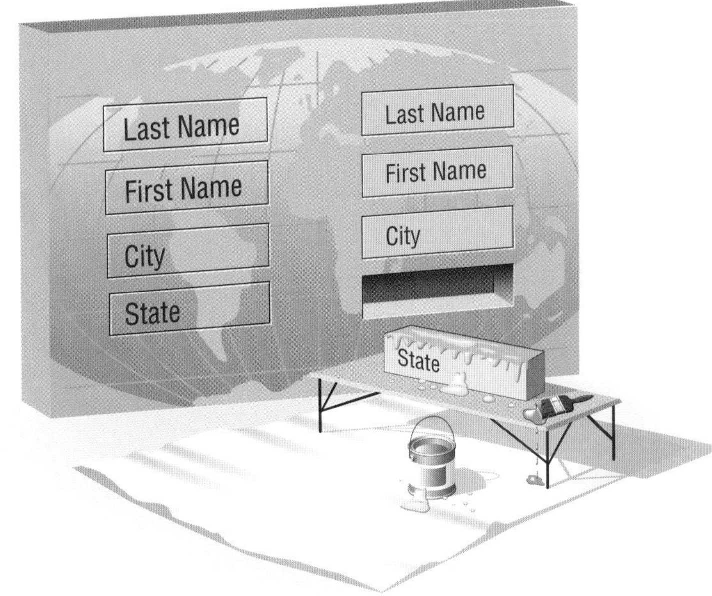

Make sure you select text and background colors that work well together. For example, red text on a blue background can be difficult to read.

CHANGE CONTROL COLOR

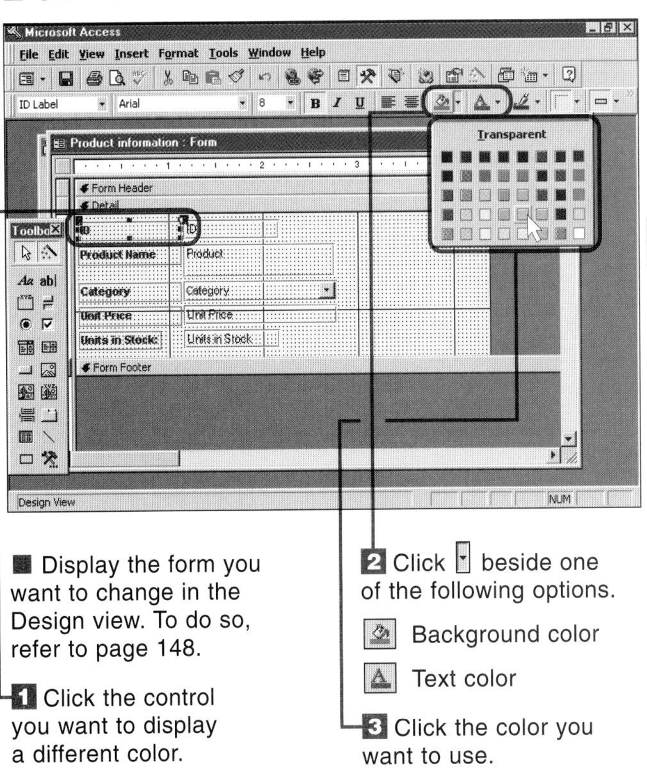

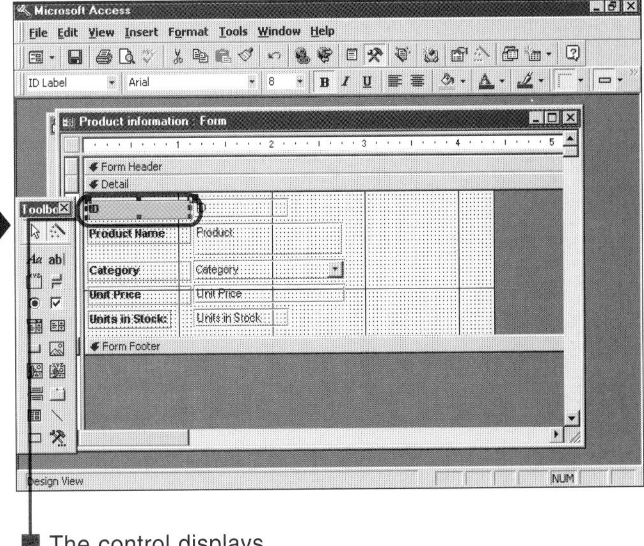

■ Display the form you want to change in the Design view. To do so, refer to page 148.

1 Click the control you want to display a different color.

2 Click ▾ beside one of the following options.

- Background color
- Text color

3 Click the color you want to use.

■ The control displays the color you selected.

ADD A LABEL

You can add a label that you want to appear for each record in a form. Labels are useful for displaying important information.

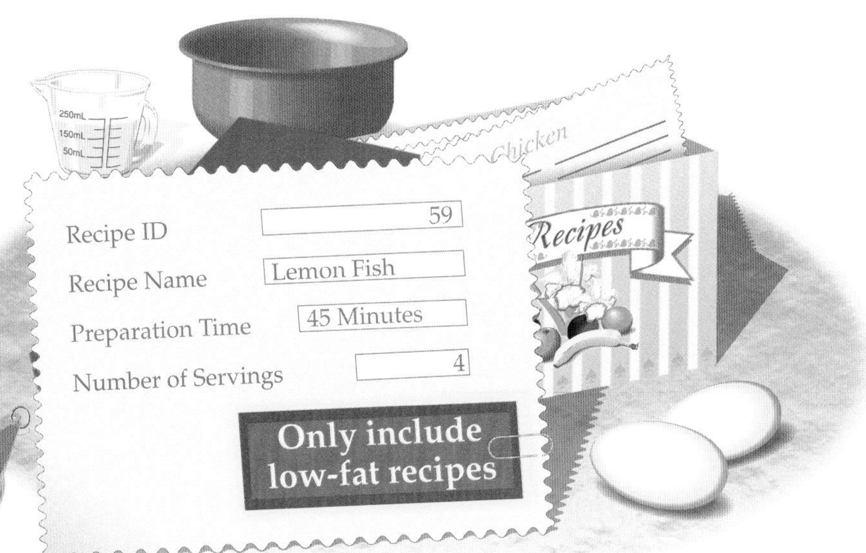

ADD A LABEL

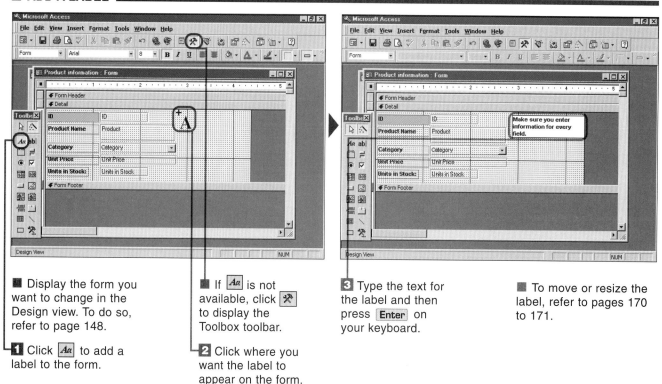

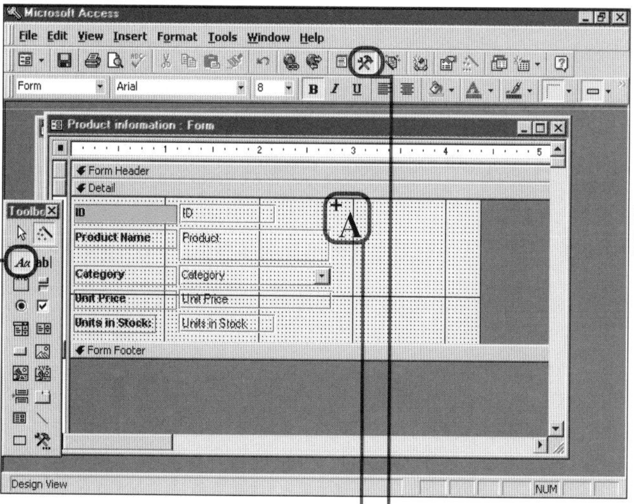

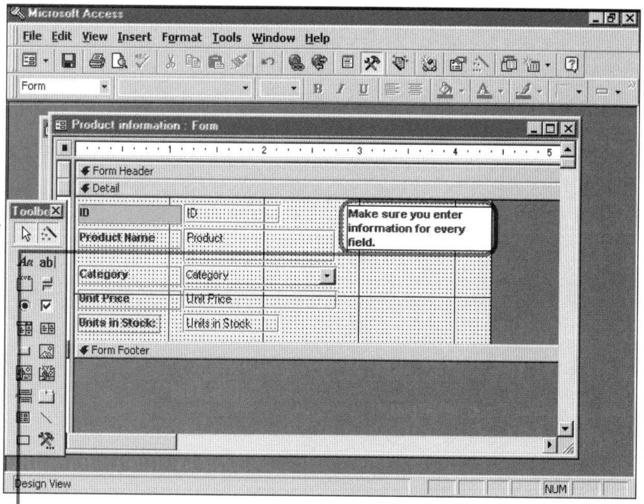

■ Display the form you want to change in the Design view. To do so, refer to page 148.

1 Click Aa to add a label to the form.

■ If Aa is not available, click the Toolbox button to display the Toolbox toolbar.

2 Click where you want the label to appear on the form.

3 Type the text for the label and then press Enter on your keyboard.

■ To move or resize the label, refer to pages 170 to 171.

CHANGE LABEL TEXT

You can change the text in a label to make the label more descriptive.

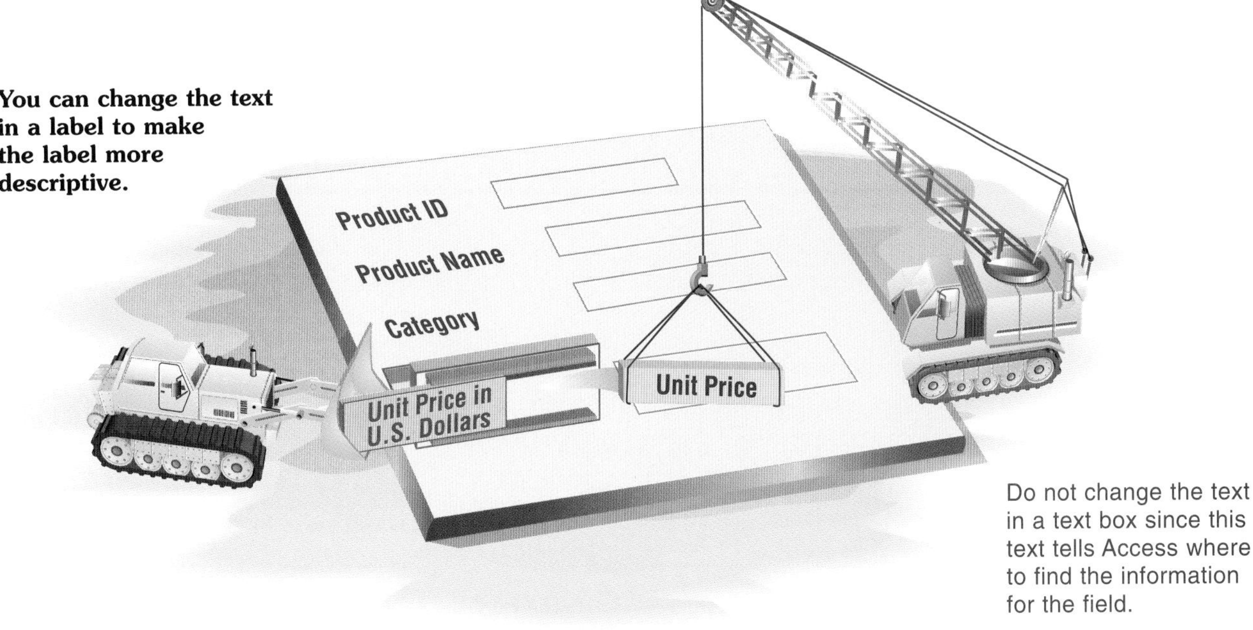

Do not change the text in a text box since this text tells Access where to find the information for the field.

CHANGE LABEL TEXT

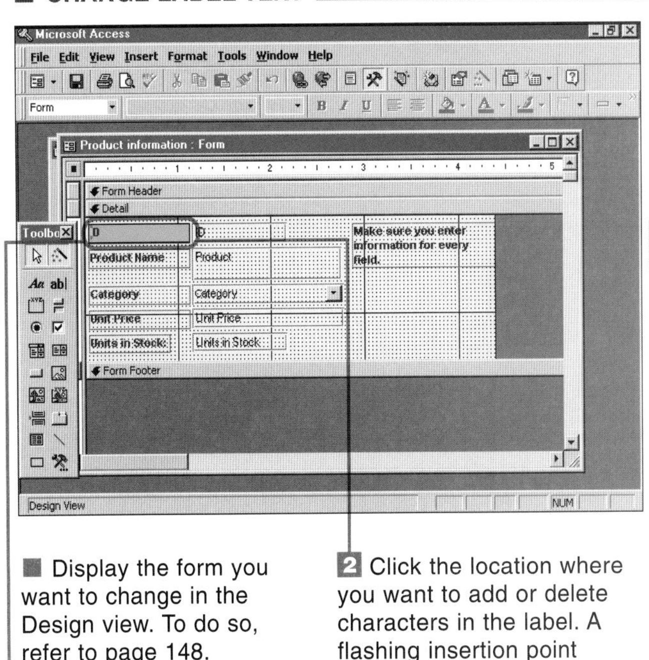

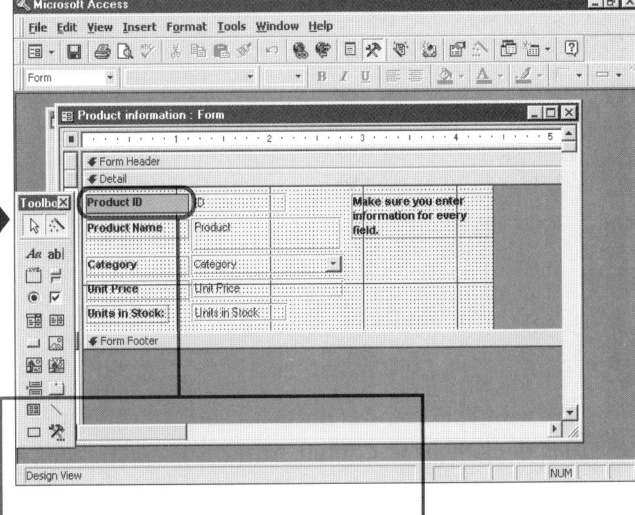

■ Display the form you want to change in the Design view. To do so, refer to page 148.

1 Click the label you want to change.

2 Click the location where you want to add or delete characters in the label. A flashing insertion point appears in the label.

Note: You can press ← or → on your keyboard to move the insertion point in the label.

3 To remove the character to the left of the insertion point, press Backspace on your keyboard.

4 To insert text where the insertion point flashes on the screen, type the text.

5 When you finish making changes, press Enter on your keyboard.

CHANGE FONTS

You can change the font, size and style of text on a form to customize the appearance of the text.

CHANGE FONTS

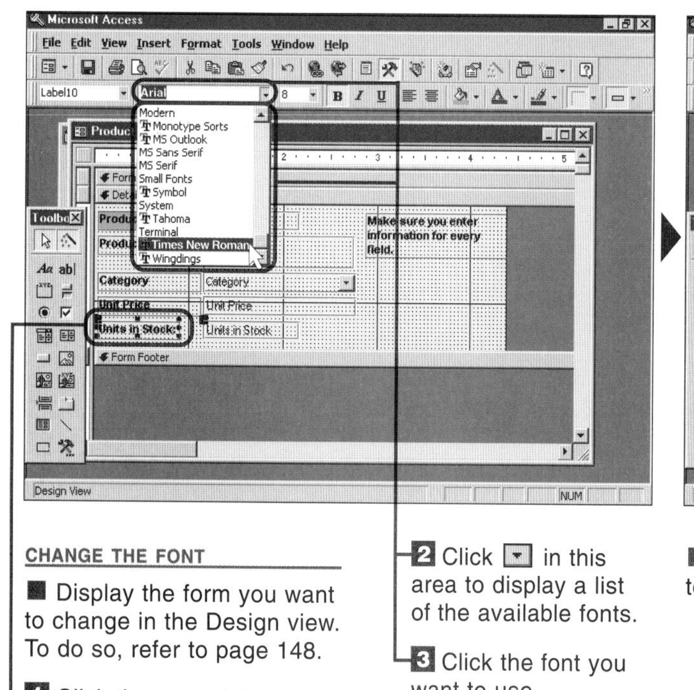

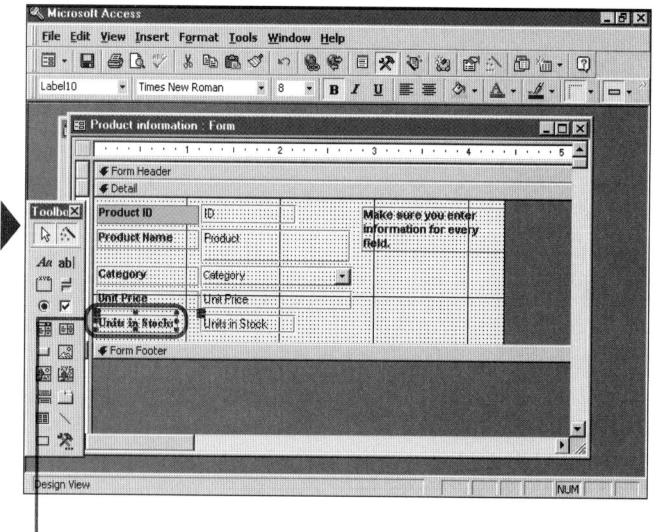

CHANGE THE FONT

■ Display the form you want to change in the Design view. To do so, refer to page 148.

1 Click the control that displays the text you want to change.

2 Click ▾ in this area to display a list of the available fonts.

3 Click the font you want to use.

■ The text changes to the new font.

When I change the font, size or style of text, the text no longer fits in the control. How can I display all of the text?

When you change the font, size or style of text, you may need to resize the control to display all of the text. To resize a control, refer to page 171.

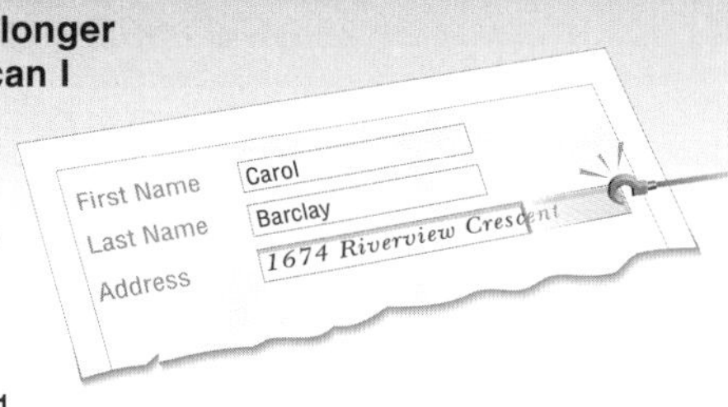

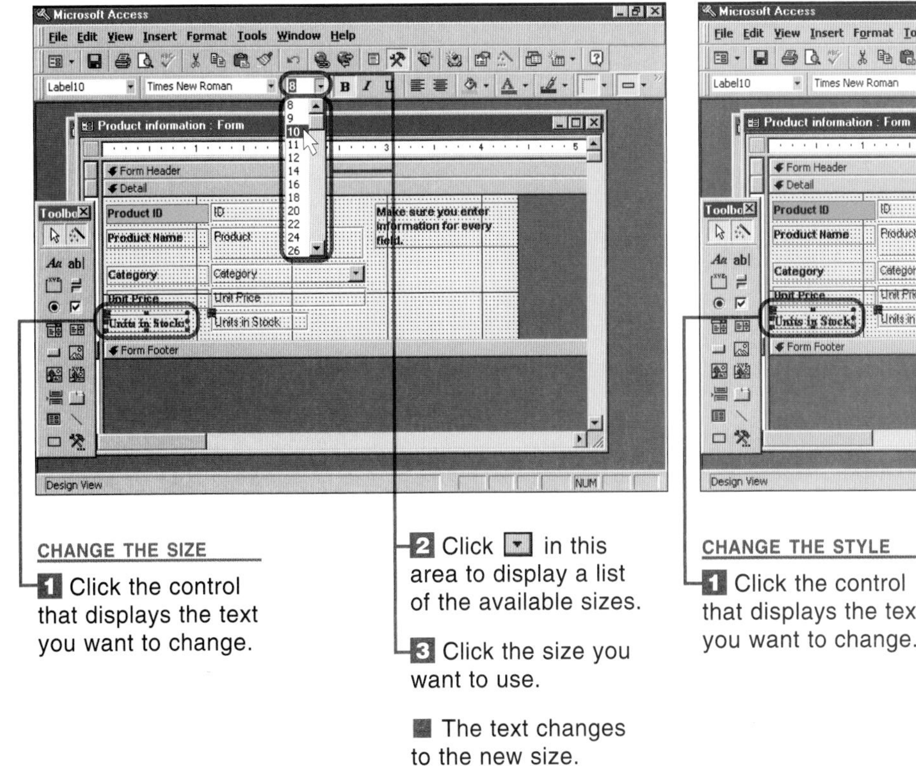

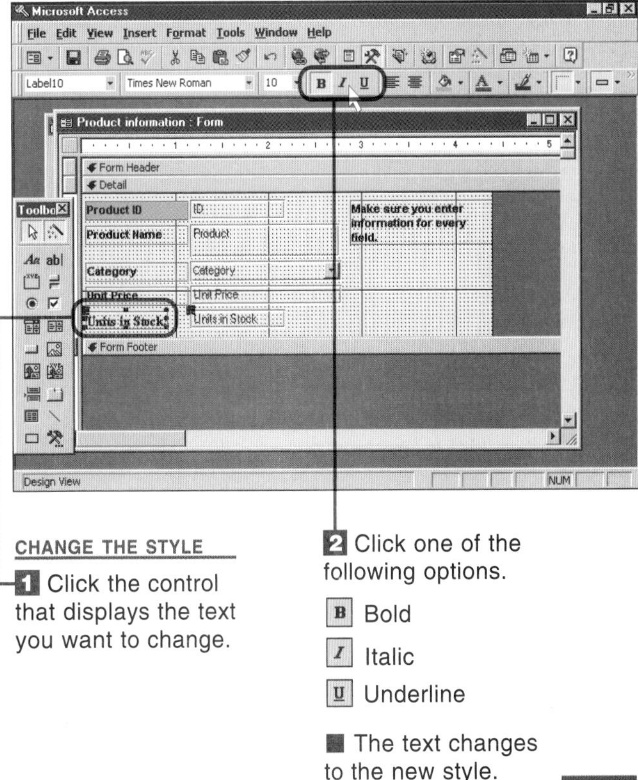

CHANGE THE SIZE

1 Click the control that displays the text you want to change.

2 Click ▼ in this area to display a list of the available sizes.

3 Click the size you want to use.

■ The text changes to the new size.

CHANGE THE STYLE

1 Click the control that displays the text you want to change.

2 Click one of the following options.

B Bold

I Italic

U Underline

■ The text changes to the new style.

CHANGE SIZE OF FORM

You can increase or decrease the size of a form. Increasing the size of a form gives you more room to add information, such as a new field or a picture.

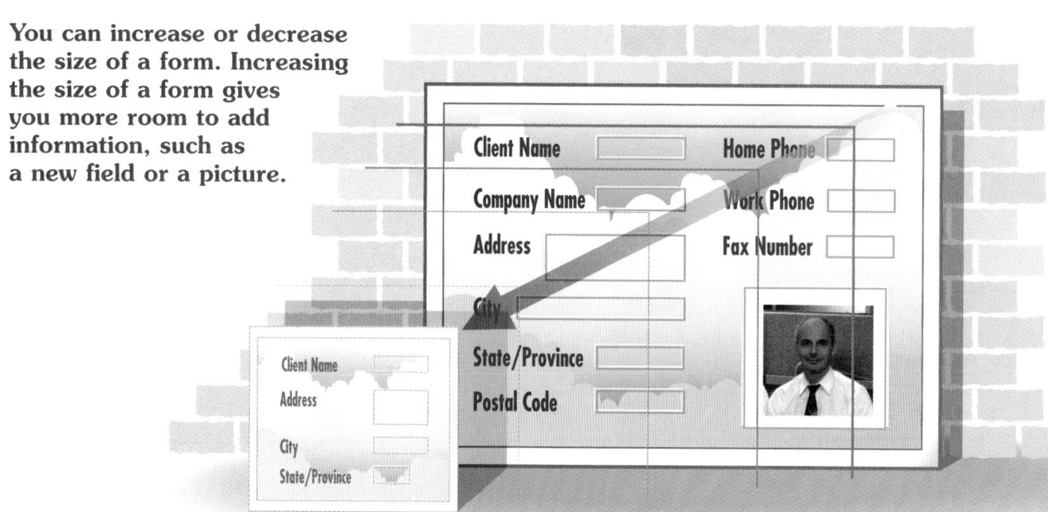

CHANGE SIZE OF FORM

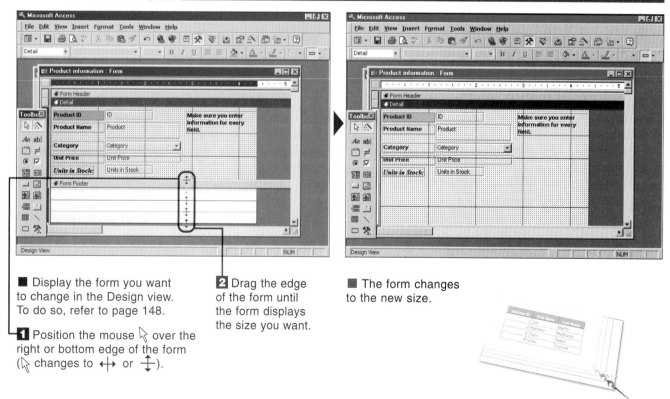

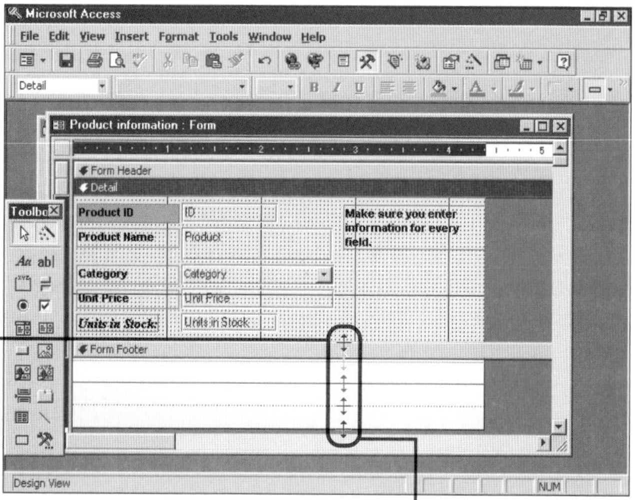

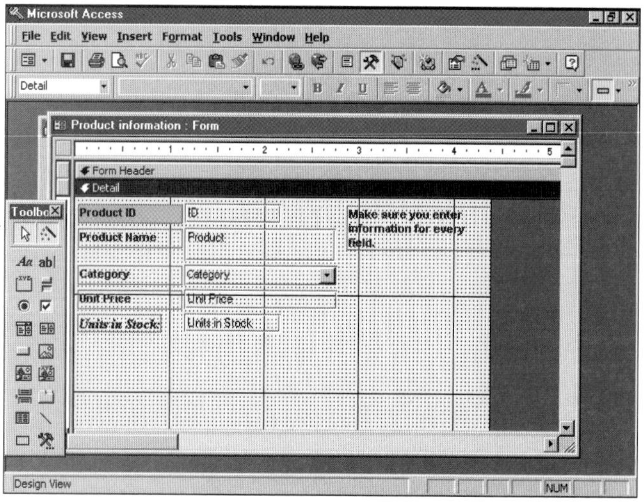

■ Display the form you want to change in the Design view. To do so, refer to page 148.

1 Position the mouse ↖ over the right or bottom edge of the form (↖ changes to ↔ or ↕).

2 Drag the edge of the form until the form displays the size you want.

■ The form changes to the new size.

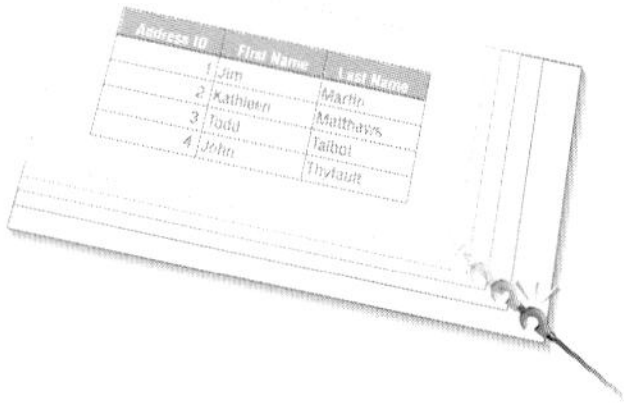

SELECT AN AUTOFORMAT

You can select an autoformat to instantly change the overall look of a form.

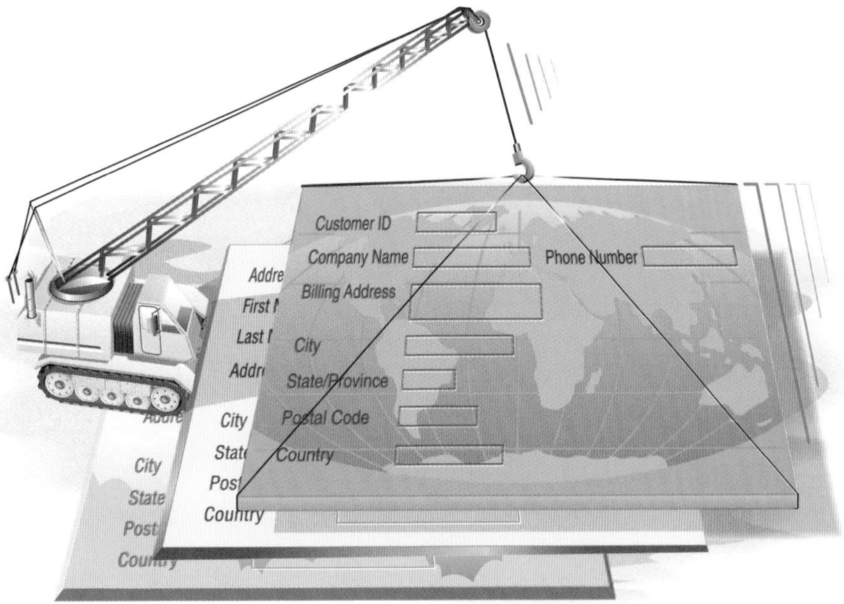

SELECT AN AUTOFORMAT

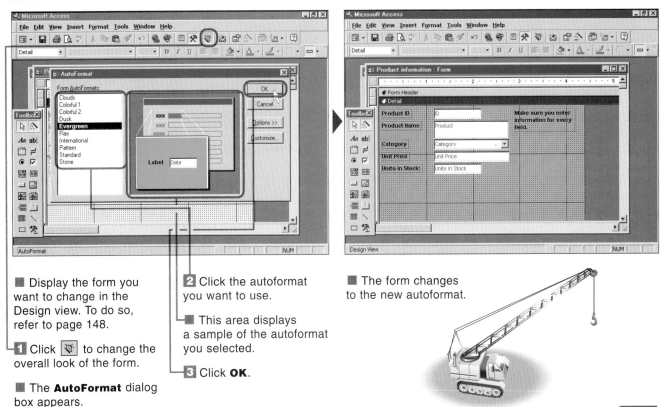

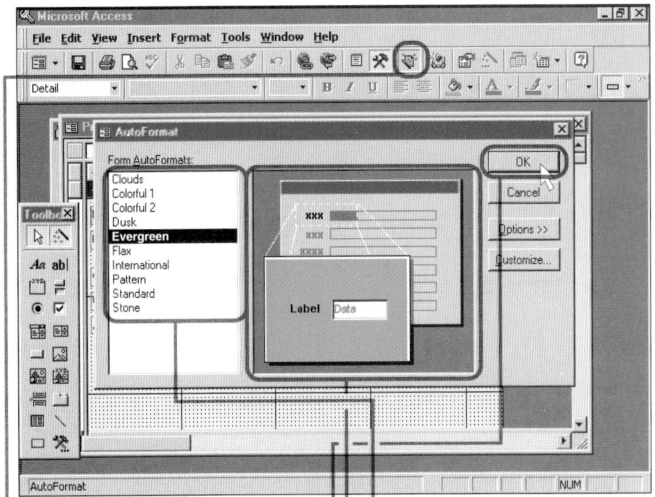

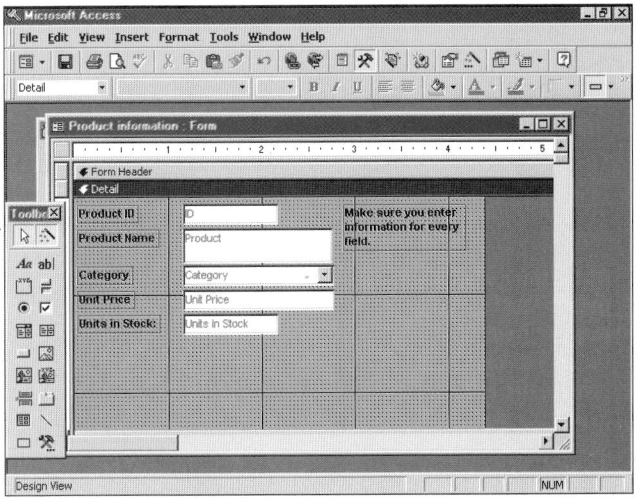

■ Display the form you want to change in the Design view. To do so, refer to page 148.

1 Click to change the overall look of the form.

■ The **AutoFormat** dialog box appears.

2 Click the autoformat you want to use.

■ This area displays a sample of the autoformat you selected.

3 Click **OK**.

■ The form changes to the new autoformat.

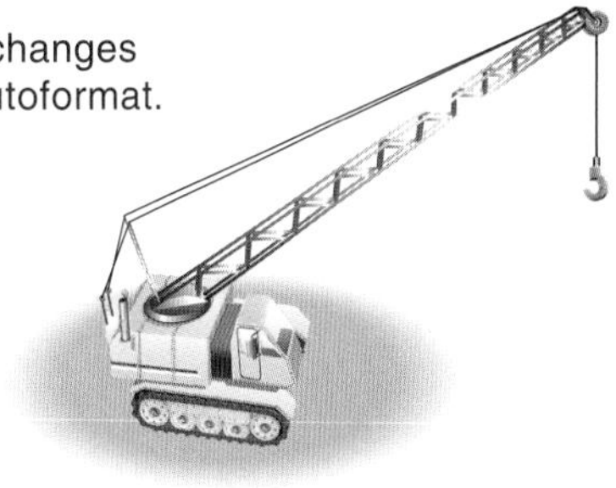

ADD A PICTURE

You can add a picture to make a form more appealing or support the data in the form. You can add pictures such as your company logo, a colorful design or a picture of your products.

If you want to display a different picture for each record, such as a picture of each employee, refer to page 126.

ADD A PICTURE

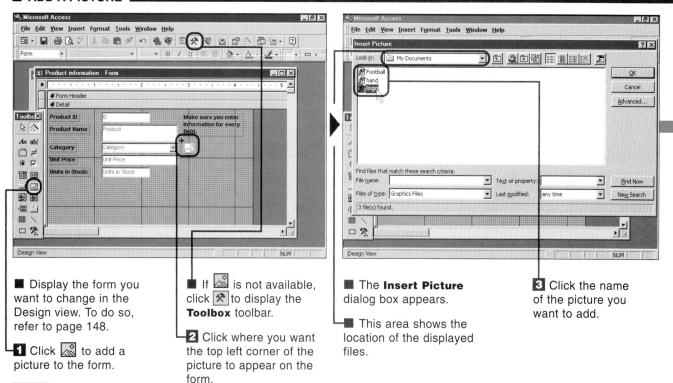

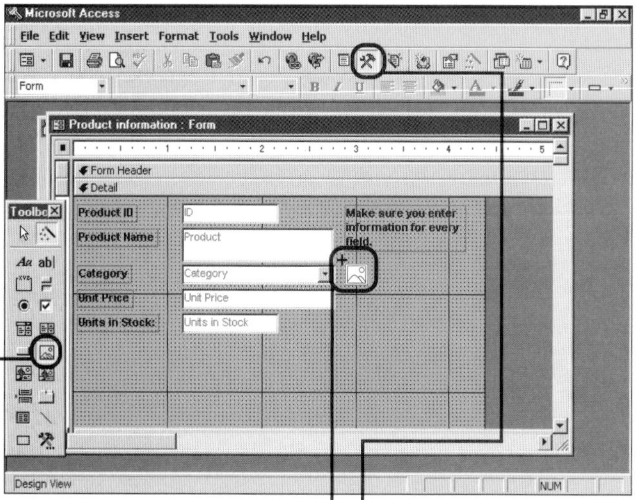

■ Display the form you want to change in the Design view. To do so, refer to page 148.

1 Click to add a picture to the form.

■ If is not available, click to display the **Toolbox** toolbar.

2 Click where you want the top left corner of the picture to appear on the form.

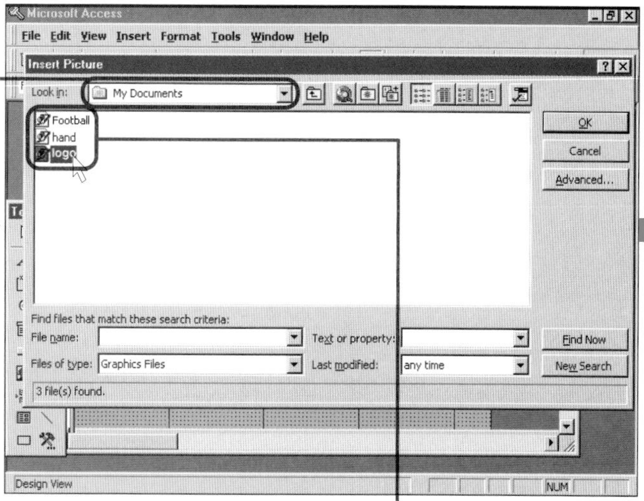

■ The **Insert Picture** dialog box appears.

■ This area shows the location of the displayed files.

3 Click the name of the picture you want to add.

Where can I get pictures to use in my forms?

You can use a drawing program to create your own pictures or use a scanner to scan pictures into your computer. You can also buy a collection of pictures, called clip art, at most computer stores. Many pages on the Web offer pictures you can use for free.

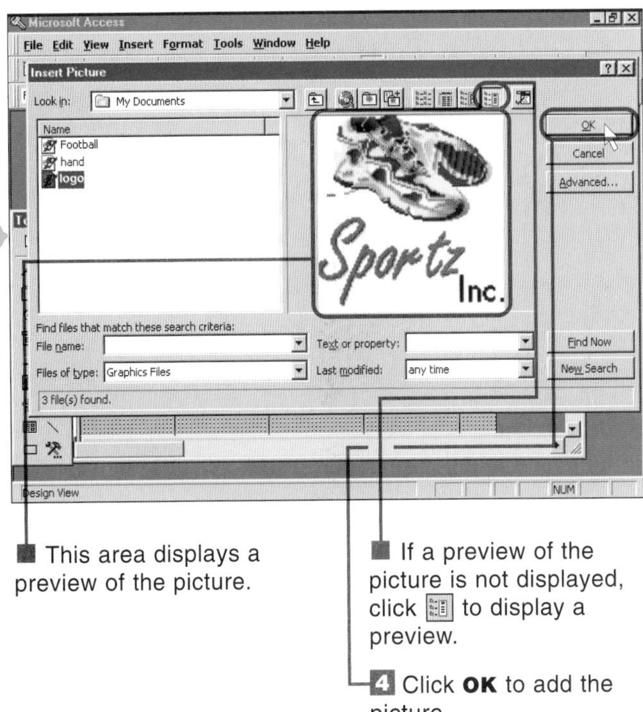

■ This area displays a preview of the picture.

■ If a preview of the picture is not displayed, click the Preview button to display a preview.

4 Click **OK** to add the picture.

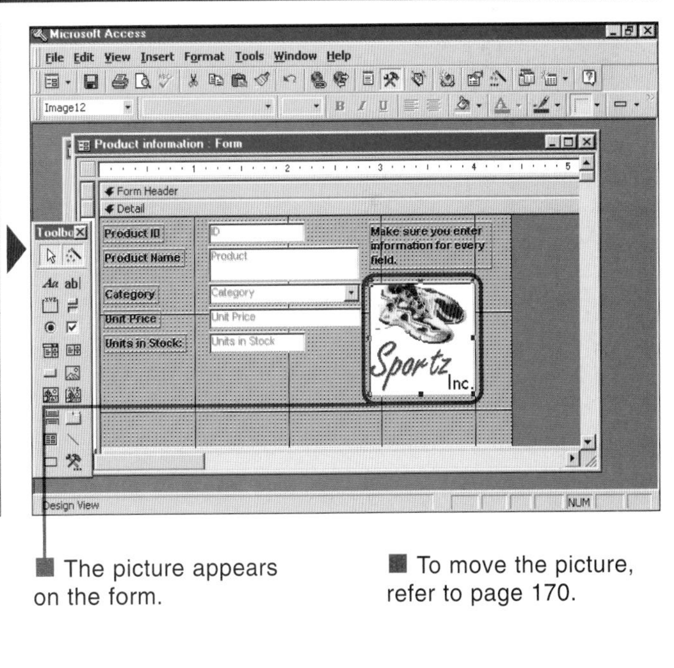

■ The picture appears on the form.

■ To move the picture, refer to page 170.

SSES - TABLE
First Name
Last Name
Address
City
State/Province
Postal Code
Addresses - Report
StateOrProvince
Last Name
Address ID
First Name
Address
City
Postal Code
ORDERS Table
Order ID
Company Name
Product
Quantity
Unit Price
F O R

Find Data

Do you want to learn how to search for and find data? This chapter teaches you how to find, replace and filter the data in your tables, forms and queries.

Find Data 186

Replace Data 188

Sort Records 190

Filter by Selection 192

Filter by Exclusion 194

Filter by Form 196

FIND DATA

You can search for records that contain specific information in your database.

Last Name
First Nam
Matheson
Smith
Inglis
Lemoine
Hyland
Mullin
Smith
Smyth
Kevin
Peter
Mike
Kelly
Adam

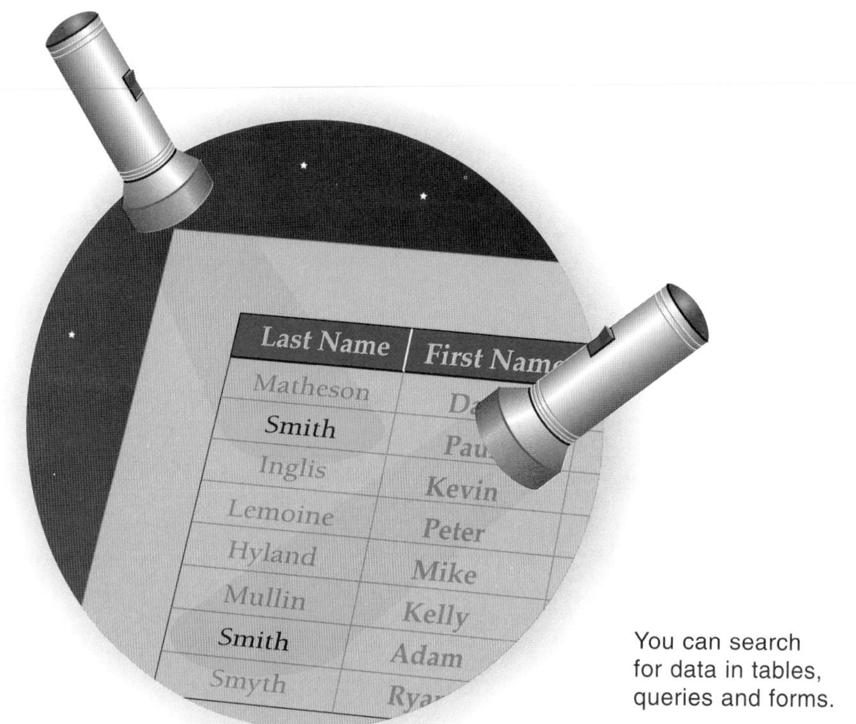

You can search for data in tables, queries and forms.

FIND DATA

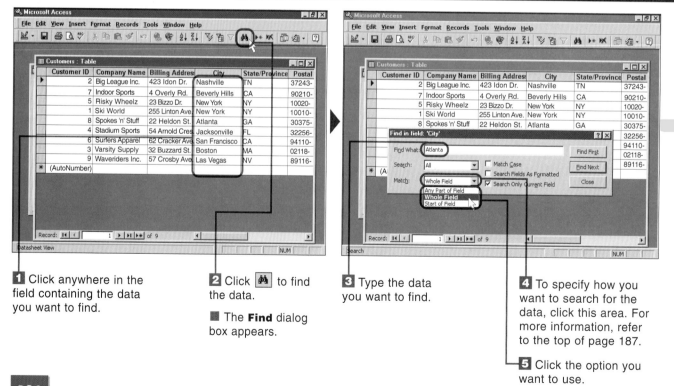

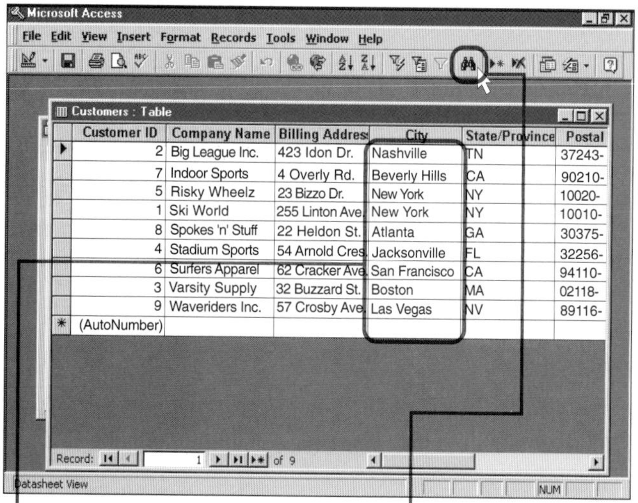

Microsoft Access
File Edit View Insert Format Records Tools Window Help
Customers : Table
Customer ID | Company Name | Billing Address | City | State/Province | Postal
2 | Big League Inc. | 423 Idon Dr. | Nashville | TN | 37243-
7 | Indoor Sports | 4 Overly Rd. | Beverly Hills | CA | 90210-
5 | Risky Wheelz | 23 Bizzo Dr. | New York | NY | 10020-
1 | Ski World | 255 Linton Ave. | New York | NY | 10010-
8 | Spokes 'n' Stuff | 22 Heldon St. | Atlanta | GA | 30375-
4 | Stadium Sports | 54 Arnold Cres. | Jacksonville | FL | 32256-
6 | Surfers Apparel | 62 Cracker Ave. | San Francisco | CA | 94110-
3 | Varsity Supply | 32 Buzzard St. | Boston | MA | 02118-
9 | Waveriders Inc. | 57 Crosby Ave. | Las Vegas | NV | 89116-
(AutoNumber)
Record: 1 of 9
Datasheet View
NUM

1 Click anywhere in the field containing the data you want to find.

2 Click 🔍 to find the data.

■ The **Find** dialog box appears.

Microsoft Access
File Edit View Insert Format Records Tools Window Help
Customers : Table
Find in field: 'City'
Find What: Atlanta
Search: All
Match: Whole Field
Any Part of Field
Whole Field
Start of Field
Match Case
Search Fields As Formatted
Search Only Current Field
Find First
Find Next
Close
Record: 1 of 9
Search
NUM

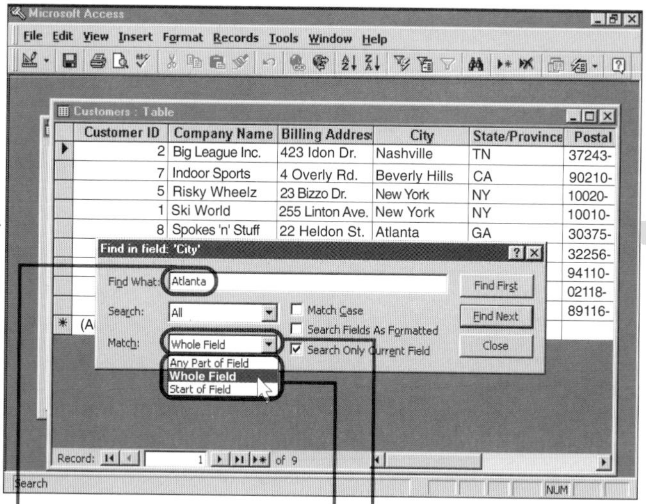

3 Type the data you want to find.

4 To specify how you want to search for the data, click this area. For more information, refer to the top of page 187.

5 Click the option you want to use.

How can Access search for data in a field?

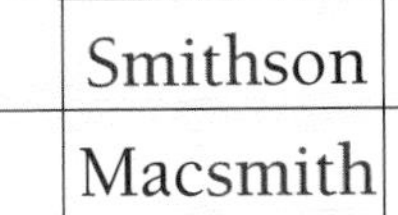

Any Part of Field

Finds data anywhere in the field. For example, **smith** finds **Smithson** and **Macsmith**.

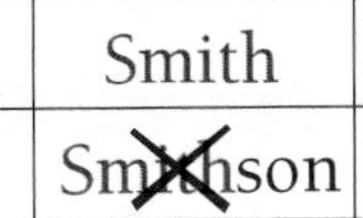

Whole Field

Finds data that is exactly the same. For example, **smith** finds **Smith**, but not **Smithson**.

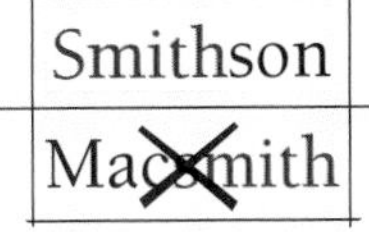

Start of Field

Finds data only at the beginning of the field. For example, **smith** finds **Smithson**, but not **Macsmith**.

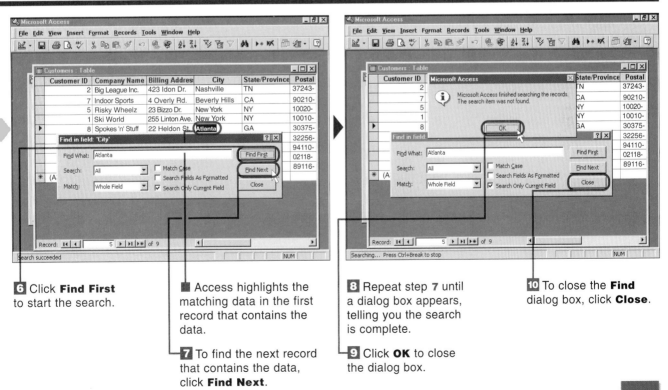

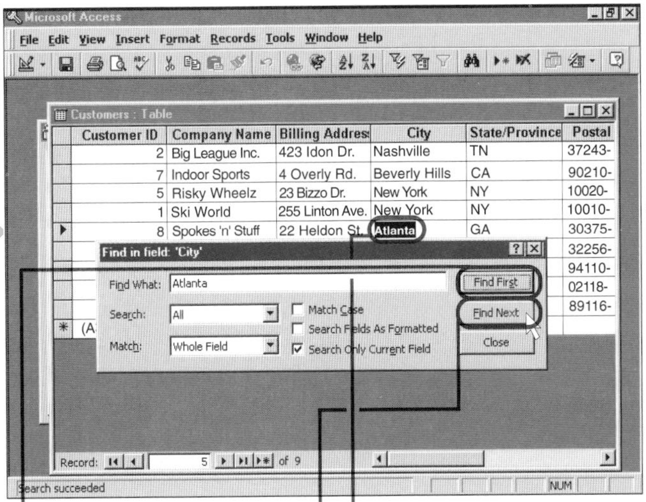

6 Click **Find First** to start the search.

■ Access highlights the matching data in the first record that contains the data.

7 To find the next record that contains the data, click **Find Next**.

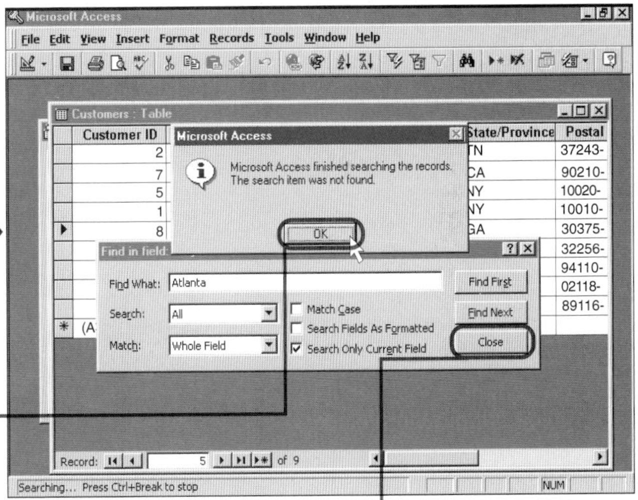

8 Repeat step **7** until a dialog box appears, telling you the search is complete.

9 Click **OK** to close the dialog box.

10 To close the **Find** dialog box, click **Close**.

REPLACE DATA

You can easily find and replace information in a table, form or query in your database. The Search and Replace feature is ideal when you want to make the same change to many records.

REPLACE DATA

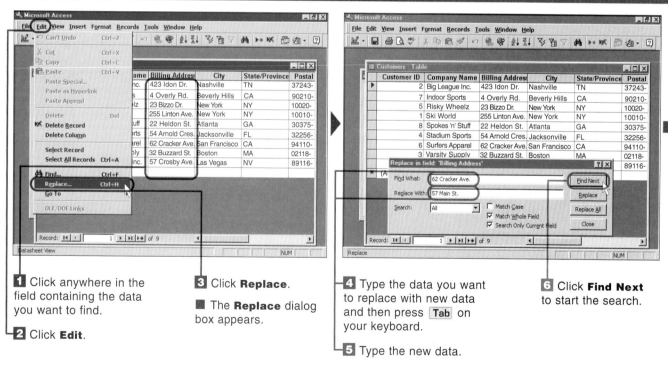

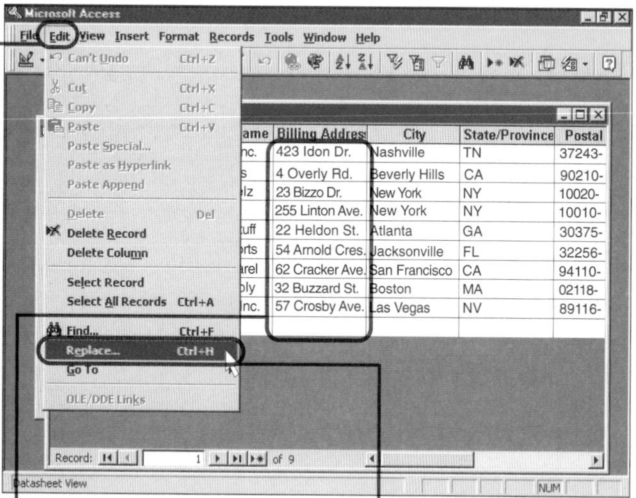

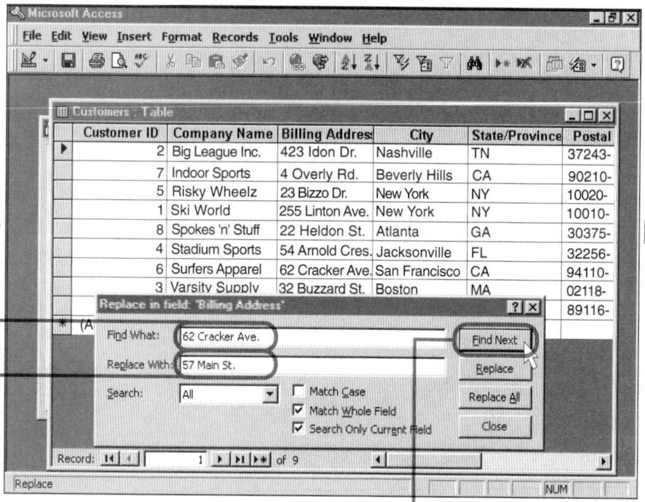

1 Click anywhere in the field containing the data you want to find.

2 Click **Edit**.

3 Click **Replace**.

■ The **Replace** dialog box appears.

4 Type the data you want to replace with new data and then press Tab on your keyboard.

5 Type the new data.

6 Click **Find Next** to start the search.

What options can I select in the Replace dialog box?

You can select one of the following options in the **Replace** dialog box.

Match Case

Find text with matching upper and lower case letters.

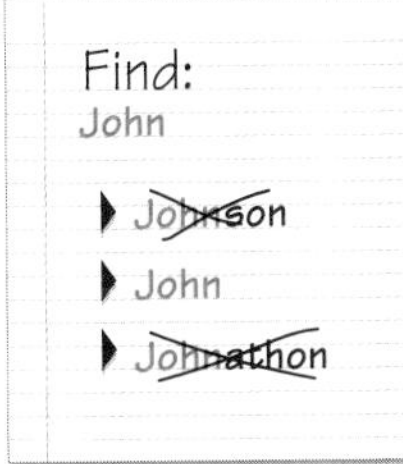

Match Whole Field

Find only whole words instead of text inside longer words.

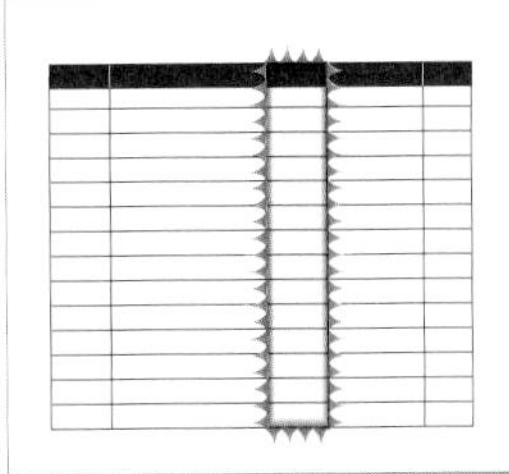

Search Only Current Field

Search only the current field instead of all the fields.

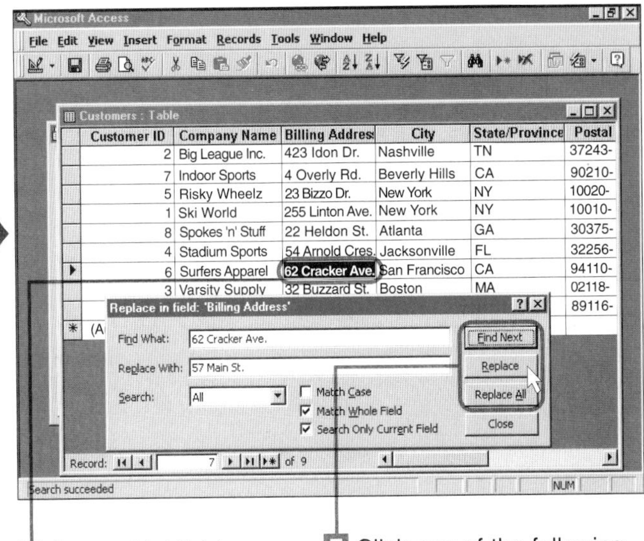

■ Access highlights the matching data in the first record that contains the data.

7 Click one of the following options.

Find Next - Find the next matching record.

Replace - Replace the data.

Replace All - Replace the data and all other matching data in the field.

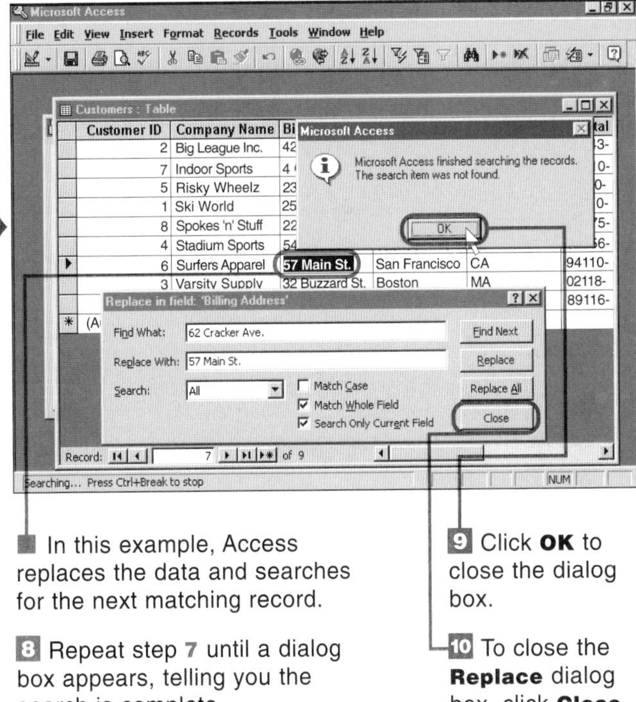

■ In this example, Access replaces the data and searches for the next matching record.

8 Repeat step 7 until a dialog box appears, telling you the search is complete.

*Note: You can click **Close** at any time to end the search.*

9 Click **OK** to close the dialog box.

10 To close the **Replace** dialog box, click **Close**.

SORT RECORDS

You can change the order of records in a table, query or form to help you find and analyze information.

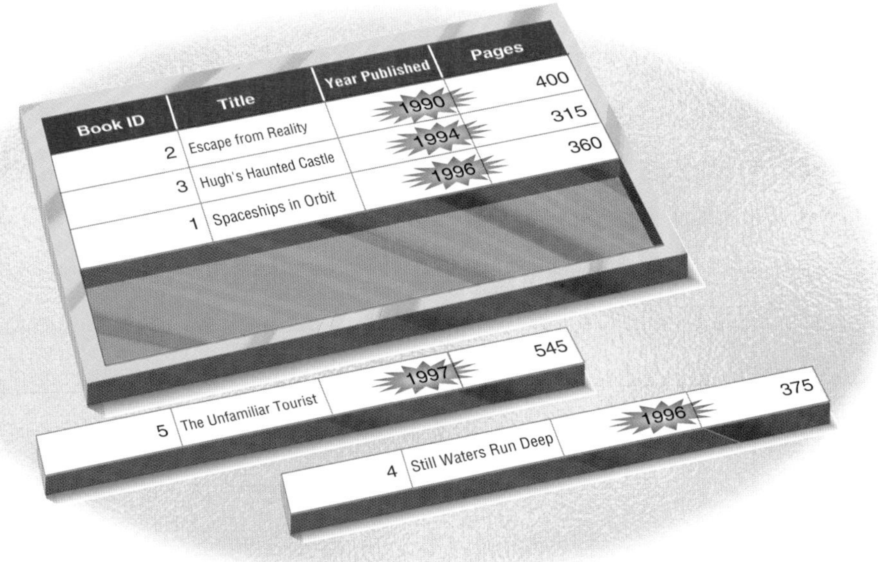

SORT RECORDS

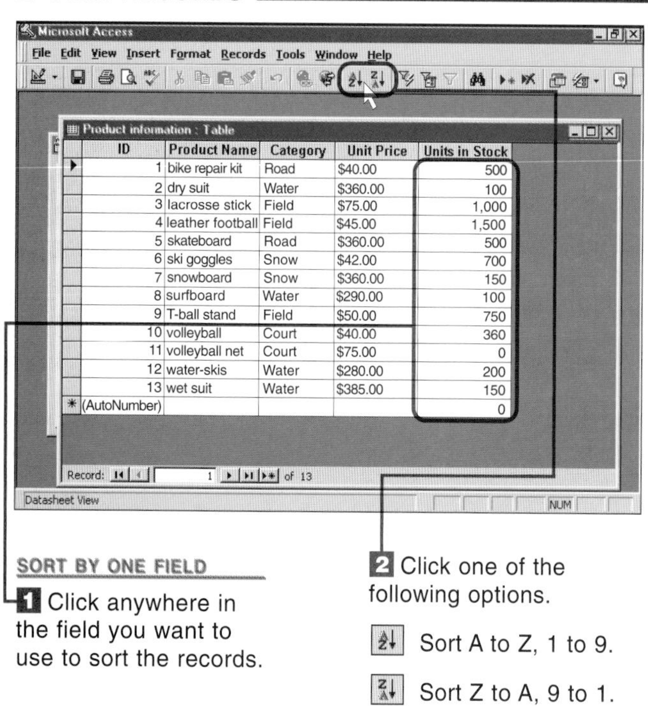

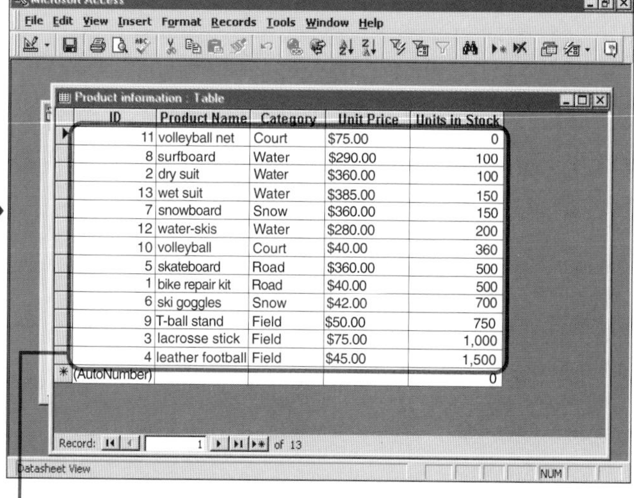

SORT BY ONE FIELD

1 Click anywhere in the field you want to use to sort the records.

2 Click one of the following options.

Sort A to Z, 1 to 9.

Sort Z to A, 9 to 1.

■ The records appear in the new order. In this example, the records are sorted by the number of units in stock.

■ When you save the table, query or form, Access saves the sort order.

?

How do I remove a sort from my records?

Access stores your records in primary key order on your computer. Sorting changes the order that the records are displayed on your screen, but does not change the order they are stored on your computer. If you no longer want to display your records in the sort order you specified, you can return your records to primary key order at any time.

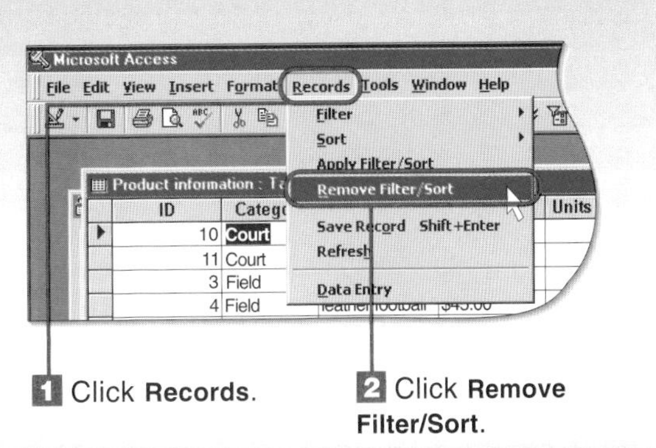

1 Click **Records**.

2 Click **Remove Filter/Sort**.

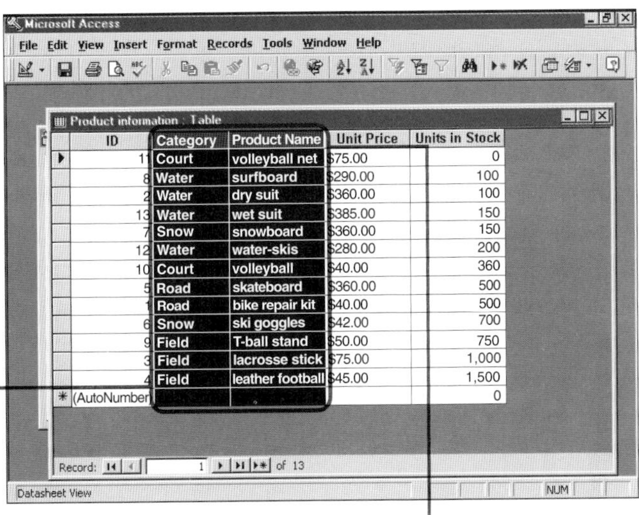

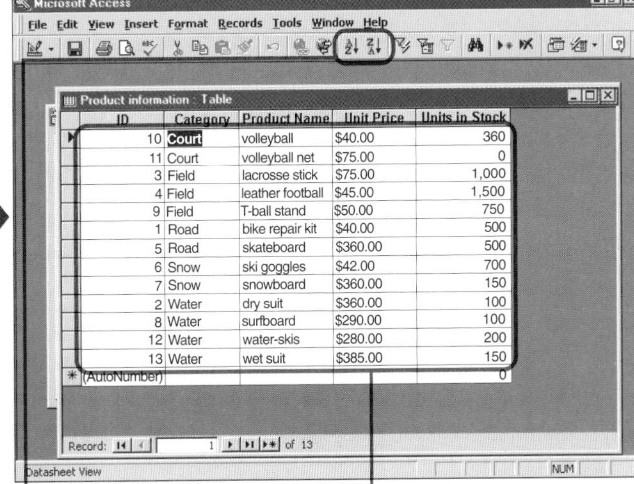

SORT BY TWO FIELDS

1 Place the fields you want to use to sort the records side-by-side. Make sure the fields appear in the order you want to sort. To rearrange fields, refer to page 41.

Note: In this example, the Category field was placed before the Product Name field.

2 Position the mouse ⬇ over the first field you want to use to sort the records. Then drag the mouse ⬇ until you highlight the second field.

3 Click one of the following options.

- Sort A to Z, 1 to 9.
- Sort Z to A, 9 to 1.

■ The records appear in the new order. In this example, the records are sorted by category. All records with the same category are also sorted by product name.

FILTER BY SELECTION

You can filter records in a table, form or query to display only specific records. Filters can help you review and analyze information in your database by temporarily hiding information not currently of interest.

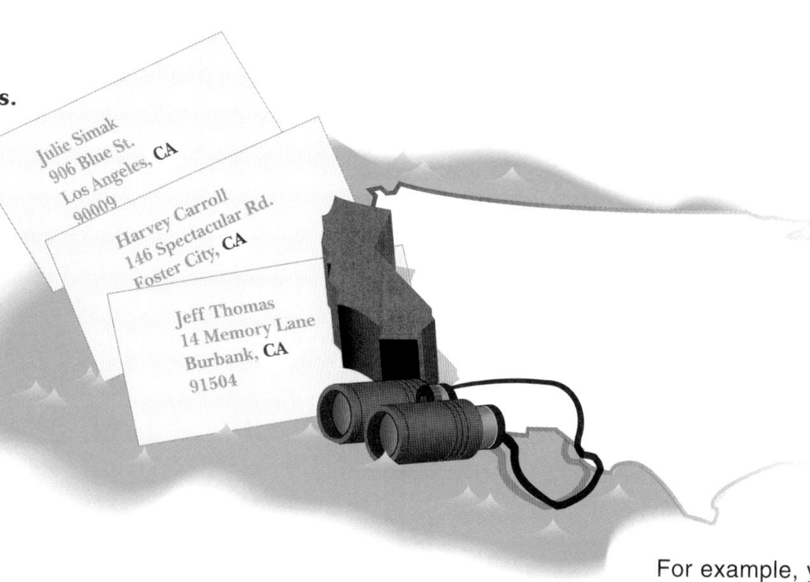

For example, you can display only the records for the clients who live in California.

FILTER BY SELECTION

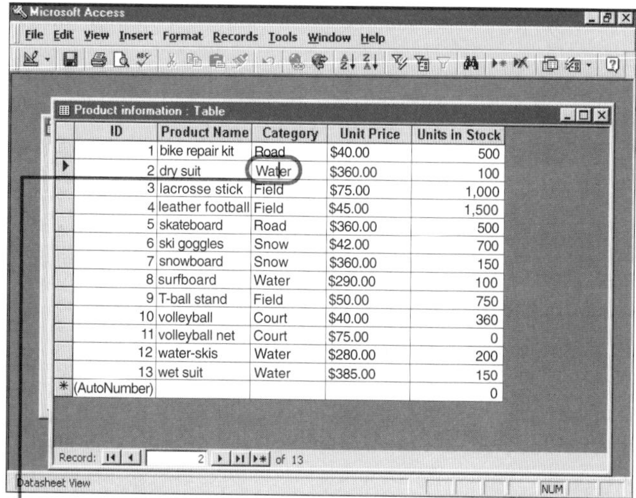

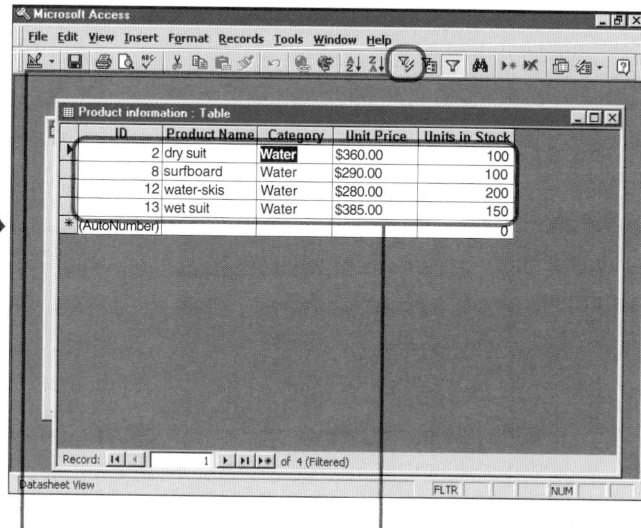

1 Click the data you want to use to filter the records. Access will find all records that contain exactly the same data.

■ You can change the way Access searches for data by dragging the mouse I to select the data you want to find. For more information, refer to the top of page 193.

2 Click [Filter By Selection button] to filter the records.

■ Access displays all the records containing matching data. All other records are hidden.

Can I change the way Access searches for data?

How you select the data determines which records Access will find.

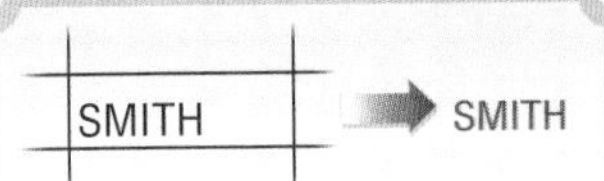

If you do not select any data, Access will find data that exactly matches. For example, **Smith** finds only **Smith**.

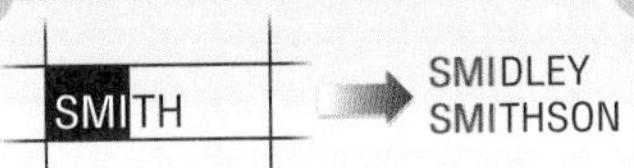

If you select part of the data starting with the first character, Access will find data that starts with the same characters. For example, **Smi**th finds **Smi**dley and **Smi**thson.

If you select part of the data after the first character, Access will find data containing the selected characters. For example, Smith**son** finds **Son**y and Ron**son**ville.

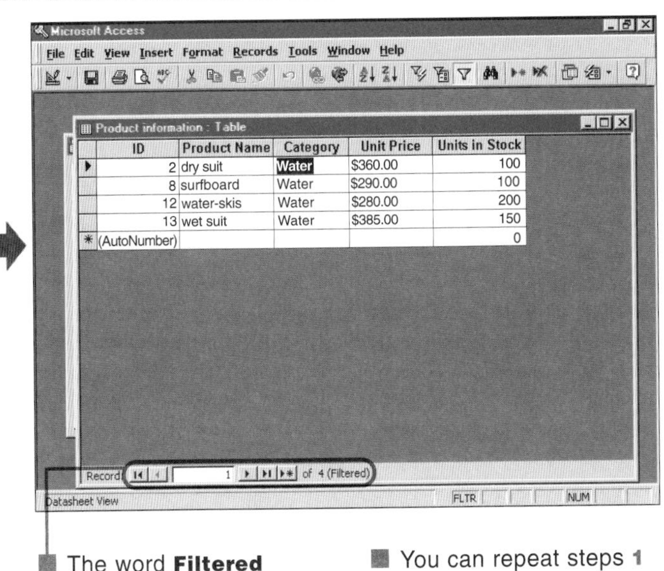

■ The word **Filtered** appears in this area to indicate that you are looking at a filtered view of the data.

■ You can repeat steps **1** and **2** to further filter the records.

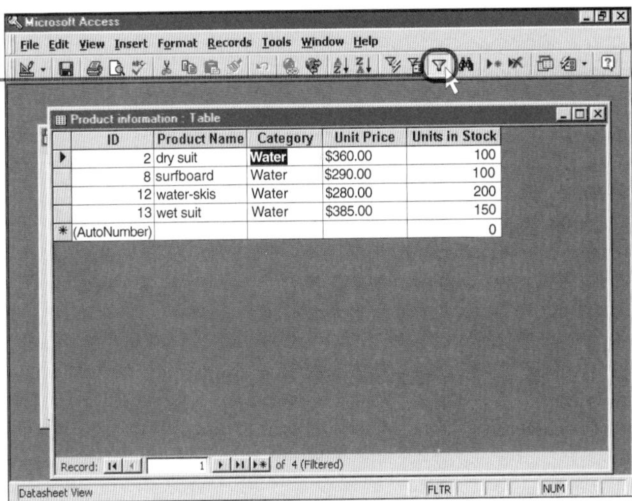

REMOVE THE FILTER

1 To once again display all the records, click [filter icon].

FILTER BY EXCLUSION

You can have Access temporarily hide records that contain specific information in a table, form or query.

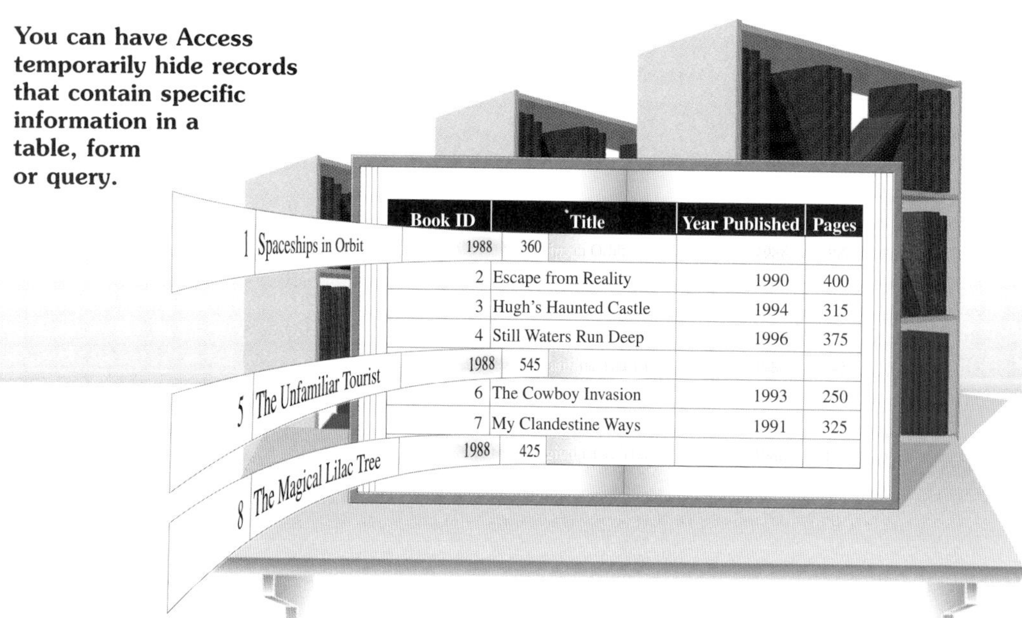

Book ID
Title
Year Published
Pages
1 Spaceships in Orbit
1988 360
2 Escape from Reality 1990 400
3 Hugh's Haunted Castle 1994 315
4 Still Waters Run Deep 1996 375
5 The Unfamiliar Tourist
1988 545
6 The Cowboy Invasion 1993 250
7 My Clandestine Ways 1991 325
8 The Magical Lilac Tree
1988 425

For example, you can have Access exclude the records for all books published in 1988.

FILTER BY EXCLUSION

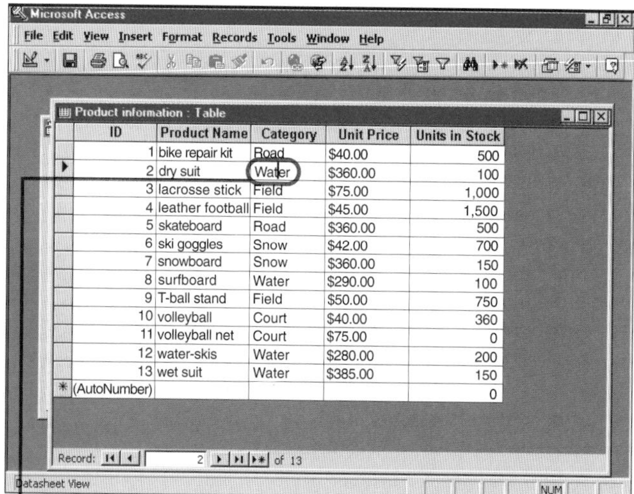

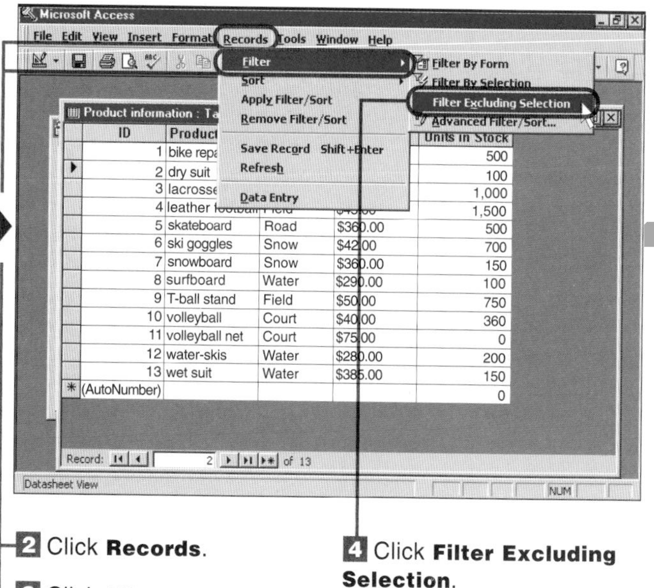

1 Click the data you want to use to filter the records. Access will hide all records that contain exactly the same data.

■ You can change the way Access searches for data by dragging the mouse I to select the data you want to exclude. For more information, refer to the top of page 195.

2 Click **Records**.

3 Click **Filter**.

4 Click **Filter Excluding Selection**.

Can I change the way Access searches for data?

How you select the data determines which records Access will hide.

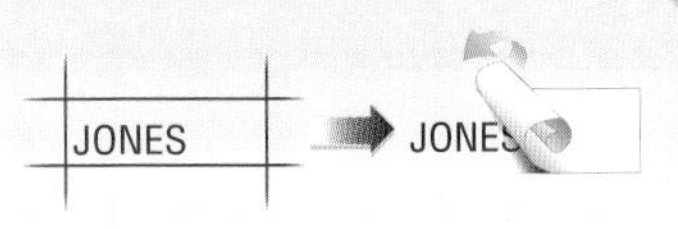

If you do not select any data, Access will hide data that exactly matches. For example, **Jones** hides only **Jones**.

If you select part of the data starting with the first character, Access will hide data that starts with the same characters. For example, **Jon**es hides **Jon**asson and **Jon**son.

If you select part of the data after the first character, Access will hide data containing the selected characters. For example, Gr**ant** hides **Ant**hony and Pl**ant**er.

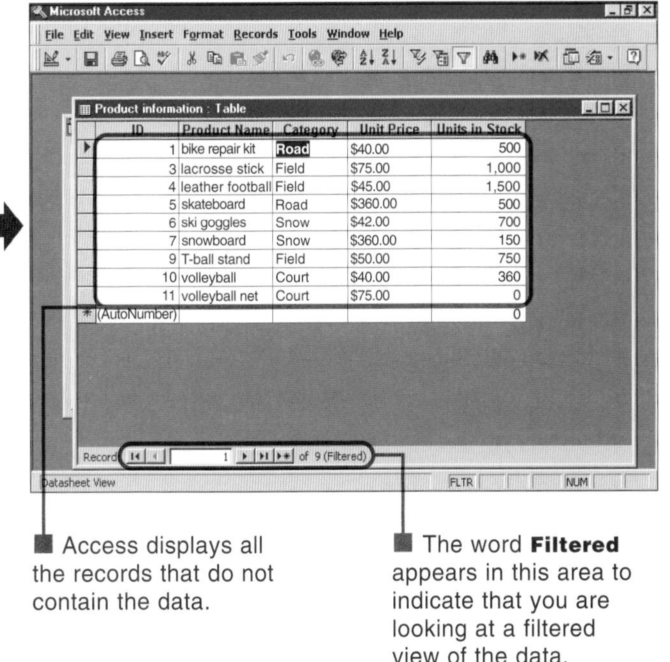

■ Access displays all the records that do not contain the data.

■ The word **Filtered** appears in this area to indicate that you are looking at a filtered view of the data.

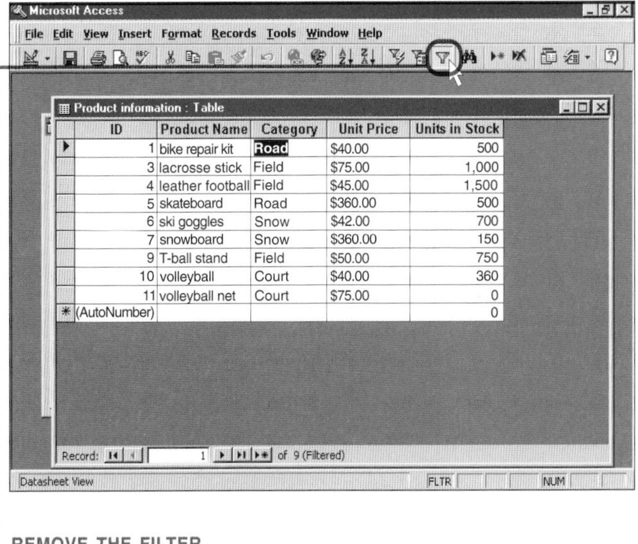

REMOVE THE FILTER

1 To once again display all the records, click [Remove Filter].

FILTER BY FORM

You can use the Filter by Form feature to perform powerful searches of a table, form or query in your database. This feature allows you to specify conditions that data must meet to be displayed.

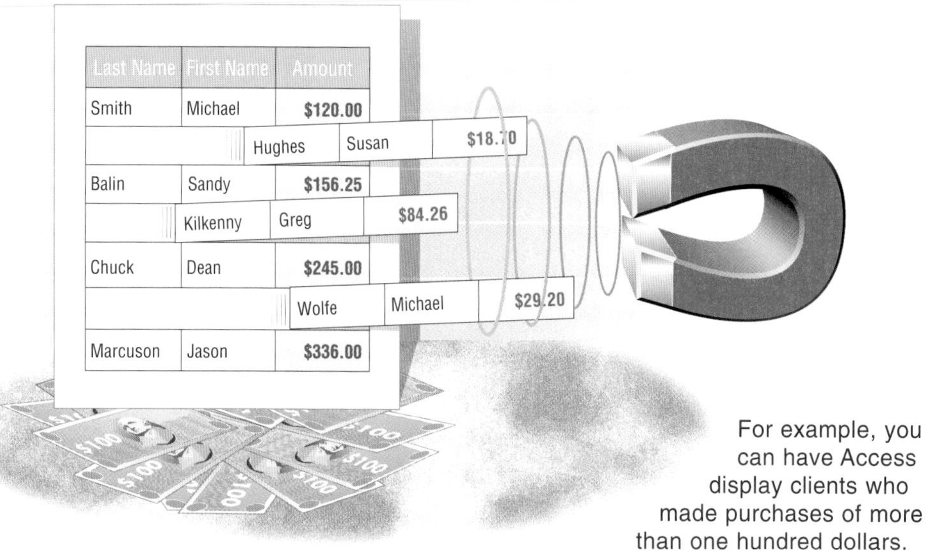

For example, you can have Access display clients who made purchases of more than one hundred dollars.

FILTER BY FORM (USING ONE CONDITION)

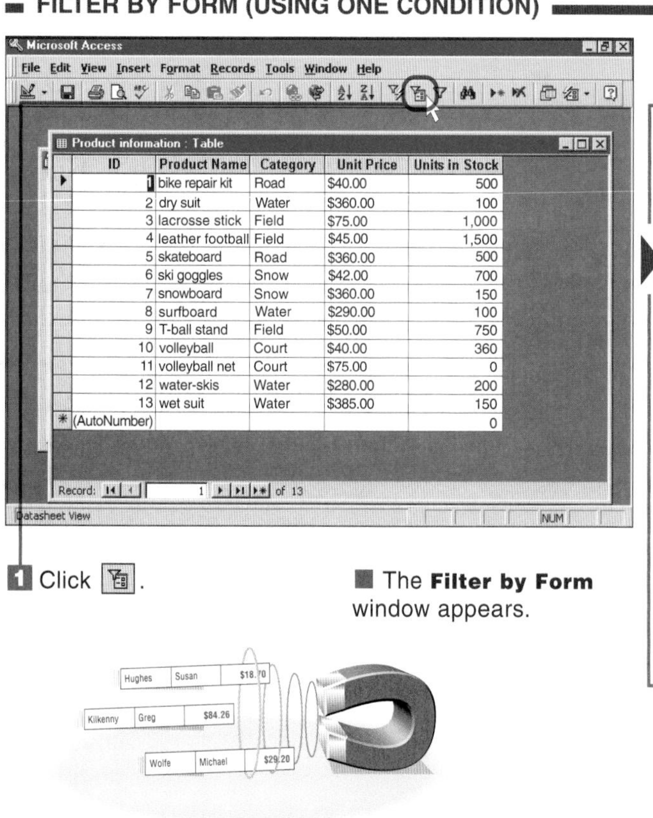

ID	Product Name	Category	Unit Price	Units in Stock
1	bike repair kit	Road	$40.00	500
2	dry suit	Water	$360.00	100
3	lacrosse stick	Field	$75.00	1,000
4	leather football	Field	$45.00	1,500
5	skateboard	Road	$360.00	500
6	ski goggles	Snow	$42.00	700
7	snowboard	Snow	$360.00	150
8	surfboard	Water	$290.00	100
9	T-ball stand	Field	$50.00	750
10	volleyball	Court	$40.00	360
11	volleyball net	Court	$75.00	0
12	water-skis	Water	$280.00	200
13	wet suit	Water	$385.00	150
(AutoNumber)				0

1 Click the Filter by Form button.

■ The **Filter by Form** window appears.

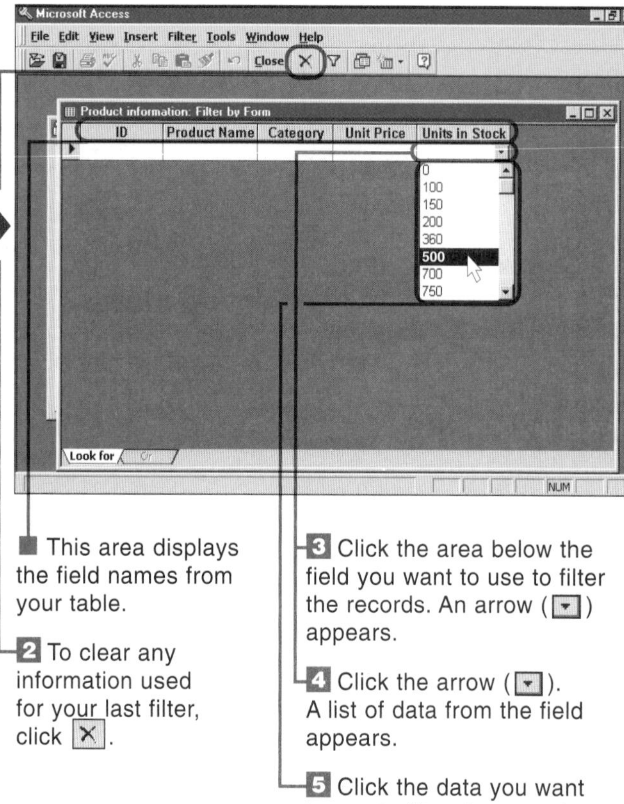

■ This area displays the field names from your table.

2 To clear any information used for your last filter, click the Clear Grid button (X).

3 Click the area below the field you want to use to filter the records. An arrow (▾) appears.

4 Click the arrow (▾). A list of data from the field appears.

5 Click the data you want to use to filter the records.

?

What conditions can I use?

Here are some examples of conditions that you can use to help narrow which records Access finds. For more examples, refer to pages 210 to 211.

Condition	Description
<1000	Must be less than 1000.
<M	Must begin with a letter before M.
>1000	Must be greater than 1000.
>M	Must begin with a letter after M.
<>California	Must not be California.
Between 100 and 200	Must be between 100 and 200.
Mar*	Must start with Mar, followed by any number of characters.
Mar???	Must start with Mar, followed by any 3 characters.
mar	Must contain the letters "mar".

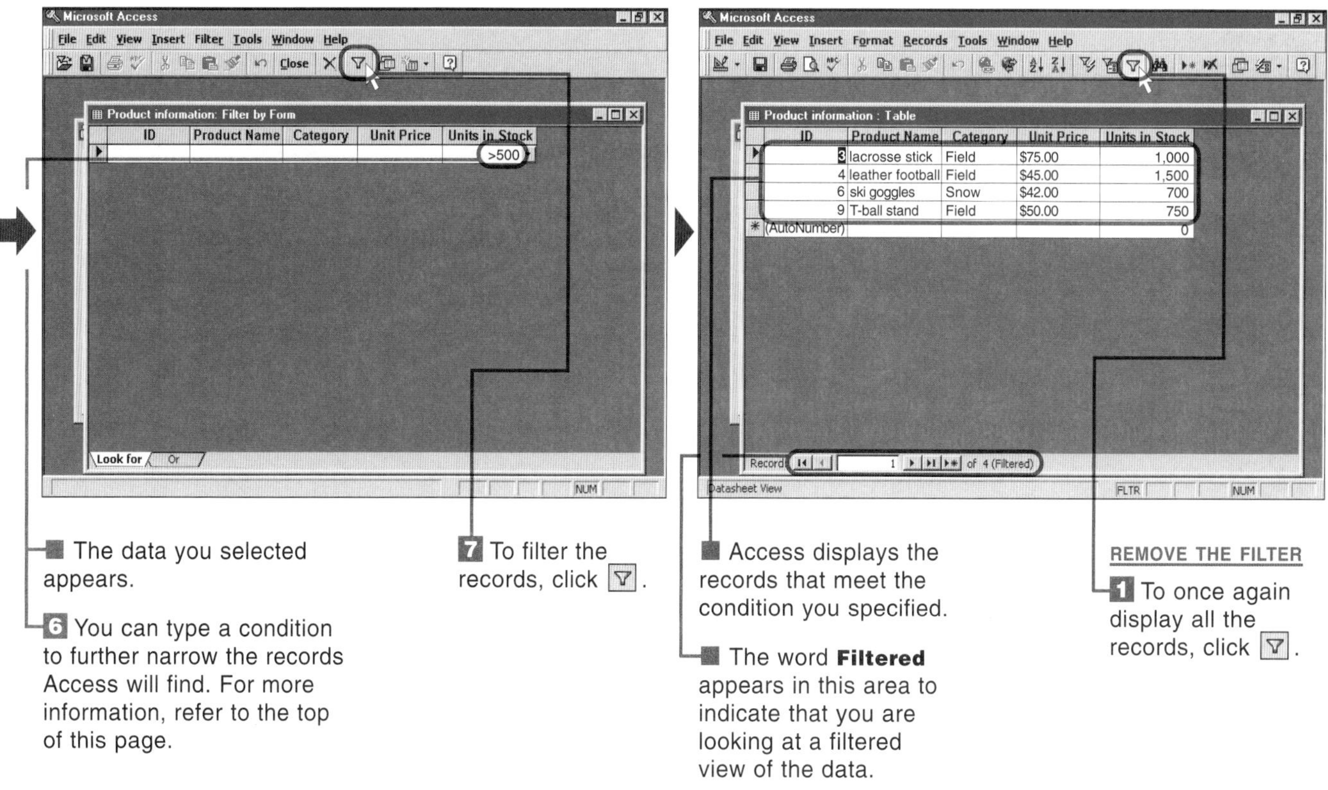

■ The data you selected appears.

6 You can type a condition to further narrow the records Access will find. For more information, refer to the top of this page.

7 To filter the records, click [filter icon].

■ Access displays the records that meet the condition you specified.

■ The word **Filtered** appears in this area to indicate that you are looking at a filtered view of the data.

REMOVE THE FILTER

1 To once again display all the records, click [filter icon].

FILTER BY FORM

You can use more than one condition to filter your records. Filtering your records allows you to quickly find and display records of interest in your database.

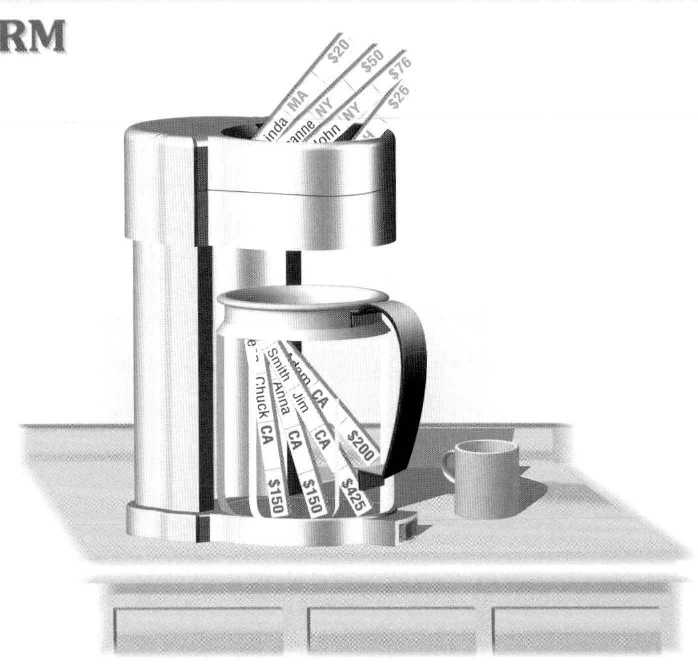

For example, you can have Access find clients living in California who made purchases of more than one hundred dollars.

FILTER BY FORM (USING MULTIPLE CONDITIONS)

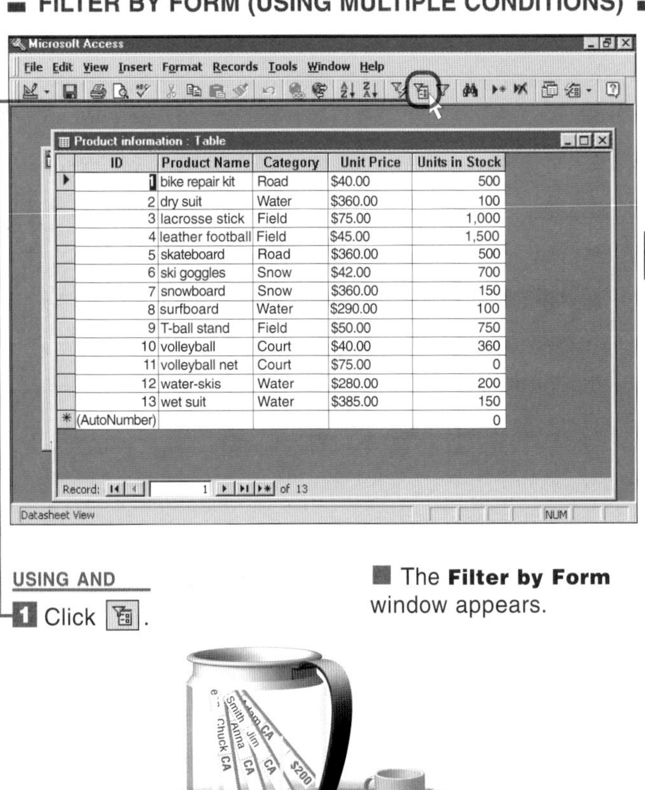

ID	Product Name	Category	Unit Price	Units in Stock
1	bike repair kit	Road	$40.00	500
2	dry suit	Water	$360.00	100
3	lacrosse stick	Field	$75.00	1,000
4	leather football	Field	$45.00	1,500
5	skateboard	Road	$360.00	500
6	ski goggles	Snow	$42.00	700
7	snowboard	Snow	$360.00	150
8	surfboard	Water	$290.00	100
9	T-ball stand	Field	$50.00	750
10	volleyball	Court	$40.00	360
11	volleyball net	Court	$75.00	0
12	water-skis	Water	$280.00	200
13	wet suit	Water	$385.00	150
(AutoNumber)				0

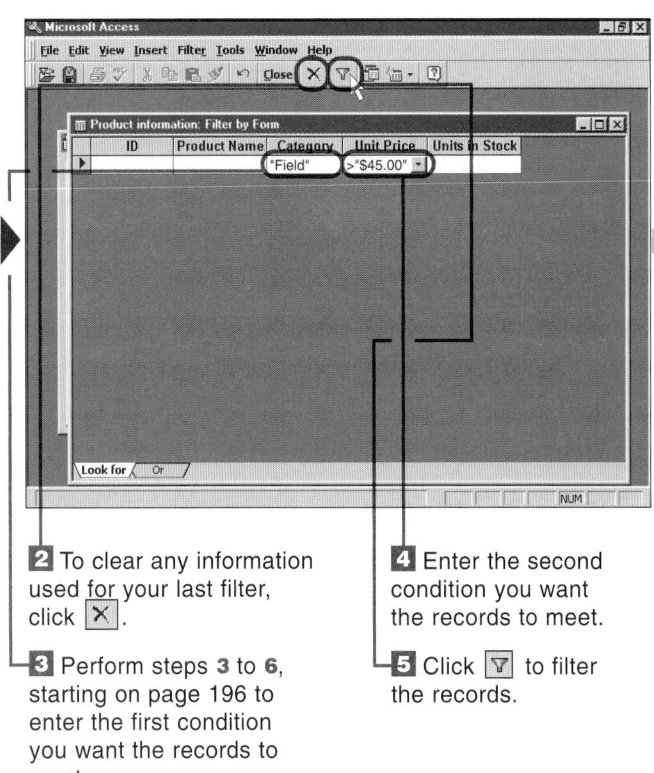

USING AND

1 Click .

■ The **Filter by Form** window appears.

2 To clear any information used for your last filter, click .

3 Perform steps **3** to **6**, starting on page 196 to enter the first condition you want the records to meet.

4 Enter the second condition you want the records to meet.

5 Click to filter the records.

? How can I use multiple conditions to find data?

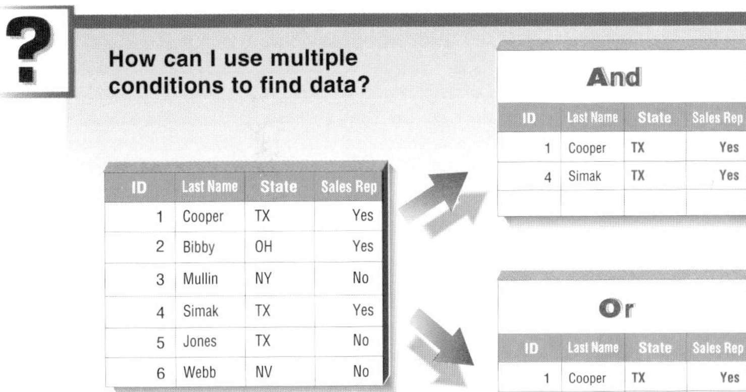

And

Access will display records that meet all of the conditions you specify. For example, you can find the names of all sales representatives living in Texas.

Or

Access will display records that meet at least one of the conditions you specify. For example, you can find the names of all sales representatives in the company as well as all employees living in Texas.

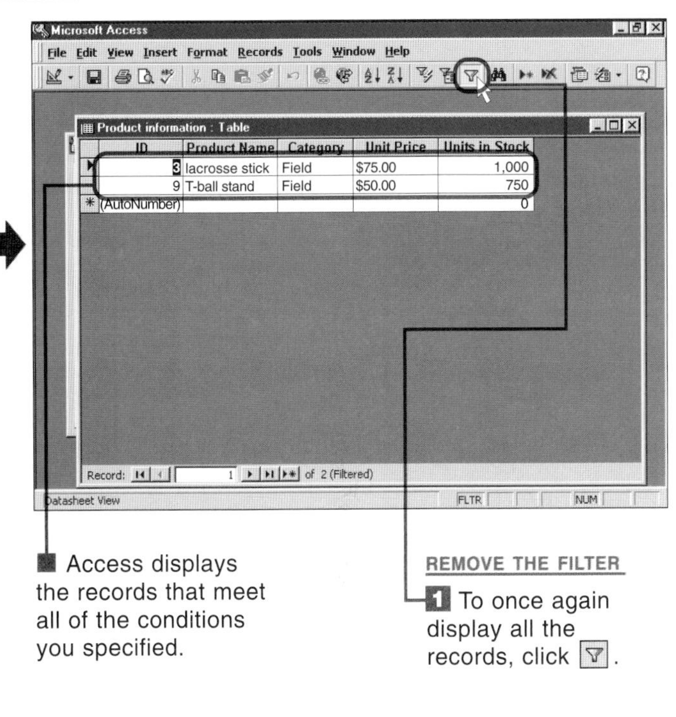

■ Access displays the records that meet all of the conditions you specified.

REMOVE THE FILTER

1 To once again display all the records, click [filter icon].

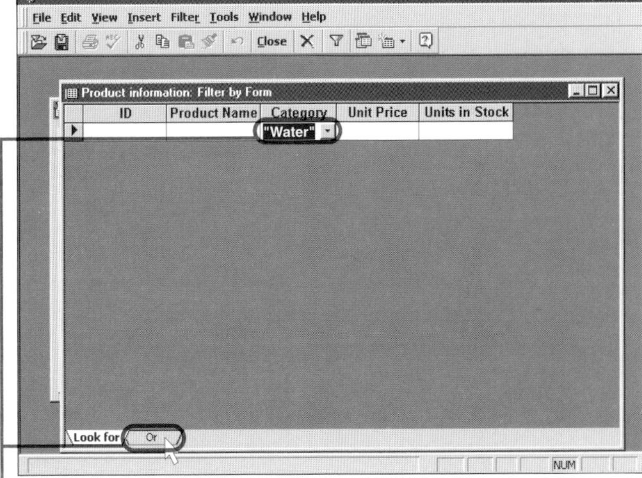

USING OR

1 Perform steps **1** to **6** on page 196 to enter the first condition you want the records to meet.

2 Click the **Or** tab. A blank row appears where you can enter the second condition.

3 Enter the second condition you want the records to meet.

4 Click [filter icon] to filter the records.

■ Access will display the records that meet one of the conditions you specified.

Which clients live in Florida?
Client ID
Last Name
State
5
Brady
Florida
6
Robertson
Florida
9
Walsh
Florida
14
Salinger
Florida

Create Queries

Are you ready to create queries? This chapter teaches you how to create a query to find information of interest in your database.

Create a Query 202

Change View of Query 206

Sort the Records 208

Set Criteria 209

Examples of Criteria 210

Delete a Field 212

Hide a Field 213

Rearrange Fields 214

Clear the Grid 215

Select All Fields 216

Close a Query 218

Open a Query 219

Rename a Query 220

Delete a Query 221

Using the Simple Query Wizard 222

CREATE A QUERY

You can create a query to find information of interest to you in your database.

Which wines were made before 1965?

When you create a query, you ask Access to find information that meets certain criteria or conditions.

CREATE A QUERY

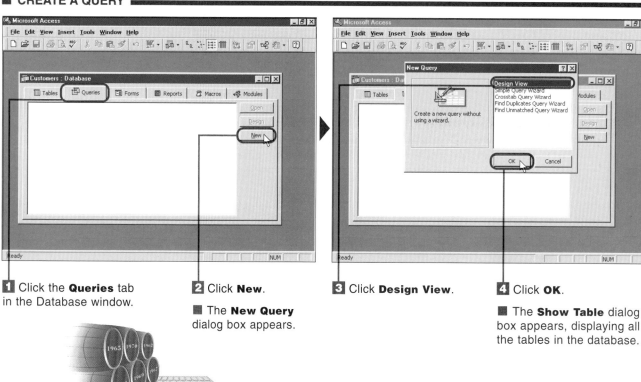

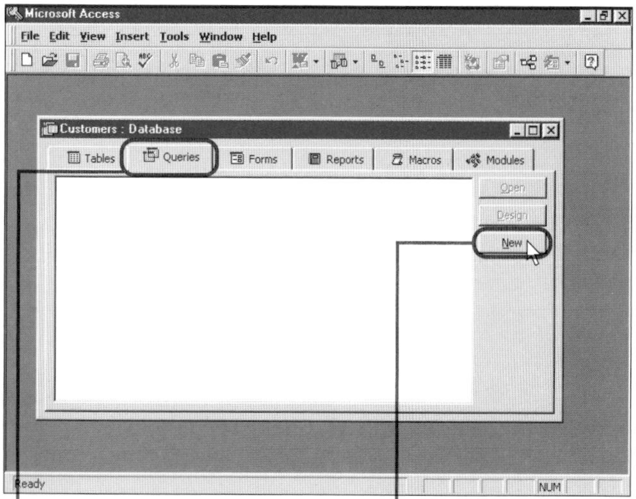

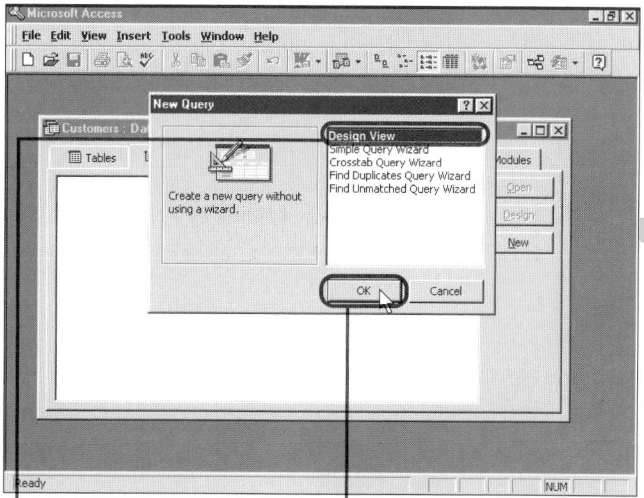

1 Click the **Queries** tab in the Database window.

2 Click **New**.

■ The **New Query** dialog box appears.

3 Click **Design View**.

4 Click **OK**.

■ The **Show Table** dialog box appears, displaying all the tables in the database.

?

Can I later add another table to the query?

You can click [Show Table button] at any time to redisplay the **Show Table** dialog box and add another table to the query.

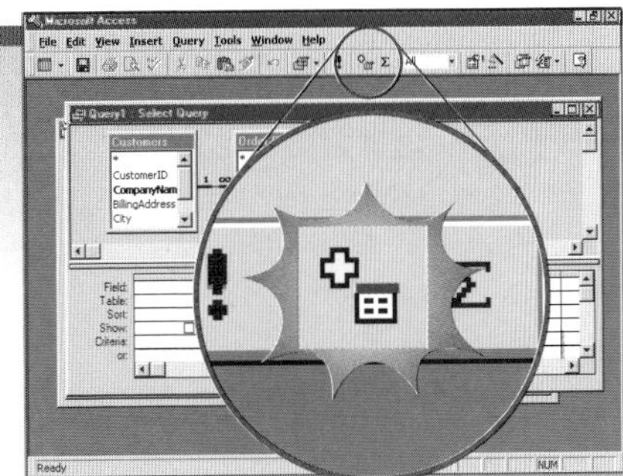

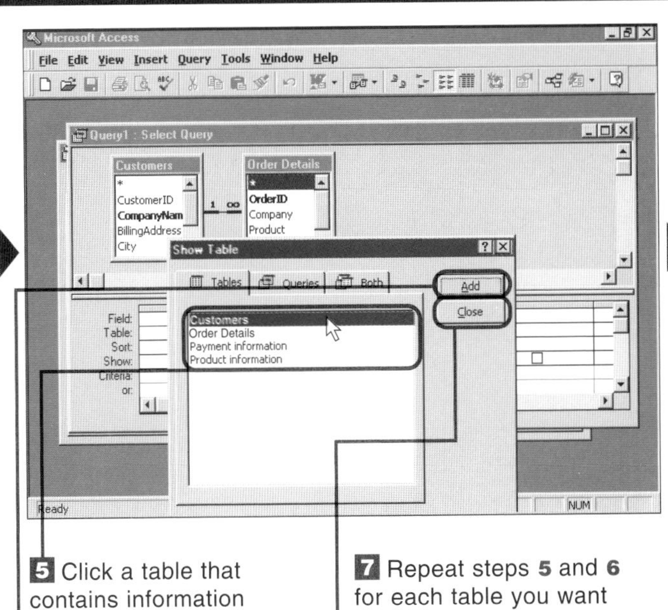

5 Click a table that contains information you want to use in the query.

6 Click **Add** to add the table to the query.

7 Repeat steps **5** and **6** for each table you want to use in the query. In this example, the Order Details table was selected.

8 Click **Close** to hide the **Show Table** dialog box.

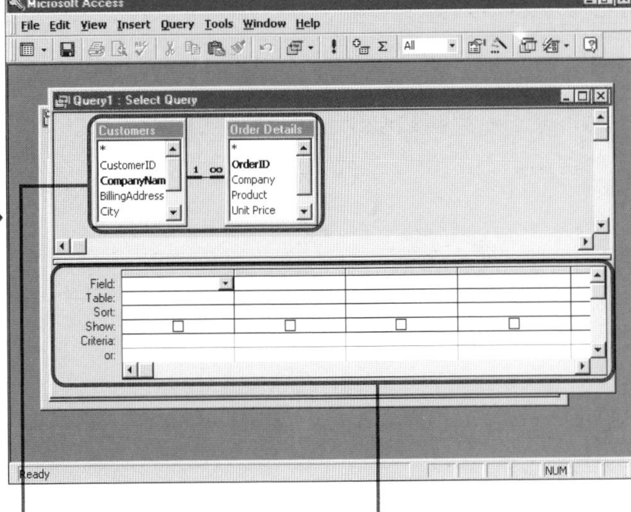

■ Each box in the **Select Query** window displays the fields from one table you added.

Note: If the tables you selected are related, Access displays a line joining the related fields. For information on relationships, refer to page 138.

■ You use this area to specify which records you want to find.

CONTINUED

You can select which fields you want to appear in the results of the query.

For example, you may want to display only the name and phone number of each client.

CREATE A QUERY (CONTINUED)

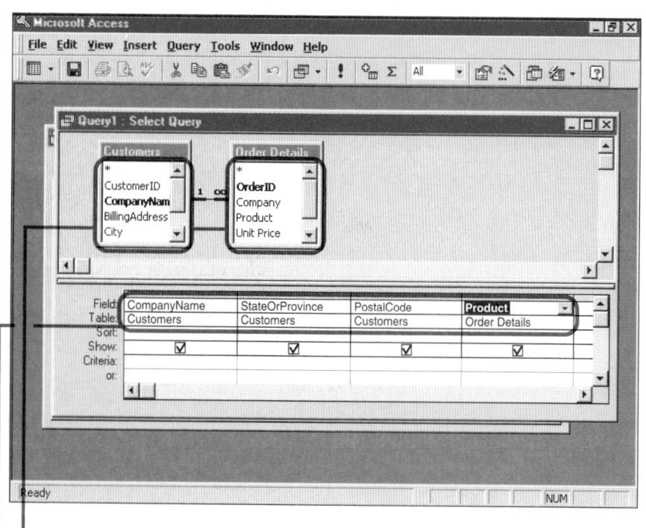

9 Double-click a field you want to include in the query.

■ This area displays the field you selected and the table that contains the field.

10 Repeat step **9** for each field you want to include.

Note: To quickly select all the fields in the table, refer to page 216.

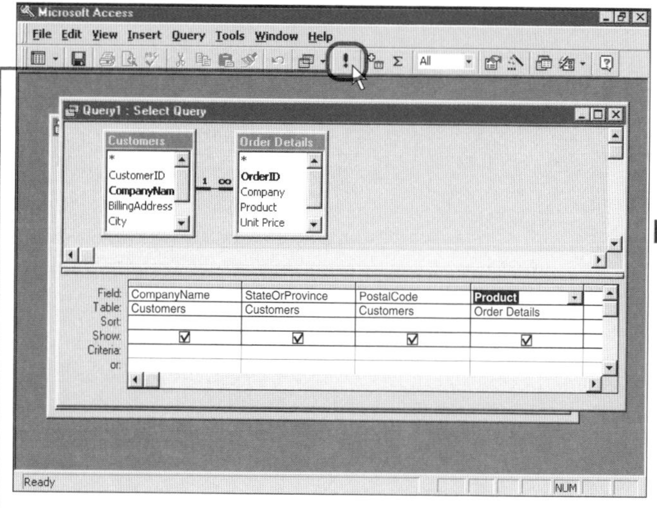

RUN THE QUERY

1 Click ! to run the query.

■ The results of the query appear.

Does a query store data?

A query gathers information from a table to answer a question you specify. When you save a query, the query does not store any data. The query stores the question so you can ask the same question again and again. For example, you can run the same query each week to display the names of the top sales reps for the week.

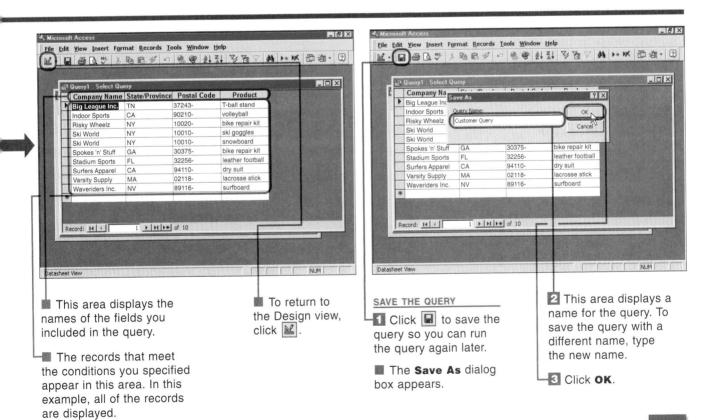

■ This area displays the names of the fields you included in the query.

■ The records that meet the conditions you specified appear in this area. In this example, all of the records are displayed.

■ To return to the Design view, click .

SAVE THE QUERY

1 Click to save the query so you can run the query again later.

■ The **Save As** dialog box appears.

2 This area displays a name for the query. To save the query with a different name, type the new name.

3 Click **OK**.

CHANGE VIEW OF QUERY

There are three ways you can view a query. Each view allows you to perform a different task.

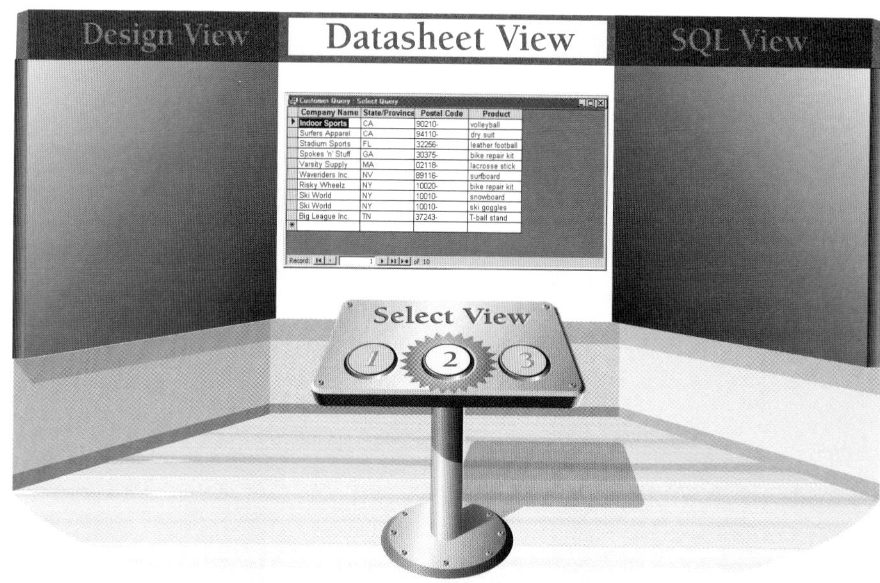

CHANGE VIEW OF QUERY

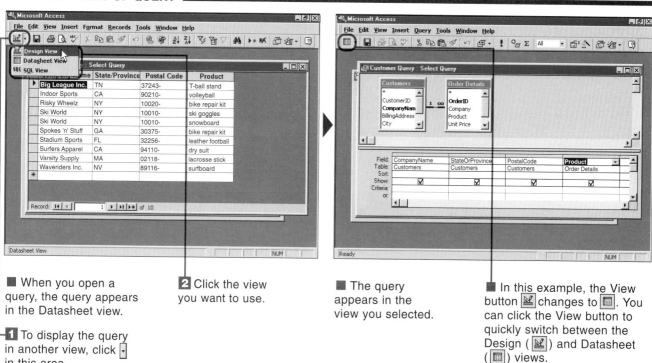

■ When you open a query, the query appears in the Datasheet view.

1 To display the query in another view, click ▾ in this area.

2 Click the view you want to use.

■ The query appears in the view you selected.

■ In this example, the View button (Design) changes to (Datasheet). You can click the View button to quickly switch between the Design ( ) and Datasheet ( ) views.

THE QUERY VIEWS

Design View

The Design view allows you to plan your query.

You use this view to tell Access what data you want to find, where Access can find the data and how you want to display the results.

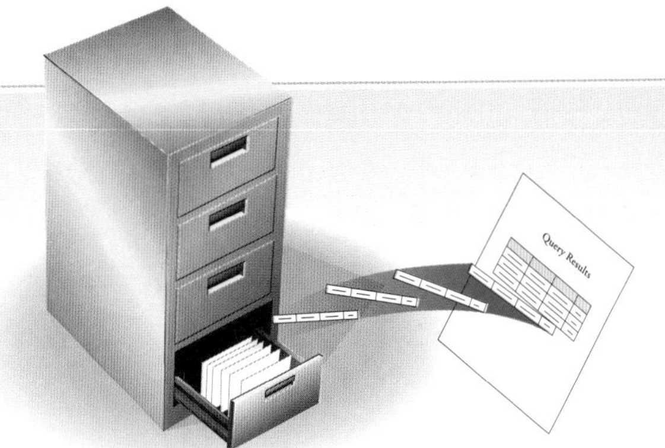

Datasheet View

The Datasheet view displays the results of the query. The field names appear across the top of the window.

Each row shows the information for one record that matches the information you are looking for.

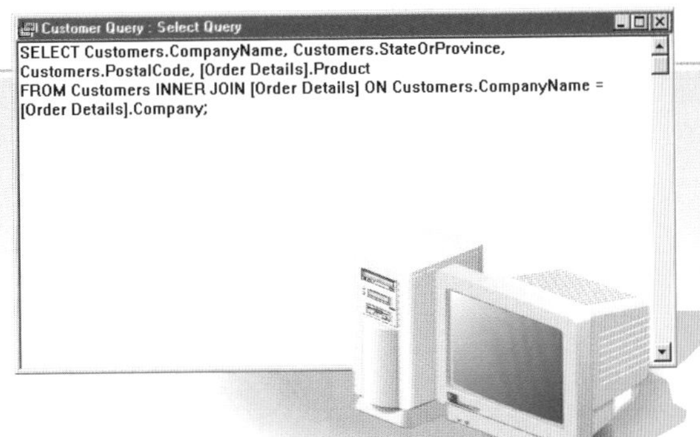

SQL View

Structured Query Language (SQL, pronounced "sequel") is a computer language. When you create a query, Access creates the SQL statements that describe your query.

The SQL view displays the SQL statements for the current query. You do not need to use this view to effectively use Access.

SORT THE RECORDS

You can sort the results of a query to help you find information of interest quicker.

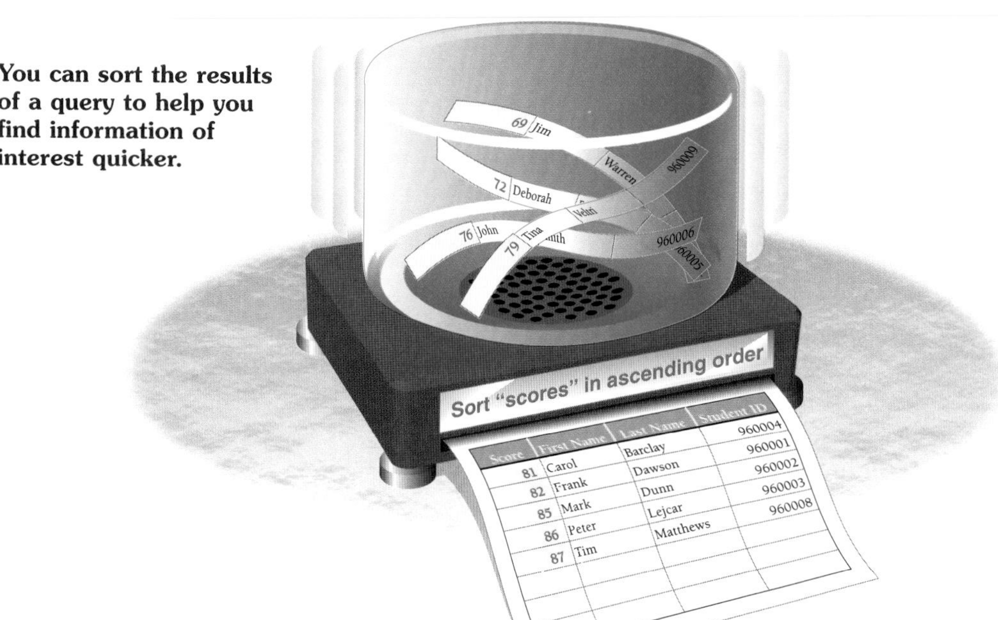

There are two ways you can sort data.

Sort Ascending
Sorts A to Z, 1 to 9

Sort Descending
Sorts Z to A, 9 to 1

SORT THE RECORDS

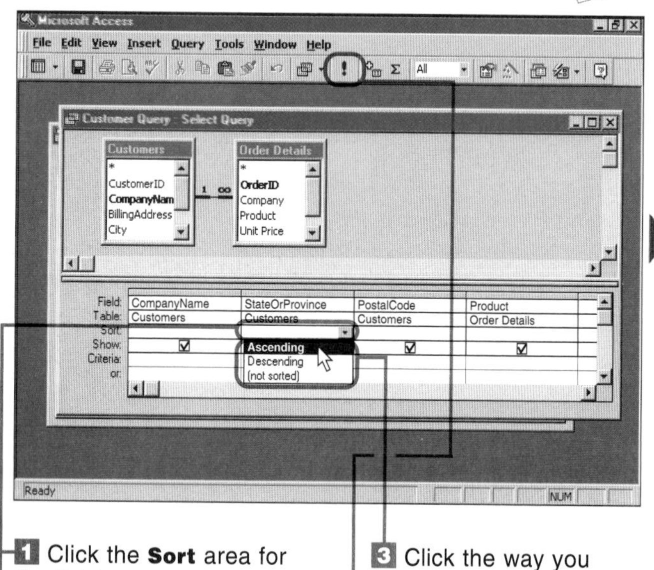

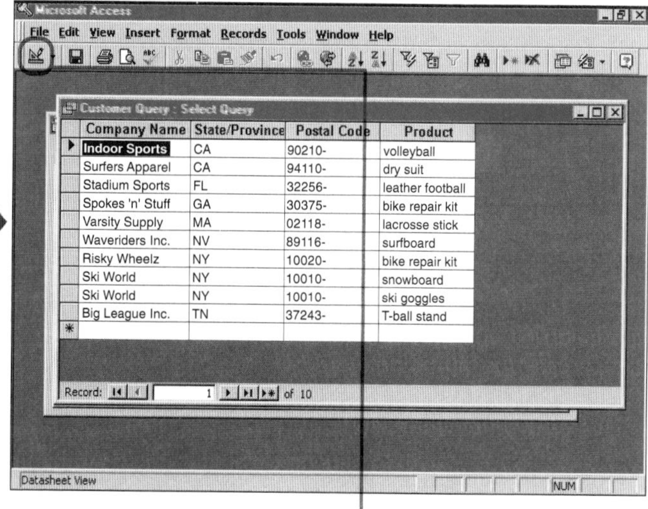

1 Click the **Sort** area for the field you want to use to sort the results of the query. An arrow (▾) appears.

2 Click the arrow (▾).

3 Click the way you want to sort the data.

4 To run the query, click !.

■ The records appear in the new order. In this example, the records are sorted alphabetically by state.

■ To return to the Design view, click the Design View button.

SET CRITERIA

You can use criteria to find specific records in your database. Criteria are conditions that identify the records you want to view.

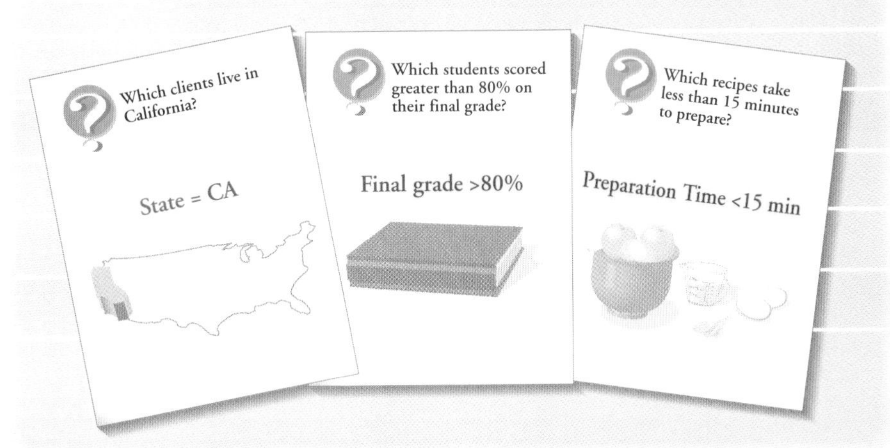

For example, you can use criteria to tell Access to find only the clients who live in California.

SET CRITERIA

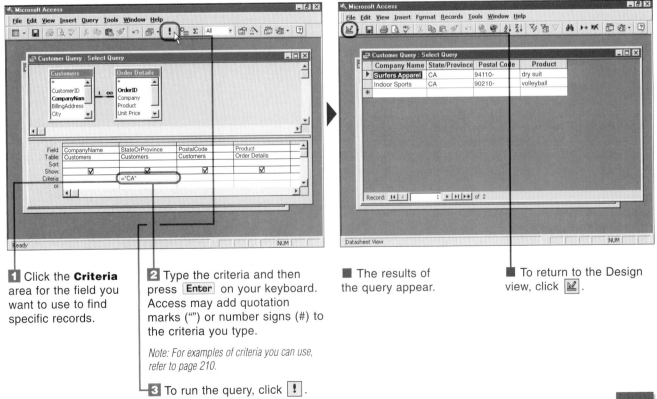

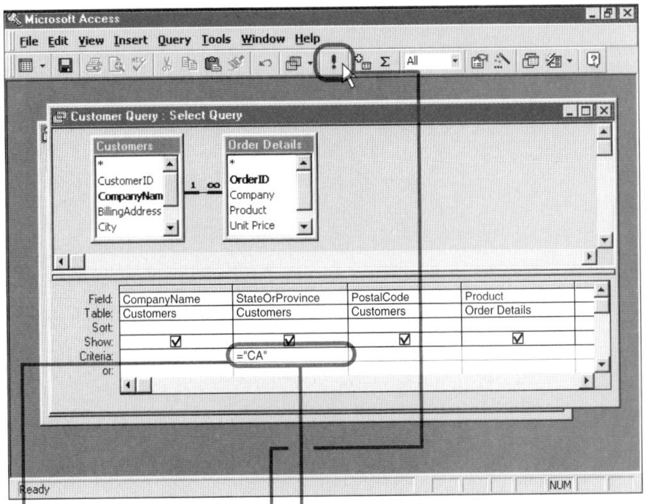

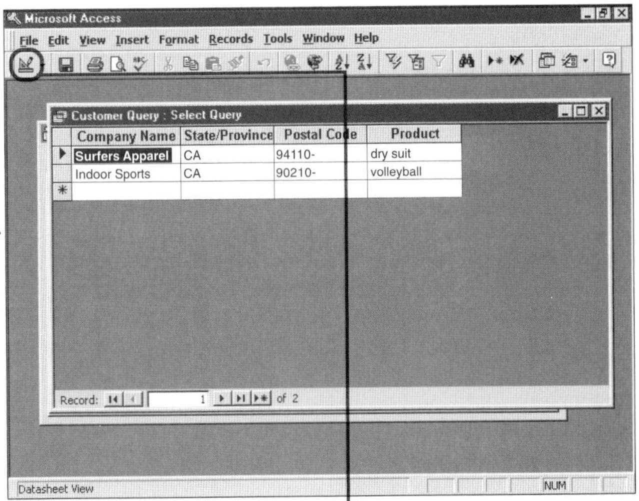

1 Click the **Criteria** area for the field you want to use to find specific records.

2 Type the criteria and then press Enter on your keyboard. Access may add quotation marks ("") or number signs (#) to the criteria you type.

Note: For examples of criteria you can use, refer to page 210.

3 To run the query, click !.

■ The results of the query appear.

■ To return to the Design view, click the Design View button.

EXAMPLES OF CRITERIA

Here are examples of criteria that you can use to find specific records in your database.

Criteria are conditions that identify the records you want to view.

Exact matches

=100	Finds the number 100.
=California	Finds California.
=1/5/97	Finds the date 5-Jan-97.

Note: You can leave out the equal sign (=) when searching for an exact match.

Less than

<100	Finds numbers less than 100.
<N	Finds text starting with the letters A to M.
<1/5/97	Finds dates before 5-Jan-97.

Less than or equal to

<=100	Finds numbers less than or equal to 100.
<=N	Finds the letter N and text starting with the letters A to M.
<=1/5/97	Finds dates before and on 5-Jan-97.

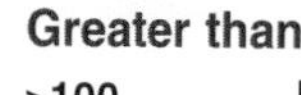

Greater than

>100	Finds numbers greater than 100.
>N	Finds text starting with the letters N to Z.
>1/5/97	Finds dates after 5-Jan-97.

Greater than or equal to

>=100	Finds numbers greater than or equal to 100.
>=N	Finds the letter N and text starting with the letters N to Z.
>=1/5/97	Finds dates after and on 5-Jan-97.

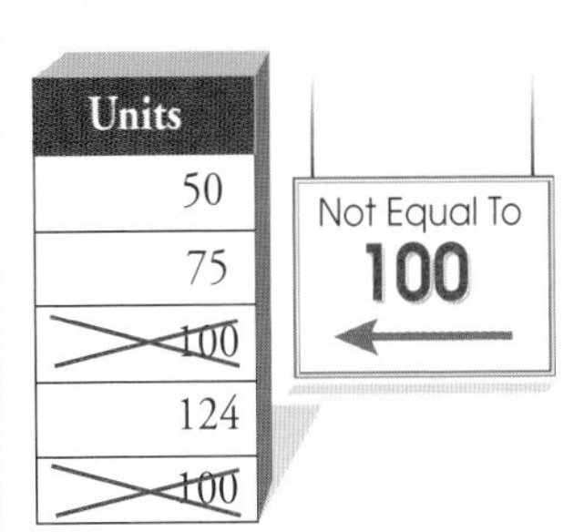

Not equal to

<>100
Finds numbers not equal to 100.

<>California
Finds text not equal to California.

<>1/5/97
Finds dates not on 5-Jan-97.

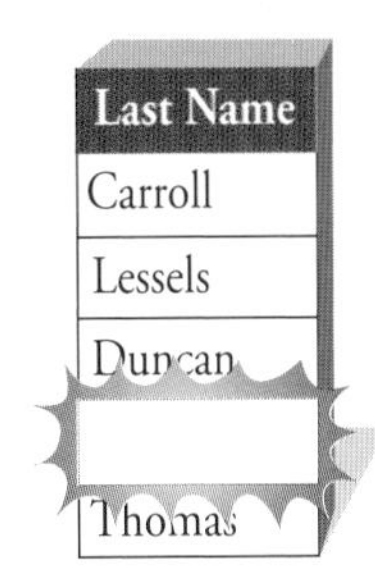

Empty fields

Is Null
Finds records that do not contain data in the field.

Is Not Null
Finds records that contain data in the field.

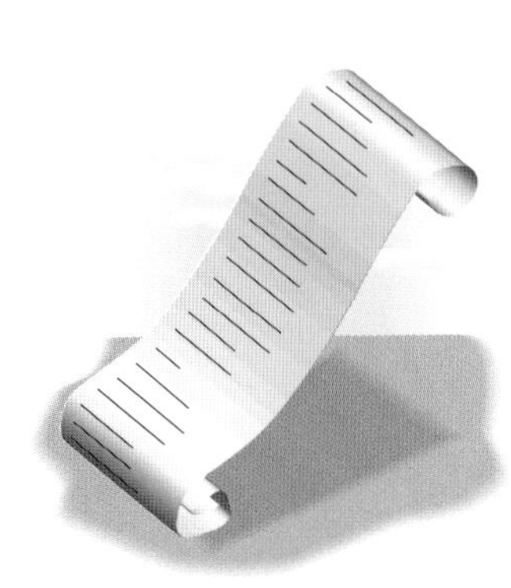

Find list of items

In (100,101)
Finds the numbers 100 and 101.

In (California,CA)
Finds California and CA.

In (#1/5/97#,#1/6/97#)
Finds the dates 5-Jan-97 and 6-Jan-97.

Between...And...

Between 100 And 200
Finds numbers between 100 and 200.

Between A And C
Finds text starting with the letters A to C.

Between 1/5/97 And 1/15/97
Finds dates between 5-Jan-97 and 15-Jan-97.

Wild cards

The asterisk (*) wild card represents one or more characters. The question mark (?) wild card represents a single character.

Like Br*	Finds text starting with **Br**, such as **Br**enda or **Br**own.
Like *ar*	Finds text containing **ar**, such as **Ar**nold or M**ar**c.
Like Wend?	Finds 5 letter words starting with **Wend**, such as **Wend**i or **Wend**y.

DELETE A FIELD

You can delete a field you no longer need to find information in your query.

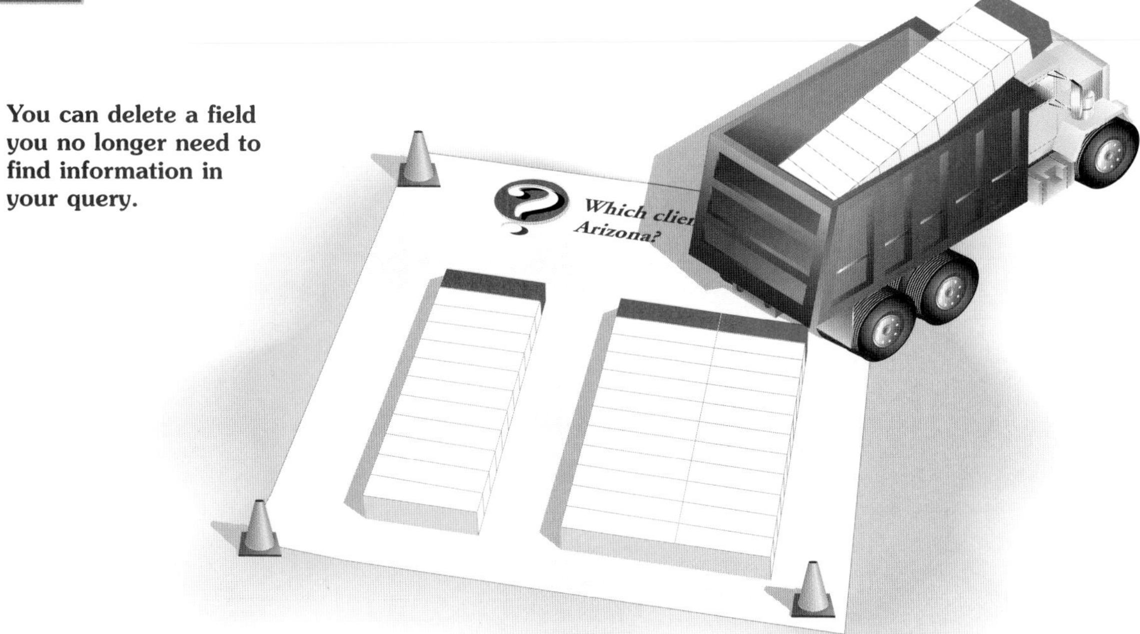

DELETE A FIELD

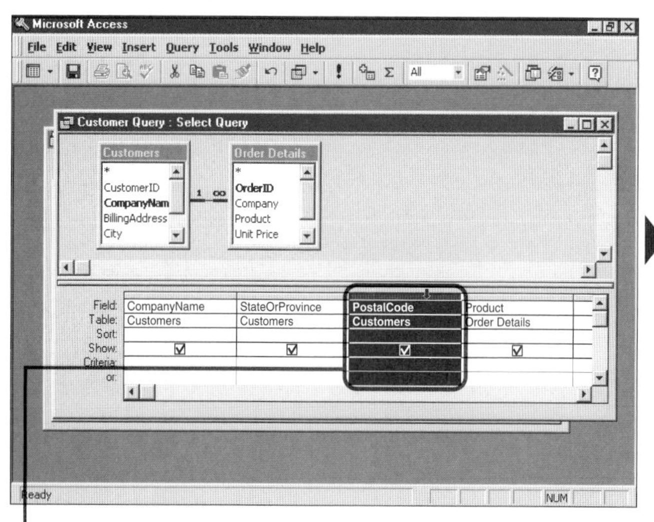

1 Position the mouse directly above the field you want to delete (changes to ⬇) and then click to select the field.

2 Press Delete on your keyboard.

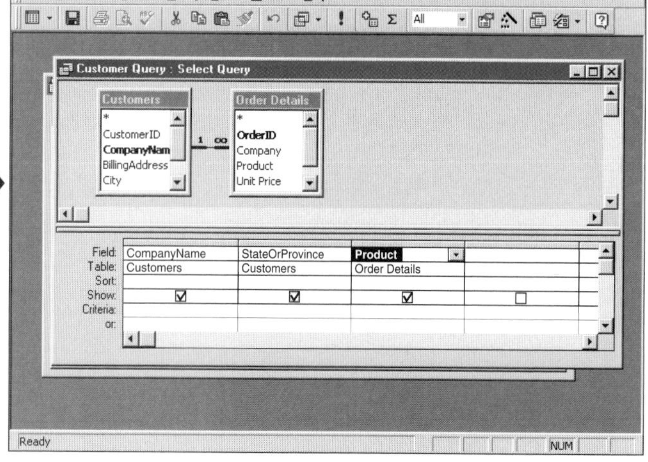

■ The field disappears.

HIDE A FIELD

You can hide a field used in a query. Hiding a field is useful when you need a field to find information in your database, but you do not want to show the field in the results of the query.

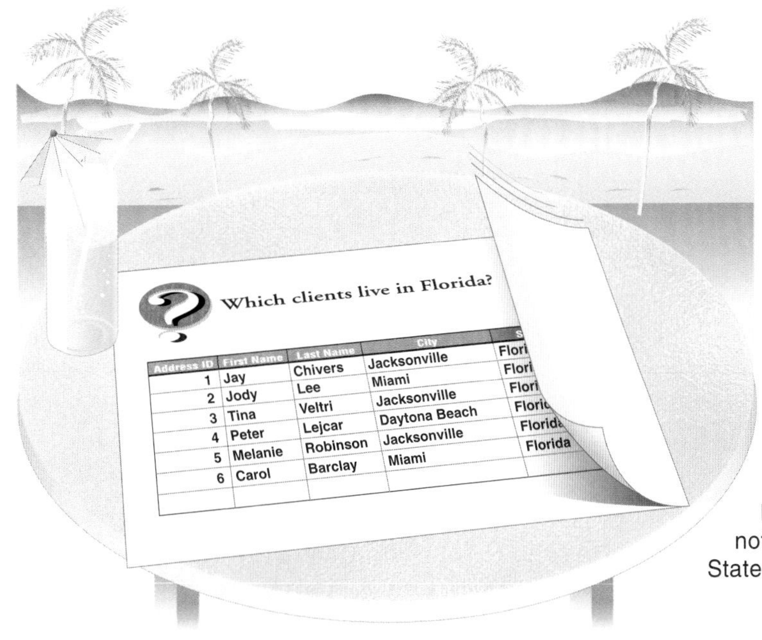

Which clients live in Florida?
Address ID | First Name | Last Name | City
1 Jay Chivers Jacksonville Flori
2 Jody Lee Miami Flori
3 Tina Veltri Jacksonville Flori
4 Peter Lejcar Daytona Beach Florid
5 Melanie Robinson Jacksonville Florida
6 Carol Barclay Miami Florida

For example, you can hide the State field if you need the State field to find clients in Florida, but you do not want to show the State field in the results.

HIDE A FIELD

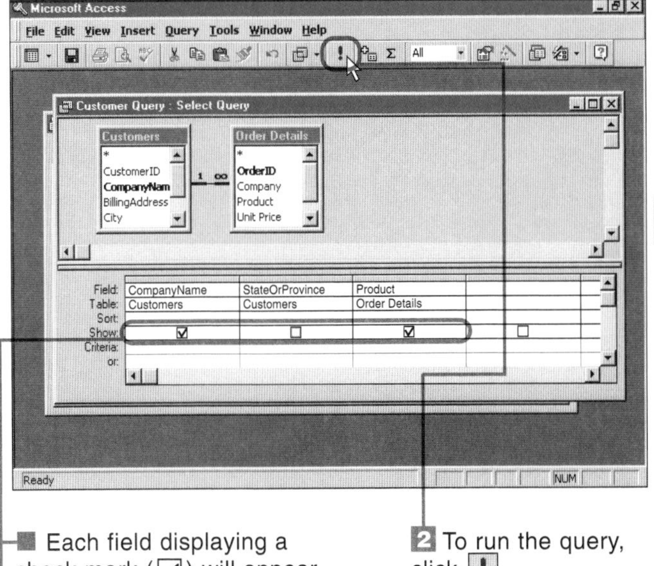

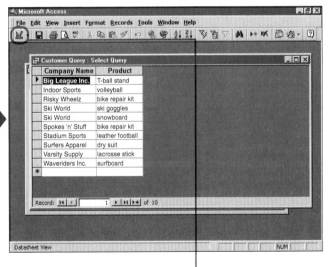

- Each field displaying a check mark (✔) will appear in the results of the query.

1 If you do not want a field to appear in the results of the query, click the **Show** box for the field (✔ changes to ☐).

2 To run the query, click !.

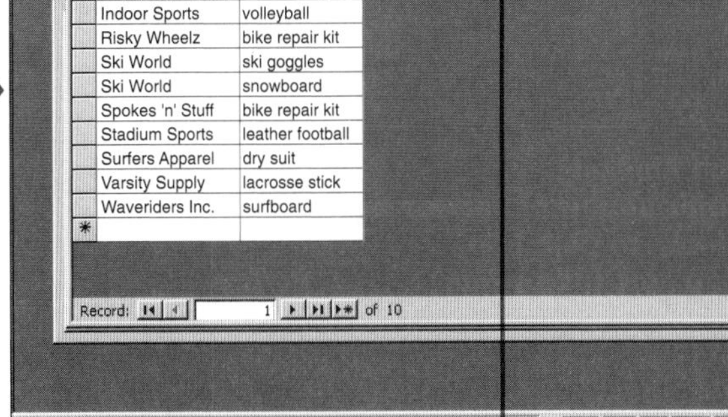

- The field does not appear in the results of the query.

- To return to the Design view, click the Design View button.

REARRANGE FIELDS

You can change the order of fields in a query. Rearranging fields in a query will affect the order that the fields appear in the results.

REARRANGE FIELDS

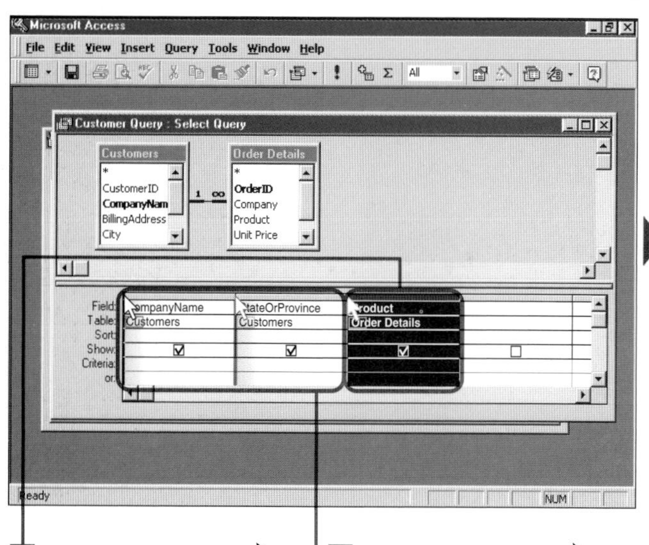

1 Position the mouse ↖ directly above the field you want to move (↖ changes to ⬇) and then click to select the field.

2 Position the mouse ↖ directly above the selected field and then drag the field to the new location.

Note: A thick black line indicates where the field will appear.

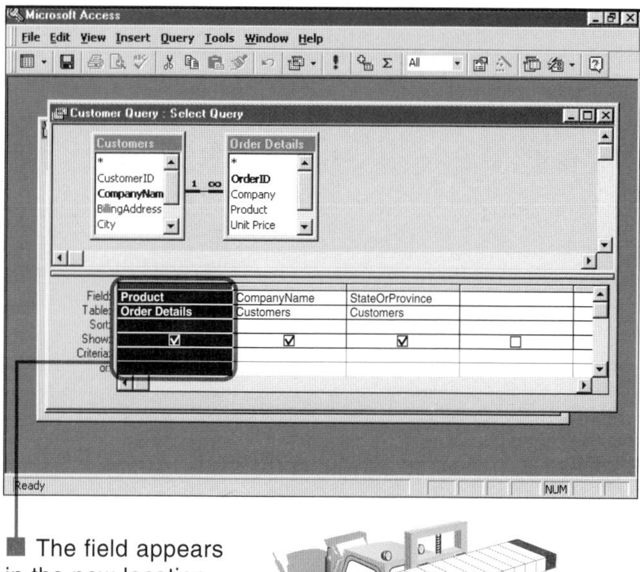

■ The field appears in the new location.

CLEAR THE GRID

If you make mistakes while entering information for a query, you can start over by clearing the grid.

CLEAR THE GRID

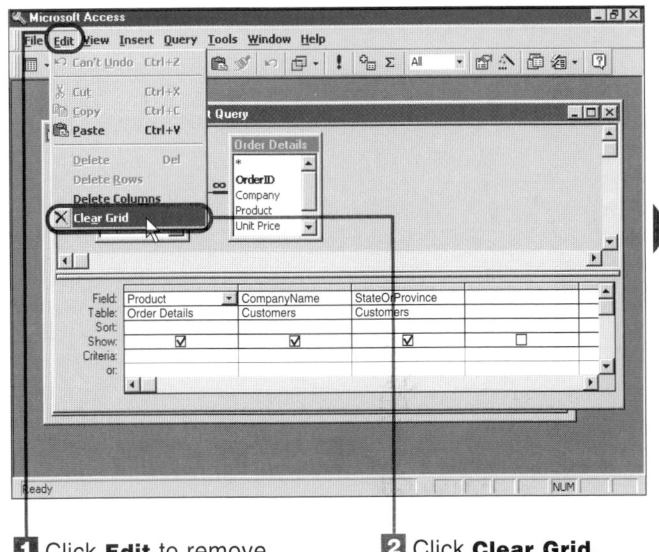

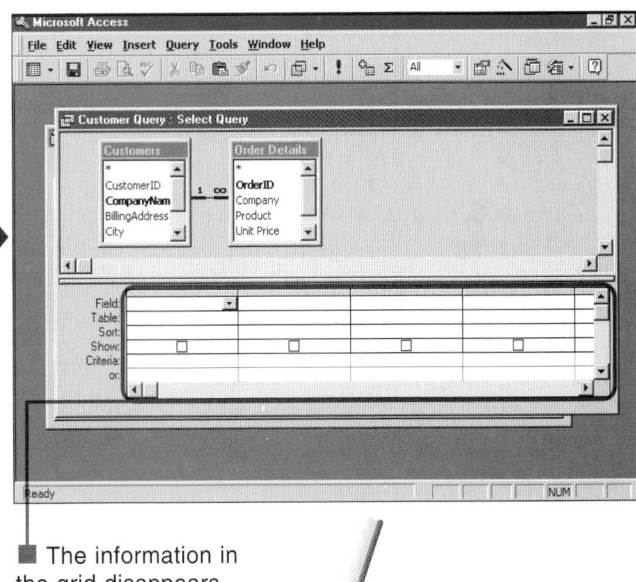

1 Click **Edit** to remove all the information from the grid.

2 Click **Clear Grid**.

■ The information in the grid disappears.

SELECT ALL FIELDS

When creating a query, you can select all the fields in a table at once. Selecting all the fields at once saves you time when adding fields to a query.

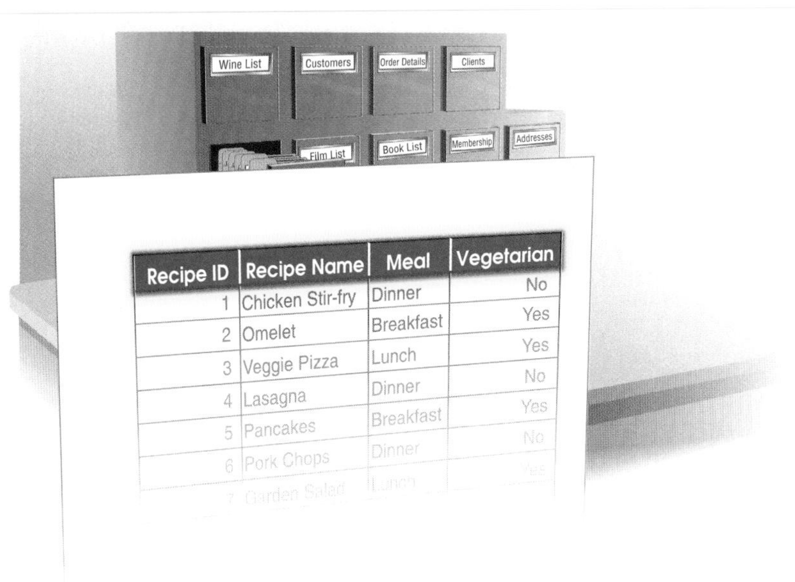

Wine List
Customers
Order Details
Clients
Film List
Book List
Membership
Addresses
Recipe ID
Recipe Name
Meal
Vegetarian
1 Chicken Stir-fry Dinner No
2 Omelet Breakfast Yes
3 Veggie Pizza Lunch Yes
4 Lasagna Dinner No
5 Pancakes Breakfast Yes
6 Pork Chops Dinner No

USING THE TABLE HEADING

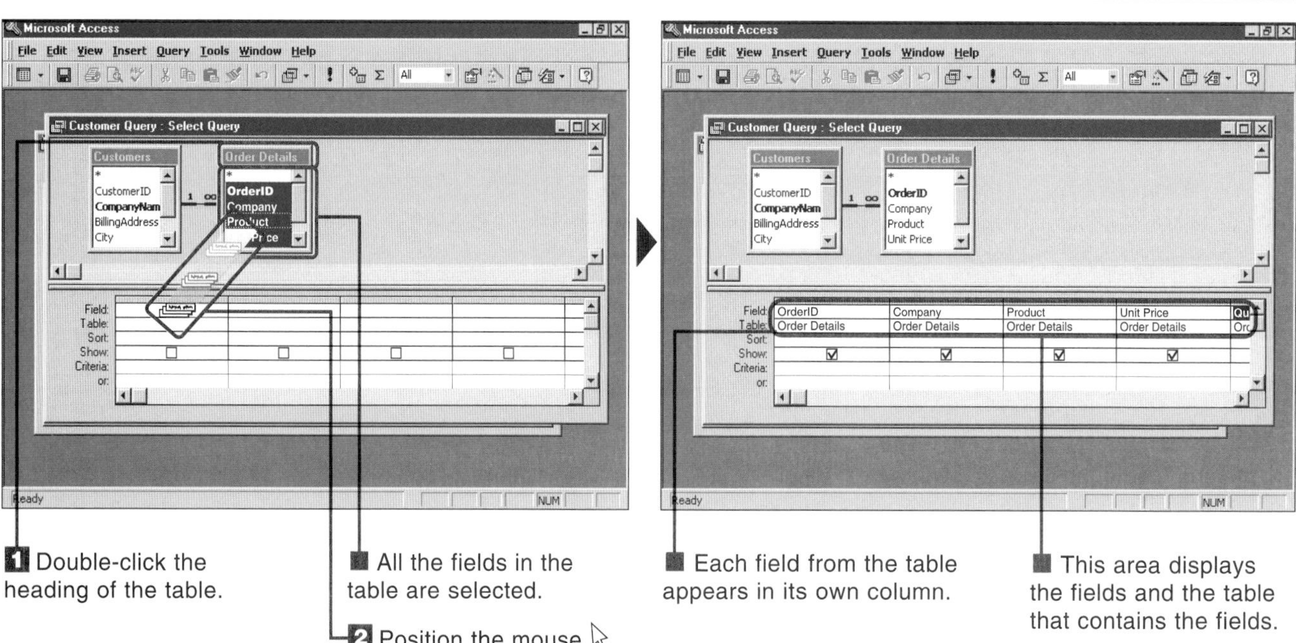

1 Double-click the heading of the table.

■ All the fields in the table are selected.

2 Position the mouse over any field and then drag the fields to the first empty column.

■ Each field from the table appears in its own column.

■ This area displays the fields and the table that contains the fields.

?

Why would I use the asterisk (*) to select all the fields?

Using the asterisk (*) tells Access that you want to use every field from a table in the query. If you later add a field to the table, Access will automatically include the new field in the query.

If you use the table heading to select all the fields and later add a field to the table, you must manually add the new field to the query.

USING THE ASTERISK

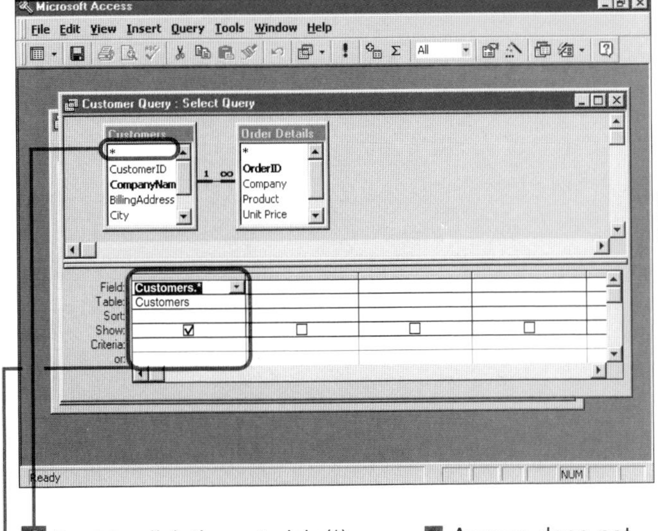

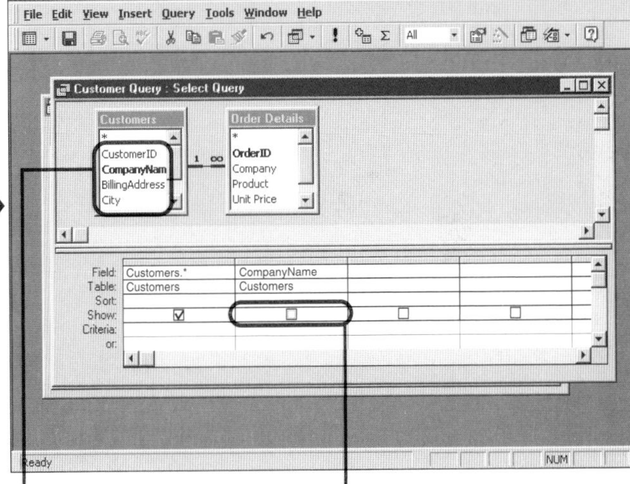

1 Double-click the asterisk (*) at the top of the field list.

■ The first column displays the name of the table followed by an asterisk (*), indicating that all the fields in the table are included.

■ Access does not display each field in a separate column, but all the fields will appear in the results when you run the query.

■ To set criteria for a specific field in the table, double-click the field to place it in a separate column. You can then set the criteria for the field.

Note: To set criteria, refer to page 209.

■ Click the **Show** box for the field (☑ changes to ☐) so the field will not appear twice in the results.

CLOSE A QUERY

When you finish working with a query, you can close the query to remove it from your screen.

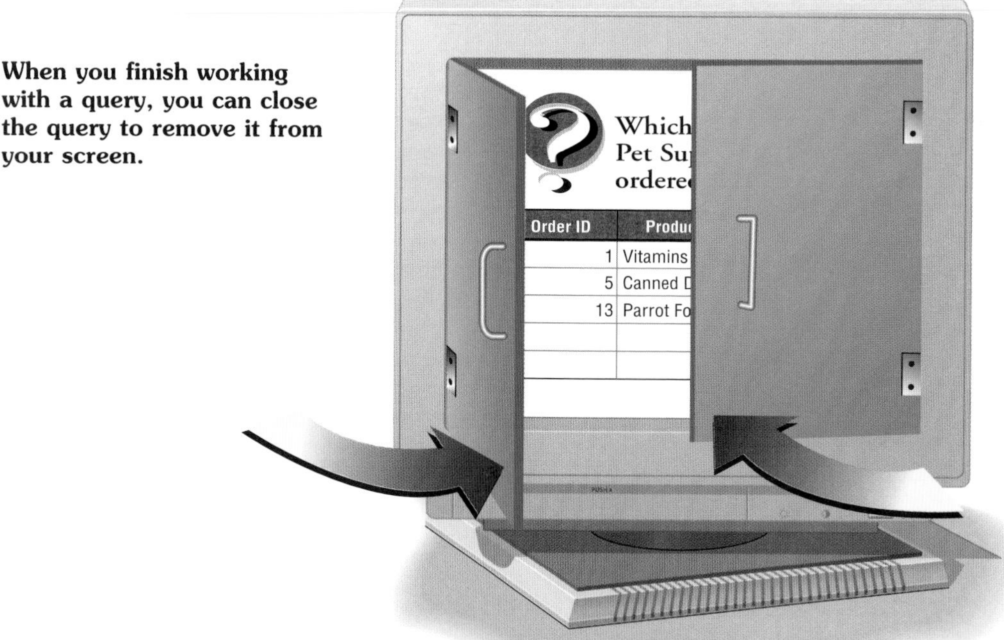

CLOSE A QUERY

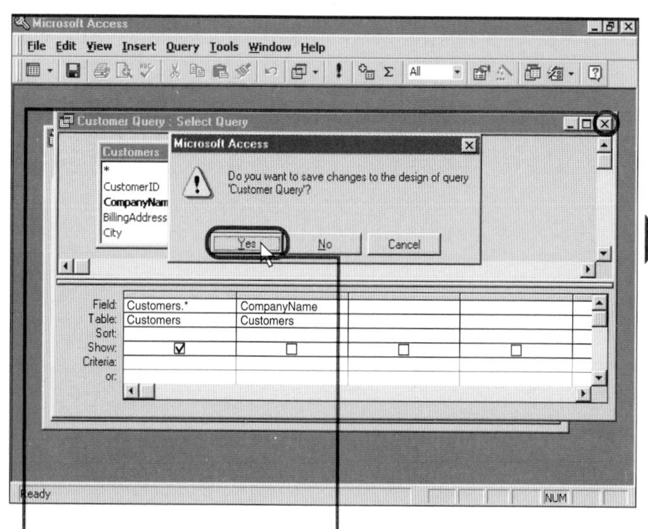

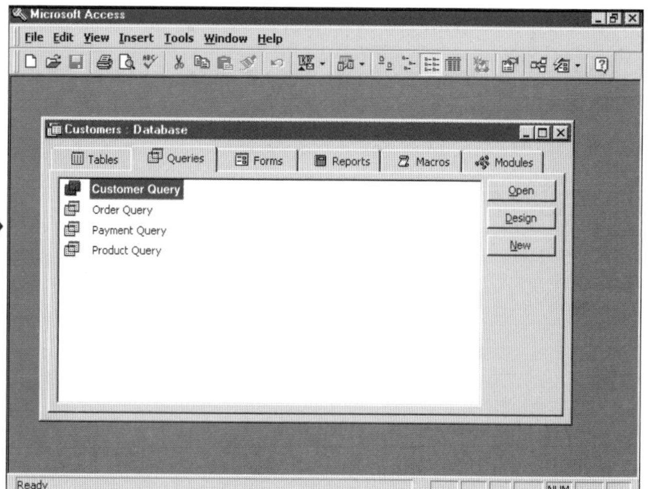

1 Click ☒ to close the query displayed on your screen.

■ A dialog box appears if you have not saved changes you made to the query.

2 To save the changes, click **Yes**.

■ The query disappears from your screen.

OPEN A QUERY

You can open a query to ask the same question again. For example, you may want to open and run a query at the end of each week to display your top-selling products.

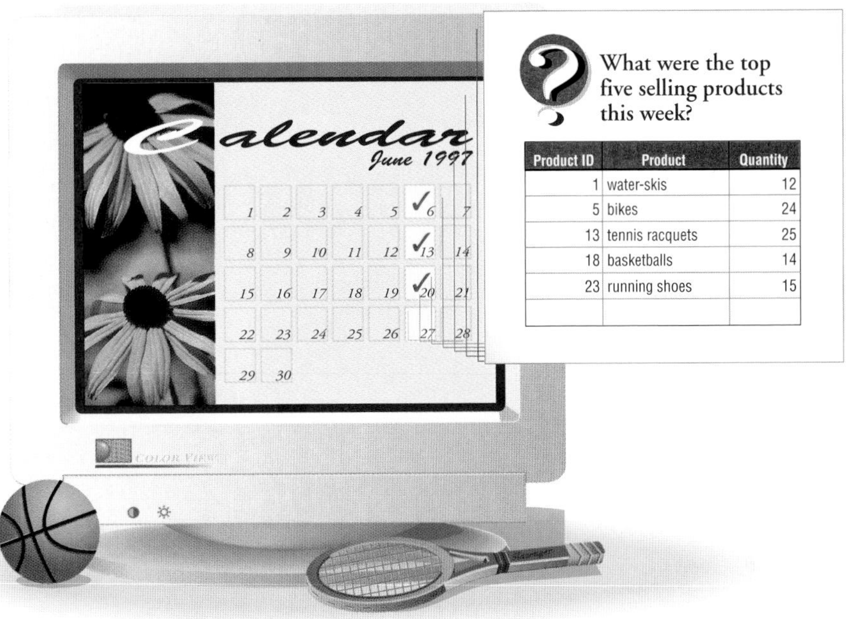

Calendar
June 1997
What were the top five selling products this week?
Product ID
Product
Quantity
1 water-skis 12
5 bikes 24
13 tennis racquets 25
18 basketballs 14
23 running shoes 15

OPEN A QUERY

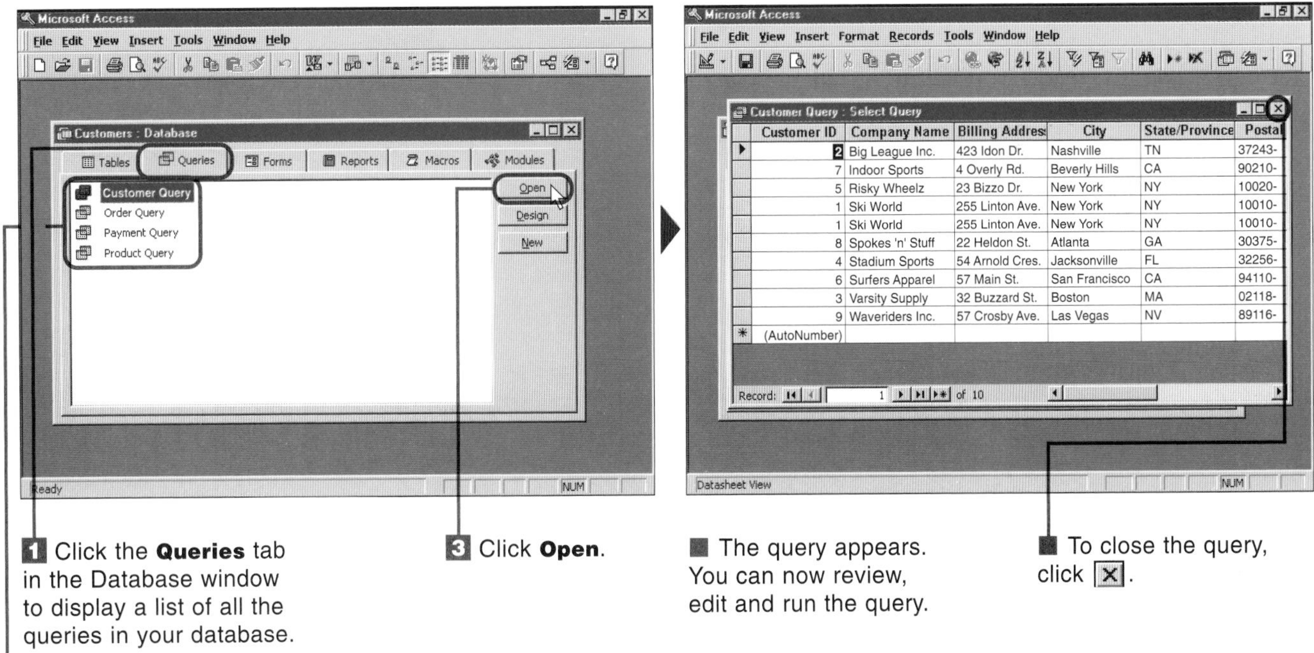

1 Click the **Queries** tab in the Database window to display a list of all the queries in your database.

2 Click the query you want to open.

3 Click **Open**.

■ The query appears. You can now review, edit and run the query.

■ To close the query, click ☒.

RENAME A QUERY

You can change the name of a query to help you remember the purpose of the query.

RENAME A QUERY

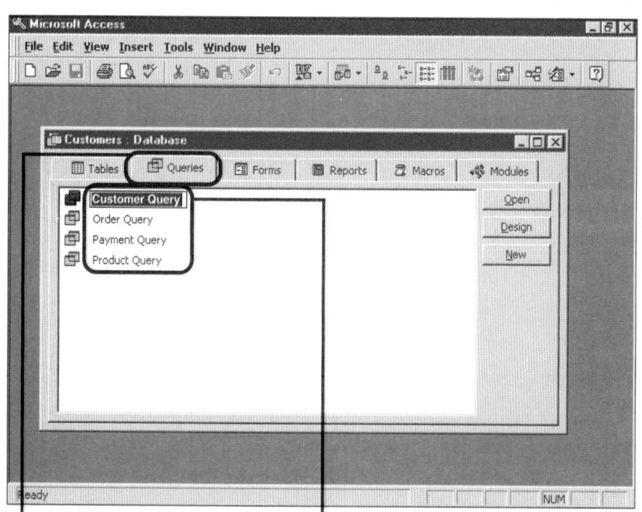

1 Click the **Queries** tab in the Database window to display a list of all the queries in the database.

2 Click the name of the query you want to change. After a few seconds, click the name of the query again. A black border appears around the name.

Note: If you accidentally double-click the name of a query, the query will open.

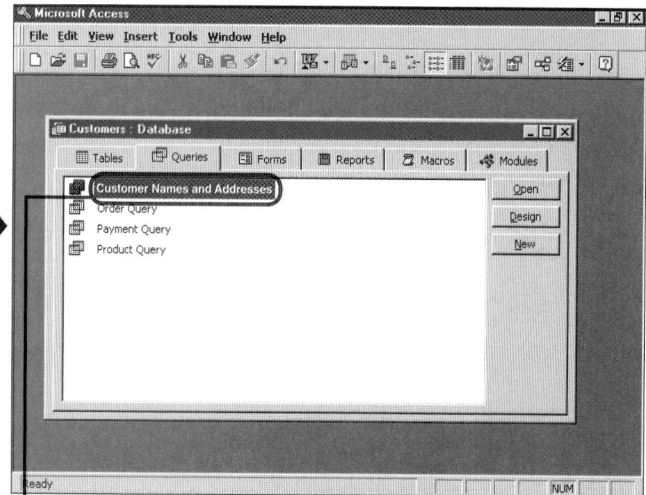

3 Type a new name for the query and then press **Enter** on your keyboard.

DELETE A QUERY

If you are sure you will not need the query again, you can permanently delete the query from your database.

DELETE A QUERY

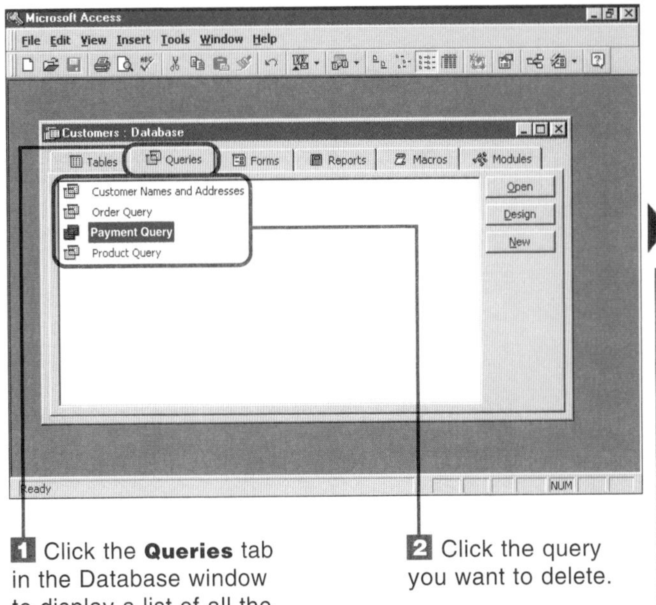

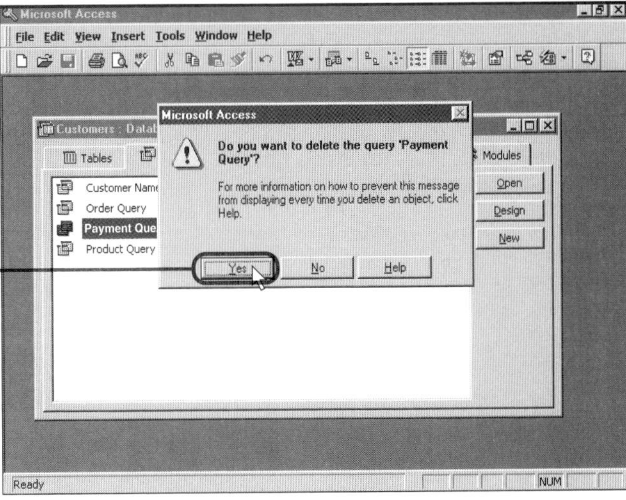

1 Click the **Queries** tab in the Database window to display a list of all the queries in the database.

2 Click the query you want to delete.

3 Press Delete on your keyboard.

■ A dialog box appears, confirming the deletion.

4 To permanently delete the query, click **Yes**.

■ The query disappears.

USING THE SIMPLE QUERY WIZARD

You can use the Simple Query Wizard to gather data from one or more tables in your database.

The Simple Query Wizard will ask you a series of questions and then set up a query based on your answers.

USING THE SIMPLE QUERY WIZARD

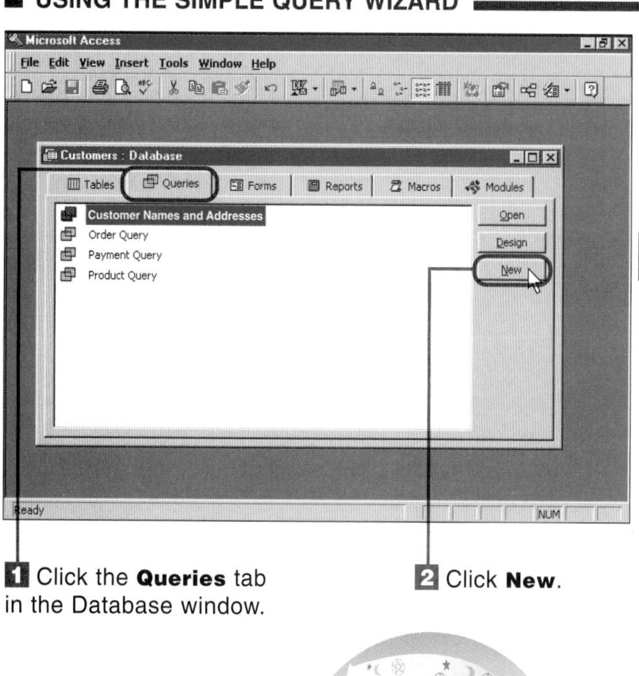

1 Click the **Queries** tab in the Database window.

2 Click **New**.

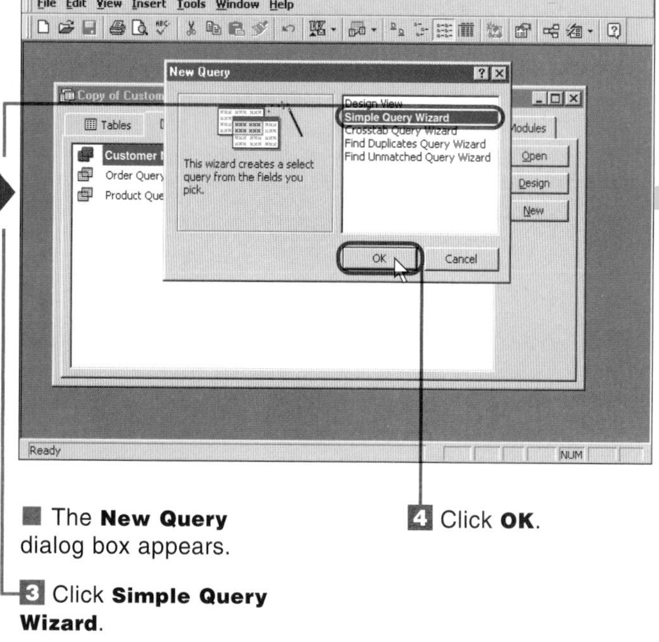

■ The **New Query** dialog box appears.

3 Click **Simple Query Wizard**.

4 Click **OK**.

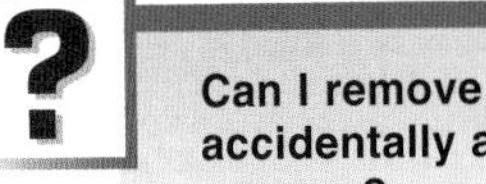

Can I remove a field I accidentally added to a query?

While creating a query with the Simple Query Wizard, you can remove a field you no longer want to include in the query.

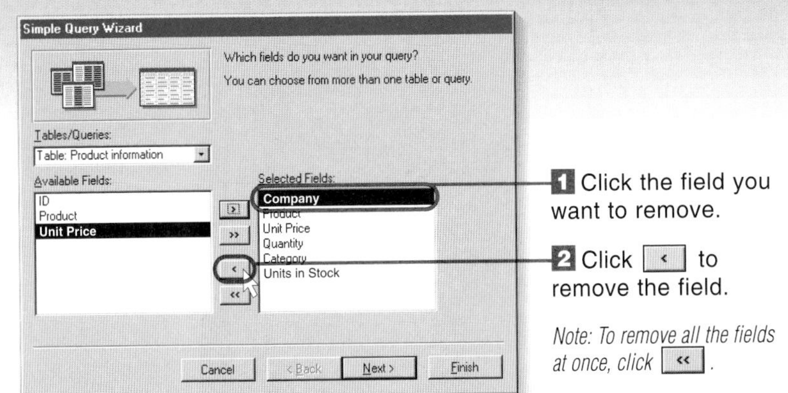

1 Click the field you want to remove.

2 Click < to remove the field.

Note: To remove all the fields at once, click <<.

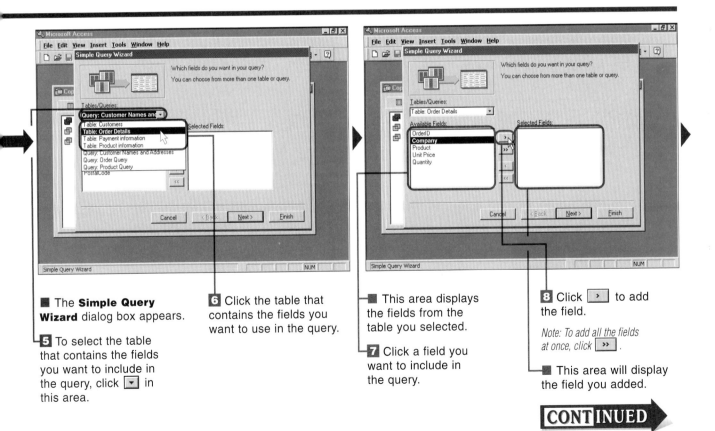

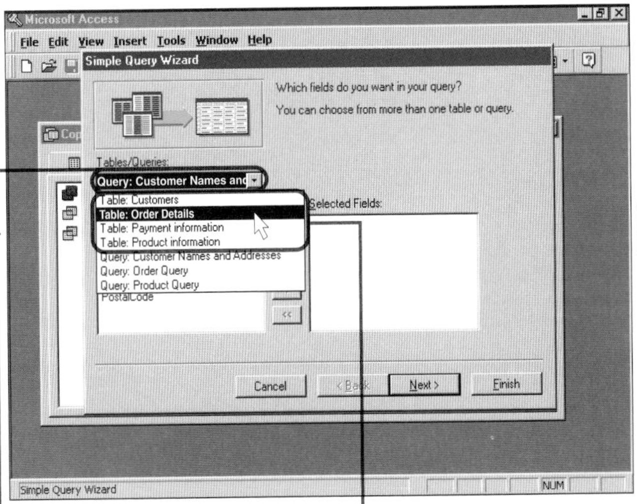

■ The **Simple Query Wizard** dialog box appears.

5 To select the table that contains the fields you want to include in the query, click ▾ in this area.

6 Click the table that contains the fields you want to use in the query.

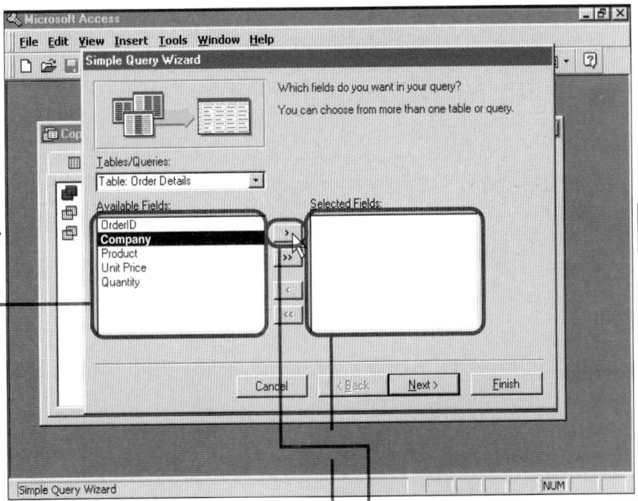

■ This area displays the fields from the table you selected.

7 Click a field you want to include in the query.

8 Click > to add the field.

Note: To add all the fields at once, click >>.

■ This area will display the field you added.

CONTINUED

If your query contains information that can be calculated, you can choose to show all the records or just the summary in the results of your query.

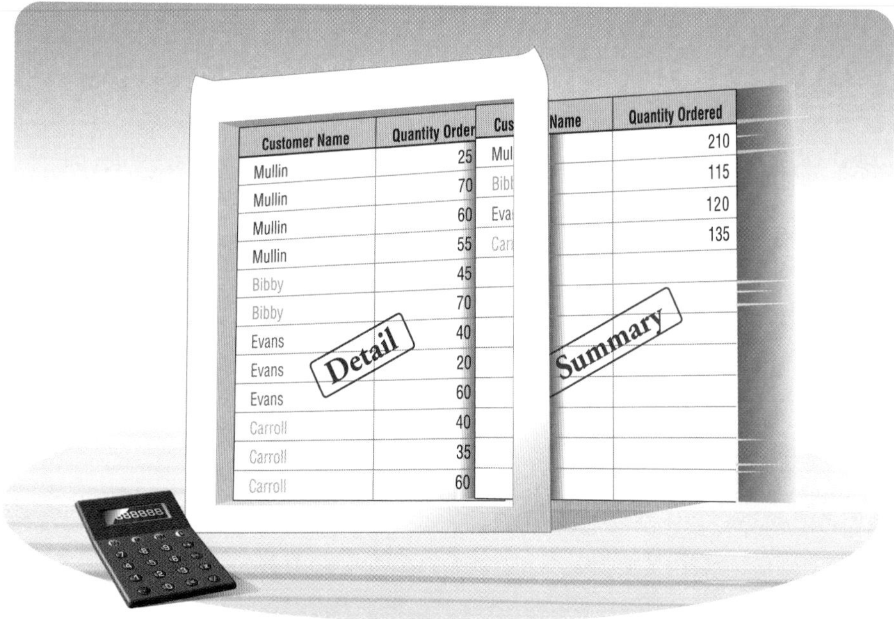

USING THE SIMPLE QUERY WIZARD (CONTINUED)

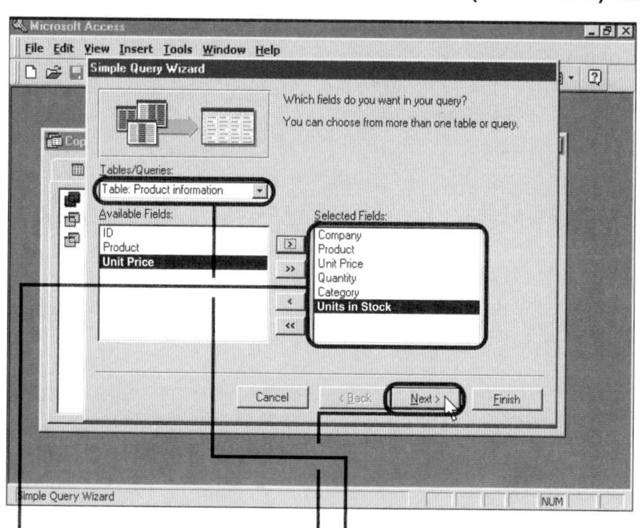

9 Repeat steps **7** and **8** on page 223 until the area displays all the fields you want to use in the query.

10 You can add fields from other tables by performing steps **5** to **9** for each table.

11 Click **Next** to continue.

Note: If you are creating a query using fields from more than one table, the tables must be related. To relate tables, refer to page 138.

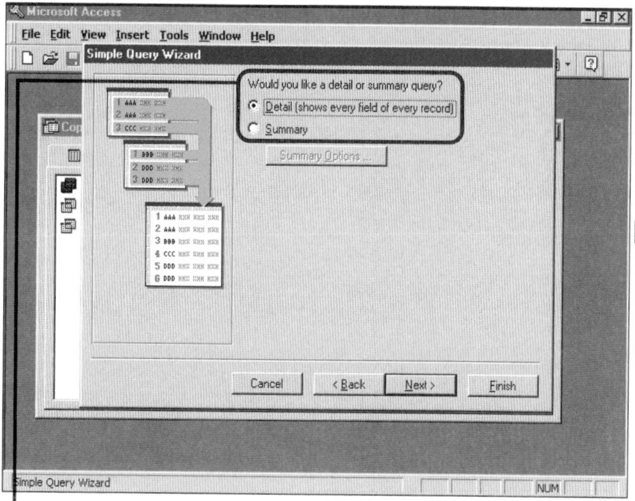

■ If your query contains information that can be calculated, you can choose how you want to display the information in the results.

*Note: If this question does not appear, skip to step **17** on page 226 to continue creating the query.*

What calculations can I perform in a query?

Sum
Adds the values.

Avg
Calculates the average value.

Min
Finds the smallest value.

Max
Finds the largest value.

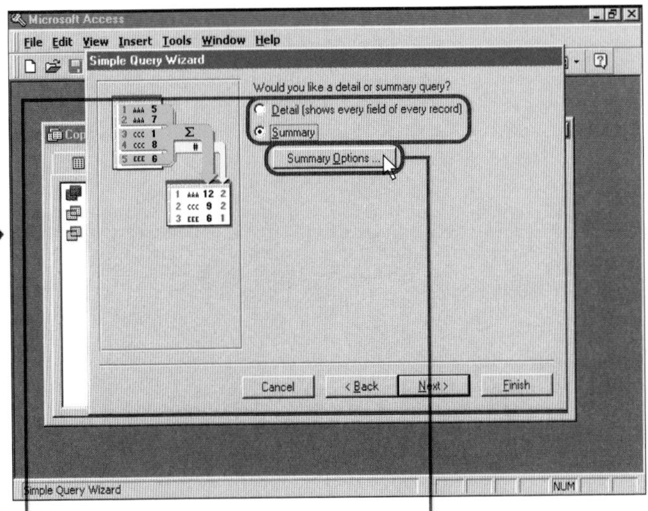

12 Click the way you want to display the information in the results (○ changes to ◉). If you select **Detail**, skip to step **17** on page 226.

13 Click **Summary Options** to select how you want to summarize the information.

■ The **Summary Options** dialog box appears.

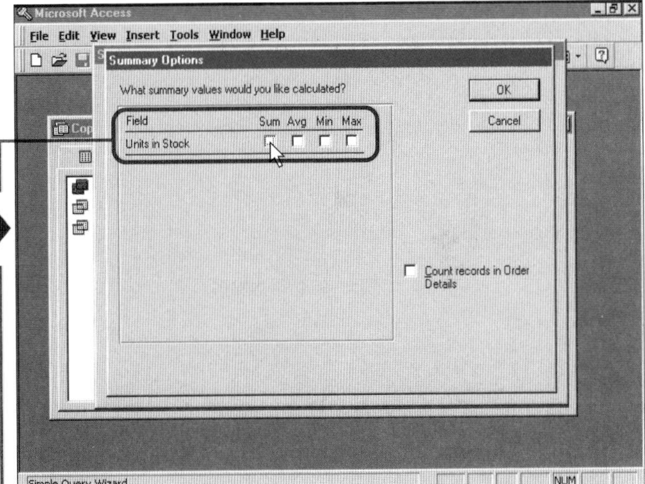

■ This area displays the fields you can perform calculations on.

14 Click the box (☐) for each calculation you want to perform (☐ changes to ☑).

Note: For information on calculations, refer to the top of this page.

CONTINUED

USING THE SIMPLE QUERY WIZARD

You can have Access count the number of records in each group that will be calculated in your query.

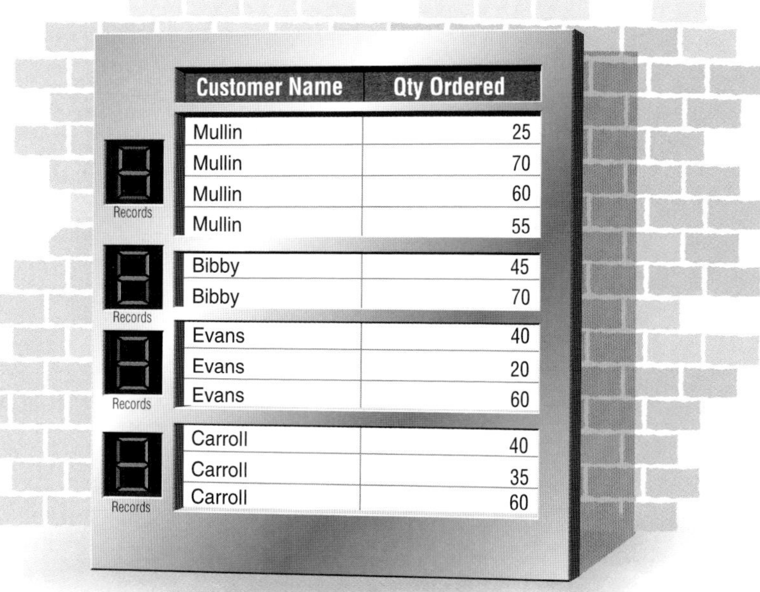

Customer Name
Qty Ordered
Mullin 25
Mullin 70
Mullin 60
Mullin 55
Bibby 45
Bibby 70
Evans 40
Evans 20
Evans 60
Carroll 40
Carroll 35
Carroll 60
Records
Records
Records
Records

USING THE SIMPLE QUERY WIZARD (CONTINUED)

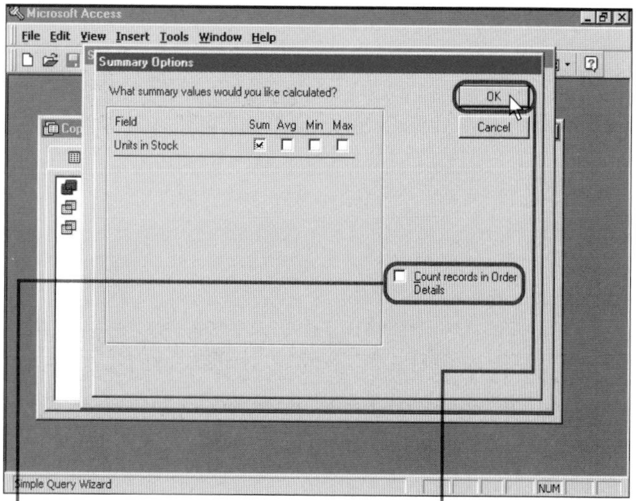

15 To count the number of records in each group that Access will calculate, you can click this option (☐ changes to ☑).

16 Click **OK**.

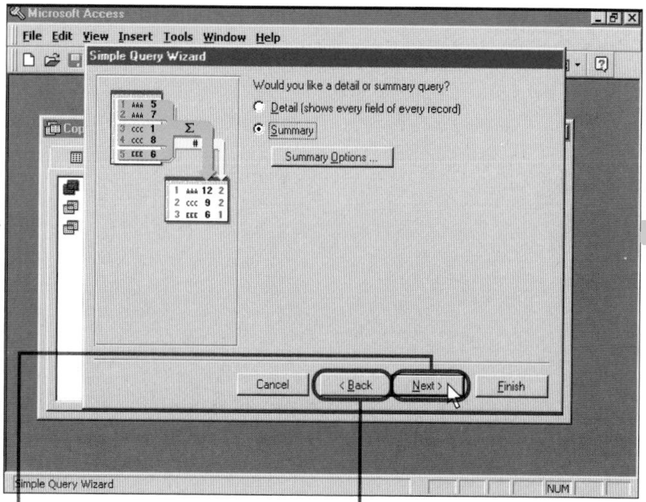

17 Click **Next** to continue.

■ You can click **Back** at any time to return to a previous step and change your answers.

How can I make changes to a query I created using the Simple Query Wizard?

You can use the Design view to make changes to any query you create. You can sort records, add and remove fields and more. To display the query in the Design view, refer to page 206.

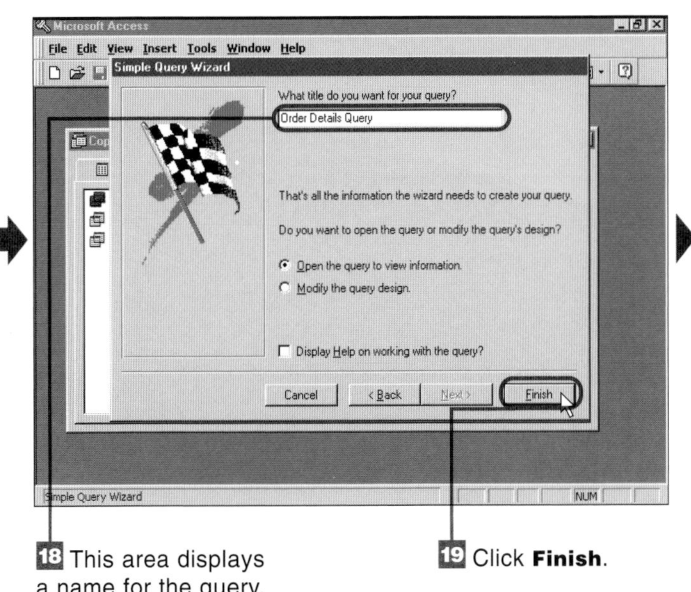

18 This area displays a name for the query. To save the query with a different name, type the new name.

19 Click **Finish**.

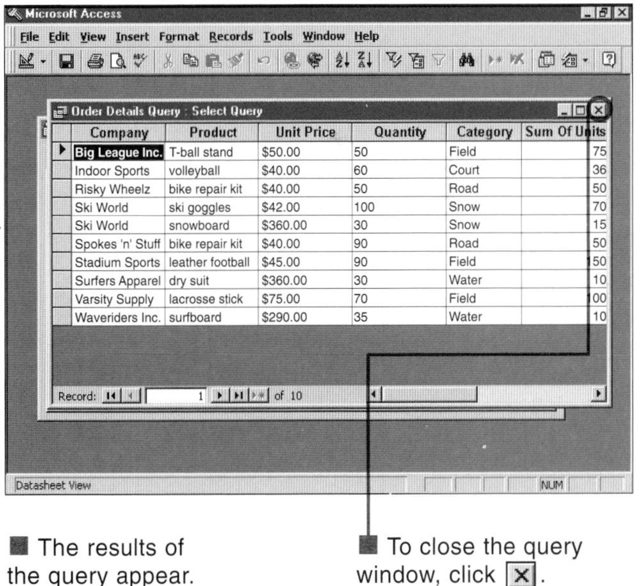

■ The results of the query appear.

■ To close the query window, click ☒.

43560
MIN
AVG
SUM
STDEV
COUNT
MAX
LAST
FIRST
VAR

Advanced Queries

Do you want to learn how to create advanced queries? This chapter shows you how to perform calculations, summarize data and much more.

Display Top or Bottom Values 230

Perform Calculations 232

Change Format of Calculated Field 234

Using Parameters 236

Change the Join Type..................................238

Using Multiple Criteria 240

Summarize Data...244

Find Unmatched Records 250

DISPLAY TOP OR BOTTOM VALUES

You can choose to display just the top or bottom values in the results of a query.

TOP 5 ORDERS
Company | Product | Total Ordered
Sports R Us | Skis | 898
Golf & Skis Inc. | Ski Pants | 742
Skis Please! | Racing Helmet | 616
#1 Skis Inc. | Ski Goggles | 425
Downhill Plus | Ski Boots | 306

Displaying the top or bottom values is useful when you want to see the top five orders or the ten lowest-selling products.

DISPLAY TOP OR BOTTOM VALUES

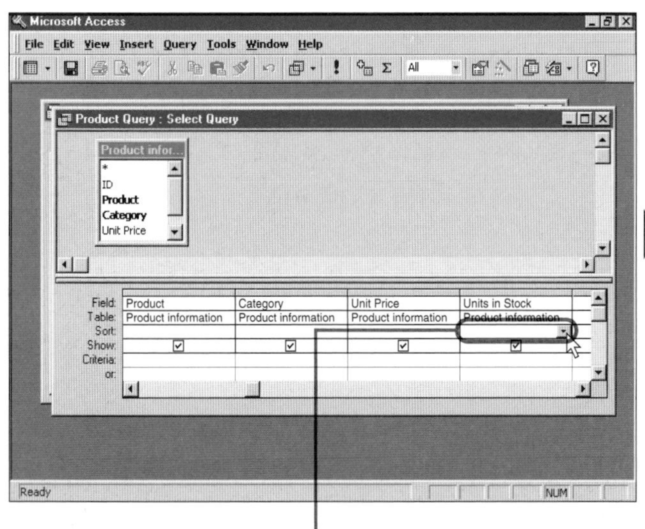

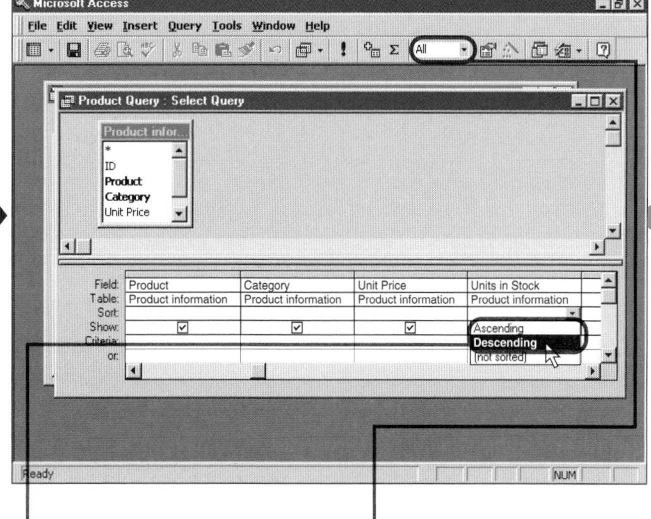

■ Display the query you want to change in the Design view. For information on changing views, refer to page 206.

1 Click the **Sort** area for the field you want to display the top or bottom values. An arrow (▾) appears.

2 Click the arrow (▾).

3 To display the top or bottom values, click the way you want to sort the data.

Ascending - Display the bottom values.

Descending - Display the top values.

4 To specify the number or percentage of records you want to display in the results, click ▾ in this area.

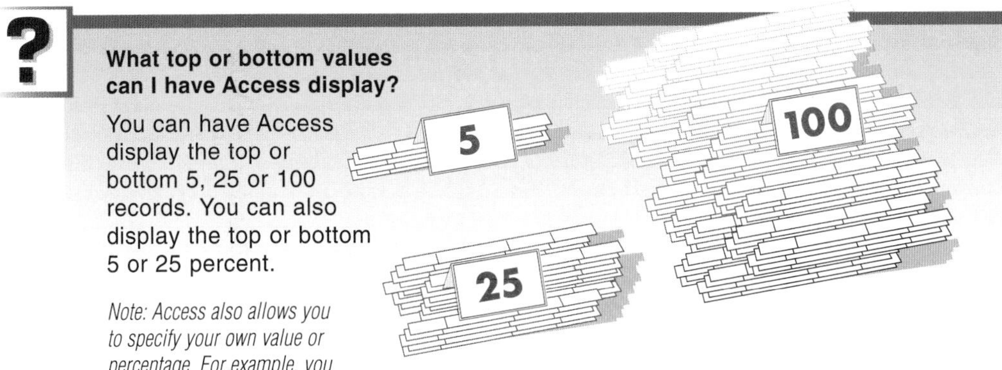

? What top or bottom values can I have Access display?

You can have Access display the top or bottom 5, 25 or 100 records. You can also display the top or bottom 5 or 25 percent.

Note: Access also allows you to specify your own value or percentage. For example, you can display the top 10 records.

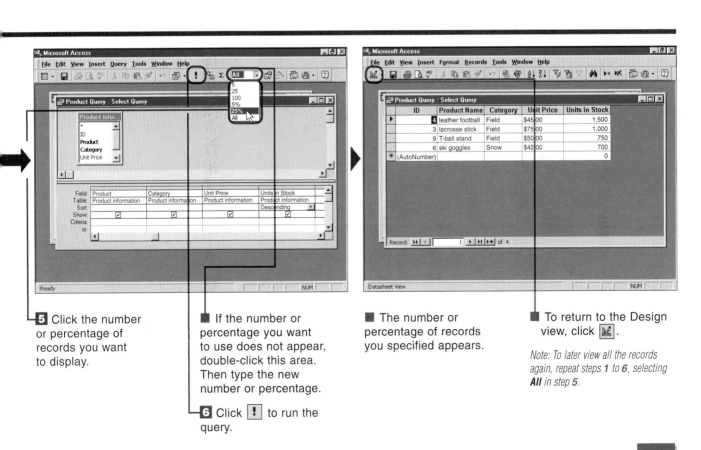

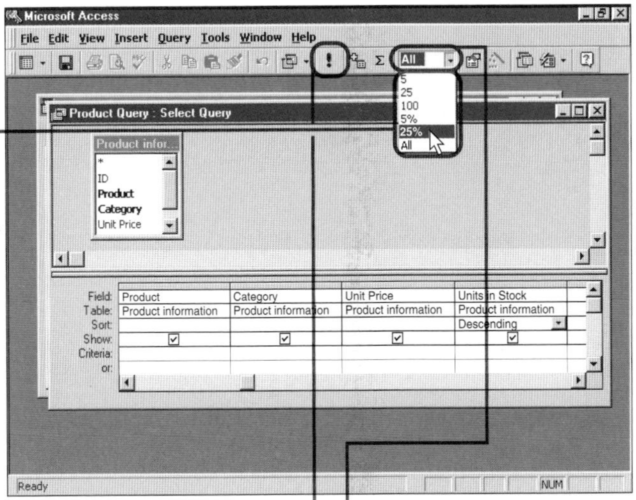

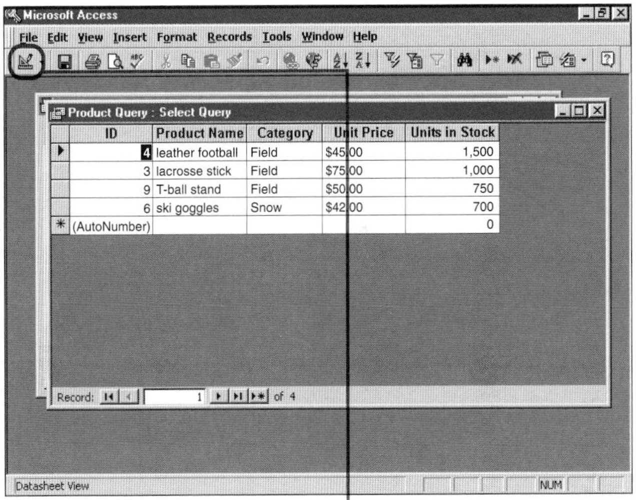

5 Click the number or percentage of records you want to display.

■ If the number or percentage you want to use does not appear, double-click this area. Then type the new number or percentage.

6 Click ! to run the query.

■ The number or percentage of records you specified appears.

■ To return to the Design view, click [Design View button].

*Note: To later view all the records again, repeat steps **1** to **6**, selecting **All** in step **5**.*

PERFORM CALCULATIONS

You can perform calculations on each record in your database. You can then review and analyze the results.

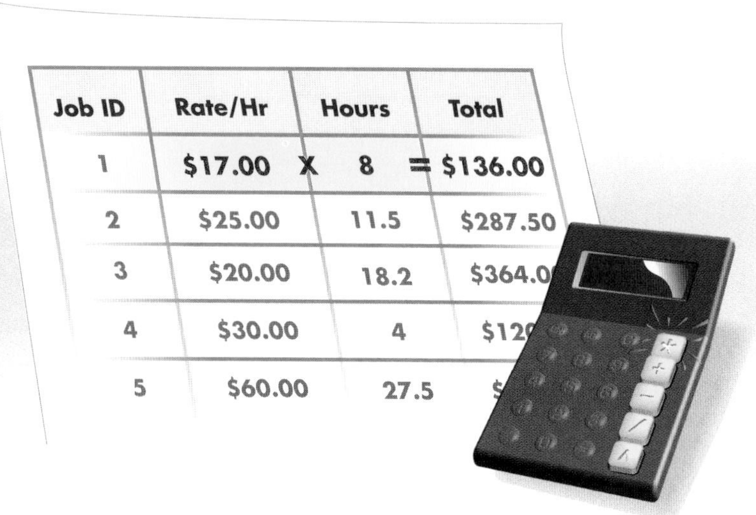

Job ID
Rate/Hr
Hours
Total
1
$17.00
X
8
=
$136.00
2
$25.00
11.5
$287.50
3
$20.00
18.2
4
$30.00
4
5
$60.00
27.5

You can use these operators in your calculations.

*	**Multiply**
+	**Add**
–	**Subtract**
/	**Divide**
^	**Raise to a power**

PERFORM CALCULATIONS

How do I enter an expression to perform a calculation?

[Products]![Quantity]*[Products]![Cost]

■ To enter a field name in an expression, type the table name in square brackets (**[Products]**) followed by an exclamation mark (!). Then type the field name in square brackets (**[Quantity]**).

Note: Make sure you type the table and field names exactly.

■ If a field name is in only one table, you do not need to enter the table name. For example, type **[Quantity]*[Cost]**.

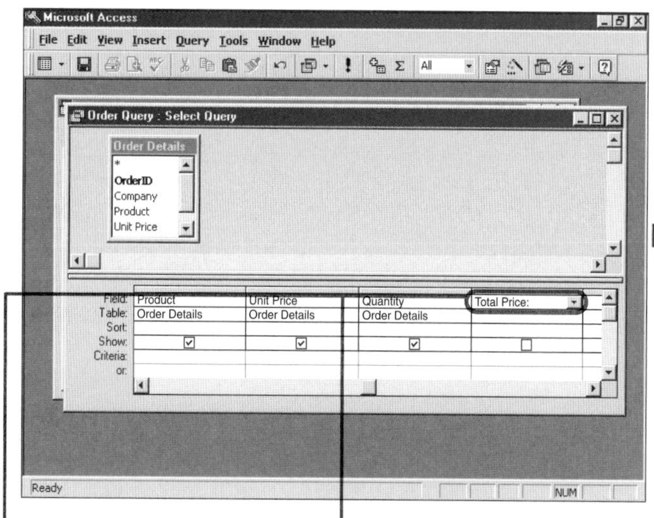

■ Display the query you want to change in the Design view. For information on changing views, refer to page 206.

1 Click the **Field** area in the first empty column.

2 Type a name for the field you want to display the results of the calculation, followed by a colon (:). Then press the **Spacebar** on your keyboard to leave a blank space.

? What types of calculations can I perform in a query?

You can calculate the total cost for each order.

Total Cost: [Quantity]*[Cost]

You can calculate the price of each product after a 15% discount.

Price After Discount: [Price]*0.85

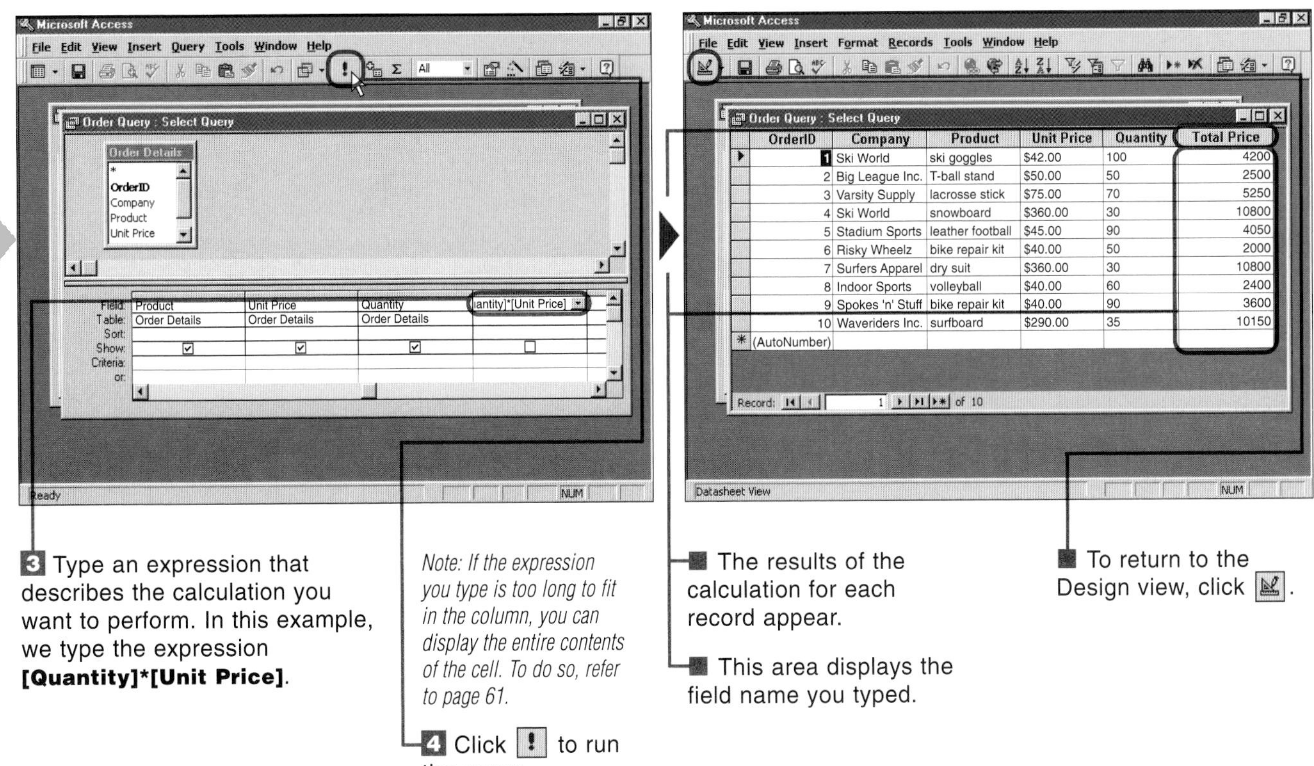

3 Type an expression that describes the calculation you want to perform. In this example, we type the expression **[Quantity]*[Unit Price]**.

Note: If the expression you type is too long to fit in the column, you can display the entire contents of the cell. To do so, refer to page 61.

4 Click ! to run the query.

■ The results of the calculation for each record appear.

■ This area displays the field name you typed.

■ To return to the Design view, click the Design View button.

CHANGE FORMAT OF CALCULATED FIELD

You can change the way calculated information is displayed in the results of a query. The format you choose depends on your personal preference.

Company Name
Amount
Waves Plus
65.79
$65.79
Sports R Us
78.79
$78.79
Golf & Skis Inc.
58.92
$58.92
Runaway Sports
89.50
$89.50
A+ Sports
120.10
$120.10

CHANGE FORMAT OF CALCULATED FIELD

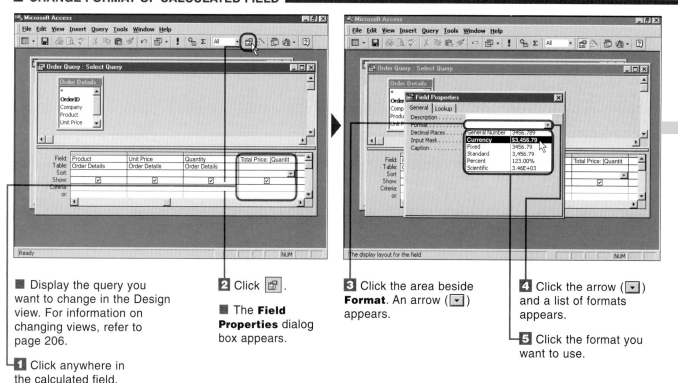

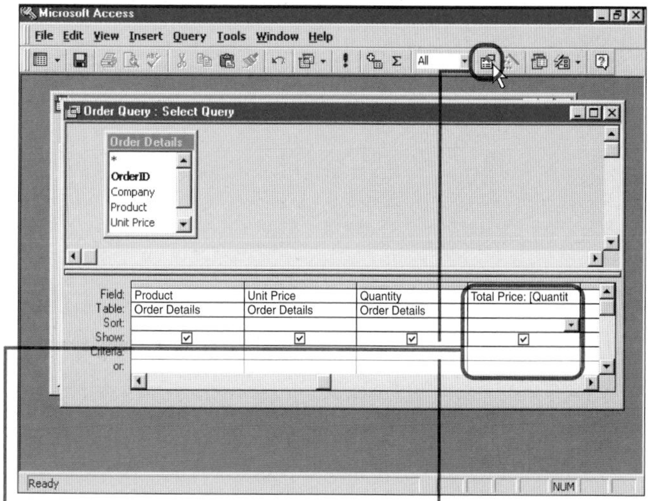

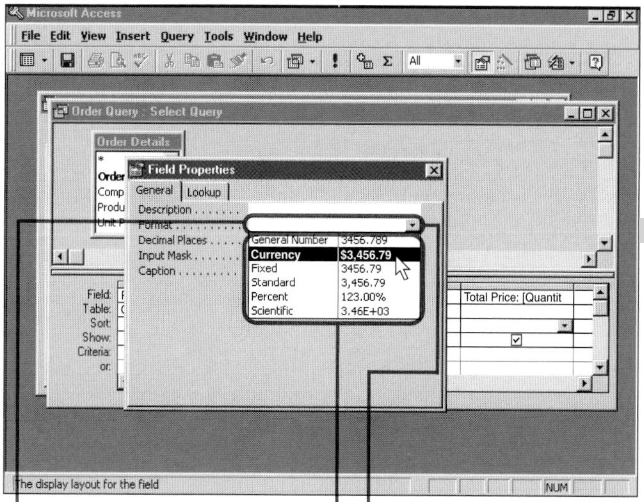

■ Display the query you want to change in the Design view. For information on changing views, refer to page 206.

1 Click anywhere in the calculated field.

2 Click [icon].

■ The **Field Properties** dialog box appears.

3 Click the area beside **Format**. An arrow ([▼]) appears.

4 Click the arrow ([▼]) and a list of formats appears.

5 Click the format you want to use.

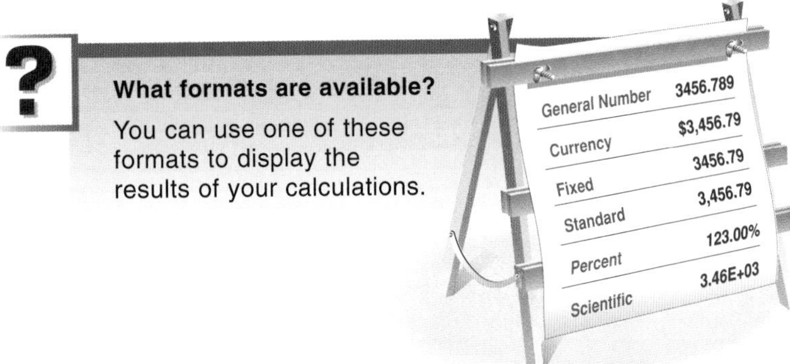

?
What formats are available?
You can use one of these formats to display the results of your calculations.
General Number 3456.789
Currency $3,456.79
Fixed 3456.79
Standard 3,456.79
Percent 123.00%
Scientific 3.46E+03

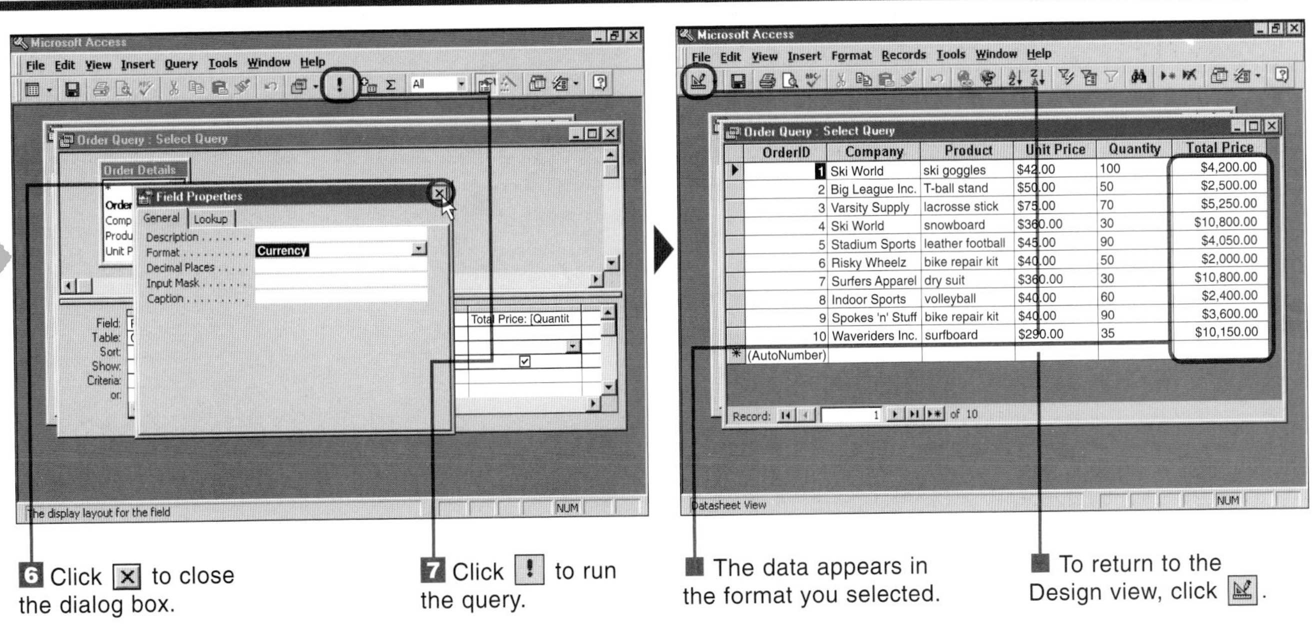

6 Click ☒ to close the dialog box.

7 Click ! to run the query.

■ The data appears in the format you selected.

■ To return to the Design view, click ☑.

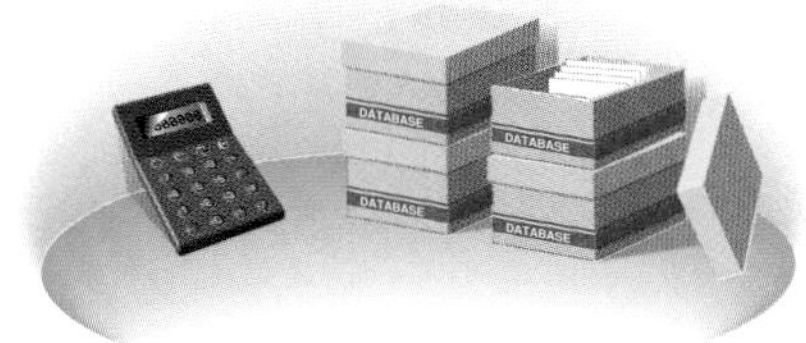

USING PARAMETERS

You can use a parameter to make your query more flexible. When you use a parameter, Access will ask you to specify which information you want to find each time you run a query.

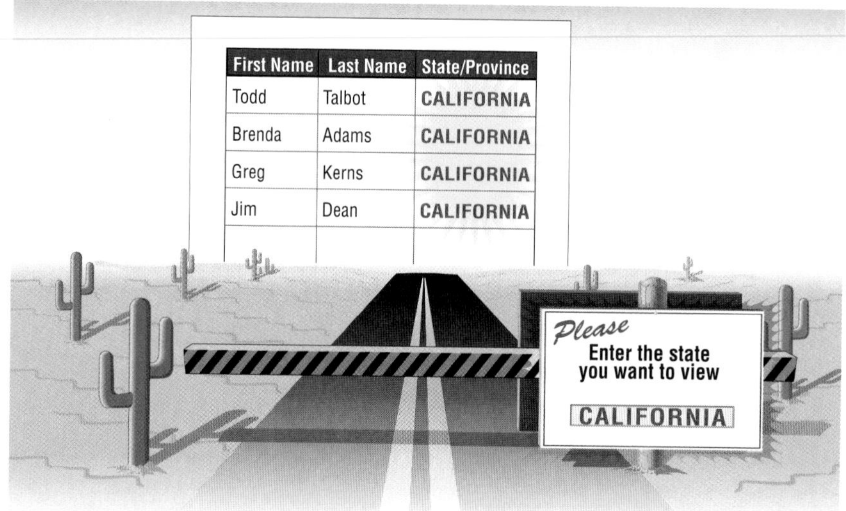

First Name
Last Name
State/Province
Todd
Talbot
CALIFORNIA
Brenda
Adams
CALIFORNIA
Greg
Kerns
CALIFORNIA
Jim
Dean
CALIFORNIA
Please
Enter the state you want to view
CALIFORNIA

For example, rather than manually changing the state for the records you want to view, you can have Access ask you for the name of the state each time you run a query.

USING PARAMETERS

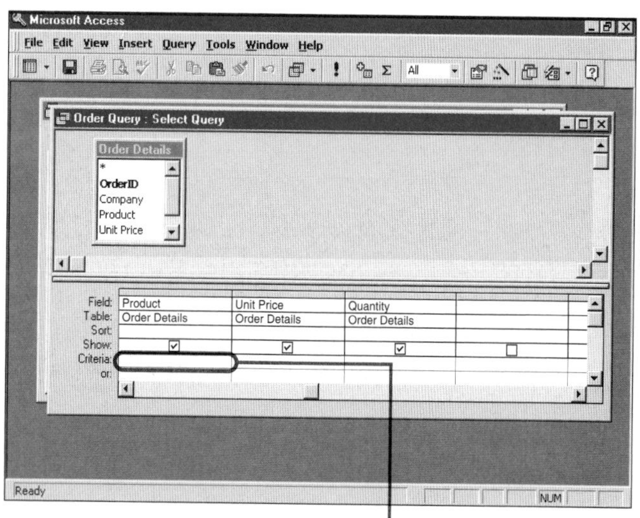

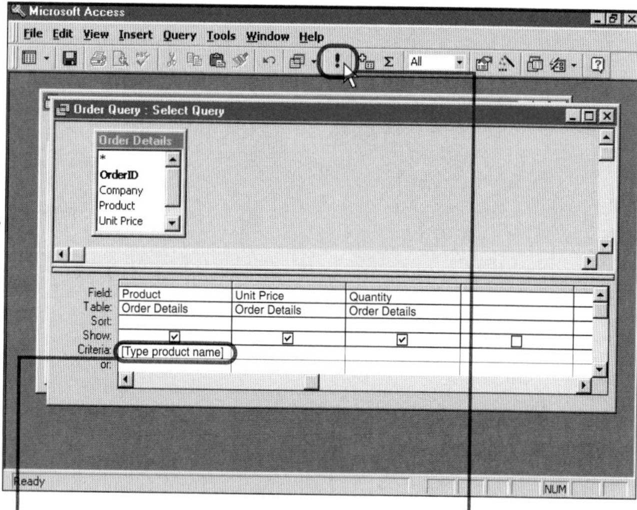

■ Display the query you want to change in the Design view. For information on changing views, refer to page 206.

1 Click the **Criteria** area for the field you want to use to find specific records.

2 Type the message you want Access to display to ask you for information when you run the query. Enclose the message in square brackets [ ].

Note: If the parameter you type is too long to fit in the column, you can display the entire contents of the cell. To do so, refer to page 61.

3 Click ! to run the query.

What types of parameters can I use in my queries?

Example	Result
<[Find records less than the value you enter]	Display the records less than this value.
Between [Type the starting date] And [Type the ending date]	Display the records between these dates.
>=[Type the smallest value you want to find]	Display the records greater than and equal to this value.

You can include other criteria with a parameter to find information in your database.

For examples of criteria, refer to pages 210 to 211.

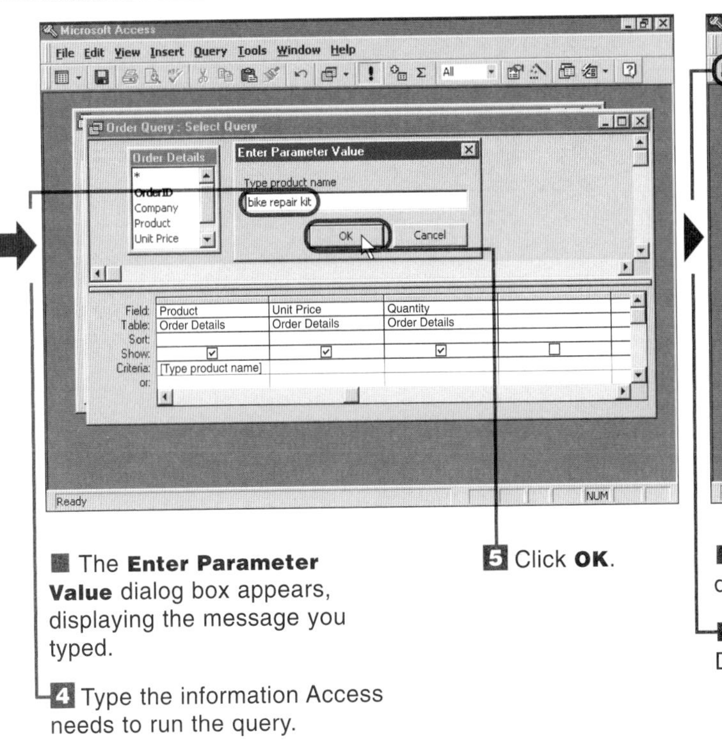

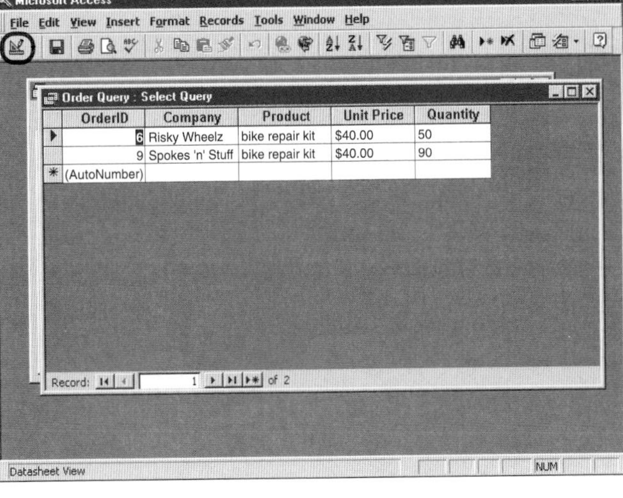

■ The **Enter Parameter Value** dialog box appears, displaying the message you typed.

4 Type the information Access needs to run the query.

5 Click **OK**.

■ The results of the query appear.

■ To return to the Design view, click .

■ You can use more than one parameter in a query. For each parameter in the query, an **Enter Parameter Value** dialog box will appear, requesting information.

CHANGE THE JOIN TYPE

You can change the way tables are joined in a query. The join type determines which records will appear in the results of a query.

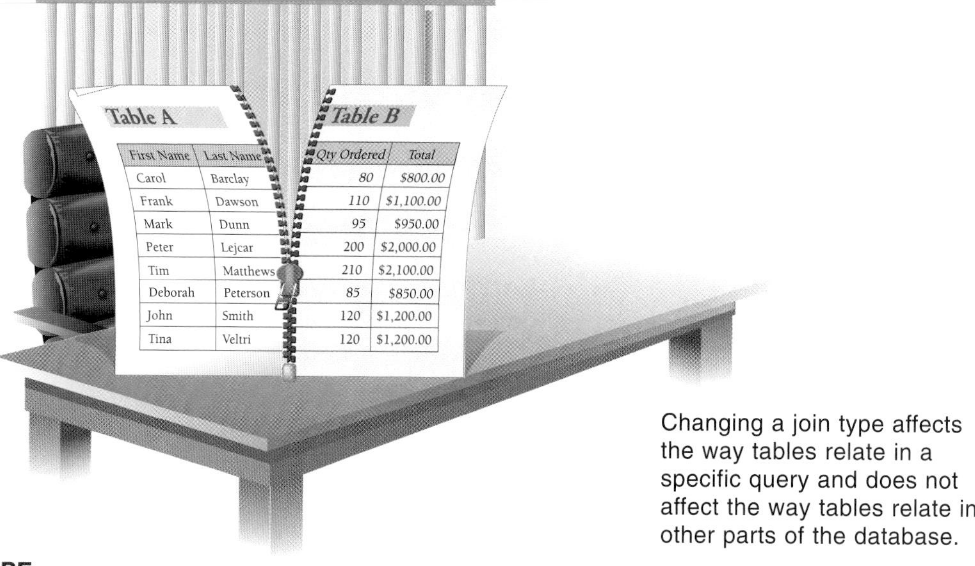

First Name	Last Name	Qty Ordered	Total
Carol	Barclay	80	$800.00
Frank	Dawson	110	$1,100.00
Mark	Dunn	95	$950.00
Peter	Lejcar	200	$2,000.00
Tim	Matthews	210	$2,100.00
Deborah	Peterson	85	$850.00
John	Smith	120	$1,200.00
Tina	Veltri	120	$1,200.00

Changing a join type affects the way tables relate in a specific query and does not affect the way tables relate in other parts of the database.

CHANGE THE JOIN TYPE

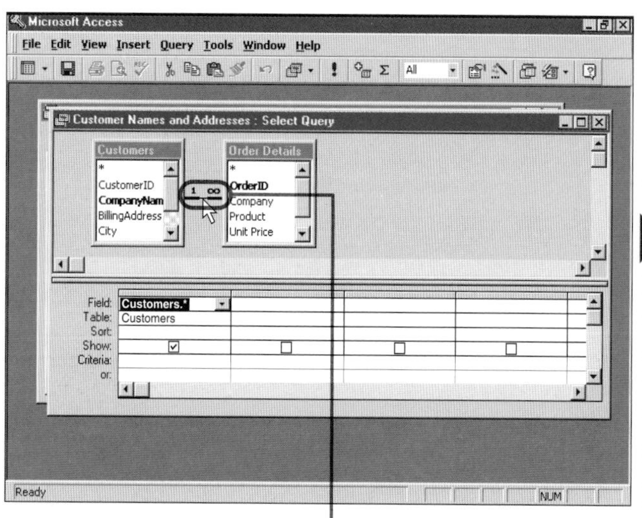

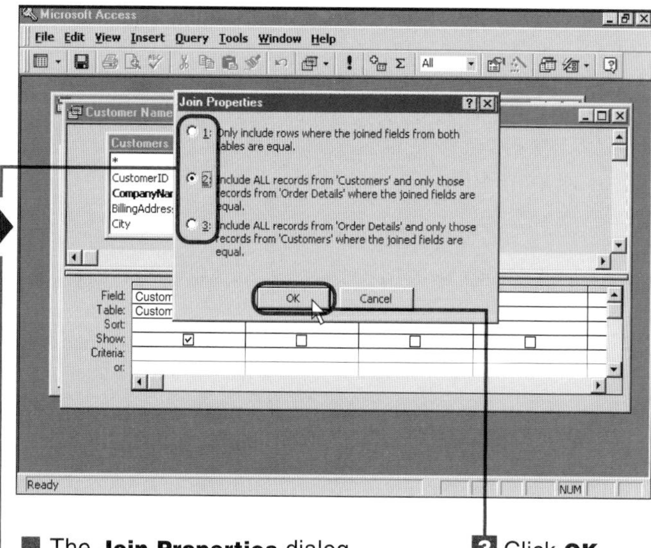

■ Display the query you want to change in the Design view. For information on changing views, refer to page 206.

■ A line connects the matching fields in the tables.

Note: If a line does not appear, the tables are not related. To create a relationship, refer to page 138.

1 To specify the type of join you want to use, double-click the middle of the line.

■ The **Join Properties** dialog box appears.

2 Click the number of the option you want to use for the query (○ changes to ◉).

3 Click **OK**.

First Name	Last Name	Quantity	Last Order
Mark	Dunn	145	3/21/96
Susan	Hughes	125	5/5/97
Carol	Barclay	120	7/12/97
Todd	Talbot	110	8/12/96
Allen	Toppins	100	4/6/97
Melanie	Robinson	95	6/30/96
Frank	Dawson	95	8/15/96

Option 1

Display all records from both tables that have matching values. This is the standard option used in most queries. For example, display only clients with orders.

First Name	Last Name	Quantity	Last Order
Mark	Dunn	145	3/21/96
Susan	Hughes	125	5/5/97
Carol	Barclay	120	7/12/97
Todd	Talbot	110	8/12/96
Allen	Toppins	100	4/6/97
Melanie	Robinson	95	6/30/96
Frank	Dawson	95	8/15/96
Jason	Marcuson		
Dorothy	Spencer		
Peter	Lejcar		

Option 2

Display all records from table A, but only matching records from table B. For example, display all records from the Clients table even if a client does not have any orders.

First Name	Last Name	Quantity	Last Order
Mark	Dunn	145	3/21/96
Susan	Hughes	125	5/5/97
Carol	Barclay	120	7/12/97
Todd	Talbot	110	8/12/96
Allen	Toppins	100	4/6/97
Melanie	Robinson	95	6/30/96
Frank	Dawson	95	8/15/96
		85	5/12/96
		80	6/17/96
		60	3/2/97

Option 3

Display all records from table B, but only matching records from table A. For example, display all records from the Orders table even if an order does not have a client. This option can help you find errors in your database design.

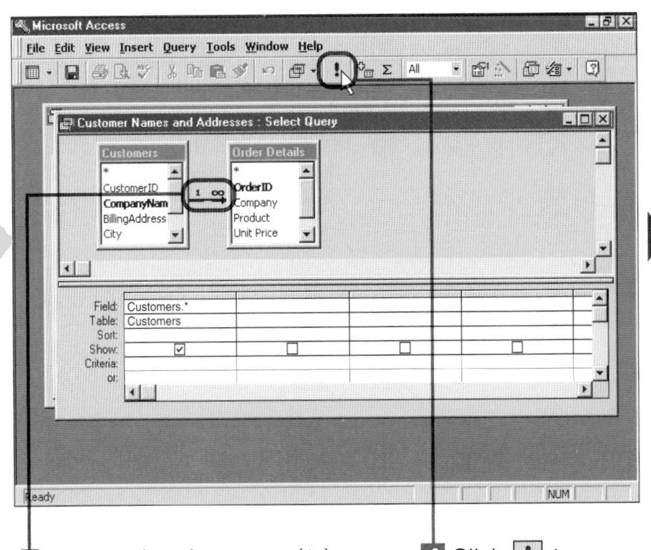

■ An arrowhead appears (▸) on the join line. The arrowhead points to the table that will display only matching records. The other table will show all records.

*Note: If you selected the first option in step **2**, no arrowhead appears on the line.*

4 Click [!] to run the query.

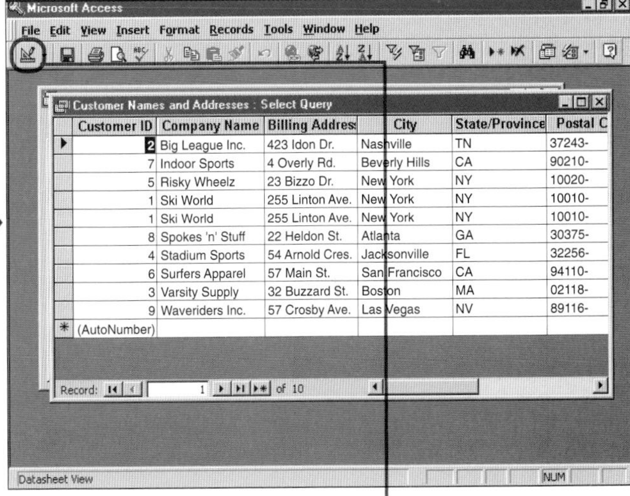

■ The results of the query appear. In this example, Access displays all records from the Customers table even if a customer does not have any orders.

■ To return to the Design view, click [Design view button].

USING MULTIPLE CRITERIA

You can use multiple criteria to find information in your database. Using the Or condition helps you find records that meet at least one of the criteria you specify.

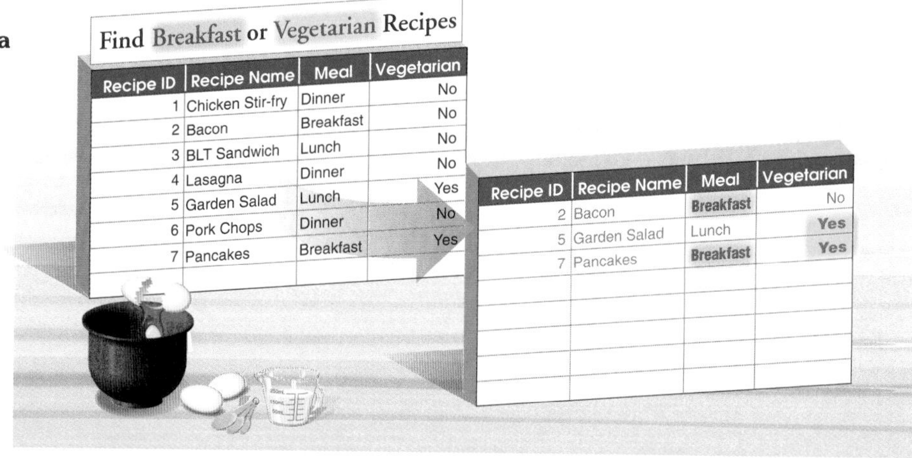

Find Breakfast or Vegetarian Recipes
Recipe ID | Recipe Name | Meal | Vegetarian
1 | Chicken Stir-fry | Dinner | No
2 | Bacon | Breakfast | No
3 | BLT Sandwich | Lunch | No
4 | Lasagna | Dinner | No
5 | Garden Salad | Lunch | Yes
6 | Pork Chops | Dinner | No
7 | Pancakes | Breakfast | Yes
Recipe ID | Recipe Name | Meal | Vegetarian
2 | Bacon | Breakfast | No
5 | Garden Salad | Lunch | Yes
7 | Pancakes | Breakfast | Yes

Access lets you use many types of criteria. For examples of criteria, refer to pages 210 to 211.

USING OR (WITH ONE FIELD)

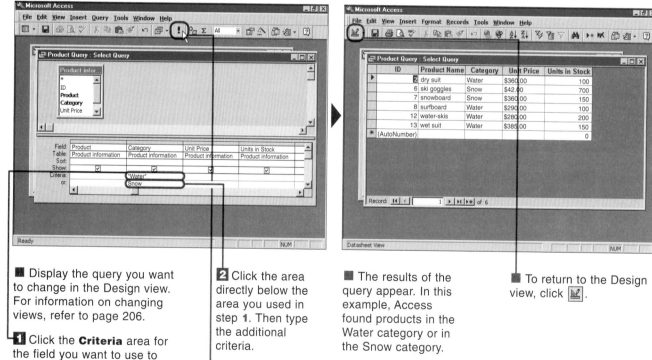

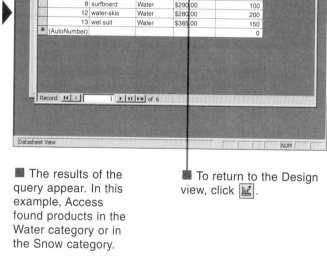

■ Display the query you want to change in the Design view. For information on changing views, refer to page 206.

1 Click the **Criteria** area for the field you want to use to find specific records. Then type the criteria.

2 Click the area directly below the area you used in step **1**. Then type the additional criteria.

3 Click [!] to run the query.

■ The results of the query appear. In this example, Access found products in the Water category or in the Snow category.

■ To return to the Design view, click [Design View icon].

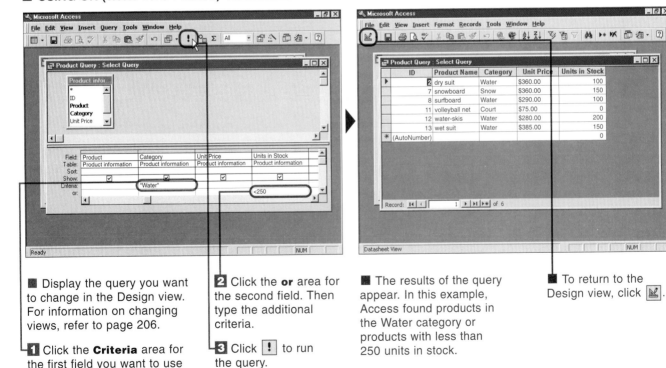

How can I use the Or condition to find information in my database?

You can use the Or condition with one or two fields.

State
CA
CA
TX
TX

One Field

California Or Texas

Finds clients living in California or in Texas.

State	Units Sold
IL	305
CA	550
IL	210
TX	325

Two Fields

Illinois Or >300

Finds clients living in Illinois or clients who bought more than 300 units of product.

USING OR (WITH TWO FIELDS)

■ Display the query you want to change in the Design view. For information on changing views, refer to page 206.

1 Click the **Criteria** area for the first field you want to use to find specific records. Then type the criteria.

2 Click the **or** area for the second field. Then type the additional criteria.

3 Click ! to run the query.

■ The results of the query appear. In this example, Access found products in the Water category or products with less than 250 units in stock.

■ To return to the Design view, click the Design View button.

USING MULTIPLE CRITERIA

Using the And condition in a query helps you find records that meet all of the criteria you specify.

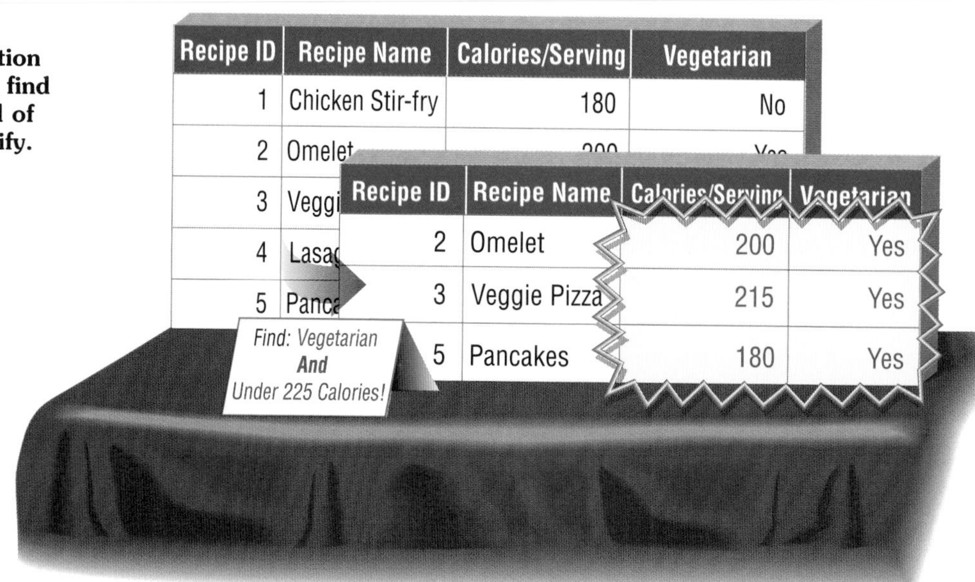

Recipe ID | Recipe Name | Calories/Serving | Vegetarian
1 Chicken Stir-fry 180 No
2 Omelet
3 Veggi
4 Lasag
5 Panca
Find: Vegetarian
And
Under 225 Calories!
Recipe ID | Recipe Name | Calories/Serving | Vegetarian
2 Omelet 200 Yes
3 Veggie Pizza 215 Yes
5 Pancakes 180 Yes

USING AND (WITH ONE FIELD)

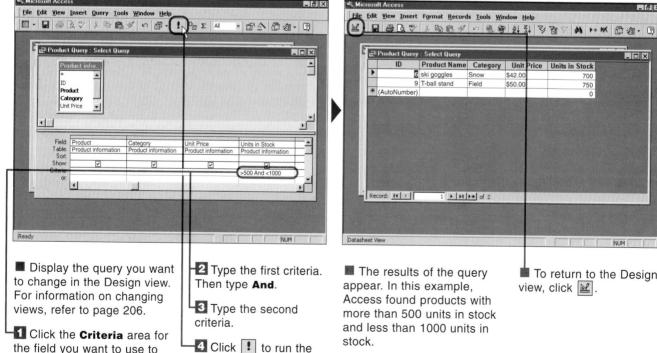

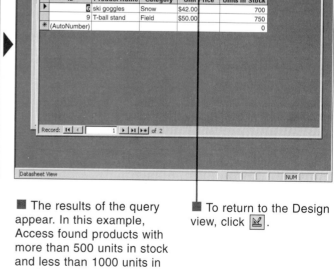

■ Display the query you want to change in the Design view. For information on changing views, refer to page 206.

1 Click the **Criteria** area for the field you want to use to find specific records.

2 Type the first criteria. Then type **And**.

3 Type the second criteria.

4 Click ! to run the query.

■ The results of the query appear. In this example, Access found products with more than 500 units in stock and less than 1000 units in stock.

■ To return to the Design view, click the Design View button.

How can I use the And condition to find information in my database?

You can use the And condition with one or two fields.

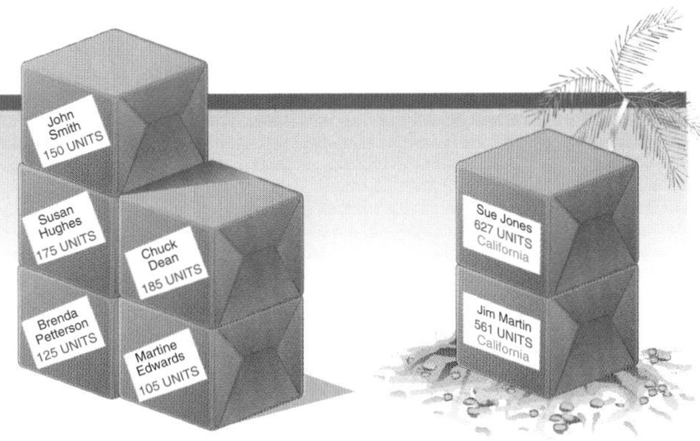

One Field

>100 And <200

Finds clients who bought more than 100 units of product and less than 200 units of product.

Two Fields

California And >500

Finds clients living in California who bought more than 500 units of product.

USING AND (WITH TWO FIELDS)

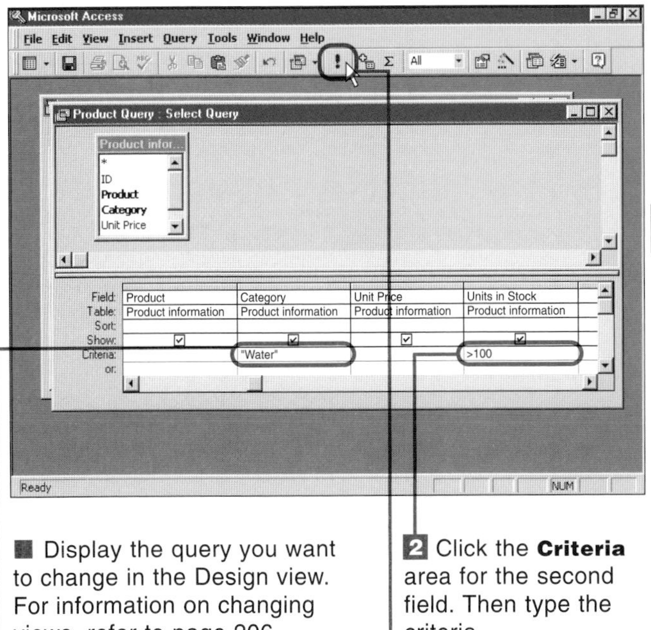

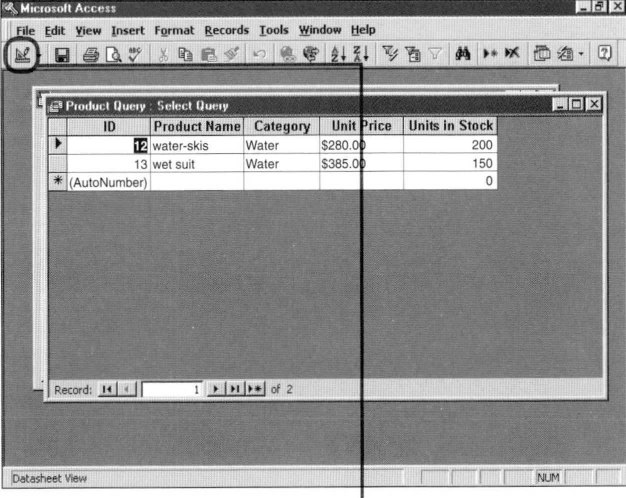

■ Display the query you want to change in the Design view. For information on changing views, refer to page 206.

1 Click the **Criteria** area for the first field you want to use to find specific records. Then type the criteria.

2 Click the **Criteria** area for the second field. Then type the criteria.

3 Click [!] to run the query.

■ The results of the query appear. In this example, Access found products in the Water category that have more than 100 units in stock.

■ To return to the Design view, click [design view icon].

SUMMARIZE DATA

You can summarize the information in your database to help you analyze the data.

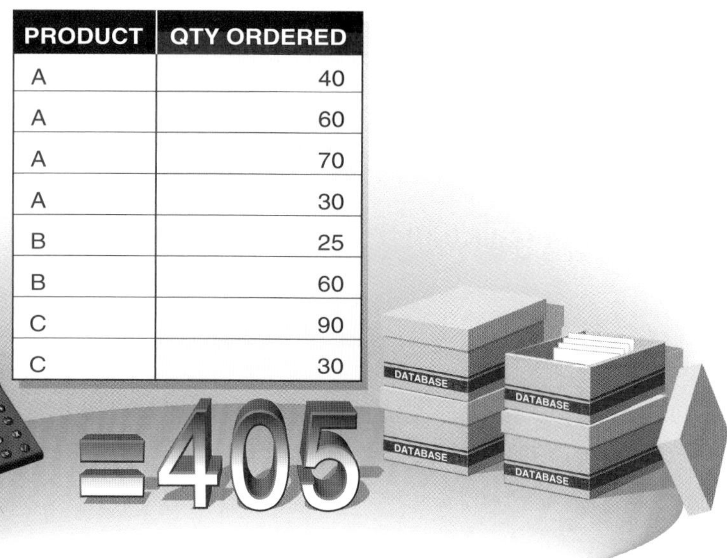

PRODUCT	QTY ORDERED
A	40
A	60
A	70
A	30
B	25
B	60
C	90
C	30

For example, you can summarize the data to determine the total number of orders.

SUMMARIZE DATA (FOR ONE FIELD)

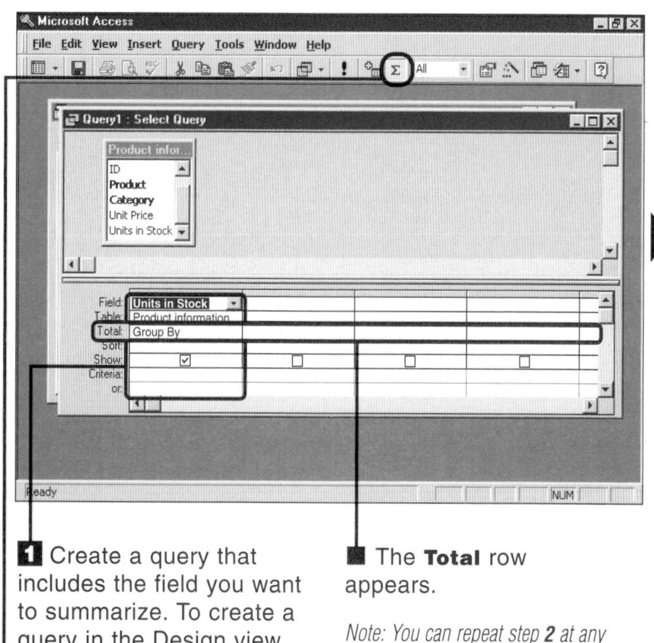

1 Create a query that includes the field you want to summarize. To create a query in the Design view, refer to page 202.

2 Click Σ to summarize the data.

■ The **Total** row appears.

*Note: You can repeat step **2** at any time to remove the **Total** row.*

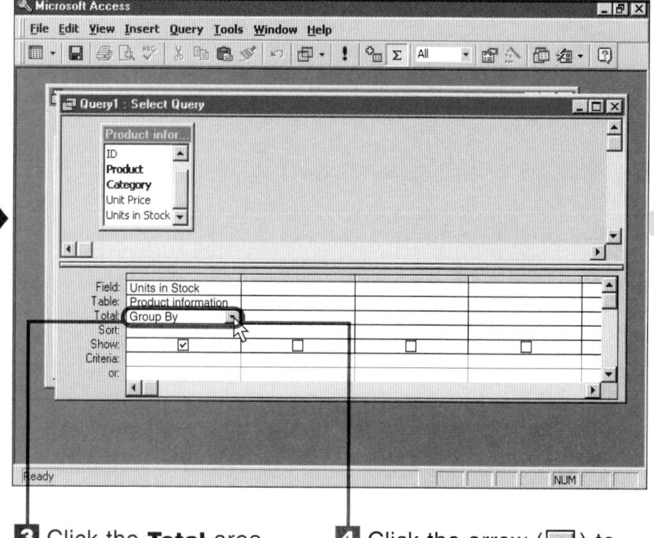

3 Click the **Total** area for the field you want to summarize. An arrow appears (▾).

4 Click the arrow (▾) to display a list of calculations you can perform.

? What calculations can I perform to summarize data?

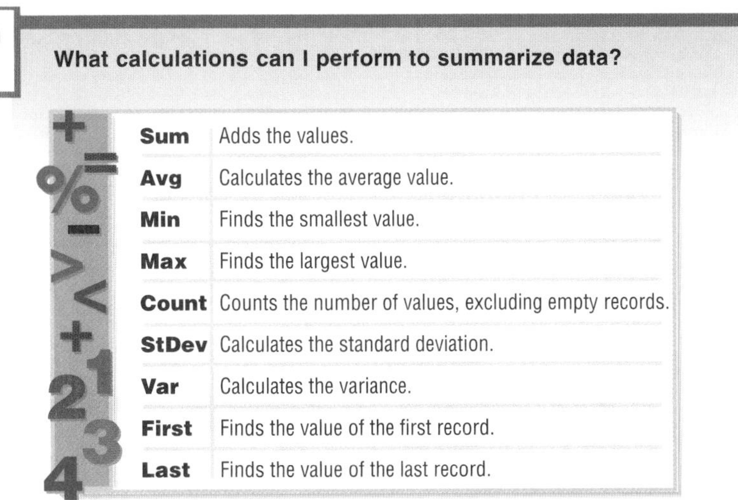

Sum	Adds the values.
Avg	Calculates the average value.
Min	Finds the smallest value.
Max	Finds the largest value.
Count	Counts the number of values, excluding empty records.
StDev	Calculates the standard deviation.
Var	Calculates the variance.
First	Finds the value of the first record.
Last	Finds the value of the last record.

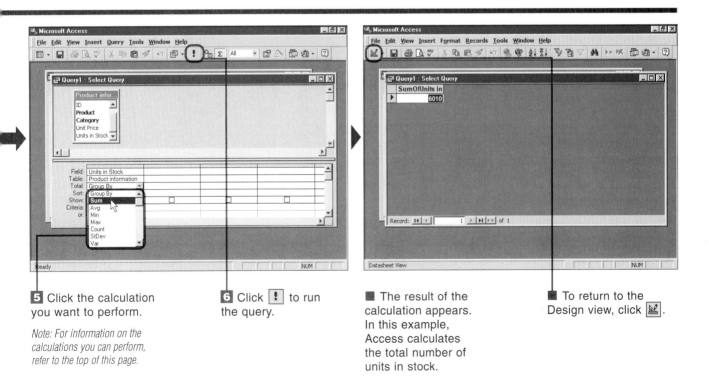

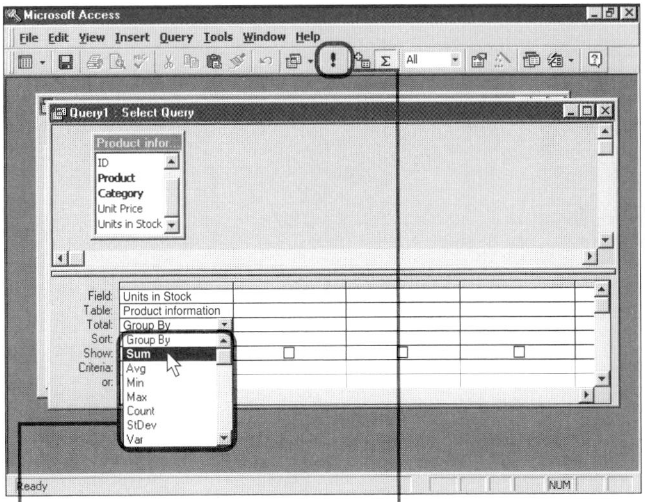

5 Click the calculation you want to perform.

Note: For information on the calculations you can perform, refer to the top of this page.

6 Click ! to run the query.

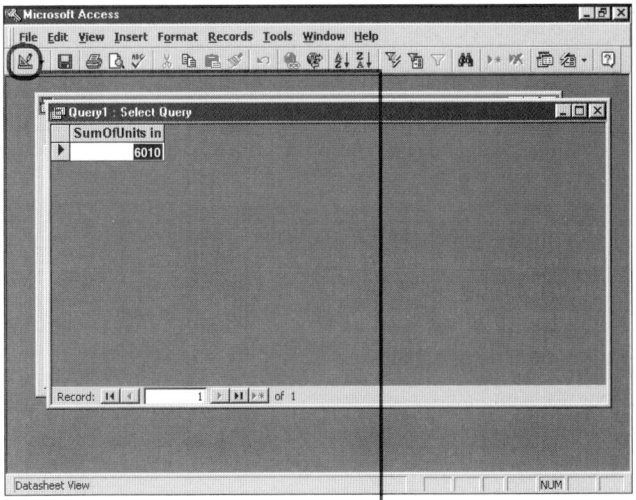

■ The result of the calculation appears. In this example, Access calculates the total number of units in stock.

■ To return to the Design view, click [Design view button].

SUMMARIZE DATA

You can separate records in your database into groups and summarize the information for each group.

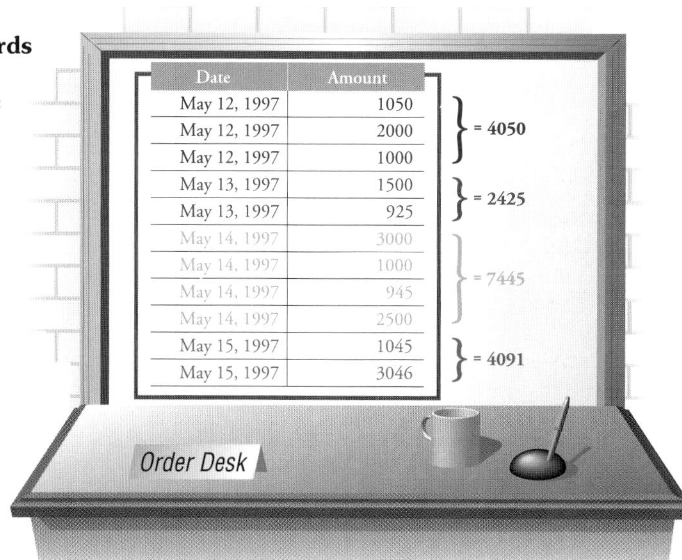

Date
Amount
May 12, 1997 1050
May 12, 1997 2000
May 12, 1997 1000
= 4050
May 13, 1997 1500
May 13, 1997 925
= 2425
May 14, 1997 3000
May 14, 1997 1000
May 14, 1997 945
May 14, 1997 2500
= 7445
May 15, 1997 1045
May 15, 1997 3046
= 4091
Order Desk

For example, you can summarize data grouped by date to determine the number of orders for each day.

SUMMARIZE DATA (FOR GROUPED RECORDS)

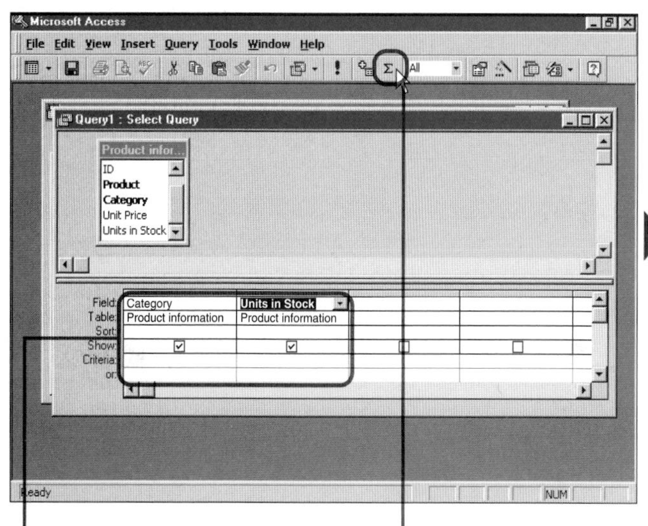

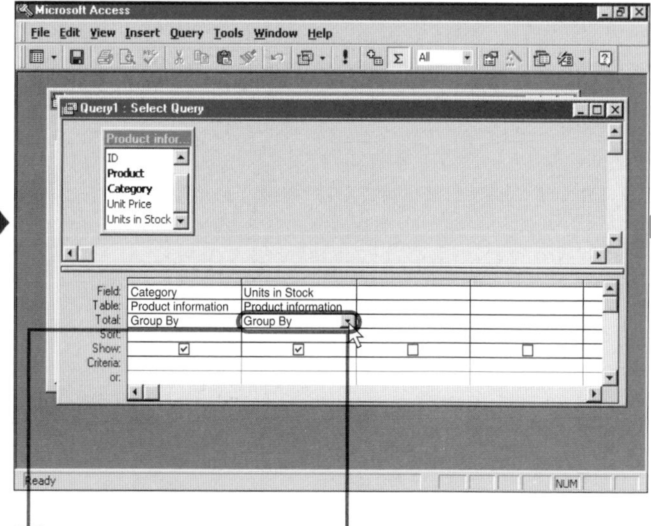

1 Create a query that includes the field you want to use to group your records and the field you want to summarize. To create a query in the Design view, refer to page 202.

2 Click Σ to summarize the data.

■ The **Total** row appears.

*Note: You can repeat step **2** at any time to remove the **Total** row.*

3 Click the **Total** area for the field you want to summarize. An arrow appears (▾).

4 Click the arrow (▾) to display a list of calculations you can perform on the field.

? Can I use more than one field to group records?

You can group records by using more than one field. For example, you may want to see the total number of each product bought by every company. Place each field in the query in the order you want to group the records.

COMPANY	PRODUCT	TOTAL QTY ORDERED	
Fitness Minds	A	40	}= 100
Fitness Minds	A	60	
Fitness Minds	C	80	}= 110
Fitness Minds	C	30	
SportStop	A	25	}= 85
SportStop	A	60	
SportStop	D	90	}= 190
SportStop	D	100	

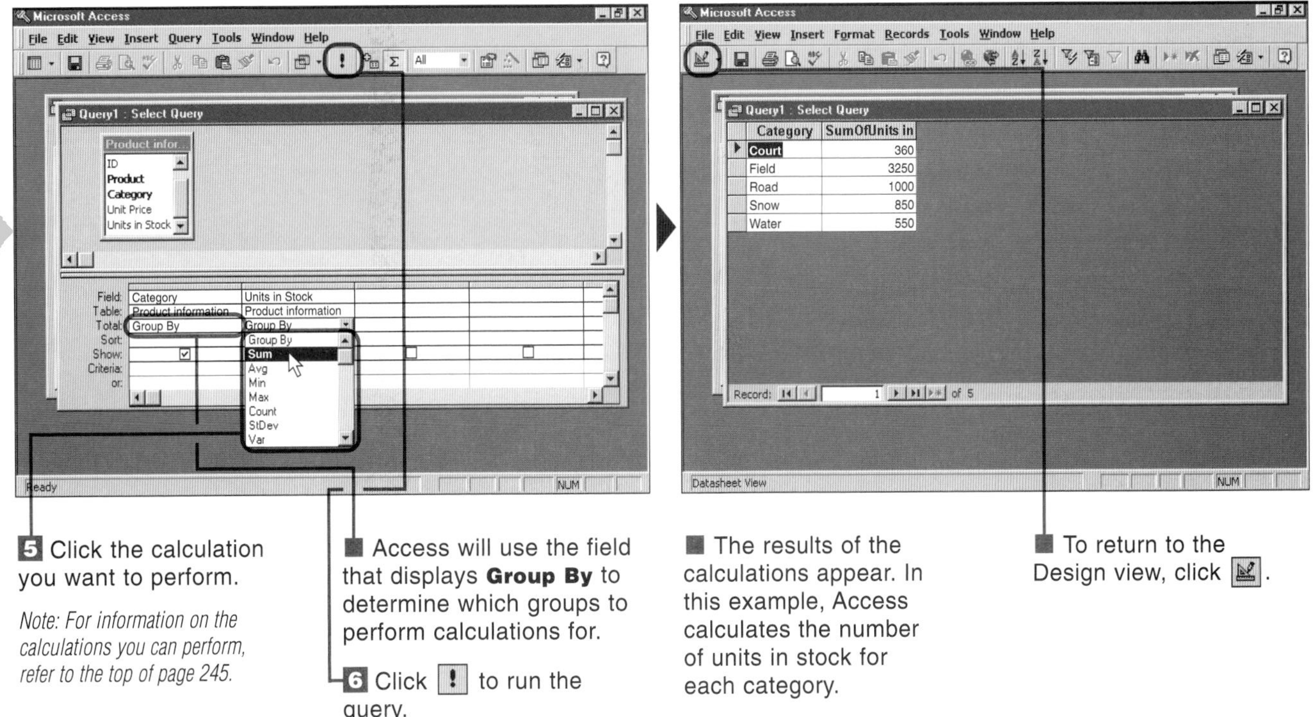

5 Click the calculation you want to perform.

Note: For information on the calculations you can perform, refer to the top of page 245.

■ Access will use the field that displays **Group By** to determine which groups to perform calculations for.

6 Click ! to run the query.

■ The results of the calculations appear. In this example, Access calculates the number of units in stock for each category.

■ To return to the Design view, click the Design View button.

When summarizing data, you can use criteria to limit the records used in a calculation. Criteria are conditions that identify the records of interest.

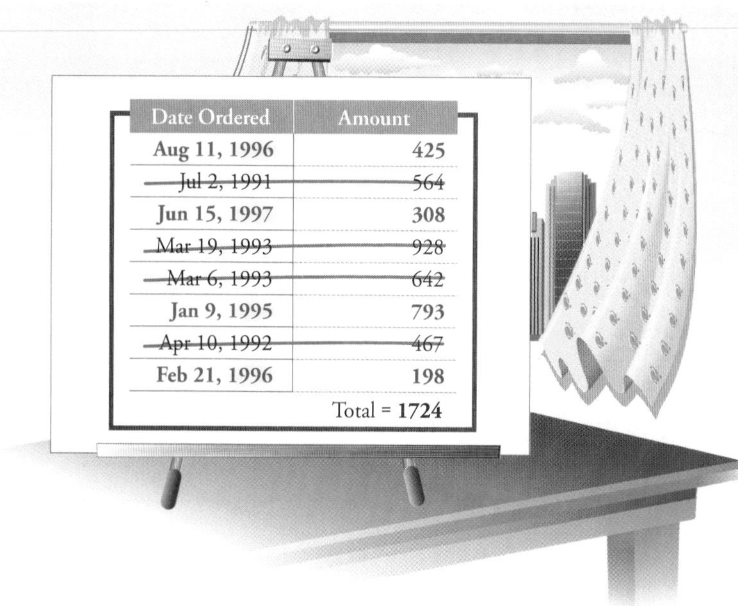

For example, you can use criteria to include only orders after 1994 in a calculation.

SUMMARIZE DATA (USING CRITERIA TO LIMIT RECORDS)

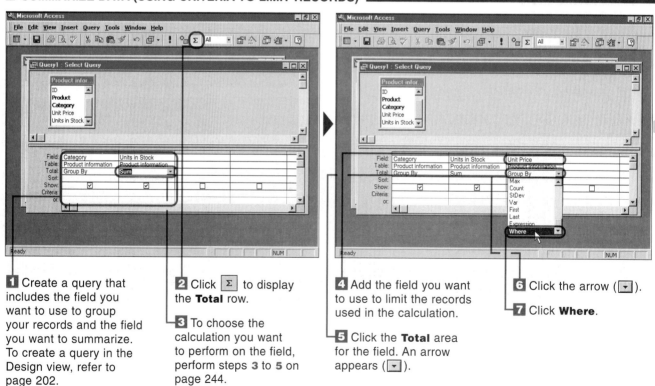

1 Create a query that includes the field you want to use to group your records and the field you want to summarize. To create a query in the Design view, refer to page 202.

2 Click Σ to display the **Total** row.

3 To choose the calculation you want to perform on the field, perform steps **3** to **5** on page 244.

4 Add the field you want to use to limit the records used in the calculation.

5 Click the **Total** area for the field. An arrow appears (▾).

6 Click the arrow (▾).

7 Click **Where**.

? Can I limit the records that appear in the results?

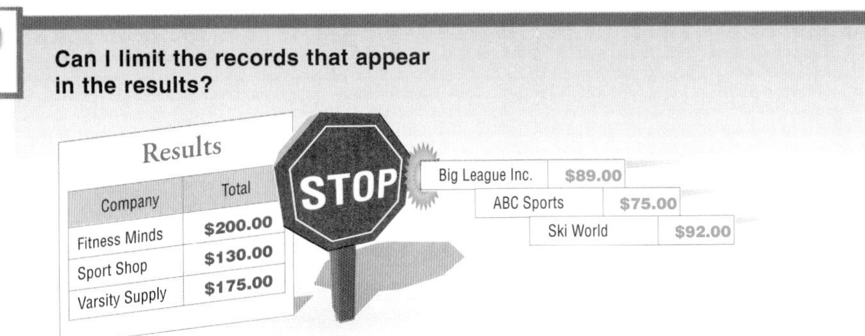

You can perform a calculation on all the records, but show only some of the records in the results. For example, you may want to display orders only if the orders total more than $100.

In the **Criteria** area of the field you are summarizing, type the criteria you want to limit the records shown in the result. For examples of criteria, refer to pages 210 to 211.

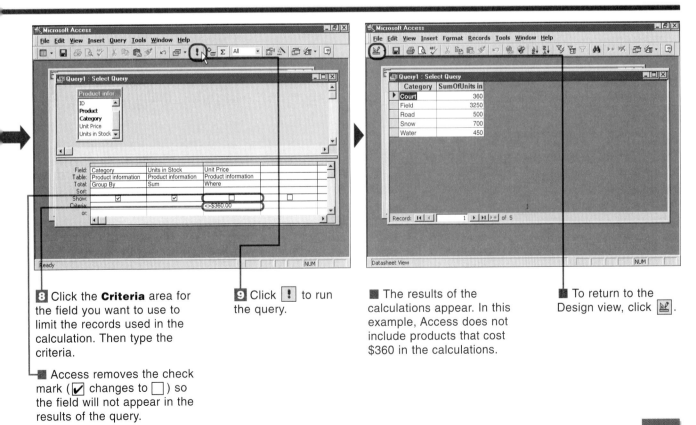

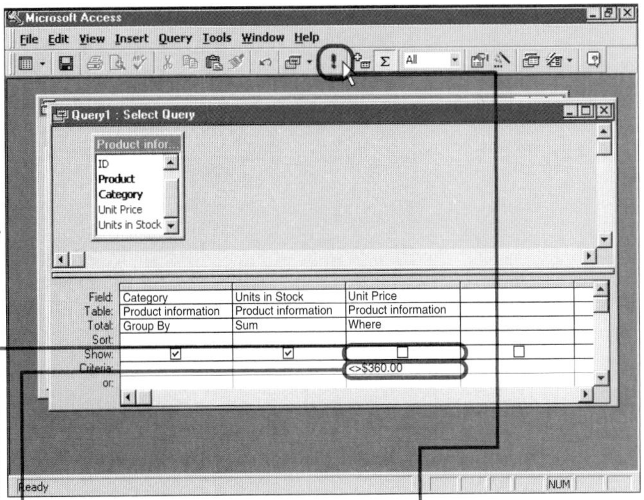

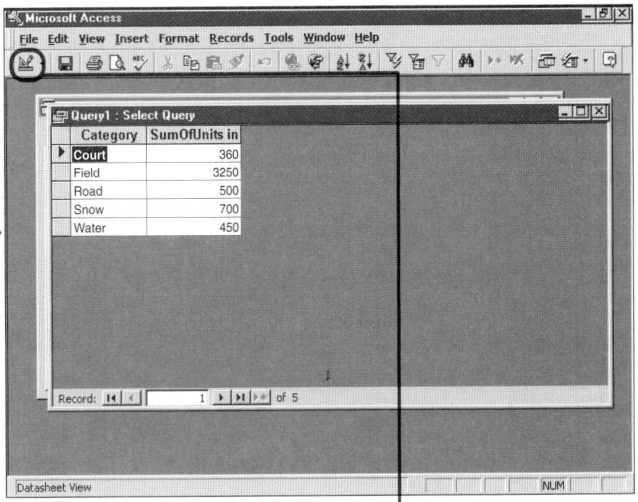

8 Click the **Criteria** area for the field you want to use to limit the records used in the calculation. Then type the criteria.

■ Access removes the check mark (☑ changes to ☐) so the field will not appear in the results of the query.

9 Click [!] to run the query.

■ The results of the calculations appear. In this example, Access does not include products that cost $360 in the calculations.

■ To return to the Design view, click [Design View].

FIND UNMATCHED RECORDS

You can easily find records in one table that have no matching records in another table.

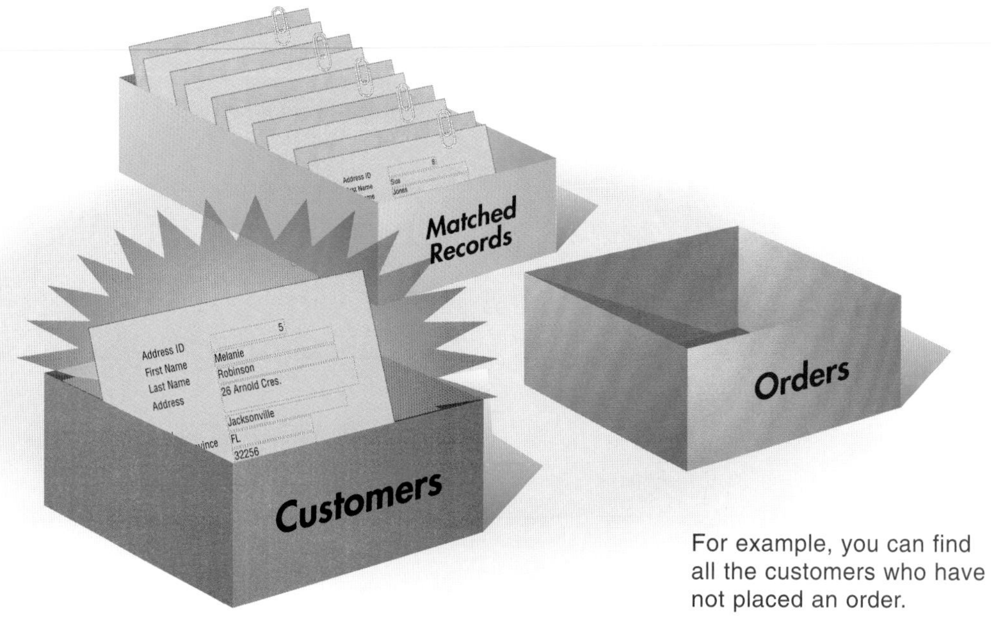

For example, you can find all the customers who have not placed an order.

FIND UNMATCHED RECORDS

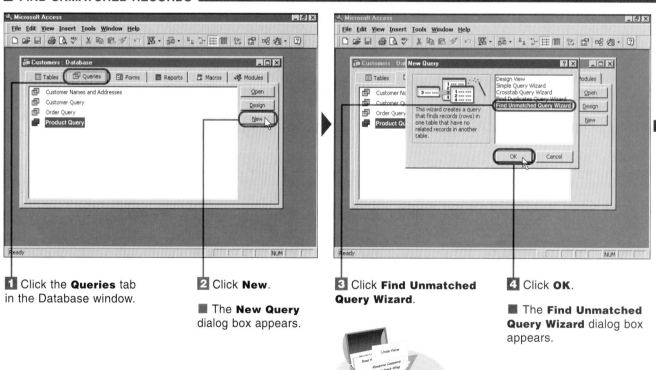

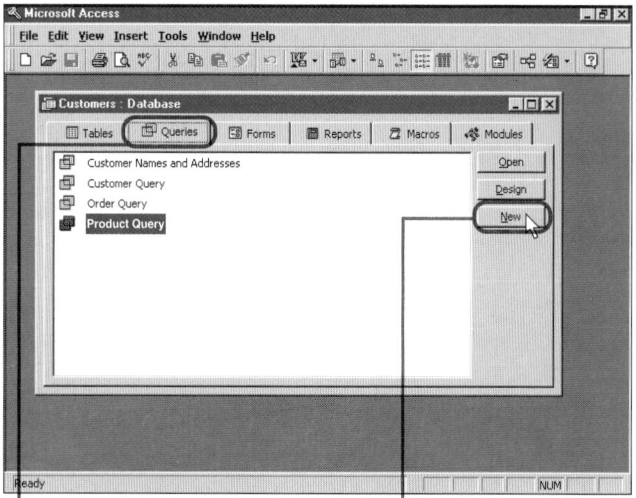

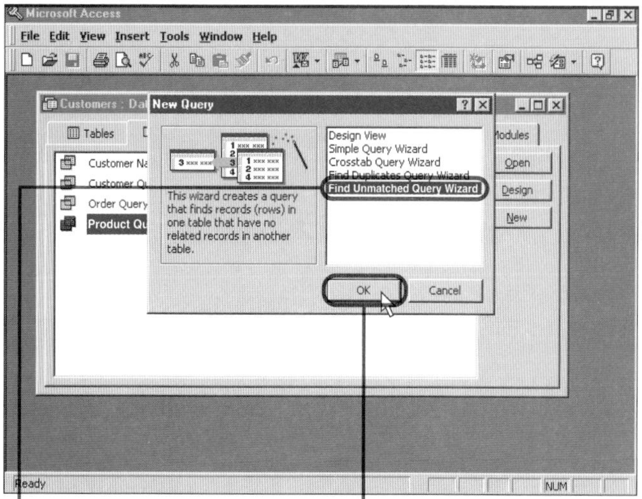

1. Click the **Queries** tab in the Database window.

2. Click **New**.

   ■ The **New Query** dialog box appears.

3. Click **Find Unmatched Query Wizard**.

4. Click **OK**.

   ■ The **Find Unmatched Query Wizard** dialog box appears.

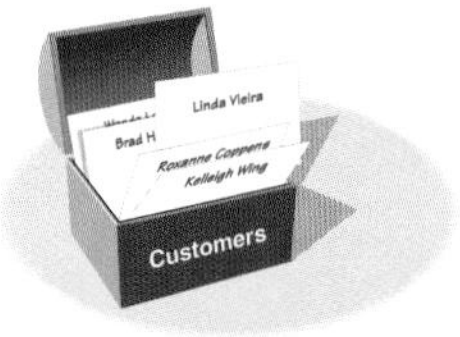

?

Why does this error message appear?

This error message appears if the Find Unmatched Query Wizard is not available on your computer. You need to install the Advanced Wizards feature from the Microsoft Access or Microsoft Office Setup program if you want to use the wizard to create a query.

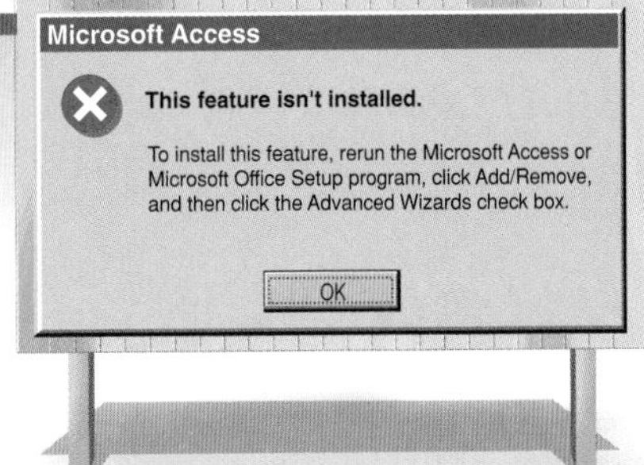

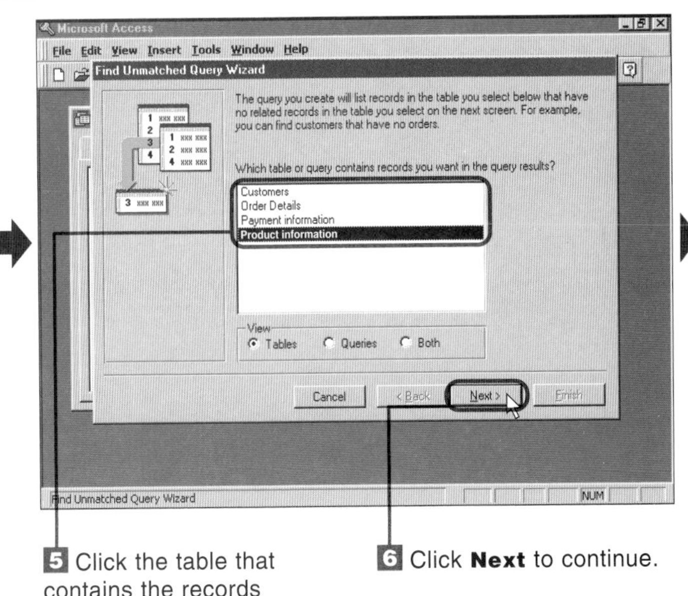

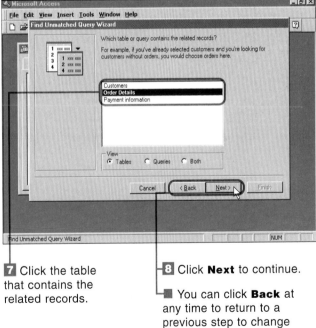

5 Click the table that contains the records you want to view if no matching records exist in the other table.

6 Click **Next** to continue.

7 Click the table that contains the related records.

8 Click **Next** to continue.

■ You can click **Back** at any time to return to a previous step to change your answers.

CONTINUED

FIND UNMATCHED RECORDS

When using the Find Unmatched Query Wizard, you need to select the field that relates the two tables in the query. The field usually has the same name in both tables.

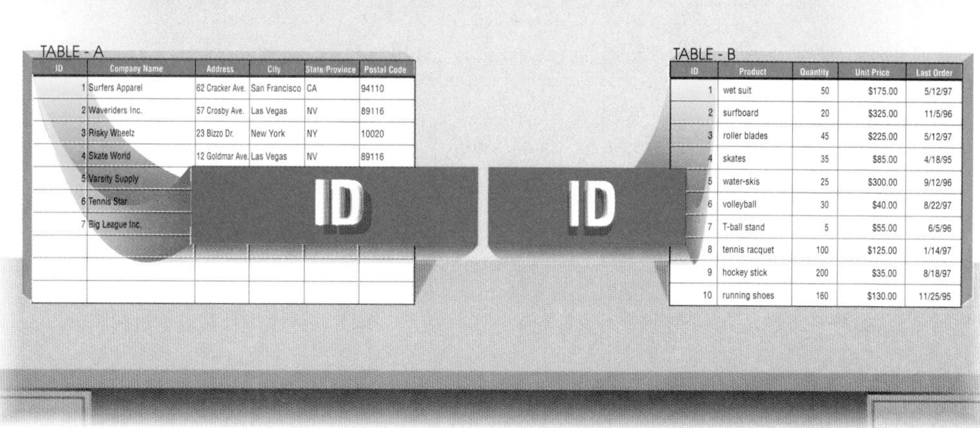

FIND UNMATCHED RECORDS (CONTINUED)

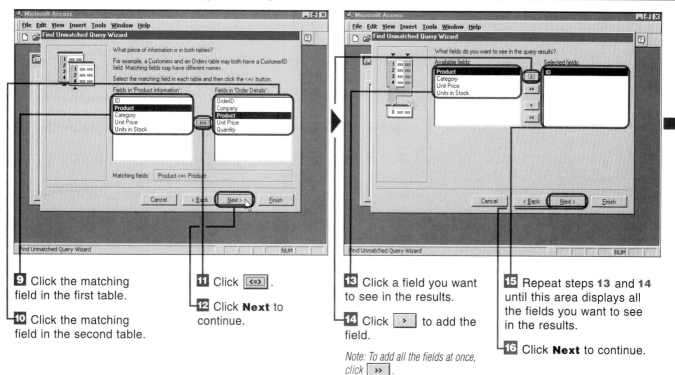

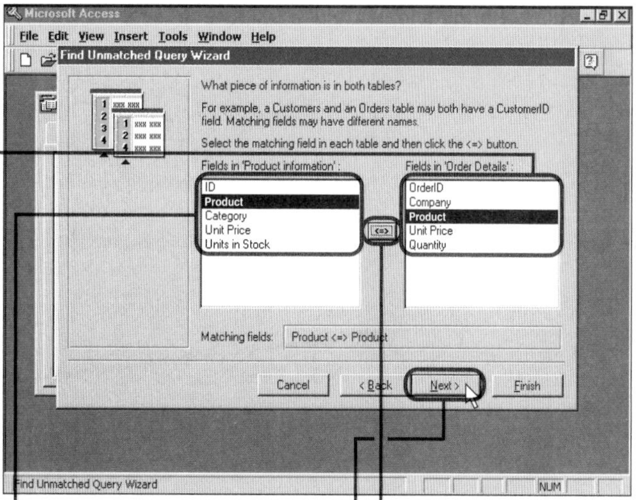

9 Click the matching field in the first table.

10 Click the matching field in the second table.

11 Click <=>.

12 Click **Next** to continue.

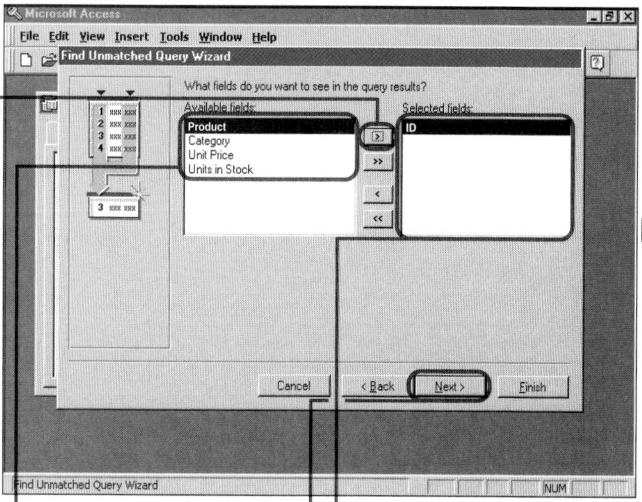

13 Click a field you want to see in the results.

14 Click > to add the field.

Note: To add all the fields at once, click >>.

15 Repeat steps **13** and **14** until this area displays all the fields you want to see in the results.

16 Click **Next** to continue.

?

Can I change a query I created using the Find Unmatched Query Wizard?

You can easily make changes to a query in the Design view. To change views, refer to page 206.

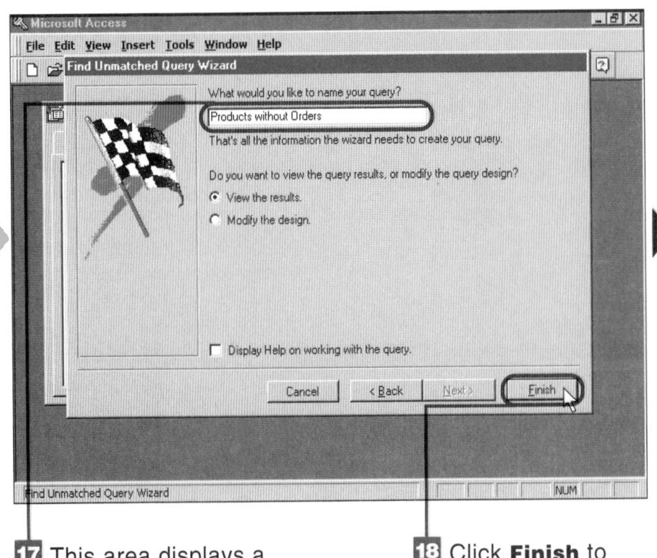

17 This area displays a name for the query. To save the query with a different name, type the new name.

18 Click **Finish** to run the query.

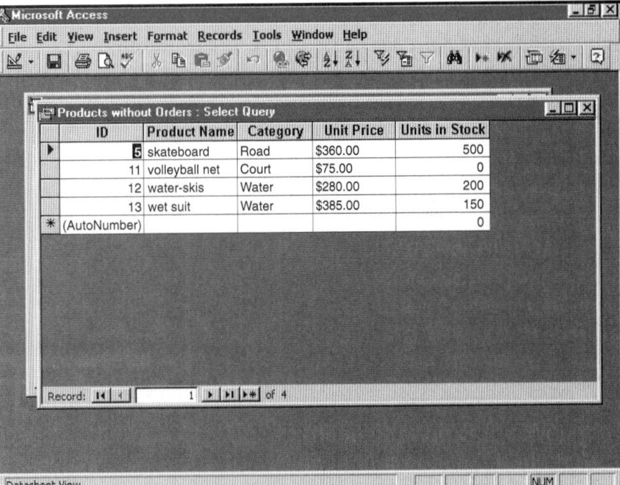

■ The results of the query appear. In this example, the results show information for each product that a customer has not ordered.

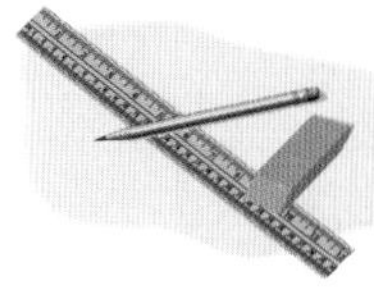

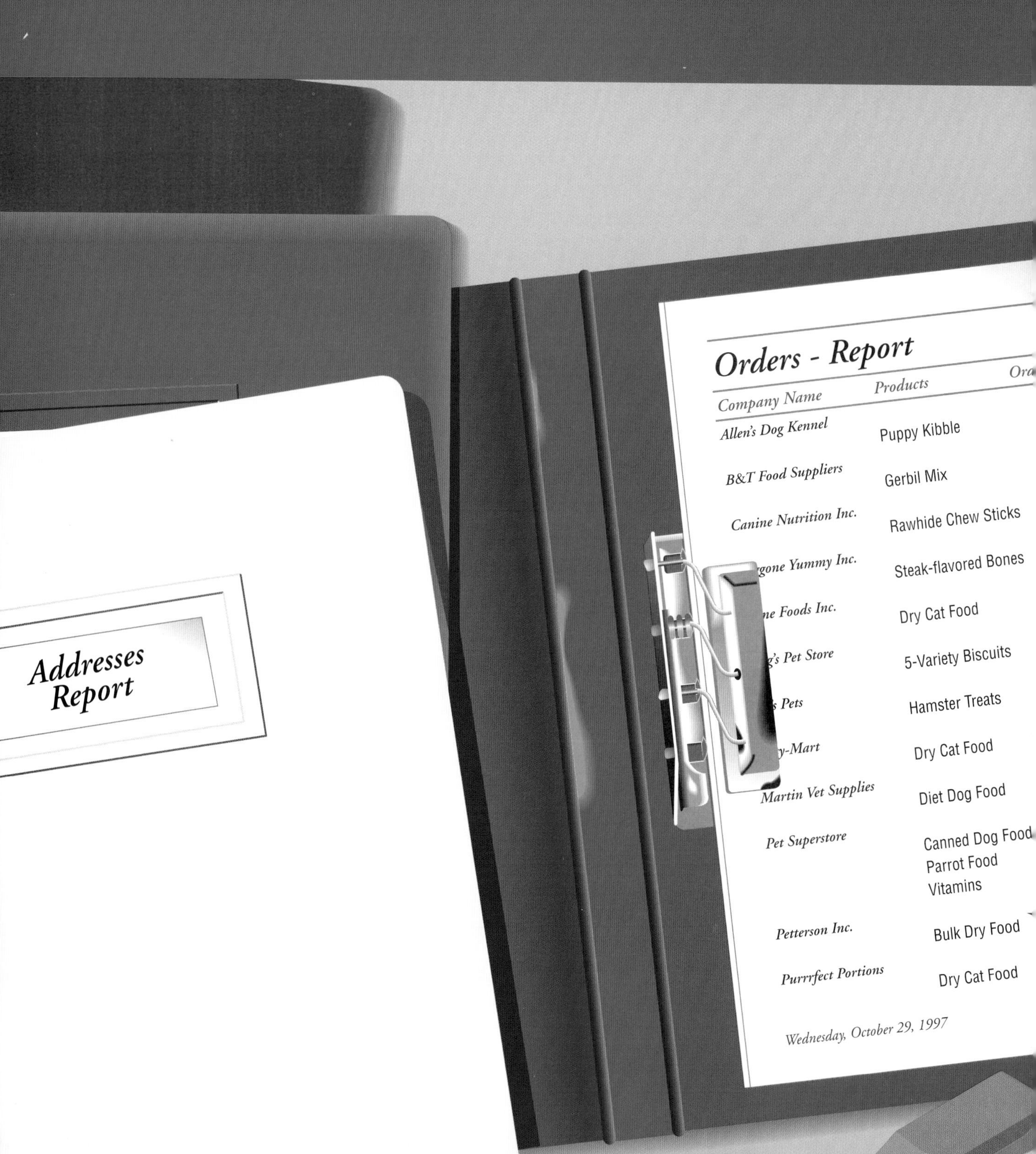
Addresses Report
Orders - Report
Company Name
Products
Allen's Dog Kennel
Puppy Kibble
B&T Food Suppliers
Gerbil Mix
Canine Nutrition Inc.
Rawhide Chew Sticks
Steak-flavored Bones
Dry Cat Food
5-Variety Biscuits
Hamster Treats
Dry Cat Food
Martin Vet Supplies
Diet Dog Food
Pet Superstore
Canned Dog Food
Parrot Food
Vitamins
Petterson Inc.
Bulk Dry Food
Purrrfect Portions
Dry Cat Food
Wednesday, October 29, 1997

CHAPTER 13

Create Reports

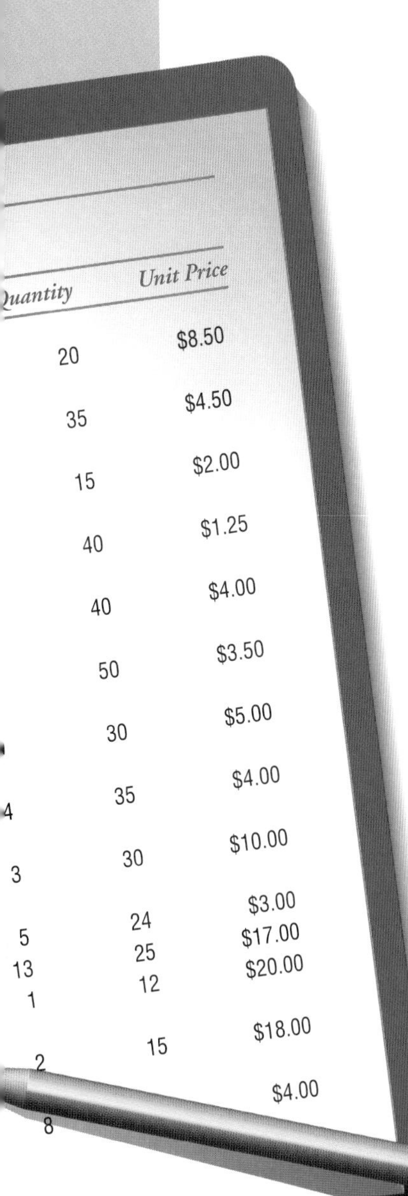

Would you like to learn how to create reports? This chapter teaches you how to use the information from your database to create personalized reports.

Create a Report Using an AutoReport 256

Change View of Report 260

Close a Report 262

Open a Report 263

Rename a Report 264

Delete a Report 265

Create a Report Using the Report Wizard........266

CREATE A REPORT USING AN AUTOREPORT

You can use the AutoReport Wizard to quickly create a professionally designed report to display information from a table.

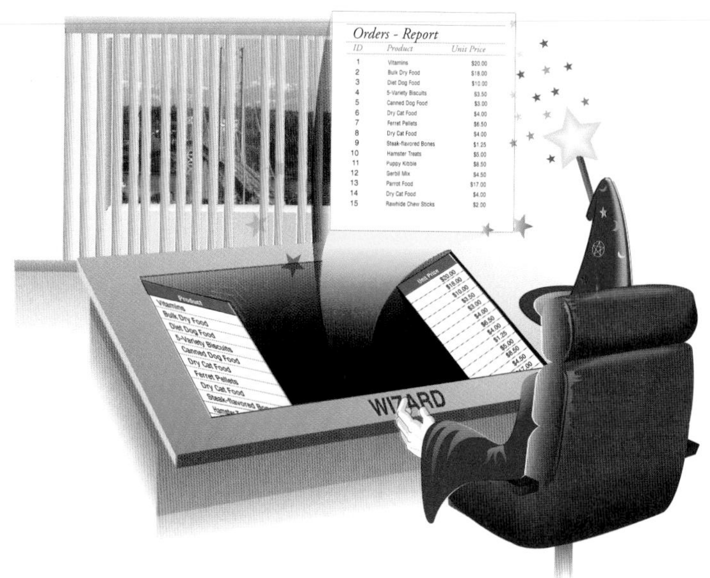

If you want to create a more sophisticated report, refer to pages 266 to 273 to create a report using the Report Wizard.

CREATE A REPORT USING AN AUTOREPORT

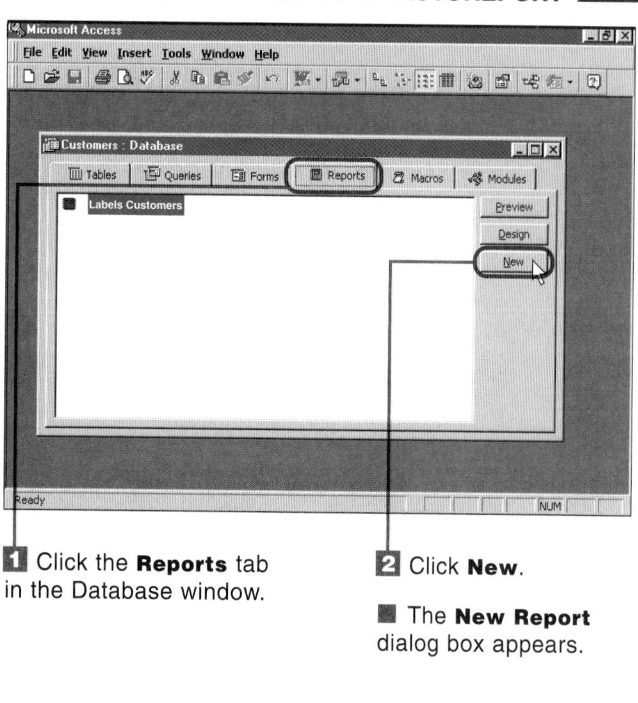

1 Click the **Reports** tab in the Database window.

2 Click **New**.

■ The **New Report** dialog box appears.

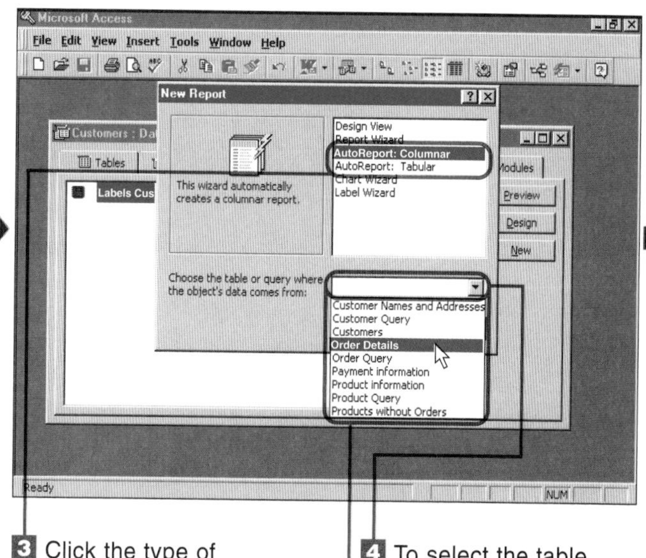

3 Click the type of AutoReport you want to create. For information on the available types, refer to the top of page 257.

4 To select the table that will supply the data for the report, click ▼ in this area.

5 Click the table that will supply the data.

?

What types of AutoReports are available?

Access offers two types of AutoReports that you can choose from.

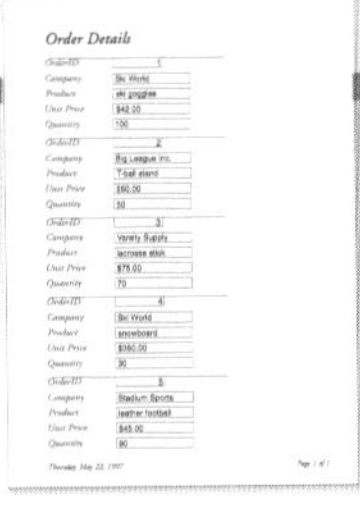

Columnar

Displays the field names down the left side of the page. The information for each record appears beside each field name.

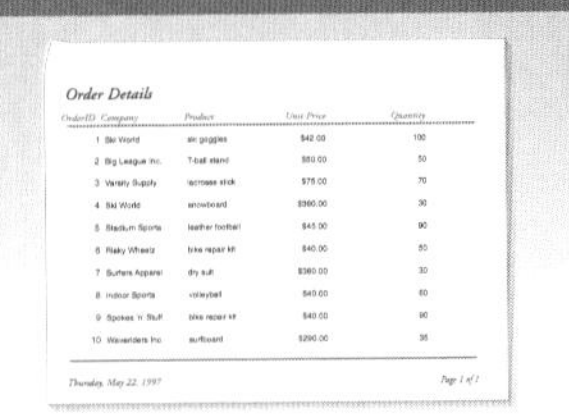

Tabular

Displays the field names across the top of the page. Each record appears on one line. The tabular format allows you to fit more records on fewer pages.

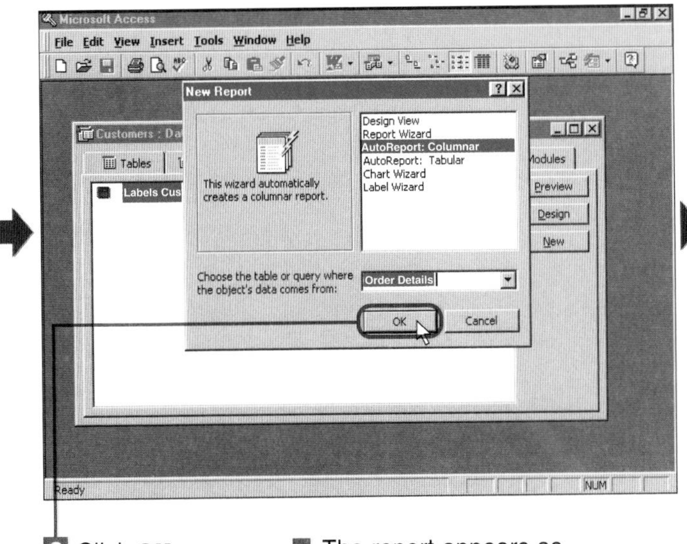

6 Click **OK**.

■ The report appears as it will look when printed.

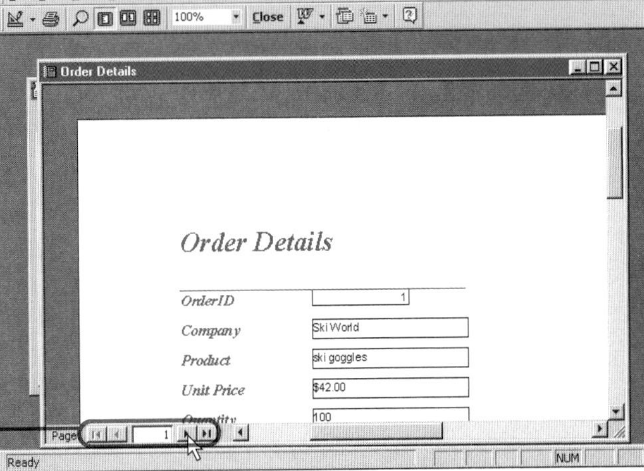

■ This area shows the number of the page displayed on your screen.

7 To display another page, click one of the following options.

Note: If an option is dimmed, the option is currently not available.

- First page
- Previous page
- Next page
- Last page

CONTINUED

CREATE A REPORT USING AN AUTOREPORT

You can display an entire page in your report to view its overall appearance or magnify an area of a page to view the data more clearly.

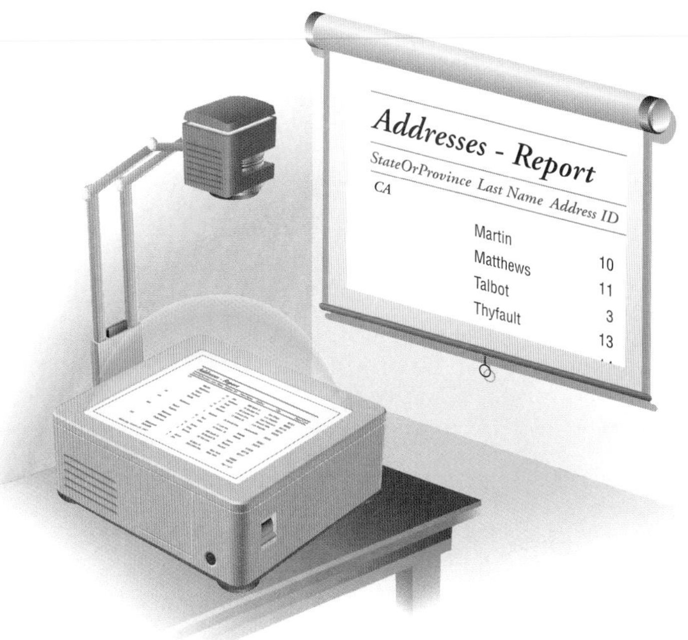

CREATE A REPORT USING AN AUTOREPORT (CONTINUED)

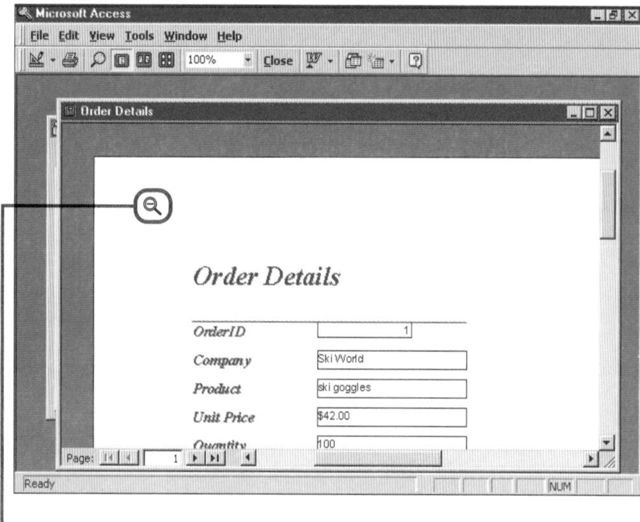

DISPLAY ENTIRE PAGE

1 To display an entire page, position the mouse anywhere on the page (changes to magnifier) and then click to display the entire page.

■ The entire page appears.

■ Access displays the date and page number on each page of the report. Access updates the date each time you open the report.

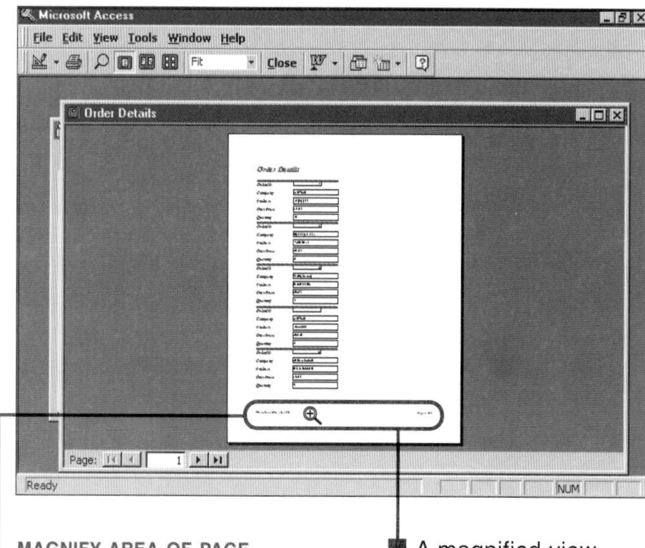

MAGNIFY AREA OF PAGE

1 To magnify an area of a page, position the mouse over the area (changes to magnifier) and then click to magnify the area.

■ A magnified view of the area appears.

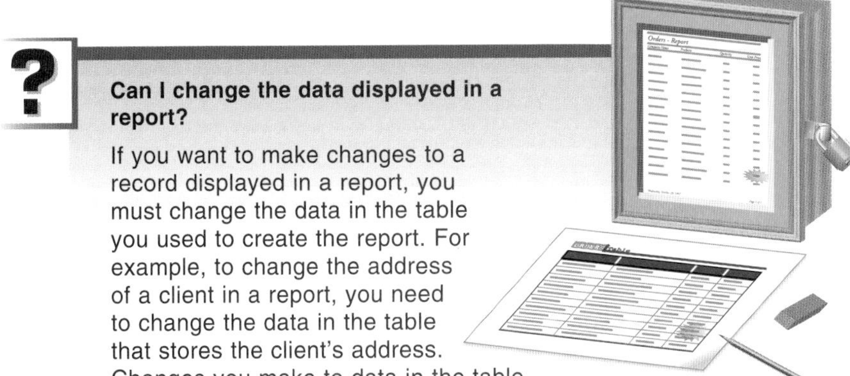

Can I change the data displayed in a report?

If you want to make changes to a record displayed in a report, you must change the data in the table you used to create the report. For example, to change the address of a client in a report, you need to change the data in the table that stores the client's address. Changes you make to data in the table will automatically appear in the report.

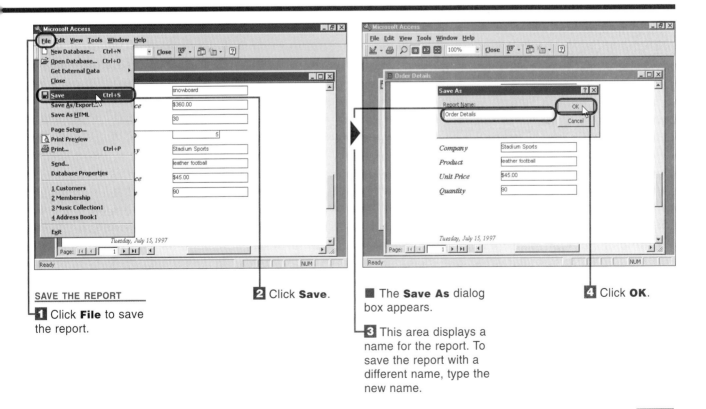

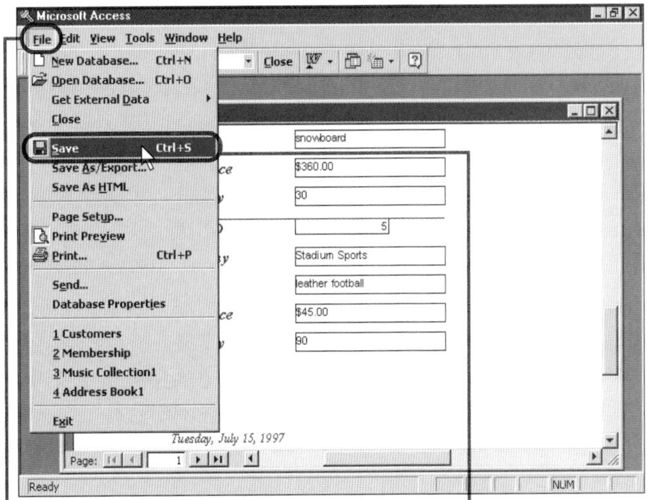

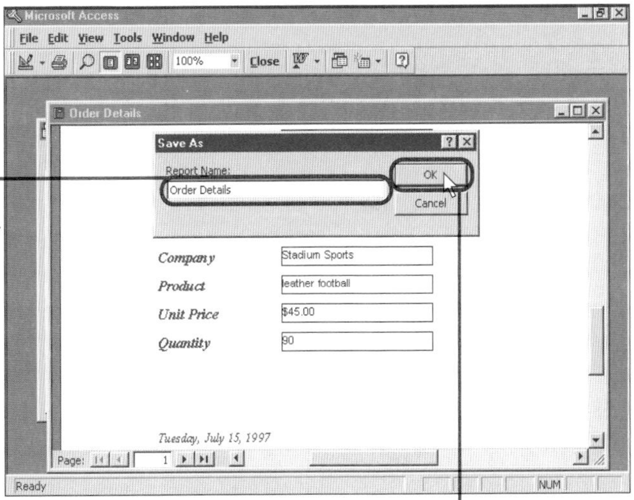

SAVE THE REPORT

1 Click **File** to save the report.

2 Click **Save**.

■ The **Save As** dialog box appears.

3 This area displays a name for the report. To save the report with a different name, type the new name.

4 Click **OK**.

CHANGE VIEW OF REPORT

There are three ways you can view a report. Each view allows you to perform a different task.

CHANGE VIEW OF REPORT

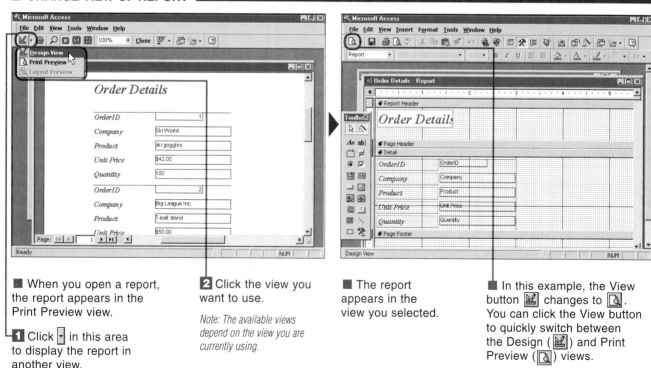

■ When you open a report, the report appears in the Print Preview view.

1 Click ▾ in this area to display the report in another view.

2 Click the view you want to use.

Note: The available views depend on the view you are currently using.

■ The report appears in the view you selected.

■ In this example, the View button changes to . You can click the View button to quickly switch between the Design () and Print Preview () views.

THE REPORT VIEWS

Design View

You can use this view to change the layout and design of a report. The Design view displays a grid of small dots (.) to help you line up items in the report.

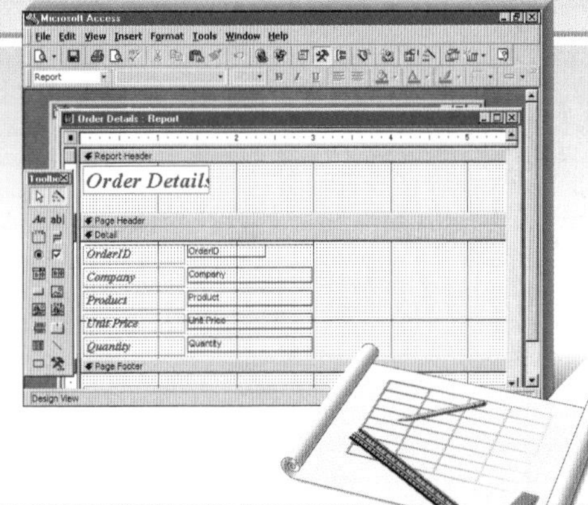

This view also displays information in several sections, such as the report header and page footer.

Print Preview View

You can use this view to see how a report will look when printed.

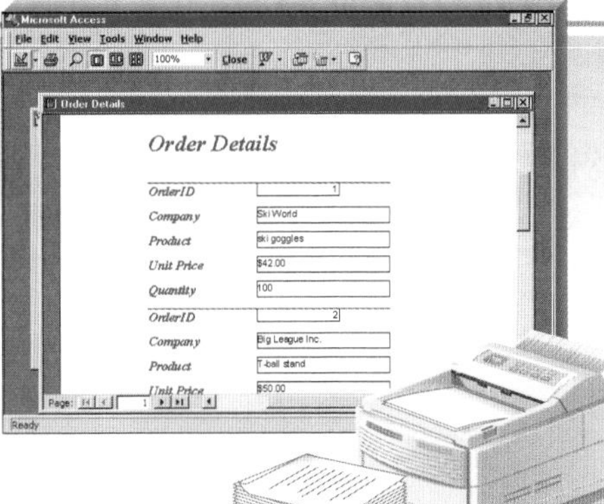

You can flip through all the pages in the report and carefully examine how each page will print.

Layout Preview View

You can use this view to quickly see how a report will look when printed. Layout Preview is usually faster than Print Preview, but only allows you to see a few pages of your report.

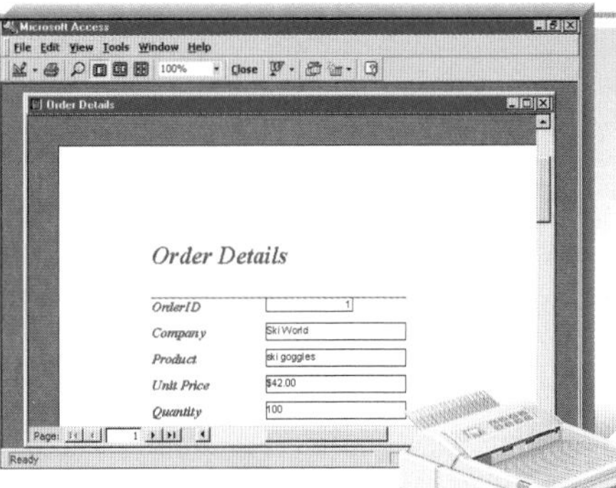

This view is useful for quickly viewing the layout and style of a report.

CLOSE A REPORT

When you finish working with a report, you can close the report to remove it from your screen.

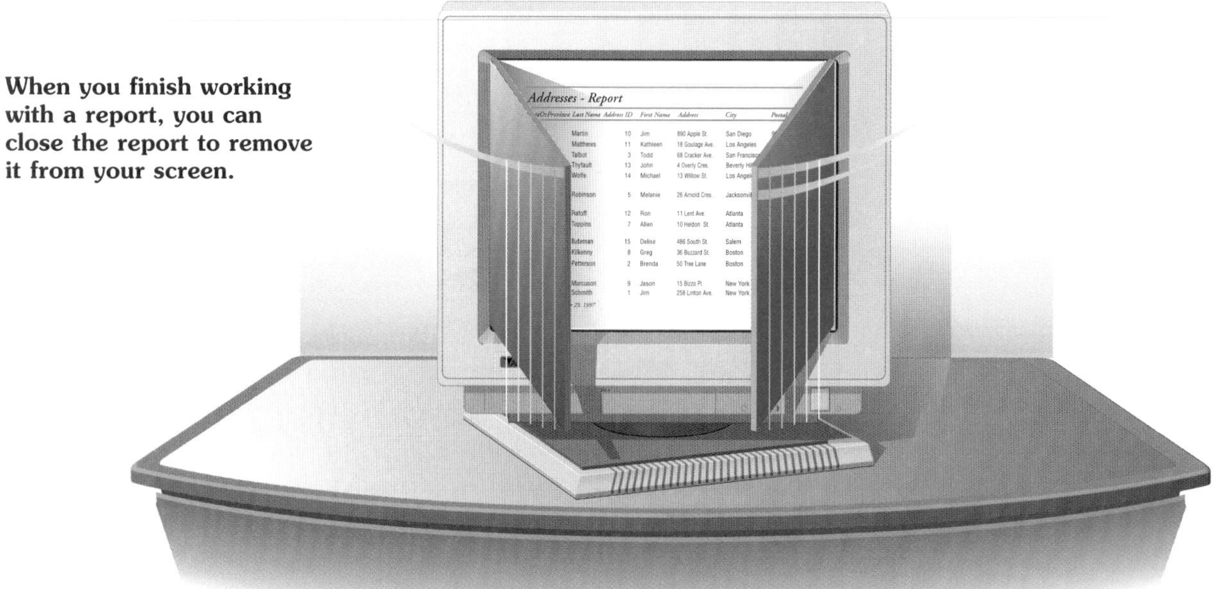

CLOSE A REPORT

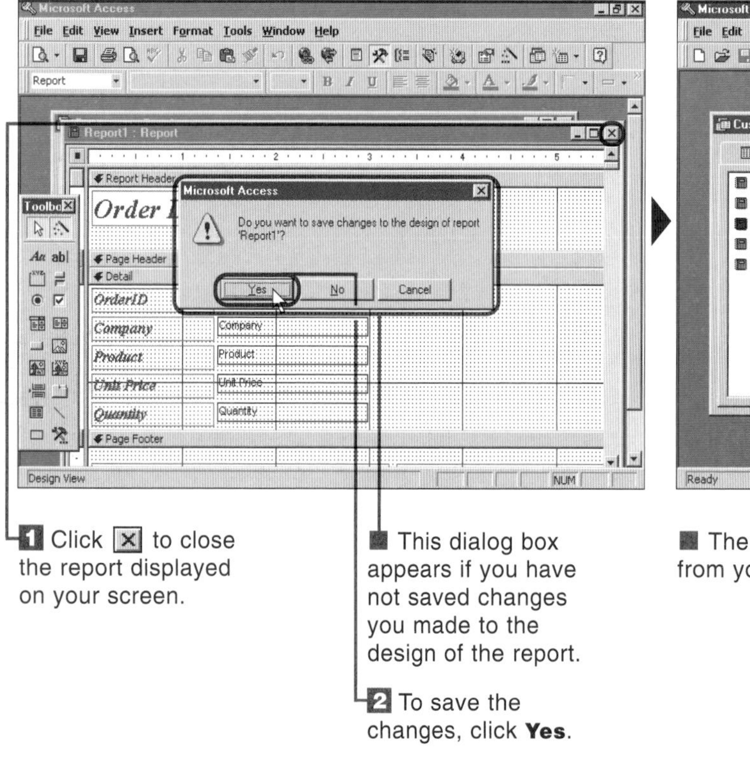

1 Click ☒ to close the report displayed on your screen.

■ This dialog box appears if you have not saved changes you made to the design of the report.

2 To save the changes, click **Yes**.

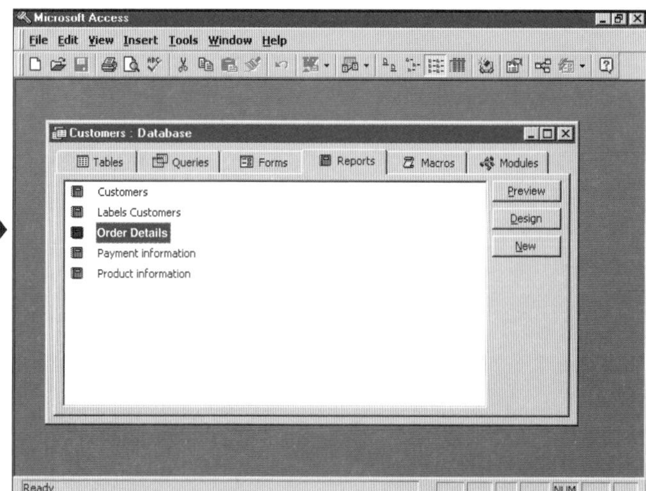

■ The report disappears from your screen.

OPEN A REPORT

You can open a report to display its contents on your screen. Opening a report lets you review the information in the report.

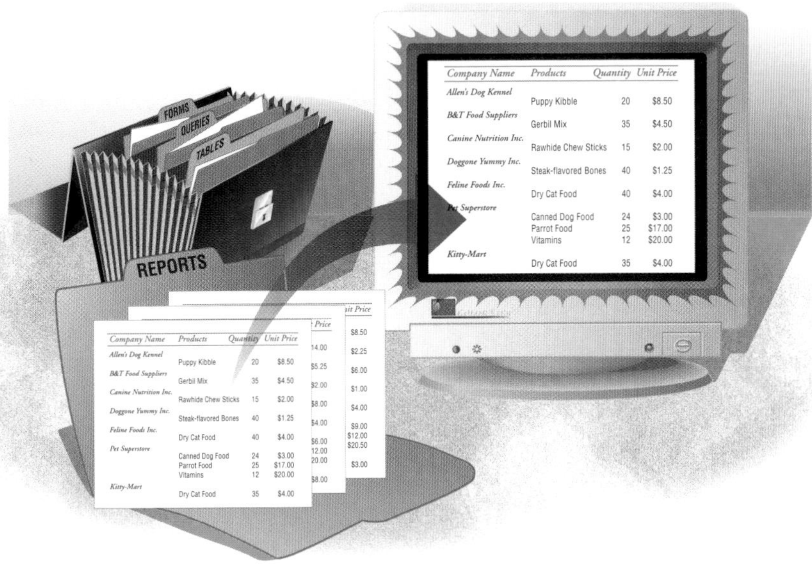

OPEN A REPORT

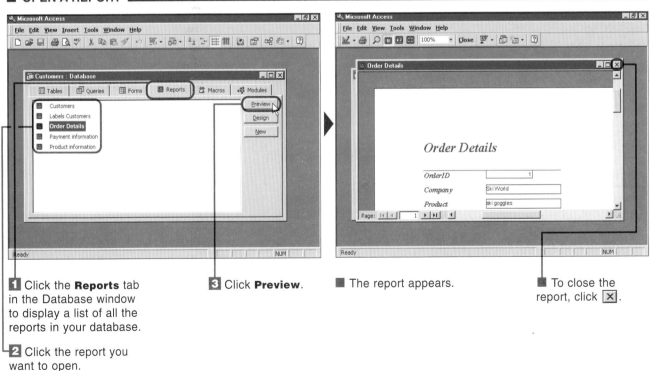

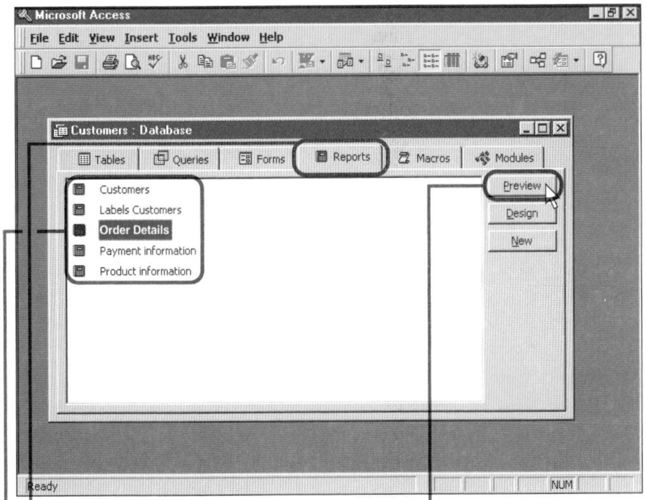

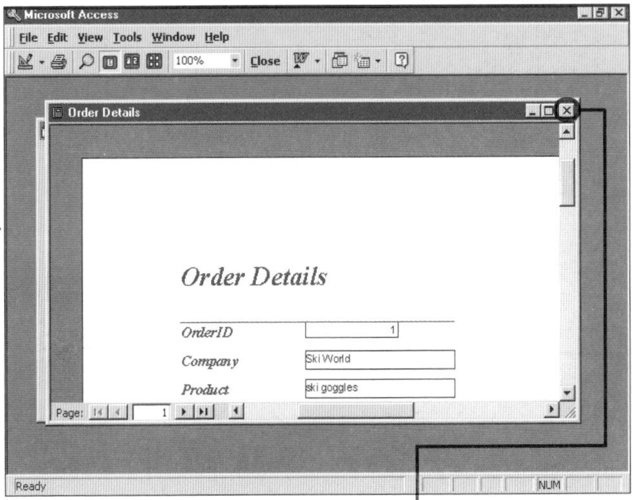

1 Click the **Reports** tab in the Database window to display a list of all the reports in your database.

2 Click the report you want to open.

3 Click **Preview**.

■ The report appears.

■ To close the report, click ☒.

RENAME A REPORT

You can change the name of a report to better describe the type of information included in the report.

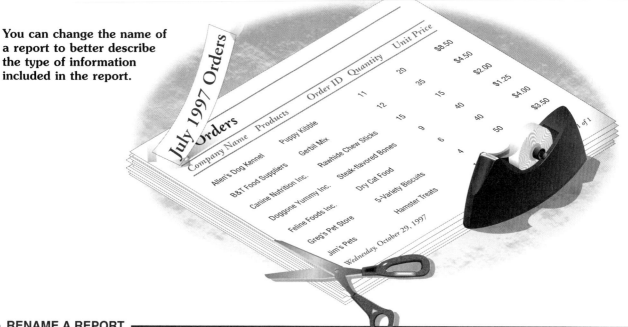

RENAME A REPORT

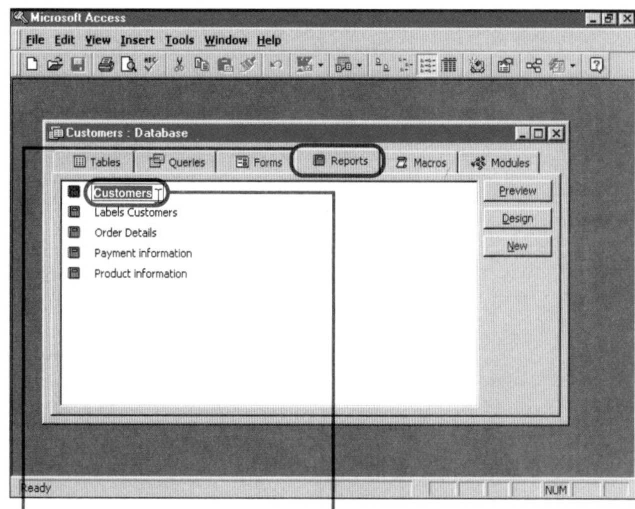

1 Click the **Reports** tab in the Database window to display a list of all the reports in your database.

2 Click the name of the report you want to change. After a few seconds, click the name of the report again. A black border appears around the name.

Note: If you accidentally double-click the name of a report, the report will open.

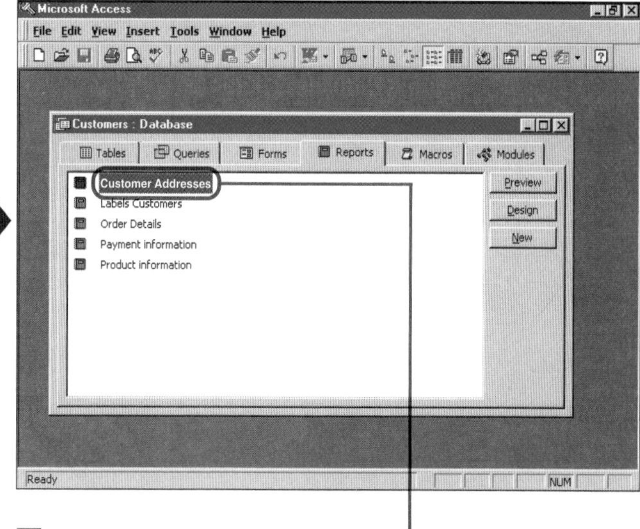

3 Type a new name for the report and then press Enter on your keyboard.

■ The new report name appears.

DELETE A REPORT

If you are sure you will no longer need a report, you can permanently delete the report from your database.

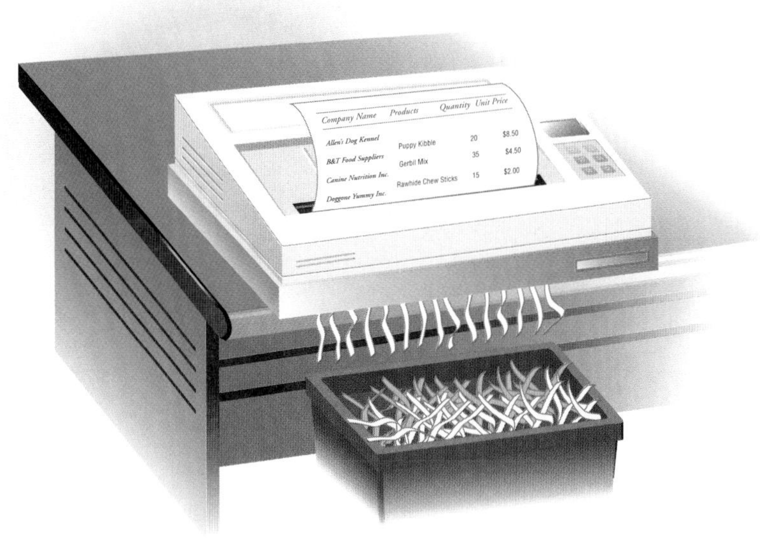

DELETE A REPORT

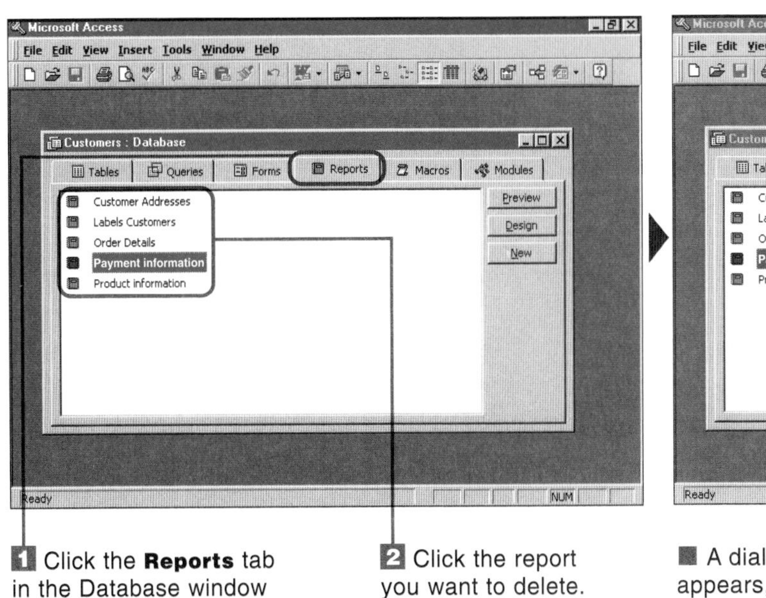

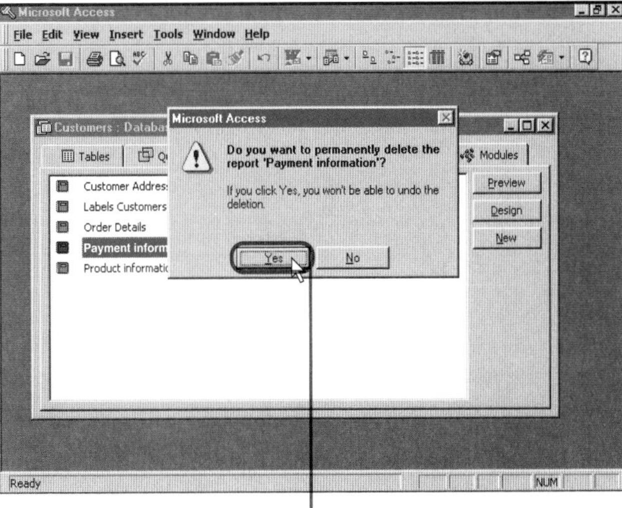

1 Click the **Reports** tab in the Database window to display a list of all the reports in your database.

2 Click the report you want to delete.

3 Press Delete on your keyboard.

■ A dialog box appears, confirming the deletion.

4 Click **Yes** to permanently delete the report.

■ The report disappears.

CREATE A REPORT USING THE REPORT WIZARD

The Report Wizard helps you create a professionally designed report to display information from one or more tables.

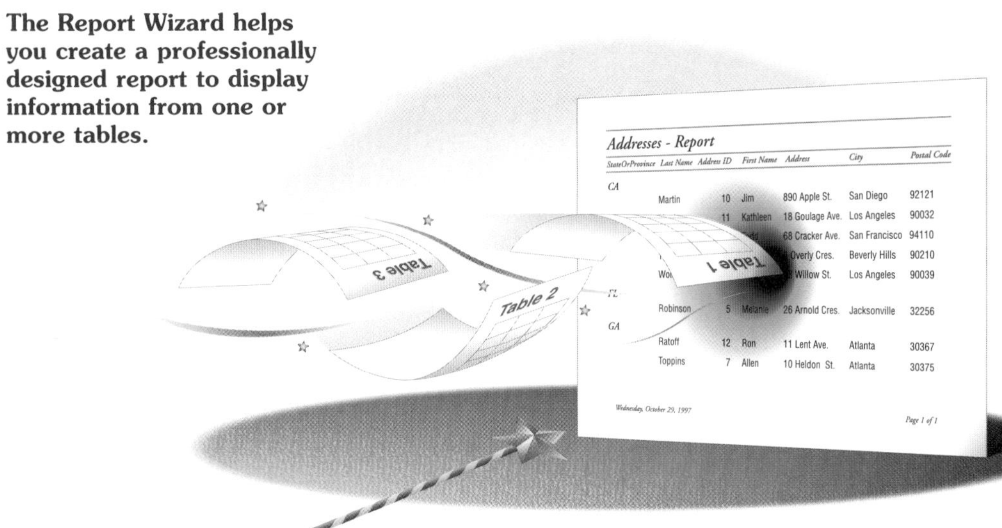

The Report Wizard will ask you a series of questions and then set up a report based on your answers.

CREATE A REPORT USING THE REPORT WIZARD

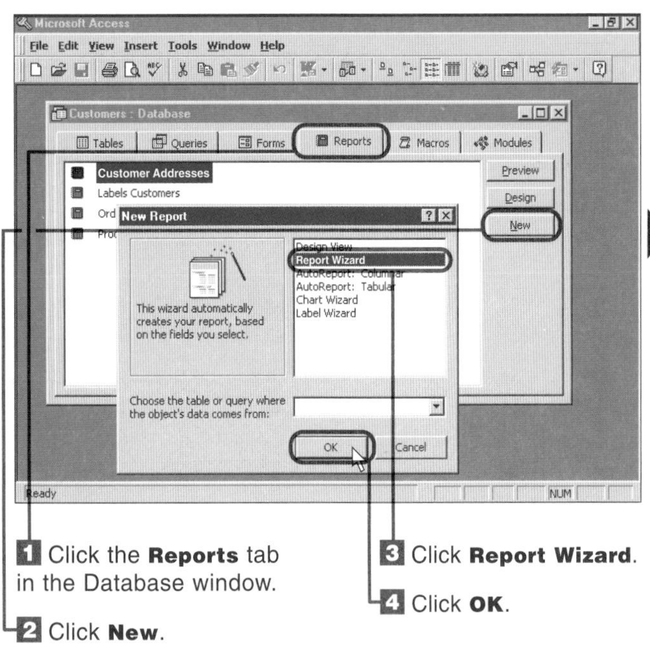

1 Click the **Reports** tab in the Database window.

2 Click **New**.

■ The **New Report** dialog box appears.

3 Click **Report Wizard**.

4 Click **OK**.

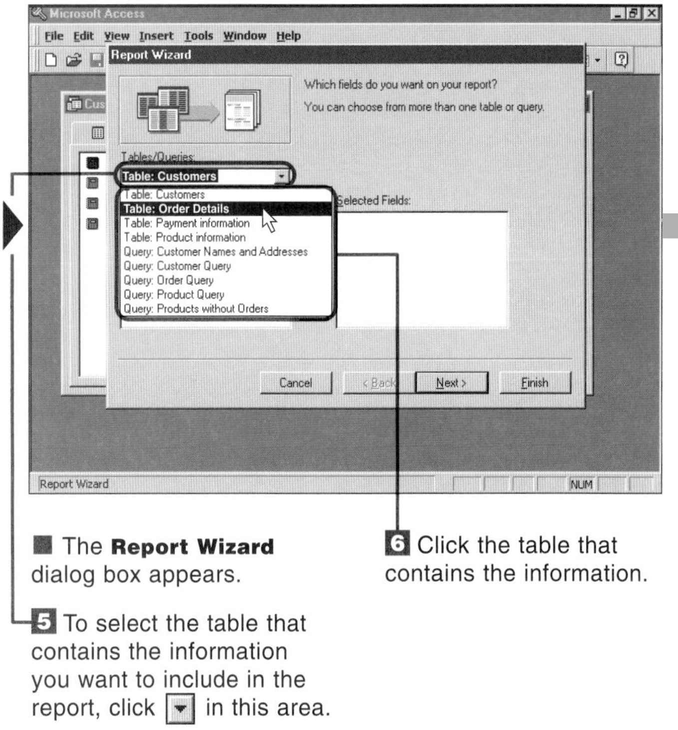

■ The **Report Wizard** dialog box appears.

5 To select the table that contains the information you want to include in the report, click ▾ in this area.

6 Click the table that contains the information.

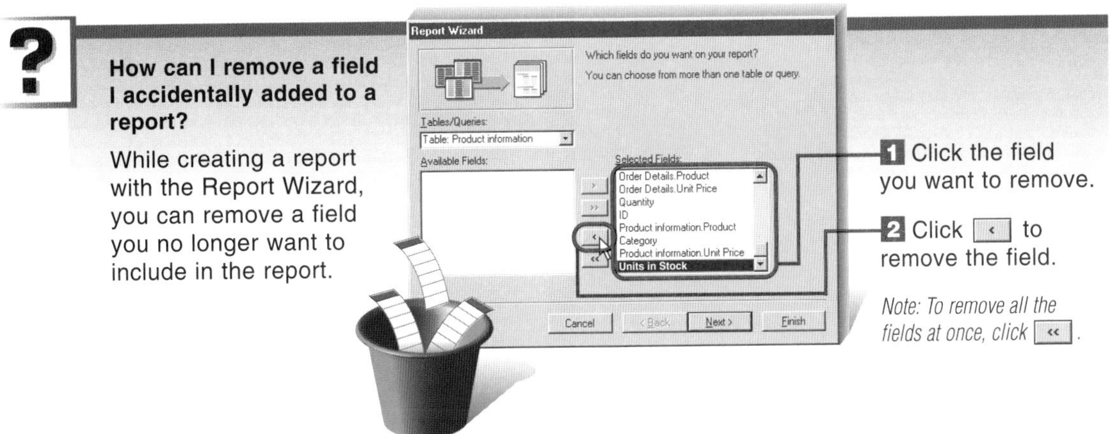

How can I remove a field I accidentally added to a report?

While creating a report with the Report Wizard, you can remove a field you no longer want to include in the report.

1 Click the field you want to remove.

2 Click < to remove the field.

Note: To remove all the fields at once, click <<.

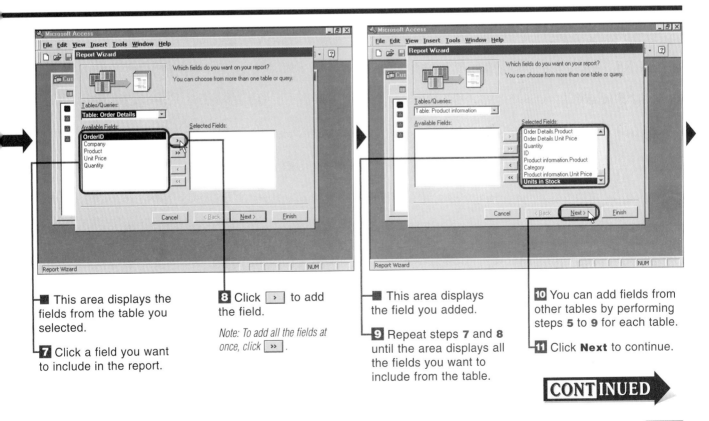

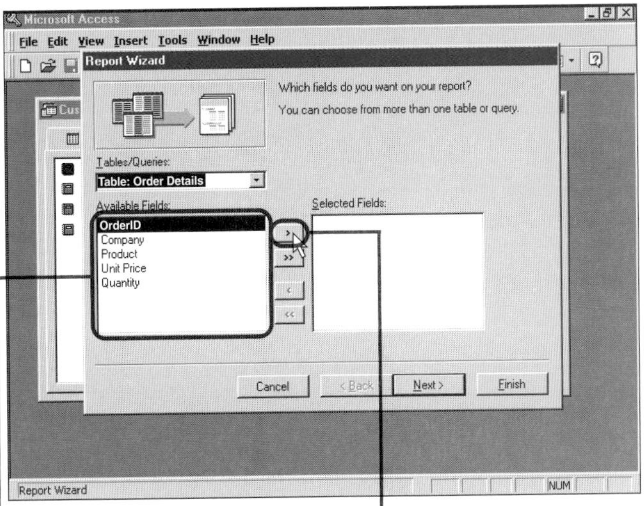

- This area displays the fields from the table you selected.

7 Click a field you want to include in the report.

8 Click > to add the field.

Note: To add all the fields at once, click >>.

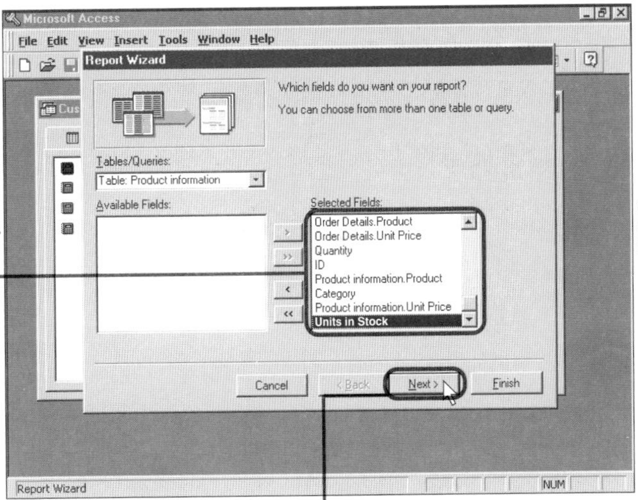

- This area displays the field you added.

9 Repeat steps **7** and **8** until the area displays all the fields you want to include from the table.

10 You can add fields from other tables by performing steps **5** to **9** for each table.

11 Click **Next** to continue.

CONTINUED

CREATE A REPORT USING THE REPORT WIZARD

You can choose how you want to organize the data in your report.

For example, you may want to place all the clients from the same state together.

CREATE A REPORT USING THE REPORT WIZARD (CONTINUED)

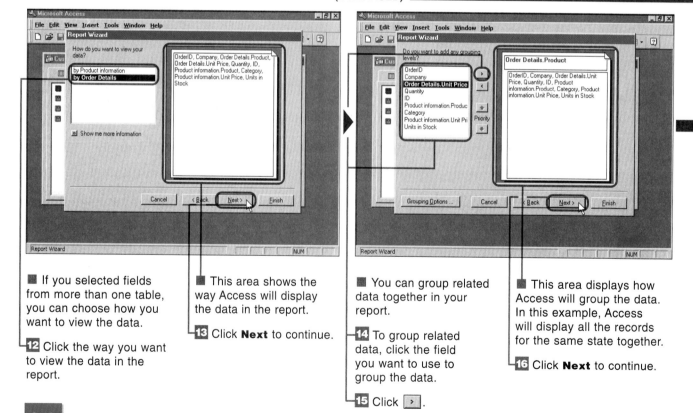

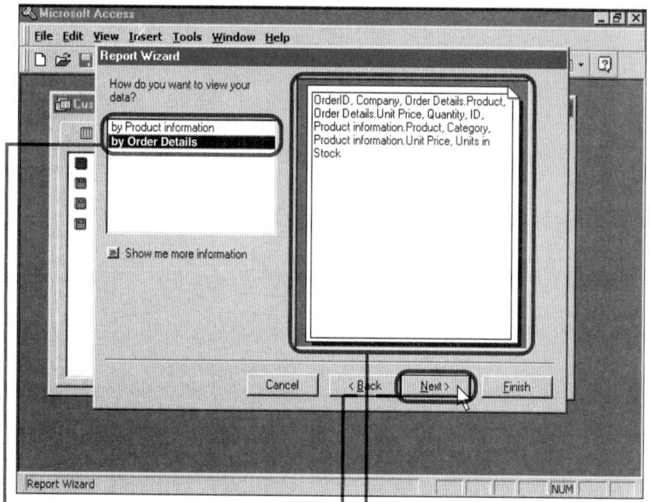

■ If you selected fields from more than one table, you can choose how you want to view the data.

12 Click the way you want to view the data in the report.

■ This area shows the way Access will display the data in the report.

13 Click **Next** to continue.

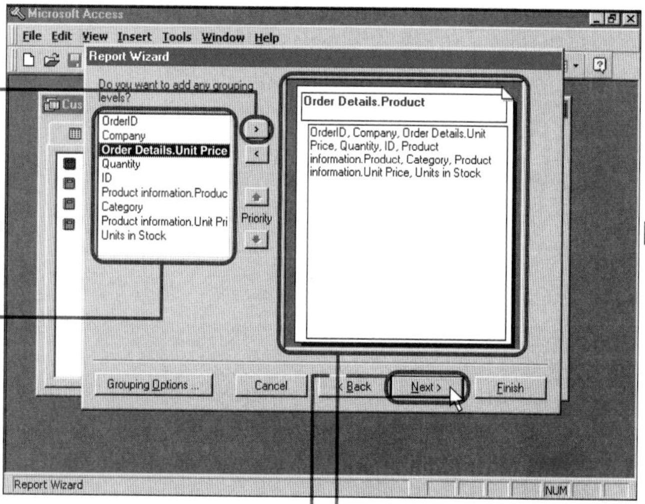

■ You can group related data together in your report.

14 To group related data, click the field you want to use to group the data.

15 Click [>].

■ This area displays how Access will group the data. In this example, Access will display all the records for the same state together.

16 Click **Next** to continue.

?

How can I sort the data in a report?

You can sort the data in a report to better organize the information. For example, you can alphabetically sort the data by last name so you can find clients of interest more easily.

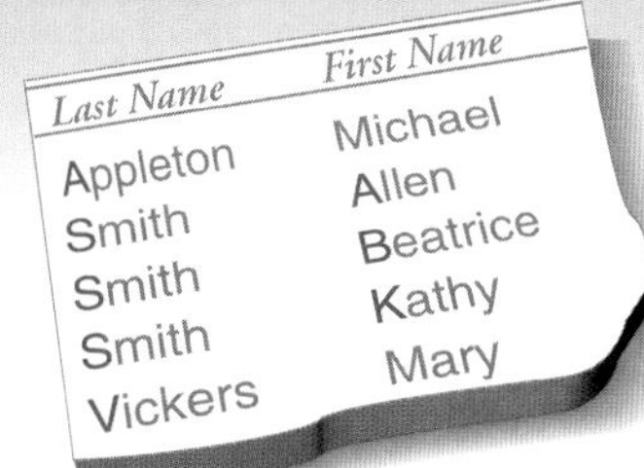

Last Name
First Name
Appleton
Michael
Smith
Allen
Smith
Beatrice
Smith
Kathy
Vickers
Mary

If a last name appears more than once, you can also sort on a second field, such as First Name.

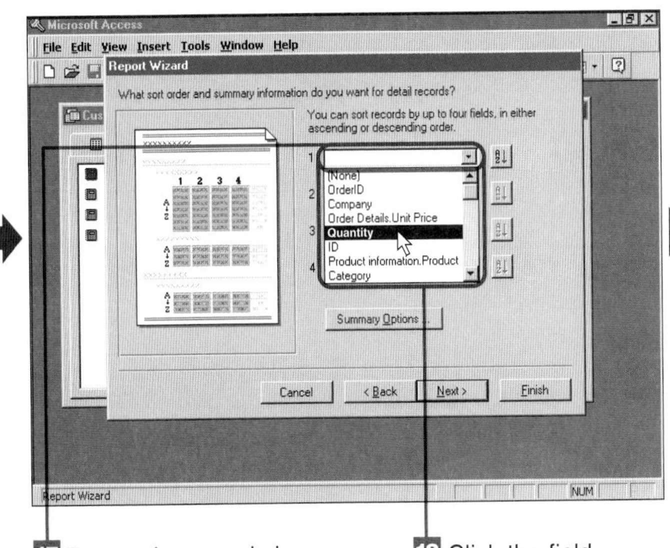

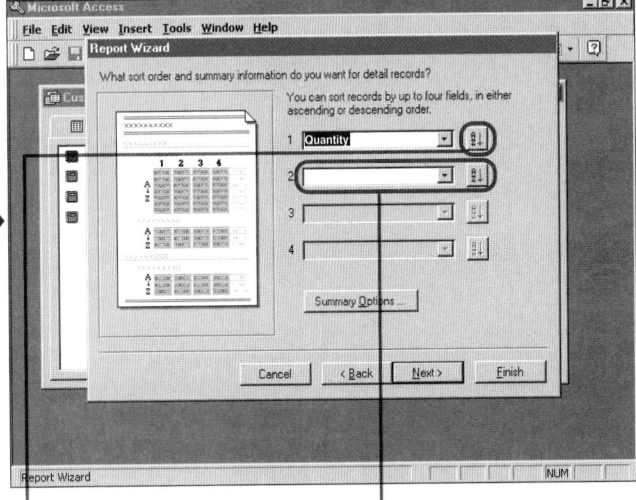

17 To sort the records in your report, click ▾ in this area.

Note: For information on sorting, refer to the top of this page.

18 Click the field you want to use to sort the records.

19 Click this button until it appears the way you want to sort the records.

- Sorts A to Z, 1 to 9
- Sorts Z to A, 9 to 1

20 To sort on a second field, repeat steps **17** to **19** in this area.

CONTINUED

CREATE A REPORT USING THE REPORT WIZARD

You can show calculations in your report to summarize your data.

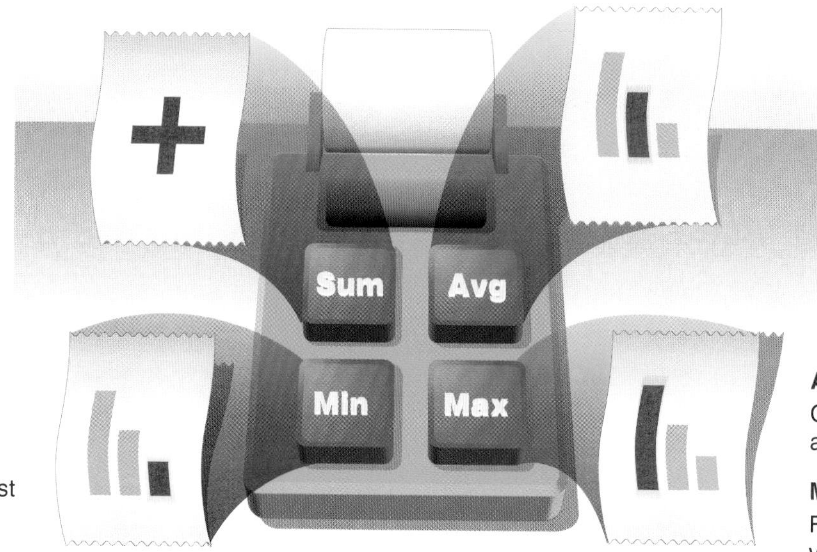

Sum
Adds the values.

Min
Finds the smallest value.

Avg
Calculates the average value.

Max
Finds the largest value.

CREATE A REPORT USING THE REPORT WIZARD (CONTINUED)

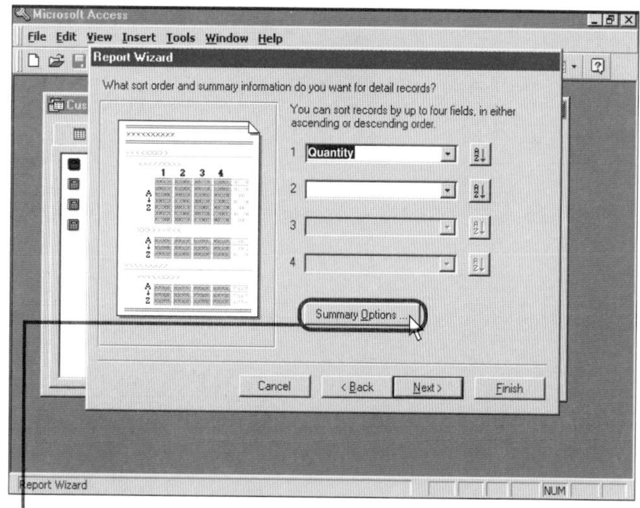

21 To show calculations in the report, click **Summary Options**.

*Note: This option may not be available for all reports. If the option is not available, skip to step **26** to continue creating the report.*

■ The **Summary Options** dialog box appears.

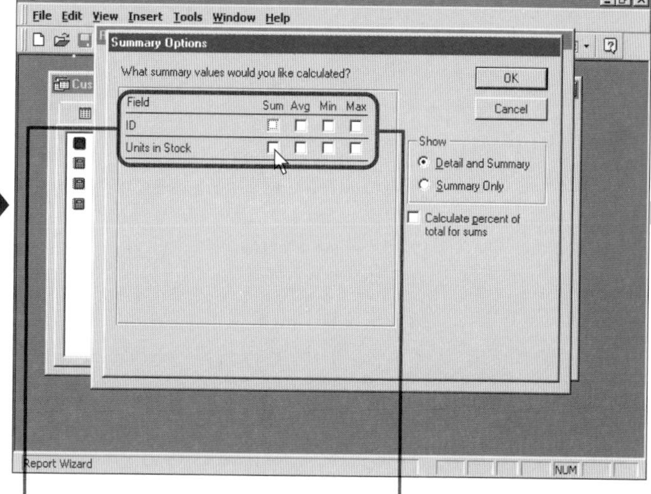

■ This area displays the fields you can perform calculations on.

22 Click the box for each calculation you want to perform (☐ changes to ☑).

How can I change the way my report displays summary information?

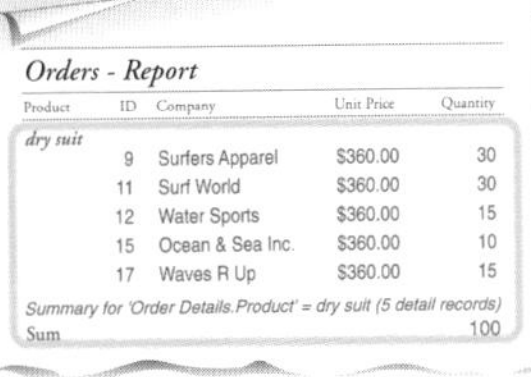

Show detail and summary

Display all the records and the summary.

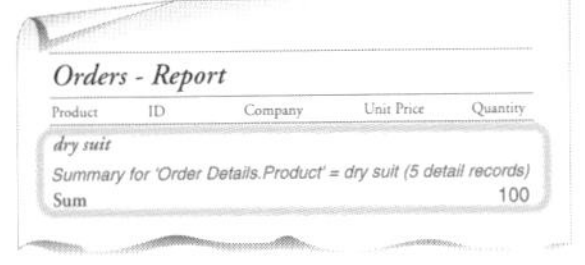

Show summary only

Display only the summary.

Calculate percent of total for sums

Display the percentage of the total that each group represents.

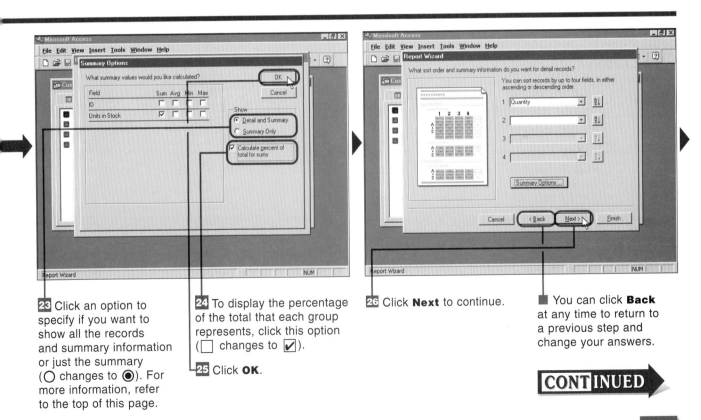

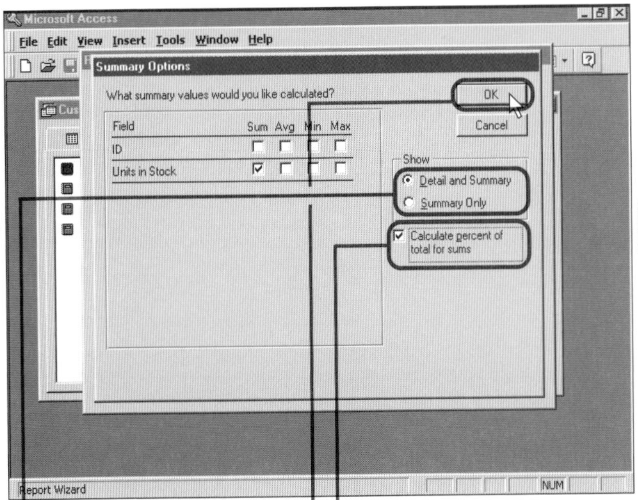

23 Click an option to specify if you want to show all the records and summary information or just the summary (○ changes to ◉). For more information, refer to the top of this page.

24 To display the percentage of the total that each group represents, click this option (☐ changes to ☑).

25 Click **OK**.

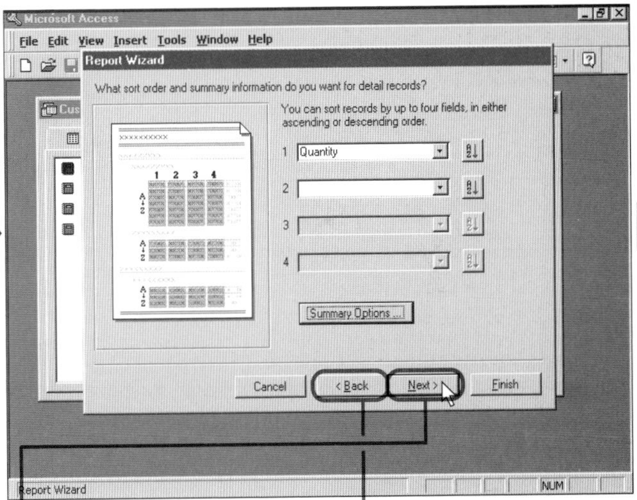

26 Click **Next** to continue.

■ You can click **Back** at any time to return to a previous step and change your answers.

CONTINUED

CREATE A REPORT USING THE REPORT WIZARD

You can choose between several layouts for your report. The layout of a report determines the arrangement and position of information in the report.

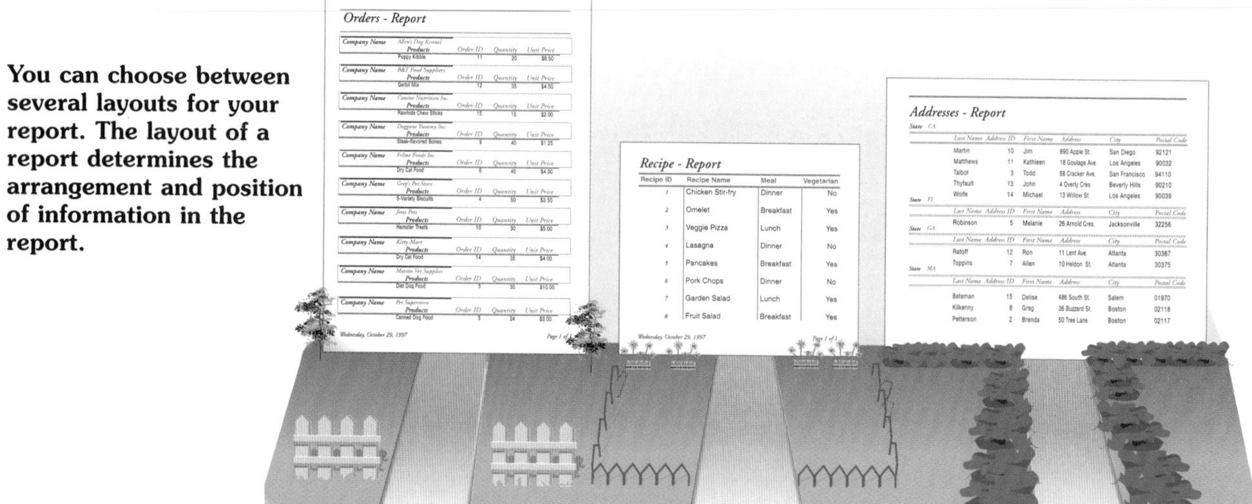

CREATE A REPORT USING THE REPORT WIZARD (CONTINUED)

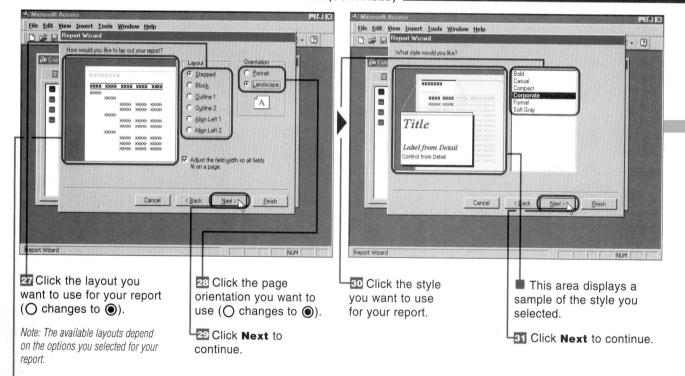

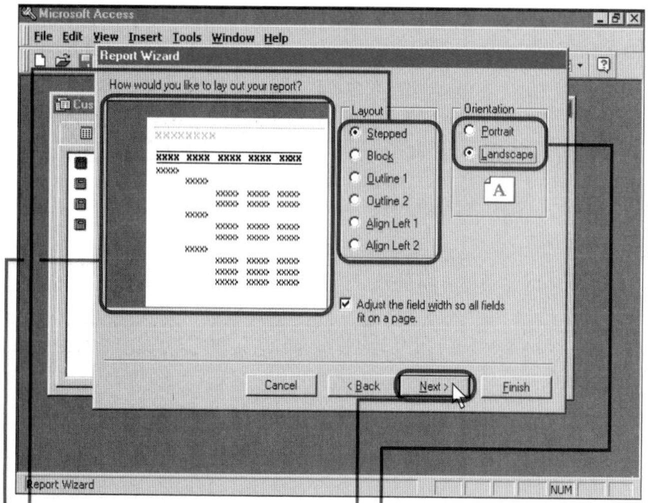

27 Click the layout you want to use for your report (○ changes to ◉).

Note: The available layouts depend on the options you selected for your report.

■ This area displays a sample of the layout you selected.

28 Click the page orientation you want to use (○ changes to ◉).

29 Click **Next** to continue.

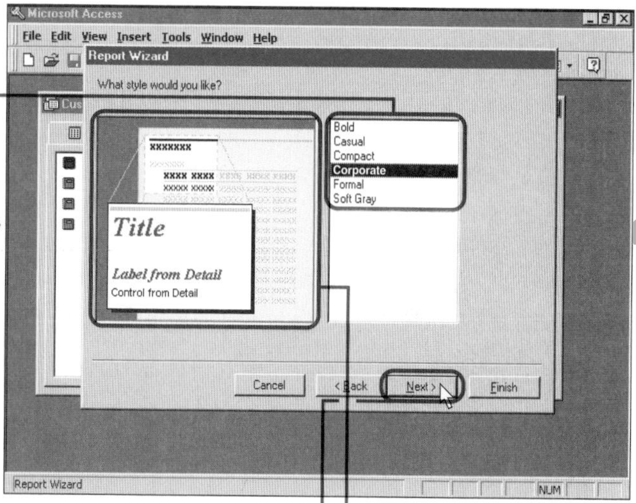

30 Click the style you want to use for your report.

■ This area displays a sample of the style you selected.

31 Click **Next** to continue.

What page orientations can I use for my report?

You can have your report print in one of two directions on a page.

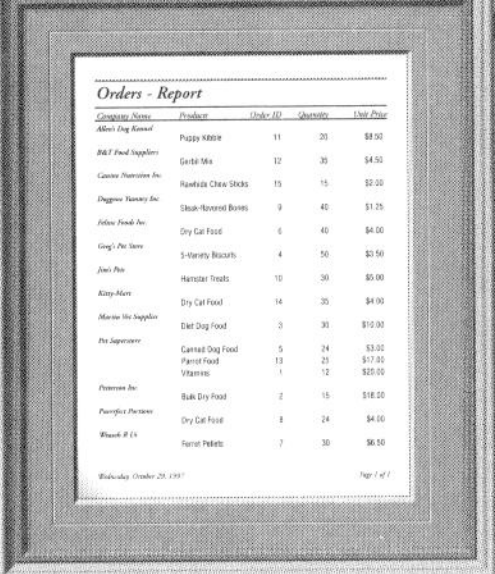

Portrait

Portrait orientation prints data across the short side of a page.

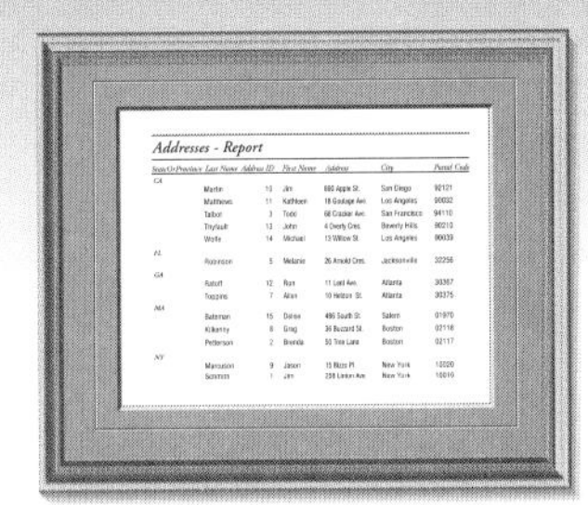

Landscape

Landscape orientation prints data across the long side of a page.

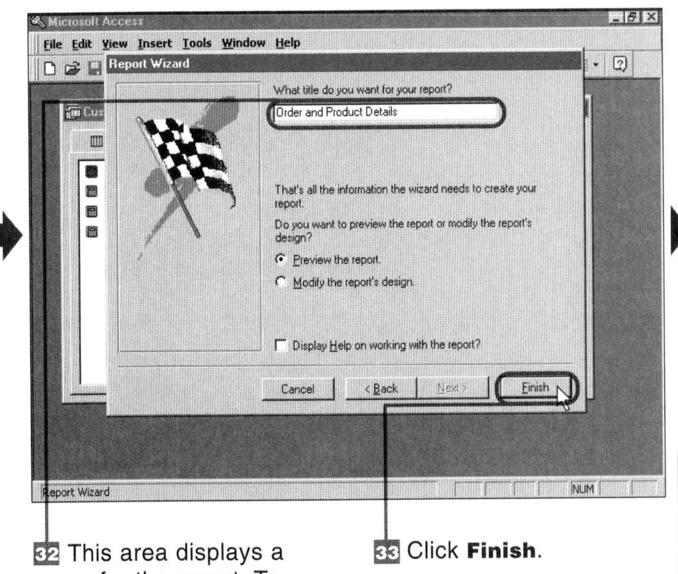

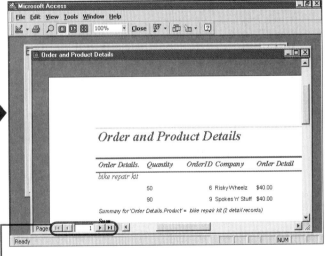

32 This area displays a name for the report. To save the report with a different name, type the new name.

33 Click **Finish**.

■ The report appears as it will look when printed.

■ This area shows the number of the page displayed on your screen.

34 To display another page, click one of the following options.

Note: If an option is dimmed, the option is currently not available.

- First page
- Previous page
- Next page
- Last page

FORM-ORDERS
Order ID
12
Order Date
20-Feb-97
Expected Shipment
21-Feb-97
Shipment Method
Speedy Delivery
Comments
Terms
Net 30 days
Customer ID
256
Contact
Jim Schmith
Billing Address
258 Linton Ave.
City
New York
State/Province
New York
Postal Code
10010
Country
USA
Phone Number
(555) 555-6974
maranGraphics - Microsoft Internet Explorer
File Edit View Go Favorites Help
Back
Forward
Stop
Refresh
Home
Search
Favoi...
Address
http://www.maran.com/
maran
Windows 95 Simplified

CHAPTER 14

Access and the Internet

Do you want to learn how to use Access and the Internet? This chapter teaches you how to insert a hyperlink, publish Web pages and much more.

Display the Web Toolbar 276

Display the Start or Search Page 277

Insert a Hyperlink 278

Move Between Documents 282

Refresh a Document 283

Open a Document 284

Stop the Connection 285

Add a Database to Favorites 286

Publish Your Database 288

DISPLAY THE WEB TOOLBAR

You can display the Web toolbar to help you browse through documents containing hyperlinks.

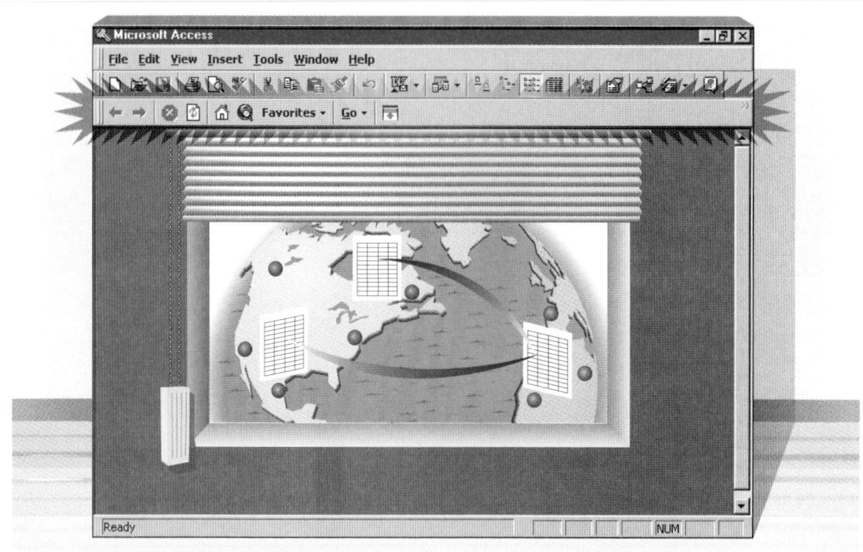

DISPLAY THE WEB TOOLBAR

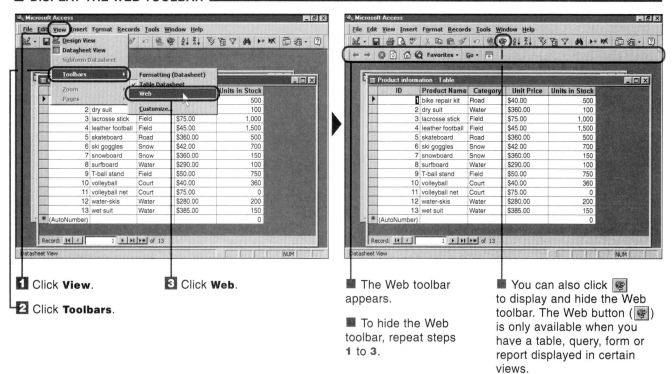

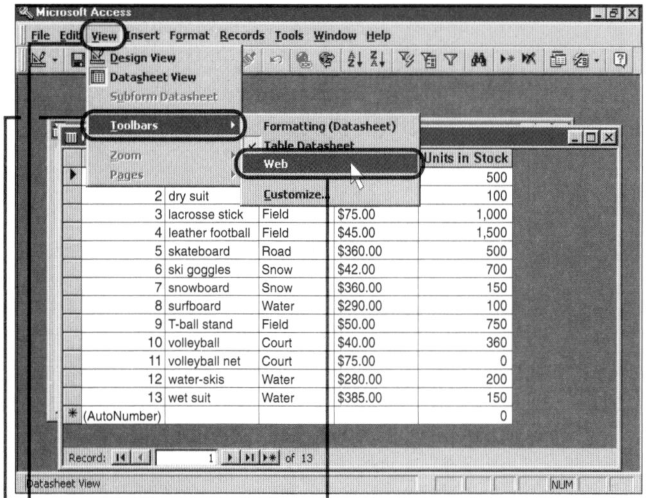

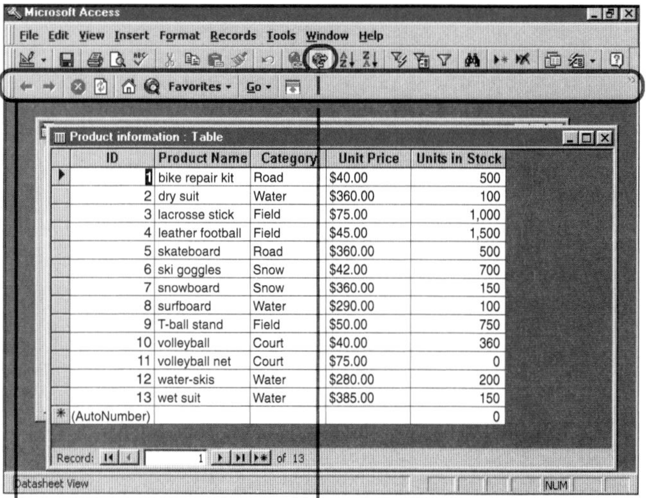

1 Click **View**.

2 Click **Toolbars**.

3 Click **Web**.

■ The Web toolbar appears.

■ To hide the Web toolbar, repeat steps **1** to **3**.

■ You can also click [Web button] to display and hide the Web toolbar. The Web button ([Web button]) is only available when you have a table, query, form or report displayed in certain views.

DISPLAY THE START OR SEARCH PAGE

You can easily display the start page or search page at any time.

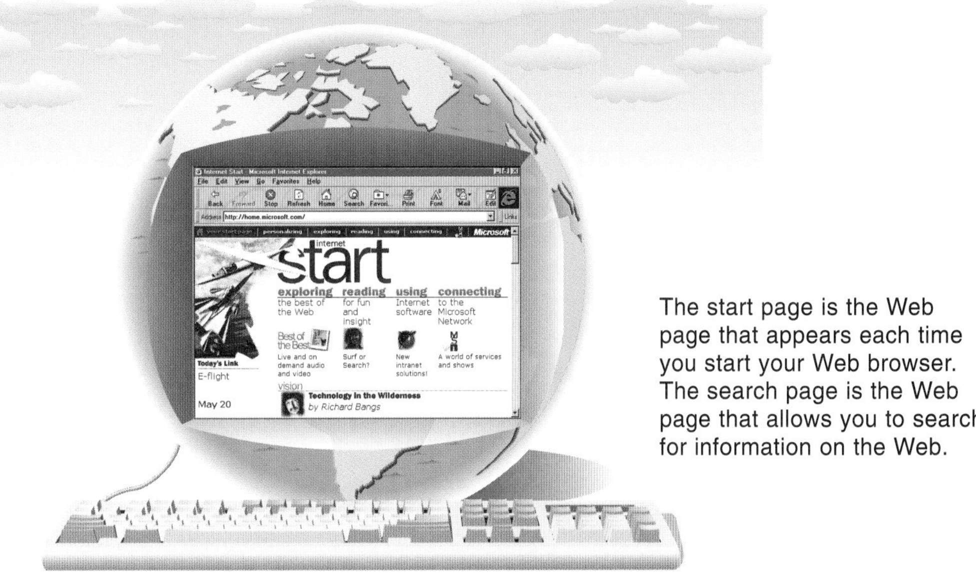

The start page is the Web page that appears each time you start your Web browser. The search page is the Web page that allows you to search for information on the Web.

DISPLAY THE START OR SEARCH PAGE

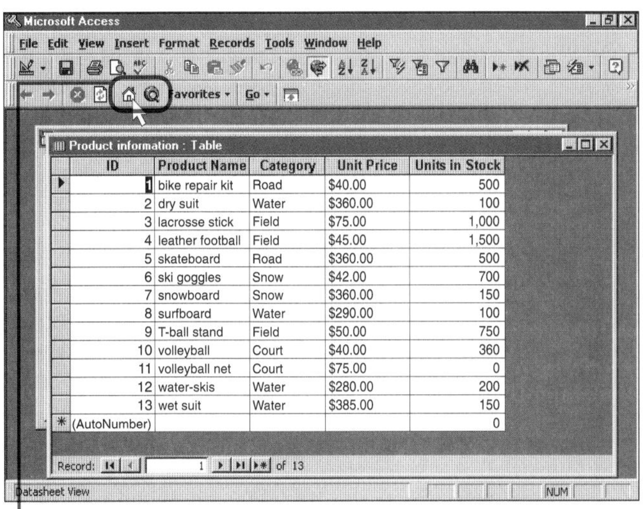

1 Click one of the following options.

Display the start page.

Display the search page.

Note: If these buttons are not available, refer to page 276 to display the Web toolbar.

■ Your Web browser opens and displays the page you selected.

INSERT A HYPERLINK

You can insert a hyperlink in a table to connect information in the table to another document. When you select the hyperlink, the other document appears. A hyperlink can be a word, phrase or graphic.

For example, you can insert hyperlinks in a table to the Web sites of your suppliers so you can quickly access product information.

INSERT A HYPERLINK

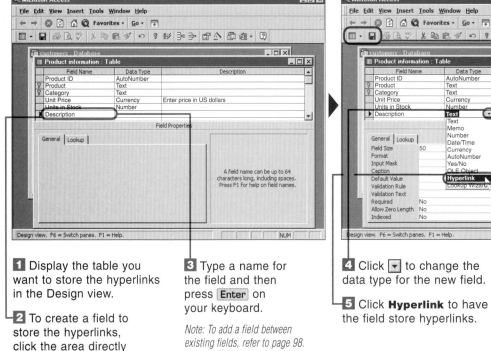

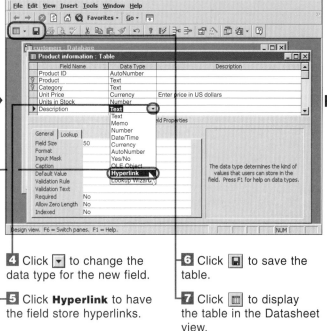

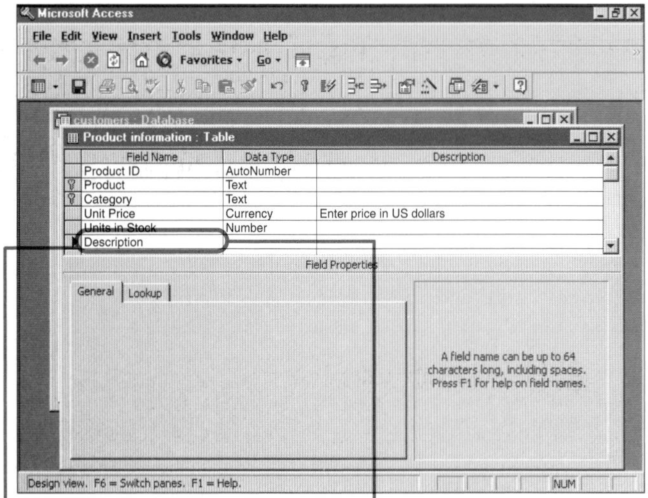

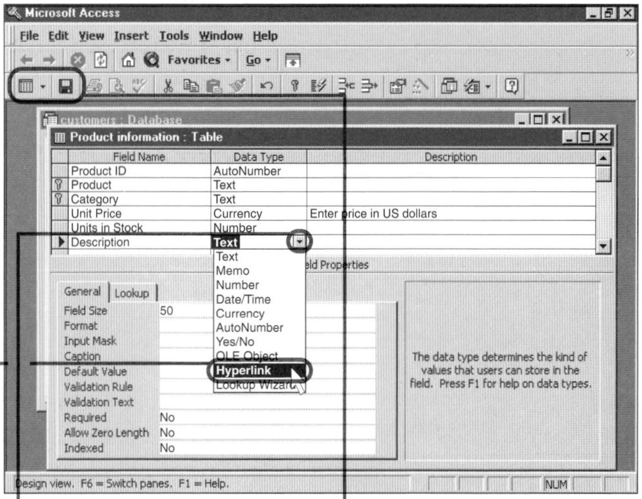

1 Display the table you want to store the hyperlinks in the Design view.

2 To create a field to store the hyperlinks, click the area directly below the last field name.

3 Type a name for the field and then press Enter on your keyboard.

Note: To add a field between existing fields, refer to page 98.

4 Click ▾ to change the data type for the new field.

5 Click **Hyperlink** to have the field store hyperlinks.

6 Click 💾 to save the table.

7 Click ▦ to display the table in the Datasheet view.

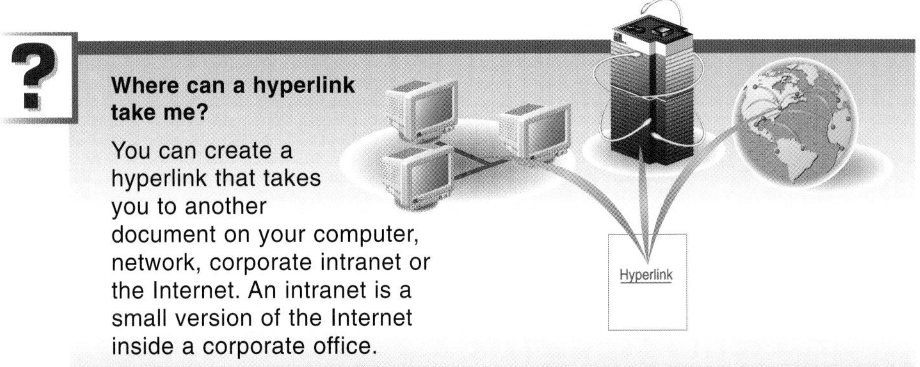

Where can a hyperlink take me?

You can create a hyperlink that takes you to another document on your computer, network, corporate intranet or the Internet. An intranet is a small version of the Internet inside a corporate office.

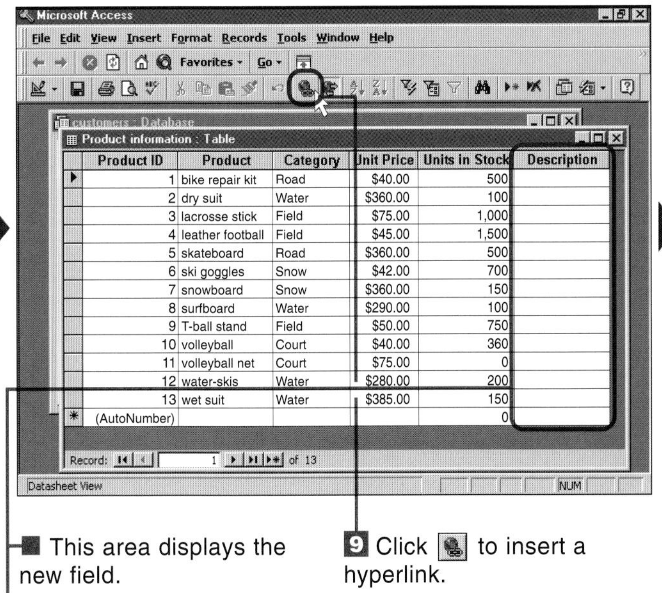

■ This area displays the new field.

8 Click the cell where you want to insert a hyperlink.

9 Click [icon] to insert a hyperlink.

■ The **Insert Hyperlink** dialog box appears.

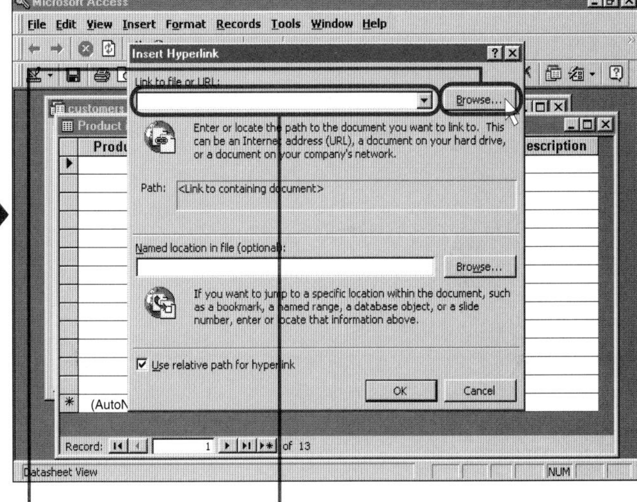

10 To create a hyperlink to a document on your computer or network, click **Browse**.

■ To create a hyperlink to a Web page, type the address of the Web page (example: http://www.maran.com). Then skip to step **13** on page 280.

CONTINUED

INSERT A HYPERLINK

You can easily see hyperlinks in a table. Hyperlinks appear underlined and in color.

Company ID	Company Name	Web Site
1	Sports Inc.	www.sportsinc.com
2	Hoop Dreams Inc.	www.hoopdreams.com
3	J.J. Sports Wear	www.jjsportswear.com
4	Total Sports Inc.	www.totalsports.com
5	Racquets-R-Us	www.racquets.com

Hyperlinks will also appear in forms that are based on tables containing hyperlinks.

INSERT A HYPERLINK (CONTINUED)

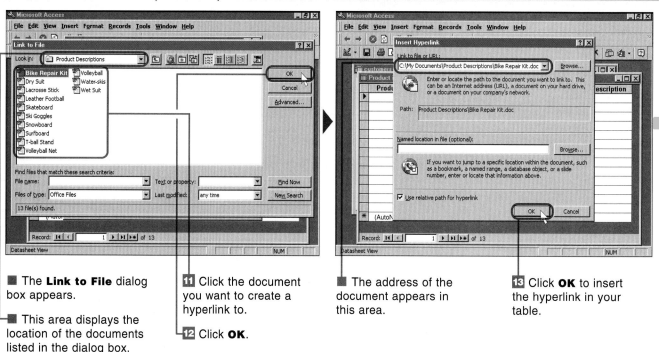

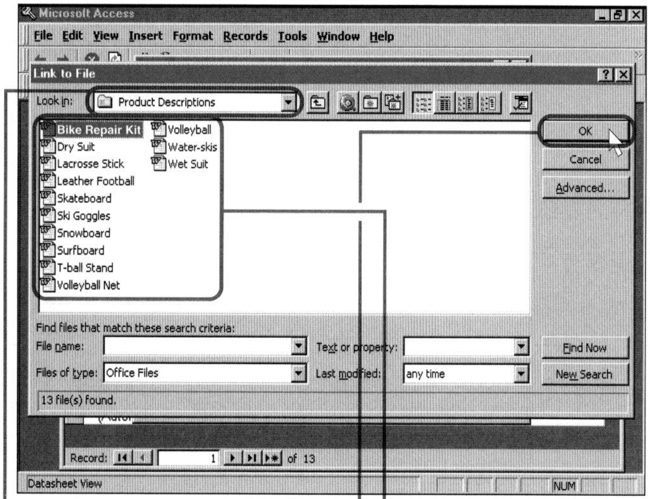

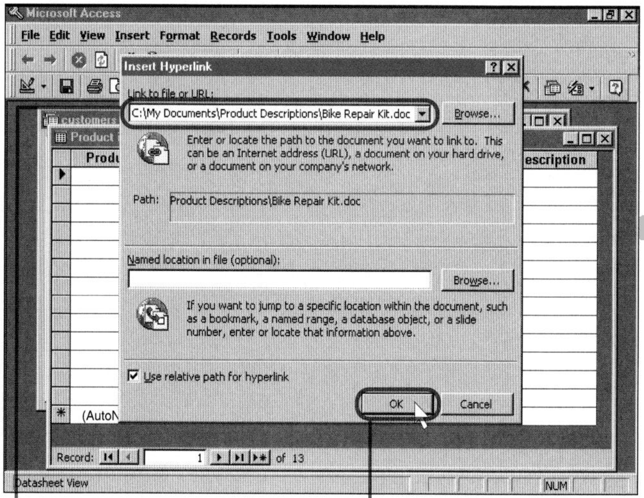

- The **Link to File** dialog box appears.
- This area displays the location of the documents listed in the dialog box.

11 Click the document you want to create a hyperlink to.

12 Click **OK**.

- The address of the document appears in this area.

13 Click **OK** to insert the hyperlink in your table.

?

Is there a faster way of entering a hyperlink?

You can type a Web page address directly into a table or form. Access will automatically display the address as a hyperlink.

When you type a Web page address, you do not need to type the **http://** part of the address.

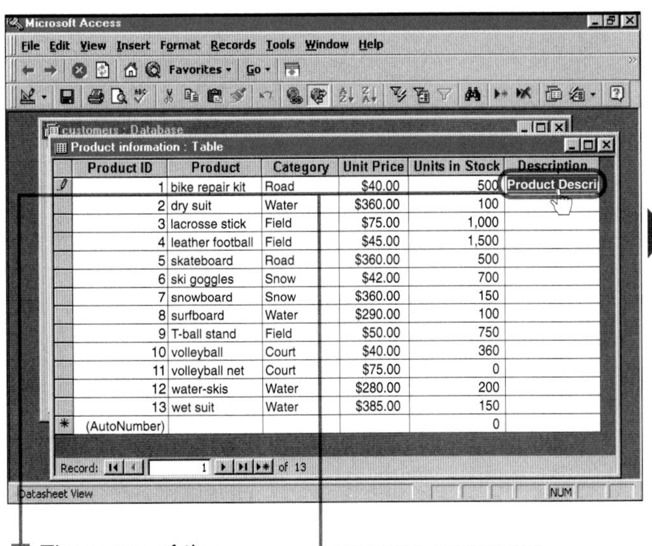

Product ID	Product	Category	Unit Price	Units in Stock	Description
1	bike repair kit	Road	$40.00	500	Product Descri
2	dry suit	Water	$360.00	100	
3	lacrosse stick	Field	$75.00	1,000	
4	leather football	Field	$45.00	1,500	
5	skateboard	Road	$360.00	500	
6	ski goggles	Snow	$42.00	700	
7	snowboard	Snow	$360.00	150	
8	surfboard	Water	$290.00	100	
9	T-ball stand	Field	$50.00	750	
10	volleyball	Court	$40.00	360	
11	volleyball net	Court	$75.00	0	
12	water-skis	Water	$280.00	200	
13	wet suit	Water	$385.00	150	
(AutoNumber)				0	

■ The name of the document or address of the Web page appears colored and underlined.

SELECT A HYPERLINK

1 Position the mouse over the hyperlink (changes to) and then click to select the hyperlink.

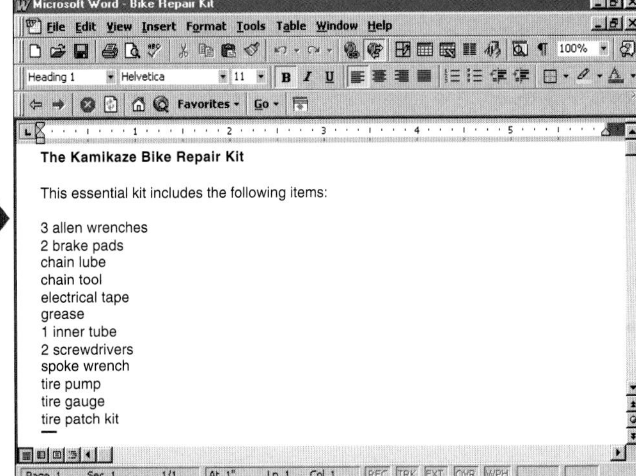

■ The document or Web page connected to the hyperlink appears.

■ If the hyperlink is connected to a Web page, your Web browser opens and displays the Web page.

MOVE BETWEEN DOCUMENTS

When you view documents by selecting hyperlinks, Access keeps track of all the documents you have viewed. You can easily move back and forth between these documents.

MOVE BETWEEN DOCUMENTS

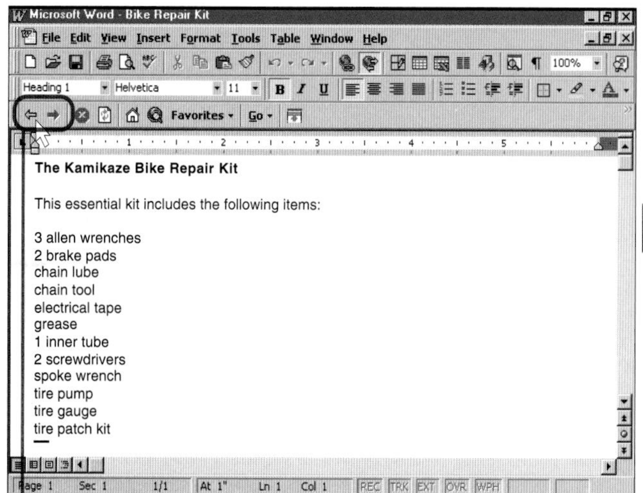

1 Click one of the following options.

⇦ Move back

⇨ Move forward

Note: If these buttons are not available, refer to page 276 to display the Web toolbar.

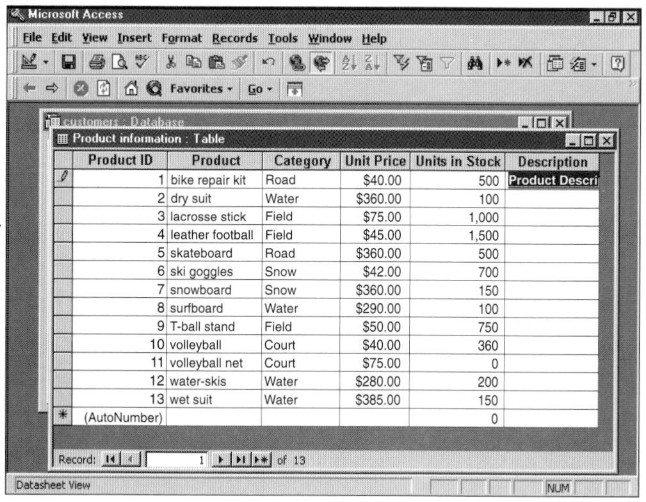

Product ID	Product	Category	Unit Price	Units in Stock	Description
1	bike repair kit	Road	$40.00	500	Product Descri
2	dry suit	Water	$360.00	100	
3	lacrosse stick	Field	$75.00	1,000	
4	leather football	Field	$45.00	1,500	
5	skateboard	Road	$360.00	500	
6	ski goggles	Snow	$42.00	700	
7	snowboard	Snow	$360.00	150	
8	surfboard	Water	$290.00	100	
9	T-ball stand	Field	$50.00	750	
10	volleyball	Court	$40.00	360	
11	volleyball net	Court	$75.00	0	
12	water-skis	Water	$280.00	200	
13	wet suit	Water	$385.00	150	
(AutoNumber)				0	

Record: 1 of 13

■ The document you selected appears.

REFRESH A DOCUMENT

While you are viewing a database shared on your network, other people could make changes to the database. You can immediately transfer a fresh copy of the database to your computer.

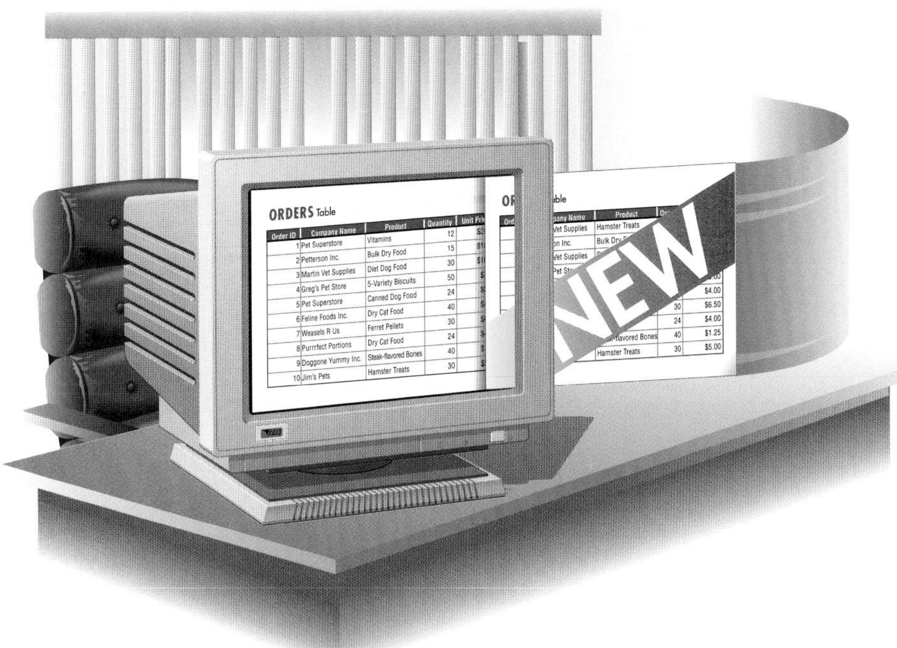

REFRESH A DOCUMENT

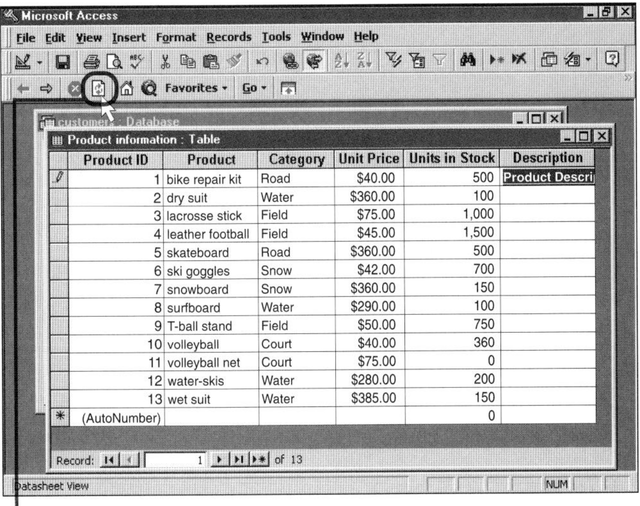

Product ID	Product	Category	Unit Price	Units in Stock	Description
1	bike repair kit	Road	$40.00	500	Product Descri
2	dry suit	Water	$360.00	100	
3	lacrosse stick	Field	$75.00	1,000	
4	leather football	Field	$45.00	1,500	
5	skateboard	Road	$360.00	500	
6	ski goggles	Snow	$42.00	700	
7	snowboard	Snow	$360.00	150	
8	surfboard	Water	$290.00	100	
9	T-ball stand	Field	$50.00	750	
10	volleyball	Court	$40.00	360	
11	volleyball net	Court	$75.00	0	
12	water-skis	Water	$280.00	200	
13	wet suit	Water	$385.00	150	
(AutoNumber)				0	

1 Click [refresh icon] to refresh the displayed database.

Note: If the Refresh button ([refresh icon]) is not available, refer to page 276 to display the Web toolbar.

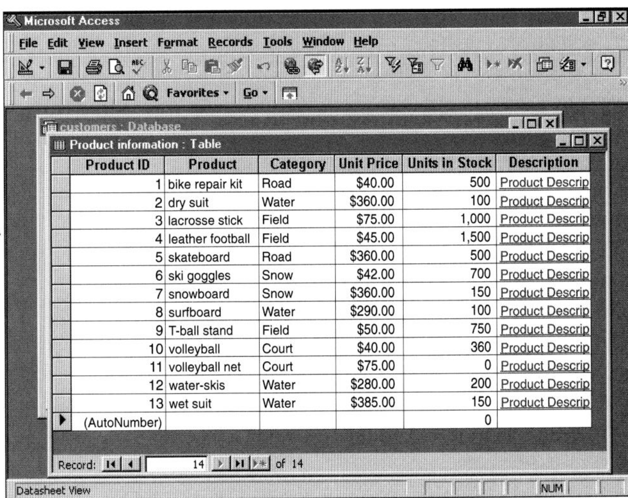

Product ID	Product	Category	Unit Price	Units in Stock	Description
1	bike repair kit	Road	$40.00	500	Product Descrip
2	dry suit	Water	$360.00	100	Product Descrip
3	lacrosse stick	Field	$75.00	1,000	Product Descrip
4	leather football	Field	$45.00	1,500	Product Descrip
5	skateboard	Road	$360.00	500	Product Descrip
6	ski goggles	Snow	$42.00	700	Product Descrip
7	snowboard	Snow	$360.00	150	Product Descrip
8	surfboard	Water	$290.00	100	Product Descrip
9	T-ball stand	Field	$50.00	750	Product Descrip
10	volleyball	Court	$40.00	360	Product Descrip
11	volleyball net	Court	$75.00	0	Product Descrip
12	water-skis	Water	$280.00	200	Product Descrip
13	wet suit	Water	$385.00	150	Product Descrip
(AutoNumber)				0	

■ An up-to-date copy of the database appears.

OPEN A DOCUMENT

You can quickly open a document stored on your computer, network, corporate intranet or the Internet.

OPEN A DOCUMENT

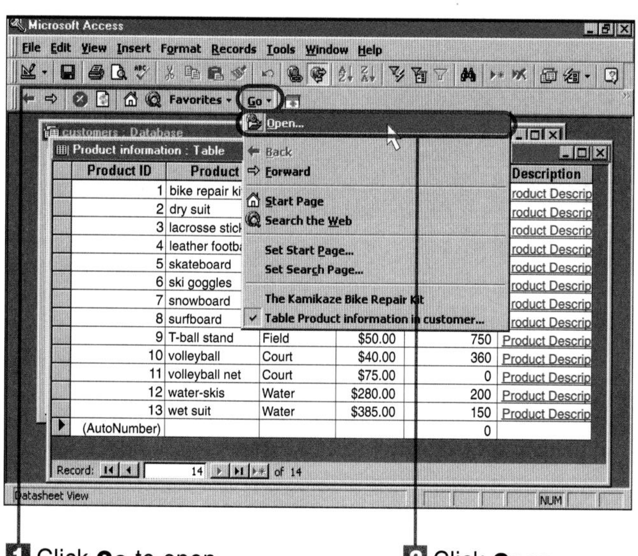

1 Click **Go** to open a document.

*Note: If the **Go** button is not available, refer to page 276 to display the Web toolbar.*

2 Click **Open**.

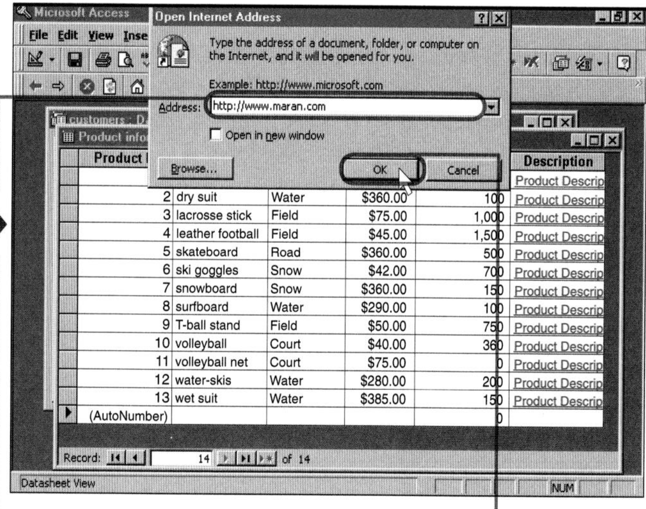

■ The **Open Internet Address** dialog box appears.

3 Type the address of the document (c:\my documents\letter.doc) or Web page (http://www.maran.com) you want to open.

4 Click **OK**.

STOP THE CONNECTION

If a Web page is taking a long time to appear, you can stop the transfer of information.

■ The document appears.

■ If you typed a Web page address in step **3**, your Web browser opens and displays the Web page.

STOP THE CONNECTION

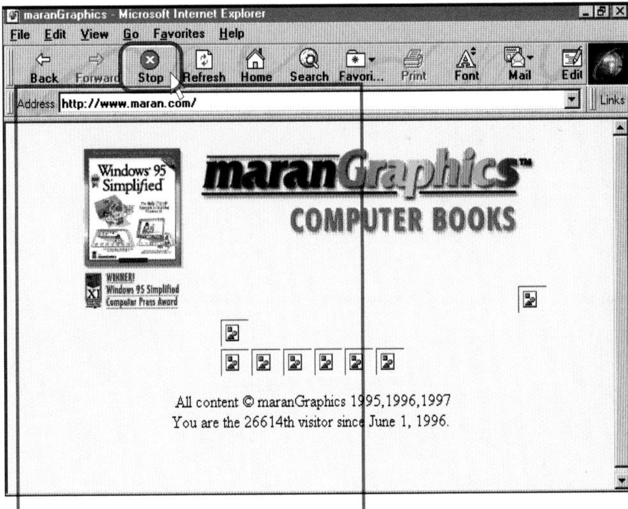

■ The Stop button is red (⊗) when information is transferring to your computer.

Note: If the Stop button (⊗) is not available, refer to page 276 to display the Web toolbar.

1 Click (⊗) to stop the transfer of information (⊗ changes to ⊗).

ADD A DATABASE TO FAVORITES

You can add databases you frequently use to the Favorites folder. You can then quickly open these databases at any time.

ADD A DATABASE TO FAVORITES

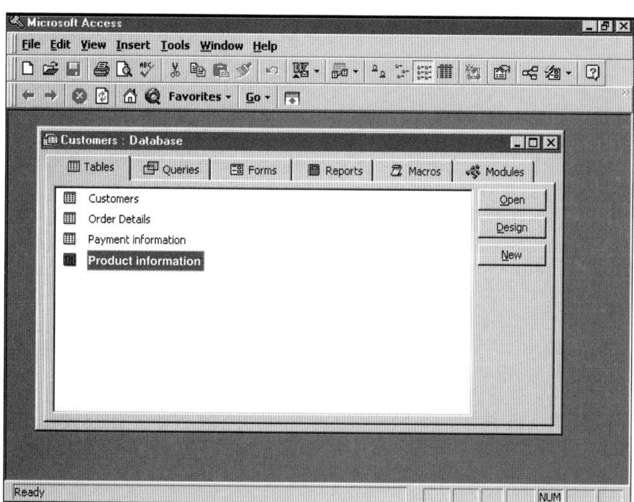

1 Open the database you want to add to the Favorites folder. To open a database, refer to page 30.

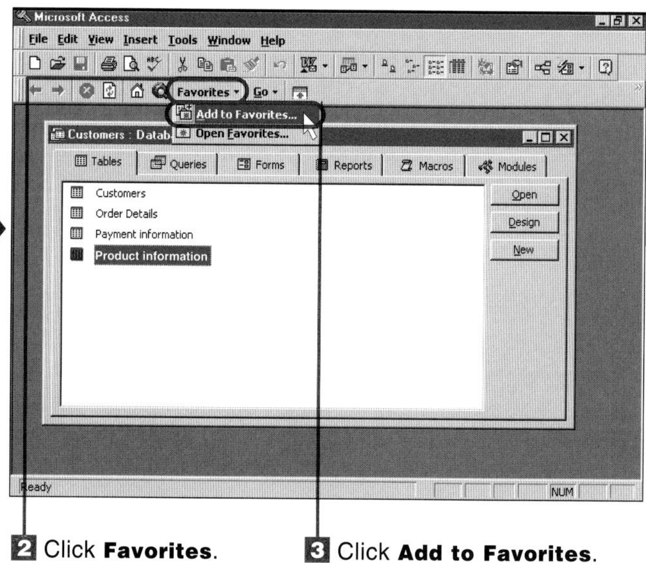

2 Click **Favorites**.

*Note: If **Favorites** is not available, refer to page 276 to display the Web toolbar.*

3 Click **Add to Favorites**.

? **When I add a database to the Favorites folder, does the database move to a new location on my computer?**

When you add a database to the Favorites folder, you create a shortcut to the original database. The original database does not change its location on your computer.

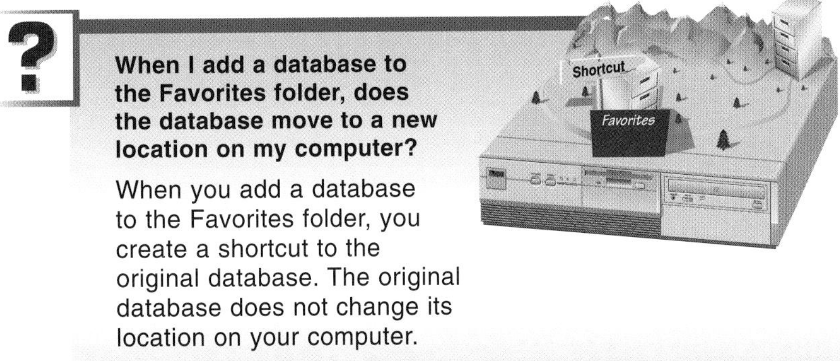

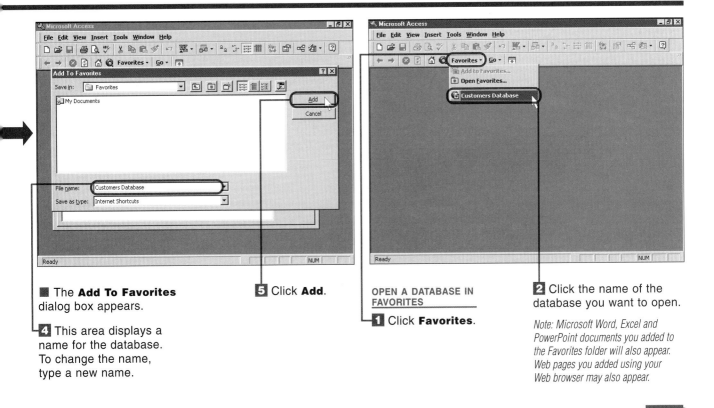

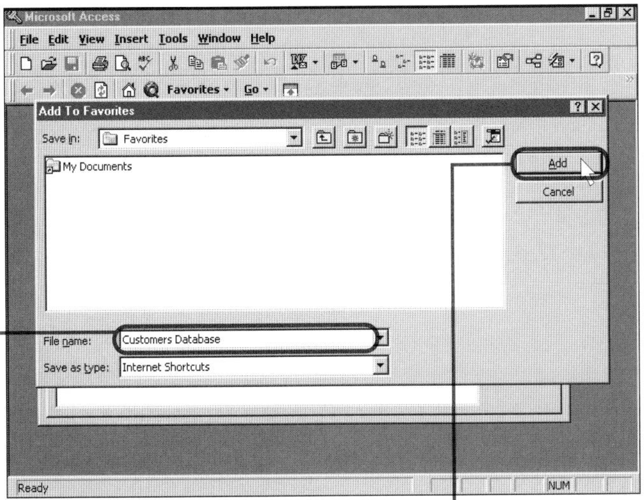

■ The **Add To Favorites** dialog box appears.

4 This area displays a name for the database. To change the name, type a new name.

5 Click **Add**.

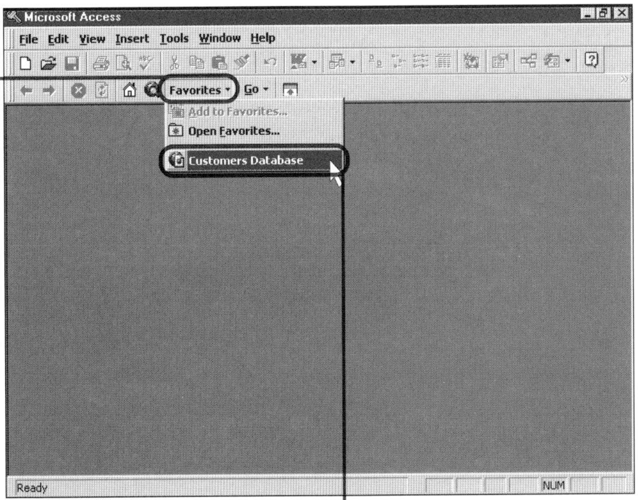

OPEN A DATABASE IN FAVORITES

1 Click **Favorites**.

2 Click the name of the database you want to open.

Note: Microsoft Word, Excel and PowerPoint documents you added to the Favorites folder will also appear. Web pages you added using your Web browser may also appear.

PUBLISH YOUR DATABASE

You can create Web pages from tables, forms, queries and reports in a database. You can place the information on the Web or on your company intranet for others to view.

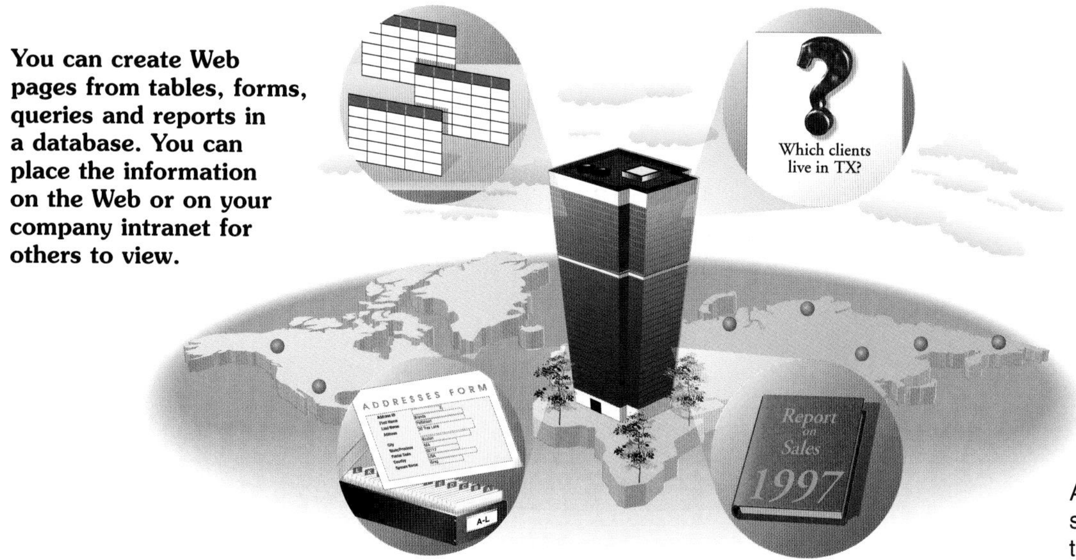

An intranet is a small version of the Internet inside a corporate office.

PUBLISH YOUR DATABASE

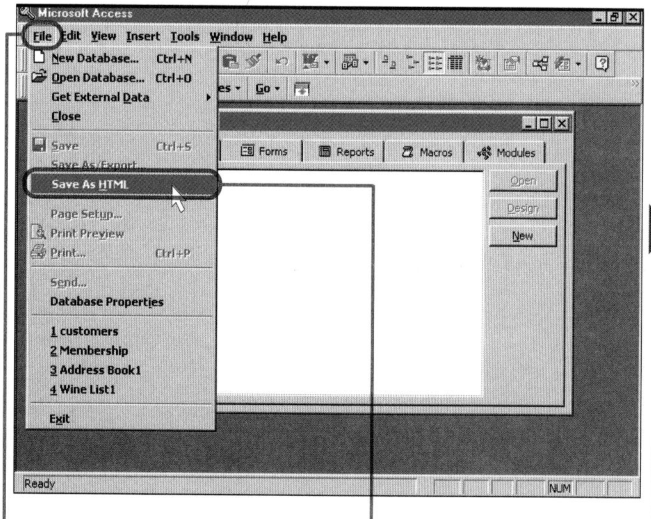

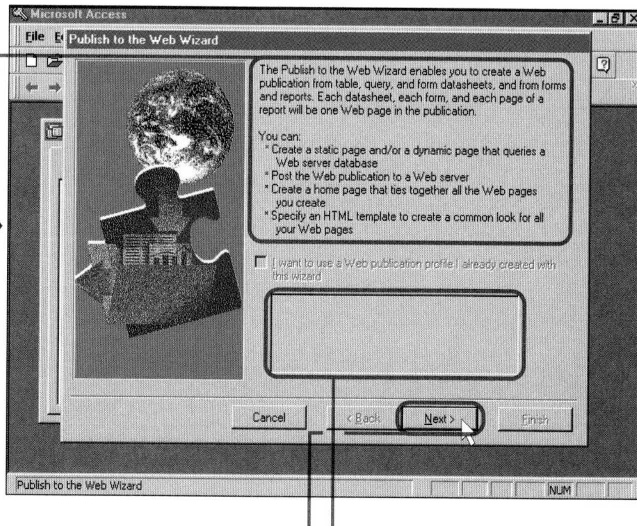

1 Open the database that contains the information you want to publish. To open a database, refer to page 30.

2 Click **File**.

3 Click **Save As HTML**.

*Note: If the **Save As HTML** command is not available, you need to add the Web Page Authoring (HTML) component from the Microsoft Access or Microsoft Office CD-ROM disc.*

■ The **Publish to the Web Wizard** dialog box appears.

■ This area describes what you can do with the wizard.

■ If you have previously used the wizard, any profiles you created appear in this area. To select one of these profiles, refer to the top of page 289.

4 Click **Next** to continue.

How do I select a profile I previously created?

A profile stores the choices you made the last time you used the wizard. You can select a profile you previously created to quickly republish information.

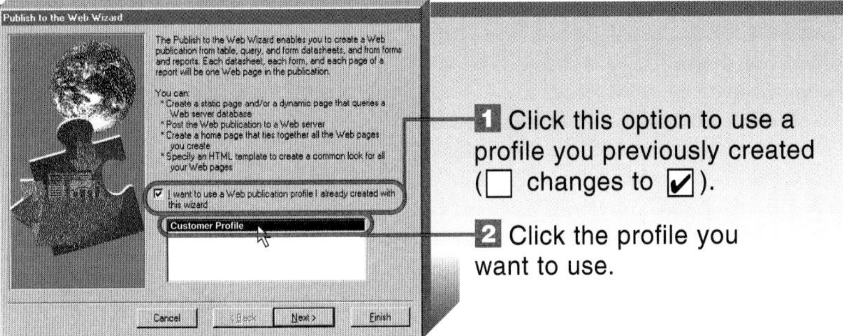

1 Click this option to use a profile you previously created (☐ changes to ☑).

2 Click the profile you want to use.

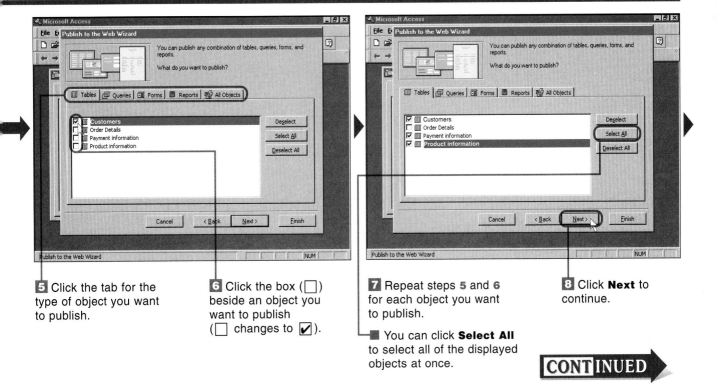

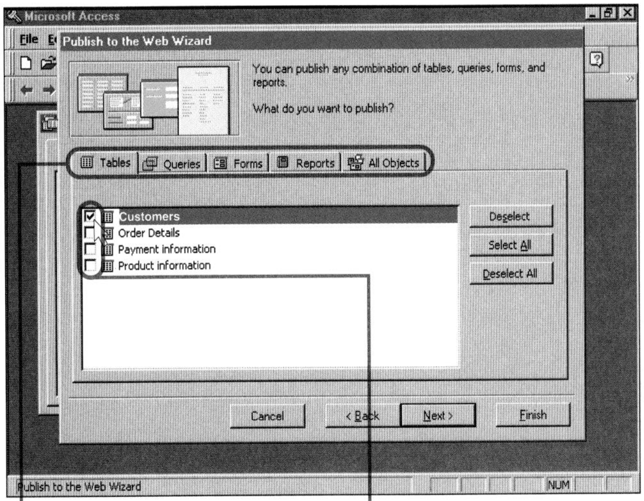

5 Click the tab for the type of object you want to publish.

6 Click the box (☐) beside an object you want to publish (☐ changes to ☑).

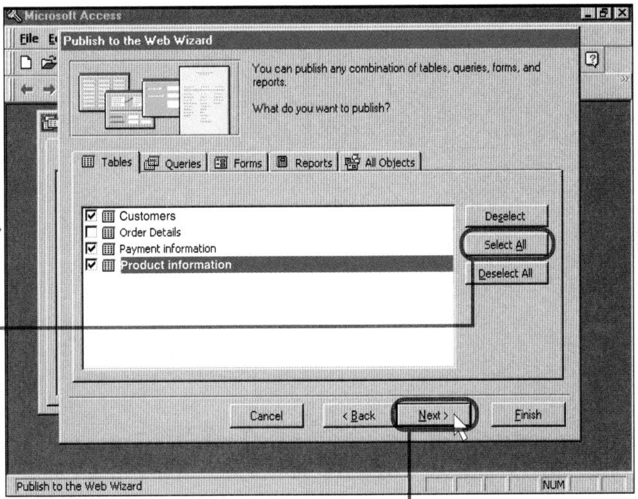

7 Repeat steps 5 and 6 for each object you want to publish.

■ You can click **Select All** to select all of the displayed objects at once.

8 Click **Next** to continue.

CONTINUED

The wizard offers templates that provide formatting for your Web pages and give the pages a consistent appearance.

PUBLISH YOUR DATABASE (CONTINUED)

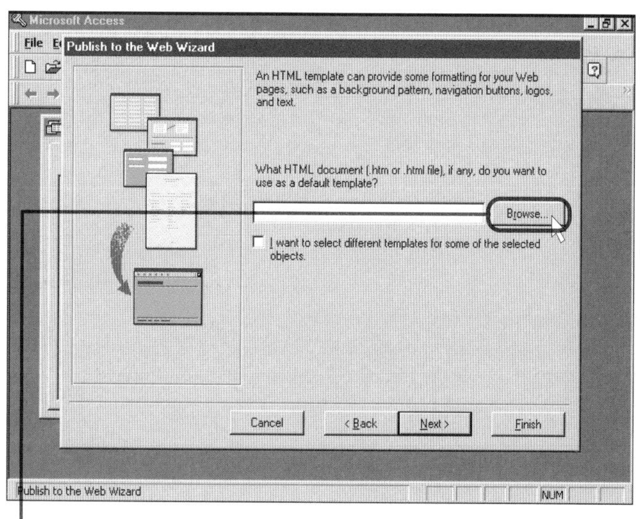

9 Click **Browse** to select the template you want to use to format your Web pages.

■ The **Select an HTML Template** dialog box appears.

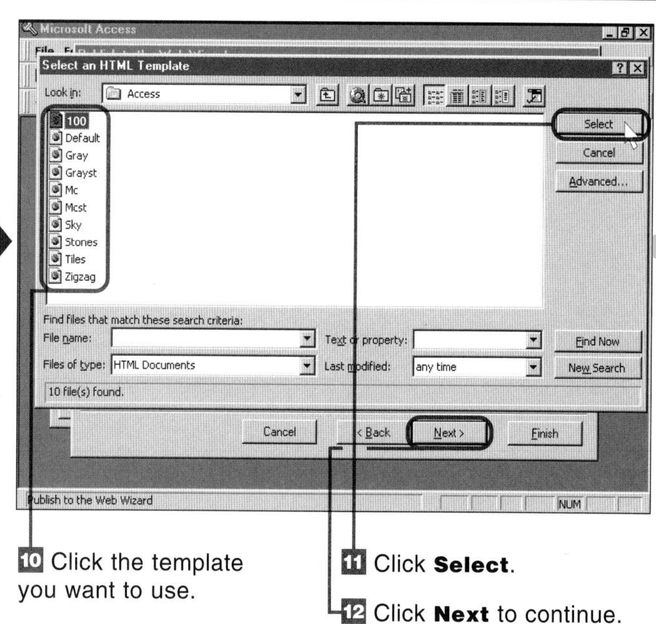

10 Click the template you want to use.

11 Click **Select**.

12 Click **Next** to continue.

What is the difference between static and dynamic Web pages?

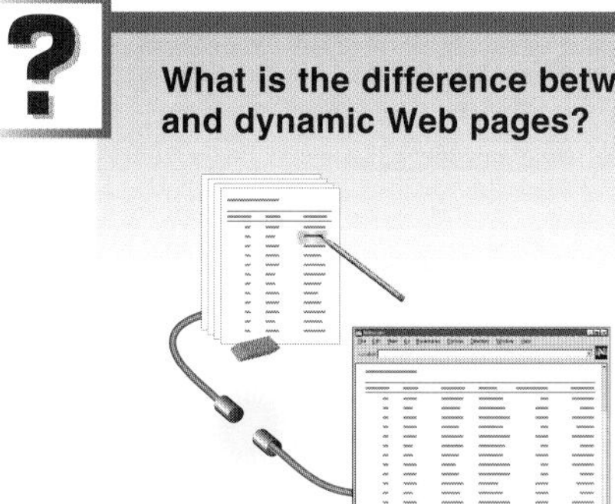

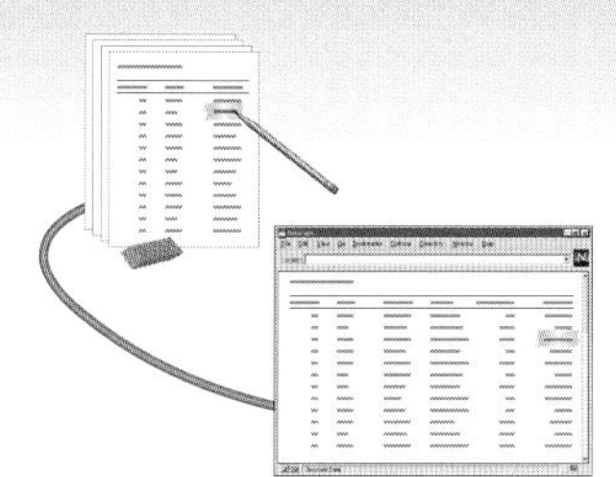

Static

Changes you make to the database **do not appear** in the Web pages. Use this type of page when your data does not frequently change.

Dynamic

Changes you make to the database **appear** in the Web pages. The pages will always display the most current information. Use this type of page when your data frequently changes.

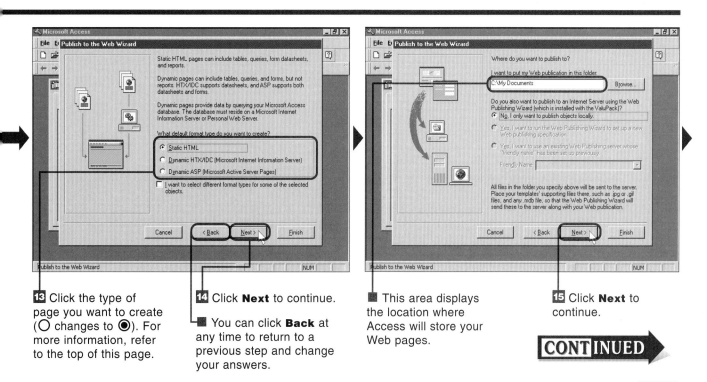

13 Click the type of page you want to create (○ changes to ◉). For more information, refer to the top of this page.

14 Click **Next** to continue.

■ You can click **Back** at any time to return to a previous step and change your answers.

■ This area displays the location where Access will store your Web pages.

15 Click **Next** to continue.

CONTINUED

PUBLISH YOUR DATABASE

The wizard can create a home page for your publication. A home page lists each table, query, form and report you published and gives you quick access to each item.

PUBLISH YOUR DATABASE (CONTINUED)

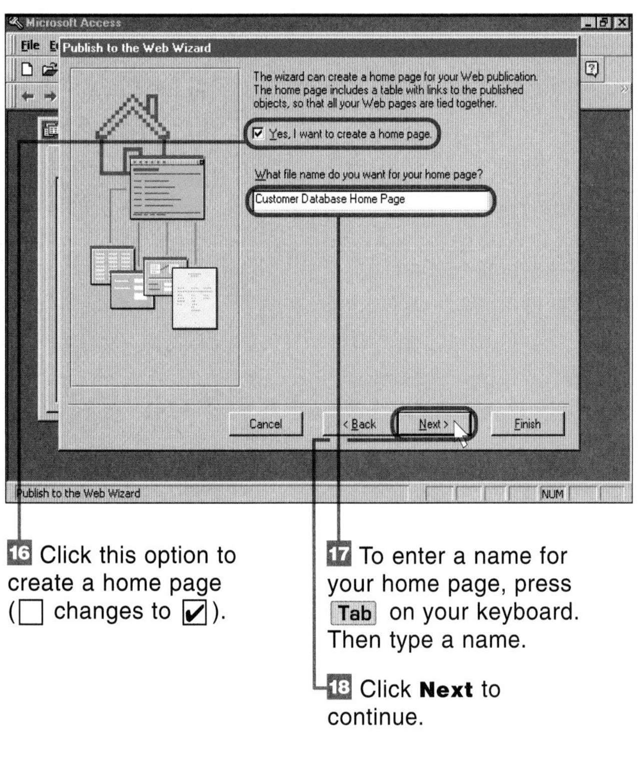

16 Click this option to create a home page (☐ changes to ☑).

17 To enter a name for your home page, press Tab on your keyboard. Then type a name.

18 Click **Next** to continue.

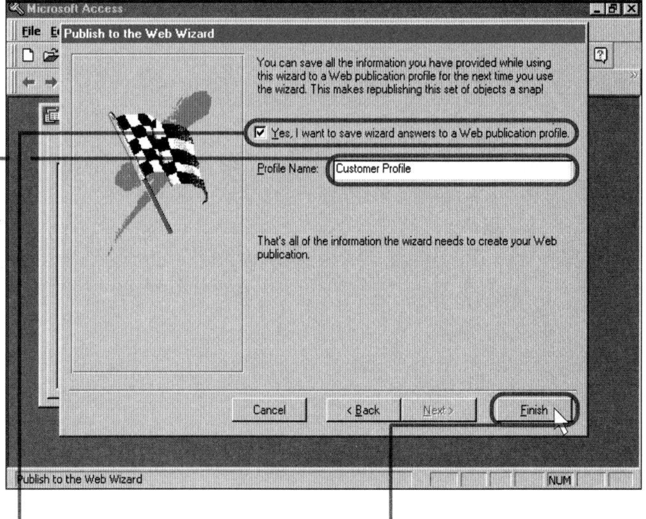

19 To save the choices you made as a profile, click this option (☐ changes to ☑).

20 To enter a name for the profile, press Tab on your keyboard. Then type a profile name.

21 Click **Finish** to create the Web pages.

■ You can now place the database on the Web or on a corporate intranet for others to view.

Why don't my Web pages display any formatting?

When creating Web pages, you can select a template that provides formatting for your pages. Each template uses two graphics files, which consist of the msaccess.jpg file and a file that is different for each template (example: sky.jpg). You need to copy these two files to the folder that stores your Web pages.

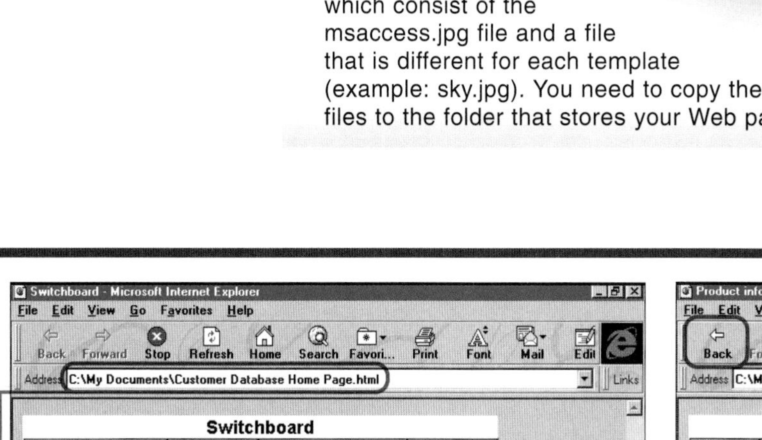

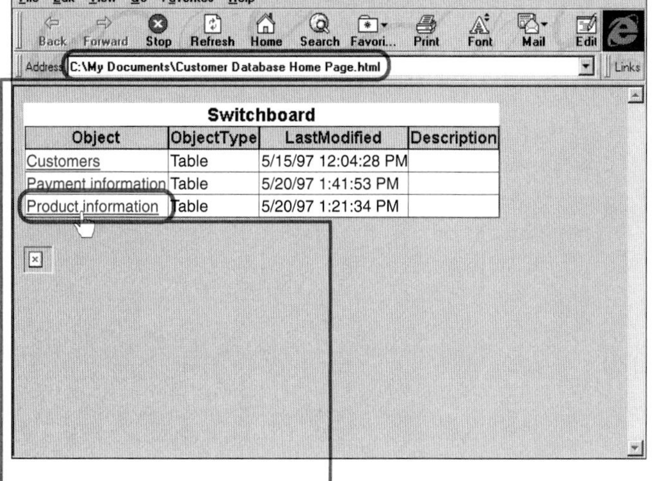

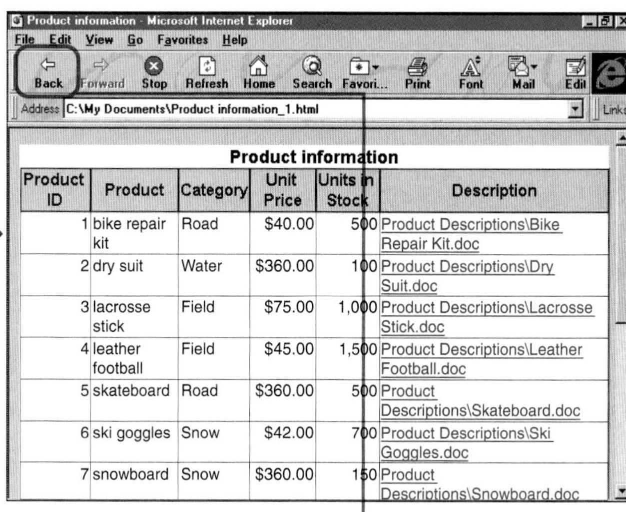

Product ID	Product	Category	Unit Price	Units in Stock	Description
1	bike repair kit	Road	$40.00	500	Product Descriptions\Bike Repair Kit.doc
2	dry suit	Water	$360.00	100	Product Descriptions\Dry Suit.doc
3	lacrosse stick	Field	$75.00	1,000	Product Descriptions\Lacrosse Stick.doc
4	leather football	Field	$45.00	1,500	Product Descriptions\Leather Football.doc
5	skateboard	Road	$360.00	500	Product Descriptions\Skateboard.doc
6	ski goggles	Snow	$42.00	700	Product Descriptions\Ski Goggles.doc
7	snowboard	Snow	$360.00	150	Product Descriptions\Snowboard.doc

You can view the Web pages in a Web browser.

1 Display the home page you created in your Web browser.

■ The home page displays a list of each table, query, form and report you published.

2 Click the name of the object you want to view.

■ The contents of the object appears.

■ You can click **Back** to return to the home page.

INDEX

A

Access. *See also specific subject or feature*
  documents. *See* databases; forms; queries; reports; tables
  exit, 27
  overview, 4-5
  start, 11
add
  captions, 110
  databases to Favorites, 286-287
  default values, 111
  fields
    description, 102
    to forms, 173
    to tables, 42, 98-99
  labels to forms, 176
  pictures
    to forms, 182-183
    to records, 126-129
  records
    to forms, 152
    to tables, 62
  validation rules, 116-117
allow zero-length strings, 114
And criteria, queries, 242-243
appearance, cells, change, 74-75
asterisk (*)
  using to select fields in queries, 217
  as wild card, 211
AutoForm Wizard, 146-147
AutoFormat, forms, select, 181
automatic correction, spelling, 69
AutoNumber
  data types, 105
  primary keys, 137
AutoReport Wizard, 256-259
AVG, calculate
  in queries, 225, 245
  in reports, 270

B

between, criteria, 211
blank databases, create, 28-29
bottom values, display in queries, 230-231
browse
  through pages in reports, 257, 273
  through records
    in forms, 150-151
    in tables, 56-57, 60
buttons, display names, 33

C

calculated fields, format, change in queries, 234-235
calculations, perform
  in queries, 225, 226, 232-233
  in reports, 270, 271
captions, add, 110
cascade
  delete related fields, 143
  update related fields, 143
cells
  appearance, change, 74-75
  effects, change, 75
  replace data, 65, 155
  select
    data, 58-59
    in tables, 59
  zoom into, 61
clear grid, 215

click, using mouse, 10
close
    Access, 27
    forms, 156
    queries, 218
    reports, 262
    tables, 44
    windows, 23
color, change
    cell background, 74
    controls, 175
    gridlines, 75
columnar reports, 257
columns
    lookup, create, 122-125
    width, change in tables, 70
connections, stop, 285
controls in forms
    color, change, 175
    defined, 170
    delete, 172
    move, 170
    resize, 171
copy
    data in tables, 66-67
    vs. move, 67
create
    databases
        blank, 28-29
        using wizard, 14-19
    forms
        using AutoForm, 146-147
        using Form Wizard, 160-163, 164-167
    home page, 292
    hyperlinks, 278-281
    indexes, 120-121
    input masks, 130-131, 132-133
    lookup columns, 122-125
    mailing labels, 88-93
    queries
        in Design view, 202-205
        using Simple Query Wizard, 222-227
    reports
        using AutoReport, 256-259
        using Report Wizard, 266-273
    tables, 36-39
        using wizard, 48-53
    Web pages, 288-293
    Yes/No fields, 118-119
criteria in queries
    examples, 210-211
    using multiple, 240-243
    set, 209
Currency, data types, 105

D

data. *See also* records; text
    calculate in reports, 270, 271
    connect to other documents, 278-281
    copy in tables, 66-67
    edit
        in forms, 154-155
        in tables, 64-65
    find, 186-187
    font, change in tables, 72-73
    format, change, 106-107
    group in reports, 268
    modify in reports, 259
    move in tables, 66-67
    preview, 82-83
    print only, 84-85
    replace, 188-189
        in cells, 65, 155
    require entry, 112-113
    scroll through in tables, 60
    select in tables, 58-59
    sort in reports, 269

INDEX

summarize
grouped records in queries, 246-247
limit records in queries, 248-249
one field in queries, 244-245
types
change, 104-105
defined, 97
Database window, using, 24-25
databases
add to Favorites, 286-287
application, 4-5
create blank, 28-29
create using wizard, 14-19
open, 30-31
in Favorites, 287
parts, 6-7
plan, 8-9
publish, 288-293
view on Web, 293
Datasheet view
forms, 149
queries, 207
tables, 97
Date/Time, data types, 105
decimal places, number, change, 115
default values, add, 111
delete
controls in forms, 172
fields
in queries, 212
in tables, 43, 100
forms, 159
queries, 221
records
in forms, 153
in tables, 63
reports, 265
tables, 47
descriptions, fields, add, 102
Design view
forms, 149
queries, 207
reports, 261
tables, 97
using to create queries, 202-205
display
button names, toolbar, 33
fields, properties, 103
pages in reports, 258
search page, 277
start page, 277
toolbars, 26
top or bottom values in queries, 230-231
Web toolbar, 276
documents on Web
move between, 282
open, 284
refresh, 283
double-click, using mouse, 10
drag and drop, using mouse, 10
dynamic Web pages, 291

E

edit data
in forms, 154-155
in tables, 64-65
effects, cells, change, 75
empty fields, criteria, 211
end relationships, 141
enforce referential integrity, 142-143
errors, clearing in queries, 215
exact matches (=), criteria, 210
exclusion, filter by, 194-195
exit Access, 27

F

Favorites
- add databases, 286-287
- open databases, 287

fields
- add
  - in forms, 173
  - in tables, 42, 98-99
- calculated in queries, format, change, 234-235
- captions, 110
- data, change
  - entry, 112-113
  - format, 106-107
  - types, 104-105
- decimal places, number, change, 115
- default values, 111
- defined, 37
- delete
  - in queries, 212
  - in tables, 43, 100
- description, add, 102
- empty, criteria, 211
- format, change in forms, 174
- freeze in tables, 78-79
- hide
  - in queries, 213
  - in tables, 76-77
- indexes, 120-121
- input masks, create, 130-131, 132-133
- lookup columns, create, 122-125
- names, defined, 37, 97
- as part of table, 6
- properties
  - defined, 97
  - displayed, 103
- rearrange
  - in queries, 214
  - in tables, 41, 101
- redisplay in tables, 77
- related
  - cascade delete, 143
  - cascade update, 143
- remove in reports, 267
- rename in tables, 40
- scroll through in tables, 60
- select
  - all in queries, 216-217
  - in tables, 58
- size, change in tables, 108-109
- validation rules, add, 116-117
- Yes/No, create, 118-119
- zero-length strings, allow, 114

files, Access. *See* databases

filter records
- by exclusion, 194-195
- by form, 196-197, 198-199
- by selection, 192-193

find
- data, 186-187
- list of items, criteria, 211
- unmatched records, queries, 250-253

Find Unmatched Query Wizard, 250-253

fonts, change
- in forms, 178-179
- in tables, 72-73

form, filter by, 196-197, 198-199

Form view, 149

format, change
- calculated fields in queries, 234-235
- data, 106-107
- fields in forms, 174

forms
- AutoFormat, select, 181
- browse through records, 150-151
- close, 156
- controls
  - color, change, 175

delete, 172
move, 170
resize, 171
create
using AutoForm, 146-147
using Form Wizard, 160-163, 164-167
data, edit, 154-155
delete, 159
fields
add, 173
format, change, 174
remove, 161
fonts, change, 178-179
labels
add, 176
text, change, 177
open, 157
as part of database, 7
pictures, add, 182-183
print, 86-87
records
add, 152
browse through, 150-151
delete, 153
rename, 158
size, change, 180
styles, 163
views, change, 148-149
freeze, fields in tables, 78-79

G

greater than (>), criteria, 210
greater than or equal to (>=), criteria, 210
grid, clear, 215
gridlines, change, 75
group, data in reports, 268

H

headings, print, 84-85
height, rows in tables, change, 71
help, 32-33
hide
fields
in queries, 213
in tables, 76-77
toolbars, 26
home page, create, 292
Hyperlink, data types, 105
hyperlinks
insert, 278-281
select, 281

I

images. *See* pictures
indexes, create, 120-121
input masks, create
personalized, 132-133
using wizard, 130-131
insert hyperlinks, 278-281
intranet, described, 288

J

join type, change in queries, 238-239

K

keyboard, using to move through records
in forms, 151
in tables, 57

L

labels
forms
add, 176
text, change, 177
mailing, 88-93
landscape orientation, reports, 273

- Layout Preview view, reports, 261
- less than (<), criteria, 210
- less than or equal to (<=), criteria, 210
- lines in tables, color, change, 75
- list of items, find, criteria, 211
- lookup columns, create, 122-125
- Lookup Wizard, data types, 105

M

- magnify, pages, reports, 258
- mailing labels, 88-93
- margins, change, 84-85
- MAX, calculate
  - in queries, 225, 245
  - in reports, 270
- maximize windows, 21
- Memo, data types, 105
- Microsoft Access. *See* Access
- MIN, calculate
  - in queries, 225, 245
  - in reports, 270
- minimize windows, 20
- modify, data in reports, 259
- mouse, using, 10
- move
  - between documents, 282
  - controls in forms, 170
  - data in tables, 66-67
  - through records
    - in forms, 150-151
    - in tables, 56-57
  - vs. copy, 67
- multiple criteria, queries, 240-243
- multiple-field primary keys, 137

N

- not equal to (<>), criteria, 211
- null, fields, criteria, 211
- Number, data types, 105
- numbers. *See also* data, records, text
  - decimal places, change, 115

O

- Office Assistant, 11
- OLE Object, data types, 105
- open
  - Access, 11
  - databases, 30-31
    - in Favorites, 287
  - documents, 284
  - forms, 157
  - queries, 219
  - reports, 263
  - tables, 45
- Or criteria, queries, 240, 241
- orientations, pages
  - change, 84-85
  - reports, 273
- override, referential integrity, 143

P

- pages
  - display
    - search, 277
    - start, 277
  - magnify, reports, 258
  - margins, change, 84-85
  - orientation
    - change, 84-85
    - reports, 273

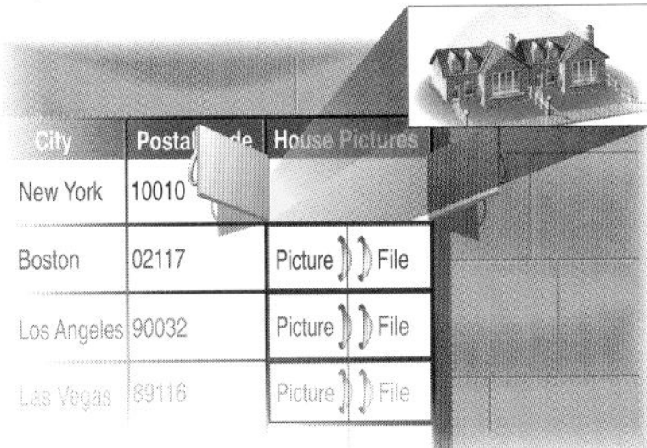

reports
display, 258
magnify, 258
setup, 84-85
Web
insert hyperlinks, 278-281
publish, 288-293
parameters, queries, 236-237
pictures, add
to forms, 182-183
to records, 126-129
portrait orientation, reports 273
preview, data, 82-83
primary keys
defined, 9, 51, 121
set, 136-137
primary table, 140
Print Preview view, reports, 261
print, 86-87
data only, 84-85
headings, 84-85
preview, 82-83
profiles, Web publishing, 289
properties, fields
defined, 97
display, 103
publish databases, 288-293

Q

queries
calculated fields, format, change, 234-235
calculations, perform, 225, 226, 232-233
close, 218
create
in Design view, 202-205
using Simple Query Wizard, 222-227
criteria
examples, 210-211
set, 209
data, summarize
grouped records, 246-247
limit records, 248-249
one field, 244-245
delete, 221
fields, 212
fields
delete, 212
rearrange, 214
select all, 216-217
Find Unmatched Query Wizard, 250-253
grid, clear, 215
hide fields, 213
join type, change, 238-239
multiple criteria, 240-243
open, 219
parameters, 236-237
as part of database, 7
print, 86-87
rename, 220
run, 204
save, 205
sort records, 208
top or bottom values, display, 230-231
unmatched records, find, 250-253
view, change, 206-207
question mark (?) as wild card, 211

R

rearrange, fields
in queries, 214
in tables, 41, 101
records. *See also* data, text

add
in forms, 152
in tables, 62
browse through
in forms, 150-151
in tables, 56-57, 60
defined, 37, 97
delete
in forms, 153
in tables, 63
enforce referential integrity, 142-143
filter
by exclusion, 194-195
by selection, 192-193
find unmatched, queries, 250-253
move through
in forms, 150-151
in tables, 56-57
as part of table, 6
pictures, add in tables, 126-129
print all, 87
save, 53
scroll through in tables, 60
select in tables, 58
sort, 190-191
in queries, 208
referential integrity, enforce, 142-143
refresh, documents, 283
relationships
defined, 9
end, 141
start, tables, 138-141
remove. *See* delete
rename
fields in tables, 40
forms, 158
queries, 220
reports, 264
tables, 46 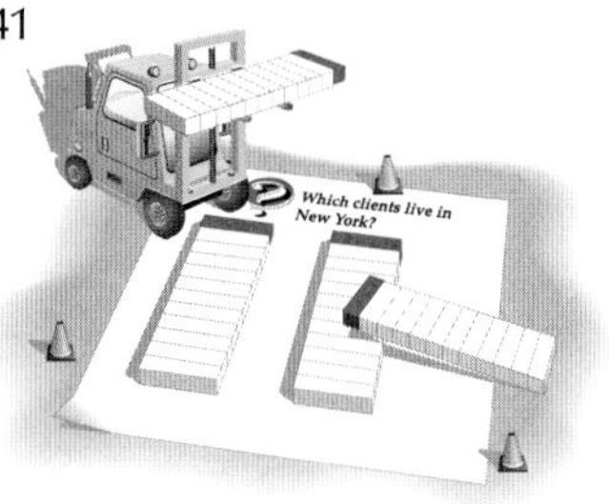
replace, data, 188-189
in cells, 65, 155
Report Wizard, 266-273
reports
browse through page, 257, 273
calculations, perform, 270-271
close, 262
create
using AutoReport, 256-259
using Report Wizard, 266-273
delete, 265
modify data, 259
open, 263
pages
browse through, 257, 273
display, 258
magnify, 258
as part of database, 7
print, 86-87
rename, 264
save, 259
sort data, 269
views, change, 260-261
resize, controls in forms, 171
rows, height, change in tables, 71
rules, validation, add, 116-117
run queries, 204

S

save
queries, 205
records in tables, 53
reports, 259
screen displays, styles, 17
scroll through data in tables, 60
search. *See* find
search page, display, 277

select
- all fields in queries, 216-217
- data, 58-59
- formats, 106-107
- hyperlinks, 281
- tables, 59

selection, filter by, 192-193

set
- criteria in queries, 209
- primary keys, 136-137

setup, pages, change, 84-85

single-field primary keys, 137

size, change
- controls in forms, 171
- fields in tables, 108-109
- forms, 180

sort
- data
  - in queries, 208
  - in reports, 269
- records, 190-191

spelling
- check, 68-69
- errors, automatic correction, 69

SQL (Structured Query Language) view, queries, 207

start. *See also* open
- Access, 11
- relationships, 138-141

start page, display, 277

static Web pages, 291

stop connections, 285

strings, zero-length, allow, 114

styles, forms, change, 181

subforms, 165-167

SUM, calculate
- in queries, 225, 245
- in reports, 270

summarize, data
- grouped records in queries, 246-247
- limit records in queries, 248-249
- one field in queries, 244-245

switch between windows, 22

switchboard, using, 18-19

T

tables
- as part of database, 6
- cells
  - appearance, change, 74-75
  - zoom into, 61
- close, 44
- columns, width, change, 70
- create, 36-39
  - using Table Wizard, 48-53
- data
  - copy, 66-67
  - edit, 64-65
  - font, change, 72-73
  - move, 66-67
- delete, 47
- fields
  - add, 42, 98-99
  - delete, 43, 100
  - freeze, 78-79
  - hide, 76-77
  - rearrange, 41, 101
  - rename, 40
  - size, change, 108-109
- join types, change, 238-239
- open, 45
- pictures, add to records, 126-129
- preview before printing, 82-83
- primary keys, set, 136-137
- print, 86-87
- records
  - add, 62
  - delete, 63
  - move through, 56-57
  - save, 53
- relationships
  - defined, 9

start, 138-141
rename, 46
rows, height, change, 71
scroll through data, 60
select, 59
data, 58-59
spelling, check, 68-69
view pictures, 129
views, change, 96-97
tabular reports, 257
Text, data types, 105
text. *See also* data, records
labels, change on forms, 177
toolbars
button names, display, 33
display or hide, 26
Web, display, 276
top values in queries, display, 230-231
types, data, change, 104-105

U

undo, changes, 155

V

validation rules, add, 116-117
values, top or bottom in queries, display 230-231
view
databases on Web, 293
pictures in tables, 129
views, change
forms, 148-149
query, 206-207
reports, 260-261
tables, 96-97

W

Web pages
create hyperlinks, 278-281
dynamic, 291
publish, 288-293
static, 291
view, 293
Web toolbar, display, 276
width, columns in tables, change, 70
wild cards, criteria, 211
windows
close, 23
Database, using, 24-25
maximize, 21
minimize, 20
switch between, 22
wizards
AutoForm, 146-147
AutoReport, 256-259
Database, 14-19
Find Unmatched Query, 250-253
Form, 160-163, 164-167
Input Mask, 130-131
Label, 88-93
Lookup, 122-125
Publish to the Web, 288
Report, 266-273
Simple Query, 222-227
Table, 48-53
wrist strain, 39

Y

Yes/No
fields, create, 118-119
data types, 105

Z

zero-length strings, allow, 114
zoom into cells in tables, 61

OVER 4 MILLION

OTHER 3-D Visual SERIES

SIMPLIFIED BOOKS

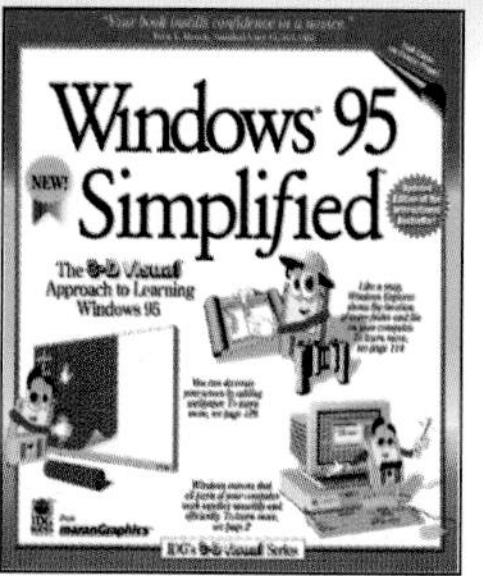

Windows 95 Simplified
ISBN 1-56884-662-2
$19.99 USA/£18.99 UK

More Windows 95 Simplified
ISBN 1-56884-689-4
$19.99 USA/£18.99 UK

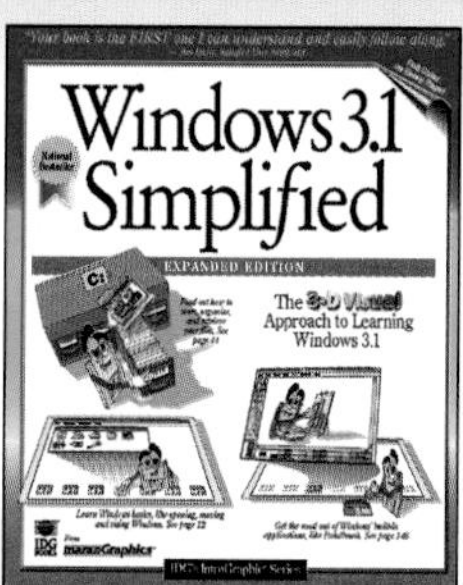

Windows 3.1 Simplified
ISBN 1-56884-654-1
$19.99 USA/£18.99 UK

Word 97 Simplified
ISBN 1-7645-6011-5
$24.99 USA/£23.99 UK

Word For Windows 95 Simplified
ISBN 1-56884-681-9
$19.99 USA/£18.99 UK

Microsoft Office 4.2 For Windows Simplified
ISBN 1-56884-673-8
$27.99 USA/£26.99 UK

Creating Web Pages Simplified
ISBN 0-7645-6007-7
$24.99 USA/£23.99 UK

World Wide Web Color Yellow Pages Simplified
ISBN 0-7645-6005-0
$29.99 USA/£28.99 UK

Internet and World Wide Web Simplified
ISBN 1-56884-658-4
$19.99 USA/£18.99 UK

Computers Simplified, Third Edition
ISBN 0-7645-6008-5
$24.99 USA/£23.99 UK

POCKETGUIDES

The Proven 3-D Visual Approach To Learning Computers In A Handy Pocket Size.

Windows 95 Visual PocketGuide
ISBN 1-56884-661-4
$14.99 USA/£13.99 UK

Word 6 For Windows Visual PocketGuide
ISBN 1-56884-666-5
$14.99 USA/£13.99 UK

ALSO AVAILABLE:

Windows 3.1 Visual PocketGuide
ISBN 1-56884-650-9
$14.99 USA/£13.99 UK

FOR CORPORATE ORDERS, PLEASE CALL: 800-469-6616

S A T I S F I E D   U S E R S !

Word 6 For Windows Simplified

ISBN 1-56884-660-6
$19.99 USA/£18.99 UK

Excel 97 Simplified

ISBN 1-7645-6022-0
$24.99 USA/£23.99 UK

Excel For Windows 95 Simplified

ISBN 1-56884-682-7
$19.99 USA/£18.99 UK

Excel 5 For Windows Simplified

ISBN 1-56884-664-9
$19.99 USA/£18.99 UK

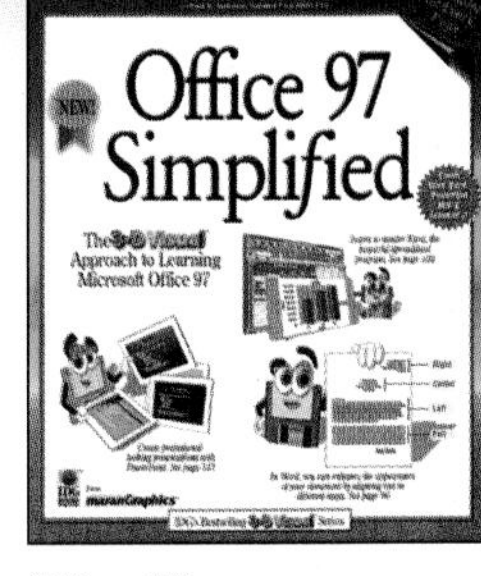

Office 97 Simplified

ISBN 0-7645-6009-3
$29.99 USA/£28.99 UK

Computers Simplified, 2nd Edition

ISBN 1-56884-676-2
$19.99 USA/£18.99 UK

Netscape 2 Simplified

ISBN 0-7645-6000-X
$19.99 USA/£18.99 UK

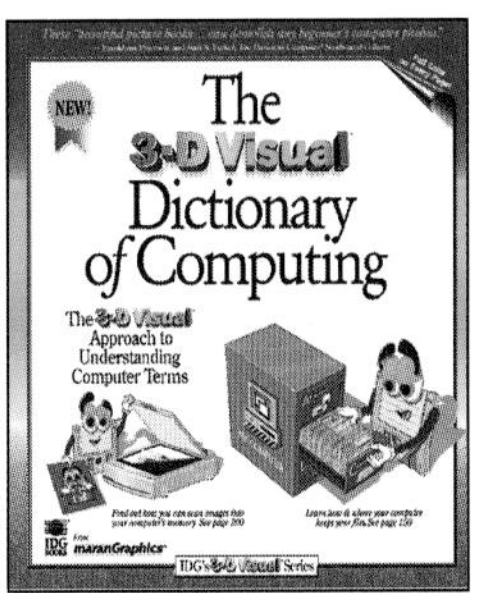

The 3-D Visual Dictionary of Computing

ISBN 1-56884-678-9
$19.99 USA/£18.99 UK

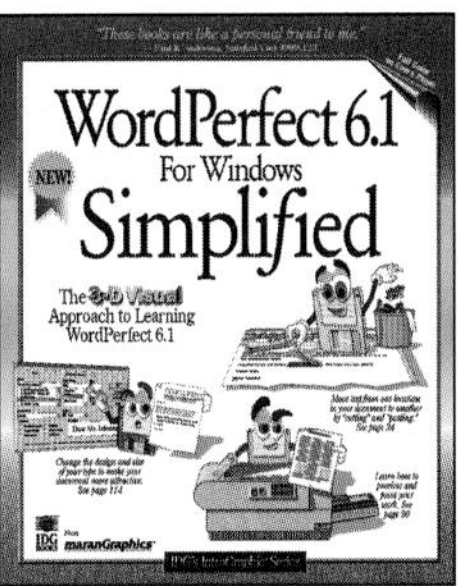

WordPerfect 6.1 For Windows Simplified

ISBN 1-56884-665-7
$19.99 USA/£18.99 UK

Lotus 1-2-3 R5 For Windows Simplified

ISBN 1-56884-670-3
$19.99 USA/£18.99 UK

Excel 5 For Windows Visual PocketGuide

ISBN 1-56884-667-3
$14.99 USA/£13.99 UK

WordPerfect 6.1 For Windows Visual PocketGuide

ISBN 1-56884-668-1
$14.99 USA/£13.99 UK

Lotus 1-2-3 R5 For Windows Visual PocketGuide

ISBN 1-56884-671-1
$14.99 USA/£13.99 UK

FOR CORPORATE ORDERS, PLEASE CALL: **800-469-6616**

SATISFIED USERS!

Visit our Web site at:
http://www.maran.com

This is what people are saying about our books...

"This book was so easy to understand that it did everything except punch the keys."
—Charles Ray Greene, Rincon, Georgia

"This series is written for people on planet Earth."
—M. Klappenberger, Elkridge, Maryland

"Your expertise in presenting information logically, understandably and completely is absolutely beyond compare."
—Rey Archambault, Phoenix, Arizona

"Beautifully illustrated. Crystal clear. Excellent for beginner to expert."
—Henry Conn, Athens, Alabama

"I have learned more since I bought your book than I did in the last 6 months on my own. Best purchase I ever made."
—Helene Jacobs, St. Petersburg, Florida

"For the first time, a book I can really understand. I can't imagine anyone not being able to learn from this book."
—Charles Kline, Catskill, New York

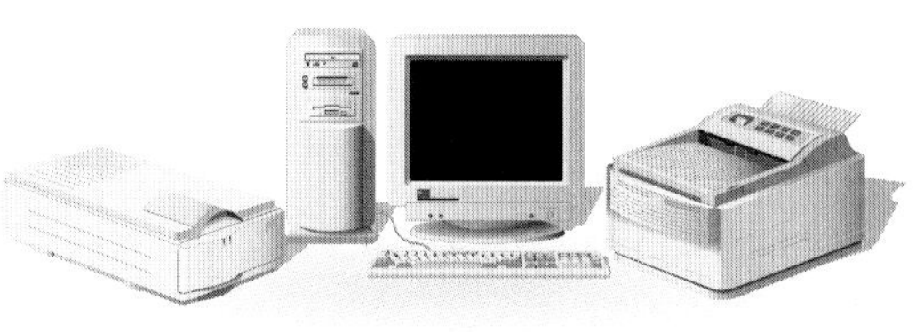

FOR CORPORATE ORDERS, PLEASE CALL: 800-469-6616

DUMMIES PRESS

DOS For Dummies,® 2nd Edition
by Dan Gookin

ISBN: 1-878058-75-4
$16.95 USA/$22.95 Canada

The Internet For Dummies™
by John Levine & Carol Baroudi

ISBN: 1-56884-024-1
$19.95 USA/$26.95 Canada

Macs For Dummies,™ 2nd Edition
by David Pogue

ISBN: 1-56884-051-9
$19.95 USA/$26.95 Canada

TRADE & INDIVIDUAL ORDERS

Phone: **(800) 762-2974**
or **(317) 895-5200**
(8 a.m.–6 p.m., CST, weekdays)
FAX : **(317) 895-5298**

EDUCATIONAL ORDERS & DISCOUNTS

Phone: **(800) 434-2086**
(8:30 a.m.–5:00 p.m., CST, weekdays)
FAX : **(817) 251-8174**

CORPORATE ORDERS FOR 3-D VISUAL™ SERIES

Phone: **(800) 469-6616**
(8 a.m.–5 p.m., EST, weekdays)
FAX : **(905) 890-9434**

Qty	ISBN	Title	Price	Total

Shipping & Handling Charges

	Description	First book	Each add'l. book	Total
Domestic	Normal	$4.50	$1.50	$
	Two Day Air	$8.50	$2.50	$
	Overnight	$18.00	$3.00	$
International	Surface	$8.00	$8.00	$
	Airmail	$16.00	$16.00	$
	DHL Air	$17.00	$17.00	$

Subtotal __________

CA residents add applicable sales tax __________

IN, MA and MD residents add 5% sales tax __________

IL residents add 6.25% sales tax __________

RI residents add 7% sales tax __________

TX residents add 8.25% sales tax __________

Shipping __________

Total __________

Ship to:

Name__________

Address__________

Company__________

City/State/Zip__________

Daytime Phone__________

Payment: □ Check to IDG Books (US Funds Only)
□ Visa □ Mastercard □ American Express

Card # __________ Exp. ______ Signature__________